Legal Practice Companion

'A woman of valour - who can find one?
Her value is far beyond pearls'

בס"ד

Book of Proverbs (Mishlei), Ch.31, v.10

I thank G'd every day that He has given me the merit to find one. This book is for my amazing wife. Dani - for you.

It is also for Eliezer and Rafi. Thank you for being good boys during waking hours - and for sleeping soundly in the late/early hours - and so allowing daddy to have the peace and quiet to write this book. May you always merit the protection inherent in the meaning of your names.

'There are three partners in [a] man -
The L'rd (Blessed be He), his [the man's] father and his mother.'

Babylonian Talmud, Tractate Niddah 31a

I thank them all. I owe all that has been achieved to them.

M.W.

For Fiona, Professor David Silk and Mr Roger Springall

- to each of whom I am extremely grateful, albeit in rather different ways.

G.F.H.M.

Legal Practice Companion

Gerald Montagu
BA (Hons), MA, Solicitor

Mark Weston
LLB (Hons), Solicitor

Twelfth edition (2006-2007)

Foreword to the
Legal Practice Companion and the
Companion series

The Right Honourable Lord Woolf
former Lord Chief Justice

Foreword to the
Legal Practice Companion

The Honourable Mr Justice Lightman

LawMatters
PUBLISHING

Twelfth edition first published in Great Britain 2006 by

Law Matters Limited
33 Southernhay East
Exeter EX1 1NX
Tel: 01392 215560
www.lawmatterspublishing.co.uk

© GFH Montagu and M Weston 2006

This publication is sold with the understanding that neither the publisher, nor the authors, are engaged in rendering legal, accounting or other professional services. If legal advice is required, the services of a competent professional person should be sought.

Eleventh edition (2005 and reprinted 2006) published by Law Matters Limited
Ninth (2003), tenth (2004 and reprinted 2005) editions published by Cavendish Publishing Limited
Eighth edition (2002) published by Oxford University Press
Fourth (1998), fifth (1999), sixth (2000) and seventh (2001) editions published by Blackstone Press Limited
First (1995), second (1996) and third (1997) editions published by CLT Professional Publishing

Gerald Montagu and Mark Weston have asserted their moral rights
under the Copyright, Designs and Patents Act 1988

The authors and publisher acknowledge Crown copyright in all statutory materials in this work

All rights reserved. No part of this publication may be reproduced, stored in a retrieval system, or transmitted, in any form or by any means, electronic, mechanical, photocopying, recording, scanning or otherwise, without the prior permission in writing of the copyright holders (or as expressly permitted by law), or under the terms agreed with the appropriate reprographics rights organisation. Enquiries concerning reproduction outside the scope of the above should be sent to the publisher at the address above.

You must not circulate this book in any other binding or cover
and you must impose the same condition on any acquirer.

British Library Cataloguing in Publication Data
Montagu, Gerald
Weston, Mark
Legal Practice Companion 2006/2007
1 Law - England 2 Law - Wales
3 Procedure (Law) - England 4 Procedure (Law) - Wales
I Title II Weston, Mark
349.4'2

Library of Congress Cataloguing in Publication Data
Data available

ISBN 1 84641029 0

978 1 84641 029 1

Typeset by Gerald Montagu and Daniella Weston

Printed by Ashford Colour Press

Foreword to the *Legal Practice Companion*

The *Legal Practice Companion* is intended as a companion, friend and guide to the student and newly qualified practitioner. Its purpose is achieved with distinction. This work sets out the principles of substantive law in the areas where the reader will need to tread; and civil procedure can no longer be a mystery to those who have this book at hand. The quality of the contents and the clarity of thought and presentation combine to enable the authors, in one volume, to provide a map and a guided tour of legal practice today. Seasoned practitioners will find it valuable to have at their elbows such an up-to-date and reliable summary, and most certainly the *Legal Practice Companion* will occupy a place on my bookshelf.

The Honourable Mr Justice Lightman

Foreword to the *Companions*

I am wholly in favour of the Companions. Legal text books are not often to the fore when it comes to presenting legal information in an attractive, readily understandable and digestible form. However, this is exactly what the Companion series achieves. The law is becoming ever more complex and there is undoubtedly a need to find new methods of communicating it to those who need to know, whether they be members of the public, law students, practitioners or for that matter judges. They will all find that it is a great advantage to have access to a Companion.

This is why the original volume in the series, The Legal Practice Companion (LPC) has proved to be a success. It is now in its twelfth edition, having been first published in 1995. The Intellectual Property and Media Law Companion, the Corporate Finance Companion and the Banking and Capital Markets Companion are worthy successors to the core volume, LPC.

Some of the subjects which are now dealt with by the Companions are not ones with which I am particularly familiar and so I was able to find out for myself in practice whether they work. I can assure the potential reader that they do work as far as I am concerned and that they are very user friendly. The very clear method of presentation both provided an overview of the subject and a step by step guide. I feel confident that they will translate well to multimedia formats since their present style will be very familiar to regular users of information technology.

My enthusiasm for the *Companion* series is in part because they complement the reforms I recommended for civil procedure and which I hope will make our Civil Justice System an appropriate one for this new century. I am very conscious that a weakness of the reforms is that in general they were confined to procedural law and left substantive law intact and in a state which means that in the majority of areas it is impenetrable to those to whom it is unfamiliar. This creates a real impediment to access to justice. The virtue of the *Companion* series is that it provides a clear path through what is so often a jungle. While the *Companion* series will usually provide all that the reader requires, when this is not the case they will be a solid base from which to embark on a more detailed investigation of the tangled undergrowth of the law.

That I find the *Companion* series refreshing is no doubt due to the fact that the authors are (by judicial standards) younger and obviously very bright. Having been schooled in the law and practice in more recent times, they know the needs of others in their position and how the existing texts do not always meet those needs. They have decided that something can and should be done to provide a solution. LPC was the start and the other *Companions* followed. They deserved to achieve the success that they have done and I believe that they will continue to succeed in meeting that need. I congratulate the team on their initiative and on what they are achieving and I look forward to the continued growth of the *Companion* series.

The Right Honourable, Lord Woolf

former *Lord Chief Justice*

Introduction

Welcome to the *Legal Practice Companion*!

To the Practitioner

This book aims to help provide a guide to law and practice beyond your areas of specialisation. It sets out the context, general 'feel' and basic concepts of an area of English law. Its purpose is to serve as a prelude to detailed research. The numerous references aid 'mapping out' research, before clients are given more considered advice based on that research.

The book is intended to provide an *overview* for the practitioner. It is *not* comprehensive; there are numerous specialist works on particular topics that are intended for that purpose. For example, the demands of converting highly complex statutes into digestible points have forced us to focus on those points that seem most relevant. When giving advice, original sources should *always* be checked. For example, we set out in the criminal sections the law applying to adults only and without taking into account the special provisions for sexual offences.

Meeting the needs of practitioners has required an original approach. After discussions with solicitors and trainees, we have evolved a novel format that represents something of a departure for legal publishing. This is reflected in both the choice of material and its presentation.

In this book:

1. Procedures are often broken down into steps or flowcharts, so that they can easily be followed.

2. The law is set out schematically and areas are linked together as appropriate. For example, the *Business* section gives an integrated overview of the legal framework within which businesses operate, dealing with corporate governance, employment, and commercial agreements.

3. All this is packaged in one convenient volume. Therefore, for example, the conveyancer will find an outline of the possible tax treatment of the transaction a few pages away - the importance of which has been highlighted by Lightman J.'s judgment in *Hurlingham Estates Ltd v Wilde & Partners* [1997] STC 627).

4. This book also flags statutes which have received Royal Assent (or will shortly receive it), which are not yet in force but are awaiting orders to bring them into force. This should help maintain an awareness of how the law *will* work (as well as how it *does* work).

We believe that this book will become a valued tool. It is a trusty companion for the practitioner whom will, we hope, keep a copy within reach of his or her desk.

Introduction

Welcome to the *Legal Practice Companion*!

To the Student

The **Legal Practice Course** moves the worlds of work and law school closer together than ever before. This volume is intended to help in both.

Information required for the compulsory topics and the pervasive topics on the LPC (under the Law Society's Legal Practice Course Board's Written Standards) is presented here in one volume. After you complete the course, the source references to lay the basis for your research in practice are included in a format which will quickly become familiar.

Other books and materials usually contain unwieldy blocks of text, which are often split over numerous pages and volumes. This often hinders grasping masses of information which appears unconnected and unclear. The Legal Practice Companion breaks new ground by presenting the relevant law and practice in a step by step format - it is all in one volume, and frequently one topic is presented per page. Charts, flow charts and summaries provide an accessible, clear and straightforward overview of modern legal practice. Please note that the book does assume some prior knowledge and comprehension of basic concepts - it is aimed at students undertaking a Legal Practice Course, or equivalent professional examinations - but can also be used at a wholly different level (using the referenced sources) when you get to practice. The Legal Practice Companion, for example, will not define a 'shelf' company or an 'either way' offence, but it will summarise what to do with respect to them and the procedures that apply to them.

This book is intended:

1. To explain complex parts of the course that you have already covered.
2. To provide a breakdown (aiding comprehension) for parts of the course that you are about to tackle.
3. To present an area of law coherently in one place (for example, taxation and conduct are grouped in their own sections).
4. To split topics up so that they appear where they fit best (such as EU law in *Business*).

For you, the student, this book is intended to cover the core material that you need for your courses, and to help you beyond into the world of work. No doubt your annotations will soon cover the pages. This is entirely suitable and to be encouraged, not least because the precise focus of what is taught and examinations varies from course to course. For those who can take books into examinations (or who chop the pages out, hole-punch them and then pop them into their files), this presentation of the course, together with your annotations, should be invaluable in helping you pass your exams well.

Acknowledgements

Access to ... the law ... and to justice

In 1995, the *Legal Practice Companion* was launched into the stormy debate over legal education. Since then, some 37,000 copies have been sold. With Lord Woolf's civil justice reforms now well entrenched, we hope that regular users of this book have found the civil litigation section useful. With the rapid changes in criminal law, we express the same sentiments for the criminal litigation section to those regular users undergoing the stresses of coping with keeping up to date. Also, with ever more rapid change in the law generally and with the increasing demands of clients, we suspect that more rough seas lie ahead. We hope to continue to tackle those seas and this has been possible so far due to the many who deserve our thanks. We start by thanking our readers, the former Lord Chief Justice and Mr Justice Lightman for their whole-hearted support and encouragement.

Continuing growth...

A fifth edition of the *Banking and Capital Markets Companion*, and a fourth edition of the *Intellectual Property and Media Law Companion* are now in preparation. The *Companions* continue to meet what, judging from the response, is a very real need both in the legal profession and further afield.

Our thanks go to all at Law Matters, and in particular, to Jeremy Stein.

Behind the scenes ...

We would like to thank (as always) Mark's wife, Daniella, for her typesetting, proof reading, RSI-busting typing and her continual support and madness at putting up with it all - while juggling work, home and life in general. Fiona Montagu has put her hand to the tiller and kindly cast a sharp eye over some of the drier aspects (!) of the text.

Mark is also particularly grateful to his mother, Diana Weston for everything she does and to the whole Estrin clan who have had all sorts of trials and tribulations over the past year (and particularly in respect of Jonny who has made us focus on what is really important in life and to whom we wish a Refuah Sheleimah - a complete recovery).

We would also like to thank Catherine Hughes and Ruth Kent at Matthew Arnold & Baldwin (mab) for organising Mark's life between 8am and 8pm, Rebecca Jenrick at Sidley Austin for her patience and the ability to magic-up a copy of the Finance Act in a twinkling, and Salpy Kouyoumjian for some helpful advice

And of course - no *Legal Practice Companion* would be complete without mentioning Gill Zeiner who developed the original typeset for our approach many moons and editions ago.

We hope that readers will continue to write to us at our firms with suggestions on how the *Legal Practice Companion* can become even more helpful.

Without which ...

And of course, many thanks to our families and friends who put up with us during the writing process and to anyone inadvertently missing ...

The law ...

As usual, we cover English law only. We have tried to reflect changes until going to press, but the law is generally as stated at 31 July 2006.

Gerald Montagu and Mark Weston,

London, 14 August, 2006.

'Many rough and cragged by-ways have been ... trodden towards the intricate problems of the Law's mysteries, but no foot-path ... [has been] plainley beaten, so that anyone could ... find the way without being subject to any Aberrations [and which] should safely conduct the Zealous Pilgrim through the sullen deserts, and over the craggy precipicies of this Herculean voyage.'

Compleat Solicitor (London, 1668)

Contents

Foreword to the *Legal Practice Companion*	v
Foreword to the *Companions*	vi
Introduction to the Practitioner	viii
Introduction to the Student	ix
Acknowledgements	x
Contents	xiii
Boxes, conventions and update	xv
Table of abbreviations	xvi
Table of authorities	xxiii

Conduct

A	Cornerstones of good conduct	2
B	Advertising, introductions and referrals	3
C	Money laundering	4
D	Taking instructions	8
E	Costs, help in funding a case and bills	15
F	Undertakings	25
G	Discipline	26
H	Financial services	28
I	Professional ethics	31
J	Human rights	34

Accounts

A	Basic bookkeeping	36
B	Advanced bookkeeping	44
C	Bank reconciliations	51
D	Partnership accounts	52
E	Interpreting accounts	56
F	*Solicitors' Accounts Rules 1998*	60
G	Keeping accounts as a solicitor	69

Taxation

A	Income tax (IT)	80
B	Capital allowances	91
C	Capital gains tax (CGT)	94
D	Inheritance tax (IHT)	100
E	Corporation tax (CT)	104
F	Distributions	111
G	Close companies	112
H	Assessment and payment of tax (IT, CGT, IHT, CT)	115
I	Value added tax (VAT)	122
J	Stamp duty	126
K	Stamp duty reserve tax (SDRT)	131
L	Stamp duty land tax (SDLT)	133
M	Some planning ideas	137

Wills, probate and administration

A	Valid wills	144
B	Contents of a will	146
C	Intestacy	151
D	Probate	154
E	Administration	160
F	Problems which can arise	167

Conveyancing

A	A chronological conveyance	174
B	Checking title and making searches	212
C	Variations to the standard contract	223
D	Leases	227
E	Security of tenure	233
F	Commonhold	239
G	Remedies	240

Business

A	Partnerships (non-tax aspects)	244
B	Limited liability partnerships (LLPs)	250
C	Private companies (non-tax aspects)	255
D	Public companies (non-tax aspects)	286
E	Converting businesses	289
F	Choice of business medium	290
G	Insolvency	292
H	Competition and trading	307
I	Commercial agreements	322
J	Employment	326

Civil Litigation

A	First steps	334
	Overview of proceedings	340
B	Court matters applicable throughout litigation	341
C	Starting proceedings	355
D	Defendant's options	365
E	Claimant's options	370
F	Applications for court orders	371
G	Interim remedies	381
H	Offers to settle / payments into court	385
I	Allocation (and automatic transfer)	392
J	Small claims track	394
K	Fast track	397
L	Multi track	399
M	Disclosure and inspection	401
N	Evidence	406
O	Trial preparations	411
P	The trial	415
Q	Costs	417
R	Enforcing judgments	423
S	Appeals	430

Criminal Litigation

	Overview of the criminal process	432
A	Criminal investigations	433
B	Arrest and interview	434
C	Court matters applicable generally	451
D	Remand and bail	454
E	Mode of trial/Allocation on an 'either way' offence	460
F	Preparations for summary trial	464
G	Summary trial	465
H	Sending for trial and committal	467
I	Preparations for Crown Court hearings and trial	474
J	Crown Court hearings and trial	475
K	Sentencing powers	478
L	Sentencing procedure and mitigation	491
M	Appeals	493
N	Disclosure	495
O	Evidence at trial	497
P	Forthcoming changes	512

Index

Index	513

Boxes, conventions and update

I Boxes

> **Legal points** and principles
> ➤ Square boxes contain information relating to a specific area of law or legal principle.

> **Practice points** and principles
> ➤ Round boxes contain information relating to information that is useful in practice.

II Legislative citations and update

➤ At the time of going to press, certain legislation awaits an order from a Minister before it comes into force (this is dependent on the drafting and approval of secondary legislation and/or regulatory codes).

- Notwithstanding that the provisions of the *FA 2006* come into force on various dates, it has been assumed that all provisions of *FA 2006* are fully in force.
- The *HIPR 2006* do not come into force until 1 June 2007.
- The *IT(DA)(EE)(A)R 2006*, which amend the *IT(DA)(EE)R 2004*, do not come into force until 1 September 2006 and have effect in relation to deaths occurring on or after 1 September 2006; we have, however, assumed that the *IT(DA)(EE)(A)R 2006* are in full force and effect.

> Where legislation is not yet in force, this is indicated by '[not yet in force]' and the presentation of text and bullets in italics.
>
> The repeal of legislation with effect from a future date is indicated by a ✂ symbol.

Table of abbreviations
Statutes

A

AA 1870	Apportionment Act 1870.
AA 1976	Adoption Act 1976.
AA 1996	Arbitration Act 1996.
ABA 2003	Anti-social Behaviour Act 2003.
ACA 2002	Adoption and Children Act 2002.
AEA 1925	Administration of Estates Act 1925.
AEA 1971	Administration of Estates Act 1971.
AE(SP)A 1965	Administration of Estates (Small Payments) Act 1965.
AIA 1996	Asylum and Immigration Act 1996.
AJA 1920	Administration of Justice Act 1920.
AJA 1952	Administration of Justice Act 1952.
AJA 1969	Administration of Justice Act 1969.
AJA 1982	Administration of Justice Act 1982.
AJA 1985	Administration of Justice Act 1985.
AJA 1999	Access to Justice Act 1999.
ANLA 1992	Access to Neighbouring Land Act 1992.
AtEA 1971	Attachment of Earnings Act 1971.
ATCSA 2001	Anti-Terrorism Crime and Security Act 2001.

B

BA 1976	Bail Act 1976.
BA 1987	Banking Act 1987.
B(A)A 1993	Bail (Amendment) Act 1993.
BEA 1998	Bank of England Act 1998.
BNA 1985	Business Names Act 1985.
BSA 1986	Building Societies Act 1986.

C

CA	Companies Act 1985.
CA 1989	Companies Act 1989.
ChA 1989	Children Act 1989.
CA 1992	Charities Act 1992.
CA 1998	Competition Act 1998.
CA 2003	Courts Act 2003.
CAA 1968	Criminal Appeal Act 1968.
CAA 1995	Criminal Appeal Act 1995.
CAA 2001	Capital Allowances Act 2001.
CCA 1974	Consumer Credit Act 1974.
CCA 1984	County Courts Act 1984.
CrDA 1971	Criminal Damage Act 1971.
CDA 1998	Crime and Disorder Act 1998.
CDDA 1986	Company Directors Disqualification Act 1986.
CDSA 2006	Criminal Defence Service Act 2006.
CEA 1898	Criminal Evidence Act 1898.
CEA 1968	Civil Evidence Act 1968.
CEA 1972	Civil Evidence Act 1972.
CEA 1995	Civil Evidence Act 1995.
CE(A)A 1997	Criminal Evidence (Amendment) Act 1997.
CIA 1994	Coal Industry Act 1994.
CICA 1995	Criminal Injuries Compensation Act 1995.
CJA 1967	Criminal Justice Act 1967.
CJA 1982	Criminal Justice Act 1982.
CJA 1987	Criminal Justice Act 1987.
CJA 1988	Criminal Justice Act 1988.
CJA 1991	Criminal Justice Act 1991.
CJA 2003	Criminal Justice Act 2003.
CJCSA 2000	Criminal Justice and Courts Services Act 2000.
CJJA 1982	Civil Jurisdiction and Judgments Act 1982.
CJJA 1991	Civil Jurisdiction and Judgments Act 1991.
CJPA 2001	Criminal Justice and Police Act 2001.
CJPO 1994	Criminal Justice Public Order Act 1994.
CL(C)A 1978	Civil Liability (Contribution) Act 1978.
CLRA 2002	Commonhold and Leasehold Reform Act 2002.
CRA 1965	Commons Registration Act 1965.
CRA 2006	Commons Registration Act 2006.
CLSA 1990	Courts and Legal Services Act 1990.

COA 1979	Charging Orders Act 1979.
CPA 1865	Criminal Procedure Act 1865.
CPA 1987	Consumer Protection Act 1987.
CPA 1997	Civil Procedure Act 1997.
CPA 2004	Civil Partnership Act 2004.
CP(AW)A 1965	Criminal Procedure (Attendance of Witnesses) Act 1965.
CPIA 1996	Criminal Procedure and Investigations Act 1996.
CRA 1965	Commons Registration Act 1965.
CRA 2006	Commons Registration Act 2006.
C(S)A 1997	Crime (Sentences) Act 1997.
C(ROTP)A 1999	Contracts (Rights of Third Parties) Act 1999.

D

DA 1996	Damages Act 1996.
DDA 1995	Disability Discrimination Act 1995.
DVCAVA 2004	Domestic Violence, Crime and Victims Act 2004.

E

EA 1851	Evidence Act 1851.
EA 1989	Electricity Act 1989.
EA 2002	Enterprise Act 2002.
EEA 1979	Estate Agents Act 1979.
EPA 1970	Equal Pay Act 1970.
EPA 1990	Enviromental Protection Act 1990.
EPAA 1985	Enduring Powers of Attorney Act 1985.
ERA 1996	Employment Rights Act 1996.
ERA 1999	Employment Relations Act 1999.

F

FAA 1976	Fatal Accidents Act 1976.
FA 1930	Finance Act 1930.
FA 1931	Finance Act 1931.
FA 1971	Finance Act 1971.
FA 1985	Finance Act 1985.
FA 1986	Finance Act 1986.
FA 1990	Finance Act 1990.
FA 1996	Finance Act 1996.
FA 1997	Finance Act 1997.
FA 1998	Finance Act 1998.
FA 1999	Finance Act 1999.
FA 2000	Finance Act 2000.
FA 2001	Finance Act 2001.
FA 2002	Finance Act 2002.
FA 2003	Finance Act 2003.
FA 2004	Finance Act 2004.
FA 2005	Finance Act 2005.
FA 2006	Finance Act 2006.
F(No.2)A 1992	Finance (No.2) Act 1992.
F(No.2)A 1997	Finance (No.2) Act 1997.
F(No.2)A 2005	Finance (No.2) Act 2005.
FIA 2000	Freedom of Information Act 2000.
FJ(RE)A 1933	Foreign Judgments (Reciprocal Enforcement) Act 1933.
FLA 1996	Family Law Act 1996.
FLRA 1969	Family Law Reform Act 1969.
FLRA 1987	Family Law Reform Act 1987.
FSMA 2000	Financial Services and Markets Act 2000.

G

H

HA 1957	Homicide Act 1957.
HA 1980	Highways Act 1980.
HA 1985	Housing Act 1985.
HA 1988	Housing Act 1988.
HA 1996	Housing Act 1996.
HA 2004	Housing Act 2004.
HPA 1964	Hire Purchase Act 1964.
HRA 1998	Human Rights Act 1998.
HSCA 2001	Health and Social Care Act 2001.
HSSA 1983	Health and Social Security Administration Act 1983.
HSWA 1974	Health and Safety at Work Act 1974.

I

IA 1978	Interpretation Act 1978.
IA and IA 1986	Insolvency Act 1986.
IA 1994	Insolvency Act 1994.
I(No2)A 1994	Insolvency (No2) Act 1994.
IEA 1952	Intestates' Estates Act 1952.
IHTA 1984	Inheritance Tax Act 1984.
IOA 1968	International Organisations Act 1968.
IOA 1981	International Organisations Act 1981.
I(PFD)A 1975	Inheritance (Provision for Family and Dependants) Act 1975.
IT(EP)A 2003	Income Tax (Employment and Pensions) Act 2003.
IT(TOI)A 2005	Income Tax (Trading and Other Income) Act 2005.

J

JA 1838	Judgments Act 1838.
JA 1974	Juries Act 1974.

K

L

LA 1976	Legitimacy Act 1976.
LA 1980	Limitation Act 1980.
LD(A)A 1888	Law of Distress (Amendment) Act 1888.
LLCA 1975	Local Land Charges Act 1975.
LPA	Law of Property Act 1925.
LPA 2000	Limited Partnership Act 2000.
LPCD(I)A 1998	Late Payment of Commercial Debts (Interest) Act 1998.
LP(JT)A 1964	Law of Property (Joint Tenants) Act 1964.
LP(MP)A 1989	Law of Property (Miscellaneous Provisions) Act 1989.
LP(MP)A 1994	Law of Property (Miscellaneous Provisions) Act 1994.
LP(R)A 1938	Leasehold Property (Repairs) Act 1938.
LRA	Land Registration Act 1925.
LRA 1967	Leasehold Reform Act 1967.
LRA 1997	Land Registration Act 1997.
LRA 2002	Land Registration Act 2002.
LR(CN)A 1945	Law Reform (Contributory Negligence) Act 1945.
LRHUDA 1993	Leasehold Reform Housing and Urban Development Act 1993.
LR(MP)A 1934	Law Reform (Miscellaneous Provisions) Act 1934.
LR(PI)A 1948	Law Reform (Personal Injuries) Act 1948.
LR(S)A 1995	Law Reform (Succession) Act 1995.
LTA 1927	Landlord and Tenant Act 1927.
LTA 1954	Landlord and Tenant Act 1954.
LTA 1985	Landlord and Tenant Act 1985.
LTA 1987	Landlord and Tenant Act 1987.
LTA 1988	Landlord and Tenant Act 1988.
LT(C)A 1995	Landlord and Tenants (Covenants) Act 1995.

M

MA 1967	Misrepresentation Act 1967.
MCA 1980	Magistrates' Courts Act 1980.
MCA 1987	Minors' Contracts Act 1987.
MCA 2005	Mental Capacity Act 2005.
MHA 1983	Matrimonial Homes Act 1983.
MntHA 1983	Mental Health Act 1983.

N

NAA 1948	National Assistance Act 1948.

O

OA 1978	Oaths Act 1978.
OAPA 1861	Offences Against the Person Act 1861.
OLA 1984	Occupiers' Liability Act 1984.

P

PA	Partnership Act 1890.
PA 1911	Perjury Act 1911.
PAA 1971	Powers of Attorney Act 1971.
PACE	Police and Criminal Evidence Act 1984.
PCA 1994	Proceeds of Crime Act 1994.
PCA 2002	Proceeds of Crime Act 2002.
PCC(S)A 2000	Powers of Criminal Courts (Sentencing) Act 2000.
PEA 1977	Protection from Eviction Act 1977.
PHA 1997	Protection from Harassment Act 1997.
PIL(MP)A 1995	Private International Law (Miscellaneous Provisions) Act 1995.
P(LBCA)A 1990	Planning (Listed Buildings and Conservation Areas) Act 1990.
POA 1985	Prosecution of Offences Act 1985.
POA 1986	Public Order Act 1986.

Q

R

ROA 1974	Rehabilitation of Offenders Act 1974.
RRA 1976	Race Relations Act 1976.
RTA 1988	Road Traffic Act 1988.
RTA 1991	Road Traffic Act 1991.
RT(C)A 1999	Road Traffic (NHS Charges) Act 1999.
RTOA 1988	Road Traffic Offenders Act 1988.

S

SA 1891	Stamp Act 1891.
SA 1974	Solicitors' Act 1974.
SLA 1925	Settled Land Act 1925.
SCA 1981	Supreme Court Act 1981.
SDA 1975	Sex Discrimination Act 1975.
SDA 1986	Sex Discrimination Act 1986.
SGA 1979	Sales of Goods Act 1979.
SG(A)A 1995	Sale of Goods (Amendment) Act 1995.
SGSA 1982	Supply of Goods and Services Act 1982.
SG(IT)A 1973	Supply of Goods (Implied Terms) Act 1973.
SG(A)A 1995	Sale of Goods (Amendment) Act 1995.

SOCPA 2005	Serious Organised Crime and Police Act 2005.
SSGA 1994	Sale and Supply of Goods Act 1994.
SS(RB)A 1997	Social Security (Recovery of Benefits) Act 1997.

T

TA 1925	Trustee Act 1925.
TA 1968	Theft Act 1968.
TA 2000	Trustee Act 2000.
TCA 2002	Tax Credits Act 2002.
TCGA 1992	Taxation of Chargeable Gains Act 1992.
TCPA 1990	Town and Country Planning Act 1990.
TDA 1999	Trustee Delegation Act 1999.
TIA 1961	Trustee Investments Act 1961.
TLATA 1996	Trusts of Land and Appointment of Trustees Act 1996.
TMA 1970	Taxes Managment Act 1970.
TULR(C)A 1992	Trade Union and Labour Relations (Consolidation) Act 1992.

U

UCTA 1977	Unfair Contract Terms Act 1977.

V

VATA	Value Added Tax Act 1994.

W

WA 1837	Wills Act 1837.
WA 1968	Wills Act 1968.
WIA 1991	Water Industry Act 1991.
WRPA 1999	Welfare Reform and Pensions Act 1999.

X

Y

YJCEA 1999	Youth Justice and Criminal Evidence Act 1999.

Z

Table of abbreviations

Statutory Instruments / Law Society codes / FSA rules

A

AIEDPO 1986	Administration of Insolvent Estates of Deceased Persons Order 1986.
AJA(DA)O 2000	Access to Justice Act 1999 (Destination of Appeals) Order 2000.
ATAO(F)R 1988	Assured Tenancies and Agricultural Occupational (Forms) Regulations 1988.

B

C

CA(CD)R 1993	Commercial Agents (Council Directive) Regulations 1993.
CA(DTP)O 2000	Competition Act (Determination of Turnover for Penalties) Order 2000.
CA(EC)O 2000	Companies Act (Electronic Communications) Order 2000.
CA(LAER)O 2004	Competition Act 1998 (Land Agreements Exclusion and Revocation) Order 2004.
CA(SACMS)R 2000	Competition Act (Small Agreements and Conduct of Minor Significance) Regulations 2000.
CBNR 1981	Company and Business Names Regulations 1981.
CC(ANEE)R 1987	Crown Court (Advance Notice of Expert Evidence) Rules 1987.
CCFAR 2000	Collective Conditional Fee Agreements Regulations 2000.
CCR	County Court Rules (CPR Sch 2).
CDA(SOPE)R 2005	Crime and Disorder Act (Scope of Prosecution Evidence) Regulations 2005.
CDS(F)O 2001	Criminal Defence Service (Funding) Order 2001.
CDS(G2)R 2001	Criminal Defence Service (General)(No.2) Regulations 2001.
CDS(RDCO)R 2001	Criminal Defence Service (Recovery of Defence Costs Orders) Regulations 2001.
CDS(ROA)R 2001	Criminal Defence Service (Representation Order Appeals) Regulations 2001.
CFAO 2000	Conditional Fee Agreements Order 2000.
CITEPPOR 2005	Charge to Income Tax By Reference to Enjoyment of Property Previously Owned Regulations 2005.
CJA(N8)O 2005	Criminal Justice Act 2003 (Commencement No.8 and Transitional and Saving Provisions) Order 2005
CJJO 2001	Civil Jurisdiction and Judgments Order 2001.
CJJ(AICS)O 2001	Civil Jurisdiction and Judgments (Authentic Instruments and Court Settlements) Order 2001.
CL(E)R 2000	Contaminated Land (England) Regulations 2000.
C(LR)R 2004	Commonhold (Land Registration) Rules 2004.
CLS(CP)R 2000	Community Legal Service (Cost Protection) Regulations 2000.
CLS(F)R 2000	Community Legal Service (Financial) Regulations 2000.
CLS(C)R 2000	Community Legal Service (Costs) Regulations 2000.
CP(DS)R 2000	Consumer Protection (Distance Selling) Regulations 2000.
CPIA(DDTL)R 1997	Criminal Procedure and Investigations Act (Defence Disclosure Time Limits) Regulations 1997.
CPR	Civil Procedure Rules 1998.
CrPR	Criminal Procedure Rules 2005.
CR 2004	Commonhold Regulations 2004.
C(SFS)R 1995	Companies (Summary Financial Statement) Regulations 1995.

CT(IP)R 1998	Corporation Tax (Instalment Payments) Regulations 1998.	IS(IC)O 1977	Intestate Succession (Interest and Capitalisation) Order 1977.
		ISR 1998	Individual Savings Accounts Regulations 1998.

D

D(RPC)O 1996	Deregulation (Resolutions of Private Companies) Order 1996.
DR	Market Abuse Directive (Disclosure Rules) Instrument 2005.

IT(DA)(EE)R 2004	Inheritance Tax (Delivery of Accounts) (Exempted Estates) Regulations 2004.
IT(DA)(EE)(A)R 2006	Inheritance Tax (Delivery of Accounts) (Exempted Estates) (Amendment) Regulations 2006.
IT(PA)R 1996	Income Tax (Payments on Account) Regulations 1996.

E

EE(A)R 2006	Employment Equality (Age) Regulations 2006.
EPLLCR 2004	European Public Limited-Liability Company Regulations 2004

J

JD(RI)) 1993	Judgment Debt (Rate of Interest) Order 1993.

K

L

LLPR 2001	Limited Liability Partnership Regulations 2001.
LRR 2003	Land Registration Rules 2003.
LR(RA)O 1999	Lay Representatives (Right of Audience) Order 1999.
LT(C)(N)R 1995	Landlord and Tenant (Covenants) Act (Notices) Regulations 1995.
LTA(N)R 2004	Landlord and Tenant Act 1954, Part II (Notices) Regulations 2004.

F

FCR 2006	Fines Collection Regulations 2006
FS(DM)R 2004	Financial Services (Distance Marketing) Regulations 2004
FSMA(CRAWB)O 2001	Financial Services and Markets Act 2000 (Carrying on Regulated Actvities by Way of Business) Order 2001.
FSMA(E)O 2001	Financial Services and Markets Act (Exemption) Order 2001.
FSMA(FP)O 2001	Financial Services and Markets Act 2000 (Financial Promotion) Order 2001.
FSMA(RA)O 2001	Financial Services and Markets Act 2000 (Regulated Activities) Order 2001.

M

MLR	Money Laundering Regulations.

N

NA(AR)R 1992	National Assistance (Assessment of Resources) Regulations 1992.
NCPR 1987	Non-Contentious Probate Rules 1987.
NPR(RO)R 2000	National Police Records (Recordable Offences) Regulations 2000.

G

GR 1998	Groundwater Regulations 1998.
GS(IU)R 1998	Gas Safety (Installation and Use) Regulations 1998.

O

H

HCCCJO 1991	High Court and County Courts Jurisdiction Order 1991.
HCCCJ(A)O 1996	High Court and County Courts Jurisdiction (Amendment) Order 1996.
HIPR 2006	Home Information Pack Regulations 2006.

P

PO(CTL)R 1987	Prosecution of Offences (Custody Time Limits) Regulations 1987.
PPC(EW)R 2000	Pollution Prevention and Control (England and Wales) Regulations 2000.
PTWDR	Part Time Worker Discrimination Regulations.

I

IA(PP)O 2003	Insolvency Act 1986 (Prescribed Part) Order 2003.
I(A)R 2002	Insolvency (Amendment) Rules 2002.
IPO 1994	Insolvent Partnerships Order 1994.
I(P)R 1971	Indictments (Procedure) Rules 1971.
IR 1971	Indictment Rules 1971.
IR 1986	Insolvency Rules 1986.

Q

R

RSC	Rules of the Supreme Court (in CPR Sch 1).
RR(BT)(EW)O 2003	Regulatory Reform (Business Tenancies)(England and Wales) Order 2003.
RR(RO20MLP)O 2002	Regulatory Reform (Removal of 20 Member Limit in Partnerships etc.) Order 2002.

S

SAR 1998	Solicitors' Accounts Rules 1998.
SCICCC 1999	Solicitors' Costs Information and Client Care Code 1999.
S(CIPS)O 2005	Solicitors (Compensation for Inadequate Professional Services) Order 2005.
SDC 1995	Solicitors' Discrimination Code 1995.
SDLTAS(PDA)R 2005	Stamp Duty Land Tax Avoidance Schemes (Prescribed Descriptions of Arrangements) Regulations 2005.
SFS(S)R 2001	Solicitors' Financial Services (Scope) Rules 2001.
SIRC 1990	Solicitors' Introduction and Referral Code 1990.
SPC 2001	Solicitors' Publicity Code 2001.
SPR 1990	Solicitors' Practice Rules 1990.
SD(EI)R 1987	Stamp Duty (Exempt Instruments) Regulations 1987.
SRO 1994	Solicitors' Remuneration Order 1994.
SSC(I)R 2000	Social Security Contributions (Intermediaries) Regulations 2000.
SSGCR 2002	Sale and Supply of Goods to Consumers Regulations 2002.
SS(RB)R 1997	Social Security (Recovery of Benefit) Regulations 1997.
SS(RB)(A)R 1998	Social Security (Recovery of Benefits) (Appeals) Regulations 1997.

T

TAS(I)R 2004	Tax Avoidance Schemes (information) Regulations 2004.
TAS(I)(A)R 2006	Tax Avoidance Schemes (information) (Amendment) Regulations 2006.
TAS(PDA)R 2006	Tax Avoidance Schemes (Prescribed Descriptions of Arrangements) Regulations 2006.
TCP(GPD)O 1995	Town and Country Planning (General Permitted Development) Order 1995.
TCP(UC)O 1987	Town and Country Planning (Use Classes) Order 1987.
TU(PE)R 2006	Transfer of Undertakings (Protection of Employment) Regulations 2006.

U

UTCCR 1999	Unfair Terms in Consumer Contracts Regulations 1999.

V

VATR 1995	Value Added Tax Regulations 1995.

W-Z

Table of authorities
Cases

Case	Page

A

Allhusen v Whittel (1867) LR 4 Eq 295 . . . . 150, 160
Aluminium Industrie v Romalpa Aluminium Ltd [1976] 2 All ER 552 316

B

Banks v Goodfellow (1870) LR 5 QB 549 144
Barclays Mercantile Business Finance Ltd v Mawson (Inspector of Taxes) [2005] STC 1 142
Barsted v Jones (1964) 124 *JP* 400 465
Bell Houses Ltd v City Properties Ltd [1966] 2 QB 656 257
Re Benjamin [1902] 1 Ch 723 169
Bevan Ashford v Geoff Yeandle (Contractors) Ltd [1999] Ch 239 22
Biguzzi v Rank Leisure [1999] 1 WLR 1926 341
Bolkiah v KPMG [1999] 2 WLR 215 (HL) 11
Re Bowes (1887) 37 Ch D 128 170
Bowman v Fels [2005] EWCA Civ 226 (CA) 6
Brady v Brady [1989] AC 755 282
Bratty v AG for Northern Ireland [1963] AC 386 497
Burns v Siemens Brothers Dynamo Works Ltd [1919] 1 Ch 225 260
Bushell v Faith [1970] 1 All ER 53 . . . . 258, 268, 269

C

Calderbank v Calderbank [1975] All ER 333 385
Callery v Gray [2002] UKHL 28 22
Charterhouse Investment Trust Ltd v Tempest Diesels Ltd [1986] BCLC 1 282
Chief Constable of Norfolk v Clayton [1983] 2 AC 473 465
Clemens v Clemens Brothers Ltd [1976] 2 All ER 268 . . . . 260, 263
Commission v Belgium [1980] ECR 3881 326
Commission v Denmark [1989] CMLR 619 314
Commission v Ireland [1982] ECR 4005 314
Commission for the New Towns v Cooper (Great Britain) Limited [1995] 26 *EG* 129 201
Corbett v Newey [1996] 2 All ER 914 CA 144

D

D v NSPCC [1978] AC 171 505
Douglas & Others v Hello! Ltd (No.1) [2001] QB 967 34
DPP v Kilbourne [1973] AC 729 505
DPP v Wood [2006] EWHC 32 495

E

Re Everest [1975] Fam 44 145

F

Flanders v Clarke (1747) 3 Atk 509 170
Foss v Harbottle (1843) 2 Hare 461 263

Case	Page

G

Gasus Dosier und Fördertechnik GmbH v Netherlands (1995) 20 EHRR 403 142
Re Goodchild (deceased) [1996] 1 All ER 670 Ch D 145
Gravier v City of Liege [1985] ECR 593 326
Greer v Downs Supply Co [1927] 2 KB 28 323
Greville v Brown (1859) 7 HLC 689 166
Griffin & Amos v Ferard (1835) 1 Curt 97 144

H

Hadley v Baxendale (1854) 9 Ex Ch 341 242
Halloran v Delaney [2002] EWCA Civ 1258 22
Halsey v Milton Keynes NHS Trust and Steel v Joy [2004] EWCA 576 335
Hart v O'Connor [1985] 2 All ER 880 195
Hart & McLean 1998 CLY 1056 442
Heyting v Dupont [1964] 2 All ER 273 263
Hobbs v Knight (1838) 1 Curt 768 145
Re Hodson *ex parte* Richardson (1818) 3 Madd 138 149
Hollins v Russell and other appeals [2003] EWCA Civ 718 23
Howe v Dartmouth (1802) 7 Ves 137 .... 150, 160
Hurlingham Estates Ltd v Wilde & Partners [1997] STC 627 viii

I

Ingram v IRC [1999] STC 9 142
Inland Revenue Commissioners v Scottish Provident Institution [2005] STC 15 142
International Drilling Fluids Ltd v Louisville Investments (Uxbridge) Ltd [1986] 1 EGLR 39 231
Re Ipswich Justices *ex parte* Callaghan 159 *JP* 748 462
IRC v Willoughby [1997] STC 995 HL 142
Re Irvine [1929] 2 IR 485 145

J

Johnson v Agnew [1979] 1 All ER 883 242

K

Re Keck and Mithouard (Joined Cases C-267/91 and C-268/91) [1993] ECR I-6097; [1995] 1 CEC 298 314
Kennewell v Dye [1949] Ch 517 169
Khatibi v DPP [2004] 168 *JP* 361 32
Kuruma, Son of Kariu v The Queen [1955] AC 197 504

L

Luisi v Ministero del Tesoro [1984] ECR 377 326

M

McCausland and Another v Duncan Lawrie Limited (1996) *The Times* 18 June CA 202
Mallalieu v Drummond [1983] 2 AC 861 .... 81, 104
Marquess of Winchester's Case (1598) 6 Co Rep 32a 144
Martin v DPP [2000] 164 *JP* 405 487
Re Midgley [1955] Ch 576 166
Re Moles [1981] Crim LR 170 455

N

National Provincial Building Society and Others v UK [1997] STC 1466 142
Nederlandse Bakkerij Stichting v Edah BV [1986] ECR 3359 314
Neptune (Vehicle Washing Equipment) Ltd v Fitzgerald [1995] 3 All ER 811 Ch D 272
North of Scotland Bank v IRC 1 SC 149 127

Case	Page

O

O'Neill v Phillips [1999] 1 WLR 1092. ...263
Re Owers, Public Trustee v Death [1941] Ch 389. ...170

P

Panorama v Fidelis [1971] 2 QB 711. ...273
Parinv (Hatfield) Limited v IRC [1998] STC 305. ...130
Parker v Felgate (1883) 8 PD 171. ...144
Parkins v Hawkshaw (1817) 2 Stark NP 239. ...505
Patel v Daybells [2001] EWCA Civ 1229 CA. ...205, 211
Re Peter Vriend [1980] ECR 327. ...314
Re Pitcairn [1896] 2 Ch 199. ...150
Practice Direction (Submission of no Case) [1962] 1 WLR 227. ...473
Procureur du Roi v Dassonville [1974] ECR 837. ...314
Prudential Assurance Co v Newman Industries Ltd (No.2) [1982] Ch 204. ...263

Q

R

Re R A Noble (Clothing) Ltd [1983] BCLC 273. ...263
R v Andrews (Donald) [1987] AC 281. ...510
R v Argent (1997) Cr App R 27. ...443
R v Balloz (1908) 1 Cr App R 258. ...497
R v Betts (2001) 2 Cr App R 16. ...443
R v Bowden (1999) 2 Cr App R 176. ...442
R v Cheema [1994] 1 WLR 147. ...502
R v Condron [1997] 1 WLR 827. ...442
R v Cowan; Gayle; Ricciardi [1995] 3 WLR 818 CA. ...443, 511
R v DPP *ex parte* Lee [1999] 2 All ER 737. ...495
R v Flax Bourton Magistrates' Court *ex parte* Commissioner of Customs & Excise (1996) 160 *JP* 481. ...462
R v Forbes [2005] EWCA Crim 2069. ...491
R v Fulling [1987] QB 426. ...508
R v Galbraith [1981] 1 WLR 1039. ...473
R v Garbett (1847) 2 C & K 474. ...505
R v Glen Parva Young Offender Institution *ex parte* G (1998) QB 877. ...458
R v Goodyear [2005] EWCA Crim 888. ...491
R v Hall (2001) 2 Cr App R 16. ...443
R v Hanson, Gilmore and Pickstone [2005] 1 WLR 3169. ...499
R v Hart & McLean 1998 CLY 1056. ...442
R v Henn and Darby [1979] ECR 3795. ...314
R v Knight [2004] 1 WLR 340. ...443
R v Makanjuola; R v Easton [1995] 2 Cr App R 469. ...502
R v Miller [1952] 2 All ER 667. ...505
R v Mills [1995] 3 All ER 865. ...510
R v Newton (1982) 77 Cr App R 13. ...492
R v Sang [1980] AC 402. ...504
R v Shaw (1888) 16 Cox 503. ...498
R v Taylor [1999] Crim LR 77. ...442
R v Taylor (2006) *The Times* 7 February. ...506
R v Turnbull [1977] QB 224. ...502
R v Turner [1995] 1 WLR 264. ...505
R v Ward (1993) 1 WLR 619. ...474
Ratten v R [1972] AC 378. ...510
Re Recher [1972] Ch 526. ...148
Rewe-Zentrale AG v Bundesmonopolverwaltung für Branntwein (Re Cassis de Dijon) [1979] ECR 649. ...314
Rewe-Zentrale GmbH v Landwirtschaftskammer [1975] ECR 843. ...314
Roberts v Pocock (1748) 4 Ves 150. ...171
Roberts v Walker (1830) 1 R & My 752. ...166
Royal Bank of Scotland v Etridge [2001] UKHL 44. ...196

Case	Page

S

Seal v Claridge (1881) 7 QBD 516 204
Re Segelman (deceased) [1995] 3 All ER 676 Ch D 168
Re Sevenoaks Stationers (Retail) Ltd [1991] Ch 164 269
Smith v Eric S Bush [1990] 1 AC 831 189
Soderman v The King [1936] 2 All ER 1138 497
Solle v Butcher [1950] 1 KB 671 242
South Australia Asset Management Corporation v York Montague Limited [1996] 3 All ER 365 HL 200
Speyer Brothers v IRC [1908] AC 92 127
Re Stevens, Cooke v Stevens [1898] 1 Ch 162 158
Stoke-on-Trent City Council v B & Q plc [1993] 1 All ER 481 314
Suleman v Shahisavari [1989] 2 All ER 460 201

T

Re Tankard [1942] Ch 69 169
Re Taylor's Estate [1969] Ch 245 166
Thomas v Bunn [1991] 1 AC 362 425
Three Rivers District Council v Bank of England (Disclosure) (No.3) [2003] EWCA Civ 474 405
Toohey v Metropolitan Police Commissioner [1965] AC 595 498
Torfaen Borough Council v B & Q plc [1989] ECR 765 314
Townson v Tickell (1819) B & Ald 31 141

U

UCB Corporate Services v Halifax (SW) Ltd [1999] CPLR 691 341
Re Unisoft Group Ltd (No.2) [1994] BCC 766 267
United Brands v Commission [1978] ECR 207 310

V

W

Walker v Symonds (1818) 3 Swan 1 170
Re Whitehead [1913] 2 Ch 56 171
Whittal v Kirby [1947] KB 194 488
Williams and another v National Life Health Foods Limited & Richard Mistlin [1998] 1 WLR 830 254
Wright v Howell (1947) 92 *Sol Jo* 26 CA 233

X–Z

Table of authorities

Statutes/Bills/European and International law

Statute	Page

A

Access to Justice Act 1999. . . . . 16, 22
    s 11. 422
    s 29. 22
    Sch 2. 16
    Sch 3. . . . . 20, 21
Access to Neighbouring Land Act 1992. 216
Administration of Estates Act 1925. 148
    s 4. 166
    s 7. 170
    s 25. . . . . 156, 160
    s 33. . . . . 151, 166
        (1)–(2). 166
        (7). 166
    s 34(1). 164
    s 35. 148
        (1). 164
    s 36. 213
        (4). 165, 213
    s 41. . . . . 150, 160
    s 42. 150
    s 44. 160
    s 46. 152
        (2A). 152
    s 47. 151
    Sch I
        Part I(i)–(ii) 166
        Part II 164
    Sch II
        Part I(i)–(ii) 166
Administration of Estates Act 1971
    s 9. . . . . 156, 160
Administration of Estates (Small Payments)
    Act 1965. 155
Administration of Justice Act 1920 423
Administration of Justice Act 1956
    s 37. 426
Administration of Justice Act 1969
    s 12. 430
Administration of Justice Act 1982
    ss 20–21. 168
Administration of Justice Act 1985 60
    s 48. 168
Adoption Act 1976 xv
Adoption and Children Act 2002. xv
    s 67. 165
    s 69(2). 165

Statute	Page

    s 72. 165
Anti-social Behaviour Act 2003
    s 87. 434
Apportionment Act 1870
    s 2. . . . . 150, 160
Arbitration Act 1996. 336
Asylum and Immigration Act 1996
    s 8. 330
Attachment of Earnings Act 1971 429
    s 7 429

B

Bail Act 1976
    s 3. 458
        (6ZA)–(6ZAA) 458
    s 3A. 450
    s 4 455
        (8) 455
        (9) 457
    s 5B. 457
    s 6 . . . . 459, 512
        (2)–(7) 459
        (10)–(12) 459
    s 6A. 458
    s 7 458
        (1)–(2) 459
    Sch I 450
        Part I 456
            para 2. . . . . 456, 457
            para 2A. 456
            paras 3–5 456
            para 6. . . . . 456, 457
            para 9. 457
            para 9AA 457
        Part II. 457
            paras 2–5 457
Bail (Amendment) Act 1993
    s 1(1). 457
Bank of England Act 1998. 199
Banking Act 1987 61
Building Act 1984 225
Building Societies Act 1986. . . . . 61, 63
    Sch 4
        para 2(3). 214
Business Names Act 1985. . . . . 244, 245, 255, 291
    ss 1–5 244
    s 7 244

C

Statute	Page
Capital Allowances Act 2001	81
Parts 3–3A	93
Part 4A	93
Parts 5–5A	93
Parts 6–10	93
s 11	
(1)	92
(4)	92
s 15(1)	92
ss 21–23	92
s 44	93
ss 45A–45J	93
ss 46–49	93
s 52	93
s 55	91
s 56	91, 93
s 61	91, 289
ss 70A-YJ	92
ss 74–89	91
s 91	93
ss 93–96	93
ss 98–100	93
s 101	91
s 102	93
s 107	91
ss 127–128	91
ss 172–204	92
ss 213–233	92
s 264	90
s 266	289
s 267(2)	289
s 271	92
ss 274–281	92
s 292	92
s 309	92
s 310	93
s 538	91
Charging Orders Act 1979	428
s 5(5)	428
Charities Act 1992	195
s 32	195
Children Act 1989	147
s 5(3)	147
s 6(3A)–(3B)	147
Civil Evidence Act 1968	
s 11	363
Civil Evidence Act 1972	
s 3(1)–(2)	408
Civil Evidence Act 1995	409
s 1	409, 410
s 2	410
s 3	409
s 5	409
s 6	409, 415, 416
s 7	409
s 9	408
(1)–(2)	410
Civil Jurisdiction and Judgments Act 1982	337, 423
Civil Partnership Act 2004	xv, 145, 171
Sch 4	
para 3	144
para 5	171
Civil Procedure Act 1997	
s 7	381
Coal Industry Act 1994	216
s 38	217
s 49	217
s 51	217
Commonhold and Leasehold Reform Act 2002	234, 239
s 1	219, 239
s 3	239
s 9	239
(3)(f)	239
s 26(b)–(c)	239
Sch 2	239
Commons Registration Act 1965	210, 216, 217
Commons Registration Act 2006	216
Companies Act 1985	9, 119, 120, 243, 253, 254, 255, 266, 269, 278, 282, 296
Part VII	253
ss 2–3	257
s 4	257, 284
s 5	257
s 8	258
s 9	258, 284
s 14	258, 260, 263
s 25	256, 289
s 26	257, 289
s 27	289
s 28	257, 284, 289
s 29	257, 289
s 30	256, 289
s 32	257
s 35	274, 275, 276
(2)	261, 274
s 35A	194, 274, 275
s 35B	274, 275
s 36A	203, 204, 253
(5)	186
s 42	257
s 43	287
s 44	286
s 45	287
s 80	258, 259, 265, 279, 284
s 80A	259
s 81	286
s 89	258, 259, 269, 279
s 91	286
s 95	284, 286
s 100	278
s 103	286
s 121	284
s 130	278
ss 135–137	281, 284

Statute	Page
s 142	286
s 151	282, 286
s 152(1)	282
s 153	282
s 155	282, 285
ss 156–158	282
ss 159–159A	281
s 162	281, 285, 286
ss 162A–162D	286
s 164	281
s 168	281
s 169	127
(4)	281
s 171	281, 286
s 173	281
s 183	280
s 185	261
s 221	253
s 224	253
(3)	259
s 225	253
s 226	253, 270, 283
s 226A	270
ss 227–232	253
s 233	253, 270
s 234	271
s 234ZA	270
ss 234ZZA–234ZZB	271
s 238	253
s 240	261
s 241	253, 270, 271
s 242	253, 270
s 244	253, 270, 271, 286
s 246	253, 270, 273
s 246A	253, 270
s 247	93, 253, 270, 273, 301
s 249A	273
s 252	259
s 263	283, 290
s 275	283
s 277	283
s 282	286
s 283	273
s 288	271
s 293	286
s 303	258, 261, 265, 268, 284
s 304(1)	268
s 305	259, 271
s 309	271
s 312	271, 285
s 317	267, 270, 272, 277
s 318	267
s 319	267, 271, 284
s 320	271, 284
s 322B	272
s 324	280
s 325	271, 280
s 330	272, 282, 286
s 331	286
s 342	286

Statute	Page
ss 348–349	253, 259
ss 350–351	259
s 352	260, 261
s 359	260
s 363	253, 254, 271
s 364	271
s 364A	271
s 366	261, 264
s 366A	259, 261, 264
s 367	261
s 368	261
(3)	261
s 369	261, 264
(3)(b)	261
(4)	259
s 370	261, 266
s 371	261
s 372	266
(3)	264
(5)	266
s 373	261, 266
s 376	261
s 378	303
(3)	259
s 379	264, 268
s 379A	259, 261, 284
(2A)	264
s 380	265, 284, 285
s 381A	261, 265
(3)	265
s 381B	265
(2)	265
(4)	265
s 382	266
(1)	272
s 382B	266
s 383	261
s 384	254, 273
s 385	254
s 385A	273
s 386	259
s 390	265
s 391	273, 284
s 392	273
s 394	273
s 395	278, 305
ss 396–397	278
s 399	253
ss 403–404	278
s 458	254, 305
s 459	261, 263
s 461(1)–(2)	263
s 463	277
s 652	297
(6)(a)	297
s 653	297
s 711	257
ss 723B–723F	267
s 725	353
s 727	274

Statute	Page
s 741	267
Sch 4	253, 270
Schs 8–8A	253, 270
Sch 15A	265
Companies Act 1989	257, 278, 430
Companies Acts	253, 256, 287
Company and Business Names (Chamber of Commerce Etc.) Act 1999	257
Company Directors Disqualification Act 1986	253, 269
s 11	296
Competition Act 1998	190, 310, 311, 313, 325
Part I	190, 359
s 6	311
ss 9–11	311
ss 25–26	313
ss 31–31E	313
s 36	313
ss 39–40	313
s 60	310
Consumer Credit Act 1974	377
Consumer Protection Act 1987	325
Contracts (Rights of Third Parties) Act 1999	246, 322
County Courts Act 1984	357, 426
s 15	357
s 23	357
s 40	358, 359
ss 41–42	359
s 51	364
ss 52–53	381, 402
s 69	363
s 74	425
Courts Act 2003	
s 97	484
Sch 5	484
Courts and Legal Services Act 1990	25
ss 21–26	27
ss 27–28	32
s 58	22
(3)(a)	22
(10)	22
s 58A(1)	22
ss 92–93	27
Sch 4	2
Crime and Disorder Act 1998	478, 512
ss 28–32	479
s 41	470
s 51	461, 467, 468
(1)	468
(3)–(5)	468
(7)–(9)	468
(11)	468
s 51A	467, 468
(3)(d)	467
s 51B	468, 469
ss 51C–51D	468
s 52(1)	469
s 52A	469
ss 65–66	434

Statute	Page
Sch 3	469
para 2	470
paras 6–7	470
Criminal Appeal Act 1968	494
ss 1–2	493
s 9	493
s 11	493
Criminal Appeal Act 1995	493, 494
Part II	494
ss 26–28	494
Criminal Damage Act 1971	
s 1(1)	479
Criminal Defence Service Act 2006	
s 1	20
ss 2–3	21
Criminal Evidence Act 1898	
s 1	503
(2)	504, 505
Criminal Injuries Compensation Act 1995	336
Criminal Justice Act 1967	
s 9	464
(1)	508
s 10	497
s 22	455
Criminal Justice Act 1982	
s 37	252, 439
Criminal Justice Act 1987	
s 4	467
Criminal Justice Act 1988	
Part IV	494
ss 23–24	473
s 30(2)	510
ss 33–34	493
ss 35–36	493, 494
s 40(1)	462
s 41(1)	462
Criminal Justice Act 2003	487, 501
Part 6	467
s 9	508
s 14(1)	456
s 15(1)	456
s 16	458
s 18	457
s 19	456
s 22	434, 512
ss 23–27	434
s 41	454, 460, 461, 462, 467, 468, 490
s 42	467
ss 98–99	499
s 100	501
s 101	499
ss 102–106	500
ss 107–108	499
ss 109–110	501
s 112	499
(2)–(3)	501
s 114	506
(d)	506, 507
(1)–(3)	506
s 115	506

Statute	Page
s 116	507
s 117	507, 509
s 118	499, 506, 510
ss 119–121	509
s 124	507
s 126	506
s 128	508
s 129	506
s 133	497
ss 137–139	497
s 142	478
s 143(1)–(3)	478
s 144	478, 491
s 145	478, 479
s 146	478
s 147	485, 486
s 148	485, 486
(1)–(2)	485
ss 149–151	485, 486
s 152(2)	480
ss 153–155	480
s 156	485
(1)	480
(3)–(5)	492
s 161	492
ss 161A–161B	478
s 162	484
s 163	439, 484
s 164	484
(1)–(3)	484
s 165	484
ss 166–173	491
s 174	492
s 177	485, 486
(1)–(3)	486
(6)	486
ss 178–180	485, 486
s 181	479, 481, 512
s 182	479, 512
ss 183–186	479
ss 189–194	482
ss 199–223	486
s 224	467
s 225	481
s 226(3)	467
s 227	480
s 228(2)	467
s 229	480
s 230	481
s 240	480
s 270	492
s 278	489
s 282	439
ss 300–301	484
s 313	494
Sch 3	454, 460, 461, 462, 471
paras 21–28	490, 492
Sch 5	480
Sch 8	485
Sch 12	482, 483
Sch 15	481
Sch 18	481
Criminal Justice and Court Services Act 2000	
s 61	490
Criminal Justice and Police Act 2001	
s 2	434
s 45	267
s 131	458
Criminal Justice and Public Order Act 1994	442, 502, 511
s 25	450, 455
s 32	502, 504
s 33	502
s 34	442, 443, 511
s 35	466, 475, 511
ss 36–37	442, 511
s 38	442, 511
(3)	443
Sch 10	
para 2	503
Criminal Procedure Act 1865	
s 3	498, 501
ss 4–6	498
Criminal Procedure (Attendance of Witnesses) Act 1965	
s 2	471
Criminal Procedure and Investigations Act 1996	460, 461, 466
Parts II–III	432
s 1	432, 464, 495
(1)–(2)	495
ss 2–4	432, 464, 495
s 5	432, 464, 495, 496
ss 5A–5D	495
s 6	432, 464, 495, 496
ss 6A–6D	495
s 6E(2)	495
s 7	432, 464, 495
s 7A	495
ss 8–9	432, 464, 495
ss 10–18	432, 464, 495, 496
ss 19–21	432, 464, 495
s 23(1)	433
ss 28–30	475, 477
s 31	475, 477
(8)	477
ss 32–38	475, 477
ss 39–43	475
s 53	489
s 66	442

D

Statute	Page
Damages Act 1996	334
s 2(4)	386
Data Protection Act 1998	329
Disability Discrimination Act 1995	329

Statute	Page

Domestic Violence, Crime and Victims Act 2004
   s 10 437
   s 14 478

E

Electricity Act 1989 60
Employment Act 2002 329
Employment Relations Act 1999 328
Employment Rights Act 1996
   s 1 328
   ss 86–97 330
   s 98 330
     (2) 330
   ss 99–181 330
Enduring Powers of Attorney Act 1985 214
   s 6 214
   s 9(4) 214
Enterprise Act 2002 297
   Part 3 308
   ss 6–8 310
   ss 71–95 308
   ss 188–202 313
Environmental Protection Act 1990
   Part IIA 189
Equal Pay Act 1970 329
Equality Act 2006 329
Estate Agents Act 1979
   s 16 198
Evidence Act 1851
   s 3 505

F

Family Law Act 1996 .... 181, 191, 220, 295
   ss 30–31 191
   Sch 4
     para 4(1)(a)–(c) 191
     para 5(1) 191
Family Law Reform Act 1969
   s 15 165
Family Law Reform Act 1987
   s 18 158
   s 19(1) 165
   s 21 158
Fatal Accidents Act 1976 ..... 359, 364, 383, 391
Finance Act 1930
   s 42 128
Finance Act 1931
   s 28 .... 186, 208
Finance Act 1971
   s 64 128
Finance Act 1985
   s 83(1) 128
   s 84(1) 128
   s 85
     (4) 128
     (6)–(7) 128
Finance Act 1986
   s 66 127

Statute	Page

   ss 75–77 128
   s 78 129
   s 79 129
     (4) 129, 131
     (5) 129
     (7A) 129
   s 86(4) 131
   s 87 132
     (1) 132
     (3) 132
     (6) 132
   ss 88A–88B 132
   s 89A 132
   s 91(1) 132
   s 92 131
   s 93
     (3)–(5) 131
     (6)(a) 131
   s 99(5) 131
   ss 102–102C 100
Finance Act 1990
   s 25 86
Finance Act 1996 106
   s 80(1) 106
   s 81 105
   s 82(2) 109
   s 83(2)–(3) 109
   s 84 105
     (1)(a) 106
   ss 85A–85C 105
   ss 87–87A 105
   ss 91A–91G 105
   s 94A 106
   Sch 8
     para 1 109
     para 3 109
   Sch 9
     para 6(1) 105
     para 13 105
Finance Act 1997
   s 39 78
Finance Act 1998 138
   Sch 18
     para 2 119
     para 3(1)–(2) 119
     paras 7–8 119
     para 11 119
     para 14 120
     paras 17–24 120
     paras 36–49 120
Finance Act 1999
   s 101(2) 127
   s 109 130
   s 112 130
   Sch 13 126
   Part I
     para 1 127
     para 3 127
     para 7 127

Statute	Page
Part III	
para 1	127
para 7	127
Part IV	129
para 2	128
para 3	129
Sch 15	126, 127
Sch 17	130
Finance Act 2000	110
Sch 15	107
Sch 20	
paras 1–16	110
Finance Act 2001	
Sch 22	104
Sch 25	250
Finance Act 2002	106, 107
Sch 12	110
Part 1	110
paras 8–11	110
Schs 26–28	106, 109
Sch 29	106
Finance Act 2003	
Part 4	136
s 3A	134
s 43	133
s 44	
(3)	133
(4)	133, 136
(5)(a)–(b)	133
(6)–(7)	133
s 44A	134
(3)	136
s 45	136
s 45A	134, 136
ss 46–47	134
s 48	133
s 49	134
s 55	135
s 57A	135
ss 60–61	135
ss 63–64	135
s 64A	134
s 65	135, 289
ss 66–67	135
s 69	135
ss 71–75	135
s 76	
(1)	136
(3)	136
s 77	136
s 79	208
(1)–(3)	136
ss 81–81A	136
s 85	136
s 87	136
s 90	136, 208
s 117	136
s 125	126
Sch 3	136
paras 1–4	134

Statute	Page
Sch 4	
paras 1–2	134
paras 7–8	134
paras 10–11	134
paras 13–15	134
para 17	134
Sch 5	
para 2	135
Schs 6–6A	135
Sch 7	
paras 1–13	135
Schs 8–9	135
Sch 10	
paras 3–5	136
Sch 12	136
Sch 15	133
Part 3	126
Sch 17A	135
Sch 19	186, 208
Sch 31	110
Finance Act 2004	126
Part 4	331
Part 7	142
s 50	105
s 55	121
ss 126–130	89
ss 131–133	109
Sch 15	139
Finance Act 2005	
ss 23–29	87
ss 30–33	87, 96, 99
ss 34–45	87
s 103	94, 102, 128
Finance Act 2006	xv, 85, 92, 139
s 155	103
Finance (No.2) Act 2005	xv, 105
Part 4	288
Financial Services and Markets Act	
2000	28, 30, 199
Part IV	29, 63
Part XX	28, 30
s 2(2)–(3)	28
ss 3–6	28
s 11	28
s 19	29
s 21	29
s 23	29, 30
ss 24–28	29
s 327	28
(6)	30
ss 328–329	30
s 332(4)	30
Sch 2	
Part II	29
Foreign Judgments (Reciprocal Enforcement) Act 1933	423
Freedom of Information Act 2000	11

G

H

Health and Safety at Work Act 1974 329
    s 37 232
Health and Social Care Act 2001
    s 55 140
Health and Social Security Administration
Act 1983
    ss 21–22 140
    s 24 140
Highways Act 1980
    s 38 226
Hire Purchase Act 1964
    s 27(5)(a) 317
Homicide Act 1957
    s 2(2) 497
Housing Act 1985
    Part II 233
    Part 5 .... 209, 210
    s 171A 209, 210
Housing Act 1988
    s 1(1) 233
    s 5(2) 233
    s 6A 233
    s 7 233
    ss 8–8A 234
    s 9A 235
    s 19A 233
    ss 20–20A 233
    s 21 .... 233, 234, 235
    Sch 2 235
    Sch 2A 233
Housing Act 1996
    s 17 235
    s 22 234
    s 81 234
    s 82A 235
    s 83 234
    ss 101–102 235
    ss 144A–144P 235
    s 148 235
    Sch 2
        Part III 235
    Sch 6 234
Housing Act 2004 183
    Part 2 234
    Part 5 183
    s 72 234
    s 148(1) 183
    s 151 183
    s 153 183
    ss 155–157 183
    s 160 183
    ss 167–168 183
    s 170 183
    Sch 8 183
Human Rights Act 1998 .... 34, 142, 329
    s 3 34
    s 4 .... 34, 359
    ss 5–6 34
    s 7(5) 34
    s 10 34
    s 19 34
    Sch 2 34

I

Immigration, Asylum and Nationality Act
2006
    s 21 330
Income and Corporation Taxes Act
1988 .... 112, 114
    s 1(2)
        (a)–(aa) 87
        (b) 87
    s 1A 111
        (1A) 111
    s 1B 111
    s 7(2) 119
    s 11(3) 119
    s 13 108
    s 13A(2) 113
    s 15 104
    s 17 106
    s 18 104
    s 34 104
    s 35 106
    s 38 106
    s 54 106
    s 74(1) 104
    s 117 89
    s 118 109
    s 118ZA 90
    ss 118ZB–118ZO 89
    ss 155–156 107
    s 208 111
    s 209(2)(d)–(e) 105
    s 219 282
        (1)(a)–(b) 282
        (2) 282
    s 220 282
        (1) 282
        (5) 282
    s 221 282
    s 222 282
        (1) 282
    ss 223–224 282
    s 231B 111, 114
    s 246(3)–(4) 90
    ss 256–257 87
    s 257A 87
        (5) 87
    s 265 87
    ss 289–312 .... 89, 137
    s 338 107
    s 338B 107
    s 339 107
    s 349(1)–(2) 82

Statute	Page
s 353	86
(2)–(3)	90
s 358	161
ss 360–360A	86, 114
s 361	86
s 362	86, 291
s 363	86, 114
s 364	86
s 379A	89
s 380	89
s 381	89
s 382(4)	89
ss 384–385	89
s 386	89, 289
s 388	89
s 392A	109
s 393	109
(5)	109
s 393A	109
ss 394–396	109
s 414	112
(5)	112
s 415	112
s 416	112, 114
(2)	114
s 417	
(1)	112
(5)	112
s 418	113
(3)	113
s 419	82, 113, 119
s 420	82, 113
(2)	113
s 421	82, 113
s 480A	82
ss 502A-502L	192
s 574	86
ss 587B–587C	86
s 686	87
(1AA)	87
(6)	161
s 686D	87
s 687	87
ss 703–709	111
s 747(4)(a)	119
s 787	105
ss 788–790	119
s 837A(2)–(6)	110
s 839	134
s 840	112, 114
s 842AA	89, 137
s 848	90
s 850	90
s 854(1)	90
Sch A	92, 104, 109
Sch D	104
case I	104, 105
case II	105
case III	105, 106
case V	104, 109

Statute	Page
case VI	104, 109
Income Tax (Earnings and Pensions) Act 2003	
Part 2	83
Part 3	83, 113
Parts 4–7	83
Parts 9–11	83
s 1	80
s 6	83
s 7	88
(4)–(6)	83
ss 9–12	83
ss 14–41	83
ss 49–56	86, 291
s 62	83
ss 70–113	84
ss 114–171	85
ss 175–177	85
ss 179–180	85
ss 192–196	85
s 197	85, 88
s 198	85
(2)	88
s 199	85, 88
s 200	85
(2)–(4)	88
s 201	85
s 202	85, 88
s 203	85
(2)	85
ss 204–207	85
ss 208–210	85, 88
ss 211–214	80, 85, 88
s 215	85, 88
s 216	84
ss 217–218	84, 88
s 219	84
s 220	84, 89
ss 229–238	85
ss 240–241	85
ss 243–248	85
ss 250–265	85
ss 271–289	85
ss 306–307	85
ss 309–311	85
s 313	85
ss 316–317	85
ss 318–318D	85
ss 319–320	85
s 320A	85
ss 321–325	85
ss 327–331	83
ss 336–341	83
s 342	83, 84
ss 343–344	84
ss 346–350	84
ss 356–358	84
s 359	83
s 367	84
ss 370–372	84
s 377	84

Statute	Page
s 380	89
ss 386–416	83
ss 471–484	83
ss 488–519	83
ss 521–541	83
s 574	86
s 677	80
s 687	86
Income Tax (Trading and Other Income) Act 2005	
Parts 2–3	80
Part 4	80, 282
Part 5	80, 161
Part 8	80
s 3	80
s 24	81
s 25	80
s 28	81
ss 32–35	81
ss 45–47	81
ss 53–55	81
ss 57–59	81
s 69	81
ss 73–76	81
ss 81–82	81
s 87	81
s 96	80
ss 148A–148J	192
ss 159–160	81
ss 221–225	81
s 242	289
s 263	80
s 266	81
s 272	81
ss 276–307	81
s 365	80
s 383	82, 113
s 397	82, 111
s 415	82, 113
ss 416–421	113
s 574	80
ss 691–692	80
s 725	80
s 727	80
s 744	80
s 751	80
s 776	80
s 785	80
s 803	80
ss 852–853	82
Inheritance (Provision for Family and Dependants) Act 1975	167, 168, 169
Inheritance Tax Act 1984	
s 2	101
s 3A	101
s 5	103
(3)	102
s 18	102
s 20	102
s 21	102, 138

Statute	Page
ss 22–26	102
ss 30–35	102
ss 46A–46B	103
s 49	101
s 49A	103, 139
s 49B	103
s 51	139
s 59	101, 137
ss 64–69	138
s 71A	103, 139
ss 71D–71F	139
s 89B	103
s 94	112
(1)	113
s 98(1)	113
ss 105–106	102
ss 115–130	102
s 141	102
s 142	141
s 160	101
s 162	102
ss 167–168	101
s 174	101
ss 178–198	101
s 199	100
s 200	100, 103
s 202(1)	113
s 204	100
(8)	100
s 211	163
s 218A	141
s 226	118
s 227	118
(4)	118
ss 233–234	118
s 239(4)	162
s 267A	254
s 268	139
s 505	102
Insolvency Act 1986	213, 254, 296, 297
ss 1–4A	301
ss 5–7	301
s 46	278
s 84	285, 303
s 85	303
s 89	303
s 91	303
s 94	303
(3)	303
ss 98–100	303
s 106	303
(3)	303
s 109	303
s 122	
(a)–(f)	304
(g)	261, 304
s 125	304
ss 131–132	304
s 136	304
(5)	304

Statute	Page
s 146	304
s 175	304
s 176A	304
s 178	305
s 183	305
s 188	304
s 201	303
s 202	304
s 213	274, 290, 305
s 214	254, 274, 290, 305
s 214A	254
ss 238–239	305
s 245	305
s 252	292
s 253	293
(5)	292
s 255(6)	293
s 256	
(1)	293
(4)	293
ss 256A–258	293
s 262	292
s 262A	293
ss 263–263A	293
s 267	294
s 272	294
s 279	294
s 281	294
s 281A	296
s 283(2)	295
s 283A	295
s 284	295
ss 287–288	294
ss 293–294	294
s 306	294
s 313A	295
ss 315–316	295
s 328	296
ss 336–338	295
ss 339–341	140, 295
ss 346–347	295
s 356	296
s 360	296
s 378	285
s 386	296
s 423	140, 295, 305
ss 424–425	140
Sch 4	304
Sch 4A	296
Sch 6	296
Sch A1	301, 302
Sch B1	
para 8(1)(a)–(b)	297
paras 10–11	298
para 12	298
(2)–(3)	298
paras 13–25	298
para 26	298
(3)	298
para 27	298

Statute	Page
para 28	298
(2)	299
paras 29–33	298
para 34	298, 299
paras 39–43	299
para 44(2)	298
para 45	299, 300
paras 46–49	300
para 52	300
paras 54–55	300
para 59	299
para 61	299
paras 65–67	299
paras 70–71	299
para 73	300
Insolvency (No.2) Act 1994	213
International Organisations Act 1968	377
International Organisations Act 1981	377
Intestates' Estates Act 1952	
s 5	153
Sch II	153

J

Judgments Act 1838	
s 17	380, 425
Juries Act 1974	
s 17(1)	475

K

L

Land Registration Act 1925	197, 217
Land Registration Act 2002	185, 197, 209, 217, 218
Part 8	218
s 3	209
s 4	209, 217
s 6	
(1)	209
(4)–(5)	209
s 7(1)–(2)	209
s 8	209
s 9(2)–(5)	218
s 10	
(2)–(3)	219
(5)–(6)	219
s 11(4)	218
ss 15–20	209
s 21	209
(1)–(3)	197
s 22	209
s 24	197
s 26	197
s 27	
(1)	210
(3)–(5)	210
ss 28–29	218
s 33	216
s 35	216
s 37	216

Statute	Page
s 40	216
s 43	216
s 58	216
s 60	178
ss 62–63	218
s 67	182, 218
s 72	220
ss 79–85	185
s 90	217
s 93	218
ss 116–117	217
s 120	218
Sch 1	217, 218
Sch 2	210
Sch 3	217
Sch 4	
para 5	217
Sch 8	217
Sch 12	217
Landlord and Tenant Act 1927	
Part I	237
ss 19–19A	231
Landlord and Tenant Act 1954	236
Part II	233, 236
s 23	236
s 24	238
(1)	236
ss 24A–24D	238
s 25	237, 238
s 26	237, 238
(6)	238
ss 27–29	238
ss 29A–29B	238
s 30(1)	238
(e)–(g)	237
ss 32–36	238
s 37	237
s 38A	236
s 43	
(1)(a)	236
(2)–(3)	236
Landlord and Tenant Act 1985	
ss 11–14	234
s 18	234
s 19	234
s 27A 234	
ss 20–30	234
Landlord and Tenant Act 1987	216
Part I	234
Landlord and Tenant Act 1988	
s 1(3)	231
Landlord and Tenant (Covenants) Act	
995	230, 232
ss 1–4	170
s 5	170, 229
(3)	231
s 6(2)	232
s 7(2)	232
s 8	232
s 9	231

Statute	Page
(2)	232
s 10	231
s 16	229
Late Payment of Commercial Debts (Interest)	
Act 1998	315, 318, 425
ss 1–2	318
s 4	318
s 5A(2)	318
s 8	318
Law of Distress (Amendment) Act 1888	
s 4	426
Law of Property Act 1925	
s 1(2)	
(a)–(b)	210
(e)	210
s 2	192, 213
s 21	150
s 24	187
s 27	192, 213
s 30	295
s 42(1)	180
s 44	212, 215
(2)	215
s 45	212
(9)	206
s 48	180
s 49(1)	240
s 52	203
(2)(d)	229
s 53	229
s 54(2)	229
s 64	215, 224
s 67	204
s 69	204
ss 73–74	186
s 76(1)	242
s 77	230
s 115	214
ss 126–128	214
s 146	227, 234
s 184	148
s 200	224
Law of Property (Joint Tenants) Act 1964	
s 1	213
Law of Property (Miscellaneous Provisions)	
Act 1989	
s 1	203
(2)	203
(a)	186
(3)	186, 203
s 2	201, 202
Law of Property (Miscellaneous Provisions)	
Act 1994	179
s 1	179
s 2	179
(1)–(2)	179
s 3	179
(1)	179
(3)	179
ss 4–5	179

Statute	Page
s 12	179
s 16	194
Law Reform (Miscellaneous Provisions) Act 1934	364, 391
Law Reform (Succession) Act 1995	
s 1	152
Leasehold Reform Act 1967	234
Leasehold Reform, Housing and Urban Development Act 1993	234
Legitimacy Act 1976	
s 5(3)–(4)	165
s 7	165
Limitation Act 1980	218, 334, 340
s 2	334
s 5	334
s 11	334, 349
s 12	349
ss 14–14A	334
s 33	334
Limited Partnership Act 2000	90, 99, 128, 186, 250, 289, 290
s 1	
(1)	250
(3)	250
s 2	251
(1)(a)–(c)	251
(2)–(4)	251
s 3(1)–(4)	251
s 5	
(1)(a)–(b)	251
(2)	252
s 6	
(1)	253
(4)	253
s 7	252
s 9	252
s 12	128
Sch 1	
Part 1	251
Limited Partnerships Act 1907	250
Local Land Charges Act 1975	
s 10	220

M

Statute	Page
Magistrates' Courts Act 1980	
s 4	472
s 5A	473
(6)	473
ss 5B–5D	473
s 6	
(1)–(2)	471, 472
(3)	454, 471
s 8	473
(2A)	473
ss 8A–8D	465
s 9	466
s 10	455
(3)	454
s 17	460, 461
s 18	450, 455, 460, 461
s 19	460, 461
(3)	460, 461
s 20	460, 461
(2)–(3)	460
(9)(b)	461
ss 21–24	460, 461
s 25	460, 461, 462
ss 26–27	460, 461
s 32	439
s 76	484
s 80(1)	484
s 83	484
s 88	484
s 97	464
s 97A	473
(9)	473
s 108	493, 494
ss 109–111	493
s 123	465
s 127	450
ss 128–128A	454
s 132	480
s 133(2)	480
s 136	484
s 142	494
Sch 1	
para 28(c)	462
Married Women's Property Act 1882	155
Matrimonial Homes Act 1983	295, 352, 355, 356, 361
Mental Capacity Act 2005	16, 214
Mental Health Act 1983	
Part VII	195
s 96(1)(g)	248
s 99	195
Minors' Contracts Act 1987	191
Misrepresentation Act 1967	
s 2(1)	242

N

Statute	Page
National Assistance Act 1948	
Part 3	140
s 56	140

O

Statute	Page
Occupiers Liability Act 1957	321
Occupiers Liability Act 1984	194
Offences Against the Person Act 1861	
s 20	479
s 47	439, 479

P

Statute	Page
Partnership Act 1890	245
s 1	244, 245
ss 5–8	246, 323
s 9	246, 247
s 10	246

Statute	Page
s 14	247
s 17	246, 247
s 23	248
s 24	
(1)	245
(3)–(8)	245
s 25	245, 248
s 26	245, 248
(2)	248
ss 28–30	246
s 32(a)–(c)	248
s 33	245
(1)–(2)	248
s 34	248
s 35	248
(b)–(f)	248
s 36	247
ss 38–39	248, 249
ss 42–44	249

Perjury Act 1911
s 13	502

Planning (Listed Buildings and Conservation Areas) Act 1990
s 3	188
ss 47–48	188
s 66	188
s 72	188
s 74	188

Police and Criminal Evidence Act 1984 .. 448, 512
s 24	435
(1)–(3)	435
(4)–(6)	435, 436
s 24A	437
(4)–(5)	437
s 29	440
s 30	
(1A)	438
(7)–(7A)	438
(8)–(9)	438
(10)–(10A)	438
(11)	438
s 30A	438, 512
ss 30B–30D	438
s 34	
(2)	440
(7)	440
s 37	
(2)	440, 512
(7)	
(a)	438
(b)	438, 512
(c)–(d)	438
ss 37A–37D	438
s 38	450
(1)	450
s 39(1)	434
s 40(3)	440
s 41	
(1)	440
(2)(a)(i)	440

Statute	Page
(7)	440
s 42(4)	440
s 43	440
s 44	440
(3)(b)	440
s 46(1)	450
s 46A	450
s 47	450
s 54A	448
s 58	449
s 60A	441
s 60AA	448
ss 61–61A	448
s 62	447
(10)	447
s 63	448
s 63B	447, 450
s 64A	448
s 65	447, 448
s 76	508
(2)	508
(4)(a)–(b)	508
(8)	508
s 76A	508
s 78	504, 506, 508
s 79	503
s 80	
(2)–(2A)	503
(3)	503
(4)–(4A)	503
(5)	503
s 81	510
s 82	
(1)	508
(3)	504

Powers of Attorney Act 1971
s 4	214
s 5	
(1)	323
(4)	214

Powers of Criminal Courts (Sentencing) Act 2000 487
s 1	489
s 3	490, 492
s 4	492
ss 12–15	487
s 36A	492
s 40A	485
s 63	490
(1)	485
s 69	490
(1)	485
s 73	490
ss 77–78	480
s 83	479
ss 89–91	490
s 97	490
s 100	490
s 111	481

Statute	Page
s 130	336, 489
(6)	489
ss 131–134	336, 489
s 137	484
s 143	489
s 146	487
(1)–(3)	487
ss 148–149	489
s 163	485
Private International Law (Miscellaneous Provisions) Act 1995	337
Proceeds of Crime Act 2002	4, 6, 11, 175
ss 6–91	489
s 327	4
s 328	4, 6
s 329	4
s 333	6
s 338	4
Prosecution of Offences Act 1985	
s 16	489
(1)	466
(7)	466
s 18	489
(1)	466
(3)	466
s 21(4A)	466
s 22	454
s 22B	454
Protection from Eviction Act 1977	
s 2	227
Protection from Harassment Act 1997	479
Public Order Act 1986	
Parts 3–3A	437
s 4	439, 479
ss 17–29N	437

Q

R

Statute	Page
Race Relations Act 1976	329
Rehabilitation of Offenders Act 1974	474
Rent Acts	169
Road Traffic Act 1988	336
ss 2–3	439
s 151	336, 339, 355, 383
s 152	336, 339, 355
Road Traffic (National Health Charges) Act 1999	335
Road Traffic Offenders Act 1988	
s 1	450
s 28(4)–(6)	487
s 35	488
(4)	488
Sch 2	439

S

Statute	Page
Sale of Goods Act 1979	316-17, 321
s 2	316
s 8	315, 316
s 10	315, 316
s 12	315
s 13	315, 317
s 14	317
(2)–(2A)	315
(3)	315
s 15	315, 316, 317
s 15A	317
ss 16–18	315, 316
s 19	316
s 20	315, 317
s 20A	317
s 21	317
ss 27–28	317
s 29	315, 317
ss 30–31	317
s 34	317
ss 35–35A	317
s 36	317
ss 41–42	317
ss 44–45	317
s 48A	317
ss 49–50	317
s 55	315
s 61(1)	316
Sale and Supply of Goods Act 1994	315
Serious Organised Crime and Police Act 2005	
s 102	5
s 104	5
Settled Land Act 1925	149, 216, 217
s 27	191
(1)	191
Sex Discrimination Act 1975	329
Sex Discrimination Act 1986	329
Social Security (Recovery of Benefits) Act 1997	334, 362, 383, 385, 386
s 1	390, 391
s 8	386
Sch 2	386
Solicitors' Act 1974	
s 22	31
s 44A	27
s 47	27
s 69	24
Sch 1	27
Sch 1A	
para 3(1)	27
Stamp Act 1891	
s 14(4)	129, 130, 180
s 15A	129, 130
(4)	130
s 15B	129
(1)–(3)	130
s 17	129, 130
s 55	126
s 57	126, 127, 128
s 117	130, 180
Stamp Acts	130

Statute	Page
Supply of Goods (Implied Terms) Act 1973	315, 321
ss 8–9	315
s 10(2)–(3)	315
s 11	315
Supply of Goods and Services Act 1982	315
s 2	315, 321
s 3	315
s 4(2)–(6)	315
s 5	315
s 7–8	315
s 9(2)–(5)	315
s 10	315
s 13	26, 315
ss 14–15	315
Supreme Court Act 1981	
ss 15–18	430
s 28A	493
s 32A	364
ss 33–34	381, 402
s 35A	334, 363
s 48	493
s 51	242
s 79(3)	493
s 81	455
s 113	157
ss 116–117	157

T

Statute	Page
Tax Credits Act 2002	87
Taxation of Chargeable Gains Act 1992	
s 2(2)(a)–(b)	95, 107
s 2A	97
(8)–(9)	97
s 3	
(2)	95
(5)	98
(7)	161
s 4	99
(1AA)	99, 161
s 10A	137
s 13	112, 113
s 15(2)	94, 106
s 17	94
ss 22–28	94, 106
s 35	94
s 38	94
ss 44–45	95, 107
s 54	95
s 58	94
s 59	99
s 59A	
(1)	99
(5)	99
s 62	
(1)(a)–(b)	161
(4)	166
(6)–(7)	141
s 100	89, 137
ss 105A–105B	98
s 106A	98, 138
ss 127–137A	107
ss 150–150C	89, 96, 137, 289
s 150D	89, 96, 137
ss 152–157	96, 107
ss 162–162A	96
s 165	96
(11)	96
s 169A	96, 99
ss 169B–169G	96
s 222	95
(2)–(5)	95
s 223	
(1)–(2)	95
(3)(a)–(c)	95
ss 225–s225A	95
s 257	94
s 260(7)	96
s 262	95, 107
s 281	
(1)(a)–(b)	99
(3)	99
s 283	116
Sch 5B	89, 96, 137, 289
Sch 5BA	89, 96, 137
para 16	98
Sch 7	96
Sch 7AC	107
Sch 8	81, 104
Sch A1	98
paras 4–6	97
paras 15–16	98
Taxes Management Act 1970	11, 115
s 7(3)–(7)	115
s 8	
(1)(a)	115
(1A)	115
s 9	90
(2)–(3)	115
s 12B(1)–(6)	115
s 28C	115
s 42	90
s 59A	116
(1)(c)–(d)	116
(2)	116
ss 59B–59C	116
s 59(D)	121
s 86	116
s 93(2)–(4)	115
s 824	116
Theft Act 1968	
ss 7–9	439
ss 12–12A	439
Torts (Interference with Goods) Act 1977	381
Town and Country Planning Act 1990	
s 55	188
ss 65–66	188
ss 91–92	188
ss 94–96	188

Statute	Page
ss 171E–171H	188
s 172	188
s 183	188
s 187A	188
Trade Union and Labour Relations (Consolidation) Act 1992	330
Trustee Act 1925	
s 19	149, 160
s 25	160, 214
s 26	170
s 27	154, 165, 169
ss 31–32	150, 151
s 36(1)	195
s 42	160
ss 61–62	170
s 68(1)	170
Trustee Act 2000	149
Part IV	149
s 1	169
s 3	169
(1)–(6)	149
ss 4–5	149
s 8	149, 169, 193
s 11	149, 160, 169, 214
s 12(3)	149
s 15	149
ss 16–17	149, 169
ss 28–29	150, 160
ss 31–32	150, 160
s 34	149, 169
Sch 1	169
Trustee Delegation Act 1999	
s 2	214
s 7	213
Trusts of Land and Appointment of Trustees Act 1996	149, 150, 151, 160, 194, 213
s 3	193
(2)–(3)	193
s 4	193, 213
ss 7–8	193
s 9	193, 208
(1)–(2)	214
(4)	214
s 10(3)	191
s 11	
(1)	192, 193
(2)–(4)	193
ss 12–13	194
s 14	193, 428
s 15	193
s 16	213
(1)–(2)	192
(4)–(5)	192
s 18	194
(3)	193
s 20	195
s 21(1)	195
Sch 1	
para 1	191

Statute	Page
Sch 2	
para 5	151
U	
Unfair Contract Terms Act 1977	320, 321
ss 2–3	321
ss 6–7	321
s 11	321
s 26	320
V	
Value Added Tax Act 1994	
ss 1–2	122
s 26A	78, 122
s 29A	123
s 30	
(2)	123
(6)	123
s 31(1)	123
s 36	78
s 49	289
ss 59–60	125
s 63	125
s 67	125
s 69	125
s 72	125
Sch 7A	123
Schs 8–9	123, 124
Sch 10	
para 2	124
para 3	124
(AA)	124
paras 4–6	124
Sch 11A	142
W	
Water Act 1989	220
Water Industry Act 1991	
s 104	226
Welfare Reform and Pensions Act 1999	
ss 75–76	86
Wills Act 1837	
s 1	144
s 9	144
s 15	144, 158
s 18	145
s 18A	145, 171
s 18B	145
s 18C	145, 171
ss 20–21	145
s 24	148
s 33	165, 171
X	
Y	
Youth Justice and Criminal Evidence Act 1999	
ss 16–18	504

Statute	Page
s 19	504, 507
ss 20–33	504
s 53	503
s 55	503
s 58	511

Z

Bills

	Page
Companies Bill 2006	243
Police and Justice Bill 2006	512

European legislation

	Page
Treaty of Rome	430
arts 28–30	314
art 39	326
(3)–(4)	326
art 43	243
art 49	243, 326
art 81	308, 309, 311, 312, 325, 359
(1)	324
(2)	308
(3)	309, 312
art 82	310, 311, 312, 313, 359

International legislation

	Page
Brussels Convention	377, 384, 423
European Convention on Human Rights	34, 142
arts 2–5	34
art 6	6, 34, 142, 451
art 7	34
art 8	34, 329
arts 9–12	34
art 14	34, 329
Protocol 1	
art 1	34
(1)–(2)	142
arts 2–3	34
Protocol 13	34
Lugano Convention	377, 384, 423

Table of authorities

Statutory instruments/European secondary legislation

Statutory instrument	Page

A

Access to Justice Act 1999 (Destination of Appeals) Order 2000 430
Administration of Insolvent Estates of Deceased Persons Order 1986 163

B

Building Regulations 2000 225

C

Charge to Income Tax by Reference to Enjoyment of Property Previously Owned Regulations 2005 139
Civil Jurisdiction and Judgments (Authentic Instruments and Court Settlements) Order 2001 423
Civil Jurisdiction and Judgments Order 2001 .. 423
Civil Procedure Rules 1998 ... 333, 335, 341, 342, 345, 375, 380, 399, 423, 425, 451
  Part 1
    r 1 341
  Part 2
    r 2.1 333
    r 2.3 .... 333, 344
    rr 2.8–2.11 345
  Part 3
    r 3.1 342
      (3) 387
      (5) 387
    r 3.2 452
    r 3.3 .... 342, 452
    r 3.4 .... 343, 377, 452
      (2) 343
        (a) 343, 419
        (b)–(c) 343
      (3)–(4) 343
    r 3.5 .... 343, 452
    r 3.6(1)–(4) 343
    rr 3.7–3.7A 344
    r 3.8
      (1)–(2) 344
      (3) 345
    r 3.9 .... 343, 345
    r 3.11 .... 344, 372
  PD 3
    paras 1.4–1.6 343

Statutory instrument	Page

    paras 2–3 343
  PD 3B 344
  PD 3C 344, 372
  Part 5
    rr 5.2–5.3 346
    r 5.5 346
  PD 5
    para 2.2 346
    para 5.3 346
  PD 5B 346
    para 6 347
    paras 8–9 347
  Part 6
    r 6.1 354
    r 6.2 354
      (2) 353
    r 6.3 353
      (2) 353
    r 6.4 354
      (4)–(5) 353
    r 6.5
      (2)–(3) 352
      (5)–(6) 352
    r 6.6 352
    r 6.7 354
    r 6.8 352
      (3) 353
    r 6.10 354
    rr 6.11–6.11A 353
    r 6.13 .... 352, 353
    r 6.14 353
  PD 6
    paras 2.1–2.2 354
    paras 3.1–3.4 354
    paras 4.1–4.2 353
    paras 6.1–6.2 353
    para 6.16 352
    para 8.1 353
    para 8.3 353
    para 9.1 352
  Part 7 .... 340, 361-2, 369, 430
    r 7.2
      (1) 340, 361
      (2) 333, 361
    r 7.3 355
    r 7.4 .... 363, 364
      (1)(a)–(b) 340
      (3) 340, 363

Statutory instrument	Page	Statutory instrument	Page
r 7.5	340	r 15.8	370, 392
r 7.8(1)	363	r 15.9	340
PD 7		r 15.10	392
para 2	357	r 15.11	340
para 3.1	340, 361	**PD 15**	
para 4	362	para 3.2A	370
paras 4.1–4.2	348	**Part 16**	
paras 5A–5C	355	r 16.2	362
para 5.1	340	r 16.3	362
para 6.1	363	(5)	375
para 8.2	333	(6)	362
PD 7A		r 16.4	363, 364
para 6	364	rr 16.5–16.6	366
PD 7E	357	r 16.7	370
Part 8	240, 340, 361, 369, 377, 428	**PD 16**	
Part 9		para 1.4	348
r 9.2	340	para 2	362
Part 10	340, 366, 369	paras 2.2–2.3	362
r 10.3	340	para 3	364
Part 11	369	para 3.1	363
r 11(3)	369	para 3.3	363
Part 12	340, 375, 377, 423	para 3.4	364
rr 12.1–12.2	377	para 3.8	364
r 12.3(1)–(3)	377	paras 4–7	364
r 12.4		para 8	364
(1)	377, 419	para 8.1	363, 364
(2)	377	para 8.2	363
r 12.5(1)–(4)	377	para 9	364
r 12.6(1)	377	paras 9.2–9.3	348
r 12.7	377	paras 11–12	366
r 12.9	377	para 13.1	366
r 12.10(a)–(b)	377	para 13.3	348
PD 12		**Part 17**	
paras 1.2–1.3	377	r 17.1	349
para 4.1	377	(1)	349
Part 13	340, 377, 380	(2)(a)–(b)	349
rr 13.2–13.3	377	rr 17.2–17.4	349
Part 14	340, 375, 423	**PD 17**	
r 14.1		para 1	349
(1)–(2)	367, 379	paras 2.1–2.4	349
(4)	367, 379	Part 18	378
(5)	367	r 18.1	343
r 14.2	379	**PD 18**	
(1)	340	paras 1.1–1.4	378
r 14.3	367, 375	para 1.6	
r 14.4	340, 367, 368, 375, 379	(a)	378
(3)	419	(2)	378
r 14.5	340, 367, 368, 375, 379, 392	para 1.7	378
(6)	419	para 2.1	378
rr 14.6–14.7	340, 367, 368, 375, 379	paras 3–5	378
r 14.8	368, 375	paras 5.5–5.8	378
rr 14.9–14.10	368, 375, 379	**Part 19**	
rr 14.11–14.13	375, 379	r 19.2	350
r 14.14	368, 375	r 19.3	355
PD 14		r 19.4	349, 350
paras 5–6	379	r 19.5(2)	349
para 16.3	348	r 19.5A	364
Part 15	340	**PD 19**	
r 15.4(1)(a)–(b)	340	paras 1.3–1.5	350
r 15.5	340	paras 3–4	350

Statutory instrument	Page
para 5.2	350
Part 20	340, 365, 366, 370, 374-5, 393
r 20.1(3)–(4)	375
r 20.2	374
r 20.3	375
(2)	375
(3)	375, 377
(4)	375
r 20.4	374, 377
rr 20.5–20.7	374
r 20.8	374
(1)(a)–(b)	374
(2)	374
r 20.9(1)–(2)	375
r 20.10(1)	374
r 20.11	375
r 20.12(1)–(2)	374
r 20.13	375
(1)–(2)	375
PD 20	
para 2	374
para 5	375
paras 5.1–5.3	375
Part 21	355, 356, 427
r 21.2	
(1)	355
(2)	356
r 21.3	
(2)	355, 356
(3)	355
r 21.5	356
r 21.9	355, 356
r 21.10	356, 367
r 21.11	356
(1)(b)	388
PD 21	355, 356
paras 1.2–1.3	355
paras 1.4–1.5	356
para 2.3	356
paras 2.4–2.4A	356
Part 22	351, 366, 372
PD 22	351
Part 23	342, 343, 359, 371, 377, 378, 382
r 23.1	371
r 23.2	371
(7)	372
r 23.3	350, 371
r 23.4	350, 372
r 23.6	372
r 23.7	
(1)	372
(4)–(5)	372
r 23.8	372
r 23.9(2)–(3)	373
r 23.10(1)–(2)	373
r 23.12	372
PD 23	
para 2.1	372
paras 2.3–2.5	372
paras 2.7–2.9	371

Statutory instrument	Page
para 2.10	371, 373
para 3	373
para 4.2	371
paras 6.1–6.1A	373
paras 6.2–6.5	373
para 11.1	372
Part 24	340, 376, 419
rr 24.2–24.4	376
r 24.5	376
(1)–(2)	376
(3)(a)–(b)	376
(4)	376
r 24.6	376
PD 24	
para 2	
(3)–(4)	376
(6)	376
para 3(1)	376
para 4	376
paras 5.1–5.2	376
para 7.1(b)	376
para 7.3	376
para 10	376
Part 25	381-3
r 25.1	381
r 25.2	
(1)	381
(2)(b)–(c)	381
(3)–(4)	381
r 25.3(1)–(2)	382
r 25.6	365, 370, 381
(1)	383
(3)–(5)	383
r 25.7	383
(1)	383
(4)–(5)	383
rr 25.8–25.9	383
r 25.11	344
rr 25.12–25.15	384
PD 25 (Interim Injunctions)	
paras 1.1–1.4	382
paras 2.1–2.4	382
paras 3.2–3.4	382
para 4	382
PD 25 (Interim Payments)	
paras 2.1–2.2	383
paras 4–5	383
Part 26	392-3
r 26.2	
(1)	392
(3)–(4)	392
r 26.3	
(1)–(4)	392
(6)–(6A)	392
r 26.4	393
r 26.5	392
(4)	392
r 26.6(1)–(6)	392
rr 26.7–26.8	393
r 26.9	392

Statutory instrument	Page
PD 26	
paras 2.3–2.4	393
para 2.5	392
para 3	393
paras 5–6	393
Part 27	394-6
r 27.4	
(1)(a)–(e)	394
r 27.5	395
r 27.6(1)	394
r 27.8(1)–(6)	395
r 27.9(1)–(4)	396
r 27.10	395
r 27.11(1)–(3)	396
r 27.14	419
PD 27	
para 3.1(2)	395
para 3.2	
(1)–(2)	395
(4)	395
para 3.3(3)	395
para 4.1(1)	395
para 4.3	395
paras 5.1–5.5	395
para 6.2	396
Appendix B–Appendix C	396
Part 28	
r 28.2(2)–(4)	397
r 28.3(1)–(2)	397
r 28.4	398
r 28.5(1)–(4)	397
r 28.6	360, 411
(2)	397
PD 28	398
para 2	397
paras 3–4	398
para 5	344
para 6	397
para 6.1	397
para 7	398
para 8.2	415
Appendix	398
Part 29	
r 29	360
r 29.2	
(1)–(2)	399
(23)	399
r 29.3	399
r 29.6	399
(1)	399
(4)	399
r 29.8	399, 411
PD 29	
para 2.6	359
para 3	399
para 4	400
para 5	399, 400
para 6	400
para 7	344
para 8	399

Statutory instrument	Page
para 8.1	399
(3)	399
(5)–(6)	399
para 9	400
Part 30	358
r 30.2(1)–(6)	358
rr 30.3–30.4	359
r 30.8	359
PD 30	
para 6	359
Part 31	401-5, 406
r 31.2	401, 403
r 31.3	404
r 31.4	401
r 31.5(1)–(3)	403
r 31.6	403
r 31.7	403
(1)–(3)	403
r 31.8	401, 403
r 31.9	401
r 31.10	403
(3)–(5)	403
(7)	403
r 31.11(1)–(2)	401
r 31.12	402
(1)–(3)	402
r 31.13	401
rr 31.14–31.15	405
r 31.19	401
r 31.20	405
r 31.21	401
PD 31	
para 1.1	403
para 1.4	403
para 2A	404
paras 3.1–3.2	403
paras 4.2–4.3	403
Part 32	407
r 32.1	406
r 32.2	406
(4)(b)	410
r 32.3	406
r 32.4(1)–(3)	407
r 32.5	
(2)	407
(5)	407
r 32.6	406
r 32.8	407
r 32.9(1)–(2)	408
r 32.10	407
r 32.13(1)–(4)	405
r 32.14	351, 406
rr 32.18–32.19	406
r 32.20	410
PD 32	407
paras 17–20	407
para 25.1	407
Part 33	
r 33.2	
(3)(a)–(c)	410

Statutory instrument	Page
(4)(a)	409
r 33.3	410
r 33.4(1)–(2)	410
r 33.5	408
(1)–(2)	410
Part 34	413
rr 34.2–34.11	413
PD 34	
para 1	413
para 3	413
Part 35	414
r 35.1	414
r 35.2(2)	414
r 35.3	414
r 35.4	
(1)–(2)	414
(4)	414
r 35.5(1)	414
rr 35.7–35.8	414
r 35.10	414
(4)	414
r 35.13	414
PD 35	414
para 4	414
para 5.3	414
Part 36	339, 346, 365, 370, 385-91, 417, 421
r 36.1(2)	385
r 36.2	
(4)	387
(5)	385
r 36.2A	386
(4)–(5)	386
(7)	386
r 36.3	
(1)	385
(2)	387
r 36.4	385
(3)	386
(4)	388
r 36.5	386
(1)–(2)	386
(3)(a)–(c)	386
(4)–(7)	386
(8)	387
r 36.6	386
(2)	
(a)–(c)	386
(e)	386
(3)	387
(5)	387
r 36.7	
(3)(a)–(c)	386
(5)–(6)	388
r 36.8	
(1)–(4)	387
(5)	388
r 36.9(1)–(2)	387
r 36.10	
(2)–(4)	389

Statutory instrument	Page
(5)	387
r 36.11	
(1)	388, 389
(2)(a)–(b)(i)	388
(3)	388
r 36.12	
(1)	388
(2)(a)–(b)(i)	388
(3)	388
r 36.13	390
(1)–(4)	390
r 36.14	390
r 36.15	
(1)–(4)	390
(6)	390
r 36.16	390
rr 36.17–36.18	389
r 36.19(2)–(3)	391
r 36.20(2)	391
r 36.21(2)–(5)	391
r 36.22(1)–(2)	386
r 36.23	386
(2)	385
(4)	391
(5)	390
PD 36	
para 4.1	387
Part 37	385-91
r 37.1(1)	387
r 37.2(1)–(3)	387
r 37.4	391
PD 37	
paras 6.1–6.2	388
Part 38	379
r 38.2(2)(a)–(c)	379
r 38.3	
(1)(a)–(b)	379
(2)–(4)	379
r 38.4(1)–(2)	379
rr 38.6–38.8	379
Part 39	360
r 39.1	360
r 39.3	360
(1)–(5)	360
rr 39.4–39.5	360, 411
r 39.6	360
PD 39	
para 3	411
Part 40	423
r 40.2(2)	423
r 40.3	
(1)	423
(3)–(4)	423
r 40.4(1)–(2)	423
r 40.5	423
r 40.6	380
(2)–(7)	380
r 40.7	423
r 40.8	425
r 40.9	423

Statutory instrument	Page
rr 40.11–40.12	423
r 40.20	380
PD 40B	
para 3.4	380
Part 41	364, 381-3, 388
r 41.1	384
r 41.2	384, 388
rr 41.3–41.10	334
Part 44	
r 44.2	417
r 44.3	418
(1)–(2)	417
(4)–(5)	417
(6)–(8)	418
r 44.3A	422
r 44.4(1)–(3)	417
r 44.5	419
r 44.7	417, 420
r 44.13	418
(1A)	418
PD 44	
paras 21–22	422
Part 45	419
r 45.16	23
Part 46	420
r 46.3(2A)	420
Part 47	
r 47.1	420
rr 47.6–47.9	421
rr 47.11–47.16	421
r 47.17	422
rr 47.20–47.23	421, 430
Part 48	422
r 48.8	24
(3)	24
Part 52	396, 430
r 52.1	430
r 52.3	430
rr 52.10–52.11	430
PD 52	
paras 2A.1–2A.2	430
para 5.8	396
para 7.7A	396
Part 54	430
Part 57	
r 57.12	168
rr 57.14–57.16	168
Part 64	
r 64	168, 169
Part 70	419, 426
Part 71	419, 424
Part 72	419, 427
r 72.3	351
r 72.7	351
Part 73	419, 428
r 73.3	351
Part 74	423
Sch 1, RSC	333
r 30	429

Statutory instrument	Page
rr 46–47	426
r 51	429
r 81	355
r 114	430
Sch 2, CCR	333
rr 16–17	402
r 26	426
r 27	429
PD Civil Appeals	430
PD Costs	
paras 4.1–4.4	421
para 4.9	421
para 4.13	421
para 6	392
para 8.3(1)	417
para 8.5	418
para 12.2	420
paras 13.1–13.2	420
para 13.5	372, 420
(4)	420
paras 13.9–13.10	422
para 19	360, 361, 365, 370
para 21	422
para 32	421
para 35.1	421
para 40	421
paras 40.11–40.12	421
Pre-action Protocols	345
Construction and Engineering Disputes	337
Defamation	337
Disease and Illness Claims	337
Housing Disrepair	337
Judicial Review	337
Personal Injury Claims	337
Professional Negligence	337
Resolution of Cliinical Disputes	337
Practice Direction	337-8
Collective Redundancies and Transfer of Undertakings (Protection of Employment) (Amendment) Regulations 1995	329
Collective Redundancies and Transfer of Undertakings (Protection of Employment) (Amendment) Regulations 1999	329
Commercial Agents (Council Directive) Regulations 1993	322, 325
regs 3–4	322
regs 6–20	322
Commonhold (Land Registration) Rules 2004	
rr 5–7	239
r 15	224
Commonhold Regulations 2004	239
reg 3	239
reg 9	239
regs 11–15	239
Sch 1	239
Schs 3–4	239
Community Legal Service (Cost Protection) Regulations 2000	422

Statutory instrument	Page

Community Legal Service (Costs)
Regulations 2000
   reg 6 384
Community Legal Service (Financial)
Regulations 2000 17
Companies Act (Electronic Communications)
Order 2000 255
Companies Act (Small Agreements and
Conduct of Minor Significance)
Regulations 2000 311
Companies (Summary Financial Statement)
Regulations 1995 261
Companies (Tables A–F) Amendment
Regulations 1985 264
   Table A 258, 260, 264
      art 2 258
      art 3 .... 258, 278, 281
      arts 4–23 258
      art 24 .... 258, 280
      arts 25–31 258
      art 32 .... 258, 279
      art 33 258
      art 34 .... 258, 264
      art 35 .... 258, 281
      art 36 258
      art 37 .... 258, 264
      art 38 .... 258, 264, 267
      arts 39–40 258
      art 41 .... 258, 266
      arts 42–45 258
      art 46 .... 258, 261, 266
      arts 47–49 258
      art 50 .... 258, 266
      arts 51–63 258
      art 64 .... 258, 267, 284
      arts 65–66 .... 258, 267
      arts 67–69 258
      art 70 .... 258, 262, 272, 276
      art 71 258
      art 72 .... 258, 262, 273
      arts 73–74 .... 258, 268
      art 75 .... 258, 260, 268
      art 76 .... 258, 267, 268, 285
      arts 77–79 .... 258, 267, 268
      art 80 .... 258, 268
      art 81 .... 258, 269, 296
      art 82 .... 258, 267, 284
      art 83 258
      art 84 .... 258, 273
      arts 85–87 258
      art 88 .... 258, 272, 273
      art 89 .... 258, 272
      art 90 258
      art 91 .... 258, 273
      art 92 258
      art 93 .... 258, 272
      arts 94–95 .... 258, 267, 269, 272
      art 96 .... 258, 267, 284
      art 97 .... 258, 284
      art 98 258
      art 99 .... 258, 273
      art 100 .... 258, 272
      art 101 258
      art 102 .... 258, 261, 283, 285
      art 103 .... 258, 261, 283
      arts 104–108 .... 258, 261
      arts 109–110 258
      arts 111–112 .... 258, 264
      arts 113–114 258
      arts 115–116 .... 258, 264
      arts 117–118 258
Company and Business Names Regulations
1981 244
Competition Act 1998 (Determination of
Turnover for Penalties) Order 2000 313
Competition Act 1998 (Land Agreements
Exclusion and Revocation) Order 2004 190
   rr 4–5 190
Conditional Fee Agreements Order
2000 22
Conditional Fee Agreements Regulations
2000 22
Consolidated Criminal Practice Direction
   Part IV.41 476
   Part IV.44 511
Consumer Protection (Distance Selling)
   Regulations 2000 .... 315, 318-19, 320
   regs 4–6 318
   regs 7–8 319
   regs 10–15 319
   reg 17 319
   reg 19 318
   reg 21 319
   regs 26–27 318
Contaminated Land (England) Regulations
2000 189
Corporation Tax (Instalment Payments)
Regulations 1998
   reg 2(3) 121
   regs 3–4 121
   reg 5(2)–(3) 121
   reg 6 121
County Courts (Interest on Judgment Debts)
Order 1991 425
Crime and Disorder Act (Scope of Prosecution
Evidence) Regulations 2005 469
Criminal Defence Service (Funding) Order
2001 19
Criminal Defence Service (General) (No.2)
Regulations 2001 .... 19, 20, 21
Criminal Defence Service (Recovery of Defence
Costs Orders) Regulations 2001 21
Criminal Defence Service (Representation Order
Appeals) Regulations 2001 20
Criminal Justice Act 2003 (Commencement No.8
and Transitional and Saving Provisions) Order
2005 486
Criminal Procedure and Investigations Act 1996
Code of Practice 432
   para 3.1 433

Statutory instrument	Page
para 5.1	433
paras 5.7–5.10	433
paras 6.2–6.4	433
para 6.6	433
para 6.8	433
para 7.1	433
Criminal Procedure and Investigations Act 1996 (Defence Disclosure Time Limits) Regulations 1997	495
Criminal Procedure Rules	471, 493
Part 1	
r 1	451
Part 2	
r 2.2	451
Part 3	
rr 3.6–3.8	453
Part 4	451
Parts 5–6	451
Part 7	451
r 7.2(2)	451
r 7.3(1)	450
Parts 8–9	451
Part 10	451
rr 10.1–10.3	472
r 10.4	471
Parts 11–20	451
Part 21	451, 460, 461
r 21.3	464
Parts 22–23	451
Part 24	451
r 24.1	474, 510
r 24.3	510
Parts 25–33	451
Part 34	451, 507
Parts 35–36	451
Part 37	451, 466
r 37.1(1)–(6)	466
Parts 38–62	451
Part 63	451
r 63	493
Parts 64–78	451

D

E

Statutory instrument	Page
Employment Equality (Age) Regulations 2006	329
Estate Agents (Accounts) Regulations 1981	
reg 7	198
European Public Limited Liability Company Regulations 2004	287

F

Statutory instrument	Page
Financial Services (Distance Marketing) Regulations 2004	318
Financial Services and Markets Act 2000 (Carrying on Regulated Activities by Way of Business) Order 2001	29
Financial Services and Markets Act 2000 (Financial Promotion) Order 2001	29
Sch 1	29
Financial Services and Markets Act 2000 (Regulated Activities) Order 2001	29, 30
art 5	29
art 6(1)(a)(iv)	29
art 7	29
art 9B	29
art 10	29
art 12	29
art 14	29
arts 19–21	29
arts 25–25A	29
art 37	29
art 40	29
art 43	29
art 45	29
arts 48–54	29
art 56	29
art 59	29
art 61	29
art 64	29
art 70	29
Financial Services and Markets Act (Exemption) Order 2001	29
Fines Collection Regulations 2006	484

G

Statutory instrument	Page
Gas Safety (Installation and Use) Regulations 1998	
reg 36(2)	232
General Product Safety Regulations 1994	325
Groundwater Regulations 1998	189
Guide to the Professional Conduct of Solicitors	2

H

Statutory instrument	Page
High Court and County Courts Jurisdiction Order 1991 (SI 1991/724)	357
art 8	426
High Court and County Courts Jurisdiction (Amendment) Order 1996	
Sch 1	426
Home Information Pack Regulations 2006	xv
Part 5	183
reg 8	183, 184
reg 9	183
regs 12–14	183
reg 18	183
reg 20	183
Schs 2–5	184
Sch 6	184
para 3	225
para 6	225
para 9	225
paras 11–15	225
paras 17–18	225
Sch 7	184, 225

Statutory instrument	Page
Schs 8–9	184

I

Income Tax (Payments on Account) Regulations 1996	116
Indictment Rules 1971	
r 4(2)	475
r 9	475
Indictments (Procedure) Rules 1971	
r 5	450, 475
Inheritance Tax (Delivery of Accounts) (Exempted Estates) Regulations 2004	
regs 3–4	117
reg 6	117
Inheritance Tax (Delivery of Accounts) (Exempted Estates) (Amendment) Regulations 2006	xv
Insolvency Act (Prescribed Part) Order 2003	304
Insolvency Rules 1986	285, 293, 306
rr 5.3–5.5	293
r 5.23	293
r 6	306
Insolvency (Amendment) Rules 2002	306
Insolvent Partnerships Order 1994	296
Intestate Succession (Interest and Capitalisation) Order 1977	153

J–K

L

Land Registration Rules 2003	224
r 5	216
rr 8–9	216
rr 21–53	209
r 58A	229
rr 64–65	216
rr 70–76	216
rr 80–82	216
r 89	216
rr 91–100	216
rr 117–123	178, 218
rr 124–125	218
r 134(1)(a)–(b)	218
r 135(1)(a)	218
r 136	208
rr 147–160	220
r 163	194
r 164	192
rr 165–166	216
r 173	185
rr 176–180	195
rr 181–185	194
Sch 1A	229
Sch 4	216
Landlord and Tenant Act 1954 Part II (Notices) Regulations 2004	237
Landlord and Tenant (Covenants) Act (Notices) Regulations 1995	231

Statutory instrument	Page
Lay Representatives (Rights of Audience) Order 1999	395
Limited Liability Partnership Regulations 2001	251, 253, 254
reg 5	296
reg 7	251, 252
(1)–(8)	252
(9)–(10)	252, 254
reg 8	251, 252
Sch 1	253
Sch 2	253
Part I	253
Sch 3	254, 296

M

Money Laundering Regulations 2003	7, 11, 175

N

National Assistance (Assessment of Resources) Regulations 1992	140
National Police Records (Recordable Offences) Regulations 2000	447
Non-Contentious Probate Rules 1987	
r 8	156
rr 13–16	168
r 20	157, 158, 159, 167, 170
r 22	157, 158, 159, 170
r 27(5)	158
r 31	157
r 32	157, 158
r 35	157, 158
r 37	158
r 44	167
r 45	168
rr 46–48	167
rr 52–53	157
r 55	168

O

P

Part Time Worker Discrimination Regulations	328
Police and Criminal Evidence Act 1984	
Codes of Practice	448, 508
Codes A–B	434
Code C	434
para 1.7	440
para 2.4	448, 464
para 3.2	439
para 6.1	449
paras 6.5–6.6	449
para 6.10	449
para 6.15	449
para 6D	449
para 10.1	439, 441
paras 10.4–10.5	439
para 10.8	439
paras 11.1–11.1A	441

Statutory instrument	Page
para 11.2	441
paras 11.4–11.14	441
para 11.15	440
para 11.18	440
para 11E	441
para 12.2	440
para 12.4	440
paras 12.6–12.8	440
para 16.1	447
para 16.2	439
para 16.5	441
Annex B	
para B3	449
Annex C	
para 2	439
Annex D	441
Code D	434
paras 3.2–3.11	444
para 3.14	444
paras 3.16–3.17	444
para 3.21	444
para 3.23	444
Annex A	444, 445
paras 2–2A	445
para 3	445
para 5	445
para 7	445
paras 10–12	445
Annex B	444, 445
paras 1–3	445
paras 9–10	445
paras 12–18	445
para 23	445
Annex C	444, 446
paras 2–6	446
para 8	446
para 10	446
paras 13–32	446
paras 35–36	446
Annex D	444, 446
paras 1–7	446
Annex E	444, 446
paras 1–2	446
para 4	446
Code E	434, 441
para 2	441
para 2.2	441
para 3.1(a)	441
Code F	434, 441
para 6.4	441
Code G	434, 435
paras 1.1–1.4	435
paras 2.1–2.3	435
para 2.4	436
para 2.8	435
para 2.9	436
para 4	437
paras 4.1–4.3	437
Code H	434
Pollution Prevention and Control (England and Wales) Regulations 2000	189
Prosecution of Offences (Custody Time Limits) Regulations 1987	
reg 4A	454
reg 5	454
Regulatory Reform (Business Tenancies) (England and Wales) Order 2003	236
Schs 1–2	236
Regulatory Reform (Removal of 20 Member Limit in Partnerships etc) Order 2002	244

Q–R

S

Statutory instrument	Page
Sale and Supply of Goods to Consumers Regulations 2002	
reg 15	318
Social Security Contributions (Intermediaries) Regulations 2000	86
Solicitors' Accounts Rules 1998	2, 27, 60-8, 70, 76, 77, 198, 201
r 1	61, 69
r 2(2)	
(c)–(d)	61, 63
(h)	61
(j)–(l)	65
(s)	65
(t)	60
(z)	62, 65
r 4(1)(b)–(c)	60
r 5(a)–(c)	60
r 5n(i)	60
rr 6–7	60
r 8	61
r 12	61
r 13	61, 74, 75
r 13n	
(i)	61
(xi)–(xii)	61
r 14(1)–(5)	63
r 15	
(1)	62, 77
(2)	62
(a)	62
(b)	67
r 16(1)	62
(a)	67
rr 17–18	62
r 19	
(1)	62
(a)	64, 72
(b)	62, 64, 72
(c)	64, 72
(d)	64
(2)–(3)	61, 62, 64
(5)	64
r 20	64, 72

Statutory instrument	Page
(2)	63
(b)	62
(3)	63
r 21	62
(1)	
(a)	65
(b)	64, 65
(2)(b)–(d)	65
(3)	65
r 22	62
(1)–(3)	62
(4)–(8)	63
r 23(1)–(2)	66
r 24	67, 68, 198
(1)–(2)	67
(4)–(5)	68
(6)	67
r 25(1)–(2)	68
r 26	67
r 27	67, 68
r 32	69, 75, 76
(1)–(2)	66
(5)	66
(6)	66, 75
(7)–(10)	66
Solicitors' Anti-Discrimination Rules 2004	13
Solicitors (Compensation for Inadequate Professional Services) Order 2005	27
Solicitors' Costs Information and Client Care Code 1999	12, 13, 15, 22, 176, 339
r 5(d)	23
Solicitors' Financial Services (Scope) Rules 2001	30
r 3	30, 176
rr 4–5	30
Solicitors' Introduction and Referral Code 1990	3, 176
r 1(2)(c)	3
r 2(9)–(11)	3
r 2A	
(3)	3
(4)(b)	3
(6)	3
r 4(2)	3
Solicitors' Investment Business Rules 1995	27
Solicitors' Practice Rules 1990	3, 11, 27, 32
r 1	2, 12, 13, 61, 177, 180
r 3	3
r 6	9, 12, 175, 200
(2)	10
(3)	10, 12
(c)	10, 12
(d)	12
(e)	10, 12
(f)	10
r 6A	9, 12, 175
r 10	3, 61, 76
r 15	12, 13, 15, 27
r 16D	
(2)–(3)	8

Statutory instrument	Page
(4)	9, 14
(5)	9
r 16E	
(2)	11
(4)	11
(5)	11, 12
(6)	12
Solicitors' Publicity Code 2001	3
Stamp Duty (Exempt Instruments) Regulations 1987	128
reg 3	128
Stamp Duty Land Tax Avoidance Schemes (Prescribed Descriptions of Arrangements) Regulations 2005	142

T

Tax Avoidance Schemes (Information) Regulations 2004	142
Tax Avoidance Schemes (Prescribed Descriptions of Arrangements) Regulations 2006	142
Town and Country Planning (General Permitted Development) Order 1995	188
Town and Country Planning (Use Classes) Order 1987	188
Transfer of Undertakings (Protection of Employment) Regulations 2006	289, 329
Transitional Information and Consultation of Employees Regulations 1999	330

U

Unfair Terms in Consumer Contracts Regulations 1999	320
regs 3–5	321
reg 6	321
(2)	321
regs 7–8	321
regs 10–15	321
Sch 2	321

V

Value Added Tax Regulations 1995	
regs 99–112	122
reg 113	122
(a)–(f)	125
(h)	125
regs 114–115	122, 125
reg 116	122
regs 165–172	78

W

Working Time Regulations 1998	330

EU secondary legislation

Directive 89/48 328
Directive 97/7/EC 318
Directive 2001/86 287
Directive 2002/65/EC 318
Directive 2004/38 328
    arts 6–7 327
    arts 16–17 327
    art 18 326
    art 23 326
    art 24 328
    art 27 326
Directive 2004/48
    art 9 381
Directive 2005/36/EC 328

Regulation 1612/68
    art 2 328
Regulation 2790/1999 .... 309, 324
Regulation 1346/2000 306
Regulation 2658/2000 309
Regulation 2659/2000 309
Regulation 44/2001 .... 384, 423
Regulation 2157/2001 287
Regulation 1/2003 312
    arts 2–3 312
    arts 5–9 312
    art 11 312
    art 13 312
    arts 16–23 312
Regulation 139/2004 (Merger Control) 307
    Recital 32 307
    Recital 34 307
    arts 1–2 307
    art 4 307
    art 6 307
    art 9 307
    art 10(1) 307
    arts 11–15 307
Regulation 772/2004 309

CONDUCT

This chapter examines:

A	Cornerstones of good conduct	2
B	Advertising, introductions and referrals	3
C	Money laundering	4
D	Taking instructions	8
E	Costs, help in funding a case and bills	15
F	Undertakings	25
G	Discipline	26
H	Financial services	28
I	Professional ethics	31
J	Human rights	34

Where to find the various rules

➤ *SPR 1990, SIRC 1990* and *SPC 2001* can all be found at:

http://www.lawsociety.org.uk//documents/downloads/Profethics_PracticeRules.pdf

A   Cornerstones of good conduct

Solicitors' Practice Rules 1990 r 1

➤ This rule is the cornerstone of good conduct.

'A solicitor shall not do anything in the course of practising as a solicitor, or permit another person to do anything on his or her behalf, which compromises or impairs or is likely to compromise or impair any of the following:

a) the solicitor's independence or integrity.

b) a person's freedom to instruct a solicitor of his or her choice.

c) **the solicitor's duty to act in the best interests of the client.**

d) the good repute of the solicitor or the solicitors' profession.

e) the solicitor's proper standard of work.

f) the solicitor's duty to the court.'

➤ Individual solicitors are liable for any breach of these rules.

➤ All partners of a law firm are jointly and severally liable for breach of these rules by any fee earner.

All basic conduct rules are soon to change!

➤ The Law Society is in the course of bringing in a new Code of Conduct which will replace The Guide to the Professional Conduct of Solicitors.

- **This new Code of Conduct is not yet in force.**

➤ The new Law Society's Code of Conduct:

- was made by the Council of the Law Society in September 2004.
- is currently undergoing a process of review by government and the judiciary under *CLSA 1990 Schedule 4*.
- is expected to come into force towards the end of 2006.
- will replace almost all of the provisions currently found in The Guide to the Professional Conduct of Solicitors, except for:
  - *SAR 1998*, *and*
  - rules relating to professional indemnity, *and*
  - rules relating to financial services, *and*
  - rules relating to the Compensation Fund.

B Advertising, introductions and referrals

    I   Advertising
    II   Introductions and referrals

I Advertising

- Advertisements must comply with the *SPC 2001*, which forbids comparisons with other firms and unsolicited intrusion upon members of the public (eg: tele-sales).
- Advertisements must not be in bad taste, must contain accurate information and nothing which is misleading and comply with the general law.

II Introductions and referrals

- Introductions by third parties are permitted (*SPR r 3*) if *SIRC 1990* and *SPR 1990* are complied with.
    - The solicitor may pay a third party for an introduction if:
        - it does not compromise the duty to act in the client's best interest (*SIRC 1990 r 1(2)(c)*), and
        - the client has been informed by the introducer of the payment before the solicitor is instructed (*SIRC 1990 r 2A(3)*), and
        - the introducer has not obtained the client by means forbidden to solicitors eg: cold-calling (*SIRC 1990 r 2A(4)(b)*).
    - Paying for an introduction in this way is not allowed for legally aided work or criminal work (*SIRC 1990 r 2A(6)*).
    - The firm must keep a written record of any agreements for the introduction of clients (*SIRC 1990 r 2(9)*).
    - Each firm should conduct a review at six-monthly intervals, which should check (*SIRC 1990 r 2(10)*):
        a) that the *SIRC 1990* has been complied with, *and*
        b) that the clients concerned have been advised impartially, *and*
        c) the income which the firm derives from each agreement with an introducer.
- Where, so far as can be reasonably ascertained, more than 20% of a firm's income during the period under review arises from a single source of introduction of business, the firm should consider whether steps should be taken to reduce that proportion (*SIRC 1990 r 2(11)*).
- A solicitor may refer a client to a third party, provided he:
    a) acts in the client's best interests (*SIRC 1990 r 4(2)*), *and*
    b) accounts to a client for commissions over £20, or retains the money with the client's prior consent (*SPR r 10*).

C Money laundering

➤ The *PCA 2002* defines 5 offences on money laundering, all carrying strict criminal penalties.

1. Concealing (s 327)

➤ **The offence:** concealing, disguising, converting or transferring criminal property or removing criminal property from England and Wales.

- 'Concealing or disguising' includes concealing or disguising its nature, source, location, disposition, movement or ownership or any rights with respect to it.

DEFENCES: See box at bottom of page.

2. Arranging (s 328)

➤ **The offence:** entering into or becoming concerned in an arrangement which he knows or suspects facilitates (by whatever means) the acquisition, retention, use or control of criminal property by or on behalf of another person.

DEFENCES: See box at bottom of page.

3. Acquiring, using and possessing (s 329)

➤ **The offence:** acquiring, using or possessing criminal property.

→ **EXTRA DEFENCE:** A person does not commit such an offence if he acquired or used or had possession of the property for adequate consideration.

DEFENCES: See box at bottom of page plus ↓

Defences to offences 1, 2 and 3 above (ss 327, 328, 329, 338)

➤ **Defences:** A person does not commit an offence under *ss 327, 328 or 329* if:

- he makes an authorised disclosure to the police or an MLO (see below) before the prohibited act and he has the appropriate consent, *or*

- he makes an authorised disclosure to the police or an MLO (see below) while the alleged offender is doing the prohibited act, and the offender began the act when (because he did not then know or suspect that the property constituted or represented a person's benefit from criminal conduct) the act was not a prohibited act, and the disclosure is made on his own initiative and as soon as is practicable after he first knows or suspects that the property constitutes or represents a person's benefit from criminal conduct, *or*

- he makes an authorised disclosure to the police or an MLO (see below) after the prohibited act and he has good reason not to disclose before and the disclosure is made on his own initiative and as soon as practicable, *or*

- he intended to make such a disclosure but had a reasonable excuse for not doing so, *or*

- the act is done in carrying out a function he has relating to the enforcement of any provision of *PCA 2002* or of any other enactment relating to criminal conduct or benefit from it, *or*

- he knows, or believes on reasonable grounds, that the relevant criminal conduct occurred in a particular country/territory outside the UK *and* the relevant criminal conduct was not, at the time it occurred, unlawful under the criminal law then applying in that country/territory, and is not of a description prescribed by an order made by the Secretary of State, *or*

- for deposit taking institutions only: they are exempt from the offence if they operate an account maintained with them and the criminal property involved is under £250 (although this amount may be varied in certain circumstances).

CONDUCT

Money laundering

4. Failing to disclose (ss 330-332) (as amended by SOCPA 2005 ss 102, 104)

➤ **The offence:** A person commits an offence if:

A he knows or suspects or has reasonable grounds for knowing or suspecting, that another person is engaged in money laundering, *and*

B the information or other matter on which his knowledge or suspicion is based, or which gives reasonable grounds for such knowledge or suspicion, came to him in the course of his business in a regulated sector (which includes legal services providers eg: lawyers), *and*

C he:
- can identify the other person mentioned in A or the whereabouts of any of the laundered property, *or*
- believes, or it is reasonable to expect him to believe, that the information or other matter mentioned in B will or may assist in identifying that other person or the whereabouts of any of the laundered property, *and*

D he does not make the required disclosure, as soon as is practicable after the information or other matter in B comes to him, to a nominated officer (ie: the Money Laundering Officer (MLO) of the firm) or to a person authorised by the Serious Organised Crime Agency (SOCA).

➤ **Defences:** A person does not commit such an offence if:
- he has a reasonable excuse for not making the required disclosure, *or*
- he is a professional legal adviser (or other relevant specified professional adviser, eg: accountant, auditor, tax adviser etc.) *and*:
  - if he knows either of (i) or (ii) below (see 'required disclosure'), he knows the thing because of information or other matter that came to him in privileged circumstances, *or*
  - the information or other matter mentioned in offence element B above came to him in privileged circumstances, *or*
- he does not know or suspect that another person is engaged in money laundering *and* he has not been provided by his employer with certain specified mandated training, *or*
- he knows, or believes on reasonable grounds, that the money laundering is occurring in a particular country/territory outside the UK, *and* the money laundering is not unlawful under the criminal law applying in that country/territory and is not prescribed by an order made by the Secretary of State, *or*
- he is employed by (or is in partnership with) a professional legal adviser (or a relevant professional adviser) to provide the adviser with assistance or support, *and* the information or other matter mentioned in offence element B above comes to the person in connection with the provision of such assistance or support, *and* the information or other matter came to the adviser in privileged circumstances.

➤ **The required disclosure is:** a disclosure of:
i) the identity of the other person mentioned in offence element A above, if he knows it, *and*
ii) the whereabouts of the laundered property, so far as he knows it, *and*
iii) the information or other matter mentioned in offence element B above.

➤ Legal privilege applies if the information or other matter comes to a solicitor when it is *not* given with the intention of furthering a criminal purpose and is communicated or given to him:
- by (or by a representative of) a client of his in connection with the giving by the solicitor of legal advice to the client, *or*
- by (or by a representative of) a person seeking legal advice from the solicitor, *or*
- by a person in connection with legal proceedings or contemplated legal proceedings.

5. Tipping off (s 333)

➤ **The offence:** A person commits an offence if he knows or suspects that a disclosure to an MLO or the police has been made and he makes a disclosure (ie: tips off the subject of the investigation) which is likely to prejudice any investigation which might be conducted following that disclosure.

➤ **Defences:** A person does not commit such an offence if:
- he did not know or suspect that the disclosure (ie: tipping off) was likely to be prejudicial, *or*
- the disclosure (ie: tipping off) is made in carrying out a function he has relating to the enforcement of any provision of *PCA 2002* or any other enactment relating to criminal conduct or benefit from criminal conduct, *or*
- he is a professional legal adviser, and the disclosure is not made with the intention of furthering a criminal purpose and the disclosure is to (or to a representative of) a client of the solicitor in connection with the giving by the solicitor of legal advice to the client or is to any person in connection with legal proceedings or contemplated legal proceedings.

Reinterpretation by *Bowman v Fels [2005] EWCA Civ 226* (Court of Appeal)

➤ **Litigation is not an 'arrangement' for the purposes of *PCA 2002 s 328*.**
➤ Lord Justice Brooke delivered the judgment of the court and said:
- *s 328* cannot have been intended to affect the ordinary conduct of litigation by legal professionals.
  - This includes any step taken by legal professionals in litigation from the issue of proceedings and the securing of injunctive relief or a freezing order up to its final disposal by judgment.
- The European/UK legislator could not have envisaged that any of these ordinary activities could fall within the concept of 'concerned in an arrangement...'.
- Legal proceedings are a state-provided mechanism for the resolution of issues according to law. Everyone has the right to a fair and public trial in the determination of his civil rights and duties which is secured by *ECHR Art 6*.
- Parliament could not have intended that proceedings or steps taken by lawyers in order to determine or secure legal rights and remedies for their clients should involve them in 'becoming concerned in an arrangement...', *even if they suspected that the outcome of such proceedings might have such an effect*.
- If the court was wrong in its interpretation of *s 328* and Parliament *had* intended to override legal professional privilege, then the legislation had to be clearer and should be amended to state this intention expressly.

CONDUCT
Money laundering

Money Laundering Regulations 2003

➤ It is necessary to have in place 3 sets of procedures to prevent and forestall money laundering:
- identification procedures, *and*
  - A solicitor always needs to check the identity of a client (eg: by asking to see a photo identification and proof of address eg: passport and recent utility bill).
- record-keeping procedures, *and*
- internal reporting procedures.

➤ A person must take 'all reasonable steps' and 'diligence' to ensure an offence is not committed.

➤ In addition to these procedures, training must be given to employees in order to facilitate identification of money laundering.

Verifying identification

➤ Reasonable measures must be taken to ensure identification if:
- a solicitor and a client agree to form a business relationship, *and*
- either:
  - the solicitor suspects money laundering, *or*
  - payment of 15,000 euros or more is or will be made to or by the client either in a one-off payment or in total payments.

➤ Identification procedures must be carried out as soon as practicable after contact.

➤ Where satisfactory evidence of identity is not obtained, the business relationship or one-off transaction must not proceed any further.

➤ If the client is acting for another person, measures must be taken to ensure their identity.
- There are exceptions to this eg: if a solicitor has received instructions from a regulated professional acting on behalf of another, satisfactory evidence of identity will already have been obtained, thus no further measures need to be taken. However it is usually safest to verify identity always.

Keeping records

➤ Where a solicitor and client have formed a business relationship, records must be retained for at least 5 years commencing with the date on which the relationship ends, or if the business relationship is regarding a one off transaction, then at least 5 years commencing with the date of the completion of all activities regarding that transaction.

➤ Records must be kept of:
- A copy of identity and information as to where a copy of that evidence is, *and*
- Documentation of all relevant business carried out by the solicitor.

➤ Records must be passed over to the relevant authoritative body if there is a suspicion of money laundering.

D Taking instructions

| I | Conflicts, disclosure and confidentiality | III | Solicitor authority |
| II | Practical matters on accepting instructions | IV | Terminating a retainer |

I Conflicts, disclosure and confidentiality

A Conflicts of interest generally

A conflict of interest (SPR r 16D(2))

➤ There is a conflict of interest if either:

a) a solictior's interests, *or*

b) the solicitor's duty to act in the best interests of 2 or more clients,

  ... conflict(s), or there is a significant risk that they may conflict, in relation to the same, or a related matter.

- A 'related matter' includes any other matter which involves the same asset or liability.

The rules on conflicts (SPR r 16D(3))

➤ Where there is conflict of interest, a solicitor must not act unless:

either i) when two different clients have a conflict/possible conflict, the different clients have a substantially common interest in relation to the matter or a particular aspect of it, *and*

ii) all the clients have given in writing their informed consent to the solicitor acting, ...

or i) the clients are competing for the same asset which, if attained by one client, will make the asset unobtainable by the other client(s), *and*

ii) there is no other conflict, or significant risk of conflict between the interests of any of the clients in relation to the matter, *and*

iii) the clients have confirmed in writing that they want the solicitor's practice to act in the knowledge that the practice may act for one or more of the clients competing for the asset, *and*

iv) unless the clients specifically agree, no individual solicitor acts for, or is responsible for the supervision of, more than one of those clients ...

and (in either case above) it is reasonable for the solicitor and the practice to act for all the clients.

'Informed consent'

➤ A client will not be regarded as having given 'informed consent' unless a solicitor:

a) draws all the relevant issues to the clients' attention before agreeing to act (or, if the solicitor is already acting, as soon as practicable when the conflict arises) and in such a way that the clients can understand the risks and issues involved, *and*

b) has a reasonable belief that the clients understand the issues, *and*

c) is reasonably satisfied that the clients are of full capacity.

Conflict arises while already acting (SPR r 16D(4))

➤ If a solicitor/practice, acts for more than one client and a conflict arises, the solicitor/practice may only continue to act for one or more of the clients if the duty of confidentiality to the other is not at risk.

Conflicts in gifts (SPR r 16D(5))

➤ If a client plans to make a gift (while alive, or on death), a solicitor must advise the client to take independent advice about the gift, where:

a) the gift is for the benefit of:
   i) the solicitor, or
   ii) a proprietor/employee of the practice, or
   iii) a family member of anyone within i) or ii), and

b) the client is a not a member of the beneficiary's family, and

c) the gift is of a significant amount of itself, or in the context of the client's estate and the reasonable expectations of the prospective beneficiaries (SPR r 16D(5)).

   - If the client refuses, the solicitor must cease to act in relation to the gift.

B Conflicts of interest (Conveyancing)

➤ A solicitor must not accept instructions where SPR rr 6-6A are not complied with.

➤ A solicitor must not act for a buyer and a seller in a 'contract race' (even if SPR r 6 would otherwise permit the solicitor to act), nor may he act for more than one buyer (SPR r 6A).

   ◆ A 'contract race' occurs when a seller of freehold or leasehold land either:

   a) instructs a solicitor to deal with more than one prospective buyer, or

   b) is known by the solicitor to be dealing with more than one prospective buyer (SPR r 6A).

SPR r 6 generally

➤ SPR r 6 applies where a solicitor is asked to act for a party in conveyancing, property selling or mortgage related services in connection with:

a) the transfer of land for value at arm's length, or

b) the grant or assignment of a lease, or some other interest in land, for value at arm's length, or

c) the grant of a mortgage over land.

   ◆ 'Arm's length' is not necessarily a market value transaction. It depends on the precise facts; usually a transaction will not be a transaction at arm's length if the parties are:
   - related by blood, adoption or marriage, or
   - the trustees of a trust and the settlor of that trust, or
   - a beneficiary of a trust (or a relative of a beneficiary) and the trustees of a trust, or
   - a beneficiary and PRs, or
   - trustees of separate trusts for the same family, or
   - a sole trader, partners, or a limited company established to incorporate their business, or
   - associated companies (ie: there is a subsidiary/holding company relationship for the purposes of CA 1985).

CONDUCT
Taking instructions

Acting for the Seller and the Buyer (SPR r 6(2))

Is it the case that:
a) the solicitor does **not** have the written consent of both parties to act, *and/or*
b) a conflict of interest exists or arises, *and/or*
c) the seller is selling or leasing as a builder or developer?

→ **Yes** → The solicitor **must not act**, or if he has begun to act **must cease to act.**

↓ **No**

The solicitor may act if ...

Or ... both parties are established clients

Or ... the consideration is £10,000 or less, *and* the transaction is **not** the grant of a lease

Or ... there is no other qualified conveyancer in the area who either the buyer or the seller could reasonably be expected to consult

Or ... separate offices in different localities represent the seller and the buyer, *and* ... different solicitors who normally work at each office conduct or supervise the transaction for each party, *and* ... no office of the practice (or an associated practice) referred either client to the office conducting that client's transaction

Or ... the solicitor is only acting for the **buyer** in providing mortgage related services

Or ... the solicitor is only acting for the **seller** in providing property selling services through a Solicitors' Estate Agency Limited (**'SEAL' - a company that does not undertake conveyancing**)

... **and** provided that ...

... different persons conduct the work for the seller from those who work for the buyer (if such persons are supervised they must be supervised by different solicitors),

and

... the solicitor **informs the seller in writing** (before accepting instructions to deal with the property selling) of services which the buyer may be offered through the same practice or an associated practice,

and

... the solicitor **explains to the buyer** (before the buyer consents to the arrangement):

a) the implications of a conflict of interest arising, *and*
b) the solicitor's financial interest in the sale going through, *and*
c) if the solicitor proposes to offer mortgage related services through a SEAL which is acting for the seller, that the solicitor cannot advise the buyer on the merits of the purchase

Acting for the Buyer and the Lender (SPR r 6(3))

A mortgage is a standard mortgage where:
i) it is provided in the normal course of a lender's activities, *and*
ii) a significant part of those activities consists of lending, *and*
iii) the mortgage is on standard terms

Is it the case that:
a) a conflict of interest exists or arises, *and/or*
b) an individual mortgage is to be granted at arm's length?
(An 'individual mortgage' is any mortgage other than a standard mortgage - see bubble left)

→ **Yes** → The solicitor **must not act**, or if he has begun to act **must cease to**

↓ **No**

The solicitor may act if ...

↓

... the mortgage is a standard mortgage ...

r 6(3)(c) lists duties

Under *r 6(3)(e)*, *r 6(3)* prevails if instructions are ambiguous or there is a discrepancy between them and *r 6(3)*

... *and*
a) the lender's instructions:
  i) do not extend beyond the limitations set out in *r 6(3)(c), (e)* (eg: as set out in the *CML Handbook*), *and*
  ii) permit the use of a certificate of title as set out in the Appendix to *r 6(3)* if a property is to be a private residence) *or* (in any other case) the City of London Law Society's land law sub-committee's certificate (see *r 6(3)(f)*), *and*
b) the solicitor first informs the lender in writing of the circumstances if:
  i) the solicitor or a member of his immediate family is a borrower, *or*
  ii) the solicitor proposes to act for the seller, the buyer and the lender in the same transaction.

C Disclosure and confidentiality

➤ A solicitor must **not** agree to act if the solicitor, or the practice, holds confidential information relating to a client/former client, and there would be a risk of breaching confidentiality on a matter where (*SPR r 16E(4)*):

  a) the information might reasonably be expected to be material, *and*

  b) that client has an interest 'adverse' (e.g. the parties are, or are likely, to oppose each other in a matter or ADR: see *Bolkiah v KPMG* ([1999] 2 WLR 215, HL)) to the client or former client,

  unless (*SPR r 16E(5)*):

  i) both clients give informed consent, *and*

  ii) the client for whom the solicitor proposes to act knows that material information which cannot be disclosed is, or may be, held by the solicitor or the practice, *and*

  iii) the solicitor has a reasonable belief that the clients understand these issus (having had them brought to their attention), *and*

  iv) both clients have agreed to set conditions for the solicitor (eg: using an information barrier), *and*

  v) it is reasonable in all the circumstances for the solicitor to act.

➤ A solicitor must maintain confidentiality owed to existing and former clients, except if disclosure is required or permitted, either by law or by the client/former client (*SPR r 16E(2)*).

  ◆ The duty of confidentiality owed under common law, and the *SPR 1990*, is distinct from the duty to maintain legal professional privilege.

  ◆ No duty of confidentiality arises:
    a) if a client is attempting to use a solicitor to perpetrate a fraud, or other crime, *or*
    b) in respect of information which is a matter of public record.

  ◆ In certain exceptional circumstances a solicitor may be required to disclose information, eg:

  • a solicitor believes it is necessary to disclose information to prevent the commission of a criminal act that the solicitor reasonably believes is likely to result in serious bodily harm.

  • a solicitor may disclose information to an appropriate authority, where children are involved if :
    i) a child reveals information indicating continuing sexual or other physcial abuse, *or*
    ii) an adult discloses such abuse.

  • where a government body is authorised by statute to require disclosure (eg: disclosure to HMRC under powers conferred under *TMA 1970*).

  • in compliance with a court order permitting seizure of confidential documents.
    ▪ If a client does not waive confidentiality, a solicitor can ask for a *sub poena* or witness summons to allow a court to determine whether privilege may be claimed.

  • information held by 'public bodies' that is required to be disclosed under *FIA 2000*.

  • money laundering reporting requirements under *PCA 2002*, terrorism legislation and *MLR 2003*.

  • where it is reasonably necessary to establish a defence to a criminal charge, or civil claim, by a client against the solicitor.

  • where conduct is being investigated by the Law Society/Solicitors Disciplinary Tribunal.

  • where a client is publicly funded, there may be a duty to report information to the LSC.

CONDUCT
Taking instructions

Conflicts of duties of confidentiality and disclosure

➤ If a conflict arises between a solicitor's duty of confidentiality and disclosure, the duty of confidentiality is paramount and the solicitor must cease to act, unless *either*:

   a) both clients consent (*SPR r 16E(5)*), *or*

   b) it is not possible to obtain informed consent from the client, or former client (*SPR r 16E(6)*), *and*:

   i) the client has agreed to the solicitor acting, or continuing to act, in the knowledge that the solicitor or the practice, holds or might hold, material to the matter which the solicitor cannot disclose, *and*

   ii) safeguards which comply with the law in force at the time put in place (eg: an information barrier), *and*

   iii) it is reasonable in all the circumstances for the solicitor to continue to act.

II Practical matters on accepting instructions

➤ On accepting instructions a solicitor should:

- take instructions directly from the client (ie: a request for advice on behalf of a potential client should be confirmed personally by the client).
- ensure a client is free to instruct whomever he wishes, and is aware of this right (*SPR r 1*).
- always comply with the Law Society's client care rules (*SPR r 15* and *SCICCC 1999*).
- in a 'contract race' for conveyancing clients, immediately inform each buyer's solicitor of the race by telephone or fax, and confirm this in writing (*SPR r 6A*).
- if acting for a buyer and a lender in respect of an institutional mortgage, where the property is to be used as a private residence and the lender has not certified that the lender's instructions comply with *SPR r 6(3)(c), (e)*, notify that lender that the certificate of title will be in the form approved under *SPR r 6* and that the solicitor's duties are limited to those duties set out in *SPR r 6(3)* (*SPR r 6(3)(d)*).

➤ On accepting instructions a solicitor should **not**:

- accept instructions on a basis which excludes the jurisdiction of the Law Society.
- act for a client where the action is malicious.

Fees, quotations and estimates

➤ If a solicitor gives a quotation instead of an estimate, he must do the job for that price.

➤ An estimate of fees should make clear how costs will be calculated; the solicitor must inform the client if it appears likely that costs will exceed the estimate.

➤ If VAT is not mentioned, the client is entitled to assume the price is inclusive of VAT.

➤ For conditional fee agreements, see pp 22-23.

CONDUCT
Taking instructions

Law Society's client care *SPR r 15* and *SCICCC 1999*

➤ Serious or persistent material breaches of *SCICCC 1999* may be a breach of *r 15* (leading to professional conduct issues and sanctions) and may also be evidence of inadequate professional service.

- Material breaches which are not serious or persistent will not be a breach of *r 15* but may be evidence of inadequate professional service (see pp 26-27).

➤ The solicitor should:

- give the client the best information possible about the likely overall costs (including a breakdown between fees, VAT and disbursements).
    - This means agreeing a fixed fee, giving a realistic estimate, giving a forecast within a possible range of costs, or explaining to the client the reasons why it is not possible to fix, or give a realistic estimate or forecast of, the overall costs, and giving instead the best information possible about the cost of the next stage of the matter.
- explain clearly to the client the time likely to be spent in dealing with a matter, if time spent is a factor in the calculation of the fees.
- (in an appropriate case), explain to a privately paying client that the client may set an upper limit on the firm's costs for which the client may be liable without further authority. Solicitors should not exceed an agreed limit without first obtaining the client's consent.
- make it clear at the outset if an estimate, quotation or other indication of cost is not intended to be fixed.
- explain what reasonably foreseeable payments a client may have to make either to the solicitor or to a third party and when those payments are likely to be needed.
- explain to the client the arrangements for updating the costs information

- explain to the client how the firm's fees are calculated except where the overall costs are fixed or clear. If the basis of charging is an hourly charging rate, that must be made clear.
    - The client should be told if charging rates may be increased.
- discuss with the client how and when any costs are to be met, and consider whether:
    - the client may be eligible and should apply for legal aid,
    - the client's liability for their own costs may be covered by insurance,
    - the client's liability for another party's costs may be covered by pre-purchased insurance and, if not, whether it would be advisable for the client's liability for another party's costs to be covered by after the event insurance (including in every case where a conditional fee or contingency fee arrangement is proposed), *and*
    - the client's liability for costs (including the costs of another party) may be paid by another person e.g. an employer or trade union.
- discuss with the client whether the likely outcome in a matter will justify the expense or risk involved including, if relevant, the risk of having to bear an opponent's costs.

Other practical matters during the retainer

➤ A solicitor should act in the client's best interests (*SPR r 1*).

➤ A solicitor must not mislead the court (*SPR r 1*).

- In a criminal case, a solicitor can put the prosecution to proof even if the client admits guilt to the solicitor. However, assisting a client to give perjured evidence would breach the solicitor's duty to the court, and the solicitor should refuse to act if a client attempts this.

- A solicitor is not obliged to inform the court if it is mistaken about a defendant's criminal record, provided the court does not request any positive representation. If a court requests information, the solicitor must advise the client to tell the truth, and must refuse to act if the client declines.

➤ A solicitor must write regularly to the client keeping him informed of what is (or is not!) happening, the costs incurred, and any action which the client ought to take (*SPR r 15*).

Solicitors' Anti-Discrimination Rules 2004

➤ A solicitor should not discriminate on grounds of race, sex or sexual orientation.

➤ A solicitor should not discriminate unreasonably or unfairly on grounds of disability.

➤ A solicitor may not refuse instructions on the above grounds, or discriminate against his staff on these grounds. If a client asks a solicitor to instruct a barrister of a particular race or sex, the solicitor should try to persuade him otherwise, and if this fails, he should refuse to act.

III Solicitor authority

➤ **Non-contentious business** (ie: before litigation is commenced): a solicitor has 'ostensible authority' to act on the client's behalf.

➤ **Contentious business:** a solicitor has 'actual authority' to act on a client's behalf and to bind a client.

- The solicitor should always obtain a client's express authority, preferably in writing, before making any commitment on their behalf, unless the matter is urgent.
- A solicitor acting without client consent may be liable to a third party for breach of warranty of authority.

IV Terminating a retainer

➤ The retainer may be terminated:
- by the client at any time, for any reason.
- by the solicitor if there is 'good reason' and reasonable notice is given.
  - When stating the 'good reason', a solicitor must not breach his duty of confidentiality.
    - Eg: if a solicitor is acting both for an insured person and that insured person's insurance company, and the solicitor becomes aware that the insured person is defrauding the insurers, the solicitor should refuse to act for both parties. The solicitor must maintain confidentiality to both clients, and must therefore not disclose any details to the insurer.
    - Eg: if a solicitor is acting for both a mortgage company and a house buyer, where the house buyer wishes to obtain a mortgage for more than the property is worth. The solicitor should refuse to act for both parties. The solicitor must maintain confidentiality to both clients, and must therefore not disclose any details to the mortgage company.
    - Circumstances which may entitle, or compel, a solicitor to end a retainer include:
      a) a conflict of interest arises (eg: a solicitor for 2 co-accused with contradictory defences should decline to act for both), *or*
         NB: where a conflict of interest does not threaten the administration of justice, and *SPR 16D(4)* is complied with, then a solicitor may continue acting for one of the parties.
      b) the client instructs a solicitor to break the law, *or*
      c) when confidence between the solicitor and the client breaks down, *or*
      d) when the client does not meet an interim bill during contentious proceedings.
- by operation of law.
  - Eg: the solicitor is declared bankrupt or is of unsound mind.

Actions on termination

➤ A solicitor should return the client's papers, unless the solicitor:
  a) holds the papers as the client's agent, *and*
  b) has a lien over them (eg: for unpaid work).

➤ If the client instructs another solicitor, the second solicitor must secure the documents by giving an undertaking as to the costs incurred by the first solicitor.
- When the client is LSC funded, there is no need for such an undertaking.

E Costs, help in funding a case and bills

> I Types of costs
> II LSC funding
> III Civil: CLS help
> IV Criminal: CDS help
> V The difference between 'contingency' and 'conditional' fee agreements
> VI Conditional fee agreements
> VII Bills

➤ A solicitor should always discuss with a client how and when costs are to be met.
  ◆ This discussion may include whether liability for their own or another party's costs may be insured using before-the-event or after-the-event insurance.

I Types of costs

➤ A client will have to bear costs. These costs fall into 2 classes:

1 **Solicitor-own-client costs:** these are all the expenses which the solicitor incurs on the client's behalf, eg: the solicitor's own fees, fees for expert opinions, applications for police accident reports, counsel's advice, etc. The solicitor usually asks for payment on account, for expenses that he expects to incur.

2 **Inter partes costs:** in a civil claim, these are expenses which other parties to a claim incur and are usually the responsibility of whichever party loses litigation (subject to the court's ruling on costs, see pp 417-422).

Contentious matters (civil) (SPR r 15 and SCICCC 1999) Solicitors must explain:	
Private clients	**Community Legal Service funded clients**
◆ the client's potential liability for his own costs and those of any other party ◆ the fact that the client will be responsible for paying the firm's bill in full regardless of any order for costs made against the opponent ◆ the probability that the client will have to pay the opponent's costs as well as the client's own costs if the case is lost ◆ the fact that even if the client wins, the opponent may not be ordered to pay or be capable of paying the full amount of the client's costs ◆ the fact that if the opponent is LSC funded, the client may not recover costs even if successful	◆ the client's potential liability for his own costs and those of any other party ◆ **the effect of the statutory charge and its likely amount** ◆ **the client's liability to pay the statutory charge and consequences of failure to do so** ◆ the fact that the client may still be ordered by the court to contribute to the opponent's costs if the case is lost even though the client's own costs are covered by the CLS ◆ the fact that even if the client wins, the opponent may not be ordered to pay or be capable of paying the full amount of the client's costs

➤ For further information on civil costs see pp 417-422.

II LSC funding

- The Legal Services Commission (LSC) provides legal funding help.
    - Ie: the LSC pays set rates to solicitors who do legal work for people who need government help to fund legal cases/advice.
    - The LSC has 11 regional offices and a number of Head Office departments.
- The Legal Services Commission is responsible for running 2 schemes (*AJA 1999*):
    - for civil matters: **the Community Legal Service (CLS)**, *and*
    - for criminal matters: **the Criminal Defence Service (CDS)**.
- For civil matters, the primary practical document to consult on the rules is the Funding Code.
    - This can be found at: http://www.legalservices.gov.uk/civil/guidance/funding_code.asp#.

III Civil: CLS help

- Solicitors can provide advice or representation funded by the LSC (via the CLS) only if they have a 'General Civil Contract' with the LSC.
    - For family cases and specialist areas like immigration and clinical negligence, only specialist firms are funded to do the work.
    - Claims for personal injury (except clinical negligence) are not funded by the LSC. Such cases can instead be pursued under conditional fee agreements between solicitors and clients (see pp 22-23).
    - Firms are audited against the Contract to ensure they continue to meet quality assurance standards.
- The CLS cannot be used to fund services (beyond the provision of general information about the law and the legal system and the availability of legal services) in relation to (*AJA 1999 Sch 2*):
    - allegations of personal injury or death, other than allegations relating to clinical negligence, *or*
    - allegations of negligently caused damage to property, *or*
    - conveyancing, *or*
    - boundary disputes, *or*
    - the making of wills, *or*
    - matters of trust law, *or*
    - defamation or malicious falsehood, *or*
    - matters of company or partnership law, *or*
    - other matters arising out of the carrying on of a business, *or*
    - certain areas under *MCA 2005*.
- The LSC funds a range of legal services. There are 6 main forms of civil legal help:

CONDUCT

Costs, help in funding a case, bills

Types of civil legal help (CLS(F)R 2000)	
Covered in this book	**Not covered in this book**
1 Legal Help 2 Help At Court 3 Legal Representation: 　Type 1: 　　◆ Investigative Help 　Type 2: 　　◆ Full Representation	4 **Help with Mediation** 　◆ Purpose: help and advice in support of Family Mediation, help in drawing up any agreement reached in mediation and help in confirming such an agreement in a court order and related conveyancing work. 5 **General Family Help** 　◆ Purpose: provides help in relation to a family dispute. 6 **Family Mediation** 　◆ Purpose: covers mediation for a family dispute.

1 **Legal Help**

➤ Purpose: advice/assistance with any legal problem. It covers general advice, writing letters, negotiating, getting a barrister's opinion, preparing a written case if going before a court or tribunal.

➤ Financial restrictions:
  ◆ Capital and income must be within certain prescribed financial limits.
  ◆ No contribution is payable by the applicant.
  ◆ A maximum level of work only (set by standard rate) is allowed to be performed under this. When this level is reached, authority for further work is needed from the LSC regional office.
  ◆ The statutory charge will apply to any money or property recovered or preserved.

➤ Age: for anyone over 16. For minors, a parent's/guardian's capital and income are assessed.

2 **Help At Court**

➤ Purpose: allows for a solicitor or adviser to speak at court hearings, without acting for the client in the whole proceedings.

➤ Financial restrictions:
  ◆ Capital and income must be within certain prescribed financial limits.
  ◆ No contribution is payable by the applicant.
  ◆ A maximum level of work only (set by standard rate) is allowed to be performed under this. When this level is reached, authority for further work is needed from the LSC regional office.
  ◆ The statutory charge will apply to any money or property recovered or preserved.

➤ Age: for anyone over 16. For minors, a parent's/guardian's capital and income are assessed.

CONDUCT
Costs, help in funding a case, bills

3   Legal Representation (2 types):

Type 1:   Investigative Help

➤ Purpose: investigation of the strength of a proposed claim where the prospects of success are not clear and the investigation is likely to be expensive. It covers the issue and conduct of proceedings only so far as these are necessary to obtain disclosure of relevant information or to protect a position in relation to an urgent hearing or a time limit for the issue of proceedings.

Type 2:   Full Representation

➤ Purpose: for representation in legal proceedings to trial and beyond.

For Type 1 or Type 2:

➤ Procedure: an organisation with an LSC contract applies on behalf of the applicant to the LSC regional office, which decides (usually within 2 weeks) whether it meets the funding criteria. The regional office can either grant or refuse the application.

- If the application is refused, there is a right of review by the LSC's regional director and ultimately by the LSC's funding review committee.
- If the application is granted and no contribution is payable, the LSC regional office sends a certificate detailing the scope of the funding.
- If the application is granted and a contribution will be payable, the LSC regional office sends an offer to the applicant (detailing the scope of the contribution), which, if accepted by the applicant, results in a certificate being sent to the applicant detailing the scope of the funding.

➤ The certificate:

- copies are sent to the applicant and the solicitor and notice of issue is served on any other parties.

  NB: No notice of any limitation or restrictions on the legal help must be given to other parties.

- if the certificate needs to be amended, an amended certificate is issued and notice must be served on all parties to the dispute.

➤ Financial restrictions:

- The calculation is based on the applicant's disposable capital and disposable income (together with a spouse's/unmarried partner's, provided that there is no conflict of interest between them).
- Capital and income must be within certain prescribed financial limits.
  - Reassessments of income/capital may happen any time while the certificate is in force.
- A contribution may be payable by the applicant.
- The statutory charge will apply to any money or property recovered or preserved.

➤ Merits restriction: the funding criteria must be satisfied: they are set out in the Funding Code.

EMERGENCIES:
It is also possible for either type of Legal Representation to be granted on an emergency basis where the matter is urgent and meets the criteria.

IV Criminal: CDS help

➤ Solicitors can carry out criminal defence work funded by the LSC (via the CDS) only if they have a 'General Criminal Contract' with the LSC or some other franchised arrangement with the LSC.

- Firms are audited against the Contract to ensure they continue to meet quality assurance standards.

➤ The LSC also directly employs some criminal defence lawyers (known as public defenders) who can provide any CDS criminal services.

- Employees of the CDS are subject to a strict code of conduct.

➤ There are 3 forms of CDS-provided help (*CDS(F)O 2001*):

1 **Advice and Assistance (this covers advice and assistance on criminal matters)**
Subcategory: Advice and Assistance if questioned by police

2 **Advocacy Assistance (this covers some advice and representation at court)**

3 **Representation for criminal offences**
Subcategory: The court duty solicitor scheme

1 Advice and Assistance

➤ **Purpose:** this covers help from a solicitor including giving general advice, writing letters, negotiating, getting a barrister's opinion and preparing a written case. It enables people of small or moderate means to get help from a solicitor but does not cover representation in court. (It is not available during criminal proceedings after charge or summons.)

➤ **Procedure:** The solicitor decides, based on the tests below, whether LSC funded help can be given. He can refuse to give advice without a reason but he may be asked to explain the reasons for his refusal by the LSC regional office.

➤ **Financial restrictions:** To qualify, disposable capital and disposable income of the applicant must be within the current financial limits, unless in receipt of certain state benefits (in which case disposable income is not looked at) (*CDS(G2)R 2001*).

- If qualified to receive advice and assistance, no contribution is payable by the applicant.
- If married (or living as a couple), the partner's capital and income will be included unless the parties live apart or there is a conflict of interest between them.

➤ **Merit restrictions:** the test is whether there is 'sufficient benefit' to the client (having regard to the circumstances of the matter, including client's personal circumstances) to justify work.

➤ **Age:** Children are eligible for Advice and Assistance, but in most cases where a child is under 17, a parent or guardian should apply on his behalf. Sometimes a solicitor can sometimes advise a child directly.

Subcategory: Advice and Assistance if questioned by police

➤ **Purpose:** If the police question an alleged offender about an offence (whether or not he has been arrested and whether or not at a police station) there is a right to free legal advice from a contracted solicitor. The police must contact a duty solicitor or the alleged offender's own solicitor or a solicitor on a police-kept list of local solicitors.

➤ **Restrictions:** None (*CDS(G2)R 2001*).

CONDUCT
Costs, help in funding a case, bills

2   **Advocacy Assistance**

➤ **Purpose:** this covers the cost of a solicitor preparing a case and *initial* representation in certain proceedings in both the magistrates' court and the Crown Court.

- It also covers representation for prisoners facing disciplinary charges before the prison governor/controller, and for discretionary and automatic lifers and those detained at Her Majesty's Pleasure whose cases are referred to the Parole Board. It also covers representation for those who have failed to pay a civil fine or obey a civil court order of the magistrates' court and are at risk of imprisonment and applications for ASBOs and some closure orders.

➤ **Procedure:** The solicitor decides whether this will be available based on the restrictions below (it is a devolved power from the LSC). The LSC pays the solicitor's bill if the merits restrictions test is met.

➤ **Financial restrictions:** There is no financial test (unless the advice and assistance is to be provided in the prison law class of work) (*CDS(G2)R 2001*).

- If qualified to receive advocacy assistance, no contribution is payable by the applicant.

➤ **Merit restrictions:** Advocacy assistance may not be granted if it appears unreasonable that approval should be granted in the particular circumstances of the case or if the case does not involve one of the *AJA 1999 Sch 3* criteria (listed overleaf).

---

3   **Representation for criminal offences**

➤ **Purpose:** Anyone charged with a criminal offence can apply. It covers the cost of a solicitor preparing a defence before going to court and represention there. It may also be available to apply for bail.

- If the case requires a barrister (particularly if in the Crown Court) that is also covered. Representation can also cover advice on appeal against a verdict or sentence of the magistrates' court or the Crown Court (or a decision of the Court of Appeal) and preparing the notice of appeal itself.

➤ **Procedure:** The solicitor assigns a Unique File Number (UFN) to the matter. He fills in the application form and sends it to the court where the case will be heard. **Details may need to be given of income and savings.** The court *[to be changed from 'court' to 'LSC' when CDSA 2006 s 1 is brought into force]* decides whether to grant Representation based on a financial and merits test (*CDS(G2)R 2001, CDS(ROA)R 2001*).

- If the application is refused, the court *[to be changed from 'court' to 'LSC' when CDSA 2006 s 1 is brought into force]* will write giving the reason for refusing Representation.
  - If the decision was to refuse Representation because it is not in the interests of justice, the applicant may make more applications (unlimited times up to the trial) to review the case.
- If the application is refused by the magistrates' court and the applicant goes to the Crown Court, he can apply to the Crown Court for Representation. *[This will change when CDSA 2006 s 1 is brought into force.]*
- In any case, if Representation is refused, a solicitor may be able to give some help in case preparation for court under Advice and Assistance.

- Financial restrictions:
    - **At present:** No contribution is payable if represented in a magistrates' court. In any other court, the judge must make a 'Recovery of Defence Costs Order' (RDCO) for the accused to pay of some or all of the cost of any representation (*CDS(G2)R 2001, CDS(RDCO)R 2001*).
    - *[When CDSA 2006 ss 2-3 are brought into force [not yet in force]:*
        - *There will be a means test.*
        - *The test will look at the applicant's gross income (which is adjusted to take into account any children of the household) in relation to upper and lower thresholds.*
            - *Applicants whose income falls below the lower threshold will automatically qualify for legal aid.*
            - *Applicants whose income falls above the upper threshold will be ineligible and expected to meet the full costs of representation before the Magistrates' Court. In the Crown Court (because of higher costs) a system of contributions will be applied.*
            - *Applicants whose income falls between these amounts will require a more detailed assessment under which the LSC will calculate the individuals's annual income (making deductions for income tax, national insurance, council tax, housing expenses, child-care costs, maintenance and living expenses). An applicant will then be eligible if the annual disposable income that remains does not exceed a fixed sum (to be specified).*
        - *There will be no right of appeal to court in relation to the application of the means test. Any complaints about miscalculation will be dealt with administratively by the LSC (although judicial review will still be an option).*
        - *Those who fail the means test may be able to take advantage of special hardship criteria.*
        - *The applicant must also fully comply with new rules as to what information he must provide.]*
- **Merit restrictions:** Representation will be granted **if it is in the 'interests of justice'** that the applicant should be represented at the LSC's expense. The decision is based on the information given in the application form. Some circumstances when it is appropriate to give LSC funding are when (*AJA 1999 Sch 3*):
    - there is a likelihood of:
        a) a custodial sentence, *or*
        b) loss of livelihood, *or*
        c) serious damage to reputation.
    - there is a substantial question of law involved (eg: evidential difficulties).
    - a disability/linguistic barrier prevents the defendant from understanding the proceedings.
    - tracing *and* interviewing of witnesses is necessary.
    - the case involves expert cross-examination of a prosecution witness.
    - it is in the interests of someone other than the accused that the accused is represented.
- **Age:** Children are eligible for Representation but, in most cases where a child is under 17, a parent or guardian should apply on his behalf.

Subcategory: The court duty solicitor scheme

- **Purpose:** If an alleged offender has to go to a Magistrates' Court and does not have his own solicitor there will usually be a duty solicitor available either at the court or on call to give free advice and representation on his first appearance.
- **Restrictions:** None (*CDS(G2)R 2001*).

V The difference between 'contingency' and 'conditional' fee agreements

Contingency fee agreements

➤ 'Contingency fee' agreements include but are wider than 'conditional fee' agreements.

➤ The term 'contingency fee' covers **all** agreements where the fee is payable only in the event of success.
- The fee may be fixed or calculated as a percentage of the proceeds recovered or otherwise.
  - Historically, 'contingency fee' agreements have become known to be where a fee is calculated as a percentage of the proceeds recovered. Such an agreement is only permissible in non-contentious matters and if a conditional fee agreement (as specified below).

Conditional fee agreements

➤ A conditional fee agreement is a special type of agreement created by statute and governed by *CFAR 2000* where certain fees are payable only in specified circumstances.
- The fee charged depends whether the case is won or lost (ie: 'no win, no fee' agreements).
  - The fee may consist of: i) basic or reduced costs, *or* ii) basic costs plus a 'success fee' of anything up to 100% of the basic costs.

VI Conditional fee agreements

Conditional fee agreements (*CLSA 1990 s 58, CFAO 2000*)

➤ *CLSA 1990 s 58* allows the use of conditional fee agreements in such types of case as the Lord Chancellor specifies by order (and subject to any requirements made by him in regulations).
- *CLSA 1990 s 58A(1)* excludes from conditional fees most criminal and family proceedings.

➤ The maximum uplift that can be charged if a lawyer is successful is 100% of the normal fees.

➤ The arrangements must be in writing *CLSA 1990 s 58(3)(a)* (but see box opposite on *SCICCC 1999*).

➤ Insurance policies are available to cover the costs of the other party and the client's own costs (including, if not a conditional fee case, the client's solicitor's fees) if the case is lost. The *AJA 1999* makes a success fee under a conditional fee agreement recoverable and also makes any premium paid for protective insurance recoverable too (*AJA 1999 s 29*).

➤ *Callery v Gray* [2002] UKHL 28 and *Halloran v Delaney* [2002] EWCA Civ 1258 give key principles:
- A claimant may enter a conditional fee agreement (CFA) and take out after-the-event (ATE) insurance on first consulting a solicitor, *before* the writing of a letter of claim and response.
- Reasonable ATE premiums are in principle recoverable as part of a claimant's costs even though a claim may be resolved without proceedings.

➤ CFAs may also apply in a case resolved by arbitration, provided all the requirements specified by regulations as to the form and content of the agreement are complied with (*Bevan Ashford v Geoff Yeandle (Contractors) Ltd* [1999] Ch. 239).

CONDUCT
Costs, helping in funding a case, bills

Abrogation of the 'indemnity principle'

- A CFA is enforceable even though the client is liable to pay his solicitor's fees and expenses only if and to the extent that the client recovers damages or costs in the action from the other party.

- For such a special type of CFA, the old 'indemnity principle' is abolished ie: the principle that the amount which can be awarded to a party in respect of costs to be paid by him to his solicitor is limited to what would have been payable by him to his solicitor if he had not been awarded costs.

- Solicitors can now agree lawfully with clients not to seek to recover by way of costs anything in excess of what the court awards, or what it is agreed will be paid.

Informing the client (SC/CCC 1999 r 5(d))

- Where a client is represented under a conditional fee agreement, the solicitor should explain:
  - the circumstances where the client may be liable for their own costs and the other party's costs,
  - the client's right to assessment of costs, wherever the solicitor intends to seek payment of any or all of their costs from the client,
  - any interest the solicitor may have in recommending a particular policy or other funding, *and*
  - if applicable, the fact that the solicitor is obliged under a fee sharing agreement to pay to a charity any fees which the solicitor receives by way of costs from the client's opponent or other third party.

A note on a CFA in road traffic cases

- For simple road traffic personal injury cases where a CFA is agreed at the outset, 12.5% is the *maximum* uplift that is allowed if the claim concludes before a trial has commenced or the dispute is settled before a claim is issued (and 100% if the claim concludes at trial) (*CPR Part 45 r 16*).

Results of a challenge to the CFA by the paying party

The party claiming costs from the paying party must:
a) disclose the CFA (subject to the removal of sensitive information from it), *or*
b) provide alternative evidence to support the claim for costs

This table is based on *Hollins v Russell* and other appeals [2003] EWCA Civ 718

VII Bills

➤ A bill must:

- be signed by a partner, and state enough to identify the matter and period to which it relates, *and*
- state whether VAT is included (NB: if it does not mention VAT, then it is taken to be included), *and*
- bill disbursements (eg: experts' fees) separately.

1 Client's remedies

➤ For non-contentious business, a client who is dissatisfied with a bill can ask the Law Society's Remuneration Certificate Department to issue a remuneration certificate *unless:*

a) the bill has already been paid, *or*

b) at least 1 month has passed since the client was told of his right to seek a certificate, *or*

c) the bill is due for a detailed assessment under a High Court order, *or*

d) the bill is over £50,000 (not including VAT and disbursements).

- A remuneration certificate is free, and if it sets a lower figure, that lower figure only is payable.

➤ Whether the matter is contentious or non-contentious, a client is also entitled to apply to the High Court for a detailed assessment (see p 421).

- If a client asks for a detailed assessment first, he cannot then ask for a remuneration certificate.
- In a detailed assessment, if the client is not LSC funded, costs are assessed on an indemnity basis (see p 417) but are presumed (*CPR r 48.8*):
  - to have been reasonably incurred if incurred with the express or implied approval of the client,
  - to be reasonable in amount if their amount was expressly or impliedly approved by the client,
  - to have been unreasonably incurred if:
    - they are of an unusual nature or amount, *and*
    - the solicitor did not tell his client that he might not recover all costs from the other party.

➤ **If a conditional fee arrangement,** where the court is considering a percentage increase, the court will have regard to all the relevant factors as they reasonably appeared to the solicitor or counsel when the conditional fee agreement was entered into or varied (*CPR r 48.8(3)*).

2 Solicitor's remedies

➤ A solicitor can sue on a bill (or threaten to do so), if:

a) the bill has been signed by a partner, *and*

b) the client has been notified in writing of the right to request a remuneration certificate, *or* if the bill is for a contentious matter, of his right to a detailed assessment at the High Court, *and*

c) 1 month has passed since the bill was delivered to the client (unless the court grants leave to sue earlier than this under *SA 1974 s 69*).

➤ A solicitor can charge interest on an unpaid bill, at the rate for judgment debts (see p 425) if:

a) 1 month has passed since the bill was delivered to the client, *and*

b) the client has been informed in writing of his right to challenge the bill, *and*

c) for non-contentious business, notice has been given of the right to charge interest, *and*

d) for contentious business, this has been agreed beforehand.

F Undertakings

    I   Undertakings generally
    II   Enforcement

I Undertakings generally

- An undertaking is '... any unequivocal declaration of intention addressed to somebody who reasonably places reliance on it.'
- An undertaking can be given by a solicitor *or* any member of his staff.
- An undertaking can be written or oral in form, and it need not use the word 'undertake'.
- An undertaking binds the firm, and all the partners are personally liable to ensure its performance (even if it was made by a member of staff without a partner's authority).

Undertakings

- To avoid incurring liability, a solicitor should follow these 5 steps before giving an undertaking.

Steps	
1	Ensure that it will be possible to fulfil the undertaking.
2	Obtain a client's authority before giving the undertaking.
3	Put the undertaking in writing.
4	Mark the client's file *on the outside* to warn everyone dealing with it of the undertaking.
5	Ask the recipient for a written discharge, and keep it on the client's file.

- It might be a good idea to observe a 'house rule' that only partners can give undertakings.
- Note:
    a) ambiguities are construed against the person who gives the undertaking.
    b) a solicitor is not released from his obligations if his default is due to circumstances beyond his control.
    c) the Law Society has drafted 'model' undertakings for use in certain situations (eg: conveyancing).

II Enforcement

- The court has jurisdiction over solicitors as they are officers of the court. The court may therefore deal with breaches of undertakings.
- Breach of an undertaking is a breach of the professional conduct rules and the Law Society may take disciplinary action. If a client suffers loss as a result, then the solicitor may be liable for damages.
- The client also has a right to complain to the Legal Services Ombudsman under the *CLSA 1990*.

G Discipline

I   Inadequate professional services/negligence
II   Disciplinary bodies

I   Inadequate professional services/negligence

➤ There is a distinction between inadequate professional services, negligence and work of low quality.

Inadequate professional services	Negligence	Low quality work

◆ These may include:
  • breach of the conduct rules
  • failure to follow instructions
  • unreasonable delays
◆ There is no need to show damage
◆ The Law Society may take disciplinary action
◆ Complaints are dealt with as indicated on the chart on the next page.
	◆ Breach of 'duty of care' to a client or a third party
	◆ Work is performed without 'reasonable skill and care' (*SGSA 1982 s 13*)
	◆ The complainant must show damage
	  • The test depends on whether the claim is in contract or tort
	◆ A civil remedy lies in contract for the client, or in tort for a third party
	◆ The Law Society *may* take disciplinary proceedings
		◆ This is to be avoided, but if it falls short of negligence and does not amount to inadequate professional services, it is not actionable

➤ A solicitor should take the following actions on discovering that there are grounds for a claim.

Steps
1. Inform the firm's insurers, and ask for their advice.
2. Advise the party concerned to seek independent legal advice.
3. Ensure all communications concerning this matter are confirmed in writing.
4. He must not admit liability without the insurer's consent.

II Disciplinary bodies

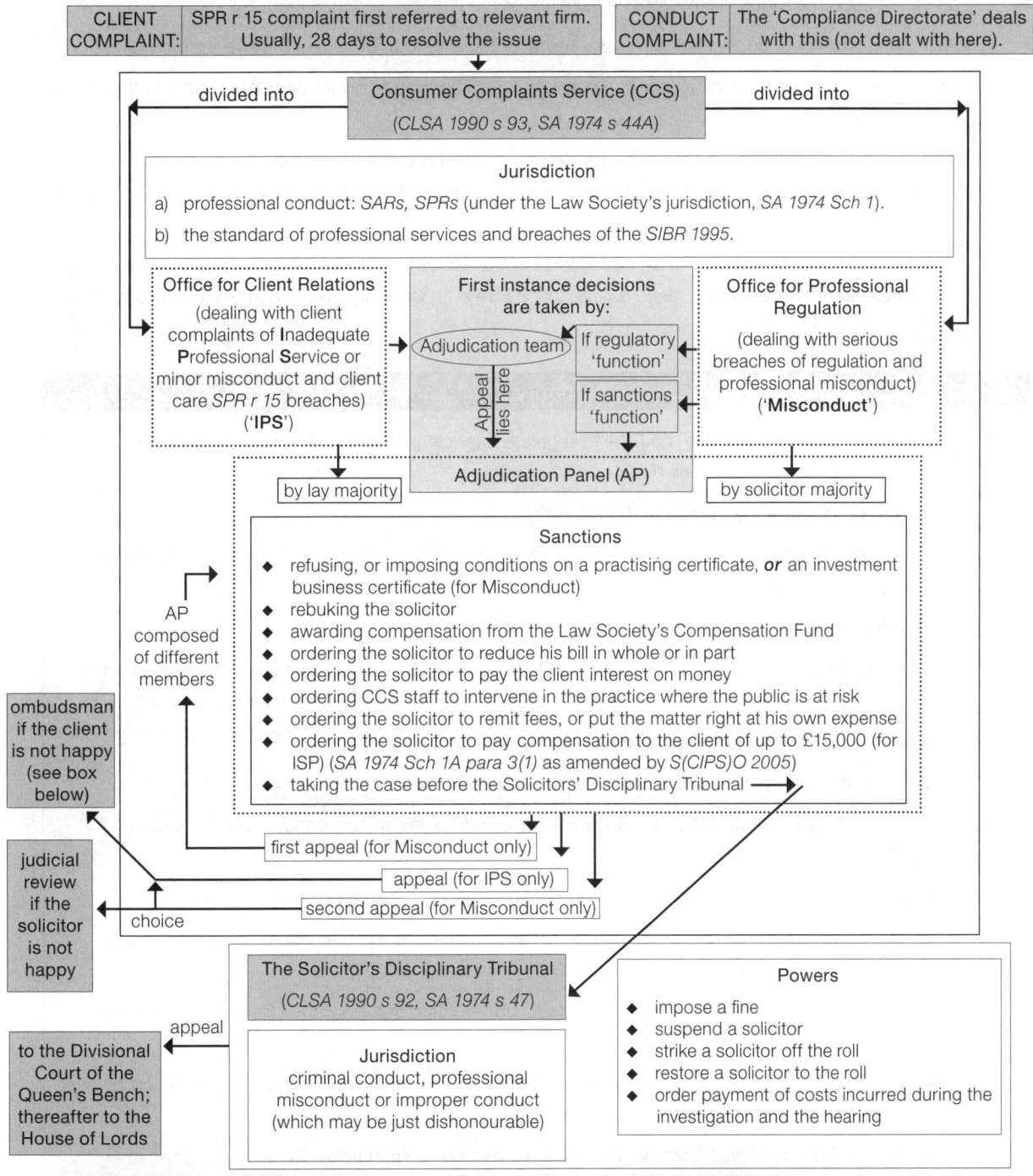

H Financial Services

➤ The *FSMA 2000* provides 'framework' legislation for the financial services industry.

➤ Placing the industry under a single regulator represented a fundamental aim of government policy.

➤ The regime set by the *FSMA 2000* and secondary legislation made under powers granted in that Act is extremely complex.

➤ The summary which follows below is no more than a very bare outline of the scheme of the legislation intended to show the broad scope of activities which may potentially be subject to regulation by the FSA.

➤ A specialised work should always be consulted before deciding whether an activity can be carried out without FSA authorisation and so as to ensure that if FSA authorisation is required FSA rules are complied with.

The Financial Services Authority ('FSA') and the *FSMA 2000*

➤ The *FSMA 2000* constitutes the FSA to regulate financial services in the UK by pursuing the following regulatory objectives (*FSMA 2000 s 2(2)*):

a) **market confidence objective** (*FSMA 2000 s 3*),

- Maintaining confidence in the financial system (eg: financial markets and exchanges and regulated activities)

b) **public awareness objective** (*FSMA 2000 s 4*),

- Promoting awareness of the benefits and risks associated with different kinds of investment and financial dealing and providing appropriate information and advice.

c) **protection of consumers objective** (*FSMA 2000 s 5*),

d) **reduction of financial crime objective** (*FSMA 2000 s 6*).

➤ In discharging its functions, the FSA must have regard to various considerations, including (*FSMA 2000 s 2(3)*):

- the desirability of achieving innovation in connection with regulated activities, *and*
- the international character of financial services and markets and the desirability of maintaining the competitive position of the UK, *and*
- the need to minimise the adverse effects on competition that may arise from anything done in discharge of its functions, *and*
- the desirability of facilitating competition between those who are subject to regulation by the FSA.
    - The FSA must also consider representations from a Practitioner Panel and a Consumer Panel (*FSMA 2000 s 11*).

➤ *FSMA 2000 Part XX* provides for the FSA to oversee the performance by members of the professions (eg: solicitors) of activities which are exempt from the general prohibition (*FSMA 2000 s 327*).

The 'general prohibition' and the 'financial promotion restriction'

'General prohibition'

➤ No person may carry on a regulated activity with respect to an investment in the UK *unless* that person is an authorised person, or an exempt person (*FSMA 2000 s 19*).

- Certain exempt persons are identified by the *FSMA(E)O 2001*.
- The FSA may grant authorisation under *FSMA 2000 Part IV*.

'Investments' (*FSMA 2000 Sch 2 Part II*)

- Securities (shares, stock, gilts, etc)
- Instruments creating/acknowledging indebtedness
- Units in collective investment schemes
- Options, futures, contracts for differences
- Contracts of insurance
- Participation in Lloyds syndicates
- Deposits
- Loans secured on land and other financial arrangements involving land

Regulated activities (*FSMA(RA)O 2001*) (see also *FSMA(CRAWB)O 2001*)

- Accepting deposits (*Art 5*) (excluding, eg: sums paid to the National Savings Bank (*Art 6(1)(a)(iv)*), or received by a solicitor (*Art 7*))
- Issuing electronic money (*Art 9B*)
- Effecting and carrying out contracts of insurance (*Art 10*)
- Dealing in investments as principal (*Art 14*)# or as agent (*Art 21*)
- Arranging deals in investments (*Art 25*)#
- Arranging regulated mortgage contracts (*Art 25A*)
- Managing investments (*Art 37*)

But not including, eg: the sale of 50% or more of the voting shares in a body corporate (*Art 70*)

- Safeguarding and administering investments (*Art 40*)
- Sending dematerialised instructions (*Art 45*)
- Establishing, etc a collective investment scheme (*Art 51*)
- Establishing, etc a stakeholder pension scheme (*Art 52*)
- Advising on investments (*Art 53*)#
- Lloyds activities (*Art 56*).
- Funeral plan contracts (*Art 59*).
- Regulated mortgage contracts (*Art 61*) (eg: mortgages over residential dwellings taken out by individuals).
- Agreeing to carry on specified activities (*Art 64*).

'Financial promotion restriction'

➤ A person must not, in the course of business, communicate an invitation or inducement to engage in investment activity (unless that person is an authorised person, or the content of the communication is approved by an authorised person) (*FSMA 2000 s 21, FSMA(FP)O 2001*).

- The *FSMA(FP)O 2001 Sch 1* employs the concepts of a 'controlled activity' and a 'controlled investment' which broadly mirror (but are not identical to) 'regulated activity' and 'investment' under *FSMA(RA)O 2001*.

- Activities not subject to the financial promotion restriction include certain communications: to persons outside the UK (*Art 12*), to an investment professional (*Art 19*), by a journalist (*Art 20*), to members or creditors of a body corporate (*Art 43*), to a certified high net worth individual (*Art 48*), to a high net worth company (*Art 49*), or to a sophisticated investor (*Art 50*), or by a PR or trustee (*Art 53-54*).

➤ Contravention of either the general prohibition in *s 19* or of *s 21* is a criminal offence punishable by a fine and up to 2 years' imprisonment (*FSMA 2000 ss 23/25*).

➤ An agreement made by (or through) a person in the course of carrying out a regulated activity in contravention of the general prohibition is unenforceable, unless a court permits otherwise (*FSMA 2000 ss 26-28*).

CONDUCT
Financial Services

The Law Society and Solicitors

➤ The Law Society is a designated professional body ('DPB') for the purposes of *FSMA 2000 Part XX*.

- A DPB is required to have rules 'designed to secure that in providing a particular service to a particular client, the member carries on only regulated activities which arise out of, or are complementary to, the provision by him of that service to that client' (*FSMA 2000 s 332(4)*).

- The Law Society has agreed with the FSA the *Solicitors' Financial Services (Scope) Rules 2001* that define 'mainstream investment advice' which solicitors may give within the DPB regime.

- Following the policy of the *FSMA 2000* that the FSA is to be the sole regulator of financial services, the FSA is empowered to disapply the exemption under the DPB regime with respect to particular firms, activities or an entire profession (*FSMA 2000 ss 328-329*).

➤ The *SFS(S)R 2001* provide that a firm must not carry out 'prohibited activities' (without FSA regulation), eg: (*SFS(S)R 2001 r 3*):

a) market-make in investments, *or*

b) buy, sell, subscribe for or underwrite investments as principal where a firm holds itself out as engaging in the business of buying such investments with a view to sale, *or*

c) buy or sell investments to stabilise or maintain the market price, *or*

d) act as stakeholder pension scheme manager, establish, operate, or wind up such a scheme, *or*

e) enter into a broker fund arrangement, *or*

f) effect or carry out a contract of insurance as a principal, *or*

g) establish, operate, or wind-up a collective investment scheme, *or*

h) manage the underwriting capacity of a Lloyds syndicate as a managing agent, or advise a person to become a member of a particular Lloyds syndicate, *or*

i) enter as a provider into a funeral plan contract, *or*

j) enter into a regulated mortgage contract as a lender, or administer a regulated mortgage contract.

➤ A firm which carries on an activity within *FSMA(RA)O 2001* must ensure that (*SFS(S)R 2001 rr 4-5*):

a) activities arise out of, or are complementary to, the provision of a particular professional service to a particular client, *and*

b) the provision of any service in the course of carrying out any regulated activities is incidental to the provision by the firm of professional services, *and*

c) the firm accounts to the client for any pecuniary reward, or other advantage, the firm receives from a third party, *and*

d) neither the activities, nor the investments are within an order under *FSMA 2000 s 327(6)* and the FSA has not made a direction or order under *FSMA 2000 ss 328-329*, *and*

e) the activity is not otherwise prohibited by the *SFS(S)R 2001* (eg: recommending a packaged product or a securities and contractually based investment (other than in certain restricted circumstances), discretionary management (unless in a capacity such as a trustee and advised by an authorised person or an exempt person), or certain corporate finance activities (eg: sponsor for securities to be admitted to trading on the London Stock Exchange)).

➤ Breach of the *SFS(S)R 2001* is a criminal offence under *FSMA 2000 s 23*.

Professional ethics

    I   Conveyancing with non-solicitors
    II   Criminal law: the prosecution's duties
    III Criminal law: the defence's duties
    IV Civil litigation

I Conveyancing with non-solicitors

➤ When dealing with a buyer or seller who is not represented by a solicitor or a licensed conveyancer, a solicitor should:

- ensure he does not inadvertently commit an offence under *SA 1974 s 22* (eg: transferring title to land, or contracting to do so for profit without authorisation from the Law Society).
- tell his client he is dealing with an unrepresented party.
- consult the Law Society's published guidelines and write to the other party warning them (tactfully!) of the law, and asking them to confirm that they are not in danger of breaching it.
- not accept undertakings as these will not be enforceable.
    - He may be negligent in his duty to his client if accepts such an undertaking.
- advise the other party to seek proper legal advice. (The solicitor does not owe a duty to the other side to explain anything to them himself.)

II Criminal law: the prosecution's duties

> **The prosecution's duties**
>
> The duty of the prosecution is to ensure all material evidence is put before the court in a dispassionate and fair manner. *All* relevant facts should be put before the court, including, after conviction, facts relevant to mitigation.

➤ There is a duty to give evidence to the defence that the prosecution does not intend to use, eg: if the prosecution has in its possession the statement of a material witness showing the innocence of the defendant, it is its duty to disclose it to the defence. (See the 'Disclosure' provisions in 'Criminal Litigation' section, see p 495).

➤ There is a duty to tell the defence if a prosecution witness gives evidence which is inconsistent with an earlier statement.

III Criminal law: the defence's duties

> **The defence's duties**
> The defence has a duty to the court and a duty to the client.

➤ **When the client admits his guilt to the solicitor,** the solicitor is unable to act by positively misleading the court. However, on a plea of 'not guilty', he can still put the prosecution to proof.

- However, it is important to remember that cases can be adjourned and reopened in the interests of justice (*Khatibi v DPP* [2004] 168 JP 361).

➤ **When the client pleads 'guilty', but has a defence,** the solicitor can act. He can put the client's defence, but must advise the client that in mitigation it may not be possible to rely on the facts constituting the defence.

➤ **When the client gives inconsistent instructions,** the solicitor can act (if there is no false evidence).

➤ The solicitor must never disclose the defence case without the client's consent.

➤ The solicitor has a positive duty to assist the court on points of law.

➤ The solicitor has a negative duty not to mislead the court on points of fact.

➤ **If the client wishes to give a false name or address to the court,** the solicitor must try to persuade the client to be truthful. If he does not succeed, the solicitor cannot act.

➤ **If the court has an incorrect list of the client's previous convictions,** the solicitor may not correct the list without the consent of the client. If there is no such consent, the solicitor must refuse to act.

➤ **If for *any* reason, the solicitor is unable to act, he may not be able to say why without breaching a client confidence.** He should just say that it is impossible for him to act, without saying why.

➤ **If the prosecution does not realise that its detention limits are about to run out,** the defence owes a duty to the client not to remind the prosecution of this (see p 454).

IV Civil litigation

➤ **The overriding duty:** the solicitor has an overriding duty to the court when appearing before it or when conducting litigation, to act with independence in the interests of justice (*CLSA s 27-28* and see also p 341).

➤ There is a statutory duty to comply with the *SPR*s and other professional rules of conduct.

➤ **Disclosure:** the solicitor should make his client aware that it is important to:

- preserve carefully all documents for disclosure whether they:
  - help the client's case, *or*
  - harm the client's case.
- be truthful when dealing with such documents because:
  - the solicitor has a duty not to mislead the court, *and*
  - from the client's point of view, if it later arises at trial that documents have been withheld, lost, or 'destroyed', it may critically prejudice the client's case.

Overview of the Law Society' Guide to Professional Conduct

➤ The Law Society's Guide to Professional Conduct was last published in 1999 and has been updated since then; for the current text see the Law Society's website at www.guide-on-line.lawsociety.org.uk.

➤ The general structure of the Guide is as follows:

- Rules and principles of professional conduct (ch 1).
- Regulatory requirements (ch 2).
- Private practice (ch 3).
- Employed solicitors (ch 4).
- Legal aid (ch 5).
- Legal expenses insurance (ch 6).
- Avoiding discrimination (ch 7).
- Obtaining instructions (ch 11).
- Retainer (ch 12).
- Client care (ch 13).
- Professional fees (ch 14).
- Conflict of interests (ch 15).
- Confidentiality (ch 16).
- Relations with third parties (ch 17).
- Professional undertakings (ch 18).
- Relations with other solicitors (ch 19).
- Relations with the Bar, other lawyers and professoinal agents (ch 20).
- Litigation and dispute resolution / ADR (chs 21-22).
- Insolvency practice (ch 23).
- Wills, administration of estates, powers of attorney and mental capacity (ch 24).
- Conveyancing (ch 25).
- Property selling (ch 26).
- Investment business (ch 27).
- Accounts (ch 28).
- Professional indemnity (ch 29).
- Office for the Supervision of Solicitors (ch 30).
- The Solicitors Disciplinary Tribunal (ch 31).
- Information packs and updated rules (ch 32).

NOTE: See the 'Practice Box' on p 2, about the forthcoming changes fo the rules!

J Human rights

- Every solicitor should be aware of the impact of human rights law on all other areas of law.
- The European Convention for the Protection of Human Rights and Fundamental Freedoms (known as the European Convention on Human Rights or ECHR) was signed in Rome on 4 November 1950.
    - The ECHR establishes a European Court of Human Rights (in Strasbourg).
- The ECHR established international protection for human rights and entitled individuals to apply to the European Court of Human Rights for enforcement. This still applies even after the *HRA 1998*.
- The ECHR is part of English law by *HRA 1998*.

European Convention for the Protection of Human Rights and Fundamental Freedoms			
Article	Content	Article	Content
2	right to life	8	right to respect for family and private life
3	prohibition of torture	9	freedom of thought, conscience and religion
4	prohibition of slavery and forced labour	10	freedom of expression
5	right to liberty and security	11	freedom of assembly and association
	◆ includes right to be brought before a judge promptly if arrested or detained	12	right to marry
	◆ includes compensation right if a victim of arrest / detention in held in contravention of this article	14	prohibition of discrimination
6	right to a fair trial (includes the presumption of innocence until proven guilty)	1st Protocol 1-3	rights to protection of property, education and free elections
7	no punishment without law (ie: victim must contravene a law in force at the time)	13th Protocol	abolition of the death penalty

Human Rights Act 1998

- The *HRA 1998* incorporates the Articles in the above table into English law.
    - The *HRA 1998* tries to balance protection of human rights with Parliamentary sovereignty.
- **New legislation:** all new legislation must comply with the convention rights above.
    - There must be a 'Declaration of Compatibility' before a second reading of a proposed Bill (*s 19*).
- **Existing legislation**
    a) All legislation must (as far as possible) be interpreted by the courts to be compatible with the ECHR (*s 3*).
    b) Courts and tribunals will have jurisdiction to hear human rights arguments.
    c) The higher courts (eg: High Court, the Court of Appeal and the House of Lords and some others) may make a 'Declaration of Incompatibility' that a law does not accord with ECHR rights (*s 4*).
        - This does not affect the validity of the law.
        - The Crown is put on notice by the court. The Crown may make a counter-argument (*s 5*).
        - A Minister may draft a remedial order amending such legislation which must be approved by Parliament within 60 days in order to be effective (*s 10 and Sch 2*).
            - In cases of particular urgency, an order may be effective immediately but lapses if not approved by Parliament within 120 days.
- It is unlawful for public authorities to act in a way incompatible with the ECHR (*s 6*).
    - Proceedings must be brought within 1 year or such other period as a Court finds equitable (*s 7(5)*).
- It is unclear if ECHR rights have horizontal effect between private parties, but Sedley LJ in *Douglas & others v Hello! Ltd (No.1)* [2001] QB 967 says that for *Art 10* rights at least, there is horizontal effect.

ACCOUNTS

This chapter examines:

A	Basic bookkeeping	36
B	Advanced bookkeeping	44
C	Bank reconciliations	51
D	Partnership accounts	52
E	Interpreting accounts	56
F	*Solicitors' Accounts Rules 1998*	60
G	Keeping accounts as a solicitor	69

Conventions in the presentation of accounts

➤ If a figure is underlined, this means it is being added or subtracted along with those *above* it.
➤ The answer may be placed in the column to the right of the underlined figure if there is one, or if there is no such column, directly below.
➤ The purpose of this is to help in the addition or subtraction of totals and subtotals.
➤ Final answers are usually double-underlined.

ACCOUNTS
Basic bookkeeping

A Basic bookkeeping

Step 1 — Produce 'T' accounts

➤ In a double entry accounting system, every transaction is recorded twice in order to produce an ongoing error check in the figures.

- ◆ 'T' accounts are used, named after the shape of the lines drawn.
  - ● These are 'fictional' devices which set out what is happening to particular items in a business.
    - ■ Items can be assets, liabilities, receipts in or payments out eg: cash, a vehicle, debtors, etc.

    NB: 'T' accounts are *not* real accounts in the sense of a bank account.

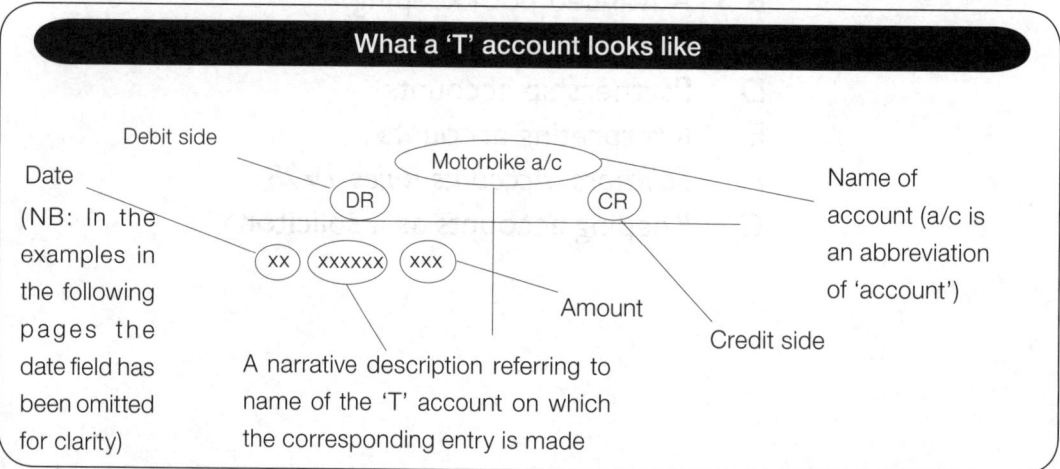

What a 'T' account looks like

➤ A debit on 1 side of a 'T' account = a credit on 1 side of another 'T' account.
- ◆ Total debits *must* equal total credits.

➤ As many 'T' accounts as necessary are used. It is easiest to start with the cash account entry.

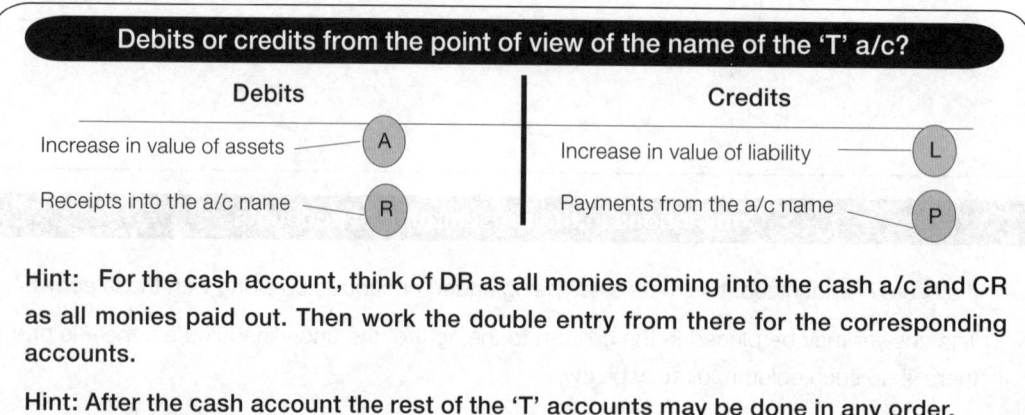

Hint: For the cash account, think of DR as all monies coming into the cash a/c and CR as all monies paid out. Then work the double entry from there for the corresponding accounts.

Hint: After the cash account the rest of the 'T' accounts may be done in any order.

➤ The collection of 'T' accounts taken together' is known as:
- ◆ the general ledger, *or*
- ◆ the nominal ledger.

ACCOUNTS
Basic bookkeeping

Step 1 — Example

Facts: Alpha and Beta start together as solicitors on 1 January 2008. Each puts £15,000 into the new partnership. In the first year the following events occur:

	DR	CR
Staff salaries	27,000	
Rent	10,000	
Company motorbike	4,000	
Office equipment bought on credit	6,500	
Misc. and general expenses	1,500	
Bills delivered		90,000

They have only collected £62,000 of bills delivered and you will see that they still owe £6,500 for the office equipment.

Hint: Start with the cash account and work through the other accounts.

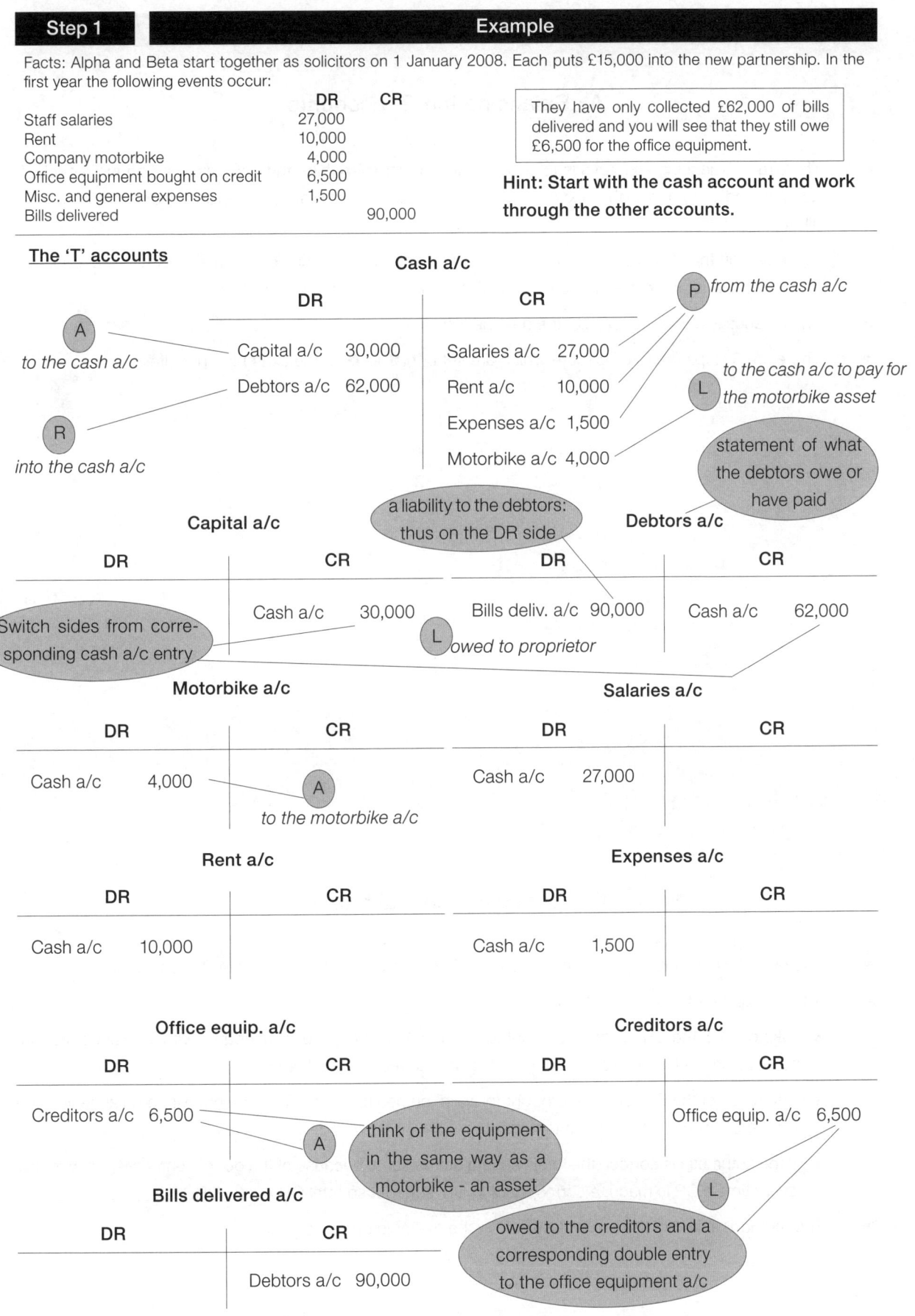

The 'T' accounts

Cash a/c
- DR: Capital a/c 30,000; Debtors a/c 62,000
- CR: Salaries a/c 27,000; Rent a/c 10,000; Expenses a/c 1,500; Motorbike a/c 4,000

P — from the cash a/c
A — to the cash a/c
R — into the cash a/c
L — to the cash a/c to pay for the motorbike asset

Capital a/c
- CR: Cash a/c 30,000

L — owed to proprietor

Switch sides from corresponding cash a/c entry

Debtors a/c
- DR: Bills deliv. a/c 90,000
- CR: Cash a/c 62,000

statement of what the debtors owe or have paid

a liability to the debtors: thus on the DR side

Motorbike a/c
- DR: Cash a/c 4,000

A — to the motorbike a/c

Salaries a/c
- DR: Cash a/c 27,000

Rent a/c
- DR: Cash a/c 10,000

Expenses a/c
- DR: Cash a/c 1,500

Office equip. a/c
- DR: Creditors a/c 6,500

A — think of the equipment in the same way as a motorbike - an asset

Creditors a/c
- CR: Office equip. a/c 6,500

L — owed to the creditors and a corresponding double entry to the office equipment a/c

Bills delivered a/c
- CR: Debtors a/c 90,000

ACCOUNTS
Basic bookkeeping

Step 2 — Balance the 'T' accounts and produce a trial balance

A Balancing the 'T' accounts

➤ The aim of balancing accounts is to draw the line under everything that has occurred so far in each 'T' account and carry on into the next period with just one figure - so starting the process for each 'T' account all over again.

➤ Balancing off the 'T' accounts is the process of adding all the entries on each side of a 'T' account and working out what the difference is and on which side that difference falls.

➤ The balance is carried forward to the next period.

➤ There are 5 steps in this procedure which are set out (❶ to ❺) in the example opposite.

B Producing the trial balance

➤ The purpose of producing a trial balance is to check the arithmetic in all of the 'T' accounts.

➤ A trial balance is produced as follows:
- take each of the DR 'balance brought forward' entries (from the 'T' accounts with a balance brought forward on the DR side) and add them together to reach a total, *and*
- take each of the CR 'balance brought forward' entries (from the 'T' accounts with a balance forward on the CR side) and add them together to reach a total, *and*
- if the arithmetic is correct, the totals should be the same because of the double entry system whereby every time a CR is made, a corresponding DR is made, so total CR = total DR.

➤ The method of setting this out is illustrated in the example opposite.

ACCOUNTS
Basic bookkeeping

Step 2 — **Example**

Facts: Continued from step 1.

NB: Only 3 'T' accounts are shown in the example below

① Add up both sides first
- DR 92,000
- CR 42,500

⑤ Check the arithmetic on each side

Cash a/c

DR		CR	
Capital a/c	30,000	Salaries a/c	27,000
Debtors a/c	62,000	Rent a/c	10,000
		Expenses a/c	1,500
		Motorbike a/c	4,000
		Balance c/f	49,500
	92,000		92,000
Balance b/f	49,500		

④ Write the figure from ③ on the other side of the double entry with the label 'Balance b/f' which means balance brought forward. This completes the double entry

② Fill in the larger of the two figures on both sides

③ Fill in the difference between the larger figure and the smaller figure with the label 'Balance c/f' which means balance carried forward on the side with the smaller total

Capital a/c

DR		CR	
Balance c/f	30,000	Cash a/c	30,000
	30,000		30,000
		Balance b/f	30,000

Debtors a/c

DR		CR	
Bills deliv. a/c	90,000	Cash a/c	62,000
		Balance c/f	28,000
	90,000		90,000
Balance b/f	28,000		

Trial Balance

	DR £	CR £
Cash a/c	49,500	
Capital a/c		30,000
Debtors a/c	28,000	
Motorbike a/c	4,000	
Salaries a/c	27,000	
Rent a/c	10,000	
Expenses a/c	1,500	
Office equip. a/c	6,500	
Creditors a/c		6,500
Bills delivered a/c		90,000
Balance	126,500	126,500

ACCOUNTS

Basic bookkeeping

| Step 3 | Produce final accounts (Profit & loss account and balance sheet) |

Stage 1: Mark up the trial balance

➤ In order to produce the 2 final accounts, it is necessary to mark every item on the trial balance as being destined for the profit & loss account or the balance sheet.
- ◆ Receipts and payments will go on the profit and loss account.
  - Receipts and payments have the nature of being ephemeral - coming and going.
- ◆ Assets and liabilities will go on the balance sheet.
  - Assets and liabilities have a more permanent nature.

➤ An example of this marking is shown in the example opposite.

Stage 2: Make any necessary adjustments as per pp 44-47

➤ The example on the right has no necessary adjustments to make.

Stage 3: Produce the profit & loss account

➤ The profit & loss account shows the profits or losses that the business has made during a particular period.

➤ The profit & loss account is part of the double entry system.
- ◆ This means that to put entries into the profit & loss account, it is necessary to close off the relevant 'T' account.

  NB: Relevant 'T' accounts are those which are relevant to the profit & loss account from the marking up of the trial balance.
  - This means writing an entry labelled 'P&L a/c' on the opposite side to the 'balance b/f' entry with the same figure.
  - Then complete the double entry in the profit & loss 'T' a/c.
- ◆ The relevant 'T' accounts for which this has been done are at zero and are said to be closed for the period in question. The new period will start from a zero balance again.

➤ There are 2 'styles' of presenting a profit and loss account.
- ◆ Style 'A' is technical and is a presentation of the profit & loss 'T' account itself.
- ◆ Style 'B' is more user-friendly and is a re-writing of the profit & loss 'T' account.

ACCOUNTS
Basic bookkeeping

Step 3 — Example

Facts: Continued from step 2.

Step 3...   **Produce final accounts (Profit & loss account and balance sheet)**

Stage 4: Produce the balance sheet

➤ The balance sheet performs 2 functions:

    a) it is a snapshot of the business's assets and liabilities at a particular date, *and*

    b) it is a check that 'Assets of the business = Liabilities of the business (ie: capital employed)'.

- The form of the balance sheet is derived from the equation as follows:

    Assets = Liabilities

    Assets = Inside liabilities (owed to the proprietor ie: capital and profit) + Outside Liabilities

    Assets = (Opening capital and profit) + Outside liabilities

    Assets - Outside liabilities = Opening capital and profit

➤ The balance sheet is *not* part of the double entry system.

- This means there is no adjustment to the 'T' accounts.

➤ The balance sheet is made up by taking the items from the marked up trial balance *and* taking the final figure from the profit and loss account and putting them into the balance sheet form. There is a pro forma balance sheet set out on p 50.

➤ The net assets [ie: (fixed + current assets) less (fixed + current liabilities)] should match the opening capital and profit. This is because it shows how the company capital is employed and tied up in assets and liabilities.

ACCOUNTS
Basic bookkeeping

Step 3... **Example (cont.)**

Stage 4

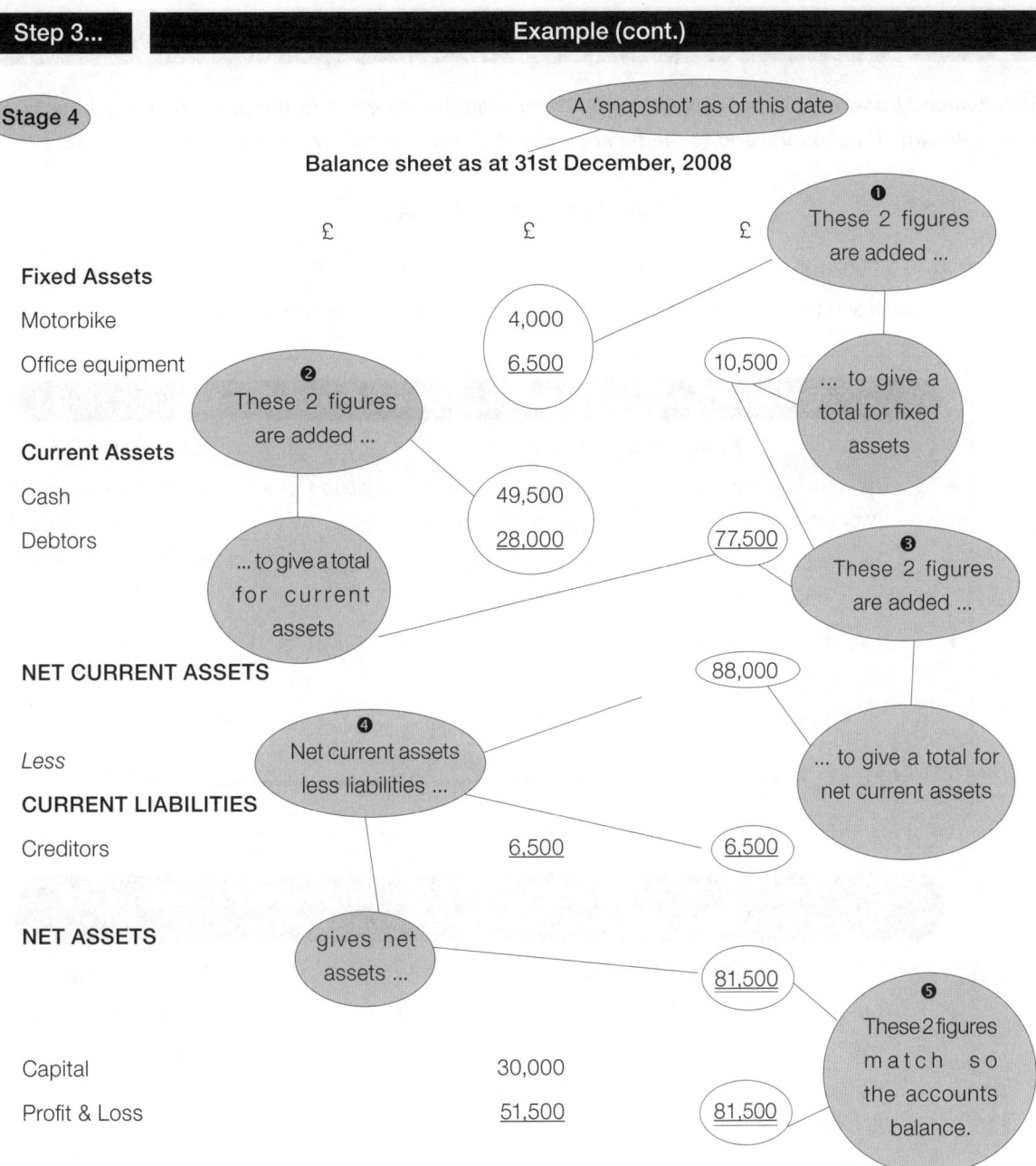

All figures used on this balance sheet are from the marked up trial balance

ACCOUNTS
Advanced bookkeeping

B Advanced bookkeeping

All advanced bookkeeping in this section (A-G) necessitates changes to the profit & loss account (and other relevant 'T' accounts) and to the balance sheet. There is a fully worked example on pp 48-49.

A Work in progress

➤ Work in progress is work that is being undertaken by the firm but which has not yet been billed.

➤ It has value and this value must be shown in the same period as the expenses spent to produce it.

End of period 1 - taking period 1 work in progress into account

Profit & loss account

- The work in progress 'T' a/c should be debited with the period 1 work in progress figure (see p 36 because it is an asset).
- The profit & loss a/c should be credited with the period 1 work in progress figure (completing the double entry).
- If presenting the account in style B (see p40), add the work in progress for period 1 to bills delivered.

Balance sheet

- Add work in progress under CURRENT ASSETS as per the pro forma on p 50.

End of period 2 - taking period 2 work in progress into account and taking out period 1 work in progress from account

Profit & loss account

- The work in progress 'T' a/c should be debited with the period 2 work in progress figure (see p 36 because it is an asset).
- The profit & loss a/c should be credited with the period 2 work in progress figure (completing the double entry).
  - The 'T' a/cs will now be accurate as the period 1 work in progress was billed and gradually paid, the necessary entries will have been made in the work in progress a/c to bring the period 1 work in progress a/c to zero.
- If presenting the account in style B (see p 40), add the work in progress from period 2 to bills delivered and subtract the work in progress from period 1 from bills delivered.

Balance sheet

- Add work in progress under CURRENT ASSETS as per the pro forma on p 50.

B Bad debts

➤ Sometimes it is obvious that specific debts will not be paid by specific debtors and it is necessary to write off those debts.

➤ Adjustments:
- the balance sheet, by amending the profit & loss figure (see below) and the current assets, *and*
- the profit & loss account and other 'T' accounts:
  - The debtors a/c is credited with an entry labelled 'bad debts a/c' and the amount.
  - The bad debts a/c is debited with an entry labelled 'debtors a/c' and the amount. This is then closed off to the profit & loss account.
    - In Style 'B' presentations, bad debts is an expense of the business.

Eg: (showing the amendments to 'T' accounts only):

The facts are as on pp 37, 39 and 41 but it becomes obvious that £1,500 will never be paid:

C Doubtful debts

➤ It is careful accounting to make a provision for doubtful debts (unlike bad debts which is knowledge that a *specific* debtor will not pay).
- The figure chosen is based on experience of debts that as a fact have not been paid in the past and is usually a percentage of total debtors.

➤ Adjustments:
- the balance sheet, by amending the profit & loss figure (see below) and the current assets (by subtracting the figure from debtors), *and*
- the profit & loss account and other 'T' accounts:
  - The doubtful debts a/c is credited with an entry labelled 'profit & loss a/c' and the amount.
  - The profit & loss a/c is debited with an entry labelled 'doubtful debts a/c' and the amount.
    - In Style 'B' presentations, the doubtful debts are an expense of the business.

D Payments in advance (prepayments)

➤ These are payments made in the current accounting period for goods/services in the following period.

➤ Adjustments:
- the balance sheet, by adding the prepayment as a current asset and amending the profit & loss figure (see below), *and*
- the profit & loss account and other 'T' accounts:
  - if the account with the prepayment is for example, rent, close off from the rent a/c to the profit & loss account the amount actually paid out for the period less the prepayment. The prepayment goes in in the CR column (of the rent a/c) (under the profit and loss a/c entry) as the 'balance c/f' figure with the corresponding double entry figure being in the DR column as the balance b/f. This is the amount brought forward into the next accounting period.

  NB: the cash a/c should always reflect the sums actually paid during the account period.
    - In Style B presentations, subtract the prepayment from the rent figure.

E Payments in arrears (accruals)

➤ These are payments that will be made in the next accounting period for goods/services used in the current accounting period.

➤ Adjustments:
- the balance sheet, by subtracting the accrual by putting it in as a current liability and amending the profit & loss figure (see below), *and*
- the profit & loss account and other 'T' accounts:
  - if the account with the accrual is for example, water, only close off from the water account to the profit & loss a/c an amount equal to the cash paid out less the prepayment. Carry forward the prepayment into the next account period.
    - In Style B presentations, add the accrual to the water figure for the period.

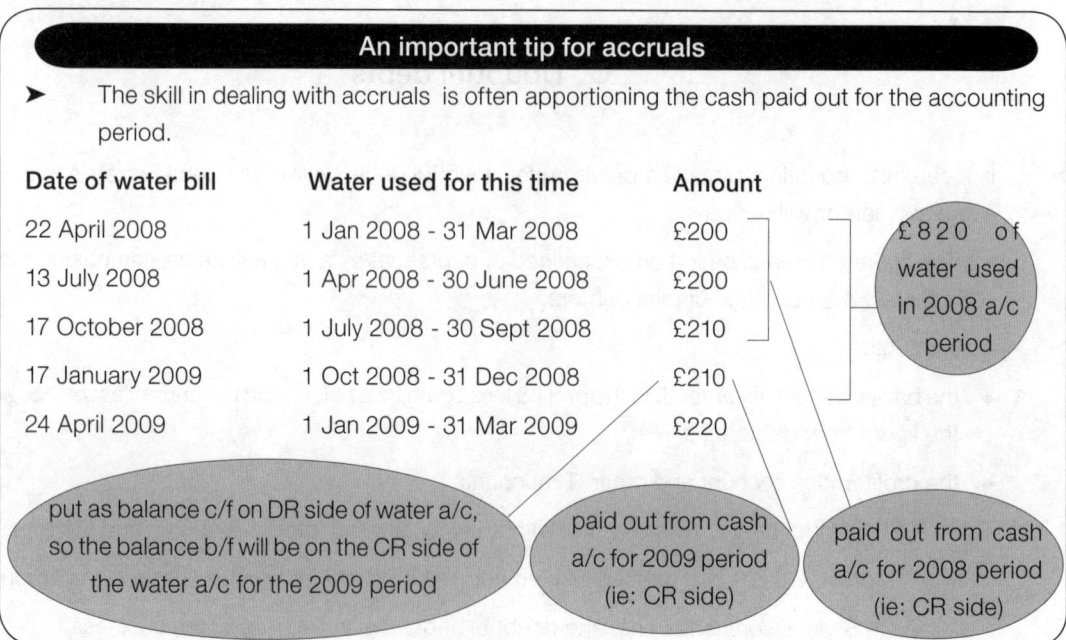

An important tip for accruals

➤ The skill in dealing with accruals is often apportioning the cash paid out for the accounting period.

Date of water bill	Water used for this time	Amount
22 April 2008	1 Jan 2008 - 31 Mar 2008	£200
13 July 2008	1 Apr 2008 - 30 June 2008	£200
17 October 2008	1 July 2008 - 30 Sept 2008	£210
17 January 2009	1 Oct 2008 - 31 Dec 2008	£210
24 April 2009	1 Jan 2009 - 31 Mar 2009	£220

£820 of water used in 2008 a/c period

put as balance c/f on DR side of water a/c, so the balance b/f will be on the CR side of the water a/c for the 2009 period

paid out from cash a/c for 2009 period (ie: CR side)

paid out from cash a/c for 2008 period (ie: CR side)

F Depreciation

➤ Depreciation is a charge made to the business each year to reflect the loss in value of an asset, eg: if a £5,000 motorbike is expected to last the business for 5 years, we will charge a cost of £1,000 per year to the business.

- The actual figure charged per year, although a 'guesstimate', is usually based on the experience of accountants.

➤ Adjustments:

- using the motorbike example above, each year on the balance sheet under the fixed asset 'motorbike' there should be an entry labelled 'accumulated depreciation'. This will be listed as £1,000 in the first year, £2,000 in the next year until it reads £5,000 in the fifth year giving an asset value of nil.
- 'T' accounts:
  - the motorbike a/c will have already have £5,000 listed on the DR side (as it is an asset, see p 36).
  - the accumulated depreciation a/c will already have the accumulated depreciation (for previous accounting years) listed on the CR side. Add to the CR side the depreciation for this year's accounting period and perform the 'balance c/f' and 'balance b/f' procedure to give a total figure for accumulated depreciation (for previous accounting periods and this accounting period) on the CR side.
  - the depreciation a/c should have this year's (and only this year's) motorbike depreciation put on the DR side and the account should be closed off to the profit & loss account.
    - In Style B presentations, this year's depreciation is an expense of the business.

G Disposal of fixed assets

➤ When a business sells assets, it will make a profit or loss on the sale.

➤ This profit is reported at the end of the profit & loss account as a separate figure from the main profit figure of the business. (Since the mainstream income of the business is not derived from the buying and selling of assets, the figure from this is listed as separate, otherwise this would confuse the true profit and loss figures.)

➤ When asset A is sold:

- put in the CR column of the asset A a/c, the label 'transfer to disposal a/c' and the cost price - this clears the asset A 'T' account, *and*
- put in the DR column of the accumulation depreciation a/c the accumulated depreciation for asset A and update the accumulation a/c by doing the balance c/f - balance b/f procedure, *and*
- put in the DR column of the fixed asset disposal a/c the label 'Asset A a/c' and the cost figure (thus completing the double entry for (a) above), *and*
- put in the CR column of the fixed asset a/c the label 'accumulated depreciation a/c' and the final accumulated depreciation figure for asset A (thus completing the double entry for (b) above), *and*

So far this has cleared off asset A from the main accounts into a special asset disposal account.

- put in the DR column of the cash account the sale price, *and*
- put in the CR column of the fixed asset disposal a/c, the sale price. Balance off the fixed asset disposal a/c and take the profit to the profit & loss a/c.
  - Style B presentations and adjustments to the balance sheet are self-explanatory.

ACCOUNTS

Advanced bookkeeping

Fully worked example

Sue, Grabbit & Run, a firm of successful solicitors in Erehwon, set up business on 1 January 1998. The accountants draw up a trial balance as at 31 December 2008 for the 2008 year of business. Produce a balance sheet and profit & loss account based on the following trial balance and extra facts:

Trial balance:	£	£
Opening capital in the business		50,000
Bank loan		80,000
Loan interest	9,000	
Balance in office account - cash	110,000	
Office equipment and computers - cost	20,000	
Office equipment and computers - accumulated depreciation		10,000
Messengers motorbikes - cost	14,000	
Messengers motorbikes - accumulated depreciation		4,000
Bills delivered		170,000
Work in progress as at 31 December 2007	80,000	
Debtors	13,500	
Creditors		8,500
Salaries	60,000	
Office rent	13,500	
Electricity	2,000	
Water	500	
	322,500	322,500

❶ Mark all items on the trial balance as destined for the BS or the P&L a/c

☐ BS

▨ P&L

Unmarked BS and P&L

- The office owes party contractors (ie: creditors) £1,000 (not yet in the account) for the 2008 office Xmas party.
- The office rent paid in advance at 31 Dec. 2008 is £2,000.
- The electricity accrued as at 31 Dec. 2008 is £400.
- The water accrued as at 31 Dec. 2008 is £100.
- It has been decided that a provision for doubtful debts of £8,500 should be made.
- Depreciation for the year is 20% of cost on office computers and equipment.
- Depreciation for the year is 15% of cost on messengers motorbikes.
- Work in progress at 31 December 2008 is £40,000.

❷ BS and P&L

Profit & Loss account for Sue Grabbit & Run for 2008 a/c period

INCOME

Bills delivered			170,000
Less: last year's work in progress			80,000
			90,000
Add: this year's work in progress			40,000
			130,000

Total income for this year

LESS:
EXPENSES

Salaries			60,000
Loan interest			9,000
Xmas party expense			1,000
Office rent	13,500		
Less: rent advance	2,000	11,500	
Electricity	2,000		
Add: electricity accrual	400	2,400	
Water	500		
Add: water accrual	100	600	
Provision for doubtful debts		8,500	
Depreciation			
2008 office/computers (20% of £20,000)	4,000		
2008 motorbikes (15% of £14,000)	2,100	6,100	99,100

See the box on p 35 on 'conventions in the presentation of accounts' to understand how the underlining of numbers works

Total expenses for this year

NET 2008 PROFIT   30,900

Fully worked example (continued)

Balance sheet of Sue, Grabbit & Run as of 31st December, 2008

FIXED ASSETS			
Office equipment and computers - cost		20,000	
Less accumulated depreciation (10,000+4,000) [pre 2008 office equipment depreciation / 2008 office equipment depreciation]		<u>14,000</u>	6,000
Messengers motorbikes - cost		14,000	
Less accumulated depreciation (4,000+2,100) [pre 2008 motorbike depreciation / 2008 motorbike depreciation]	<u>6,100</u>	<u>7,900</u>	13,900
ADD: CURRENT ASSETS			
Work in progress 2008		40,000	
Debtors	13,500		
Less provision for doubtful debts	<u>8,500</u>	5,000	
Prepayments		2,000	
Cash		<u>110,000</u>	157,000
LESS: CURRENT LIABILITIES			
Creditors	8,500		
Add creditors not yet in accounts	<u>1,000</u>	9,500	
Accruals			
Electricity	400		
Water	<u>100</u>	<u>500</u>	<u>10,000</u>
NET CURRENT ASSETS			160,900
LESS: Long term liabilities			
Bank loan			<u>80,000</u>
NET ASSETS			<u>**80,900**</u>
Capital and profit			
Capital		50,000	
Net 2008 profit		<u>30,900</u>	<u>**80,900**</u>

ACCOUNTS
Advanced bookkeeping

Pro-forma balance sheet

Balance sheet of [   ] as of [   ]

> V-W should equal AA+BB

FIXED ASSETS

Asset 1 - cost	A		
Less accumulated depreciation for asset 1	B	C (A+B)	
Asset 2 - cost	D		
Less accumulated depreciation for asset 2	E	F (D+E)	G (C+F)

ADD: CURRENT ASSETS

Work in progress current period		H	
Debtors	I		
Less provision for doubtful debts	J		
Less provision for bad debts	K	L(I+J+K)	
Prepayments (X+X+X+X+X+X+X etc.)		M	
Cash at bank		N	
Petty cash		O	P(H+L+M+N+P)

LESS: CURRENT LIABILITIES

Creditors	Q		
Add creditors not yet in accounts	R	S(Q+R)	
Accruals (X+X+X+X+X+X+X+X etc.)		T	U(S+T)

CLIENT BALANCES

Client bank account	Y		
Less client ledgers (owed to clients)	Y	NIL(Y-Y)	NIL

NET CURRENT ASSETS — V(G+P-U)

LESS: LONG TERM LIABILITIES

Bank loan — W

NET ASSETS — V-W

Capital employed

Capital	if partnership accounts, this is the partners' capital and current accounts (see p 52)	AA	
Net [year] profit		BB	AA+BB

C Bank reconciliations

➤ It is often necessary to 'reconcile' the bank statements of the business with the cash ledger (ie: the cash 'T' account) as a cheque on the double entry accounting. They may not match up because of:
- bank charges/bank interest on the statement but not in the cash book, *and/or*
- cheques received by the business but not yet paid into/credited to the bank account, *and/or*
- cheques paid out by the business but not yet cashed by those to whom they have been given, *and/or*
- error on the bank statement (quite common!) or in the cash book.

❶ Make sure the starting balances on the cash ledger and the bank statement are the same by bringing the previous month's transactions up to date. Then, cross off all similar items that appear in both the bank statement and the cash ledger and circle those that are different.

❷ Write into the cash ledger all outstanding items (see grey boxes below).

❸ Draw up a reconciliation statement to match the bank statement to the cash ledger - the end figures should be the same!

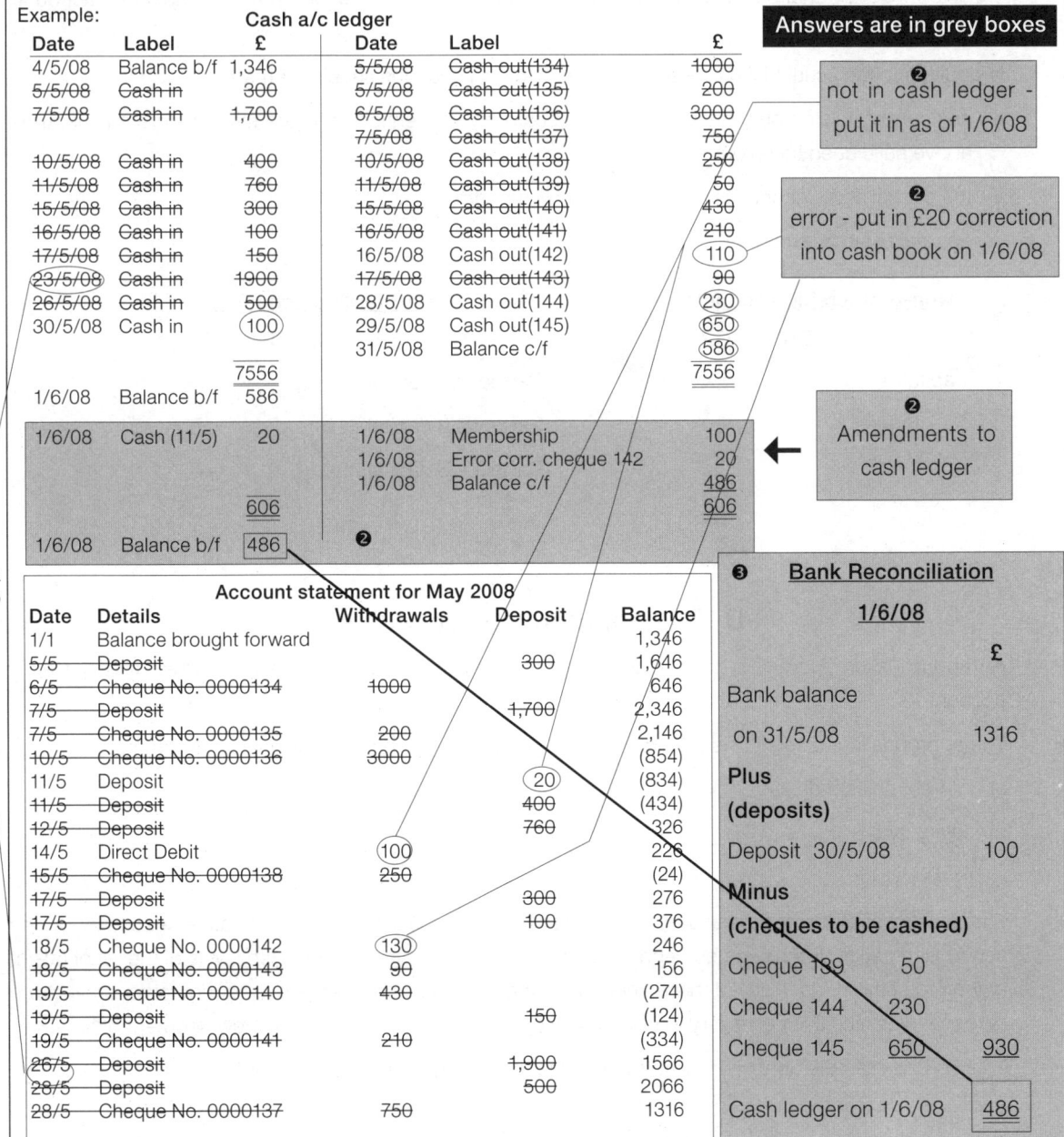

D Partnership accounts

➤ With partnership accounts, certain changes are made to the different areas of the accounts.

➤ The differences when dealing with partnerships are 4:

   a) partners may take interest on their capital contributions to the partnership, *and/or*

   b) partners may draw a salary for themselves, *and/or*

   c) partners will share profits according to a set formula (usually based on an agreed %age), *and/or*

   d) partners may take drawings from the business for themselves.

A The trial balance

➤ Remember - a trial balance is a listing of all the balances of the 'T' accounts. Although the changes below are listed from the trial balance stage, they in fact occur much earlier when the individual 'T' accounts are worked on.

➤ In addition to the usual trial balance (p 38), the following changes should be made:

   ♦ any net profit listed on the trial balance is usually, by convention, a figure taken before any of (a)-(d) above have been taken out.

   ♦ the capital account entry is split into an entry per partner:

   eg: trial balance excerpt:

Non-partnership accounts	DR	CR		Partnership accounts	DR	CR
capital		X	➡	Partner's 1 capital		A
				Partner's 2 capital		B
				Partner's 3 capital		C

B The appropriation accounts

➤ An appropriation account is a breakdown of how profit is distributed to each partner. It is not a 'T' account.

➤ The appropriation account lists the profit for the relevant period broken down into 3 elements:

   a) interest on capital, *and*

   b) salary, *and*

   c) profit division.

➤ The appropriation account is usually broken down into as many time segments as is necessary for the accounting period. Each segment represents a fixed group of partners *and* fixed levels of the list of (a)-(c) at the top of this page. If any of these change (eg: new partners are taken on, partners retire, profit share ratio changes etc.) it is necessary to start a new appropriation account for the new segment of time.

➤ The worked example opposite sets out how to set out the appropriation account.

ACCOUNTS
Partnership accounts

Fully worked example

Alpha runs his garage business but due to pressure of work he decides to take on a new partner. On 1 August 2008 he takes on Beta who in exchange for a 35% partnership and a yearly salary of £2,000, agrees to put £10,000 in to the partnership. Alpha decides to take £1,000 p.a. salary from the time Beta joins. Both partners agree to take 5% p.a. interest on capital from the time Beta joins. Below is a trial balance for the 2008 period. Draw up the appropriation account and the partners' current accounts (for current a/cs, see section C overleaf).

Trial Balance for period ending 31 December 2008

	DR £	CR £
Cash a/c	49,500	
Recovery van a/c	4,000	
Mechanical equip. a/c	6,500	
Staff salaries a/c	17,000	
Expenses a/c	12,500	
Rent a/c	10,000	
Debtors a/c	28,000	
Creditors a/c		7,500
Bills paid		139,500
Partners' capital accounts:		
Alpha		20,000
Beta		10,000
Partners' drawings:		
Alpha	45,500	
Beta	4,000	
Balance	**177,000**	**177,000**

NB: Profit for the period is bills paid (£139,500) less staff salaries (£17,000), expenses (£12,500) and rent (£10,000) = £100,000

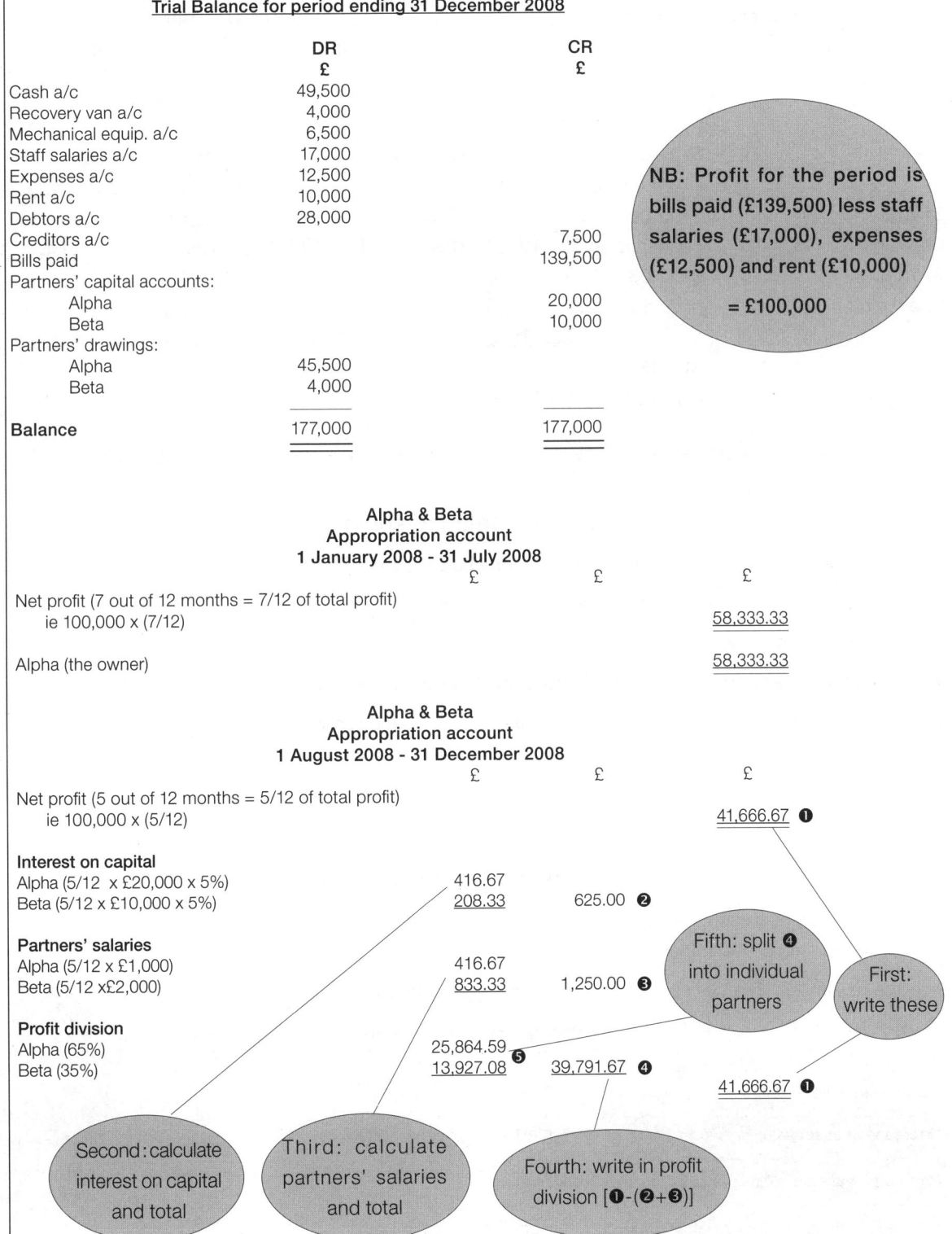

Alpha & Beta
Appropriation account
1 January 2008 - 31 July 2008

	£	£	£
Net profit (7 out of 12 months = 7/12 of total profit) ie 100,000 x (7/12)			58,333.33
Alpha (the owner)			58,333.33

Alpha & Beta
Appropriation account
1 August 2008 - 31 December 2008

Net profit (5 out of 12 months = 5/12 of total profit)
ie 100,000 x (5/12) .... 41,666.67 ❶

Interest on capital
Alpha (5/12 x £20,000 x 5%) ... 416.67
Beta (5/12 x £10,000 x 5%) ..... 208.33 ... 625.00 ❷

Partners' salaries
Alpha (5/12 x £1,000) 416.67
Beta (5/12 x £2,000) .... 833.33 ... 1,250.00 ❸

Profit division
Alpha (65%) .... 25,864.59 ❺
Beta (35%) .... 13,927.08 ... 39,791.67 ❹
.... 41,666.67 ❶

First: write these ❶
Second: calculate interest on capital and total ❷
Third: calculate partners' salaries and total ❸
Fourth: write in profit division [❶-(❷+❸)] ❹
Fifth: split into individual partners ❺

C The current accounts

➤ Each partner will have a current account, showing how much the business owes him (or how much he owes the business!).

➤ Each current account will be in a 'T' a/c format.

◆ The example below is based on the facts on the previous page:

Current a/c - Alpha

DR		CR	
		31.12.08 profit div no.1	58,333.33
		31.12.08 int. on capital	416.67
31.7.08 Drawings	45,500.00	31.12.08 partner salary	416.67
31.7.08 balance c/f	39,531.26	31.12.08 profit div no.2	25,864.59
	85,031.26		85,031.26
		31.7.08 balance b/f	39,531.26

Current a/c - Beta

DR		CR	
		31.12.08 int. on capital	208.33
31.7.08 Drawings	4,000.00	31.12.08 partner salary	833.33
31.7.08 balance c/f	10,968.74	31.12.08 profit div	13,927.08
	14,968.74		14,968.74
		31.7.08 balance b/f	10,968.74

➤ The current accounts are also presented in a certain format as notes to the balance sheet (see D be-

D The balance sheet

➤ The 'capital employed' section of the pro forma balance sheet (p 50) is made up of:

◆ the partners' capital accounts, *and*

◆ the partners' current accounts.

➤ A note to the balance sheet lists the make-up of the current accounts.

➤ ALWAYS do the capital account first, followed by the balance sheet, even though they are displayed the other way round.

➤ An example based on the facts from the previous example is on the facing page.

E Revaluations of assets

➤ A revaluation of each asset is usually carried out on a change in the partnership or a change in the profit-sharing ratio between them.

➤ A revaluation 'T' a/c is opened and the following adjustments are made:

	Revaluation a/c	Asset a/c	Partner capital a/c
Increase in asset value	CREDIT	DEBIT	
Decrease in asset value	DEBIT	CREDIT	
Profit on revaluation (close revaluation a/c)	DEBIT		CREDIT
Loss on revaluation (close revaluation a/c)	CREDIT		DEBIT

any credits/debits are in the agreed partner ratio of sharing profits and losses

ACCOUNTS

Partnership accounts

Fully worked example (continued)

Balance sheet of Alpha and Beta as of 31st December 2008

	£	£	£
FIXED ASSETS			
Recovery van - cost		4,000	
Mechanical equipment - cost		6,500	10,500
ADD: CURRENT ASSETS			
Debtors		28,000	
Cash at bank		49,500	77,500
LESS: CURRENT LIABILITIES			
Creditors		7,500	7,500
NET CURRENT ASSETS			**80,500**
NET ASSETS			**80,500**
Capital employed			
Capital accounts			
Alpha	20,000		
Beta	10,000	30,000	
Current accounts (see note 1)			
Alpha	39,531.26		
Beta	10,968.74	50,500	80,500

Do the balance sheet after the current accounts

Notes to the balance sheet
Note (1)
Current accounts

Do this first

Put these figures into the balance sheet

	Alpha	Beta
Interest on capital	416.67	208.33
Partners' salaries	416.67	803.33
Profit division no. 1	58,333.33	0.00
Profit division no. 2	25,864.59	13,927.08
	85,031.26	14,938.74
Less drawings	45,500.00	4,000.00
Balance	39,531.26	10,938.74

55

E Interpreting accounts

I	Generally
II	Ratios

I Generally

➤ When compiling accounts, accountants use guidance which the accountancy profession produces under the auspices, in the UK, of the Accounting Standards Board. ASB guidance sets out UK generally accepted accounting practice ('UK GAAP').

➤ For accounting periods beginning on or after 1 January 2005:

  a) an EU company with listed equity securities is required to draw up group accounts in accordance with International Financial Reporting Standards ('IFRS') (overseen by the International Accounting Standards Board) as endorsed by the EU Commission, *and*

  b) other companies and LLPs incorporated under English law may elect to adopt IFRS.

   • For more on this, see the *Banking & Capital Markets Companion*.

➤ Where a feature of the accounts is unusual, or requires explanation, it should be explained in the 'Notes' found at the back of the accounts. These 'Notes' are an important aid to understanding accounts.

➤ In addition to information to be found in the 'Notes' the use of ratios provides a rough and ready way to:

   ◆ identify trends in a business (by comparing ratios in successive sets of accounts), *and/or*

   ◆ compare a business with other businesses in the same sector, or of a similar size.

➤ Some frequently used ratios, which are examined below, are designed to measure:

  a) profitability, *or*

  b) financial risk, *or*

  c) cashflow.

   • Ratios should be used with caution - like all statistics they are misleading if looked at in isolation. Ratios are best used as a stimulus to ask questions about an enterprise (eg: why is 'dividend cover' so low?) rather than as a source of objective information.

II Ratios

A Profitability

➤ The ratios which are used to assess a business's profitability, including the following:

1 Return on capital employed ('ROCE')

➤ This ratio relates 'profit before interest and tax' ('PBIT') to the working capital invested in a business.

➤ ROCE can be expressed as:

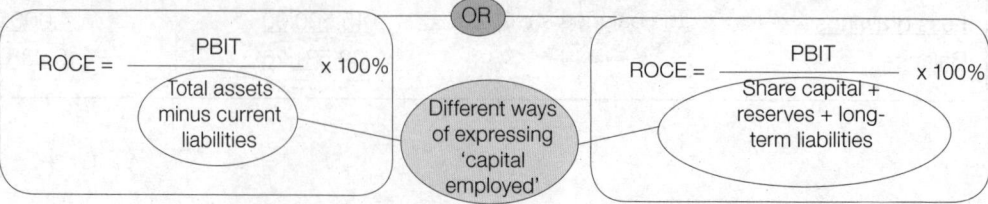

$$\text{ROCE} = \frac{\text{PBIT}}{\text{Total assets minus current liabilities}} \times 100\%$$

OR

$$\text{ROCE} = \frac{\text{PBIT}}{\text{Share capital + reserves + long-term liabilities}} \times 100\%$$

Different ways of expressing 'capital employed'

2 Asset turnover

➤ This ratio indicates the volume of sales the enterprise is generating using its assets/capital.

➤ The formula is:

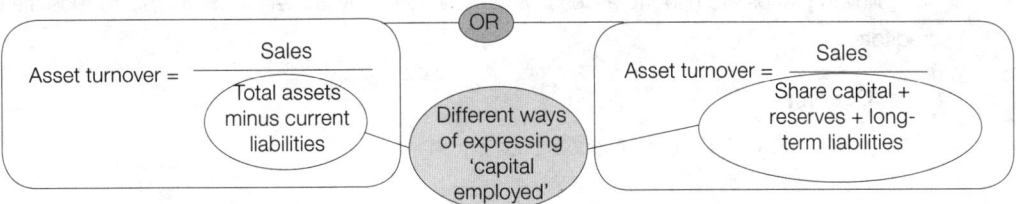

$$\text{Asset turnover} = \frac{\text{Sales}}{\text{Total assets minus current liabilities}} \quad \text{OR} \quad \text{Asset turnover} = \frac{\text{Sales}}{\text{Share capital + reserves + long-term liabilities}}$$

(Different ways of expressing 'capital employed')

3 Profit margin

➤ This ratio can be used to measure an enterprise's gross profit margin (before general expenses are deducted) or net profit margin (after general expenses are deducted).

$$\text{Gross margin} = \frac{\text{Gross profit (sales less cost of sales)}}{\text{Sales turnover}} \times 100\%$$

$$\text{Net margin} = \frac{\text{Net profit (sales less all costs)}}{\text{Sales turnover}} \times 100\%$$

4 Ratios for companies with share capital

➤ Earnings per share ('EPS'): this shows how much profit is earned on each share.

$$\text{Earnings per share} = \frac{\text{Profit}}{\text{Number of issued shares}}$$

- ◆ EPS has in the past frequently been used (indeed over used) as an indicator of whether shares are under or over priced.
  - • EPS is open to abuse, as the calculation of 'profit' or the use of complex capital structures mean that it can be manipulated.
  - • Note also the importance of cultural/economic influences when interpreting EPS as, for instance, the EPS is traditionally lower in the UK and the USA (eg: 10x-15x) than stock markets than on the Japanese market (eg: 20x-25x) while an internet ('.com') stock may have a large market capitalisation running into billions of dollars but generate no profit (or even incur a loss).

➤ Dividend cover: this relates the dividends a company pays to the profits the company earns.

$$\text{Dividend cover} = \frac{\text{Earnings per share}}{\text{Dividend per share}}$$

- ◆ Note that a dividend cover of less than 1 means that the company is paying dividends out of retained profits earned in previous years, a cover of 1 or more indicates dividends are being paid out of current earnings.
  - • Public companies often maintain a dividend cover of 1.5 to 3 (eg: in the latter case £1 paid out for every £3 of profits).

B Financial risk

➤ The following ratios are used to assess whether a company is likely to be unable to meet its obligations to its creditors.

1 Gearing

➤ Gearing relates debt finance to equity finance.

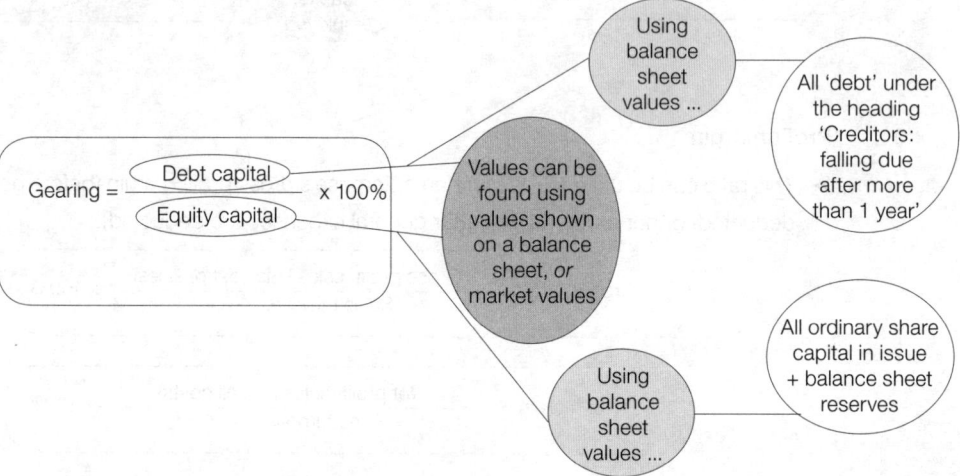

- Gearing can be measured in a number of different ways. For example, 'Total capital' can be used instead of equity capital.

➤ Whether 'gearing' (also known as 'leverage') is too high, or too low, depends on market conditions and the business sector in which the enterprise is operating. The higher the gearing, the more the equity capital may be perceived to be at risk.

2 Interest cover

➤ This ratio is a measure of credit risk - it shows how comfortably an enterprise can meet its interest obligations to creditors.

$$\text{Interest cover} = \frac{\text{PBIT}}{\text{Interest charges}}$$

3 Working capital

➤ This ratio reflects the amount of capital which is used to finance the enterprise from day-to-day.

$$\text{Working capital} = \text{'Current Assets'} - \text{'Current Liabilities'}$$

- Put another way, 'working capital' equals 'net current assets'.

C Cashflow

➤ Cashflow is essential to any enterprise. Without sufficient liquidity to pay its liabilities as they fall due even an enterprise which on paper is extremely profitable will go bust.

➤ The following ratios offer a measure of how liquid an enterprise is:

1. **Stock turnover ratio**

    ➤ This ratio shows the average number of days it takes an enterprise to turn its stock over.

    $$\frac{\text{Stock in hand}}{\text{Costs of goods sold}} \times 365$$

2. **Debtor days**

    ➤ This ratio reveals the average number of days' credit which the enterprise's customers are allowed.

    $$\frac{\text{Trade debtors}}{\text{Sales}} \times 365$$

3. **'Acid test' ratio**

    ➤ This ratio can be useful if an enterprise necessarily has a slow stock turnover and it should normally exceed 1:1.

    $$\frac{\text{Current assets minus stock in hand}}{\text{Current liabilities (ie: Creditors falling due in under 1 year)}}$$

4. **Current ratio**

    ➤ This ratio demonstrates whether an enterprise can meet its current liabilities.

    $$\frac{\text{Current assets}}{\text{Current liabilities (ie: Creditors falling due in under 1 year)}}$$

F   Solicitors' Accounts Rules 1998

   I   Generally
   II   Interest

I   Generally

'Solicitor', for the remainder of this section, refers to anyone subject to the SARs in their entirety

1 **Responsibility for compliance** (*r 6*)

   ➤ A principal (and a director of a recognised body) must ensure compliance by him or herself and everyone employed in a practice (and, in the case of a director, by the recognised body).

2 **Duty to remedy breaches** (*r 7*)

   ➤ Any breach must be remedied promptly upon discovery.

   ◆ This includes the replacement of money improperly withheld or withdrawn from client account - if necessary by the principals in the practice using their own resources.

ACCOUNTS
Solicitors' Accounts Rules 1998

General Principles (r 1)

➤ A solicitor must:

a) comply with the requirements of *SPR r 1*, and

b) keep other people's money separate from money belonging to the solicitor *or* the practice, *and*

c) keep other people's money safely in a 'bank' *or* 'building society' account identifiable as a client account except where the rules specifically provide otherwise, *and*

- A 'bank' is an institution authorised under the *Banking Act 1987*, the Post Office, or the Bank of England (*r 2(2)(c)*).
- A 'building society' is a society within the meaning of the *Building Societies Act 1986* (*r 2(2)(d)*).

d) use each client's money for each client's matters only, *and*

e) use controlled trust money for the purposes of that trust only, *and*

f) establish and maintain proper accounting systems, and proper internal controls over those systems, to ensure compliance with the *SARs*, *and*

g) keep proper accounting records to show accurately the position with regard to the money held for each client and each controlled trust, *and*

h) account for interest on other people's money in accordance with the rules, *and*

i) deliver annual accountant's reports as required by the rules.

Money a solicitor holds or receives in the course of practise is either (r 13):

Client money
Money held and received from a client and all other money which is not controlled trust money or office money

Controlled trust money
Money held or received for a controlled trust

Office money
Money which belongs to the solicitor or the practice

Includes money held or received:

a) as agent, bailee, stakeholder, donee of power of attorney, liquidator, trustee in bankruptcy, Court of Protection receiver, *or*
b) for payment of unpaid professional disbursements, *or*
c) for payment of stamp duty, Land Registry/court fees etc, where the solicitor has not already incurred an obligation to the pay the sum, *or*
d) as a payment on account of costs generally, *or*
e) as commission (unless the client has given prior authority to retain it under *SPR r.10* or it is below £20 (*r 13 n(i)*).

For a detailed definition of when a controlled trust arises see *SAR r 2(2)(h)*. Broadly, a controlled trust arises when a solicitor is a sole trustee, or is a co-trustee only with one or more of his partners or employees

Includes (*r 13 n(xi)*):
a) money held or received in connection with running a practice (PAYE, VAT, firm's fees), and
b) interest on general client accounts, *and*
c) payments received in respect of:
   ♦ fees due against a bill or written notification of costs (see *r 19(2)*).
   ♦ disbursements already paid.
   ♦ disbursements incurred (but not paid) (excluding professional disbursements).
   ♦ money paid for or towards an agreed fee, *and*
d) money held in client account and earmarked for costs under *r 19(3)*.

Money held for a principal of the practice (as a solicitor cannot act as his own client) (*r. 13 n.(xii)*) (But this does not include money held jointly for a principal and their spouse which is client money)

➤ Controlled trust money is treated as client money, except where the rules require otherwise (*r 8*).

➤ The *SARs* do not affect a solicitor's rights by way of lien, set off, counterclaim or otherwise against money standing to the credit of client account (*r 12*).

ACCOUNTS
Solicitors' Accounts Rules 1998

Categories of money *paid into* client account

May be paid into client account	a) the solicitor's own money to open or maintain the account, *or* b) an advance from the solicitor to fund payment on behalf of a client or controlled trust (being in excess of money held for that client or controlled trust), *or* c) money paid in to replace money that has been withdrawn in breach of the *r 22*, *or* d) a sum in lieu of interest which is paid into client account instead of directly to the client (*r 15(2)*).
Must be paid into client account	▶ Client money (*r 15(1)*) ◆ This must be done 'without delay', ie: in normal circumstances, the day of receipt or, if that is not possible, the next working day (*r 2(2)(z)*).
May be withheld from client account	▶ Client money which is (*r 17*): a) cash received and without delay paid in cash in the ordinary course of business to the client, or on the client's behalf to a third party, *or* b) a cheque or draft received and endorsed over in the ordinary course of business to the client, or on the client's behalf to a third party, *or* c) it is money which the client instructs the solicitor not to pay into client account, for the client's own convenience, and instructions are given in writing or are given by other means and confirmed by the solicitor to the client in writing (*SAR r.16(1)*), *or* d) unpaid professional disbursements included in a payment of costs under *r 19(1)(b)* or *r 21*, *or* e) withheld on the written authorisation of the Law Society.

▶ Controlled trust money which is (*SAR r 18*):

a) cash received and without delay paid in cash in the execution of the trust to a beneficiary/third party, *or*

b) a cheque/draft received and endorsed without delay in the execution of the trust to a beneficiary/third party, *or*

c) money which in accordance with the trustee's powers is paid into or retained in the account of the trustee (which is not client account) or properly retained cash in the performance of the trustee's duties, *or*

d) on the written authorisation of the Law Society.

Categories of money *withdrawn* from client account

Client money	Office money	Controlled trust money

a) properly required for a payment to or on behalf of a client (or another person on whose behalf the money is being held), *or* b) properly required for the payment of a disbursement on behalf of the client, *or* c) properly required in full or partial reimbursement of money spent by the solicitor on behalf of the client, *or* d) transferred to another client account, *or* e) withdrawn on the client's instructions, provided the instructions are for the client's convenience and are given in writing or by other means and confirmed by the solicitor to the client in writing, *or* f) a refund to the solicitor of an advance no longer required to fund a payment on behalf of a client, *or* g) money paid in breach of the rules, *or* h) withdrawn on the written authorisation of the Law Society (*r 22(1)*).	a) properly required in the execution of a particular trust, *or* b) properly required for payment of a disbursement of a particular trust, *or* c) properly required in full or partial disbursement of money spent by the solicitor on behalf of the particular trust, *or* d) transferred to another client account, *or* e) transferred to an account other than a client account, but only if the trustees powers permit, or to be properly retained as cash in the performance of the trustee's duties, *or* f) a refund to the solicitor of an advance no longer required to fund a payment on behalf of a controlled trust, *or* g) money paid in in breach of the rules, *or* h) withdrawn on the written authorisation of the Law Society (*r 22(2)*).

a) paid in to open the account or maintain it under *r 15(2)(a)*, *or*
b) properly required for payment of the solicitor's costs under (*r 19(2)-(3)*), *or*
c) the whole or part of a payment into client account under *r 19(1)*), *or*
d) part of a mixed payment placed in client account under *r 20(2)(b)* (*r 22(3)*).

ACCOUNTS
Solicitors' Accounts Rules 1998

A Types of client account

➤ A solicitor who holds or receives client or controlled trust money must generally keep a client account at a bank or a building society, and the naming of the account must comply with certain formal requirements (*r 14(1)-(3)*).

- ◆ A bank account or building society account must be at a branch or head office in England and Wales (*r 14(4)*).
- ◆ A building society account must be a deposit or share account (*r 14(4)*).
  - A bank means an institution with permission to accept deposits under *FSMA 2000 Part IV* (including a UK branch of an EEA firm permitted in another EC member state to accept deposits), the Post Office, or the Bank of England. A building society means a building society for the purposes of the *BSA 1986* (*r 2(2)(c)-(d)*).

➤ A client account may be either (*r 14(5)*):

a) a separate designated client account - a deposit or share account relating to a single client, or a current, deposit or share account relating to a single controlled trust, *or*

b) a general client account.

B Mixed payments into client account

➤ A mixed payment includes both client money or controlled trust money and office money..

➤ A mixed payment must either be (*r 20(2)*):

a) split as appropriate, *or*

b) placed without delay in client account (in which case all office money must be transferred out of client account within 14 days of receipt (*r 20(3)*)).

C Withdrawing money from client account

➤ Money paid into client account in breach of the rules must be withdrawn promptly on discovery (*r 22(4)*).

➤ Money withdrawn from a general client account must not exceed the money held on behalf of the particular client or controlled trust in all the solicitor's general client accounts unless:

a) sufficient money is held for that client or controlled trust in a separate designated client account, *and*

b) the appropriate transfer from the separate designated client account to a general client account is made immediately (*r 22(5)-(6)*).

➤ Money held for a particular client or controlled trust must not be used for payments for another client or controlled trust (*r 22(7)*).

➤ A client account must not be overdrawn except in the following circumstances (*r 22(8)*):

a) a separate designated client account for a controlled trust, if the controlled trustee makes payments on behalf of the trustee (eg: for IHT) before realising sufficient assets to cover the payments, *or*

b) a sole practitioner dies and his or client accounts are frozen, in which case the solicitor-manager can operate client accounts which are overdrawn to the extent of money held in the frozen accounts.

D Receipt and transfer of costs

➤ A solicitor must first give or send a bill of costs, or other notification of costs, to the client or paying party (*r 19(2)*).

♦ When this has been done, money earmarked for costs becomes office money and must be transferred out of client account within 14 days (*r 19(3)*).

➤ Where a fee is fixed (this does not include a fee that can be varied upwards or that is dependent on a transaction being completed) it must be paid into office account (and the fee must be evidenced in writing) (*r 19(5)*).

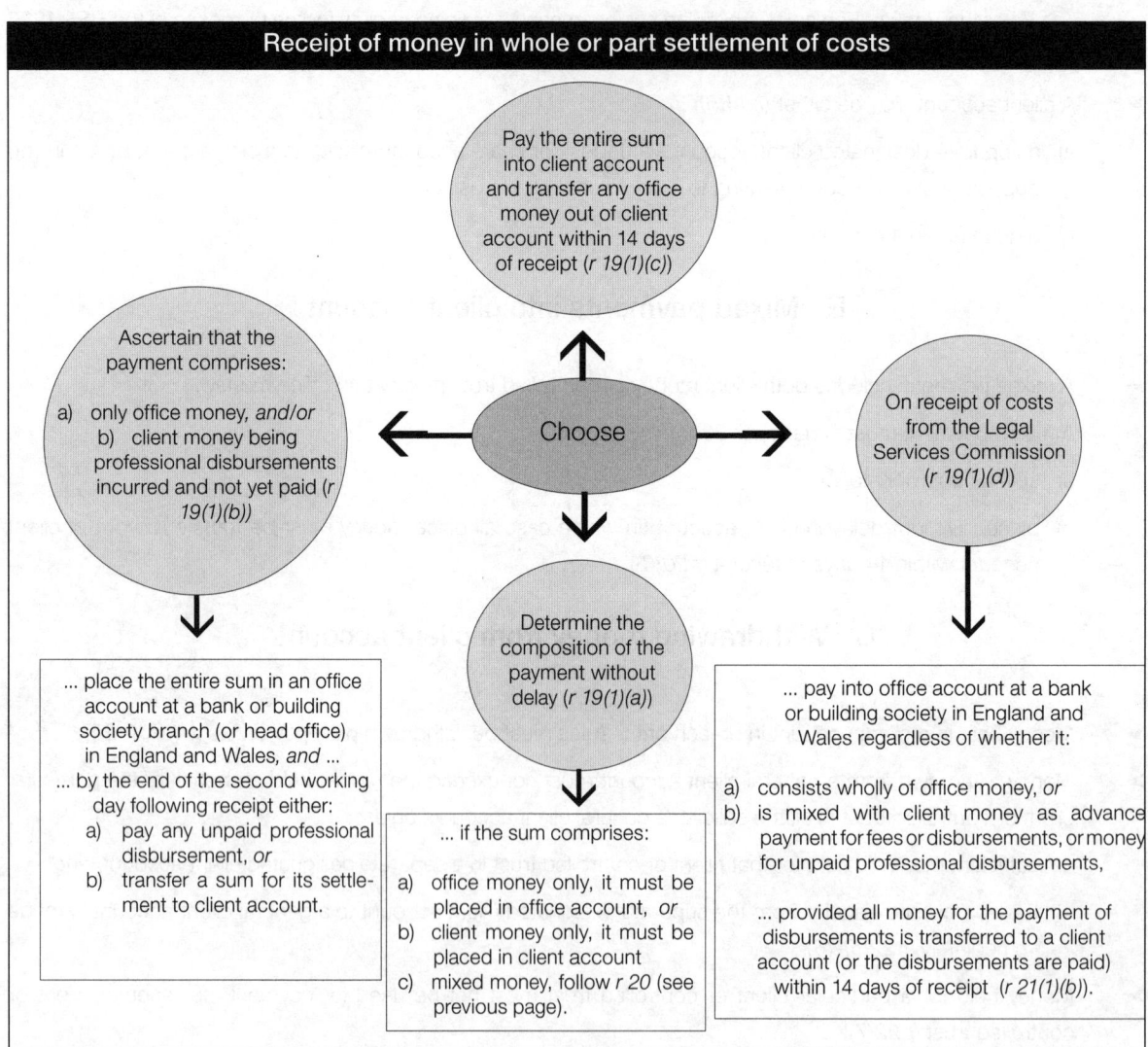

E Payments to Legal Help practitioners

1. **Payments from the Legal Services Commission (the 'Commission')**

   ➤ An advance in anticipation of work to be carried out (although client money) may be placed in office account (*r 21(1)(a)*).

   ◆ This may be done only if the Commission instructs in writing that it may be done.

   ➤ A payment for costs may be paid into office account (*r 21(1)(b)*) (see previous page).

   ➤ A payment for regular work (eg: monthly payments under civil or legal aid contracting arrangements) must be paid into office account at a bank or building society in England and Wales (*r 21(2)(b)*).

   ➤ Within 28 days of submitting a report to the Commission notifying completion of a matter (or, if permitted by the Commission to notify at other stages, on submitting such a report), a solicitor must either:

   a) pay any unpaid professional disbursements, *or*

   b) transfer to client account an amount equivalent to the unpaid professional disbursements relating to that matter (*r 21(2)(c)-(d)*).

2. **Payments from a third party**

   ➤ Payments which are no regular payments (*r 21(3)*):

   a) paid costs to a solicitor or to a previously nominated solicitor ('green form' costs, advance payments or interim costs), *or*

   b) paid professional disbursements direct and costs, *and* ....

   ... costs are subsequently settled by a third party:

   ▪ the entire third party payment must be paid into client account, *and*

   ▪ a sum representing payments made by the Commission must be retained in client account, *and*

   ▪ any balance belonging to the solicitor must be transferred to an office account within 14 days of the solicitor sending a report to the Commission containing details of the third party payment, *and*

   ▪ the sum retained in client account (as representing payments made by the Commission) must be either:

   i) recorded in the individual client's ledger account and identified as the Commission's money, *or*

   ii) recorded in a ledger account in the Commission's name and identified by reference to the client or matter, *and*

   ... kept in the client account until notification from the Commission that it has recouped an equivalent sum from subsequent legal help payments due to the solicitor (the retained sum must be transferred to office account within 14 days of notification).

Some definitions in the *SARs*

'without delay' in normal circumstances, either the day of receipt or the next day (*r 2(2)(z)*)
'costs' fees and disbursements (*r 2(2)(j)*)
'disbursement' any sum spent or to be spent by a solicitor on behalf of a client or controlled trust (incl. VAT) (*r 2(2)(k)*)
'professional disbursement' the fees of counsel, lawyer, or of a professional or agent instructed by a solicitor (*r 2(2)(s)*)
'fees' a solicitor's own charges or profit costs (incl. VAT) (*r 2(2)(l)*)

Record keeping

➤ A solicitor must keep a properly written up record of all dealings with client money (ie: client money received, held or paid by the solicitor) *(r 32(1))*.

- The record (ie: a client ledger) must also distinguish a particular client's money from other money held in client account.

- Each client ledger must show a current balance (but there is no requirement to keep a historic record of previous balances) *(r 32(5))*.

- Transfers between client ledgers must be recorded through the cash account, or a separate record (often known as a transfer journal, or 'TJ') *(r 32(2))*.

- A solicitor must keep a record of all bills of costs (distinguishing between profit costs and disbursements), and must record all bills and intimations of costs delivered to clients *(r 32(8))*.

➤ There is no obligation to keep a separate client ledger for a borrower and lender in a conveyancing transaction provided that *(r 32(6))*:

a) the funds belonging to each client are 'clearly identifiable' (eg: the fact that an amount represents a mortgage advance from a particular lender must be clearly stated in the borrower's ledger), *and*

b) the lender is an institutional lender providing mortgages in the normal course of its activities. (Consequently, this relaxation of the general rule does not apply if the lender is a private individual.)

➤ At least once every 5 weeks (at least once every 14 weeks for controlled trust money held in pass-book operated designated client accounts) a solicitor must *(r 32(7))*:

a) compare the balances in client ledgers with the cash account balance, *and*

b) prepare a reconciliation showing the cause of any difference between the two balances and reconcile the cash account with balances shown on client account pass books or statements and money held elsewhere.

➤ A withdrawal from client account must not be made unless there is specific authority signed by *(r 23(1))*:

a) a solicitor with a current practising certificate, *or*

b) a person employed by the solicitor, being ...

   i) a solicitor, *or*

   ii) a fellow of the Institute of Legal Executives (of not less than 3 years' standing), *or*

   iii) a licensed conveyancer if an office deals solely with conveyancing, *or*

c) a registered foreign lawyer who is a partner or (in the case of a recognised body) a director of the practice.

- This rule does not apply to transfers from one general client account to another general client account at the same bank or building society *(r 23(2))*.

- A solicitor must keep all cheques and copies of authorities (other than cheques) signed under SAR r 23(1) for at least 2 years, or must seek written confirmation from a bank or building society that it will retain them for at least 2 years *(r 32(10))*.

➤ A solicitor must keep all accounts, books, ledgers, records, and bank statements as printed and issued by a bank or building society, for at least 6 years from the date of last entry in each document *(r 32(9))*.

II Interest

A When interest must be paid

1. **Money in a separate designated client account (r 24(1))**

   ➤ A solicitor must account for all interest on a designated deposit account to:
   - a client, if a solicitor holds money in such an account for a client, *or*
   - a person funding all or part of the solicitor's fees, if the solicitor holds money for such a person.

2. **Money held in general client account (r 24(2))**

   ➤ A solicitor must account for a sum in lieu of interest (even if money should have been held in client account but was not):
   - to a client, *or*
   - to a person funding all or part of the solicitor's fees, ...

     ... unless any of the following 6 exemptions applies:

     a) the amount calculated is £20 or less, *or*

     b) the solicitor holds an amount for a period set out below, *or*

Amount	Period
➤ Not exceeding £1,000	➤ Not exceeding 8 weeks
➤ Not exceeding £2,000	➤ Not exceeding 4 weeks
➤ Not exceeding £10,000	➤ Not exceeding 2 weeks
➤ Not exceeding £20,000	➤ Not exceeding 1 week
➤ Exceeding £20,000	➤ For under 1 week or less if this is 'fair and reasonable' having regard to all the circumstances

     c) money is held for payment of counsel's fees, after counsel has requested a delay in settlement, *or*

     d) money held for the Legal Services Commission, *or*

     e) an advance from the solicitor (under *r 15(2)(b)*) to fund a payment on behalf of the client in excess of funds held for that client, *or*

     f) there is agreement to contract out of this rule under *r 27*.

3. **Money held outside client account on the client's instructions, or which a solicitor has been instructed to hold outside client account (but has not done so), under *r 16(1)(a)* (*r 24(6)*)**

   ➤ A solicitor must account:
   - for all the interest earned on the account, *or*
   - if the solicitor has failed to comply with instructions under *r 16(1)(a)*, for a sum *in lieu* of any net loss of interest suffered by the client (or a person funding all or part of the solicitor's fees).

4. **Stakeholder money (*r 26*)**

   ➤ A solicitor must pay interest, or a sum *in lieu* of interest, in accordance with *r 24* to the person to whom the stake is paid.

> **Contracting out (r 27)**
>
> ➤ A solicitor may come to a different arrangement from that set out in *r 24* if the solicitor enters into a written agreement:
>
> a) with a client (and there are appropriate circumstances), *or*
>
> b) with a client and the other party to the transaction, if the solicitor acts as stakeholder.

B Amount of interest / *in lieu* of interest

1 Separate designated deposit account

➤ A solicitor must obtain a reasonable rate of interest (*r 25(1)*).

A sum is 'in lieu' of interest if it is not interest but paid in respect of interest

2 General client account

➤ A solicitor must account for a fair sum in lieu of interest (*r 25(1)*).

- This need not necessarily reflect the highest rate of interest obtainable, but it is unacceptable to look only at the lowest rate of interest obtainable.
- The sum must be calculated (*r 25(2)*):
  - on the balance[s] held over the whole period for which cleared funds are held, *and*
  - at a rate not less than the higher of:
    - a) the rate of interest payable on a separate designated client account for the amount[s] held, *or*
    - b) the rate of interest payable on the relevant amount[s] if placed on deposit on similar terms by a member of the business community, *and*
  - at the bank or building society where the money is held.

➤ If sums are held intermittently, and the sum in lieu of interest is £20 or less, a sum in lieu of interest should be paid if it is fair and reasonable in the circumstances to aggregate the sums in respect of the various periods (*r 24(4)*).

➤ If, for part of a continuous period during which money is held:

- money is held in a designated deposit account, *and*
- the sum in lieu of interest for the period during which it was held in general client account is £20 or less, ...

... a sum *in lieu* of interest should be paid if it is fair and reasonable to do so (*r 24(5)*).

G Keeping accounts as a solicitor

I   Generally
II   Particular entries

I Generally

➤ In order to comply with *SAR r 1*, a solicitor must use separate bank accounts for client money and office money. Separate cash account ledgers must be kept for each bank (or building society) account (these show amounts paid into / withdrawn from each account).

➤ A solicitor must keep a separate ledger for each client (*SAR r 32*) (these show amounts received from/paid out for each client).

  ◆ Since there are two separate cash accounts (one for office money and the other for client money), each client effectively has two ledgers - one dealing with that client's 'client money' and the other with that client's 'office money'.

➤ The diagram below shows how the 2 sets of ledgers relate to each other.

  ◆ The Cash Account shows two separate accounts kept with a bank or building society (client account and office account). The Client Ledger shows the money which the firm is liable to the client for (client money) and which the client owes to the firm (office money).

  ◆ Note that double entries are never made between the 'office' and 'client' ledgers, but between the those ledgers and the related ledgers in the Cash Account (for instance, when money is paid out of one account and into the other, eg: when a bill of costs is settled).

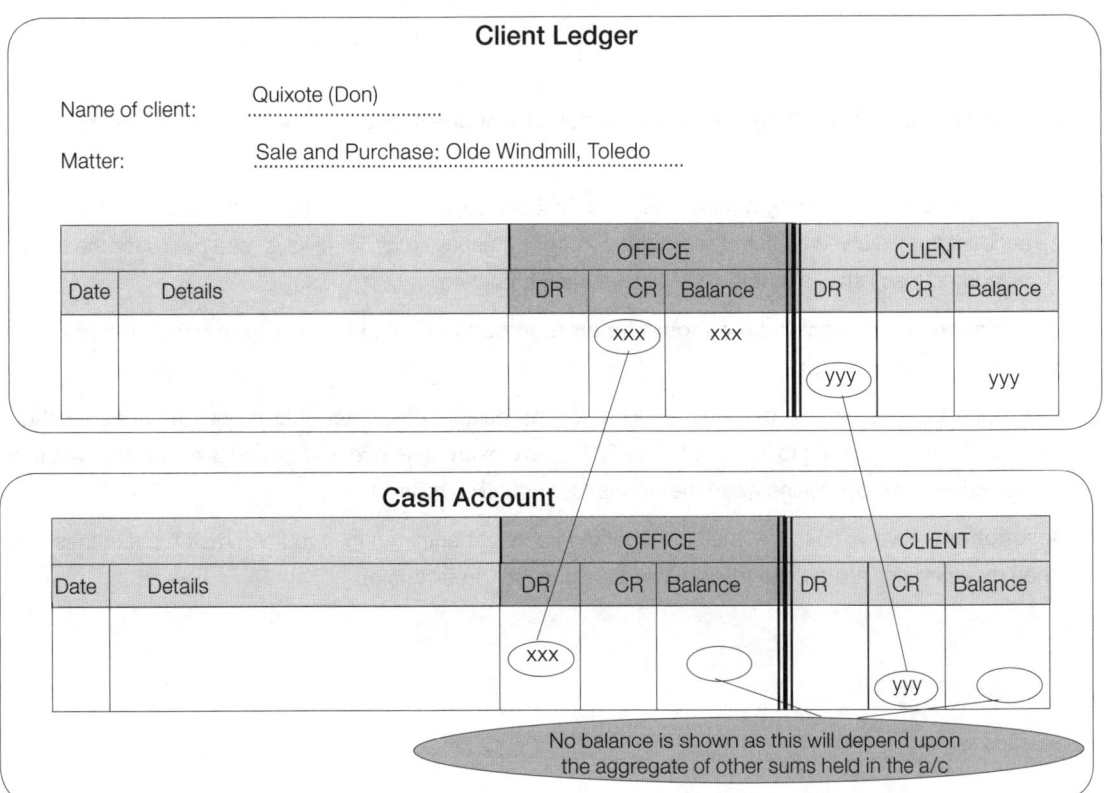

➤ Various formats can be used for ledgers, but the example below illustrates some important features of a Client Ledger comprising two separate sets of 'T' accounts (known as 'ledgers'), one showing office money and the other client money:

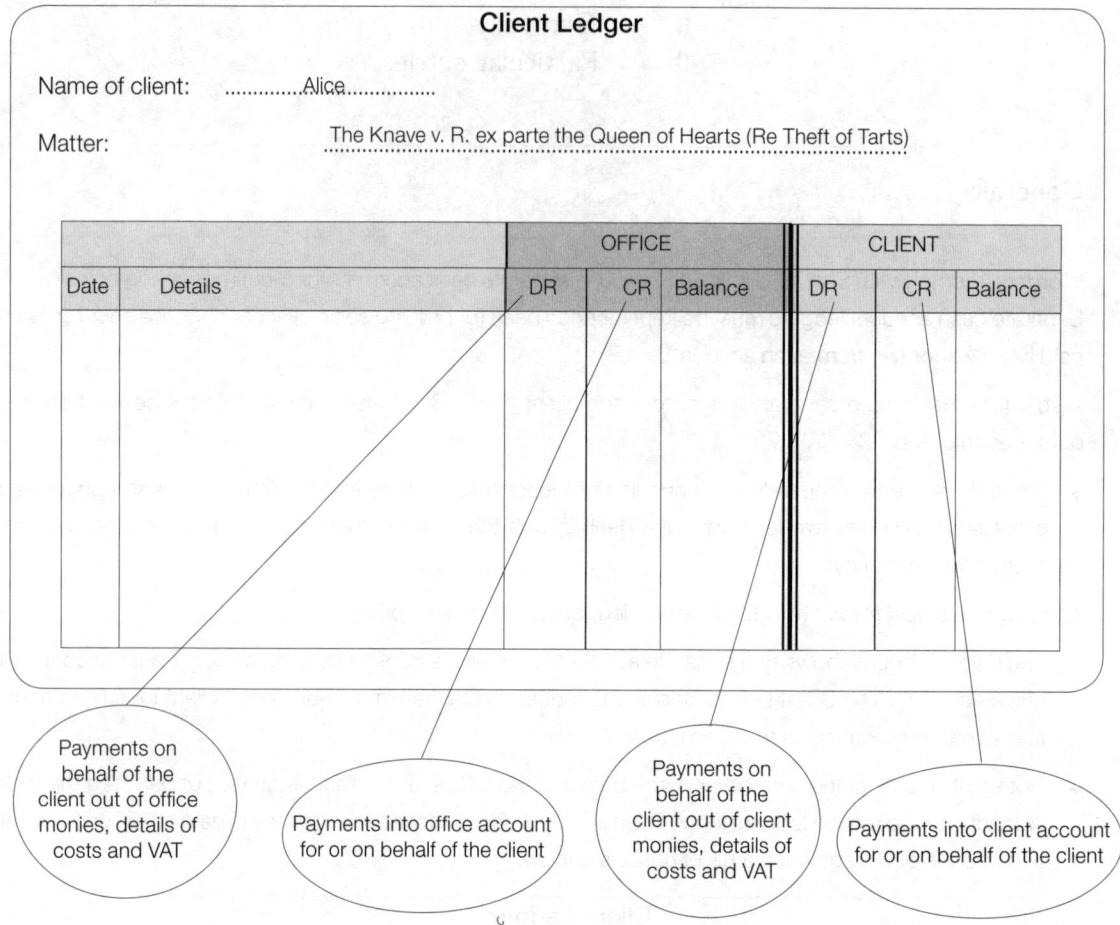

➤ **The balance in the office ledger should be a debit balance** - it indicates how much the client owes the firm for costs, disbursement etc.

   ◆ A credit balance (shown by putting 'CR' after the balance) indicates that more has been paid into the office account than is owed by the client to the solicitor - it usually (but not always, see below for the treatment of 'agreed fees') shows that the *SARs* have been breached.

➤ **The balance in the client ledger should be a credit balance** - it indicates how much money the solicitor holds on the client's behalf.

   ◆ A debit balance (shown by putting 'DR' after the balance) indicates that money has been withdrawn which does not belong to the client - the *SARs* have been breached and remedial action should be taken immediately (ie: by making good the deficiency with office money).

➤ **Description** - always 'describe' the corresponding account entry (so that you can match the entries to each other) then add any further information (see next page for an example).

ACCOUNTS
Keeping accounts as a solicitor

A note on terminology

In the following pages the word 'Ledger' (with an upper case 'L') is used to refer to the Client Ledger recording office and client money associated with a particular client. It is also used to refer to Cash Account and other ledgers recording client or office monies (eg: Profit Costs a/c). A 'ledger' ('l' in lower case) dealing with 'client money' or 'office money' is called a 'column'. This is purely to avoid the confusion sometimes occasioned by accounting terminology which uses the term 'ledger' in more than one context. Thus, the 'columns' are themselves 'ledgers' (ie: separate 'T' accounts) relating respectively to 'office money' and 'client money' which are written up, for the sake of convenience, in the same 'Ledger'.

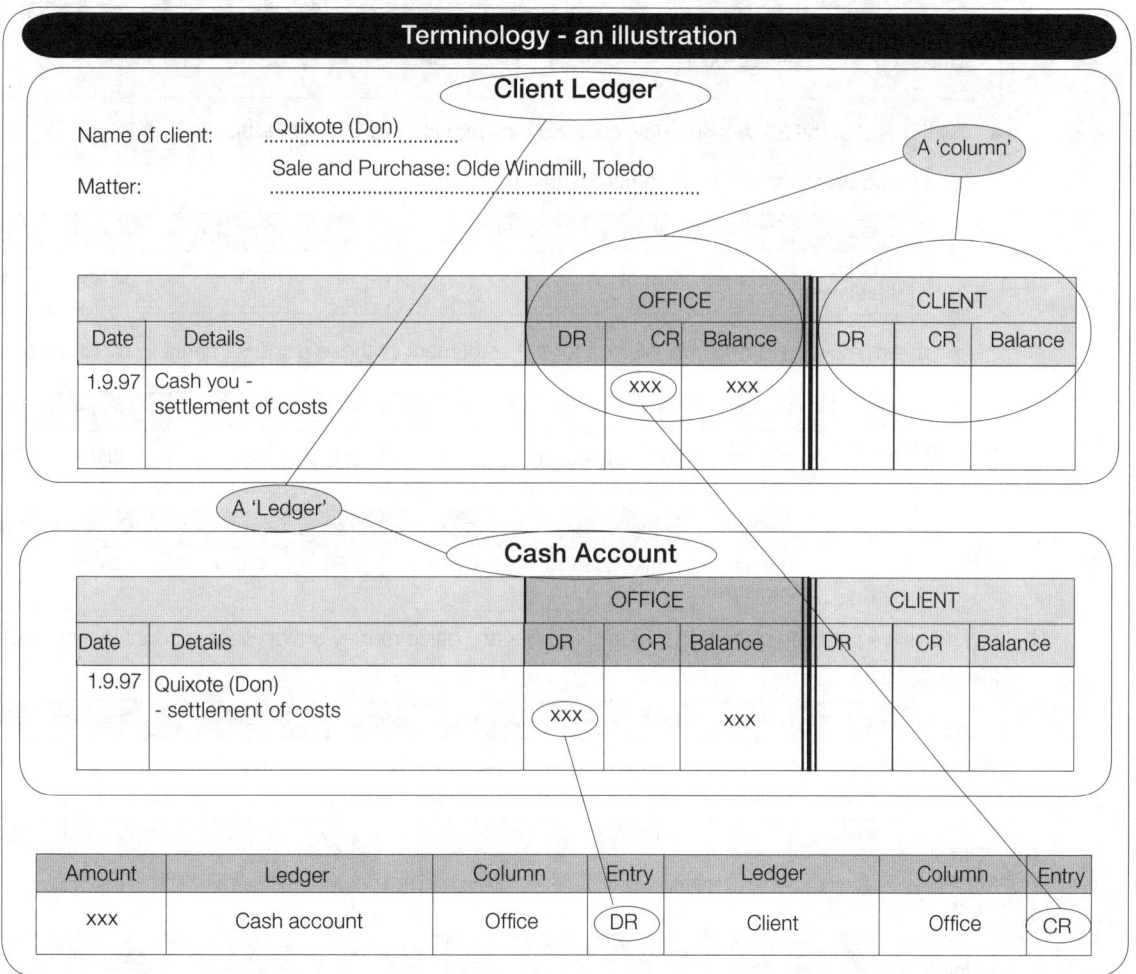

Terminology - an illustration

Client Ledger

Name of client: Quixote (Don)
Matter: Sale and Purchase: Olde Windmill, Toledo

Date	Details	OFFICE DR	OFFICE CR	OFFICE Balance	CLIENT DR	CLIENT CR	CLIENT Balance
1.9.97	Cash you - settlement of costs		xxx	xxx			

Cash Account

Date	Details	OFFICE DR	OFFICE CR	OFFICE Balance	CLIENT DR	CLIENT CR	CLIENT Balance
1.9.97	Quixote (Don) - settlement of costs	xxx		xxx			

Amount	Ledger	Column	Entry	Ledger	Column	Entry
xxx	Cash account	Office	DR	Client	Office	CR

Problem solving hints

➤ Get into the habit of thinking of entries in a particular order with its own logic, eg: (following the cash)

    a) is it client money or office money? (This dictates which 'column' is correct)

    b) is it a receipt into Cash Account (always DR) or a payment out of Cash Account (always a CR)?

    c) which Ledger should the corresponding CR entry (or DR entry) go in?

    ... does the column 'balance' as it should, or would the proposed entries breach the *SARs*?

I Particular entries

1 Costs and disbursements

➤ When a bill of costs is delivered to a client the following entries are made:

Amount	Ledger	Column	Entry	Ledger	Column	Entry
Costs	Client	Office	DR	Profit costs account	Office	CR

➤ When the bill is paid either:

a) the payment should be paid into office account as office money (*SAR rr 19(1)(a)-(b)*), or

Amount	Ledger	Column	Entry	Ledger	Column	Entry
Costs	Cash account	Office	DR	Office	Office	CR

- By the end of the 2nd working day following receipt, either (*SAR r 19(1)(b)*):

  - unpaid professional disbursements must be paid, *or*

Amount	Ledger	Column	Entry	Ledger	Column	Entry
Unpaid disbursement	Cash account	Office	CR	Office	Office	DR

  - a sum must have been transferred for the settlement of those disbursements to client account.

    Out of office a/c

Amount	Ledger	Column	Entry	Ledger	Column	Entry
Unpaid disbursement	Cash account	Office	CR	Office	Office	DR

    In to client a/c

Amount	Ledger	Column	Entry	Ledger	Column	Entry
Unpaid disbursement	Cash account	Client	DR	Client	Client	CR

b) pay the entire sum into client account and transfer any office money out of client account within 14 days (*SAR r 19(1)(c)*).

Into client a/c

Amount	Ledger	Column	Entry	Ledger	Column	Entry
Payment	Cash account	Client	DR	Client	Client	CR

Out of client a/c

Amount	Ledger	Column	Entry	Ledger	Column	Entry
Costs	Cash account	Client	CR	Client	Client	DR

Into office a/c

Amount	Ledger	Column	Entry	Ledger	Column	Entry
Costs	Cash account	Office	DR	Client	Office	CR

c) if the payment is mixed with other monies which are client money, and the solicitor does not split the cheque, the cheque should be paid into client account and the relevant amount subsequently transferred to office account (*SAR rr 19(1)(a), 20*). (The entries are as in b) above)

- Note that it is very unusual to 'split' a cheque as cheques are nowadays often crossed 'a/c payee' and so cannot be split. If a cheque is 'split', both portions are accounted for as separate payments into office and client account.

➤ Disbursements and sums paid on the client's behalf may be paid from client account if there is a sufficient balance and the solicitor has express or implied authority to make the payment. If there is not enough money in client account, then office money must be used.

2 Sums received on account of costs

➤ These are client money and should be entered on the client account.

Amount	Ledger	Column	Entry	Ledger	Column	Entry
Costs	Cash account	Client	DR	Client	Client	CR

3 VAT

➤ These are client money and should be entered on the client account.

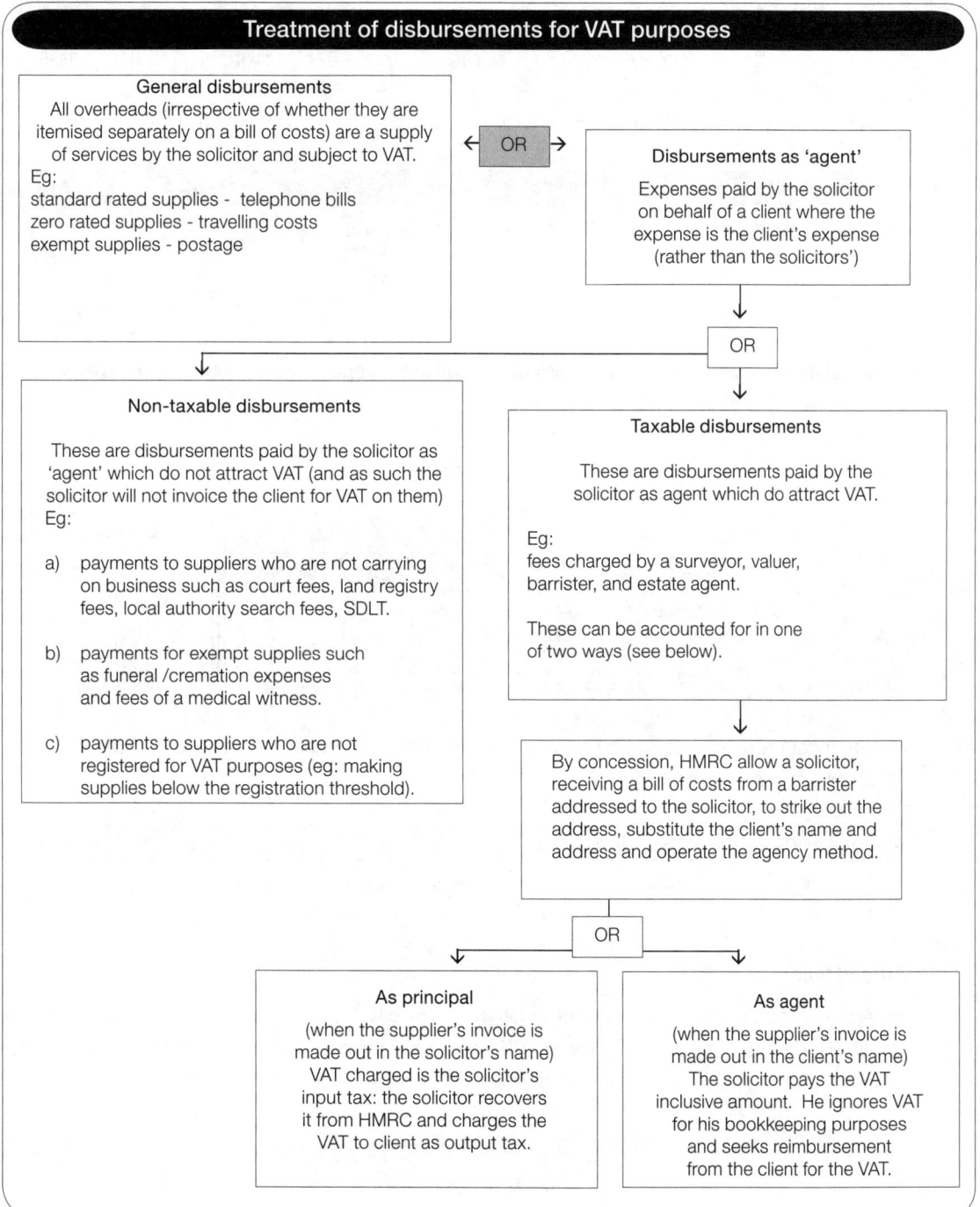

- A solicitor, like any taxable person, is obliged to charge VAT ('output tax') on supplies of services and may recover VAT ('input tax') on supplies attributable to taxable supplies which he or she makes.
- A taxable person's liability to HMRC is recorded in an HMRC account.
- When a bill of costs is delivered to a client the following double entries must be made:

Amount	Ledger	Column	Entry	Ledger	Column	Entry
Costs (ex VAT)	Client	Office	DR	Profit costs account	Office	CR

Amount	Ledger	Column	Entry	Ledger	Column	Entry
VAT	Client	Office	DR	HMRC a/c	Office	CR

- When an expense is paid (including VAT) the following double entries must be made:

Ledger	Column	Entry	Amount	Ledger	Column	Entry
Cash account	Office	CR	Expense including VAT →	Nominal expenses	Office	DR
				HMRC		

  - In order to ease a subsequent bank reconciliation the apportionment between the expense and the VAT is recorded as in the following example:

Cash Account

			OFFICE			CLIENT		
Date	Details		DR	CR	Balance	DR	CR	Balance
1.1.1998	Mousetraps VAT	240 42 282					282	

- When net VAT is paid to HMRC (ie: output tax exceeds input tax for the accounting period) the following double entries must be made:

Amount	Ledger	Column	Entry	Ledger	Column	Entry
Net VAT	Cash account	Office	CR	HMRC a/c	Office	DR

4   Agreed fees

- A payment from a client in respect of agreed fees is office money and should not be paid into client account (*SAR r 13*). (This may create a credit ('CR') balance in the office account - but this will be cancelled by a corresponding debit ('DR') in the office account when the solicitor issues his bill.)

5 Deposits (Conveyancing transactions)

➤ A deposit can be held as agent for the seller, or as stakeholder. In both cases a deposit is 'client money' (*SAR r 13*).

➤ The accounting treatment differs depending on how deposit monies are held.

- **As agent:** the solicitor may account immediately to the client for the deposit.

Amount	Ledger	Column	Entry	Ledger	Column	Entry
Deposit	Cash account	Client	DR	Client	Client	CR

- **As stakeholder:**

  a) The solicitor should not account immediately to the client for the deposit - the deposit is recorded in a separate ledger, the 'stakeholder account'.

Amount	Ledger	Column	Entry	Ledger	Column	Entry
Deposit	Cash account	Client	DR	Stakeholder a/c	Client	CR

  b) On completion, a transfer is made from the 'stakeholder account' to the client's ledger account. This transfer between the 'stakeholder account' and the client's ledger is a transfer between client ledgers and although there is therefore no need to record the transfer in the cash account (as no money is being withdrawn from client account), the transfer must be noted in both client accounts *(SAR r 32)*, stating in both cases 'transfer of deposit TJ' (for 'transfer journal')

Amount	Ledger	Column	Entry	Ledger	Column	Entry
Deposit	Stakeholder a/c	Client	DR	Client	Client	CR

- One 'stakeholder account' ledger will suffice for all stakeholder monies held by a solicitor (as it is all 'client money'); there is no need to have a separate ledger for each client in relation to whom the solicitor is a stakeholder.

6 Mortgages

➤ A solicitor may either treat an institutional lender as a separate client, or may take advantage of *SAR r 32(6)* and simply record a mortgage advance in the buyer's ledger noting the lender's interest.

ACCOUNTS
Keeping accounts as a solicitor

7 **Insurance premiums**

- When a solicitor receives an insurance premium from a client, prior to accounting to an insurance company for the net premium (ie: the gross premium less the solicitor's commission), the insurance company is treated as the solicitor's client for the purposes of the *SAR*s.

- A commission of less than £20 may be paid into office account if the solicitor has the client's permission to retain it (*SPR r 10*), otherwise it is 'client money'.

- If the solicitor receives commission **without accounting to policyholder** for it the double entries are:

    a) On payment by the policyholder:

Amount	Ledger	Column	Entry	Ledger	Column	Entry
Commission	Client (Insurance Co)	Office	DR	Commission account	Office	CR

Amount	Ledger	Column	Entry	Ledger	Column	Entry
Gross premium	Cash account	Client	DR	Client (Insurance Co)	Client	CR

    - Note that there is no entry in the ledger account of the policyholder (assuming the policyholder is a client of the solicitor) as the payment is received as 'client money' held on behalf of the insurance company.

    b) On payment by the solicitor to the insurance company.

	Amount	Ledger	Column	Entry	Ledger	Column	Entry
Out of client a/c	Net premium	Cash account	Client	CR	Client (Insurance Co)	Client	DR

	Amount	Ledger	Column	Entry	Ledger	Column	Entry
Out of client a/c	Commission	Cash account	Client	CR	Client (Insurance Co)	Client	DR

	Amount	Ledger	Column	Entry	Ledger	Column	Entry
Into office a/c	Commission	Cash a/c	Office	DR	Client (Insurance Co)	Office	CR

    - The commission account is an office ledger - at the end of the year the balance will be closed off to the solicitor's profit and loss account as income.

- If the solicitor receives commission **for which he is obliged to account to policyholder**.

Amount	Ledger	Column	Entry	Ledger	Column	Entry
Gross premium	Cash account	Client	DR	Client (Insurance Co)	Client	CR

Amount	Ledger	Column	Entry	Ledger	Column	Entry
Commission	Client ledger (Insurance Co)	Client	DR	Client (Policyholder)	Client	CR

    - There is an entry in the ledger account of the policyholder as the payment is received as 'client money' for which the solicitor must account to the policyholder.

        - Mark the entry as being 'a transfer of commission TJ' as a transfer between client ledgers (*SAR r 32*).

- No entries are made in the Commission account as the commission is accounted for to the policyholder as 'client money'. An internal transfer between client ledgers is made (which does not therefore go through the cash account as no money is drawn out of client account.

Amount	Ledger	Column	Entry	Ledger	Column	Entry
Net premium	Cash account	Client	CR	Client (Insurance Co)	Client	DR

8 Returned cheques

➤ A solicitor must record a cheque received from a client in that client's ledger without delay (*SAR r 15(1)*). Consequently, a client ledger may show uncleared funds as well as cleared funds.

Amount	Ledger	Column	Entry	Ledger	Column	Entry
Cheque	Cash account	Client	DR	Client	Client	CR

➤ If a client's cheque bounces the solicitor must make entries in the client's ledger and cash account showing that the cheque has been returned (ie: these reverse the entries made when the money was received).

Amount	Ledger	Column	Entry	Ledger	Column	Entry
Returned cheque	Cash account	Client	CR	Client	Office	DR

➤ If the solicitor has drawn on uncleared funds there will have been a breach of the *SAR*s as the money drawn from client account will effectively belong to other clients of the solicitor. The solicitor must immediately make good this breach by making a compensating transfer from office account into client account.

- Note that drawing on uncleared funds is not itself a breach of the *SAR*s.

9 Deposit interest

➤ The accounting treatment depends upon whether interest is held on a separate designated deposit account (ie: an account in the client's name, solely for holding money belonging to the named client), or the solicitor accounts to the client for interest.

➤ If a designated deposit account is used:

a) the solicitor must record the transfer of money to the designated deposit cash account.

Amount	Ledger	Column	Entry	Ledger	Column	Entry
Payment in	Cash account	Client	DR	Design. deposit a/c	Client	CR

b) on an interest payment by the bank:

Amount	Ledger	Column	Entry	Ledger	Column	Entry
Interest	Desig. deposit a/c	Client	DR	Client	Client	CR

c) in order to draw money from the designated deposit account the solicitor will have to transfer monies from the designated deposit account to general client account (ie: an account containing mixed client monies) as there will not generally be a cheque book facility on a designated deposit account. This involves reversing the entries in a) above

Amount	Ledger	Column	Entry	Ledger	Column	Entry
Payment out	Cash account	Client	CR	Design. deposit a/c	Client	DR

- If money is transferred to a designated deposit account no entry need be actually made in the client ledger (as the credit balance indicating the funds owed to the client does not change), but it is good practice to record on the ledger that money has been placed in a designated deposit account

➤ If a solicitor pays money *in lieu* of interest:

a) the solicitor must make a payment out of his own funds in lieu of interest. This can be done either:

- by a transfer from office account to client account, *or*

Amount	Ledger	Column	Entry	Ledger	Column	Entry
Interest	Cash account	Office	CR	Interest paid a/c	Office	DR

Amount	Ledger	Column	Entry	Ledger	Column	Entry
Interest	Cash account	Client	DR	Client	Client	CR

- by an office account cheque paid to the client.

Amount	Ledger	Column	Entry	Ledger	Column	Entry
Interest	Cash account	Office	CR	Interest paid a/c	Office	DR

10 Abatements and bad debts

➤ When a solicitor reduces a bill (known as 'abatement'), the client ledger must record the abatement and corresponding entries must be made in respect of VAT relating to the amount written off. The double entries are as follows:

Amount	Ledger	Column	Entry	Ledger	Column	Entry
Write off	Client	Office	CR	Costs abatement a/c	Office	DR

Amount	Ledger	Column	Entry	Ledger	Column	Entry
VAT on write off	Client	Office	CR	HMRC a/c	Office	DR

➤ If client debt which has been outstanding for more than 6 months is written off, a solicitor may generally claim VAT relief in respect of the 'output tax' that the solicitor will have paid to HMRC one month after the end of the accounting period during which the supply to which the debt relates was made (*VATA 1994 ss 26A, 36*, see also *VATR 1995 rr 165-172*). A successful claim will be recorded by the following double entries:

Amount	Ledger	Column	Entry	Ledger	Column	Entry
VAT relief	Client	Office	CR	HMRC a/c	Office	DR

➤ Any bad debt is treated on the same principles as an abatement.

TAXATION

This chapter examines:

A	Income tax (IT)	80
B	Capital allowances	91
C	Capital gains tax (CGT)	94
D	Inheritance tax (IHT)	100
E	Corporation tax (CT)	104
F	Distributions	111
G	Close companies	113
H	Assessment and collection of tax (IT, CGT, IHT, CT)	115
I	Value added tax (VAT)	122
J	Stamp duty	126
K	Stamp duty reserve tax (SDRT)	130
L	Stamp duty land tax (SDLT)	133
M	Some planning ideas	137

Income or capital?

Income is usually a receipt or expense which recurs, eg: rent money or buying paperclips.

Capital is usually a one-off payment for an asset, eg: paying for office furniture.

Individuals are presumed to be domiciled, resident and ordinarily resident in the UK.

Companies are presumed to be resident solely in the UK and trading in the UK

A Income tax (IT)

References in this section are to the IT(TOI)A 2005, unless otherwise stated.

I Calculation

A Individuals as private persons

Steps

1. Calculate 'statutory income'
2. Calculate 'total income' (ie: subtract 'charges on income')
3. Calculate 'taxable income' (ie: subtract 'personal reliefs')
4. Calculate tax payable on the 'taxable income'

Step 1 — Calculate 'statutory income'

➤ Different rules govern assessment in respect of each category of income. A loss under a category gives a nil assessment for that category.

Types of income
Profits of a trade, vocation, or profession (*s 3, Part 2*)
Profits from a property business (*s 263, Part 3*)
Savings, and investment income (*s 365, Part 4*)
Employment, pension and social security income (*IT(EP)A 2003 s 1*)
Miscellaneous income (*s 574, Part 5*)
NB: Special rules, beyond the scope of this book, apply to relevant foreign income (*Part 8*)

Some exemptions from income tax (not exhaustive)

- Interest on National Savings certificates (*s 692*)
- The first £70 of interest earned on National Savings Bank deposits (*s 691*)
- Payments to adopters (*s 744*), and foster carers with respect to certain foster care receipts (*s 803*)
- Interest on personal injury damages or death damages (*s 751*)
- Certain social security benefits (eg: child benefit) (*IT(EP)A 2003 s 677*)
- Certain annual payments under an immediate needs annuity (*s 725*)
- Scholarship income (*s 776*), provided it is not chargeable under *IT(EP)A 2003 ss 211-214*
- Gross income up to £4,400 from letting a furnished room in a 'main residence' (*s 785*)
- Maintenance from a former spouse/civil partner under a court order or written agreement (*s 727*)

➤ Where tax is deducted at source, 'gross up' the income to its value *before* tax was deducted to arrive at the 'statutory income' (eg: multiply by 100/80 if income tax has been deducted at the lower rate of 20%).

Profits from a trade, etc

➤ The profits of a trade are calculated in accordance with generally accepted accounting practice, subject to any adjustment required or authorised by law (*s 25*).

- Whether an amount is income is a question of fact, determined in accordance with case law (rather than accounting practice). NB: an amount which is capital, rather than income, is not brought into account (*s 96*).

- A deduction is not allowed, eg:
  - for items of a capital nature (*s 33*), *or*
  - for expenses not incurred wholly and exclusively for the purposes of a trade (*s 34*, *Mallalieu v. Drummond* [1983] 2 AC 861), *or*
  - for a debt, unless the debt is bad, estimated to be bad, or released as part of an insolvency arrangement (*s 35*), *or*
  - for providing entertainment or gifts in connection with a trade (*s 45*) (subject to limited exceptions in *ss 46-47*), *or*
  - for social security contributions (other than an employer's Class 1 contribution, a Class 1A contribution, or a Class 1B contribution) (*s 53*), *or*
  - for any penalty or interest incurred in relation to certain provisions relating to income tax, capital gains tax, corporation tax, VAT, excise duties, insurance premium tax, climate change/aggregates levy, landfill tax, or SDLT (*s 54*), *or*
  - crime-related payments (*s 55*).
- A deduction is allowed in respect of certain expenses, eg:
  - pre-trading expenditure (as if expenses were incurred on the first day of the trade) (*s 57*), *and*
  - certain incidental costs of obtaining loan finance (*ss 58-59*), *and*
  - a payment for a restrictive employment undertaking (*s 69*), *and*
  - counselling, or retraining (*ss 73-75*), *and*
  - redundancy/approved contractual payments (*s 76*), *and*
  - personal security (*s 81*), *and*
  - contributions to enterprise organisations, or urban regeneration companies (*s 82*), *and*
  - scientific research and development (*s 87*).
- A charge arising under *CAA 2001* is treated as a receipt of a trade, and an allowance arising under that Act is treated as an expense of a trade (*s 28*).

➤ Profits from a profession or vocation, are generally calculated in the same way as profits from a trade (*ss 24, 32*).
- Special rules apply for ministers of religion (*s 159*), barristers of not more than 7 years call (*s 160*), and creative artists, and farmers whose profits fluctuate (*ss 221-225*).

Profits from a property business

➤ Income generated from land by exploiting an estate, interest or right in or over land as a source of rents or other receipts (*s 266*).

➤ The amount of income is generally calculated in the same way as the profits of a trade (*s 272*).
- Part of a premium received on the grant of a lease with a term not exceeding 50 years, or on the surrender or variation / waiver of a lease (even if the original term exceeded 50 years), may be treated as an income receipt and as a part disposal for CGT purposes (see also *TCGA 1992 Sch 8* for CGT treatment) (*ss 276-307*).

TAXATION
income tax

Savings and investment income

➤ Sources of income arising on or after 6 April 1994 are assessed on the current year basis (ie: the tax year in which income accrues), although for a partnership with savings or investment income its basis period serves as the period of assessment if this differs from its accounting period (*ss 852-853*).

◆ An individual receives interest from a UK bank or UK building society (*TA s 480A*), and annual interest from other UK companies (*TA s 349(2)*), net of lower rate tax (currently, 20%) (ie: for £100 of interest, the individual receives £20 and the payer accounts to HMRC for £80).

Non-taxpayer	10% and 22% taxpayer	40% taxpayer
↓	↓	↓
Full rebate (20%)	No more tax to pay	20% more tax to pay

● Bank/Building Society interest: a non-taxpayer can receive the gross amount, without a deduction at source, if he or she sends the correct form to the bank/building society.

● National Savings certificates and accounts: tax is not deducted at source; interest is paid gross.

◆ Annual payments are subject to a deduction at source at the basic rate of tax (currently, 22%) (*TA s 349(1)*).

◆ Deduction at source (also known as a 'withholding tax') makes tax collection easier/more reliable and gives the Government a cashflow advantage as institutions account for tax quarterly (*viz*: before payment of tax falls due under self assessment).

➤ Although no deductible expenditure is permitted in calculating savings and investment income, if a debenture holder borrows to lend money to a company then the interest may be a 'charge on income'.

➤ Distributions (*ss 383, 397*): for a fuller explanation see p 111:

Non-taxpayer	10% and 22% taxpayer	40% taxpayer
↓	↓	↓
No more tax to pay - no rebate	No more tax to pay	32.5% more tax to pay

➤ A close company writes off a loan to a participator: the amount written off is 'grossed up' so that the income is treated as having been subject to tax at the dividend ordinary rate (10%), and the participator is assessed on the gross income (*s 415*).

◆ Since the company has already (*TA ss 419-421*), with the payment to HMRC, satisfied the shareholder's liability for basic rate tax, the shareholder has effectively postponed liability for higher rate tax.

Non-taxpayer, 10% and 22% taxpayer	40% taxpayer
↓	↓
No more tax to pay	32.5% more tax to pay

➤ A company repurchases its own shares: the difference between the original issue price of the shares and their value on sale may be taxed as if it were a dividend. Alternatively, the gain may be subject to CGT if conditions set out on p 282 are fulfilled.

TAXATION
Income tax

Employment income, pensions income and social security income
References are to the IT(EP)A 2003, unless stated otherwise

➤ Tax is imposed on 'employment income' (*Parts 2-7*), pensions income (*Part 9*) and social security income (*Part 10*) and deducted from pay under 'pay as you earn' (known as PAYE) (*Part 11*).

➤ 'Employment income' is divided into 'general earnings' and 'specific employment income' (*s 6*).

- 'General earnings' includes any salary, wages, or fee, any benefit if it is money or money's worth, and any other emolument of employment (*s 62*).
- 'Specific employment income' includes income in *Part 6* (*Income which is not earnings or share related*) and is not exempt under *Part 4* (*Exemptions*) or subject to *Part 7* (*Share related income*) (*ss 7(4)-(6)*).
  - *Part 6* imposes tax on payments to and benefits from unapproved pension schemes (*ss 386-400*) and payments and benefits on the termination of employment in excess of £30,000 (*ss 401-416*).
  - *Part 7* provides that tax is chargeable on a gain on the exercise of a share option (*ss 471-484*).
    - There is an exemption for: any gain on the exercise of an option granted under an approved share incentive plan (*ss 488-515*), an approved SAYE scheme (*ss 516-519*), an approved CSOP scheme (*ss 521-526*), or an enterprise management incentive ('EMI') (*ss 527-541*).

➤ An individual is chargeable to tax in respect of employment income on the amount of his/her 'net taxable earnings' and 'net taxable specific income' (*ss 9-10*).

- 'Net taxable earnings' and ''net taxable specific income' are calculated by deducting from 'taxable earnings'/'taxable specific income' deductions which are allowed (*ss 11-12*) (see 'Deductions' below).
- 'Taxable earnings': where an individual is resident, ordinarily resident and domiciled in the UK this is calculated in accordance *ss 14-19*, otherwise *ss 20-41* apply (the rules relating to individuals not resident, ordinarily resident and domiciled in the UK are beyond the scope of this book).

Deductions

➤ Deductions:
   a) are not allowed from earnings from other employments, *and*
   b) may not exceed earnings, must not be in duplicate for the same costs or expenses (*ss 327-330*), *and*
   c) are allowed in the order resulting in the greatest reduction in the liability to tax (subject to special rules for chargeable overseas expenses and seafarers) (*s 331*).
➤ A deduction for an employee's expenses, broadly, is allowed if *either*:
   A: a) an employee is obliged to incur and pay an amount as holder of the employment, *and*
      b) the amount is incurred wholly, exclusively and necessarily in the performance of the duties of employment (*s 336*), *or*
   B: travel expenses are incurred in certain specific circumstances, eg:
      a) where an employee is obliged to incur and pay an amount, eg: incurred in travelling in performance of employment duties, for necessary attendance at a place in performance of employment duties, *or* between employments by companies which are members of the same group of companies (*ss 337-340*), *and*
      b) at the start or finish of an overseas employment, and travel between employments when duties are performed abroad (*ss 341-342*), *and*
      c) where a company vehicle is not used and no mileage allowance payment is made and no mileage allowance relief is available (*s 359*).

TAXATION
income tax

> **Deductions (cont.)**
>
> C: travel costs and expenses are incurred where duties are performed abroad (*ss 370-372*).
>
> D: certain fees and annual subscriptions (eg: professional fees) are incurred (*ss 342-344*).
>
> E: liability is incurred to discharge an employment related liability, proceedings are conducted in respect of such a liability, or a premium is paid for insurance in respect of such a liability (*ss 346-350*).
>
> F: business entertainment and gift expenses are incurred which are *either*:
>
>   a) not deductible for an employer, *or*
>
>   b) are:
>
>   i) also provided for others, *and*
>
>   ii) their provision for employees is incidental to their provision for others (*ss 356-358*).
>
> ➤ A fixed sum is allowable as a deduction in relation to certain annual expenses incurred in respect of the repair and maintenance of work equipment (*s 367*).
>
> ➤ A deduction is allowed in respect of personal security assets and services where a special threat to personal physical security arises wholly or mainly because of employment (*s 377*).

➤ Benefits in non-cash form are taxed under the 'benefits code'.

- Certain benefits (marked in the 'Benefits code' box below with a '†') are not taxable in the hands of an employee who earns less than £8,500 a year, *and* is *either*:

  a) not a director, *or*

  b) a director who does not own a material interest (5%) in the company, *and either*

    i) is a full time working director, *or*

    ii) the company is non-profit making or established for charitable purposes (*ss 216-220*).

- An amount equal to the cost to an employer of providing a benefit is usually taxable, although special rules, some of which are outlined in the 'Benefits code' box below, apply to certain types of benefit.

> **Benefits code**
>
> ➤ The following are taxable benefits under the benefits code:
>
> a) sums in respect of expenses (*ss 70-72*)†.
>
> b) cash vouchers (*ss 73-81*) and non-cash vouchers/credit tokens (*ss 82-96*).
>
>   • There is an exception for: vouchers/tokens made available to the public generally (*ss 78, 85, 93*), cash vouchers issued under an approved scheme (*s 79*), and cash vouchers where payment of a sum would have been exempt from tax (*s 80*).
>
> c) living accommodation (*ss 97-113*).
>
>   • There is an exception for: certain accommodation provided by a local authority, accommodation provided for the better performance of duties where it is customary for employers to provide such accommodation, and accommodation provided as a result of a security threat (*ss 98-100*).
>
>   • Special rules govern the tax assessable with respect to cost of providing accommodation where that cost exceeds £75,000 (*ss 103-107*).

Benefits code (cont.)

d) cars, vans and related benefits (ss 114-171)[†].

- The cash equivalent of cars is calculated by reference to CO^2 emissions (ss 133-142).
- There is an exemption in respect of:
  - mileage allowance payments (ss 229-236), and passenger payments (ss 233-236).
  - provision of workplace parking (s 237).
  - modest private use of a heavy goods vehicle (s 238).
  - support for public bus services (s 243).
  - cycles and cyclist's safety equipment (s 244),
  - travelling and subsistence during public transport strikes (s 245).
  - disabled employees' work/home transport (ss 245-246), provision of cars (s 247).
  - late night transport home (s 248).

e) taxable cheap loans (s 175).[†]

- The cash equivalent is calculated by reference to interest saved by comparison with an official rate which is set periodically.
- There is an exception for: a loan on ordinary commercial terms (s 176), a loan qualifying for tax relief (s 177), an advance for necessary expenses (s 179), and loan under £5,000 (s 180).

f) notional loans for the acquisition of shares (ss 192-197) and a disposal of shares for more than market value (ss 198-200).[†]

g) other benefits (ss 201-215).

- There is an exception for:
  - an expense 'made good' by the employee (s 203(2)).
  - incidental overnight expenses (£5 for each night wholly in the UK, else £10) (ss 240-241).
  - work related training (ss 250-254), contributions to individual learning accounting training (ss 255-260).
  - subsidised meals (s 317), eye tests and corrective appliances (s 320A).
  - recreational benefits (ss 261-263), annual party to £150 a head (s 264), third party entertainment (s 265).
  - childcare (ss 318-318D).
  - a (single) mobile telephone for an employee (s 319 as substituted by FA 2006).
  - removal expenses not exceeding £8,000 (ss 271-289).
  - certain repairs to living accommodation (s 313), and accommodation, supplies and services used in performing duties of employment (s 316).
  - overseas medical treatment (s 325).
  - pension provision (ss 306-307).
  - up to £1,000 if service not less than 20 years (s 323), small gifts from third parties not exceeding £250 (s 324), encouragement award to £25 and financial suggestion award to £5,000 (ss 321-322).
  - redundancy payments (s 309).
  - counselling on termination of employment and outplacement (s 310), retraining courses (s 311).

➤ PAYE generally obliges employers to pay tax directly to HMRC within 14 days of the fifth of the month following the month in which either the payment takes place, or the benefit is conferred.

Private service providers

➤ An individual is treated as receiving a deemed employment payment (*IT(EP)A 2003 ss 49-50*):

   a) If an individual (the 'worker') personally performs, or is under an obligation personally to perform, services for another person (the 'client'), *and*

   b) the services are provided not under a contract directly between the client and the worker but under arrangements involving an intermediary (the 'intermediary'), *and*

   c) if the services were provided under a contract directly between the client and the worker, the worker would be regarded for tax purposes as the client's employee, *and if the intermediary is*:

      i) a company in which the worker has a material interest (eg: more than 5% of the company's ordinary share capital, a right to more than 5% of the company's distributions, *or* more than 5% of the company's assets on a winding-up) (*IT(EP)A 2003 s 51*), or

      ii) a partnership and the worker (and his relatives) are *either* entitled to 60% or more of partnership profits, *or* most of the partnership profits derive from the client and its associates, *or* the profit share of any of the partners is based on the income generated by that partner by the provision of services within a)-c) above (*IT(EP)A 2003 s 52*), or

      iii) an individual and payment/benefit is received or receivable by the worker directly from the intermediary and can reasonably be taken to represent remuneration for services provided by the worker to the client (*IT(EP)A 2003 s 53*).

➤ These provisions (known as 'IR 35' after the press release announcing them) were introduced to counter perceived avoidance of PAYE and NICs (see also *WRPA 1999 ss 75-76*, *SSC(I)R 2000*).

   ◆ The deemed payment is calculated by *IT(EP)A 2003 ss 54-55* and PAYE applies *IT(EP)A 2003 s 56*.

Miscellaneous income

➤ This covers income listed in *s 574*, including the 'full amount' of any income not caught elsewhere (*s 687*).

Step 2   'Total income' = 'statutory income' minus 'charges on income'

➤ Charges on income

   a) Interest on qualifying loans which the taxpayer takes out (*TA s 353*):

      • as a PR to pay inheritance tax (*TA s 364*).

      • to invest in a partnership (*s 362*): buy a share in, lend or contribute capital to a partnership/LLP.

         ▪ This is subject to restrictions in *TA s 363*, and provided, in the case of a LLP, that it is not an investment LLP whose purpose consists wholly or mainly in making investments.

      • to invest in a close company (not a close investment holding company) (*TA ss 360-360A*) (subject to restrictions in *TA s 363*).

      • to invest in an 'employee controlled company' (subject to restrictions in *TA s 363*).

         ▪ An 'employee controlled company' is a company in which: 50%+ of the voting rights, or ordinary shares, are held by employees, which is not quoted on the FSA's Official List within 12 months of the company becoming an employee controlled company (*TA s 361*).

         ▪ The taxpayer works full time for the company (or a 51% subsidiary) and *either*:
            i) lends money to a trading company or the holding company of a trading group, *or*
            ii) acquires ordinary shares in such a company or pays off a loan financing such an acquisition.

   b) A 'qualifying donation' to charity and the donor makes a gift aid declaration (*FA 1990 s 25*).

   c) A disposal of a qualifying investment to charity (*TA ss 587B-C*).

   d) A loss on the sale of shares in a qualifying unquoted trading company (eg: for shares issued on or after 6 April 1998, EIS shares) for which the individual was the original subscriber (*TA s 574*).

TAXATION
Income tax

Step 3	'Taxable income' = 'total income' minus 'personal reliefs'

➤ These reliefs depend on the individual's personal circumstances.

Personal relief (TA s 257): dependent on age		
Under 65	£5,035	
Over 65, but under 75*	£7,280	
Over 75*	£7,420	
Additional relief for married couples/civil partners if born before 6 April 1935 (TA s 257A)		
Either spouse or civil partner over 65 and under 75*†	£6,065	The couple/civil partners live together for part of the year. By default this relief goes to a husband, unless the couple elect before the beginning of the tax year to share it differently
Either spouse or civil partner over 75*†	£6,135	The spouse or civil partner can claim any allowance unused by the other spouse/partner at the end of the year
* Relief is *only* available on income up to £20,100 (TA s 257A(5))		
Other *additional* relief		
Blind person (TA s 265)	£1,660	If the taxpayer is registered blind. A husband and a wife, or civil partners, can both claim this relief
† Relief is restricted to 10% (TA s 256)		

> The complex provisions relating to the Children's Tax Credit and the Working Tax Credit are beyond the range of this book (TCA 2002).
> For a summary of the credits see www.hmrc.gov.uk/rates/taxcredits.htm; for eligibility, see www.taxcredits.hmrc.gov.uk/HomeIR.aspx

Step 4	Calculate tax payable on the 'taxable income'

➤ Taxable income £0 - £2,150:   taxed at the 'starting rate' of 10% (TA s 1(2)(aa)).

➤ Taxable income £2,151 - £33,300:   taxed at the 'basic rate' of 22% (TA s 1(2)(a)).

➤ Taxable income over £33,300:   taxed at the 'higher rate' of 40% (TA s 1(2)(b)).

Trustees

➤ UK resident trustees of discretionary trusts generally pay income tax at the rate applicable to trusts, currently 40% (TA ss 686-687).

  ◆ Distributions are taxable at the dividend trust rate of 32.5% (TA s 686(1AA)).

   • Income that does not exceed £1,000 is not chargeable at the rate applicable to trusts, or the dividend trust rate. Instead, it is chargeable at the rate of 20% (on savings income) or 22% (on other income) (s 686D).

   • If a beneficiary is a 'vulnerable beneficiary', and a valid election is made, trustees may claim relief so that the tax payable is reduced to the amount that would have been payable if the income had arisen directly to the beneficiary (FA 2005 ss 23-45).

     ▪ A 'vulnerable beneficiary' is a person who is disabled, or a person under 18 at least one of whose parent's has died (FA 2005 ss 38-39).

➤ Trustees of fixed interest trusts have tax at 20% deducted at source on savings income, and are subject to basic rate tax at 22% on other income.

➤ Trustees have no personal allowances, but may claim capital allowances and loss relief in respect of any trade they carry on as trustees.

TAXATION
income tax

B Individuals as sole traders/partners

Follow the 4 steps in 'A. Individuals as private persons',

BUT use these additional rules.

Step 1   Set the 'accounting date'

➤ The profits chargeable in respect of a tax year, are the profits of the 'basis period' for that year (s 7).

- A 'basis period' is the period of 12 months ending with the 'accounting date' falling in a tax year (s 198), unless special circumstances set out in s 198(2) arise, eg:

  a) the first years in which a person carries on a trade.

  - Special rules set the basis period during the first 3 years of a trade. During the first year, the basis period runs from commencement to the following 5 April (s 199). Thereafter, the rules align the basis period with the accounting period as quickly as possible.

    - Alignment happens in year 2 if *either*:

      i) there are 12 months or more between commencement and the accounting date (s 200(3)), or

      ii) there is a change of accounting date between years 1 and 2 (s 214), ...

      ... in which case the basis period is the 12 months to the new accounting date.

    - Alignment happens in year 3 if *either*:

      i) there are 12 months or less between commencement and the accounting date (s 200(2)), or

      ii) the accounting date is changed in years 1 or 2 so that the new date is less than 12 months after the business began (s 215), or

      iii) the basis period for year 2 actually ends in year 3 (s 200(4)), ...

      ... in the case of i) and ii) the basis period in year 2 is the first 12 months, but for iii) the basis period is the tax year itself.

  b) the final tax year in which a person carries on a business (s 202).

  c) the accounting date is changed and conditions set out in ss 217-18 are satisfied (including that the change is made for commercial reasons).

➤ The 'accounting date' is the date in a tax year to which accounts are drawn up (or, if there are 2 dates, the later of them) (s 197).

- Special rules apply if:

  - an accounting date falls on one of 7 (or in February, 8) consecutive days,; these rules allow the taxpayer to elect that the fourth of those dates is to be treated as the accounting date (ss 211-13), or

  - an accounting date falls on 31 March-4 April, or there is no accounting date in a tax year (ss 208-210).

TAXATION
Income tax

Step 2	Claim any 'overlap relief'

➤ When basis periods overlap, 'overlap relief' is available. The profit from the preceding year attributable to the overlapping days is apportioned, and used as a deduction to prevent a double liability (s 220).

➤ A loss cannot be used more than once, so overlap relief cannot be used to recycle any other form of loss relief such as relief under s 380 (TA s 382(4)).

Step 3	Claim any loss relief

➤ *References in this Step are to the TA, unless otherwise stated.*

	Period	Loss claimed on ...	Use on ...
Start-up relief s 381	First 4 tax years	... over the 3 tax years before the year in which the loss incurred	... any income
Terminal loss relief s 388	Final year	... the final tax year and the 3 years preceding it	... trading income
UK property relief s 379A	Any accounting year	... the next tax year of taxable income, any excess in future years	... UK property business income
Carry across relief s 380, subject to restrictions, s 384		... the tax year in which the accounting year of the loss ends, and the preceding year	... any income
Carry forward relief s 385		... the next tax year with taxable profit; any excess in future years	... trading income

➤ Using s 380 wastes personal reliefs as this relief must be used on the whole of income
➤ Using s 385 allows personal reliefs to be set off against other income
➤ s 385 can be claimed whether s.380 is used or not
➤ If s 385 is used with a s 380 loss, then s 385 can only be claimed to the extent that a loss remains unused after s 380 has been claimed

Relief on incorporation of a business s 386

If a trading loss is unrelieved when the business is transferred to a company 'wholly or mainly in return for the issue of shares' (ie: shares form at least 80% of the consideration), this loss can be carried forward and provide relief against dividends *or* salary which the former trader or partner gains from the company in future years

➤ Relief which an individual who is a partner (s 117), or an individual who is a member of a LLP (ss 118ZB-ZO), can claim for interest and trading losses against other income is restricted to that partner's/member's capital contribution to the partnership/LLP and its entitlement to undistributed profit.

　◆ A charge to income tax is imposed where an individual has made a claim for relief under ss 380-381, disposes of a licence acquired in carrying on a trade, and receives non-taxable consideration (FA 2004 ss 126-130).

➤ For R & D tax credits, see p 110.

> The detailed rules relating to tax efficient investments such as venture capital trusts (TA s 842AA, TCGA 1992 s 100), the Enterprise Investment Scheme (TA ss 289-312, TCGA 1992 ss 150-150D, Sch 5B-BA) and ISAs, are beyond the scope of this book, however, for an outline see pp 137-138

C Partnerships

Steps
1. Send in the partnership return
2. Split the profit or loss amongst the individual partners

Step 1 — Send in the partnership return

➤ The partnership must send in a return giving details of the firm's business for an accounting period (eg: partnership income, profit allocation and any capital allowances claimed) (*TMA 1970 s 9*).

➤ Claims for expenditure and capital allowances etc which affect profits and losses of the partnership are made when the partnership return is completed (*TMA 1970 s 42*).
  - Expenditure incurred by a partner must be included on the partnership return; a claim as an individual will be disallowed.
  - Claims for allowances for plant and machinery owned by a partner, and used by the partnership, must generally be made on the partnership return (*CAA 2001 s 264*).

Step 2 — Split the profit or loss amongst the individual partners

➤ Profit and loss are calculated for the partnership as a whole (*s 848*).

➤ Partners complete individual self assessments, each being liable for their own share of the profits under the profit sharing ratio during the period of assessment concerned (net of any deductions successfully claimed by the partnership) (*s 850*).
  - Partners are generally not jointly and severally liable for taxation arising on the profit earned by each other (*ss 246(3)-(4), 353(2)-(3), 854(1)*).

Continuance of partnerships

➤ Under the old rules, before the introduction of self assessment on 6 April 1994, a partnership was deemed to discontinue if its membership changed, unless the partners elected for it to continue.

➤ If the membership of a partnership changes on or after 6 April 1994, then it is deemed to continue unless none of the partners continues in the business (*ss 246(3)-(4), 353(2)-(3)*).

D Limited liability partnership incorporated under the *LPA 2000*

➤ A trade, profession or business carried on by a LLP with a view to profit is treated as a partnership carried on by its members (and not the LLP itself) (*TA s 118ZA*).
  - The property and income of a LLP are treated as the property or income of the members of the LLP.

TAXATION
Capital allowances

B Capital allowances

I   What allowances are and how they may be used
II Who can claim allowances
III What allowances can be claimed

I What allowances are and how they may be used

A What allowances are

➤ Capital allowances allow the depreciation of capital assets to be brought into account for taxation purposes and offset against income profit (earned by traders, partners and companies).

➤ Different methods of depreciation are used for different types of asset, eg:

4% straight line		25% reducing balance		
Period	Straight line depreciation	Period	Reducing balance	Depreciation
1	£4	1	£100	£25 (25% of £100)
2	£4	2	£56.25	£18.75 (25% of £75)
3	£4	3	£42.19	£14.06 (25% of £56.25)

and so on ... until allowances reach £100. The majority of the value of a 25% allowance is extracted over 7 years, thereafter the allowance becomes less significant

B How allowances may be used

➤ A capital allowance may be set against 'income profits' and used to create a loss for the purposes of income tax, or corporation tax in respect of income.

   ◆ If there is more than one item of plant /machinery, an allowance is granted on a 'pool'.

     • Separate single asset pools may exist, eg: for 'short life' assets (*CAA 2001 ss 83-89*), cars expenditure on which exceeds £12,000 (*CAA 2001 ss 74-82*), ships (*CAA 2001 ss 127-128*), contribution allowances (*CAA 2001 s 538*).

     • Expenditure on 'long life' assets (*CAA 2001 s 101*) is allocated to a class pool (ie: a pool which may contain expenditure relating to more than one asset).

➤ When a 'disposal event' occurs in respect of a capital asset, the sum written down against the capital allowance is compared with the disposal value to determine whether a balancing charge or allowance arises (*CAA 2001 ss 55-56*).

   ◆ If the sale proceeds (or original cost if less) exceed the sum written down (in respect of the asset, or the pool if there is a pool), a balancing charge arises on the excess taxed as a chargeable receipt of the trade/UK property business, etc.

   ◆ If the proceeds are less than the sum written down, the shortfall is deductible as a balancing allowance from the chargeable receipts of the trade/UK property business, etc.

     • A 'disposal event' includes where a person ceases to own plant or machinery, a qualifying activity is permanently discontinued, or equipment is destroyed (*CAA 2001 s 61*).

TAXATION
Capital allowances

II Who can claim allowances

1 Plant and machinery

➤ For plant and machinery, the general rule is that a person may claim capital allowances if that person carries on a 'qualifying activity' and incurs 'qualifying expenditure' (*CAA 2001 s 11(1)*).

- A 'qualifying activity' includes a UK property business (for IT purposes), a Schedule A business (for CT purposes), a trade, profession or vocation, or special leasing of plant or machinery (*CAA 2001 s 15(1)*).

- 'Qualifying expenditure' exists where there is:
    a) i) capital expenditure on the provision of plant or machinery wholly or partly for the purposes of a qualifying activity carried on by the person incurring the expenditure, *and*

        ii) the person owns the plant or machinery as a result of incurring the expenditure (*CAA 2001 s 11(4)*), *and*

    b) expenditure which is not excluded, see eg: *CAA 2001 ss 21-23* (expenditure on buildings, etc is excluded).

➤ Special rules govern how allowances may be claimed in respect of expenditure incurred on plant or machinery which becomes a fixture to land (*CAA 2001 ss 172-204*).

➤ Anti-avoidance rules can restrict, or deny allowances. These can apply, for example, in relation to finance leases or sale and leaseback transactions (eg: *CAA 2001 ss 213-233*).

➤ *FA 2006* introduced special rules in respect of 'long funding leases' (*CAA 2001 ss 70A-YJ, TA ss 502A-L* (for CT purposes), *IT(TOI)A 2005 ss 148A-J* (for IT purposes)).

- Under these rules allowances go to the lessee (rather than the lessor).

2 Industrial buildings

➤ For industrial buildings, the general rule is that a person can claim a writing down allowance if (*CAA 2001 s 309*):

a) qualifying expenditure is incurred on a building, *and*

- 'Qualifying expenditure' is defined in *CAA 2001 s 292*.

b) at the end of a chargeable period that person is entitled to a relevant interest in a building in relation to that expenditure, *and*

c) at the end of that chargeable period, the building is an industrial building.

- An 'industrial building' is a building or structure which is, or is to be (*CAA 2001 s 271*):
    i) in use for the purposes of a qualifying trade (*CAA 2001 ss 274-278*), *or*
    ii) a qualifying hotel (*CAA 2001 s 279*), *or*
    iii) a qualifying sports pavilion (*CAA 2001 s 280*), *or*

TAXATION
Capital allowances

III What capital allowances can be claimed

▶ A capital allowance can be claimed at:

a) 25% on a reducing balance basis for plant and machinery (*CAA 2001 s 56*).

b) 6% on a reducing balance basis for certain plant and machinery which constitute 'long life assets' that can reasonably be expected to have a useful economic life of at least 25 years (*CAA 2001 ss 91,102*). This treatment does not apply to:

   i) a person (other than a lessor) who incurs expenditure during a chargeable period of 12 months not exceeding £100,000 (*CAA 2001 ss 98-100*).

   ii) expenditure on any of the following:
   - machinery or plant which is a fixture in, or provided for use in, any building which is wholly or mainly for use as a dwelling house, retail shop, showroom, hotel or office (*CAA 2001 s 93*).
   - a car (*CAA 2001 s 96*).
   - prior to 1 January 2011 certain types of ship (basically seagoing vessels) (*CAA 2001 s 94*).
   - prior to 1 January 2011 the provision of a railway asset wholly and exclusively for the purposes of a railway business (*CAA 2001 s 95*).

c) 4% on a straight line basis for industrial buildings (*CAA 2001 s 310*).

d) in certain cases allowances are accelerated and/or offered on special terms, eg: in enterprise zones (*CAA 2001 Part 3*), renovating business premises in deprived areas (*CAA 2001 Part 3A*), agriculture and forestry (*CAA 2001 Part 4*), conversion or renovation of flats for rental over shops or commercial premises (*CAA 2001 Part 4A*), mineral extraction (*CAA 2001 Parts 5-5A*), research and development (*CAA 2001 Part 6*), know-how (*CAA 2001 Part 7*), patents (*CAA 2001 Part 8*), dredging (*CAA 2001 Part 9*) and assured tenancies (*CAA 2001 Part 10*).

▶ A small or medium sized enterprise may claim:

a) a 40% first year allowance for expenditure incurred on plant or machinery (*CAA 2001 ss 44, 52*), *and/or*
   - Not for leasing/hiring cars, long-life assets, sea-going ships or railway assets (*CAA 2001 s 46*).
   - For 2006/2007 a 50% first year allowance can be claimed by a small business.

b) a 100% allowance for expenditure on energy-saving plant or machinery, environmentally beneficial plant or machinery, cars with low CO_2 emissions, etc (*CAA 2001 ss 45A-J, 52)*).

Definition of a 'small or medium-sized enterprise'	
Company	Business
▶ A company which is: a) 'small or medium sized' for the purposes of *CA s 247* during the financial year of the company in which the expenditure is incurred, *and* b) is not a member of a large group when the expenditure is incurred (*CAA 2001 ss 47, 49*)	▶ A business which, were one to take all its trades together and prepare its accounts as if it were a hypothetical company, would qualify as 'small or medium sized' for the purposes of *CA s 247* (*CAA 2001 s 48*)
'Small or medium sized' for the purposes of *CA s.247*	
▶ A company is 'small or medium' sized for the purposes of *CA s 247* if, broadly speaking, it satisfies at least 2 of the following conditions: a) turnover of not more than £22.8 million (£5.6 million for a 'small' enterprise), *or* b) assets of not more than £11.4 million (£2.8 million for a 'small' enterprise), *or* c) not more than 250 (50 for a 'small' enterprise) employees	

C Capital gains tax (CGT)

References in this section are to the Taxation of Chargeable Gains Act 1992, unless stated otherwise.

I Calculation

Steps

1. Identify the disposal
2. Calculate the 'chargeable gain' or 'allowable loss' on *a* disposal
3. Calculate the 'taxable gain' for the tax year on **all** disposals of chargeable assets, taking due account of exemptions and reliefs
4. Calculate the tax due

Step 1 — Identify the disposal *(ss 22-28)*

➤ A sale *or* gift of a 'chargeable asset' (*s 15(2)*). Note that a disposal to a spouse (*s 58*), civil partner (*FA 2005 s 103*), or charity (*s 257*), does not give rise to a 'chargeable gain' or an 'allowable loss' for CGT purposes.

Step 2 — Calculate the 'chargeable gain' or 'allowable loss' on *a* disposal

Steps

1. Take either the market value of the asset on its 'disposal' (*s 17*) or the consideration on its sale.
2. Subtract the 'allowable expenditure'.

   'Allowable expenditure'

   ➤ Allowable expenditure is calculated by adding up the following:
   - the initial cost of the asset. If the asset was acquired before 31 March 1982, then use *either*:

     a) its value on that date, *or*

     b) the cost of acquisition, whichever produces a smaller loss or gain (*s 35*).
   - any expense 'wholly and exclusively' incurred in enhancing the asset's value (not routine maintenance) (*s 38*).
   - the cost of establishing title to the asset, and any costs incurred in disposing of it (*s 38*).

3. Apply indexation (if appropriate). (Note that taper relief may also be available.)

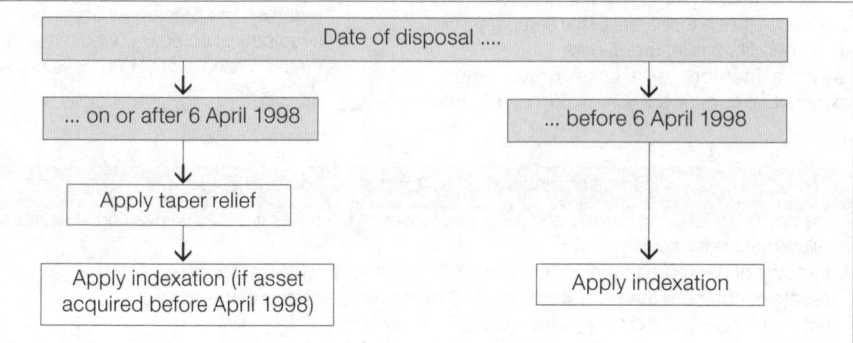

94

TAXATION
Capital gains tax

'Indexation allowance'
➤ The 'indexation allowance' accounts for the impact of inflation on a gain (prior to April 1998). 　◆ Where an asset was owned on 31 March 1982, the indexation allowance can be taken *either*: 　　a) from the asset's value on 31 March 1982, *or* 　　b) from the 'actual expenditure' on the asset (ie: acquisition, maintenance, etc), whichever carries a higher indexation (*s 54*). 　　NB: since 30 November 1993, this allowance has only reduced or extinguished a gain, it may not be used to increase the size of a loss, nor to convert a gain into a loss.

Step 3 — Calculate the 'taxable gain' for the tax year

➤ Add up the total 'chargeable gains' for the tax year and deduct:

- any 'allowable losses' from that tax year (*s 2(2)(a)*), and
- any 'allowable losses' from previous tax years not previously brought into account for CGT (*s 2(2)(b)*).

➤ Ensure that relevant exemptions and reliefs are left out of account:

Exemptions
➤ Annual exemption of £8,800 for the tax year 2006/2007 (*s 3(2)*) (£4,400 for trustees). ➤ 'Wasting assets' which have a life of under 50 years (*ss 44-45*). ➤ Tangible moveables if the consideration is less than £6,000 (*s 262*). ➤ A private dwelling house which is used as a 'main residence' (or which has been used as such during the period of ownership) and land up to half a hectare (*s 222*). 　◆ The following periods of absence are permitted: 　　• the first year of ownership (*Extra Statutory Concession D49*). 　　• up to 3 years' absence for any reason, split over relevant periods (*s 223(3)(a)*). 　　• for as long as the owner is employed outside the UK (not self-employed) (*s 223(3)(b)*). 　　• up to 4 years of absence within the UK at the reasonable behest of an employer (*s 223(3)(c)*). 　　• the last 3 years of ownership (*s 223(1)*). 　◆ Married couples/civil partners can only use this exemption for one house - if they own more than one, they must choose which qualifies for the exemption (*s 222(5)*). 　◆ The exemption will be reduced proportionately to the extent the property is used for business purposes (*s 223(2)*). 　◆ Trustees of a settlement can claim exemption from CGT so long as the occupier was entitled to occupy the house *either*: 　　a) as tenant for life, *or* 　　b) under the terms of the trust (*s 225*). 　◆ PRs can claim exemption if certain conditions are satisfied (*s 225A*). 　◆ Land over half a hectare will not come within the exemption unless the owner can show it is for the 'reasonable enjoyment' of the house (*s 222(2)-(3)*). 　◆ If land of up to half a hectare is sold off, but the house is retained, the exemption will apply to the land sold (*s 222(4)*).

Reliefs (other than taper relief)

Roll-over relief on the replacement of 'qualifying assets' (ss 152-157)
 	
Qualifying assets: a) goodwill *and* b) land *and* c) fixed plant and machinery.
 	
➤ A replacement is acquired *either* within 1 year prior to the disposal *or* within 3 years after the disposal.
➤ The replacement asset does not have to be of the same kind as the asset disposed of.
   NB: For a shareholder the assets must be used by a personal trading company.
   NB: Relief is restricted if the asset is not used in the seller's trade throughout the period of ownership *or* if the whole proceeds are not reinvested in a new qualifying asset.

Roll-over relief on EIS investments (ss150-150D, Sch 5B-BA)
 	
➤ Any gain on the disposal of assets sold to subscribe for shares issued by an EIS company.
➤ A company may be a 'qualifying company' for the EIS if:
   a) it has gross assets of less than £15 million before an investment and no more than £16 million after the investment, *and*
   b) it is not an excluded company. It should not be excluded if it carries on a 'qualifying trade' or is the parent company of a trading group.
 	
Note that certain activities such as property backed activities are excluded, eg: farming, operating or managing nursing or residential care homes, property development and forestry.
 	
◆ The replacement shares are acquired within 1 year prior to the disposal *or* within 3 years after it.

Roll-over relief on the incorporation of a business (s 162)
 	
➤ The business is transferred to a corporate body as a going concern.
   ◆ The business is transferred with all its assets (ignore cash).
   ◆ The relief only applies to the proportion of the gain for which the consideration is in shares.
➤ It is possible to elect for this relief not to apply (s 162A). This may be preferable in order to maximise taper relief

Hold-over relief on gifts of business assets (s 165, Sch 7) Qualifying assets: a) used by the business, *or* b) shares in a personal trading company, *or* c) unquoted shares. ➤ The disposal is a gift, *or* at below market value - *and* the transferee is not a settlor interested settlement. ➤ If a qualifying asset is shares or securities, relief is not available if the transferee is a company. ➤ There must be a joint election for relief by the donor and the donee.   NB: any IHT due is deductible from CGT as an 'expense' (s 260(7), s 165(11)). Relief is denied, or may be clawed back, if a gift is made to the trustees of a settlement in which the donor has an interest or arrangements exist, or arrangements subsist under which such an interest may be acquired by the donor (ss 169A-169G).
Relief for trustees in respect of a gain arising in respect of a vulnerable beneficiary (FA 2005 ss 30-33) ➤ A beneficiary is a 'vulnerable beneficiary', and a valid election is made. ➤ Trustees can claim relief so that the tax charge is reduced to that which it would have been if the chargeable gain had arisen directly to the vulnerable beneficiary (FA 2005 ss 30-33).

TAXATION
Capital gains tax

Taper relief (*s 2A*) (disposals on or after 6 April 2003)

➤ Calculate the 'qualifying holding period' (*ss 2A(8)-(9)*).

  ◆ If an acquisition took place before 5 April 1998, this is *either*:

   a) the period after 5 April 1998 for which an asset is held on its disposal, *or*

   b) where an asset was acquired before 17 March 1998, the period after 5 April 1998 for which a non-business asset is held on its disposal plus one year (there is no 'extra' year for a business asset).

  ◆ If an acquisition took place after 5 April 1998, it is the period between acquisition and disposal.

➤ Ascertain whether an asset is a business asset. The following are business assets:

Shares, or an interest in shares (*Sch A1 paras 4, 6*)	Other assets (*Sch A1 para 5*)

➤ Shares, or an interest in shares, in a company which is a 'qualifying company' in relation to an individual
 	
➤ A company is a 'qualifying company' if it is *either*:
  a) a non-trading company and an employee does not have a material interest of more than 10% in the company, *or*
  b) a trading company or the holding company of a trading group *and either*:
    i) the company is unlisted (AIM is not 'listing' for these purposes), *and/or*
    ii) the individual is an officer or employee of the company, or a company having a relevant connection with it, *and/or*
    iii) not less than 5% of the voting rights are exercisable by the individual.
	➤ An asset used wholly or partly for the purposes of:
	  a) a trade carried on by an individual or by a partnership of which an individual was at the time a member, *and/or*
	  b) a trade carried on by a company which at the time was a 'qualifying company', or a company the holding company of which was a 'qualifying company' in relation to an individual, *and/or*
	  c) an office or employment held by that individual with a person carrying on a trade.

NB: special rules apply in certain circumstances, eg: an asset is held by a PR or trustee, *or* is used as a business and a non business asset at the same time or at different times	

➤ If an asset was not a business asset prior to a date on which the legislation has been amended, an apportionment is made to reflect the proportion of the qualifying holding period during which the asset is a business asset.

➤ Apply the taper to arrive at the percentage of a gain which is chargeable to tax.

Taper - % of gain chargeable to tax		
Number of whole years in the qualifying holding period	Business assets	Non-business assets
1	50	100
2	25	100
3	25	95
4	25	90
5	25	85
6	25	80
7	25	75
8	25	70
9	25	65
10 or more	25	60

TAXATION
Capital gains tax

Application of taper relief

➤ The taper is applied to 'adjusted net gains' (*s 3(5)*).

   ◆ This means that the taper is applied *then*:

   a) any losses for the tax year in which the gain is realised are deducted from the gain, *and*

   b) any losses carried forward from previous tax years are deducted from the gain (but not so as to displace the annual exemption), *and*

   c) the annual exemption (£8,800 in 2006/2007) is deducted.

➤ The following special rules govern the interaction of taper relief with other reliefs (*Sch A1*):

   Transfer between spouses/civil partners
   - If an asset is transferred between spouses/civil partners, the taper relief on a subsequent disposal is based on the period of combined ownership by both spouses/civil partners (*para 15*).

   No-gain No-loss transfer / Hold-over relief on gifts
   - The taper takes into account the period of ownership of the owner after the no-gain no-loss transfer / the gift (*para 16*).

   Relief reducing the cost of a replacement asset (eg: roll-over relief on 'qualifying assets')
   - The taper operates by reference to the period for which the new asset is held (*para 16*).

   Relief defers a gain on a disposal (eg: reinvestment in a VCT, or EIS shares)
   - The taper is governed by the holding period of the asset on which the deferred gain arose, if EIS shares disposed of after 5 April 1999 are rolled over into more EIS shares the holding period over which the EIS shares are held is aggregated (*para 16, Sch 5BA*).

➤ The taper requires each acquisition on or after 6 April 1998 to be recorded and segregated (rather than pooled, as previously). When a disposal is made after 5 April 1998, it will be identified with acquisitions in this order (*s 106A*, but it is possible to elect for alternative treatment for shares acquired on the same day as shares as an EMI or under an approved share scheme (*ss 105A-B*)):

   a) same day acquisitions, *then*
   b) acquisitions within the following 30 days, *then*
   c) other acquisitions after 5 April 1998. The most recent acquisition is identified first (ie: a 'last in first out basis applies), *then*
   d) shares in the pool on 5 April 1998, *then*
   e) shares held on 5 April 1982, *then*
   f) shares acquired prior to 6 April 1965, *then*
   g) subsequent acquisitions.

Interaction of other roll-over and hold-over reliefs

➤ If hold-over relief or roll-over relief is used, the annual exemption may not be used with respect to the asset concerned. Taper relief can, however, be used with any other exemption.

➤ Roll-over relief treats the disposal as representing neither a gain nor a loss; it reduces the value of the consideration for the new asset by the amount of the gain realised on the disposal of the old asset.

➤ Hold-over relief holds any gain over so as to reduce the consideration which the transferror would have received on a sale at market value, and reduces the consideration for which the transferree acquires the asset by the same amount.

| Step 4 | Calculate the tax due |

➤ **Individuals:** tax is chargeable on the 'chargeable gains' for the year of assessment at 20% (if income tax is paid at the 'starting rate' or 'basic rate') or 40% (if income tax is paid at the 'higher rate') (s 4).

➤ **Trustees / PRs:** trustees of settled property and PRs pay tax at the rate of 40% (s 4(1AA)).

➤ If a beneficiary is a 'vulnerable beneficiary', and a valid election is made, trustees can claim relief so that the tax charge is reduced to that which it would have been if the chargeable gain had arisen directly to the vulnerable beneficiary (FA 2005 ss 30-33).

➤ **Partnerships:** calculate the 'chargeable gain' by subtracting a partner's share of an asset's acquisition cost from that partner's share of the asset's disposal value. It is the individual responsibility of each partner to ensure that his CGT is paid (s 59).

➤ **LLPs:** Where a LLP carries on a trade or business with a view to profit, assets held by a LLP are treated for CGT purposes as being held by its partners and tax on a disposal of such assets is assessed and charged on the partners separately (and not on the LLP) (s 59A(1)).

➤ If a LLP ceases to carry on a trade or business with a view to profit (eg: it goes into liquidation) tax is assessed and charged on (s 59A(5)):

- the LLP in respect of any chargeable gains accruing on the disposal of its assets, *and*
- on the LLP's members in respect of chargeable gains accruing on the disposal of their capital interests in the LLP (see also s 169A).

Equivalent tax rates (%) (for disposals on or after 6 April 2002)

Number of complete years after 5 April 1998 for which asset held	Business assets		Non-business assets	
	Higher rate taxpayer	Lower rate taxpayer	Higher rate taxpayer	Lower rate taxpayer
0	40	20	40	20
1	20	10	40	20
2	10	5	40	20
3	10	5	38	19
4	10	5	36	18
5	10	5	34	17
6	10	5	32	16
7	10	5	30	15
8	10	5	28	14
9	10	5	26	12
10 or more	10	5	24	11

Instalment option

➤ The instalment option enables tax to be paid in 10 annual instalments, where:

a) the disposal was a gift (s 281(1)(a)), and

b) hold-over relief is not available, as opposed to not claimed (s 281(1)(b)), and

- Normally, the 'instalment option' is not available for sole traders/partners/members of a LLP incorporated under the *LPA 2000* as there is 'hold over' relief.

c) the property disposed of was (s 281(3)):

- land, *or*
- a controlling shareholding in a quoted or unquoted company, *or*
- a minority holding in an unquoted company.

D Inheritance tax (IHT)

> *References in this section are to the Inheritance Tax Act 1984, unless otherwise stated.*

I Liability
II Calculation

I Liability

Property	Liability for IHT		Burden (if a will is silent)
Vesting in the PRs	PRs: are liable to the extent that resources fall into their hands or would do so but for their default (ss 200, 204)		Residuary beneficiary
Jointly and nominated			Beneficiary
LCTs, PETs	Donor and donee (s 199)	PRs for IHT which is unpaid after 1 year after the end of the month of death (s 204(8))	Donee
GBRs			
Life interest in possession	Donee and trustees (s 199)		Donee and trust fund

II Calculation

During life (L)

Steps

L1 Identify a 'transfer of value' which reduces the estate's value
L2 Value the transfer
L3 Deduct any exemptions or reliefs
L4 Cumulate transfers over 7 years and calculate the tax due

On death (D)

Steps

D1 Identify property deemed to pass on death: 'the free estate'
D2 Value the 'free estate'
D3 Deduct any exemptions, reliefs or deductible property
D4 Calculate IHT on death, on pre-death chargeable transfers (LCTs, PETs, GBRs)

> 'PET' - Potentially Exempt Transfer
> 'LCT' - Lifetime Chargeable Transfer
> 'GBR' - Gift in respect of a which a donor Reserves a Benefit under *FA 1986 ss 102-102C*

Step L1/L4 — Identify the lifetime transfer and calculate the tax due

Lifetime transfers which are potentially chargeable

Transfer	Definition	Tax on transfer	Cumulation on death	Tax on death
Lifetime chargeable (s.2)	a) To a trust (other than for a disabled person) b) To a company	Up to £285,000 at 0% Over £285,000 at 20% Cumulate LCTs over 7 years prior to the LCT	LCTs and chargeable PETs over 7 years prior to death	Tapering relief: year 6-7: 8% year 5-6: 16% year 4-5: 24% year 3-4: 32% Otherwise death rate at 40% Credit is given for tax already paid
Potentially exempt (s.3A)	To an individual	Nil, unless the donor dies within 7 years, then cumulate LCTs over 7 years prior to the PET	If a PET becomes chargeable, add it to the cumulative total	Tapering relief applies (as above)

Step L2/D2 — Value the transfer and/or the 'free estate'

➤ The value of a lifetime transfer is the value of the asset transferred at the time of the transfer (s 160).

➤ The probate value of the free estate is the value of the death estate minus any lifetime transfers of value.

Valuation

Bank, building society a/c	The balance of the account and interest which has accrued to the date of death
Debts	Sums owed to the deceased. Overpaid income tax is reclaimed and accounted for on *IHT 30* (s 174)
Life interest in trust	The capital value of the beneficial interest which the deceased enjoyed *and* income accrued but unpaid at death (s 49)
Insurance	If a policy matures on the deceased's death and the estate is beneficially entitled, the sum it produces on maturity. If it matures on another event, the value of premiums paid less any sum paid to surrender rights under the policy before death (s 167)
Quoted shares	In accordance with the Stock Exchange's *Daily Official List* on the day of death. The value is the 'sell' price plus one quarter of the difference between the 'sell' and the 'buy' price. Prices are usually quoted 'cum div.' (ie: with the right to the next dividend). If the dividend has been declared but not paid, the price is quoted 'ex div.' as only those registered on the company's Register of Members when the dividend is declared are entitled to receive the dividend. If the testator dies before payment of the dividend, his estate is entitled to any declared dividend. The dividend is treated as a separate asset in the estate, and the estate's gross value is calculated by adding the dividend to the 'ex div.' price of the shares
Unquoted shares	The open market value. The firm's accountants and the firm itself will advise on a valuation. The latest annual accounts should be consulted as a guide (s 168)
Land	The open market value. Estate agents will advise on this. The figure must be agreed with the local district valuer before the estate is wound up (s 160)

Loss relief on death

➤ For some assets, the sale price may replace the probate value *if* it is less than their aggregate probate value.

➤ Sale within 1 year of shares and securities quoted on a recognised stock exchange at death, or of units in an authorised unit trust (ss 178-189).

  Note: if qualifying investments are cancelled (and not replaced by the institution which issued them), they are treated as having been sold.

➤ Sale within 4 years of land (ss 190-198).

TAXATION
IHT

Step L3/D3 — Deduct any exemptions, reliefs and (on death) deductible property

Exemptions *available on lifetime transfers only per tax year*

- £3,000 per annum, which can be carried forward for 1 year so that £6,000 becomes available in a given year.
- Normal expenditure (*s 21*).
  - Regular payments + the transfer is from income + the transferor retains sufficient income to maintain his standard of living.
- PETs which are not yet chargeable *or* have become extinct as they occurred more than 7 years before death.
- £250 small gift exemption for gifts up to this sum to any particular individual (*s 20*).
- Marriage: a) up to £5,000 from a parent, b) up to £2,500 from a remoter relation, c) up to £1,000 from a non-relation (*s 22*).

Exemptions and reliefs *on lifetime transfers and on death*

Exemptions		➤ Gift to spouse (*s 18*) or civil partner (*FA 2005 s 103*)
		  ◆ The transfer of a lifetime interest in possession is treated as capital within this exemption
		  ◆ On death, a gift qualifies for exemption if it is immediate *or* conditional on survivorship for up to 1 year
		➤ Gift to charity (*ss 23-26*)
		➤ Gift for the public benefit (*ss 30-35*). Providing that:
		  a) the Treasury classes the asset as being as of national, artistic, historic or scientific interest, *and*
		  b) an undertaking is given that the asset will i) remain in the UK, *and* ii) be preserved, *and* iii) be open to public access

Business property relief (*s 105*)	Relief is at 100%	➤ A business *or* an interest in a business property ➤ Any shares in an unquoted company
	Relief is at 50%	➤ Quoted shares if the transferor had control of the company immediately before the transfer ➤ The transferor is a partner or controls a company *and* transfers land, buildings, machinery or plant which were wholly or mainly used for the business
	Property must be owned for 2 or more years before the transfer takes place (*s 106*)	
Agricultural property relief (*ss 115-24*)	Relief is at 100%	➤ The transferor used the property for agriculture for 2 years prior to the transfer, *or* ➤ The transferor owned land used for agricultural purposes during the last 7 years and is entitled to occupy it within 1 year (or the land is let under an agricultural tenancy granted on or after 1 September 1995)
	Relief is at 50%	➤ The transferor owned land used for agricultural purposes during the last 7 years and the land is subject to a tenancy granted before 1 September 1995

Exemptions, reliefs and deductible items *available on death only*

Quick succession (*s 141*)	Relief is a fraction of the tax already paid on a previous transfer:
	  1-2 years before death: 80%
	  2-3 years before death: 60%
	  3-4 years before death: 40%
	  4-5 years before death: 20%
		➤ Tax paid on a chargeable transfer to the deceased within the last 5 years
		➤ Tax is payable on the deceased's estate

Woodlands (*ss 125-130*)	Timber is exempt	➤ Timbered land not qualifying for agricultural property relief ➤ Timber itself (not the land) is exempt provided the land was bought at least 5 years before death
Funerals (*s 162*)	Fully deductible	➤ Reasonable burial expenses are deductible
Debts (*s 505*)		➤ Debts incurred for money or money's worth are deductible
Liabilities are deductible (*s 5(3)*) unless the deduction is excluded (*s 162*) (More complex liabilities are not dealt with here)		

Step L3/D3	Deduct any exemptions, reliefs and (on death) deductible property

Identifying the 'free estate' on death (*IHTA 1984 ss 5, 200*)

➤ Assets to which the testator is beneficially entitled and which pass under the will or on intestacy

➤ Assets passing outside the will or intestacy:
  - to which the deceased is beneficially entitled under property law: joint tenancies, nominated property
  - (Friendly societies, Industrial and Provident societies, some TSB accounts, with deposits up to £5,000) to which the deceased is deemed to be beneficially entitled to for IHT purposes: a GBR, a life interest in possession whch is an immediate post-death interest (*s 49A*), a disabled person's interest (*s 89B*) or a transitional serial interest (*s 49B*).

➤ The free estate does **not** include an interest in settled property which is held in trust for a bereaved minor (*s 71A*), or certain life assurance policies written in trust prior to 22 March 2006 (*ss 46A-B*).

Step D4	Calculate IHT on death and on pre-death chargeable transfers

Calculation of IHT on the death estate

LCTs and PETs	Any of these occurring within 7 years prior to the death represent additional liability	(See *Step L1*, p 101)
Tax rate on 'free estate' (after taking account of exemptions/reliefs)	Not exceeding £285,000 (£312,000 in 2008/09, £325,000 in 2009-10) in at 0% Exceeding £285,000 (£312,000 in 2008/09, £325,000 in 2009-10) at 40% (*FA 2006 s 155*)	

Note
In calculating these bands, cumulate LCTs and PETs which occurred in the 7 years prior to death

Apportionment of IHT over the estate

Subject to instructions to the contrary in the will, the IHT burden is 'apportioned' over the whole estate by the formula:

$$\text{Estate rate} = \frac{\text{Tax payable}}{\text{Taxable estate}}$$

The tax due on each asset is calculated by multiplying the value of the asset by the 'estate rate'.

E   Corporation tax (CT)

References in this section are to the Income and Corporation Taxes Act 1988, unless otherwise stated.

    I   Calculation
    II   Loss relief/R&D tax relief

I   Calculation

Steps

1. Calculate the 'income profit'
2. Calculate the 'chargeable profit'
3. Calculate 'total profit'
4. Deduct charges on income
5. Calculate the corporation tax due on profits

Step 1   Calculate the 'income profit'

(Profit under Schedules A and D) plus (Profit on 'loan relationships', foreign exchange ('forex'), derivative contracts and intangible property) less (any available losses)

Schedule A income (from the exploitation of land in the United Kingdom) (s 15)

➤ Income received on or after 1 April 1998 is calculated on Schedule D Case I principles (*s 15*).

  ◆ Remediation relief (at the rate of 150% of the actual expenditure incurred) may be claimed for expenditure incurred in cleaning up contaminated land (*FA 2001 Sch 22*).

➤ Part of a premium received on the grant of a lease with a term not exceeding 50 years, or on the surrender or variation / waiver of a lease (even if the original term exceeded 50 years), may be treated as an income receipt and as a part disposal for CGT purposes - for the apportionment see *s 34* (see also *TCGA 1992 Sch 8* for CGT treatment).

➤ Subtract any capital allowances, or add any balancing charges see p 91.

Schedule D Case I trading income ('chargeable receipts' minus 'deductible expenditure') (s 18)

➤ Chargeable receipts a) derive from income not capital, *and* b) derive from the company's trade.

➤ Deductible expenditure: expenses of an income nature that are 'wholly and exclusively' incurred for the purposes of a trade, profession, or vocation are deductible (*s 74(1)*). Case law governs whether expenses are deductible (see eg: *Mallalieu v. Drummond* [1983] 2 AC 861).

➤ Subtract any capital allowances, or add any balancing charges see p 91.

Schedule D Case III, income from loan relationships, annuities, annual payments (s 18)

Schedule D Case V, income from foreign possessions (other than loan relationships) (s 18)

Schedule D Case VI, other income (s 18)

Profits on 'loan relationships' (derivative contracts in outline)

➤ A company has a 'loan relationship' when:

a) it stands in the position of a creditor or a debtor as respects a money debt, *and*

b) the debt arises from a transaction for the lending of money (*FA 1996 s 81*) (eg: not a trade debt).

- A 'money debt' is a debt which is, or at any time has been, a debt in any currency which falls (or may at the option of the debtor or creditor fall), to be settled by the payment of money, *or* the transfer of a right to settlement of a debt which is a money debt, disregarding any other option exercisable by either party (*FA 1996 s 81*).

NB: *FA(No2)A 2005* introduced *FA 1996 ss 91A-91G* which provide for a preference share to be treated as a creditor relationship in certain circumstances.

➤ Profits and losses are calculated in accordance with generally accepted accounting practice (*FA 1996 ss 85A-C*; 'generally accepted accounting practice' is defined by *FA 2004 s 50*):

- An amortised cost basis of accounting (rather than fair value accounting) must be used in certain circumstances (eg: *FA 1996 ss 87-87A* (parties to a loan relationship are 'connected').

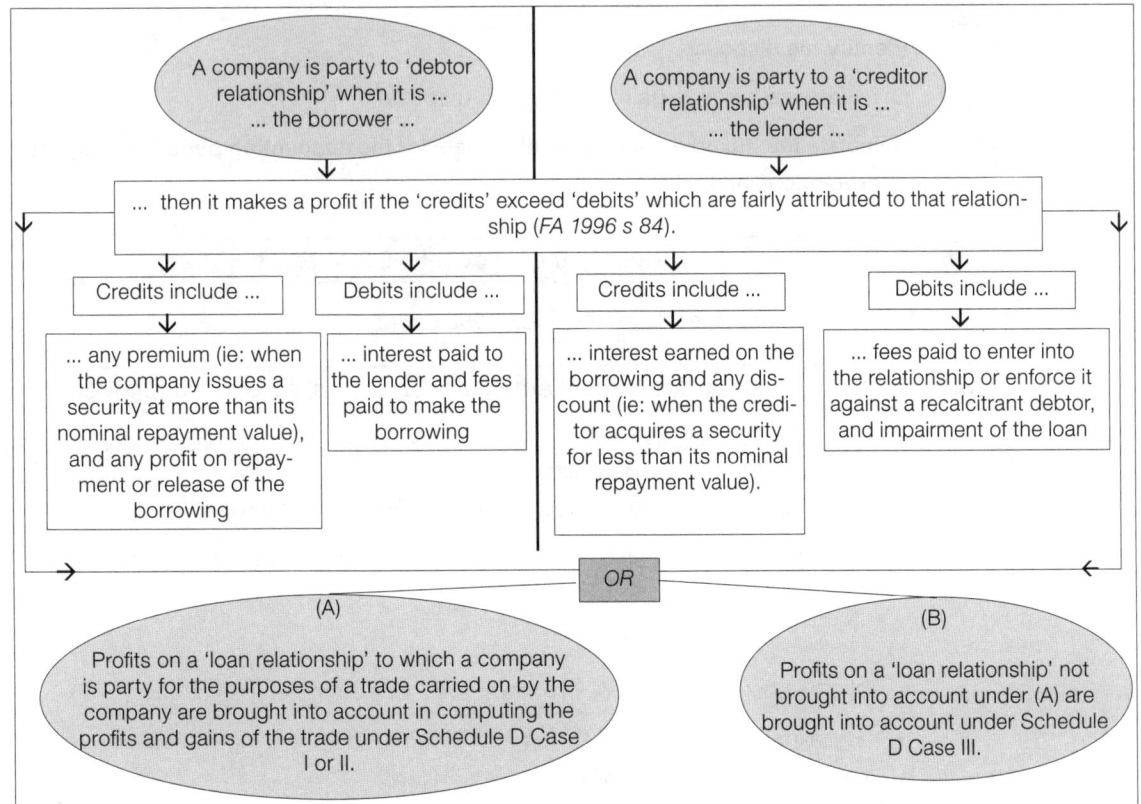

➤ Various anti-avoidance provisions may prevent a company gaining deductions in respect of interest or other 'debits'. Details are beyond the scope of this book.

- Provisions of general application include *TA s 209(2)(d)-(e)*, *TA s 787* and *FA 1996 Sch 9 para 13*.

- There are also rules which apply in particular circumstances, eg: *FA 1996 Sch 9 para 6(1)* which restricts the availability of 'debits' when an impairment loss (eg: a bad debt) arises for a creditor when a debt is between parties which have a connection.

TAXATION
Corporation tax

- ➤ The general intention is that 'capital' gains and losses (as well as 'income' profits and losses, and including forex gains and losses) on a money debt should be taxed and relieved as income (*FA 1996 ss 80(1), 84(1)(a)*).
- ➤ Gains and losses on derivative contracts (eg: options, swaps and derivatives) are brought into account under legislation which aims to follow generally accepted accounting practice (*FA 2002 Sch 26-28*).
  - ◆ Where a company is permitted or required under generally accepted accounting practice to recognise rights as being divided between rights and liabilities under a loan relationship, and rights and liabilities under a derivative financial instrument, the host loan relationship comes within *FA 1996* and the derivative (referred to as an 'embedded derivative') is addressed by *FA 2002 Sch 26* (*FA 1996 s 94A*).

Profits from intangible property (including goodwill and intellectual property)

- ➤ 'Capital' gains and losses (as well as 'income' profits and losses) may be taxed and relieved as income following generally accepted accounting practice (*FA 2002 Sch 29*).
  - ◆ Prior to the *FA 2002* regime, it was not possible to obtain a deduction in respect of goodwill.

Step 2	Calculate the ' capital profit'

Steps	
I	Identify the disposal
II	Calculate the 'taxable gain' or loss on *a* disposal
III	Calculate the 'taxable gain' on all disposals for the accounting period, taking account of exemptions and reliefs

Step I	Identify the disposal (*TCGA 1992 ss 22-28*)

- ➤ A sale *or* gift of a 'chargeable asset' (*TCGA 1992 s 15(2)*).

Step II	Calculate the 'taxable gain' or 'allowable loss' on disposal

- ➤ Take *either* the market value of the asset on its 'disposal' (*s 17*) *or* the consideration on its sale, and subtract the 'allowable expenditure'.
  - ◆ The allowable expenditure is calculated by adding up the following:
    - the initial cost of the asset. If the asset was acquired before 31 March 1982, use *either*:
      a) its value on that date, *or*
      b) the cost of acquisition, whichever produces a smaller loss or gain (*s 35*).
    - any expense 'wholly and exclusively' incurred in enhancing the asset's value (not routine maintenance) (*s 38*).
    - the cost of establishing title to the asset, and costs incurred in disposing of it (*s 38*).
- ➤ Then subtract the 'indexation allowance', which accounts for the impact of inflation on the gain.
  - ◆ Where an asset was owned on 31 March 1982, the allowance can be taken *either*
    a) from the asset's value on 31 March 1982, *or*
    b) rom the 'actual expenditure' on the asset (ie: acquisition, maintenance, etc), whichever carries a higher indexation (*s 54*).
  - NB: since 30 November 1993, this allowance only serves to reduce or extinguish a gain, it cannot be used to increase the size of a loss, nor to convert a gain into a loss.

TAXATION
Corporation tax

| Step III | Calculate the 'taxable gain' for the accounting period |

➤ Add up the total 'chargeable gains' for the accounting period.

➤ Then deduct:

- any 'allowable losses' from that accounting period (*TCGA 1992 s 2(2)(a)*), *and*
- any 'allowable losses' from previous accounting periods not brought into account to corporation tax (*TCGA 1992 s 2(2)(b)*).

➤ Ensure relevant exemptions and reliefs are left out of account:

Exemptions
'Wasting assets' which have a life of under 50 years (*TCGA 1992 ss 44-45*)
Tangible moveables if the consideration is less than £6,000 (*TCGA 1992 s 262*)
Substantial shareholdings (*TCGA 1992 Sch 7AC* inserted by *FA 2002*)
➤ A trading company disposes of a substantial (10% or more) shareholding in a trading company or a holding company of a trading group, *and* ➤ The investing company has held 10% or more of the ordinary shares in the company invested in for at least 12 months in the 2 years before the disposal

Reliefs
Roll-over relief on the replacement of 'qualifying assets' (*TCGA 1992 ss 152-157*)
Qualifying assets: a) goodwill *and* b) land *and* c) fixed plant and machinery (*ss 155-156*) ➤ A replacement is acquired *either* within 1 year prior to the disposal *or* within 3 years after the disposal ➤ The replacement asset does not have to be of the same kind as the asset disposed of NB: Relief is restricted if the asset is not used in the seller's trade throughout the period of ownership *or* if the whole proceeds are not reinvested in a new qualifying asset
Roll-over relief on paper for paper transactions (*TCGA 1992 ss 127-137A*)
Corporate venturing scheme (*FA 2000 Sch 15*)

| Step 3 | 'Total profits' = 'income profit' + 'capital profit' |

| Step 4 | Deduct any 'charges on income' |

➤ The following charges on income are deductible (*ss 338-338B*):

a) qualifying charitable donations (eg: those falling within *s 339*), *and*

b) amounts allowed in respect of gifts of shares, etc to charities.

TAXATION
Corporation tax

| Step 5 | Calculate the corporation tax due on profits (*TA ss 13*) |

➤ The rates are fixed for a financial year (1 April to 31 March): if the rate changes during the accounting period, the taxable profit is apportioned across the applicable tax rates.

Full rate of 'mainstream corporation tax':   30%   on profits over £1,500,000.

Tax on profits between £300,000 and £1,500,000:   32.75% — relief is effectively given at this marginal rate

Tax on profits not exceeding £300,000:   19% — the 'small companies rate' of corporation tax

➤ Franked investment income is ignored when paying tax, but it is included when calculating the rate of tax applicable.

II Loss relief / R&D tax relief

➤ Companies may use their losses in a number of ways.

	Loss can be claimed ...	Use on ...

Carry-across and carry-back relief *s 393A*	a) ... for the accounting period, *and*
	b) ... any unrelieved loss may be carried back against any profits from an accounting period in the previous 1 year, *provided*:
	  i) the company is carrying on the same trade as it had been in the earlier year, *and*
	  ii) the loss is set against later year(s) first
		... total profits

Losses (trading) other than terminal losses *s 393*	... following accounting periods, against losses of the trade, for as long as the company carries on the trade	... trading income
Losses from a Schedule A business *s 392A* (from 1 April 1998)	a) ... for the accounting period, *and* b) ... any unrelieved loss may be carried forward if the company continues to carry on the Schedule A business in that succeeding period	... total profits

NB: special rules apply for losses on a Schedule D Case V trade (*s 393(5)*) and Schedule D Case VI losses (*s 396*). Further rules, which are beyond the scope of this book, apply (e.g. to restrict relief to the capital contributed by the company to the partnership and undistributed profit to which the company is entitled) if a company is a member of a partnership and seeks to claim loss relief (*s 118, FA 2004 ss 131-133*).

NB: a company which is a member of a group of companies can claim group relief (see the *Banking & Capital Markets Companion*)

Loan relationships and derivative contracts

➤ Special rules govern the use of losses on 'loan relationships'.

- 'Debits' on 'loan relationships' to which a company is a party for the purposes of a trade carried on by it are deductible in computing the profits of that trade (*FA 1996 s 82(2)*) and losses may be relieved under the normal rules for the set-off of losses on income (ie: *ss 393-396*).

- All the 'debits' and 'credits' on 'loan relationships' to which a company is party otherwise than for the purposes of trade carried on by it are aggregated respectively together. If the 'non-trading debits' exceed the 'non-trading credits', a company has a 'non-trading deficit' on its 'loan relationships'. A 'non-trading deficit' may be dealt with in one of 4 ways (*FA 1996 s 83(2)*):

  a) set-off against profits from the same accounting period (in the priority required by *FA 1996 Sch 8 para 1*).

  b) relieved through group relief (see the *Banking & Capital Markets Companion*).

  c) carried back against profits which are attributable to loan relationships taxed under Schedule D Case III and earned over the previous 1 year (*FA 1996 Sch 8 para 3*).

  d) carried forward against profits for the next accounting period (provided the profits are not classed as trading income within *s 393A*) - this option is used to the extent that the others are not claimed (*FA 1996 s 83(3)*).

➤ These rules also apply to derivative contract (*FA 2002 Schs 26-28*) losses.

TAXATION
Corporation tax

R&D tax relief

'Small and medium sized enterprises' (*FA 2000 Sch 20 para 1*)

➤ R&D is an activity that is treated as research and development under guidelines published by the DTI in March 2004 (*TA s 837A(2)-(6)*).

➤ An R&D tax credit should be available if a company (*FA 2000 Sch 20 para 1*):

  a) is a 'small or medium sized enterprise' in an accounting period, *and*

   - A 'small or medium sized enterprise' is defined in Commission recommendation 2003/361/EC (*FA 2000 Sch 20 para 2*).

  b) incurs 'qualifying R&D expenditure' and 'qualifying subcontracted R&D expenditure' in that accounting period which are not in aggregate less than £10,000 and are allowable as a deduction in computing the profits of a trade carried on by a company (or would have been so allowable if the company had been carrying on a trade at the time).

   - 'Qualifying R&D expenditure' is (*FA 2000 Sch 20 paras 3-12*), eg:
     i) not of a capital nature, *and*
     ii) attributable to R&D carried on by the company or on its behalf, *and*
     iii) incurred on staff costs/consumable stores, *and*
     iv) such that any IP is or will be vested (at least in part) in the company, *and*
     v) incurred on R&D related to a trade carried on by the company, or from which it is intended that a trade carried on by the company will be derived.
   - For 'qualifying subcontracted R&D expenditure' see *FA 2002 Sch 12 paras 8-10*.

➤ If a company is (*FA 2000 Sch 20 paras 13-14*):

  a) trading and has qualifying R&D expenditure which is allowable as a deduction it may deduct an amount equal to 150% of its qualifying R&D expenditure in computing the profits of that trade, *or*

  b) not trading, but has qualifying R&D expenditure which would have been allowable if at that time it had been carrying on a trade consisting of the activities in respect of which the expenditure was incurred, it may elect to be treated as if it had incurred a trading loss in that period equal to 150% of the amount of its qualifying R&D expenditure.

   - Where a company under a) has an unrelieved loss, or a company is treated as having an unrelieved loss under b), it may claim a credit equal to 16% of that loss (*FA 2000 Sch 20 paras 15-16*).

Large companies (*FA 2002 Sch 12*)

➤ A company which: ...

  ◆ qualifies as a large company (ie: not small or medium sized) throughout a period, *and*

  ◆ incurs 'qualifying R&D expenditure' of not less than £10,000 in a 12 month accounting period (*FA 2002 Sch 12 Part 1*) ...

  ... is entitled to an additional deduction (ie: in addition to a deduction available under general principles) equal to 25% of such qualifying expenditure (*FA 2002 Sch 12 para 11*).

   ■ For this purpose 'qualifying R&D expenditure' comprises qualifying expenditure on direct R&D, 'subcontracted R&D expenditure' and contributions to independent R&D (NB: the tests are not the same as under the *FA 2000* rules for' small and medium sized enterprises').

TAXATION
Distributions

F Distributions

References in this section are to the Income and Corporation Taxes Act 1988, unless otherwise stated.

➤ A distribution by a UK resident company carries a tax credit of one nineth.

➤ The position of a shareholder depends on the status of the shareholder:

   a) an individual.

The tax credit
Distribution (of £100) on or after 6 April 1999
$1/9^{th\dagger}$ (£8.89) of the net distribution (£80) received by the shareholder
† This is equivalent to 10% of the gross distribution (£88.89) which the shareholder receives

- an individual who is a non-taxpayer (and a person benefiting from a tax exemption, eg: a charity or a pension fund) is not entitled to a repayment of the tax credit.

- an individual who is a starting (10%) and basic rate (22%) taxpayer has no further income tax liability in relation to the distribution (*IT(TOI)A 2005 s 397*).   Liability is at the 'dividend ordinary rate' - 10% of the gross distribution (*s 1A(1A)*), and the tax credit satisfies this liability.

- an individual who is a higher-rate (40%) taxpayer owes an extra 32.5% more tax at the 'dividend upper rate' (*ss 1A, 1B*).

Higher rate taxpayer's liability		
	Distributions on or after 6 April 1999	
		£
Distribution		80.00
Tax credit	(10% of 88.89, or $1/9^{th}$ of 80)	8.89
Gross income		88.89
Higher rate tax	(32.5% of 88.89)	28.89
After tax income		60.00

   b) a company receives 'franked investment income' (FII).

   - The term FII refers to both the distribution *and* the tax credit.

   - FII is taken into account in working out the rate of corporation tax applicable to a company for an accounting period, but is ignored when calculating the tax actually due (*s 208*).

➤ Note that HMRC may restrict or deny a tax credit in certain circumstances, for instance if a distribution is abnormally large and not commercially justified (*ss 703-709*).

   ◆ Anti-avoidance provision, *s 231B*, has been introduced to counteract arrangements designed to pass on the value of a tax credit to a person who would not (without such arrangements) be entitled to it.

G Close companies

  I Generally
  II Taxation of a 'close company' and its 'participators'

I Generally

➤ For corporation tax purposes, a 'close company' is a company that is *either*:

 a) 'controlled' by 5 or fewer 'participators', *or*

 b) 'controlled' by 'participators' who are its directors, *or*

 c) has amongst its shareholders 5 or fewer 'participators', or directors who are 'participators' *and* on a winding-up of the company these 'participators' would be entitled to receive the greater part of the company's assets.

- 'Control' means control as defined in *TA s 416*.
  - For the definition of 'control' in *TA s 416*, and also for the (different) definition of 'control' in *TA s 840*, see p 114. (Both definitions are used in the *Taxes Act* and it is important to make sure that the correct definition is used in the right context.)
- A 'participator' is a person who has a share or interest in the capital or the income of a company and specifically someone entitled to acquire capital or voting rights, or to ensure income or assets will be deployed for his benefit, or entitled to distributions or the proceeds of a premium or redemption paid by the company, or certain loan creditors (*TA s 417(1)*).
- The definition of 'director' is a wide one, and focuses on substance rather than the title (*TA s 417(5)*).

➤ Companies which may not be close companies for corporation tax purposes include:

- companies not resident in the UK (*TA s 414*).
- quoted companies, if shares bearing not less than 35% of the votes at a general meeting have been unconditionally allotted or acquired so that members of the public enjoy them beneficially (*TA s 415*).
- companies controlled by one or more non-close companies and which could only be treated as a close company by including a non-close company as one of the 5 participators, or by including non-close loan creditors on a liquidation (*TA s 414(5)*).

➤ The definition of a 'close company' is different in respect of the taxation of individuals who hold shares in such companies.

- For IHT purposes, the definition of a 'close company' is the same as for corporation tax purposes except that:

 a) it includes non-resident companies, *and*

 b) the test for a 'participator' disregards the interests of loan creditors (*IHTA 1984 s 94*).

- For capital gains tax purposes, the definition includes non-resident companies (*TCGA 1992 s 13*).

TAXATION
Close companies

II Taxation of a 'close company' and its participators

➤ The taxation treatment of a 'close company' depends on whether it is also a 'close investment holding company'.

➤ The rules in **A 'Close companies'** apply to all 'close companies', the additional rules in **B 'Close investment holding companies'** apply only to 'close investment holding companies'.

> ### Definition of a 'close investment holding company'
>
> ➤ A close company is a 'close investment holding company' unless it exists during an accounting period 'wholly or mainly' for one of 6 purposes.
>
> ◆ These purposes include carrying on a trade on a commercial basis, and investing in land provided the land is not intended to be let to connected persons (*TA s 13A(2)*).

A 'Close companies'

1 Loans to 'participators' (*TA ss 419-421, IT(TOI)A 2005 ss 415-421*)

➤ A company pays tax (at the rate of 25%) to HMRC in respect of a loan to a participator (eg: if the company wishes to lend £100 gross it pays £25 tax to the HMRC and the participator receives £75).

➤ This does not apply if *either*:

a) the loan is in the usual course of business for a company whose business is money lending, *or*

b) the following conditions are fulfilled:

  i) the company's total loans to the 'participator' stand at less than £15,000, *and*

  ii) the 'participator' owns 5% or less of the shares in the company, *and*

  iii) the 'participator' works full time for the company (*s 420(2)*).

➤ If a claim for repayment of the tax is made within 6 years of the end of the accounting period in which the repayment of the loan is made, HMRC refund the tax to the company.

2 Expenses of 'participators', and their 'associates', taxed as distributions (*TA s 418*)

➤ An expense to benefit a 'participator' or their 'associate' (eg: a spouse, or civil partner), is a 'qualifying distribution' on which the participator is taxed under *IT(TOI)A 2005 s 383*.

➤ A charge to tax under this section is excluded if the 'participator' is taxed on the benefit under *IT(EP)A 2003 Part 3* (*TA s 418(3)*).

3 Attribution of capital gains to a 'participator' (*TCGA 1992 s 13*)

➤ Capital gains made by a non-resident company (which would be close if UK resident) are apportioned to 'participators' in that company in proportion to their beneficial interest in the company.

4 Liability to IHT on a transfer of value by a 'close company' (*IHTA 1984 s 94(1)*)

➤ A transfer at an undervalue by a close company is treated as a transfer out of a 'participator's' estate and is chargeable to IHT. Liability rests primarily on the company, although limited recovery is possible from each 'participator' or the transferee (*IHTA 1984 s 202(1)*).

◆ Altering the rights of unquoted share or loan capital is treated as a transfer (*IHTA 1984 s.98(1)*).

5 Relief on interest on loan to, or to buy ordinary shares in, a close company (ss 360-360A, 363)

➤ The individual:

a) has a 'material interest' (he or an associate controls more than 5% of the ordinary shares or would be entitled to more than 5% of the assets of the company distributable amongst 'participators' in the company), *or* he (or his associate) already owns shares in the close company, *and*

b) the taxpayer spends the majority of time working for the company when the interest is paid, *and*

- lends money to a close company, *or*
- borrows money for the close company to use in the course of its business, *or*
- borrows to purchase ordinary shares in a close company.

B 'Close investment holding companies'

1 Rate of corporation tax

➤ Tax is paid at the full corporation tax rate of 30% (eg: not the smaller companies' rate of 19%).

2 Abuse of tax credit

➤ Anti-avoidance rules deny the benefit of a tax credit where arrangements are entered into under which a person obtains a payment representing a tax credit and those arrangements are entered into for an unallowable purpose (*TA s 231B*).

Principal definitions of 'control' in the *Taxes Act*

s 416 'control'

➤ The test is complex, but involves establishing that a person exercises, is able to exercise or entitled to acquire, direct or indirect control over a company's affairs.

♦ Examples of such control include the possession of, or entitlement to acquire:

a) the greater part of a company's issued share capital or of the voting power in a company.

b) enough of the company's issued share capital as would entitle that person to receive the greater part of the income of the company if that income were to be distributed amongst the 'participators' in the company.

c) on a winding-up of the company, to receive the greater part of the assets of the company which would be available for distribution amongst the 'participators' in the company (*s 416(2)*).

s 840 'control'

➤ A person 'controls' a company (the 'relevant company') if that person has power to secure ...

a) by means of the holding of shares or the possession of voting power in or in relation to the relevant company or any other company, *or*

b) by virtue of any powers conferred by the articles of association or other document regulating the relevant company or any other company, ...

... that the affairs of the relevant company are conducted in accordance with the wishes of that person.

TAXATION
Assessment & payment

H Assessment and payment of tax (IT, CGT, IHT, CT)

- I Self assessment of income tax and capital gains tax
- II Payment of income tax and capital gains tax
- III Assessment of IHT on death
- IV Payment of IHT
- V Self assessment of corporation tax
- VI Payment of corporation tax

I Self assessment of income tax and capital gains tax

References in this section are to TMA 1970, unless otherwise stated.

1 **Notification of chargeability**

➤ An individual is under a duty to notify HMRC of any chargeable income or capital gain within 6 months of the taxable event in respect of which tax falls due, unless the individual is exempt as:

- no chargeable income and gains arise in the year of assessment (above the exempt amount), *and*
- his net income tax liability is nil *or* tax deducted at source covers any liability (*s 7(3)-(7)*).

2 **Filing a tax return**

➤ An individual must submit a tax return stating his liability to income tax and capital gains tax (*s 8(1)(a)*).

➤ The filing date depends on whether the individual completes a self assessment.

- If he only wishes to supply information, without completing a self assessment, he must submit the return on or before 30 September following the end of the tax year, or if a notice is issued after 31 July following the end of the tax year within 2 months of the notice being issued (*s 9(2)*).
- If he is prepared to assess his own tax, then he must submit the return on or before 31 January following the end of the tax year, unless the return is issued to him late (after 31 October) in which case he has 3 months from when the return is issued (*ss 8(1)(a), 8(1A)*).
  - If a return is submitted, but the self assessment is not completed, HMRC are under a duty to complete it (*s 9(3)*).

➤ Penalties for failing to file a return on time are hefty.

- £100 automatically if a return is not submitted on time, *and*
- a further £100 if it is still outstanding 6 months later, *and*
- then up to £60 a day (*ss 93(2)-93(4)*).

➤ If no return is submitted, HMRC may, within 5 years of the end of the year of assessment, estimate the tax and make a determination stating the tax due (*s 28C*).

3 **Records**

➤ Records relevant to calculating tax liability must be kept: there is a fine of up to £3,000 for non-compliance (*s 12B(1)-(6)*).

	Individual	Sole trader/partner
Time the return is issued ...	... within 1 year of the filing date	... within 5 years of the filing date
Obligation to keep records expires	1 year after the filing date	5 years after the filing date, or when a formal HMRC enquiry is finished or becomes impossible

TAXATION
Assessment & payment

Overview of income tax and CGT calculations

Income tax	CGT

Calculate 'statutory income'
 	
Income according to the rules of each category.
 	
  Income from a UK property business
  Income from trade, etc
  Employment income
  Savings and investment income
NB: certain income is exempt.
	Identify a 'disposal' of a 'chargeable asset'
	↓
	Calculate 'chargeable gain'/'allowable loss'
	
	Market value or consideration on disposal ...
	... less allowable expenditure (ie: cost (or 31 March 1982 value) + expenses of enhancement and establishing title)
	... *less indexation allowance.*

↓	↓
Calculate 'total income' *Deduct charges on income from statutory income.*	**Calculate 'taxable gain' for tax year** *All chargeable gains ...* .. less allowable losses .. less exemptions/reliefs ... less taper relief ... less annual exemption
↓	
Calculate 'taxable income' *Deduct personal reliefs from total income.*	
↓	↓
Calculate tax liability *Apply tax at the appropriate rate.* Dividend rate (10%), Dividend higher rate (32.5%) Lower rate (20%) for savings (other than a dividend from a UK resident company) Starting (10%), basic (22%) and higher rate (40%)	**Calculate tax liability** Apply rate of top rate of income tax applicable to taxpayer (known as 'top slicing', ie: starting, basic or higher rate. NB: consider whether the installment option applies
↓	
Calculate tax to pay/reclaim *Deduct tax already paid* Eg: lower rate tax (20%) withheld on interest PAYE *Add tax overpaid* Eg: in respect of pension contributions	

II Payment of income tax and capital gains tax

➤ Tax assessed under self assessment is payable 'on account' on 31 January during the year of assessment, and on 31 July following the end of the year. Any corrective 'balancing' payment is due on the next 31 January (*TMA 1970 s 59A(2)*).

- No payment need be made on account if the income tax due is *either:*

    a) less than £500, *or*

    b) less than 20% of the taxpayer's total income tax liability for the year (ie: including income from which tax has been deducted at source) (*TMA 1970 s 59A(1)(c)-(d), IT(PA)R 1996*), ...

    ... in which case tax is payable on 31 January following the year of assessment.

- The taxpayer may opt for tax to be deducted under PAYE if the tax due is less than £1,000.

➤ Interest runs on tax due 'on account', or as a balancing payment (*TMA 1970 ss 59A-59B*) from the date the payment is due (*TMA 1970 s 86*). Interest on overpaid tax is paid to the taxpayer (*s 824, TCGA s 283*).

➤ A surcharge of 5% is levied on tax outstanding 28 days after it falls due, and there is a further 5% surcharge if the tax is still unpaid 6 months after it is due (*TMA 1970 s 59C*).

TAXATION
Assessment & payment

III Assessment of IHT on death

➤ A PR is not required to deliver an account in respect of an 'excepted estate' (*IT(DA)(EE)R 2004 r 3*).

- ◆ If an estate is an 'excepted estate' *form IHT 205* must be completed and delivered with an application for probate (*IT(DA)(EE)R 2004 r 6*). The Probate Office send *form IHT 205* to HMRC.

➤ An estate is an 'excepted estate' if (*IT(DA)(EE)R 2004 r 4*):

a) the deceased was domiciled in the United Kingdom immediately before death, *and*

b) the value of the estate is attributable wholly to property passing under a will/intestacy, *or* nomination taking effect on death, *or* under a single settlement in which the deceased was entitled to interest in possession, *or* by survivorship in a beneficial joint tenancy, *and* of such property:

   i) not more than £150,000 represented value attributable to settled property, *and*

   ii) not more than £100,000 represented value attributable to assets outside the United Kingdom, *and*

c) any chargeable lifetime transfers ('specified transfers') within 7 years of death were only cash, shares, quoted securities, chattels, *or* land (not subject to a GBR) with a total value not exceeding £150,000, *and*

d) the deceased was not a person by reason of whose death an alternatively secured pension provision (*IHTA 1984 ss 151A-C*) applies;

e) *either:*

   i) the value of the 'gross estate' (including any specified transfers and 'specified exempt transfers' (eg: to a spouse/civil partner, or charity)) did not exceed the 'IHT threshold' (currently £285,000), *or*

   ii) the value of the gross estate (as in i) above) did not exceed £1 million, and no tax is payable because the net chargeable value of the estate, after deduction of liabilities and the spouse/civil partner or charity exemption only, does not exceed the IHT threshold.

   - The 'gross estate' includes the deceased's share in any jointly owned assets and is calculated before debts, administrative expenses or IHT reliefs or exemptions are deducted.

➤ If an estate is not an excepted estate, complete *form IHT 200,* then *form IHT 200* and *D18* must be sent to HMRC Capital Taxes (the Court Service will not issue a grant until *form D18* has been authorised by HMRC).

Filling in a reduced *form IHT 200*

➤ Leaflet *IHT 19* sets out when and how a reduced *form IHT 200* may be submitted, eg: when:

a) the deceased was UK domiciled, *and*

b) assets passing by will or intestacy mostly go to exempt beneficiaries (spouse or charity), *and*

c) the gross value of:

   i) the estate passing to non-exempt beneficiaries, *and*

   ii) assets not passing by will or on intestacy but which are chargeable on death (eg: property passing on survivorship), *and*

   iii) the chargeable value of transfers made within 7 years of death ...

   ... does not exceed the IHT threshold.

IV Payment of IHT

References in this section are to IHTA 1984, unless otherwise stated.

➤ IHT is payable:

   a) 6 months from the end of the month of a chargeable transfer, *or*

   b) for lifetime transfers made between 5 April and 1 October, 30 April in the next following year (*s 226*).

➤ IHT on 'installment property' is payable in 10 equal annual installments, with the first due 6 months from the end of the month of death, rather than on delivery of HMRC account (*s 227*). It is available for:

   a) land, *and*

   b) an interest in a business, *and*

   c) shares (quoted and unquoted) which entailed control of a company immediately prior to death, *and*

   d) unquoted shares if *either*:

   - they form a large holding (10% of the nominal capital of a company worth £20,000 or more), *or*
   - HMRC accepts 'undue hardship' would follow if payment was due immediately, *or*
   - IHT on the installment option exceeds 20% of the total IHT due on the estate as a whole.

   ◆ If installment property is sold, tax and interest are both payable immediately (*s 227(4)*).

➤ Interest runs ...

   ... 6 months after a chargeable transfer: on non-instalment property vesting in PRs, land that is 'installment property', GBRs, LCTs, PETs (on death) and life interests in possession (*s 233*).

   ... from the installment date: sums unpaid on the date they are due under the installment option (*s 234*).

Paying IHT on non-installment option property

➤ Tax which falls due immediately can be funded:

   a) by assets for which a grant of representation is not needed, *and/or*

   b) by a building society/ bank holding a deceased's current account and willing to release funds, *and/or*

   c) by loans from ...

   ... beneficiaries: they may be in position to help, particularly if they are the assignees or nominees of an insurance policy maturing on the deceased's death.

   ... banks: they demand a commercial rate of interest.

➤ Interest on a loan for personalty vesting in PRs may be offset against the estate's income tax.

➤ A bank may require an undertaking from PRs to repay a loan as soon as the property is available.

   ◆ A voluntary scheme endorsed the British Bankers' Association and the Building Societies' Association enables funds held at the time of death to be used to pay IHT (*Inland Revenue Press Release, 27 March 2003*).

   - PRs enquire if an institution is willing to assist, and if it is then, when PRs are ready to apply for probate, they send a form *D20* and the estate's IHT number (obtained by contacting the CTO) to the institution which makes a payment direct to the CTO.

➤ For guidance with respect to using National Savings or British Government stock (gilts) held on the Bank of England Register to pay IHT, see HMRC's leaflet *IHT 11*.

V Self assessment of corporation tax

References in this section are to FA 1998 Sch 18, unless otherwise stated.

Self assessment for corporation tax applies to accounting periods ending on or after 1 July 1999 (the law relating to accounting periods ending before 1 July 1999 is not dealt with here).

1 Notification of chargeability

➤ A person within the charge to corporation tax must notify HMRC if it is chargeable to corporation tax for an accounting period and it has not received a notice requiring a company tax return (*para 2*).

- A company must notify HMRC within 12 months of the end of the accounting period (or face a penalty not exceeding the tax payable in respect of that accounting period).

2 The company tax return

➤ HMRC may require a person to submit a 'company tax return' (*para 3(1)*) (*Form CT 603*).

- The term 'company tax return' (*Form CT 600*) includes such relevant information, accounts, reports, statements as may be reasonably required (*para 3(2)*).
  - Where *CA 1985* requires a company to produce accounts for a period, the power to require the delivery of accounts is limited to those accounts (*para 11*).
- A company tax return must include a self assessment of the amount of corporation tax payable by the company for an accounting period (*para 7*).
  - The corporation tax payable is calculated according to four steps (*para 8*):

Steps

1–2 ➤ Calculate the tax due on the company's profits, then give effect to any other reliefs or set offs available against corporation tax chargeable on profits:

  a) any double taxation relief under *TA ss 788-790* (tax credits in respect of foreign tax), *and*

  b) any set off in respect of shadow ACT (beyond the scope of this book).

3 Add amounts assessable or chargeable as though they were corporation tax:

  a) any amount due in respect of a loan to a participator under *TA s 419*, *and*

  b) any sum chargeable as the profits of a 'controlled foreign company' ('CFC') under *TA s 747(4)(a)*.

  - A CFC is a company which during an accounting period is controlled by a company within the charge to corporation tax and is subject to a lower level of taxation (less than 75% of tax payable in the UK) in the territory in which it is resident.
  - Unless an exemption applies the company submitting the self assessment must pay tax on the CFC's income profit, in proportion to its interest in the CFC.

4 Deduct any amounts to be set off against a company's overall tax liability for a period under *TA s 7(2)* or *s 11(3)* (income tax borne by deduction)

TAXATION
Assessment & payment

3 Filing a company tax return

➤ The filing date for a company tax return is whichever of the following periods is last to end (*para 14*):

   a) 12 months from the end of the period for which the return is made, *or*

   b) if the relevant period of account is not longer than 18 months, 12 months from the end of that period, *or*

   c) if a company's period of account is longer than 18 months, 30 months from the beginning of that period, *or*

   d) three months from the date on which the notice requiring the return is served.

➤ If a company is required to deliver a company tax return and does not do so by the filing date, it is liable to a flat rate penalty of (*para 17*):

   a) £100 if the return is delivered within 3 months of the filing date, *and*

   b) £200 in any other case, *unless ...*

   ... it has an excuse for late filing (because it is not required to deliver accounts under *CA 1985* for that period and the return is delivered no later than the last date allowed by *CA 1985* for delivering accounts to Companies House) (*para 19*).

   - On the third successive failure, the figures in a) and b) are increased to £500 and £1,000 respectively.

➤ If a company is required to deliver a company tax return and fails to do so *either*:

   a) within 18 months of the end of the accounting period for which the return is required, *or*

   b) the filing date, if the filing date is later than the period in a) ...

   ... it is liable to a tax-related penalty (*para 18*).

   - A tax-related penalty is:
     - 10% of the unpaid tax if the company tax return is submitted within 2 years of the end of the period in respect of which the return is required, *or*
     - 20% of the unpaid tax, in any other case.

➤ If company does not deliver a company tax return, HMRC can determine (to the best of their information and belief) the tax due (*paras 36-49*).

4 Information and records

➤ A company must preserve such records (*para 21*), or information (*para 22*), as are needed to enable it to complete a correct and complete return for an accounting period.

➤ The duty to preserve records or information exists (*para 21*):

   a) for 6 years from the end of a period in respect of which a company may be required to submit a company tax return, *or*

   b) if a company is required to submit a company tax return before the end of the 6 year period in a) until *either*:

      i) any HMRC enquiry into that return is completed, *or*

      ii) if there is no enquiry, HMRC no longer have power to enquire into the return (broadly, if a return is submitted on or before the filing date (and is not subsequently amended), within 12 months of the filing date (*para 24*)).

   ◆ A company which fails to keep records required under *para 21* is liable to a penalty not exceeding £3,000 (*para 23*).

VI Payment of corporation tax

References in this section are to CT(IP)R 1998, unless otherwise stated.

➤ Corporation tax falls due 9 months after the end of each accounting period (*TMA 1970 s 59(D)*), unless a company is a 'large company'.

- A company is a 'large company' if (*r 3*):
    a) its profits in an accounting period exceed £1.5 million, *and*
    b) its total corporation tax liability for that accounting period exceeds £10,000 (or a proportion of £10,000 if the accounting period is less than 12 months), *and*
    c) it was a large company in the 12 months preceding that accounting period or its profits for that accounting period exceed £10 million.

➤ If a company is a 'large company' during an accounting period then the corporation tax for that period, broadly speaking, is due and payable:

a) where the length of the accounting period so allows, in installments (not exceeding 4) at intervals of 3 months beginning on the date which is 6 months and 13 days from the start of the accounting period and ending on the date which is 3 months and 14 days from the end of the accounting period (*r 5(3)*), or

b) in other cases on a date 3 months and 14 days from the end of the accounting period (*r 5(2)*).

  Eg: for an accounting period ending 31 December 2005, the payment dates are: 14 July 2005, 14 October 2005, 14 January 2006 and 14 April 2006.

➤ Where tax is payable in installments, the amount due on each installment is (*rr 4,6*):

$$\frac{3}{\text{The number of whole calendar months falling within the accounting period PLUS the number of days falling outside the accounting period divided by 30}} \times \text{Total corporation tax liability (as defined in r 2(3))}$$

First accounting period - duty to notify

➤ A company must give written notice to HMRC of the beginning of its first accounting period (*FA 2004 s 55*).

I Value added tax (VAT)

    I   Generally
    II   VAT and land - the election to tax
    III Capital goods scheme
    IV Penalties (outline)

I Generally

➤ A registered person accounts periodically to HMRC for VAT on 'output' (sales) of goods and services in the course of business, and any VAT on 'inputs' (*VATA s 1*).

➤ VAT is designed, in theory, to pass a tax charge on the value added by manufacturers and suppliers to the final customer (a non-taxable person, or one who makes exempt supplies).

➤ A taxable person who can attribute all his inputs to taxable supplies (ie: all supplies other than exempt supplies) pays no tax insofar as he reclaims 'input' tax he has paid to his suppliers against 'output' tax which he receives from his customers. The attribution of 'inputs' to 'outputs' is governed by *VATR 1995 rr 99-116*.

➤ A taxable person pays HMRC the amount by which a business's 'output' exceeds its 'input', unless 'input' exceeds 'output' in which case he claims a rebate of the excess 'input' tax.

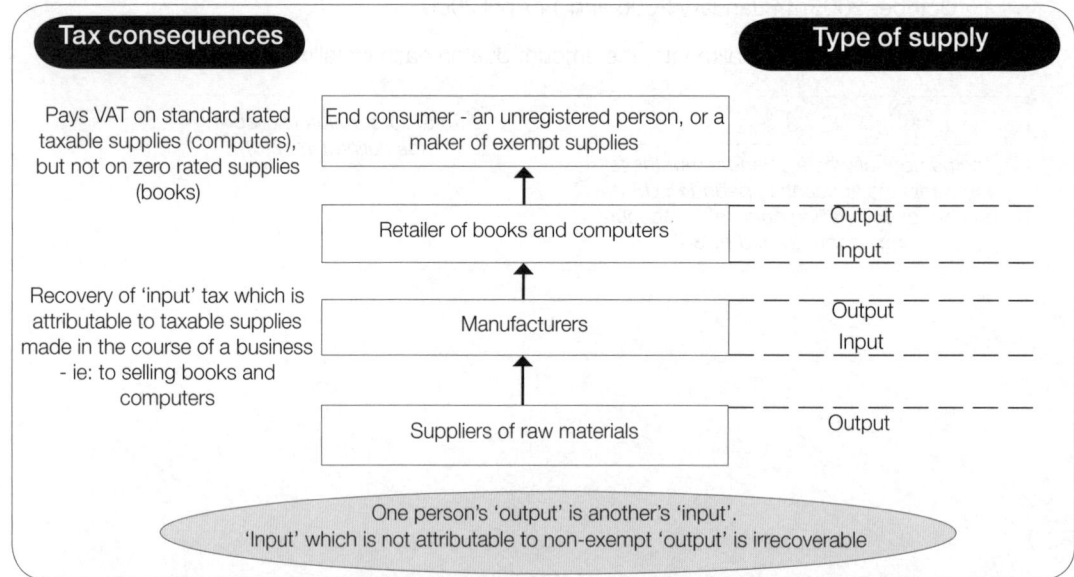

➤ A small business (annual taxable turnover not exceeding £150,000 and total turnover not exceeding £187,500) may opt to account for VAT under the 'flat rate scheme' (*VATA s 26A*).

◆ Under this scheme, a taxable person is liable to account to HMRC for a VAT on a percentage of the business's turnover. By removing the need to attribute inputs to outputs, the intention is to ease the administration and lighten the compliance burden on small businesses.

➤ A sole trader, partnership, or company which makes 'taxable supplies' of goods or services in the course of a business exceeding £61,000 a year must register for VAT with HMRC as a 'taxable person' (*VATA 1994 s 2*). Partners and trustees must register jointly. For lower turnovers registration is optional; it is only advisable if reclaimable 'input' tax outweighs the extra cost to customers of the VAT which must be charged to them, and the administrative burden is not judged too inconvenient.

TAXATION
VAT

➤ Supplies of goods and services are standard rated at 17.5% unless they fall within the categories set out in the boxes below.

Exempt supplies (*VATA 1994 s 31(1), Sch 9*)

➤ Some grants (including assignments and surrenders) of interests in or over land (*Group 1*).
  ◆ Supplies which do not fall within this exemption are listed in *Items 1(a)-(n)* in *Group 1*. They include supplies which are zero rated and some which are standard rated.
  ◆ If the option to tax is exercised, the exemption does not apply.
➤ Insurance and reinsurance services (*Group 2*).
➤ Postal services (*Group 3*).
➤ Betting, gaming and lotteries (*Group 4*).
➤ Finance (*Group 5*).
  ◆ Supplies within this group include transactions in money, transactions in securities, underwriting security transactions, running current, deposit or savings accounts, and managing unit trust schemes.
➤ Education (*Group 6*).
  ◆ This exemption embraces education services by 'eligible bodies', examination services, certain private tuition, services provided by youth clubs, research and vocational training.
➤ Health and welfare services (*Group 7*).
➤ Burial services (*Group 8*).
➤ Trade union subscriptions (*Group 9*).
➤ Sporting services (*Group 10*).
➤ Works of art (*Group 11*).
➤ Fund-raising events (*Group 12*).

Zero rated (*VATA 1994 s 30(2), Sch 8*)

➤ Food (*Group 1*).
  ◆ Certain foods are, however, standard rated, eg: supplied in the course of a catering business, hot takeaways, or food sold for consumption on the premises where the supply is made, pet food, luxury and 'frivolous' foods.
➤ Sewage and water services (*Group 2*).
➤ Books and newspapers (*Group 3*).
➤ Talking books and wireless sets (*Group 4*).
➤ Certain buildings and civil engineering works (*Group 5*).
  ◆ This includes the first grant of a 'major interest' in land (ie: of a freehold or a lease with a term exceeding 21 years) by a person who:
    i) constructs a building designed as a dwelling, or converts a building or part of a building into one or more dwellings.
    ii) constructs a building, or converts a non-residential building or part of a building, for a 'relevant residential purpose'.
    iii) constructs a building for a 'relevant charitable purpose'.
➤ Supplies of and in relation to certain protected buildings that are listed buildings or scheduled monuments (*Group 6*).
➤ Certain international services (*Group 7*).
  ◆ Services on goods obtained in, or imported into, EEC States and for export from the EEC:
    a) i) by or on behalf of the supplier, or ii) where the recipient of the services belongs in a place outside the EEC.
  ◆ Making arrangements for i) the export of goods from the EEC, ii) a supply of services of the description in item a), or iii) any supply of services which is made outside the EEC.
➤ Transport (*Group 8*).
  ◆ This includes supplies of ships and aircraft, passenger transport services and some freight transport.
➤ Caravans and houseboats (*Group 9*).
➤ Gold (*Group 10*).
➤ Bank notes (*Group 11*).
➤ Drugs medicine and aids for the disabled (*Group 12*).
➤ Certain imports/exports (*Group 13*).
➤ Supplies to or by charities (*Group 15*).   (*Group 14* has been repealed)
➤ Clothing and footwear including pedal cycle helmets (*Group 16*).
➤ Commodities traded on terminal markets such as futures transactions (*VAT(TM)O 1973*).
➤ Goods exported to third countries (*VATA 1994 s 30(6)*).

Supplies rated at 5% (*VATA 1994 s 29A, Sch 7A*)

➤ Fuel and power (for domestic use, or use by a charity other than in the course of a business).
➤ Installation of energy saving materials
➤ Grant funded installation of heating equipment, security goods or connection of gas supply.
➤ Women's sanitary products and contraceptive products.
➤ Children's car seats.
➤ Supplies in the course of a residential conversion or renovation.
➤ Welfare advice and information.

II VAT and land - the option to tax

➤ A taxable person may waive the exemption from VAT in respect of a supply of land which he would otherwise make as an exempt supply under *VATA 1994 Sch 9, Group 1*.

➤ This is known as the 'option to tax' and is governed by *VATA 1994 Sch 10 paras 2-6*. It is subject to some restrictions in that it:

- does not apply in relation to zero rated supplies within *VATA 1994 Sch 8*, *and*
- if made in respect of part of a building, it covers the whole building, *and*
- does not apply if at the time of the grant there is an intention or expectation that the land will become 'exempt land' and it is bought by a developer, financier or a connected person (broadly, land other than land used by a taxable person wholly or mainly for making supplies which are not exempt) (*VATA Sch 10 para 3(AA)*).

➤ An election must fulfil the following conditions (with effect from 1 March 1995):

- it may be in any form, *but*
- it must be notified in writing to HMRC within 30 days of its being made (there is discretion to extend this period).

➤ If a taxable person wants to elect and he has already made exempt supplies in relation to the land, he should seek clearance by writing to his VAT office, unless the circumstances fall within *HMRC's Notice 742 para 8.6* which lists when permission will be granted automatically.

➤ From 1 March 1995, an election can be revoked, with the written permission of the Commissioners, if it is done *either*:

- within 3 months of the election becoming effective provided that no input tax has been recovered and the land has not been sold as part of a TOGC (Transfer of a business as a going concern), *or*
- 20 years or more after the election took effect.

Some advantages and disadvantages of opting to tax	
✓ VAT on developing or purchasing the land or building will be recoverable	✗ Compliance costs associated with issuing VAT invoices etc
✓ Input tax will be recoverable on the landlord's overheads attributable to the taxable supply	✗ A future disposal of the building may be adversely affected as: a) the disposal may be standard rated, so SDLT will be paid on a greater amount, *and* b) even if the disposal is part of a TOGC (so that VAT will not fall due) the buyer will also have to opt to tax
✓ A landlord will be able to recover VAT on continuing maintenance costs such as expenditure on service charges	
✓ If a tenant is fully taxable, it will be able to recover VAT on service charges (this is impossible if the service charge is an exempt supply)	✗ Some tenants, whose business activities are not fully taxable, will have to bear the cost of VAT which they will be unable to recover (eg: insurers or underwriters who carry out exempt business)
	✗ The capital value of the property may be affected if local market conditions discriminate for or against buildings which are taxable

III Capital goods scheme

➤ Under this scheme 'input tax' recovered in respect of a capital item is adjusted over a period of 5 (if under a) below) or 10 (if under b) below) years. (Further adjustments are made if, during the period over which the adjustment is made, the item is sold, lost or stolen, the taxable person de-registers, or a lease in respect of the item expires.) (*VATR 1995 rr 114-115*).

➤ A capital item qualifies for the scheme if it is:

a) of a value not less than £50,000 and is computer equipment (*VATR 1995 r 113(a)*), or

b) of a value not less than £250,000 and is:

 i) an interest in land, a building (or part of a building), a civil engineering work (or part of civil engineering work) acquired as a standard rate supply (*VATR 1995 r 113(b)*), or

 ii) an interest when the taxable person changes the use of a building (or part of a building) which was previously used for a residential or charitable purpose (*VATR 1995 r 113(c)*), or

 iii) an interest in a building (or part of a building) when the taxable person either makes an exempt supply or ceases to be completely taxable (*VATR 1995 r 113(d)*), or

 iv) a building (or part of a building) which the owner constructed and used for the first time on or after 1 April 1990 (*VATR 1995 r 113(e)*), or

 v) a building which has had its floor area increased by not less than 10% (*VATR 1995 r 113(f)*).

c) a building refurbished or fitted out by the owner if the expenditure on taxable supplies (other than zero rated supplies) of services and of goods fixed to the building is not less than £250,000 (*VATR 1995 r 113(h)*).

IV Penalties (outline)

Penalties for evading VAT			
Offence	Statute	Penalty	Punishment
Default surcharge	VATA s 59	Civil	Failure to send in the 3 monthly return within 1 month of the end of each quarter: the surcharge rises to as much as 20% of the tax due over this period
Dishonest conduct	VATA s 60	Civil	Fine equal to the tax evaded by dishonestly acting *or* omitting to act, so as to avoid paying tax
Misdeclaration or neglect	VATA s 63	Civil	Fine equal to 15% of the tax the offender attempts to avoid by *either* understating his liability, *or* overstating the rebate due to him, *or* not taking reasonable steps to draw an error to HMRC's attention (subject to *de minimis* limits)
Failure to register	VATA s 67	Civil	Fine equal to 10%-30% of the tax due, on a rising scale relative to the length of time during which the offender was unregistered (for up to 18 months)
Breach of regulations	VATA s 69	Civil	Failure to keep certain records is punishable by a fine of up to £500. Other infringements carry a daily penalty
Fraudulent evasion	VATA s 72	Criminal	It is an indictable offence knowingly or deceitfully to avoid VAT. The penalty may be an unlimited fine and imprisonment for up to 7 years

J Stamp duty

I	Calculation
II	Collection and penalties

I Calculation

Steps

1. Is there a dutiable instrument?
2. What is the head of charge and what is the rate of charge?
3. Is there an exemption or relief?
4. Does duty have to be paid, or can it be deferred?

(This section focuses on stamp duty on selected heads of charge, as they apply on or after 1 December 2003)

Step 1 — Is there a dutiable instrument?

A Is there an 'instrument'?

➤ Stamp duty is a charge upon 'instruments'.

- ◆ Note that because stamp duty is chargeable on 'instruments', stamp duty can be avoided altogether if an agreement is oral and transfer is by delivery.
    - However, in such cases care must be taken that the terms of the agreement are not subsequently recorded in a memorandum of agreement, as such a memorandum will be stampable (this is known as the 'memorandum rule').
    - If the agreement relates to shares or securities consider whether there is an SDRT charge.

B Does the 'instrument' relate to stampable property?

➤ A stamp duty charge only arises when an instrument relates to 'property' for which 'stampable consideration' is given.

- ◆ From 1 December 2003, stamp duty is only chargeable with respect to (*FA 2003 s 125*) stock or marketable securities (*FA 1999 Sch 13*) and bearer instruments (*FA 1999 Sch 15*).
- ◆ For the transfer of an interest in land to/from a partnership, or the transfer of a partnership interest, see special rules in *FA 2003 Sch 15 Part 3* (as amended by *FA 2004*).

C Is there 'stampable consideration'?

➤ Stampable consideration comprises money, stock/marketable securities (*SA 1891 s 55*) and debts (*SA 1891 s 57*).

Step 2 — What is the head of charge and what is the rate of charge?

A Generally

➤ Depending on which head of charge applies, duty is either:

a) 'fixed' (£5), *or*

b) calculated by reference to the value of the stampable consideration passing under the instrument (known as '*ad valorem*' duty).

B Heads of charge

➤ An instrument liable to stamp duty under 2 heads of charge may be charged to the higher (*Speyer Brothers* v. *IRC* [1908] AC 92). But an instrument chargeable under a specific head of charge is not usually charged with greater duty under a more general head (*North of Scotland Bank* v. *IRC* 1 SC 149).

Heads of charge	
Head of charge	Rate of charge, etc
Transfer on sale (*FA 1999 Sch 13 Part I para 1*)	0.5% (*FA 1999 Sch 13 Part I para 3*)
Contracts or agreements for sale (*FA 1999 Sch 13 Part I para 7*)	➤ An agreement relating to an equitable interest is chargeable at the same rate as a transfer on sale. ♦ If such an agreement is stamped, and an instrument of transfer is subsequently executed in accordance with the agreement, there is no double charge to duty (but any excess consideration is chargeable to duty).
Transfer other than on sale (*FA 1999 Sch 13 Part III para 1*)	Fixed duty (£5) (*FA 1999 s 101(2)*).
Repurchase of own shares by a company	➤ Duty is payable at the rate of 0.5% per £100 (*FA 1986 s 66*). ♦ When a company files a return at Companies House within 28 days of receiving the shares (*CA 1985 s 169*), the return is treated as an 'instrument'.
Release or renunciation	£5, unless on a transfer on sale (*FA 1999 Sch 13 Part III para 7*).
Bearer instruments (On issue or first transfer) (*FA 1999 Sch 15*)	The details are beyond the range of this book

> When any property is conveyed:
> a) in consideration of a debt due to that person, *or*
> b) subject to the payment of money (whether secured or unsecured) (eg: a mortgage) ...
> ... the debt is treated as the consideration for the conveyance and is chargeable with *ad valorem* duty at the rate of 0.5% (*SA 1891 s 57*).

TAXATION
Stamp duty

Step 3 — Is there an exemption or relief?

1. **Exemptions under *SD(EI)R 1987* from the head 'transfer on sale'**

   ➤ An instrument falling under one of the following categories is exempt if it provides for:

   a) the vesting of property subject to a trust in the trustees of the trust on the appointment of a new trustee, or in the continuing trustees on the retirement of a trustee.

   b) the transfer of property the subject of a specific devise or legacy to the beneficiary named in the will (or his nominee).

   c) the transfer of property which forms part of an intestate's estate to the person entitled on intestacy (or his nominee).

   d) the appropriation of property in satisfaction of a general legacy of money, or in satisfaction of any interest of surviving spouse and in Scotland also of any interest of issue within *FA 1985 s 85(4), (6), (7)*.

   e) the transfer of property which forms part of the residuary estate of a testator to a beneficiary (or his nominee) entitled solely by virtue of his entitlement under the will.

   f) the transfer of property out of a settlement in or towards satisfaction of a beneficiary's interest, not being an interest acquired for money or money's worth, being a transfer constituting a distribution of property in accordance with the provisions of the settlement.

   g) the transfer of property on and in consideration only of marriage.

   h) the transfer of property in connection with divorce (within *FA 1985 s 83 (1)*), or dissolution of a civil partnership (*FA 2005 s 103*).

   i) the transfer by the liquidator of property which formed part of the assets of the company in liquidation to a shareholder of that company (or his nominee) in or towards satisfaction of the shareholder's rights on a winding-up.

   j) the transfer of property operating as a voluntary disposition *inter vivos* for no consideration in money or money's worth nor any consideration referred to in *SA 1891 s 57*.

   k) the transfer of property by an instrument varying a disposition on death within *FA 1985 s 84(1)*.

   - Note that these regulations only apply to instruments executed on or after 1 May 1987 and the nature of the instrument must be certified in accordance with *SD(EI)R 1987 r 3*, which requires a certificate stating that the donor / transferor or his solicitor, or someone authorised to do so (using their own knowledge), certifies that the instrument falls in a category [A-M] above.

   - If there is no certificate of exemption, duty of £5 is due.

2. **Mortgages granted after 1 August 1971**

   ➤ Mortgages granted after 1 August 1971 are exempt (*FA 1971 s 64, FA 1999 Sch 13 Part IV para 2*).

3. **Corporate reorganisations - under the head 'transfer on sale'** (*FA 1986 ss 75-77*)

4. **Transfer to a LLP incorporated under the *LPA 2000* (*LPA 2000 s 12*)**

   ➤ A transfer to a LPP in connection with its incorporation within 1 year of incorporation (if, broadly, there is no change in the partner's beneficial ownership in the assets) is exempt.

5. **Associated companies** (*FA 1930 s 42*)

6   **Loan capital (*FA 1986 s 79, FA 1999 Sch 13 Part IV para 3*)**

   ➤ 'Loan capital' includes any debenture stock, corporation stock or funded debt, by whatever name known, issued by a body corporate or other body of persons (*FA 1986 s 78*).

   ➤ *FA 1986 s 79* provides an exemption for an instrument on transfer of 'loan capital' from all stamp duties (*FA 1986 s 79(4)*) unless:

   a) at the time the instrument is executed, the instrument carries a right (exercisable then or later) of conversion into shares or other securities, or to the acquisition of shares or other securities, including loan capital of the same description (*FA 1986 s 79(5)*), or

   b) at the time the instrument is executed or any earlier time, it carries or has carried a right (*FA 1986 s 79(5)*):

   - to interest the amount of which exceeds a reasonable commercial return on the nominal amount of the capital, or

   - to interest the amount of which falls or has fallen to be determined to any extent by reference to the results of, or of any part of, a business or to the value of any property (see also s 79(7A)), or

   - on repayment to an amount which exceeds the nominal amount of the capital and is not reasonably comparable with what is generally repayable under the terms of issue of loan capital listed in the FSA's Official List.

7   **Examples of general exemptions (*FA 1999 Sch 13 Part IV*)**

   ➤ Transfers of shares in, or of, government stocks or funds or strips.

   ➤ Testaments, testamentary dispositions and dispositions *mortis causa* in Scotland.

   ➤ Renounceable letters of allotment (if rights renounceable not later than 6 months after issue).

Step 4 — Does duty have to be paid, or can it be deferred?

➤ An instrument must be correctly stamped if it relates to any property situated or any matter or thing done or to be done in the UK, otherwise it will be inadmissible in evidence before a civil court in the UK (*SA 1891 s 14(4)*) and may not be registered (*SA 1891 s 17*).

➤ If an instrument is executed outside the UK (and does not relate to land in the UK), the 30 day period (after which a penalty becomes due) only begins to run when the instrument is first received into the UK (*SA 1891 s 15B*).

➤ Consequently, if an instrument does not need to be received into the UK (eg: for production in evidence before a civil court, or enrolment in the UK (eg: on a share register)) (and does not relate to land in the UK), the payment of duty can be deferred indefinitely or at least until it becomes necessary to bring the instrument into the UK. To this extent, stamp duty is sometimes referred to as a voluntary imposition.

   ◆ Executing (and retaining) an instrument outside the UK can be an element in planning, although care must be taken that execution does not take place in a jurisdiction with higher stamp duty than the UK (and that no counterpart or memorandum of the agreement is made in or brought into the UK).

   NB: interest runs from 30 days after the date on which an instrument is executed (irrespective of where execution takes place) (*SA 1891 s 15A*).

II Collection and penalties

▶ Duty may be paid without a penalty becoming payable within 30 days of the instrument being executed.

- ◆ If an instrument is executed outside the UK and does not relate to land in the UK, the 30 day period runs from when the instrument is first received into the UK.

- ◆ If an instrument relates to land in the UK, the 30 day period runs from the date of execution (irrespective of where the instrument is executed) (SA 1891 s 15B(1)).

▶ Late (or insufficient) stamping invites the following sanctions (in addition to the stamp duty due):

- ◆ if an instrument is not stamped within 30 days of execution, interest: (at a rate set by the Treasury) from the end of that 30 period to the day on which the instrument is stamped (but interest is not payable if an amount less than £25 is due) (SA 1891 s 15A as introduced by FA 1999 s 109), and

- ◆ a penalty; if there is no 'reasonable excuse' for late stamping. The maximum penalty is:
  - the lesser of £300 and the unpaid duty - if the instrument is stamped within 1 year after the 30 day period ends, or
  - the greater of £300 and the unpaid duty - if the instrument is stamped 1 year after the end of the 30 day period (SA 1891 s 15B(2)-(3)).

▶ The *Stamp Acts* do not provide any general statements of who is liable to pay duty. However, an unstamped document may not generally be produced in evidence before a court (SA 1891 s 14(4), Parinv (Hatfield) Limited v. IRC [1998] STC 305), or enrolled on a register (SA 1891 s 17) (eg: a share register) so the onus is usually on whoever wishes to prove title (usually the transferee/buyer) to pay duty.

- ◆ Any arrangement or undertaking for assuming liability on account of the absence or insufficiency of stamp, or any indemnity against such liability, absence or insufficiently is void (SA 1891 s 117).
  - Attempts are sometimes made to circumvent this prohibition by covenanting to pay duty if and when an instrument executed outside the UK is received into the UK. Opinion is divided as to whether such a covenant is enforceable.

▶ Different heads of charge used to have various fines and penalties. *Sch 17* to the *FA 1999* replaced fines with penalties which are recoverable by the Commissioners.

> For instruments executed on or after 1 October 1999:
> a) amounts of stamp duty on a 'conveyance or transfer on sale' are rounded up to the nearest £5 (*FA 1999 s 112*), and
> b) interest is are rounded down to the nearest £5 (s 15A(4)).

K Stamp duty reserve tax ('SDRT')

I Generally
II The principal charge

Generally

➤ Stamp duty reserve tax ('**SDRT**') is *not* a stamp duty. It is a separate tax.

➤ SDRT is a tax on agreements relating to 'chargeable securities'.
- A 'chargeable security' includes:
  - stocks, shares or loan capital, *and*
  - interests in, or dividends, arising from stocks, shares, or loan capital, *and*
  - rights to allotments of, or to subscribe for, or options to acquire, stocks shares or loan capital, *and*
  - units under a unit trust scheme (*FA 1986 s 93(3)-6)(a)*), ...
    - ... *unless* the securities are issued by a body corporate not incorporated in the UK *and* the securities are:
      - not registered in a register kept in the United Kingdom by or on behalf of the body corporate by which the securities are issued, *or*
      - in the case of shares they are not paired with shares issued by a body corporate incorporated in the United Kingdom (*FA 1986 s 93(4)*).
- Loan capital which is exempt from all stamp duties under the loan capital exemption in *FA 1986 s 79(4)* (see p 129) is not a 'chargeable security' (*FA 1986 s 99(5)*).

➤ SDRT arises on an agreement, not the instrument of transfer. Where there is an SDRT charge and within 6 years of the SDRT charge arising:
a) a transfer is executed in relation to the securities to which the agreement related, *and*
b) stamp duty paid on the transfer ...
   ... the SDRT charge is cancelled (*FA 1986 s 92*).

➤ On an agreement to transfer 'chargeable securities' an SDRT charge arises irrespective of whether:
a) the agreement, transfer, issue or appropriation in question is made or effected in the UK or elsewhere, *and*
b) any party to the agreement is resident or situate in any part of the UK (*FA 1986 s 86(4)*).
   - Note that an oral agreement is within the charge to SDRT.

II The principal charge

➤ The 'principal charge' to SDRT is imposed when one person (A) agrees with another (B) to transfer (whether or not to B) 'chargeable securities' for money or money's worth (*s 87(1)*).

- There is an SDRT charge:

    a) if the agreement is conditional, on the day on which the condition is satisfied, *and*

    b) if the agreement is unconditional on the day on which the agreement is made (*s 87(3)*).

- Tax is charged at 0.5% (*s 87(6)*). Liability to the SDRT charge falls upon (B) (*s 91(1)*).

➤ The precise requirements for the various exemptions are beyond the scope of this book, but note that the following 2 exemptions in particular exist:

1 **Intermediaries (*FA 1986 ss 88A-88B*)**

   ➤ Agreements entered into by 'intermediaries' effected on an EEA exchange or a recognised foreign exchange are exempted from a *s 87* charge.

   - An 'intermediary' is, broadly speaking, a member of an EEA exchange or a recognised foreign exchange who is recognised as an intermediary by the exchange and who carries out a bona fide business of dealing in chargeable securities but does not carry on an 'excluded business'.

       - An 'excluded business' includes any business which consists wholly or mainly in the making or managing of investments or any business which consists of the insurance business or acting as trustee/managing investments on behalf of a pension fund.

2 **Public issues of securities (*FA 1986 s 89A*)**

   ➤ This exemption applies to various categories of issuing houses and intermediaries who enter into agreements, conditional on the admission of the securities concerned to the Stock Exchange's Official List, for the transfer of chargeable securities in order to facilitate the offer of the securities to the public.

➤ There are other SDRT charges, in addition to the 'principal charge', but these are beyond the scope of the book, as are the precise requirements for the other exemptions to the 'principal charge' (see the *Banking & Capital Markets Companion*).

L Stamp duty land tax ('SDLT')

References in this section are to the FA 2003, unless otherwise stated.

I   Calculation
II   Collection and penalties

I   Calculation

Steps
1. Identify a 'land transaction'
2. Is there a 'chargeable transaction'?
3. Calculate the amount of tax due

(SDLT applies, subject to transitional rules which are not dealt with here to transactions entered into on or after 1 December 2003; the special rules in Sch 15 relating to partnership transactions are beyond the scope of this book)

Step 1 — Identify a 'land transaction'

➤ A 'land transaction' is the acquisition of a 'chargeable interest' (*s 43*).

- ◆ A 'chargeable interest' is:
  - a) an estate, interest, right or power in or over land in the United Kingdom, *or*
  - b) the benefit of an obligation, restriction or condition affecting the value of any such estate, interest, right or power ...
    - ... other than an exempt interest (ie: a security interest, a licence to use or occupy land, or a tenancy at will, an advowson, franchise or manor) (*s 48*).

➤ If a contract for a land transaction is entered into, and that transaction is to be completed by conveyance, then:

  a) if the transaction is completed without previously having been 'substantially performed', the contract and the transaction are treated as parts of a single land transaction (*s 44(3)*).
  - The 'effective date' of the transaction is when completion takes place (*s 44(3)*).

  b) if the transaction is 'substantially performed' without having being completed, the contract is treated as if it were the land transaction (*s 44(4)*.
  - The 'effective date' of the transaction is when the contract is substantially performed (*s 44(4)*).

➤ A contract is 'substantially performed' when *either*:

  a) the purchaser, or a person connected with the purchaser, 'takes possession' of the whole, or substantially the whole, of the subject matter of the contract (*s 44(5)(a)*), *or*
  - 'Possession' includes receipt of rents and profits or the right to receive them (it is immaterial whether it is under the contract or license/lease of temporary character) (*s 44(6)*).

  a) a 'substantial amount' of the consideration is paid or provided (*s 44(5)(b)*):
  - A 'substantial amount' means (*s 44(7)*):
    - ❶ where there is no rent: all or substantially all the consideration is paid or provided, *and*
    - ❷ where all the consideration is rent: when the first payment of rent is made, *and*
    - ❸ when there is rent and other consideration: when ❶ or ❸ takes place.

➤ The acquisition of an option binding on the grantor, or a right of pre-emption preventing the grantor from entering into, or restricting the right of the grantor to enter into, a land transaction is a separate land transaction (ie: distinct from any land transaction resulting from the exercise of the option or right) (*s 46*).

➤ Where a land transaction is entered into by a purchaser in consideration of another land transaction as vendor, then each transaction is treated as a separate the distinct land transaction (*s 47*).

➤ Special rules apply where a contract provides for a conveyance to a third party (*s 44A*), or if rights under such a contract are subject to an assignment (*s 45A*).

Step 2 — Is there a 'chargeable transaction'?

➤ A 'chargeable transaction' is any land transaction, other than a transaction which is exempt (*s 49*).

- The following transactions are exempt:

  a) a land transaction for which there is no 'chargeable consideration' (eg: a gift) (*Sch 3, para 1*).

  #### 'Chargeable consideration'

  ➤ The general rule is that 'chargeable consideration' is any consideration in money or money's worth given for the subject matter of a chargeable transaction by the purchaser or a person 'connected' (for the purposes of *TA s 839*) with the purchaser (*Sch 4 para 1*).

    ◆ 'Chargeable consideration' includes VAT (except for VAT chargeable by virtue of an option to tax exercised after the effective date of the transaction) (*Sch 4 para 2*).

  ➤ Debt as consideration: if the chargeable consideration includes the satisfaction or release of a debt due to the purchaser or owed by the vendor, or the assumption of an existing debt by the purchaser, the amount satisfied, released or assumed is treated as chargeable consideration (*Sch 4 para 8*).

  ➤ Non-monetary consideration (other than money or debt) is the market value of that consideration at the effective date of the transaction (*Sch 4 para 7*).

  ➤ Special rules apply in particular circumstances, eg:

    a) the carrying out of works (*Sch 4 para 10*, see also *para 17*).

      • This is chargeable consideration except to the extent that:

        i) the works are carried out after the effective date of the transaction, *and*

        ii) the works are carried out on land acquired under the transaction or other land held by the purchaser (or a person connected with the purchaser), *and*

        iii) it is not a condition of the transaction that the works are carried out by the vendor or a person connected with the vendor.

    b) the provision of services (*Sch 4 para 11*).

    c) an indemnity given by the purchaser (not chargeable consideration) (*Sch 4 paras 13-15*).

  b) the grant of certain leases of registered social landlords (*Sch 3, para 2*).

  c) a transaction in connection with divorce/dissolution of a civil partnership (*Sch 3, para 3*).

  d) the variation of a testamentary disposition, if carried out within 2 years of death and for no consideration in money or money's worth (*Sch 3, para 4*).

  e) an initial transfer of assets to the trustees of a unit trust scheme (*s 64A*).

  f) an acquisition under an assent/appropriation by a PR (*s 3A*).

Step 3 — Calculate the tax due

➤ The amount of tax is a percentage of the chargeable consideration for the transaction; the percentage depends on the type of land (*s 55*).

Consideration	Residential	Consideration	Non-residential or mixed
Not more than £125,000	0%	Not more than £150,000	0%
More than £125,000 and not more than £250,000	1%	More than £150,000 and not more than £250,000	1%
More than £250,000 and not more than £500,000	3%	More than £250,000 and not more than £500,000	3%
More than £500,000	4%	More than £500,000	4%

➤ Tax is also chargeable in respect of so much of the chargeable consideration as includes rent (*Sch 5 para 2*, see also *Sch 17A*).

◆ That tax is a percentage of the net present value of the rent payable over the term of the lease.

Relevant rental value	Residential	Relevant rental value	Non-residential or mixed
Not more than £125,000	0%	Not more than £150,000	0%
More than £125,000	1% over £120,000	More than £150,000	1% over £150,000

➤ The following reliefs from SDLT are available:

a) a land transaction with respect to residential land in a disadvantaged area: residential land may be exempt if the relevant consideration does not exceed £150,000 (*Sch 6*), *and*

b) where a vendor and purchaser are members of the same group of companies (*Sch 7 paras 1-6*), *and*

c) reconstruction relief, where a company acquires the undertaking of another company (*Sch 7 paras 7-13*), *and*

d) charities relief, where the purchaser is a charity (*Sch 8*), *and*

e) for a right to buy transaction (*Sch 9*), *and*

f) certain acquisitions of residential property (for employment, by a property trader, etc) (*Sch 6A*), *and*

g) sale and leaseback transactions (*s 57A*), *and*

h) compulsory purchase facilitating development (*s 60*), *and*

i) compliance with planning obligations (*s 61*), *and*

j) on demutulisation of an insurance company or a building society (*ss 63-64*), *and*

k) on incorporation of a LLP (*s 65*), *and*

l) a transaction involving a public body (*s 66*), *and*

m) a land transaction in consequence of reorganisation of parliamentary constituency (*s 67*), *and*

n) on an acquisition by a body established for national purposes (*s 69*), *and*

o) certain acquisitions by a registered social landlord (*s 71*), *and*

p) alternative property finance: land sold to financial institution and leased, or resold, to an individual (*ss 72-73*), *and*

q) a land transaction on the collective enfranchisement of leaseholders (*s 74*), *and*

r) a land transaction with respect to a crofting community's right to buy (*s 75*).

II Collection and penalties

➤ The purchaser is liable for tax (s 85).

➤ The purchaser must, in the case of a 'notifiable transaction', deliver a land transaction return to HMRC before the end of the period of 30 days after the effective date of the transaction (s 76(1)).

> ♦ A 'notifiable transaction' is (s 77):
>
> a) *Either* i) the grant of a lease if the lease is for a term of 7 years or more and is granted for chargeable consideration, *or*
>
> ii) the grant of a lease is for a term of less than 7 years and *either*:
>
> ❶ the chargeable consideration is/includes a premium in respect of which tax is chargeable at a rate of 1% or higher (or would be chargeable but for a relief), *or*
>
> ❷ the chargeable consideration is/includes rent in respect of which the chargeable consideration is 1% or higher (or would be chargeable but for a relief).
>
> b) the assignment of a lease, if the grant of such a lease would be notifiable, or the consideration is chargeable at the rate of 1% or higher (or would be chargeable but for a relief), *and*
>
> c) any other acquisition of a major interest in land (ie: in England, a fee simple absolute (s 117)), *unless* the transaction is exempt under *Sch 3, or* all the land is residential property and the chargeable consideration for the transaction and any linked transaction is less than £1,000, *and*
>
> d) an acquisition of a chargeable interest in land, other than a major interest in land, if the chargeable consideration is 1% or higher (or would be chargeable but for a relief).

♦ The return must be in the prescribed form and include a declaration by the purchaser that the return is, to the best of the purchaser's knowledge, correct and complete.

♦ If the consideration is contingent or uncertain and falls (or may fall) to be paid on one or more occasions at least one of which is more than 6 months after the effective date of the transaction (and does not relate to rent), the purchaser can apply to defer payment of SDLT (s 90).

♦ A land transaction return includes a self-assessment of the tax that, on the basis of the information in the return, is chargeable and is accompanied by payment of the amount of tax chargeable (s 76(3)).

• The return and assessment are sent to HMRC's central processing centre at Netherton.

♦ A further return must be delivered where a relief (relief on an acquisition of residential property, group relief, reconstruction or acquisition relief, or charities relief) is withdrawn as a result of a disqualifying event (s 81), or as a result of a further linked transaction (s 81A).

➤ HM Land Registry will not register a land transaction (s 79(1)-(2)) unless *either*:

a) an application for registration is accompanied by a certificate of compliance with *FA 2003 Part 4, or*

> • A certificate of compliance must be *either*:
>
> i) a certificate by HMRC that a land transaction return has been delivered, *or*
>
> ii) a certificate by the purchaser (see further *Sch 12*) that no land transaction return is required (s 79(3)).

b) the entry is required to be made without any application, *or* the entry relates to an interest or right other than the chargeable interest acquired by the purchaser under the land transaction that gives rise to the application, *or*

c) a transaction treated as taking place under *s 44(4)* or *s 44A(3)* (or as applied respectively by *s 45* or *s 45A*).

➤ If tax is not paid before the end of the 30 day period, interest is payable (s 87) and penalties will be due (Sch 10 paras 3-5).

TAXATION
Planning

M Some planning ideas

➤ Often a transaction incurs liability for more than one tax - the transfer of an asset may incur CGT and IHT, and have income tax implications. Set out below are some approaches to tax-planning for individuals.

I During a client's lifetime

➤ Submit self assessment returns and make payments on account on time, to avoid penalties/interest.

➤ If a taxpayer is not resident in the UK (see *IR 20* and note the CGT provisions (*TCGA 1992 s 10A*) bringing chargeable gains realised by certain temporary non residents into charge), or may be able to establish a non-UK domicile (eg: birth outside the UK, or he regards another country as real home to which he intends to return), take specialist advice about possible tax savings.

➤ Make full use of income tax loss reliefs.

➤ Make full use of a married couple's/civil partner's personal allowances and their individual basic rate bands. If the marriage/partnership is stable, consider transferring assets from one party to the other so that they receive income more tax efficiently. (There is no CGT to pay, as transfers between cohabiting spouses or civil partners do not give rise to a 'chargeable gain' or an 'allowable loss'.)

➤ Consider investing in Enterprise Investment Scheme ('EIS') shares, a Venture Capital Trust (VCT), or an Individual Savings Account ('ISA') for various advantages with regard to both income tax and CGT.

The EIS (outline) (*TA ss 289-312, TCGA 1992 ss 150-150D, Schs 5B-BA*)

➤ If a company raises money for a qualifying activity, and both the individual and the issuing company meet certain conditions for the relevant periods, then:

   a) a chargeable gain can be rolled over into a subscription for eligible shares, *and*

   b) any capital gain realised on a disposal of the eligible shares after 3 years is tax free, *and*

   c) income tax relief (at 20%) is granted at the time of the subscription for the shares, *and*

   d) if there is a loss on the disposal of EIS shares further income tax relief is available.

➤ An individual cannot invest more than £400,000 in a tax year under the EIS.

The VCT (outline) (*TA s 842AA, TCGA 1992 s 100*)

➤ Investment in a VCT may entitle the investor to:

   a) income tax relief (at the rate of 30%) on subscription for *new* shares in a VCT (for subscriptions up to £200,000 in a tax year) if the shares are retained for at least 5 years, *and*

   b) CGT exemption on the disposal of such shares (a loss on such a disposal will not be an allowable loss), *and*

   c) exemption from income tax on dividends in respect of ordinary shares (either purchased or subscribed for, at up to £200,000 in a tax year).

➤ A VCT does not pay tax on chargeable gains which it makes.

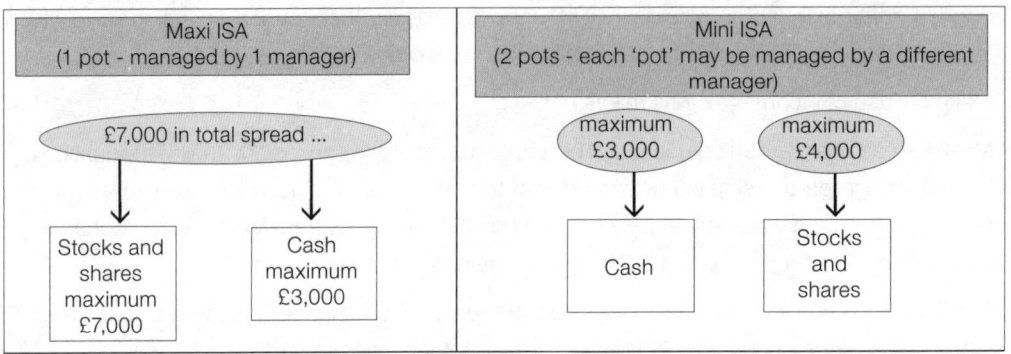

Individual savings accounts 'ISAs' (outline)

➤ An individual can invest up to £7,000 a year in an ISA.

➤ ISA accounts will be retained until 5 April 2010.

➤ Investments in an ISA are described 'tax free'. In practice, this means that:

   a) interest and dividends are not subject to tax, *and*

   b) any gains are not subject to CGT (but any loss is not an 'allowable loss').

➤ Withdrawal can be instant and will not lead to the forfeiture of tax benefits (although if the maximum subscription for a tax year has been made more cannot be subscribed in that year).

➤ An investor may choose, for a tax year, either up to 2 'mini ISAs', or a 'maxi' ISA:

➤ Make full use of CGT 'allowable losses' and use exemptions or reliefs (roll-over or hold-over).

   ◆ Complex identification rules (*TCGA 1992 s 106A*) have been introduced by *FA 1998* with the intention of frustrating 'bed and breakfasting' - the practice of selling shares and buying them back on the same or the following day to crystallise a chargeable gain while harvesting the annual CGT allowance. The new rules match disposals with acquisitions made within 30 days of a disposal.

   ◆ Chargeable gains with the least taper should be set against allowable losses so as to make best use of taper relief on gains where the relief will bring the most benefit.

➤ Where 'related property' (property which is jointly owned) is valued for IHT, ensure it is discounted to reflect the unsaleability of the share concerned by itself - discounts of, eg: 10%-30% can be allowed.

➤ When making lifetime gifts, make full use of exemptions and reliefs.

   ◆ Time gifts to gain the benefit of tapering relief for IHT (eg: plan gifts while still in good health, and do not wait until approaching 100).

   ◆ On death, the value of the transfer is frozen at the value at the time of the *inter vivos* transfer.

      • PETs: if the donor survives 7 years they are exempt.

      • If a donor has plenty of disposable income, make regular gifts using the exemption under *IHTA 1984 s 21* - unlike a PET these gifts are completely exempt irrespective of whether the donor survives for 7 years.

TAXATION
Planning

➤ As a result of changes introduced by *FA 2006, a*n *inter vivos* gift to a trust will, unless the transfer is to a disabled person's trust, be subject to an IHT charge at the rate of 20%.

- ◆ A further IHT charge arises arises:

    a) on each 10th anniversary of the original transfer (this charge is currently effectively capped at 6%); *and*

    b) when property ceases to be subject to the trust (known as an 'exit charge') (eg: on being distributed to a beneficiary).

    - The tax chargeable on 'exit' is a fraction of the (6%) 10 yearly charge; the applicable rate is determined by reference to the number of complete quarters which have elapsed since the transfer, or the date of the last 10 year anniversary of the transfer.

➤ A transfer to a trust for a bereaved minor which is established on the death of a parent (step parent, or person with parental responsibility for a child) is not a LCT, and no exit charge/10 year charge arises if various conditions are satisfied, including that the child becomes absolutely entitled at 18 (*IHTA s 71A*).

- ◆ If a child does not become absolutely entitled at 18, but will become absolutely entitled no later than 25, a charge to IHT will arise not arise until 18 (and the IHT charge is effectively capped at 4.2% at current tax rates) (*IHTA 1984 ss 71D-F*).

➤ Unlike an *inter vivos* gift to a trust, an 'immediate post-death interest' arising under a will or on intestacy, and giving rise to an immediate interest in possession, is not subject to the 10 year/exit charge (*IHTA s 49A*) (although a charge to tax will arise on the surrender of an immediate post-death interest or the death of the beneficiary entitled to the interest in possession) (*IHTA s 51*).

➤ Use the IHT nil rate band fully.

➤ Avoid making gifts and reserving the benefit (GBRs).

- ◆ Note that, with effect from 2006/2007, where an individual (a 'chargeable person'):

    a) owned an interest in land, a chattel, or certain intangible property, on or after 17 March 1986, *and*

    b) disposed of that interest otherwise than through an excluded transaction (eg: arm's length sale, or where the transferee is a spouse/civil partner), *and*

    c) in the case of land that land is occupied by the chargeable person, or in the case of a chattel the chargeable person has use or possession of that chattel,

    ... that chargeable person is chargeable to income tax by reference to the value of the land (ie: by reference to a notional market rent), chattel or intangible property, *unless either:*

    i) the chargeable person elects to take advantage of transitional rules under which the property is treated as having been subject to a GBR, *or*

    ii) the aggregate of certain amounts (eg: the notional value of the income to which the property is treated as giving rise) does not exceed £5,000 (*FA 2004 Sch 15*, see also *CITEPPOR 2005*).

➤ Do not resort to 'associated operations' (ie: a series of operations concerning a particular asset or a series of operations carried out by reference to each other which are designed to escape IHT). They will be ineffective as IHT is due under the anti-avoidance provisions (*IHTA 1984 s 268*).

➤ Retain property necessary to maintain the donor's standard of living and security. If advising a client who is elderly, see the Law Society's guidelines 'Legal services for elderly people - gifts of property: implications for future liability to pay for long-term care' (*Professional Standards Bulletin No. 15, March 1996*).

➤ Advise elderly clients considering disposing of their home of the consequences if they subsequently need residential care.

- The local authority determines the level of fees which the resident must contribute by reference to means testing under *NA(AR)R 1992 (as amended)*.

    - Means testing does not cover a minimum charge which is payable by the resident, and leaves the resident a personal allowance. The test relates to income and capital. Broadly, a resident is only entitled to have fees subsidised if their capital does not exceed £21,000, and he/she qualifies for a tapering subsidy below that figure. A home is taken into account unless:

        a) the property is occupied by a spouse, partner or relative who is *either*:

            i) incapacitated, *or*

            ii) aged 60 or over, *or*

            iii) a child under 16 whom the resident is obliged to maintain, *or*

        b) someone else occupies the property *and* the local authority uses its discretion, *or*

        c) the person's stay in care is only a temporary one.

- If the gift prevents the donor from funding care, the local authority may only fund a basic level of care. This may leave the donor dependent on others to supplement fees for better care.

- Where a resident is liable to pay for accommodation under *NAA 1948 Part 3* a local authority may enter into a deferred payment agreement with a resident which may provide for a resident to make deferred payment for care (and may include granting a charge over the resident's property) (*HSCA 2001 s 55*).

- The anti-avoidance provisions are formidable:

    - if a 'significant' motivation for a gift is to prevent a local authority imposing a charge on the client's home to pay for care, the authority can:

        a) place a charge on property transferred to a third party while the donor is in care, or within 6 months of the donor going into care (*HSSAA 1983 s 21*), or

        b) place a charge on property owned by a resident in a care home (interest runs from the date of death) (*HSSAA 1983 ss 22, 24*), or

        c) recover fees as a civil debt in the Magistrates' Court (*NAA 1948 s.56*).

    - When outstanding fees reach £750, a local authority can take insolvency proceedings and have the transaction set aside as a transaction at an undervalue, or as a transaction intended to defraud creditors (*IA 1986 ss 339-341, 423-425*).

TAXATION
Planning

II On a client's death

➤ Alter gifts in a will by a disclaimer or a variation.

Disclaimers

➤ A disclaimer is a refusal of a gift (*Townson v. Tickell* (1819) B & Ald 31). It:
- may relate to part of a gift provided the disclaimed part is severable and is not onerous (but it need not affect a separate gift under the same will).
- may not take effect if a beneficiary has benefited from property, but can be revocable.
- does not allow a disclaimor to determine property's destination unless a will permits this.

➤ The disclaimed property falls into residue (if residue is disclaimed, the property passes according to the intestacy rules) provided that there is no contrary intention in the will.
- Where an interest under the intestacy rules is disclaimed, the property is apportioned amongst the rest of the class who are entitled (or if there are none, to those next entitled).

Variations

➤ A variation enables a beneficiary to determine the destination of property.

➤ Written notice must be given to HMRC (whereas a disclaimer can be by conduct).

Some tax implications of disclaimers and variations

➤ The disclaimer or variation will not amount to a PET (*IHTA 1984 s 142*), nor will it be a chargeable transfer for CGT purposes (*TCGA 1992 s 62(6)*) if:

a) it is made within 2 years of the death, *and*

b) it is not for money or money's worth (except consideration for varying other dispositions), *and*

c) if a variation, an election is in writing *and* that election is made within 6 months of the variation.

➤ The IHT and CGT elections are entirely independent of each other. If an election is made, the property is treated as if the alteration had been made by the testator, or written into the statutory trusts governing an intestacy. If election(s) are not made, the transfer is treated as an ordinary *inter vivos* gift by the beneficiary, which qualifies as a PET/LCT and/or is subject to CGT on the gain realised by the donor on the disposal.

IHT elections

➤ A beneficiary making a variation must notify HMRC within 6 months of electing to vary the gift if the estate incurs additional IHT and the PRs should join that election (*IHTA s 218A*).

➤ In the case of a disclaimer, no election need be made (*IHTA 1984 s 142*).

CGT elections

➤ The PRs do not have to join in the election in the case of a variation, and HMRC need not be told of the election, although the instrument must contain a statement that it is intended to take effect for CGT purposes (*TCGA 1992 s 62(7)*).

➤ Make efficient use of IHT and CGT loss reliefs.

➤ Dispose of property so as to make full use of the 3 CGT annual exemptions which are available.

Anti-avoidance

➤ There is a fundamental distinction between:

a) tax evasion (which is illegal and is not dealt with here), *and*

b) tax avoidance (which is legal) (see, for example *IRC v Willoughby* [1997] STC 995, HL, *Ingram v IRC* [1999] STC 9).

◆ *Part 7* of *FA 2004* requires either the promoter of, or a party to, certain tax avoidance arrangements (specified in *TAS(PDA)R 2006*) to notify HMRC of those arrangements (giving information specified in *TAS(I)R 2004* as amended by *TAS(I)(A)R 2006*).

- From 1 August 2005 the disclosure obligation under *FA 2004 Part 7* has been extended to cover SDLT, where arrangements relate to land which does not consist wholly of residential property, the land has a market value of at least £5 million, and the arrangements are not excluded (*SDLTAS(PDA)R 2005*).

- There are provisions, equivalent to those in *FA 2004 Part 7*, with respect to VAT in *VATA 1994 Sch 11A* requiring notification to HMRC of certain VAT arrangements.

➤ Counter-measures to restrict avoidance generally take 2 forms:

a) specific statutory provisions designed to block perceived 'loopholes', *and*

b) the development, by the judiciary, of principles of statutory construction under which certain transactions without a business purpose are disregarded for tax purposes.

- For the House of Lords rulings which have shaped this judicial approach to a purposive interpretation of tax statutes, see *Barclays Mercantile Business Finance Ltd v Mawson (Inspector of Taxes)* [2005] STC 1 and *IRC v Scottish Provident Institution* [2005] STC 15.

Tax and the *Human Rights Act 1998*

➤ The following provisions of the European Convention on Human Rights may be particularly relevant to tax.

◆ Every ... person is entitled to the peaceful enjoyment of his possessions. No one shall be deprived of his possessions except in the public interest and subject ... to law. (*First Protocol, art 1(1)*) (On the construction of this article see, *National Provincial Building Society and others v UK* [1997] STC 1466.)

- This is subject to the proviso that this principle does not:

'in any way impair the right of the State to enforce such law as it deems necessary to control the use of property in accordance with the general interest or to secure the payment of taxes or other contributions or penalties' (*First Protocol, art 1(2)*).

(On the breadth of a State's prerogative in relation to tax, see *Gasus Dosier und Fördertechnik GmbH v Netherlands (1995) 20 EHRR 403.*)

◆ In tax appeals, consider *art. 6*: 'In the determination of his civil rights and obligations or of any criminal charge against him, everyone is entitled to a fair and public hearing within a reasonable time by an independent and impartial tribunal established by law'.

WILLS, PROBATE AND ADMINISTRATION

This chapter examines:

A	Valid wills	144
B	Contents of a will	146
C	Intestacy	151
D	Probate	154
E	Administration	160
F	Problems which can arise	167

WILLS

Valid wills

A Valid wills

A Generally

➤ There are three requirements for a valid will.

1 The testator has testamentary 'Capacity'.

2 The testator has general *and* specific 'Intention' to make the will.

3 The testator's signature and the form of the will must comply with the required 'Formalities'.

	Requirements	Presumed to be satisfied ...	Safeguards
1 Capacity (must have both a) and b))	a) 'Soundness of mind, memory, and understanding' (*Marquess of Winchester's Case* (1598) 6 Co Rep 32a)	... if the testator comprehends: the nature of the act, *and* the general extent of his property, *and* the moral claims on the estate. ... the will appears to be rational *and* the testator generally has capacity. ◆ A mental state is presumed to persist, so if the testator generally lacks capacity, it must be shown that he possessed it when making the will	➤ Obtain a written medical opinion on the testator's capacity, and ask the person giving this opinion to witness the will ➤ Make a detailed file note of the circumstances
	b) over 18 years of age*		
2 Intention	a) General: intention to make *a* will and b) Specific: intention to make *this particular* will The testator must intend a will to be valid unconditionally on execution (*Corbett v. Newey* [1996] 2 All ER 914, CA)	... if the testator has capacity when he executes the will. However, this presumption does not arise if: a) the testator is blind or illiterate, *or* b) 'suspicious circumstances' exist: the testator did not give free approval due to force, fear, undue influence, or because he mistook the will's contents	➤ Explain the meaning of all the clauses ➤ Ensure the client reads the will, and that it is as he wishes. If necessary, read it aloud in the presence of the witnesses, and alter the attestation clause to record this act ➤ If a gift to the solicitor is 'significant' (over £2,000 *or* 10% of the estate), recommend the client takes independent legal advice
	Intention and Capacity must be present *either*: a) when the will is executed (*Banks v. Goodfellow* (1870) LR 5 QB 549), *or* b) when the solicitor is instructed to prepare a will if a) these instructions are followed in the will, *and* b) when the testator executes the will, he comprehends that he previously gave instructions to draw it up (*Parker v. Felgate* (1883) 8 PD 171)		

3
 	
Formalities*
	➤ A will may be handwritten, typed or printed
	➤ The will is properly executed if:
	  ◆ a testator, or another at his direction, signs anywhere on the will, *and*
	  ◆ the signature is intended to validate the will, *and*
	  ◆ 2 people witness the signature by signing the will *or* acknowledge the testator's mark in his presence *(WA 1837 s 9)*
	Note:
	a) a witness must be physically and mentally present at execution, and able to give evidence of this, eg: a child must understand the significance of acting as a witness
	b) a witness does not have to see the testator sign, or know the document is a will
	c) both witnesses must be present at the same time
	d) the testator need not see the witnesses sign
			➤ An attestation clause is evidence that these requirements are met
			➤ A witness who is blind, drunk, or mentally unsound is not suitable
			➤ A witness should not *either* be a beneficiary, *or* married to/a civil partner of, a beneficiary at the time, or a gift to that person lapses. A partner must not witness a will with a charging clause for his firm (*WA 1837 s 15, CPA 2004 Sch 4 para 3*).
			But if 2 capable witnesses sign, a signature by a beneficiary or their spouse/civil partner will not cause a gift to lapse (*WA 1837 s 1*)

	Burden of proof: with the person relying on the will - the 'propounder' of the will (*Griffin & Amos v. Ferard* (1835) 1 Curt 97)		

* Not applicable to 'privileged' wills made by members of the armed forces on active service, or sailors at sea.

B Alterations

Wills Act 1837 s 21	Presumptions

➤ Before execution alterations are valid
➤ After execution alterations are void unless *either*:
   a) the testator and the witnesses initial the alteration in the margin, *or*
   b) a subsequent codicil republishes the will and confirms the alteration
	➤ Completed blanks predate execution (eg: date)
	➤ Other alterations postdate execution

Problems

If the alteration is void and the original wording is:
a) legible: the alteration is disregarded and the original is admitted to probate
b) illegible: probate is granted as if there is a blank, unless *either*:
   i) there is evidence that the testator intended to revoke the wording if the substitution was valid ('conditional revocation'), *or*
   ii) the testator had no intention to revoke the original wording, in which case the original wording is effective if extrinsic evidence reveals it, or if the original script can be successfully revealed

C Revocation

➤ There are 6 ways to revoke the whole *or* part of a will.

1 **Express revocation (*WA 1837 s 20*)**

   ➤ The insertion of suitable words in a subsequent will or a codicil executed as a will.

2 **Implied revocation**

   ➤ When a disposition is inconsistent with an earlier will, the original disposition is revoked and superseded in so far as it is incompatible with the subsequent disposition.

3 **Dependant relative revocation (*Re Irvine* [1929] 2 IR 485)**

   ➤ When the replacement of a disposition is conditional on a specified event: if the event does not occur, the earlier disposition remains valid, otherwise the conditional disposition is substituted for it.

4 **Marriage (*WA 1837 ss 18, 18B*)**

   ➤ Marriage, or the formation of a civil partnership, revokes a will, unless the will shows contrary intention.

   ➤ A will made on or after 1 January 1983 in anticipation of marriage, or after the *CPA 2004* comes into force in anticipation of the formation of a civil partnership, with a clause displaying the testator's intent that the will (or part of it) should remain valid after marriage/formation, is valid, *provided that*:

     a) the will names a particular person as the intended spouse/civil partner, and this person is married/a civil partnership is formed with that person, *and*

     b) the testator's intention 'appears from the will . . . at the time it was made'; extrinsic evidence is inadmissible.

   ➤ Marriage does not revoke a mutual will as a trust arises on the death of the first to die, and this trust is not revoked by a subsequent marriage (*Re Goodchild (deceased)* [1996] 1 All ER 670, Ch D).

5 **Divorce (*WA 1837 ss 18A, 18C*)**

   ➤ If a marriage/civil partnership ends in divorce, dissolution, or annulment, the appointment of an ex-spouse/civil partner as executor *or* trustee, or a gift to the spouse/civil partner, take effect as if the former spouse/civil partner died on the day of the dissolution or annulment.

6 **Destruction (*WA 1837 s 20*)**

   a) Burning, tearing *or* otherwise destroying the will, *and*

   b) destruction by the testator *or* by some person in his presence and by his direction, *and*

   c) destruction with the intention of revoking the will.

     ◆ Destruction must be physical - crossing a will out, or writing 'revoked' across it is insufficient.

     ◆ Symbolic destruction is not sufficient. Destruction of part may revoke only the part destroyed; this depends on the condition of any remains and quite which part of the will is destroyed.

       ● Destruction of a signature revokes the whole will (*Hobbs v. Knight* (1838) 1 Curt 768).

       ● If parts are cut out, only those parts are revoked (*Re Everest* [1975] Fam 44).

     ◆ The presumption is that a missing will is intentionally destroyed.

B Contents of a will

    I   Common clauses
    II   Hints on drafting and interpretation

I Common clauses

1 Commencement

- States the testator's name and address.
- The words 'last will and testament' are evidence of an intention to make a will.

2 Revocation of previous wills

- Quite what is revoked depends on the wording of the clause.
    - Wills' refers to wills and codicils.
    - Testamentary dispositions' covers wills, codicils and privileged wills.

3 Disposal of remains

- This is a request, it does not bind the executors.
- If organ donation or medical research are envisaged, the testator should carry a donor card and inform his family. Details should be kept with the will of how to contact HM Inspector of Anatomy (organ donation) and/or the Department of Health (research).

4 Appointment of executors

- Individuals
    - These should be suitable, willing and capable of taking a grant of representation (not a minor, a convicted criminal, or a bankrupt). Private individuals will not charge, but they may need to engage professionals who will bill the estate. It is advisable to appoint a minimum of 2 people.
- Trustees
    - A maximum of 4 may apply for a grant of probate, so avoid appointing more than this.
- Banks and trust corporations
    - For large complex estates, where the extra expense involved is justified, and the slightly more impersonal approach which may be taken is not a concern.
- Solicitors
    - An individual partner may retire or cease to practice, so appoint the firm in the alternative.
        - i) Ensure the will appoints partners acting at death, rather than those at the time of the will, *and*
        - ii) provide for the firm's amalgamation, change of name, or future incorporation.
- Public trustee
    - This is expensive and inconvenient, but available if there is no alternative.

5   **Appointment of guardians (*ChA 1989*)**

➤ A parent with 'parental responsibility' may appoint a guardian for a minor under the age of 18.

- An unmarried father does not have 'parental responsibility' unless he is granted it by a court order.
- If both parents have 'parental responsibility', then an appointment is effective on the death of both parents; where both appoint different guardians, the responsibilities are shared between them.

➤ An appointment must be written, dated and signed; it can be revoked in the same fashion *even* if the original appointment was by will *s 5(3)*. No codicil is needed to revoke an appointment, but divorce and annulment of a marriage, and dissolution or annulment of a civil partnership, revoke the appointment unless the appointment shows a contrary intention (*ChA 1989 s 6(3A)-(3B)*).

- Ensure both parents appoint the same guardian and that the person consents.
- Financial provision for the care of the children should be made by appointing the guardian trustee of a fund, with power to spend income and capital for a child's benefit.

6   **Legacies**

➤ These are classified as 'General', 'Demonstrative', 'Specific', 'Pecuniary' or 'Residuary' (see p 148).

7   **Administrative powers**

➤ PRs and trustees have powers under the general law to administer trust funds.

➤ The will may extend powers granted under the general law (see pp 149-150).

8   **Attestation clause**

➤ This is not compulsory, but it is evidence that the will has been properly executed.

Note: a space for the date is left either in the 'Commencement', or in the 'Attestation' clause.

II   Hints on drafting and interpretation

Class closing rules

Unless the will excludes the class closing rules, these will determine how a class gift is construed.

Vested gifts

a)   'To the children of X' - if there are members of the class alive at the time of the testator's death, the class closes then, otherwise it remains open until X dies.

b)   'To S for life, remainder to the children of X' - as in a), but the class *may* close from S's death.

Contingent gifts

c)   'To the children of X who attain the age of 21' - if the contingency has been fulfilled, the class closes at X's death, and it includes any children alive at the testator's death who have reached, or who may in the future reach 21. Otherwise the class closes as soon as one of X's children fulfils the contingency.

d)   'To S for life, remainder to the children of X who attain the age of 21' - as in c), but the class *may* close from S's death.

Gifts to individuals within a class: 'to *each* of the children of X' - the class closes on the testator's death.

Early closing: the class in b) and d) may close immediately the prior interest fails, then the gift operates like a) or c) respectively.

WILLS
Contents of a Will

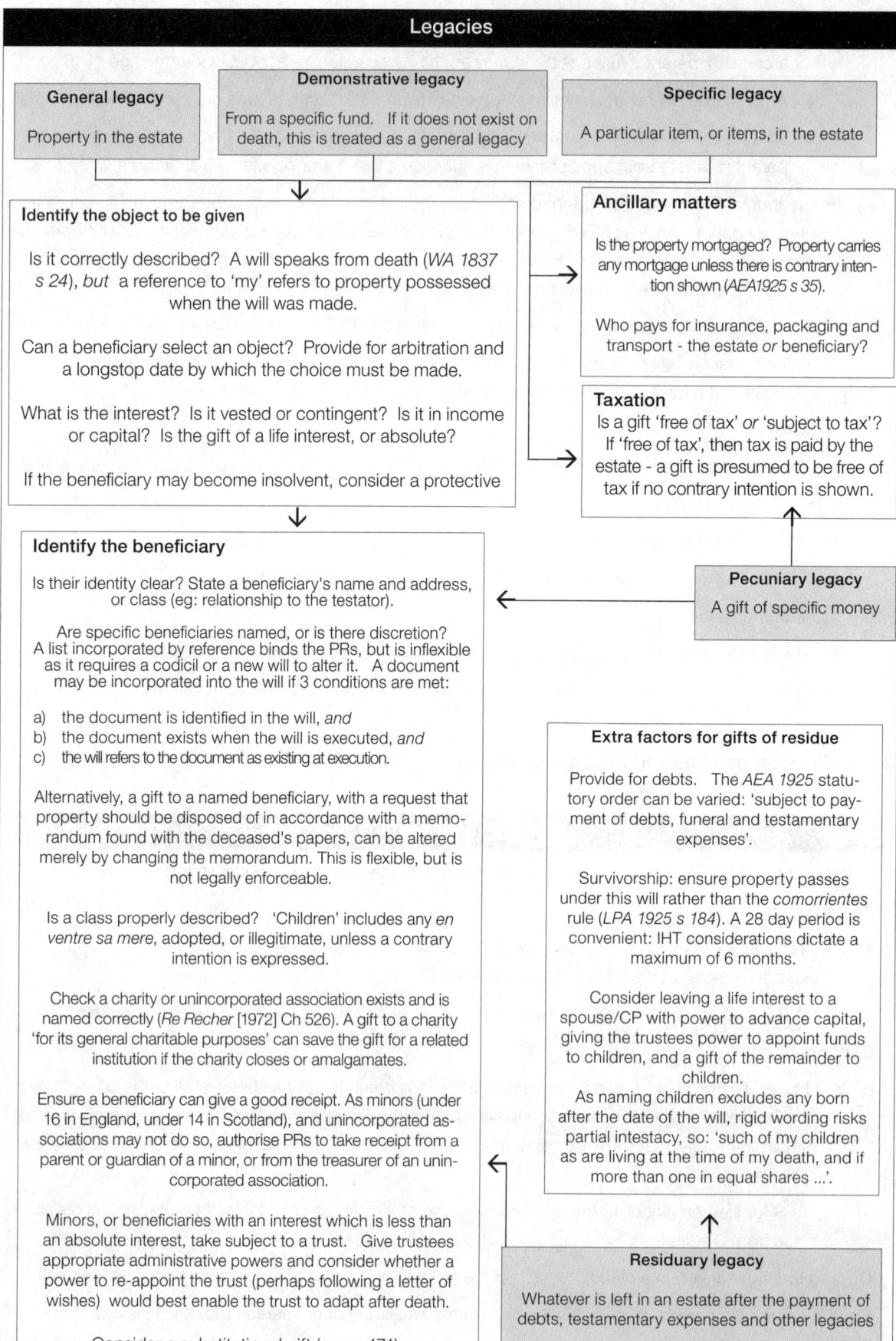

Legacies

General legacy
Property in the estate

Demonstrative legacy
From a specific fund. If it does not exist on death, this is treated as a general legacy

Specific legacy
A particular item, or items, in the estate

Identify the object to be given

Is it correctly described? A will speaks from death (*WA 1837 s 24*), *but* a reference to 'my' refers to property possessed when the will was made.

Can a beneficiary select an object? Provide for arbitration and a longstop date by which the choice must be made.

What is the interest? Is it vested or contingent? Is it in income or capital? Is the gift of a life interest, or absolute?

If the beneficiary may become insolvent, consider a protective

Ancillary matters

Is the property mortgaged? Property carries any mortgage unless there is contrary intention shown (*AEA1925 s 35*).

Who pays for insurance, packaging and transport - the estate *or* beneficiary?

Taxation
Is a gift 'free of tax' *or* 'subject to tax'? If 'free of tax', then tax is paid by the estate - a gift is presumed to be free of tax if no contrary intention is shown.

Identify the beneficiary

Is their identity clear? State a beneficiary's name and address, or class (eg: relationship to the testator).

Are specific beneficiaries named, or is there discretion? A list incorporated by reference binds the PRs, but is inflexible as it requires a codicil or a new will to alter it. A document may be incorporated into the will if 3 conditions are met:

a) the document is identified in the will, *and*
b) the document exists when the will is executed, *and*
c) the will refers to the document as existing at execution.

Alternatively, a gift to a named beneficiary, with a request that property should be disposed of in accordance with a memorandum found with the deceased's papers, can be altered merely by changing the memorandum. This is flexible, but is not legally enforceable.

Is a class properly described? 'Children' includes any *en ventre sa mere*, adopted, or illegitimate, unless a contrary intention is expressed.

Check a charity or unincorporated association exists and is named correctly (*Re Recher* [1972] Ch 526). A gift to a charity 'for its general charitable purposes' can save the gift for a related institution if the charity closes or amalgamates.

Ensure a beneficiary can give a good receipt. As minors (under 16 in England, under 14 in Scotland), and unincorporated associations may not do so, authorise PRs to take receipt from a parent or guardian of a minor, or from the treasurer of an unincorporated association.

Minors, or beneficiaries with an interest which is less than an absolute interest, take subject to a trust. Give trustees appropriate administrative powers and consider whether a power to re-appoint the trust (perhaps following a letter of wishes) would best enable the trust to adapt after death.

Consider a substitutional gift (see p 171).

Pecuniary legacy
A gift of specific money

Extra factors for gifts of residue

Provide for debts. The *AEA 1925* statutory order can be varied: 'subject to payment of debts, funeral and testamentary expenses'.

Survivorship: ensure property passes under this will rather than the *comorrientes* rule (*LPA 1925 s 184*). A 28 day period is convenient: IHT considerations dictate a maximum of 6 months.

Consider leaving a life interest to a spouse/CP with power to advance capital, giving the trustees power to appoint funds to children, and a gift of the remainder to children.
As naming children excludes any born after the date of the will, rigid wording risks partial intestacy, so: 'such of my children as are living at the time of my death, and if more than one in equal shares ...'.

Residuary legacy
Whatever is left in an estate after the payment of debts, testamentary expenses and other legacies

Administration
Insurance (*TA 2000 s 34 substituting TA 1925 s 19*)
➤ **Power to insure** trust property against loss or damage and pay premiums from income or capital
Investment
➤ A general **power of investment**: power to make any kind of investment as if the trustee were absolutely entitled to the trust assets (*TA 2000 s 3(1)-(2)*).
♦ This power does not permit a trustee to make an investment in land, other than in loans secured on land (*TA 2000 s 3(3)-(6)*).
♦ A trustee must have regard to the standard investment criteria, which are (*TA 2000 s 4*):   i) the suitability to the trust of investments of the same kind as any particular investment proposed to be made or retained and of that particular investment as an investment of that kind, *and*   ii) the need for diversification of investments, in so far as is appropriate to the trust's circumstances.
♦ Unless a trustee reasonably concludes that it is unnecessary or inappropriate, he must obtain and consider proper advice before exercising the power of investment and when reviewing investments (*TA 2000 s 5*).
➤ A **power to acquire freehold or leasehold land in the UK**: as an investment, for occupation by a beneficiary, or for any other reason (*TA 2000 s 8*).

Land, etc	
Powers under the general law	Drafting considerations
➤ Prior to 1 January 1997, land was held on a strict settlement under *SLA 1925* unless it is given to a trustee on an 'immediate binding trust for sale'. *TLATA 1996* prevents new strict settlements arising and creates a system of 'trusts of land'.	Consider how to achieve the testator's wishes under *TLATA 1996*, see further pp 183-184. *TLATA* only gives trustees of land a power to sell, so consider a power to sell personalty

Operate a business	
Powers under the general law	Drafting considerations
➤ PRs can only run a business to preserve its sale value. They are restricted to using assets the business relied on at the testator's death (*Re Hodson, ex parte Richardson* (1818) 3 Madd 138)	PRs can be permitted to use assets from the general estate to run the business, or the business and assets used to carry on the business may be left as a specific legacy

Delegation, agency, etc
➤ **Power to authorise any person to exercise delegable functions as their agent** (*TA 2000 s 11*).
♦ A beneficiary may not act as an agent (*TA 2000 s 12(3)*) (for 'delegable functions', see p 160).
♦ An agent's authorisation in relation to asset management functions must be evidenced in writing and be accompanied by guidance (known as a 'policy statement') (*TA 2000 s 15*).
➤ **Power to appoint a nominee** (*TA 2000 s 16*) or **custodian** (*TA 2000 s 17*) (*TA 2000 Part IV*).
♦ The appointment must be evidenced in writing.
➤ Professionally drafted wills may continue to include express powers and duties. The statutory framework provided by *TLATA 1996/TA 2000* offers a 'safety net' in cases where specific provision is not made.

Administration (cont.)

Remuneration / Reimbursement

➤ An **entitlement to receive payment in respect of services** (*TA 2000 s 28*).

- This applies to a trust corporation or a trustee acting in a professional capacity if the trust instrument confers an entitlement to payment out of trust funds in respect of services provided by the trustee; it applies even if the services are capable of being provided by a lay trustee.

➤ An **entitlement to receive reasonable remuneration for services to the trust** (*TA 2000 s 29*).

- This applies to a trust corporation, or a trustee acting in a professional capacity (but not the trustee of a charitable trust) where no provision for remuneration has been made in the trust instrument.
- If a trustee acts in a professional capacity, each of the other trustees must agree in writing.

➤ An **entitlement to reimbursement of/payment for a trustee's expenses** (*TA 2000 s 31*).

➤ A **power to remunerate an agent/nominee/custodian** (*TA 2000 s 32*).

Distribution

Appropriation

Powers under the general law	Drafting considerations
➤ PRs can appropriate property to pay a pecuniary legacy provided that (*AEA 1925 s 41*): a) a beneficiary does not suffer, *and* b) that beneficiary consents	Relieve PRs of the duty to obtain a beneficiary's formal consent

Apportionment

Powers under the general law	Drafting considerations
➤ *Howe v. Dartmouth* (1802) 7 Ves 137: 'wasting, hazardous and unauthorised' assets, and those which produce no income are sold, so that a life tenant benefits from capital ➤ *Allhusen v. Whittell* (1867) LR 4 Eq 295: debts, administration and tax are apportioned between capital and income *AA 1870 s 2*: rent/dividends are income arising daily: they are treated as capital before death, and income thereafter	These complex bureaucratic rules can be expressly excluded to assist the administration of the trust If the will creates a trust of land under *TLATA 1996*, then the rule in *Howe v. Dartmouth* may be automatically excluded (*Re Pitcairn* [1896] 2 Ch 199). However, this will only occur if a will trust contains land so exclude the rules expressly

Receipt

Powers under the general law	Drafting considerations
➤ A married minor can only give receipt for income (*LPA s 21*) ➤ PRs can accept receipt on behalf of minors with an absolute interest from trustees who may be appointed for this purpose (*AEA 1925 s 42*).	Authorise PRs to accept receipt from a parent/guardian of a minor under 16, to avoid appointing trustees Cater for receipt if a minor's interest is contingent, *or* if a married minor receives capital

Income / Capital

Powers under the general law	Drafting considerations
Income for 'maintenance, education or benefit', acting 'reasonably' and with regard to other resources (*TA 1925 s 31*) ➤ At 18 a beneficiary of an absolute or contingent interest is entitled to income ➤ Accumulated income is released if a beneficiary has a life interest in capital, otherwise accumulations and capital are retained until the gift vests absolutely Capital for 'advancement or benefit' whether an interest is absolute or contingent (*TA 1925 s 32*) ➤ Payments are subtracted when capital vests absolutely ➤ A holder of a prior life interest must consent in writing ➤ Only half a presumptive/ vested interest may be advanced	Give the trustees discretion to make payments as they think fit NB: the rule against cumulation imposes a long-stop of 21 years after the testator's death, after which the beneficiary must be allowed access to the capital Postpone a beneficiary's right to receive income, and/or capital, until after the statutory age of 18 Increase the capital which trustees can advance Give the trustees discretion to distribute capital without making deductions in respect of prior advancements

C Intestacy

Steps

1. Discover the extent of the estate passing on intestacy
2. Property passes to the PRs on statutory trusts *(AEA 1925 s 33)*
3. Deduct funeral, testamentary and administrative expenses and debts
4. Set aside a pecuniary legacy fund
5. Work out who is entitled to the property (apply the statutory order of entitlement)
6. Consider whether the spouse/civil partner wishes to exercise his/her rights

Step 1 — Discover the extent of the estate passing on intestacy

➤ Only property capable of passing by will can pass on intestacy.

Step 2 — Property passes to the PRs on the statutory trusts

➤ Property passes to PRs on the statutory trusts *(AEA 1925 s 47)*.

➤ The terms of the trust dictate that the gift is construed as being:
- to those entitled within a class, in equal shares, *and*
- to all 'living' persons within the class, including any children *en ventre sa mere*, *and*
- on the death of a member of a class who was entitled on the intestate's death, to that beneficiary's issue in equal shares, *and*
- contingent on the beneficiary marrying *or* reaching the age of 18.

Note: if a contingency is not met, the failed interest is disregarded, and the distribution of the estate is reassessed as if the failed interest had never existed.

➤ The trustees have:
- powers of maintenance and advancement given by the *TA 1925 ss 31-32*, *and*
- (from 1 January 1997), power to sell.
  - Prior to 1 January 1997 trustees were under a duty to sell with a power to postpone sale and a direction that the deceased's 'personal chattels' should not be sold without a 'special reason' such as the payment of debts and administration expenses *(AEA 1925 s 33)*.
    - When *TLATA* came into force on 1 January 1997 the duty to sell and convert ceased to apply *(TLATA 1996 Sch 2 para 5)*.

Step 3 — Deduct funeral, testamentary and administrative expenses

Step 4 — Set aside a fund from which to pay pecuniary legacies

WILLS
Intestacy

Step 5 — Work out who is entitled to property

The statutory order of entitlement

➤ A surviving spouse/civil partner ('CP') takes priority over anyone else. Depending on the size of the estate, the spouse/CP may share an interest with one class of kinsmen (see the chart below); if one class exists those classes further down the line are excluded (AEA 1925 s 46).

➤ If there is no spouse/CP, blood kin take in the statutory order:

a) issue, *then*

b) parents, *then*

c) brothers and sisters of whole blood, *then*

d) brothers and sisters of half-blood, *then*

e) grandparents, *then*

f) uncles and aunts of whole blood, *then*

g) uncles and aunts of half-blood, *then*

h) bona vacantia goes to the Crown, the Duchy of Lancaster, or the Duke of Cornwall; there is discretion to provide for those for whom an intestate 'might reasonably have been expected to make provision'.

➤ For deaths on or after 1 January 1996, the spouse/civil partner is treated as not having survived the intestate if he or she dies within a period of 28 days beginning on the day of the intestate's death (AEA

	Size of estate	Spouse/CP's entitlement	Others' entitlement
Spouse/CP alone		Everything passing on intestacy	Nothing
Spouse/CP and issue	Estate under £125,000	Everything (including personal chattels)	Nothing
	Estate over £125,000	Personal chattels absolutely £125,000 statutory legacy* Life interest in half the residue	On the statutory trusts: ➤ half the residue, *and* ➤ interest in remainder of residue
Spouse/CP, no issue† but other kin	Estate under £200,000	Everything (including chattels)	Nothing
	Estate over £200,000	Personal chattels absolutely £200,000 statutory legacy* Half the residue absolutely	On the statutory trusts: ➤ half the residue
No spouse/CP			Everything on statutory trusts

† Issue: children and other descendants including adopted, legitimated and legitimised children

* Statutory legacy:
  a) this is paid free of tax and costs. It also includes interest from the date of death until the legacy is paid to the spouse/civil partner
  b) the value of any personal chattels is not taken into account in establishing whether the estate is worth £125,000 or £200,000

Step 6 — Consider whether the spouse/CP wish to exercise his/her rights

1. **A spouse's/CP's right to redeem a life interest**
   - The spouse/civil partner may choose to convert the life interest into a lump sum.
   - The spouse/civil partner must notify the PRs within 1 year of the date when the grant of representation is issued.

     a) All those entitled to the remainder may, if they are *sui juris*, agree the value of the life interest in writing with the spouse/civil partner. Otherwise the sum is calculated according to *IS(IC)O 1977*.

     b) The entitlement of other beneficiaries is recalculated.

     c) IHT is recalculated and the spouse/civil partner bears any resulting charge.

2. **A spouse/civil partner's right to appropriate the matrimonial or civil partnership home (*IEA 1952 s 5 and Sch II*)**
   - The spouse/CP can demand that PRs transfer the house to him/her as part of the inheritance to which he/she is absolutely entitled.

   Steps
   1. The spouse/civil partner must notify the PRs within 1 year of the date when the grant of representation is issued.
   2. The house is valued at the time of appropriation, not death. If its value exceeds the spouse's/CP's entitlement, he or she can pay the difference to the estate as 'equality money'.

   NB: if the spouse/CP is the sole surviving PR, then the President of the Family Division must be notified of an intention to invoke either of these statutory rights. This is done by lodging the notification together with the original grant at the Probate Registry so that this intention can be recorded on the grant.

D Probate

I Overview of solicitor's role
II Applying for a grant of representation

I Overview of a solicitor's role

A solicitor's duty to PRs

1 Advise on succession and revenue law.
2 Prove the testator's will.
3 Administer the estate.
4 Prepare estate accounts.

How to carry out this duty

1 Take instructions directly from the PR.
2 Obtain the deceased's will (and ensure PRs each have a copy).
3 Attend to the deceased's wishes as regards cremation, organ donation, etc, in consultation with the PRs.
4 Secure property (ie: check an empty house is locked and insured, locate and safeguard documents of title to assets).
5 Attend to financial arrangements (ie: loans to support a family pending grant of probate or during the administration of the estate).
6 Obtain the death certificate.
7 Compile a list of the deceased's assets and liabilities. This list should be continuously updated during the administration of the estate, to show their state at any given time and what steps have been or are being taken with regard to them.
8 Discover details of all the beneficiaries (ie: ages and addresses).
9 Protect PRs from personal liability against unknown or missing creditors or beneficiaries (eg: place advertisements in good time for the purposes of *TA s 1925 s 27*, see p 169).
10 Prepare the oath and the HMRC account.
11 Obtain a grant and make office copies of the grant.
12 Collect and realise assets.
13 Pay debts.
14 Pay legacies.
15 Ascertain and distribute residue.

I   Administering property immediately after death

➤ The executor's first duty, after making suitable arrangements for a funeral, is to ascertain what assets and liabilities there are in the estate.

- Certain assets can be paid to someone who appears to be beneficially entitled to them without sight of a grant (which may take a little time to obtain) - this is a discretion to be exercised by whomever holds the assets, PRs cannot demand payment as of right.

Type of property	Comments
Salaries of public sector employees	The PRs can administer such property if (AE(SP)A 1965):
Some pensions	
National Savings bank accounts, TSB accounts	➤ payment is at the discretion of the trustees, *and*
National Savings certificates and premium bonds	➤ the asset is not worth more than £5,000, *and*
Building society and Friendly society accounts	➤ the applicant appears to be beneficially entitled to the asset
Life assurance policy held on trust	A death certificate is needed to gain access to the proceeds of the policy The proceeds are paid to whomever was assigned the benefit of the policy, or in the case of a *MWPA* policy in favour of children, to the trustees who were appointed under the terms of the policy
Property held under a joint tenancy	A death certificate establishes a tenant's right to take through survivorship Only if a survivor murders another tenant will he not be entitled to the property
Chattels	Although a grant is theoretically necessary to prove title, in practice it is not usually necessary to produce one

- These assets can be used to meet debts and to pay for funeral expenses and IHT.
- National savings investments and British Government Stocks on the Bank of the England register can be used to pay IHT; funds can be transferred directly to HMRC to meet an IHT liability, although this can take up to 4 weeks (HMRC leaflet, *IHT 11*).

➤ The executors should write to institutions holding assets, quoting whatever details they possess about the assets and inquiring about:

a) the value of the asset(s) on the date of death (including accrued interest), *and*

b) the daily interest which is accruing on the asset(s), *and*

c) whether the institution holds any other assets on behalf of the deceased.

- It is usual to *either* request a cheque for the sum due *or* to ask for the relevant papers needed to close the account.
- The PRs should send appropriate evidence of their title, eg: to claim an insurance policy written into trust, send a certified copy of the trust instrument and any appointments/resignations of trustees plus a certified copy of the death certificate.

II   Applying for a grant of representation

➤ A PR's duty is (*AEA 1925 s 25* as amended *AEA 1971 s 9*): 'to collect and get in the real and personal estate of the deceased and administer it according to law'.

➤ A grant of representation is necessary to administer the rest of the deceased's estate as the executor(s) will need to be able to prove that he/they are entitled to sell or dispose of assets.

➤ The procedure for 'Swearing the oath' and 'Applying for the grant' is as follows:

Steps
1. Decide what sort of grant is appropriate.
2. Ascertain who is entitled to take a grant.
3. Ascertain who is entitled to take a grant.
4. Fill in the oath.

Swearing/affirming the oath

➤ Executors complete the jurat before an independent solicitor with a current practicing certificate or commissioner for oaths (*not* an executor or connected with a firm acting for the PRs).

➤ If the oath is affirmed, rather than sworn, an executor does not need to hold a Bible/the New Testament and simply states 'I do solemnly sincerely and truly declare and affirm ...'

➤ Executors and a solicitor, or a commissioner for oaths, initial the will and any codicils.

Applying for the grant

➤ Send to the Probate Registry (using a District Registry may minimise publicity):
   ◆ the oath (*NCPR r 8*), *and*
   ◆ the will, *and*
   ◆ the court fee, *and*
     • The basic fee is calculated by reference to the value of the net estate. Add to this the photocopy for each office copy of the grant of representation requested. (Work out how many copies to ask for by reference to the number of assets for which the grant will need to be produced.)
   ◆ a fee sheet showing how the fee was calculated *and*
   ◆ the HMRC account (unless the estate is 'excepted').

➤ The Probate Registry usually issues the grant in 5 to 15 days.

➤ Where an estate is 'excepted', HMRC has 35 days after the grant is issued in which to demand the production of an account.

➤ If the PRs discover other assets, making it necessary to submit a corrective account, then they must send *form C4* to HMRC within 6 months of making this discovery.

WILLS

Probate

Step 1		Decide what sort of grant is appropriate	

➤ A straightforward grant of probate *or* letters of administration is usually sought:

Grant	Circumstances	Effect of grant	PRs identified
Grant of probate	The executor appointed in a valid will is willing *and* able to act (even if the estate actually passes under the intestacy rules)	➤ It confirms the appointment made in the will ➤ It is conclusive evidence that the PRs have title to the estate *and* that the will is valid	In the will
Letters of administration with will annexed	The appointment of executors in the will fails as *either* it is invalid *or* they are unwilling to act	➤ It confers authority on the PRs ➤ It vests title to the estate in PRs	Following *NCPR r 20*
Simple administration	Total intestacy		Following *NCPR r 22*

➤ However, in certain circumstances, a different form of grant of representation will be appropriate:

Type of grant	Circumstances: when ...
Grant for the use and benefit of a person who is mentally incapacitated NCPR r 35	... a sole executor or only potential administrator is mentally incapacitated. Grant to a capable adult in the following order: a) adult authorised by the Court of Protection to apply for a grant b) lawful attorney of the incapacitated person, with registered enduring power of attorney c) the deceased's residuary legatee or devisee
Administration for the use and benefit of a minor NCPR r 32	... a minor is the sole executor, or the only administrator in the category with highest priority. The grant is made to an adult, often the minor's guardian
Grants over specified property NCPR r 53	... a will appoints an executor in respect of particular property *or* the court exercises its discretion to make a grant over part of the estate (*SCA 1981 s 113*)
Grant *ad litem* SCA 1981 s 116	... an estate is a party to legal proceedings and there is no PR
Administration with litigation pending SCA 1981 s 117	... assets need safeguarding while a probate action takes place. This requires the consent of all parties to the action
Administration *ad colligenda bona* NCPR r 52	... a person with an interest in the estate seeks to ensure the collection and preservation of its property - this grant does not permit distribution, and ceases when a full grant is made
Attorney grants NCPR r 31	... a letter of administration is granted to the lawful attorney of someone who is entitled to a grant
Double grant of probate *	... power is reserved - it operates in tandem with the original grant
Cessate grant *	... a grant which was made for a limited time expires - it is a regrant to an executor of what remains of the estate
Grant *de bonis administrandum* *	... a sole surviving PR dies so that the chain of representation is broken

* With applications for such grants submit *Form A5-C* to the probate registry (no need to first send *Form A5-C* to HMRC)

WILLS
Probate

Step 2 — Ascertain who is entitled to take a grant

➤ Applicants for grants must satisfy the following criteria:

	Executors	Administrator
Mentally incapable	Not suitable (*NCPR r 35*)	
Renunciation (*NCPR r 37*)	If the executor has not 'intermeddled' with the estate (actively administered the estate) (*Re Stevens, Cooke v. Stevens* [1898] 1 Ch 162) he may renounce. When this is done he may not apply for a grant. A renunciation must be in writing, signed, witnessed *and* filed at the probate registry	
Minor	Not suitable, until majority is reached, when a cessate grant can be sought. If an adult is appointed, power can be reserved to a minor. If only a minor is appointed, parents or a guardian take letters of administration with the will annexed	Not suitable, until majority is reached, when a cessate grant can be sought. A parent or guardian can apply for a minor's 'use and benefit' (*NCPR r 32*); anyone entitled in the same degree takes in preference to a guardian (*NCPR r 27(5)*)
Former spouse/ civil partner	Not suitable, *unless* the will indicates an intention that, despite the divorce/dissolution, the appointment should stand (*WA 1837 s 15*)	Not suitable
Power reserved	Yes, if an appointee entitled in the same degree requests it. Notice must be given to all those entitled	No power may be reserved
Number needed	Up to 4 (reserve power if a future vacancy is likely)	At least 2 if there is a minority or life interest; unless the court permits one

NCPR r 20

➤ NCPR r 20 allows the appointment of administrators if:
- the appointment is void, *or*
- the appointee is incapable.

a) Any executor
↓
b) A residuary legatee holding in trust for any other person
↓
c) A residuary legatee: a vested interest takes in priority to a contingent one, and those entitled to residue take priority over any entitled under a partial intestacy
↓
d) A PR of any residuary legatee, or of one entitled to residue under the intestacy rules, provided the deceased beneficiary had an absolute interest (eg: not a life interest)
↓
e) Any legatee, or creditor. A legatee of a vested interest takes priority over one entitled to a contingent interest
↓
f) A PR of any legatee (with an absolute interest) or creditor

NCPR r 22

➤ NCPR r 22 sets out the entitlement to administer the estate on an intestacy.

A beneficiary under the will who is ...

a) a surviving spouse/civil partner
↓
b) children, or their issue if they are dead
↓
c) father and mother
If the couple are not married, there is a presumption the father is dead, unless they live together or the father is in contact with the child (*FLRA 1987 ss 18,21*)
↓
d) brothers and sisters of whole blood, or their issue if they are dead
↓
e) brothers and sisters of half-blood, or their issue if they are dead
↓
f) grandparents
↓
g) uncles and aunts of whole blood, or their issue if they are dead
↓
h) uncles and aunts of half-blood, or their issue if they are dead
↓
i) a creditor may apply, or the Treasury Solicitor claims the estate as *bona vacantia*

➤ An applicant for a grant under *NCPR r 20* or *r 22* must swear why those with priority are unable or unwilling to apply for the grant - this is known as 'clearing off'.

Step 3 — Complete form *IHT 200* (unless the estate is 'excepted')

WILLS
Probate

Step 4 — Filling in the oath

Consider (and fill in or delete as appropriate) ...

... when preparing an oath for an executor

➤ details (in the top left hand corner) of the solicitor's firm lodging the oath.

➤ the deceased's name, plus any alias (and the reason for such an alias).

➤ the deceased's date of death and age at death. If the date of death is uncertain, the time when the deceased was last seen alive and the date on which the body was found are sworn.

➤ the deceased's last address and the address of the deceased when the will was made if this differs.

➤ whether any settled land was vested in the deceased.

➤ whether power is reserved and, if so, to whom.

➤ the gross and net value of the estate and whether it is 'excepted'.

♦ If an executor has renounced, ensure a Form of Renunciation is annexed to the oath.

... additionally when preparing an oath for an administrator with a will annexed

➤ if a minority arises under the estate, *or* the deceased at his death had an interest in land under a strict settlement, 2 administrators will be needed (one executor could have acted alone).

➤ details of the applicant's right under the *NCPR r 20* to seek a grant of representation:

  a) an explanation of why an executor is not applying, ie: none was appointed, renunciation, or death, *and*

  b) the applicant's capacity to take a grant - eg: 'residuary legatee and the devisee under the said will', 'specific legatee and devisee named in the said will'.

... additionally when preparing an oath for an administrator of an intestate

Marital status	Single	Married/CP	Divorced/Dissolved	Judicially separated	Annulled
Fill in	Bachelor/spinster	Married/CPed man/woman, or widow/er			Status before annulment
			The court which implemented the divorce/dissolution, date of the order (if the court was outside England and Wales, provide an office copy of the decree)		
			That the deceased did not re marry/partner	That the separation continued until death	

➤ Clear off those with a prior entitlement under *NCPR r 22* (but not those in the same category). Mention any renunciation and clear off using the following terms depending how the deceased died.

- Spouse/CP: abachelor/spinster, widow(er), single man/woman
- Children: without issue
- Parents
- Brothers, sisters/issue: (or) brother or sister of [whole/half] or issue thereof
- Grandparents: (or) grandparent
- Uncle, aunt/issue: (or) uncle or aunt of [whole/half] blood or issue thereof

➤ If a spouse/civil partner survives, and there are no issue qualifying for a share in the estate, the words 'or any other person entitled in priority to share in [his/her] estate by virtue of any enactment' remain - otherwise delete them.

➤ State the applicant's relationship to the deceased.

- Spouse/CP: lawful husband/widow/civil partner
- Child: son/daughter (whether or not parents were married at birth)
- Grandchild: grandson/daughter (state that the applicant's parents have died)
- Brother/Sister: brother/sister of [whole/half] blood
- Parent: father/mother
- Grandparent: grandfather/grandmother
- Cousin: cousin german of [whole/half] blood (state that the applicant's parents have died)

➤ State why the applicant is entitled to a share in the estate, eg: 'the only person entitled to the estate', 'one of the persons entitled to share in the estate'.

E Administration

I	Collecting in all the deceased's assets
II	Ensuring the estate meets its tax liability
III	Paying debts
IV	Paying legacies
V	Obtaining a discharge

I Collecting in all the deceased's assets

➤ A PR's duty is (*AEA 1925 s 25* as amended *AEA 1971 s 9*): 'to collect and get in the real and personal estate of the deceased and administer it according to law'.

➤ PRs should write to institutions holding the deceased's assets, enclosing an office copy of the grant together with any other appropriate documents (eg: building society pass-book if the account is to be closed, insurance policy) and requesting details of the assets.

- Ask for the office copies of the grant to be returned, to reduce costs.

➤ PRs and trustees have statutory powers, and may receive additional powers in the will.

PRs' statutory powers, rights and duties
Pay an agent: *TA 2000 s 32*.
Appropriate property in the estate amongst the beneficiaries (*AEA1925 s 41*).
Insure the estate's assets: *TA1925 s 19*.
PRs (and trustees) can **delegate the exercise of powers or discretions** for up to 1 year. ◆ This is useful if renunciation is impossible but the PR is going abroad, etc) (*TA 1925 s 25*). PRs can **employ agents** to exercise 'delegable functions' (*TA 2000 s 11*); these are any function other than: a) any function relating to whether or in what way any assets of the trust should be distributed, *or* b) any power to decide whether any fees or other payment due to be made out of trust funds should be made out of income or capital, *or* c) any power to appoint a person to act as trustee of the trust, *or* d) any power conferred by any other enactment or trust instrument which permits the trustees to delegate any of their functions or to appoint a person t act as a nominee or custodian.
Reimbursement of/payment of expenses: *TA 2000 s 31*.
Charging: *TA 2000 ss 28 -29*.
Apportionment: sell wasting assets (*Howe v. Dartmouth*), pay debts fairly (*Allhusen v. Whittell*), *AA 1870 s 2*.
Running a business: duty to run the business to maintain its value as an asset for sale.
Power and duties in respect of land forming part of the estate during the administration: ◆ In respect of estates arising due to deaths on or after 1 January 1997 when *TLATA 1996* came into force PRs have the same powers and duties as trustees of land (see p 191), except that they will not be bound to obtain the beneficiaries' consent before selling land.
Power to invest (see p 149)
Power to appoint trustees who will be able to give the PRs valid receipt on behalf of a minor who is absolutely entitled (*TA 1925 s 42*).
Power to postpone distribution even if the will specifies payments within a time-frame (*AEA1925 s 44*). If payment is delayed beyond a year after death, interest is payable from that date. If the testator specifies a date or contingency upon which payment is to be made, interest runs from that point. The rate of interest is 6% per annum, *or* as laid down in the will.

II Ensuring the estate meets its tax liability

➤ PRs should complete a self assessment tax return for the deceased's income and capital gains from 6 April to his death. Any reliefs and allowances available for the full year may be claimed. Any liability or repayment forms part of the estate, and must be met or accounted for by the PRs during the administration.

➤ Throughout each tax year during the administration, the PRs must make tax returns on behalf of the estate.

1 Income tax

➤ This is chargeable on the deceased's income and is a debt due from the estate.

➤ Interest on a loan for paying IHT is deductible as a 'charge on income' (*TA s 358*).

➤ Personal allowances are available for the tax year in which death occurs, but not for the remainder of the administration.

➤ The dividend ordinary rate (10%), or dividend upper rate (32.5%), apply to distributions from companies. Interest is taxed at the lower rate (20%) and other income is subject to tax at the basic rate (22%) (*TA s 686(6)*).

- If a beneficiary is entitled to income, PRs supply a certificate of deduction of tax (*Form 185E*).
  - When a beneficiary prepares his self assessment he uses *Form 185E*.
  - A beneficiary is liable for tax on the gross income (*IT(TOI)A 2005 Part 5 Ch 7*).

2 Capital gains tax

➤ As death is not a disposal, no charge to CGT arises on death (*TCGA 1992 s 62(1)(b)*).

➤ The probate value becomes the base value (ie: rather than the original acquisition value) (*TCGA 1992 s 62(1)(a)*).

➤ Tax is due at the rate of 40% on chargeable gains realised during administration (*TCGA 1992 s 4(1AA)*).

- Taper relief is available.

➤ The PRs are entitled to use an annual exemption (£8,800 for 2006/2007) (*TCGA 1992 s 3(7)*):

- for the year of death (*in addition* to the deceased's exemption accruing before his death), *and*
- for 2 subsequent years.

➤ Losses may be carried back 3 years and forward during the administration period, but not after it.

3 Loss relief for capital gains tax and inheritance tax

➤ PRs may opt either for:

- IHT loss relief at up to 40% (preferable if an estate is in the nil rate band/exempt), *or*
- CGT loss relief at 40% (advisable in most other circumstances).

Final adjustments

➤ PRs should retain sufficient assets to discharge any outstanding IHT liability, including provision for the payment of tax on instalment option property, and the need to meet any further liability from:

- LCTs or gifts with benefit reserved where the donee does not pay what he owes.
- newly discovered LCTs or PETs which the deceased made within 7 years of death, and which alter cumulation and tapering relief.
- valuations which are agreed with HMRC at a level different from the probate value.
- the discovery of assets or liabilities which were unknown on probate.
- any agreement with HMRC on the deceased's pre-death liability for income tax or CGT.
- sales which qualify for IHT 'loss relief' (see p 99).
- post-death variations or disclaimers.

Steps

1. **The PRs send a corrective account to the CTO.**

   For minor adjustments the PRs may write a letter to the CTO, otherwise they complete a Form Cap D3, and send it to the CTO, who prepare a final assessment.

2. **The PRs send the CTO 2 copies of *Form IHT 30*, requesting a clearance certificate.**

3. **The CTO return the form with an endorsement.**

➤ The certificate discharges the PRs of liability and extinguishes any charge over the estate for unpaid IHT.

➤ Where instalments are outstanding, the discharge is partial: on their fulfilment PRs should seek a full certificate.

➤ The certificate provides only limited protection, as HMRC may re-open the account if:

a) there has been fraud or failure to disclose material facts, *or*

b) additional assets are later shown to have been included in the transfer, *or*

c) further tax becomes payable as a result of statutory amendments after issue of the certificate (*IHTA 1984 s 239(4)*).

III Paying debts

➤ The rules depend on whether an estate will be A. Insolvent, or B. Solvent, after the payment of:

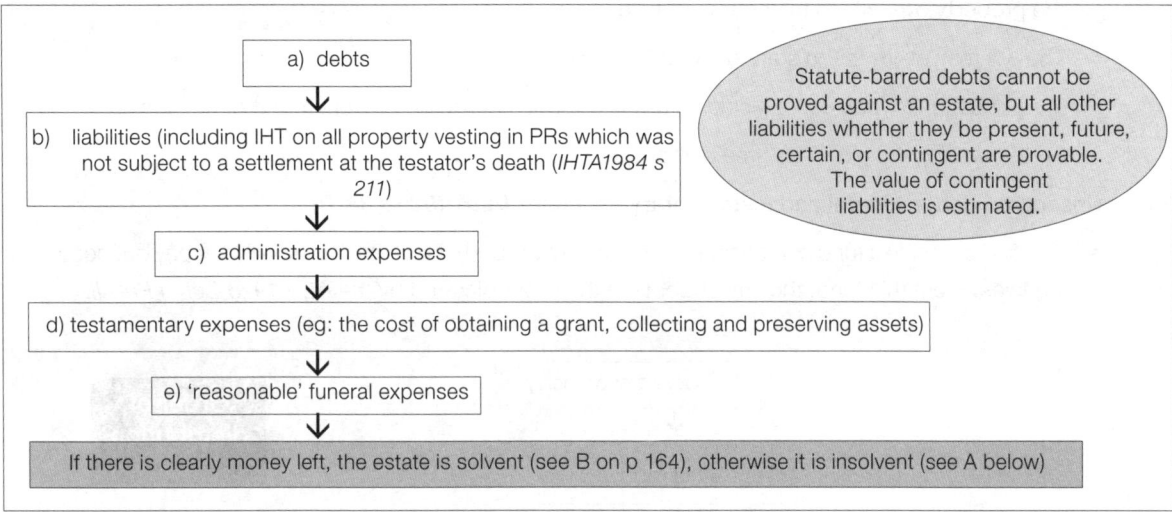

A Insolvent estates (or where solvency is doubtful)

1 **Secured creditors**

   ➤ They have three options:

   a) sell the secured asset and seek to recover outstanding liability as unsecured creditors, *or*

   b) value the security and seek any outstanding balance as unsecured creditors, *or*

   c) simply rely on the fixed charge and collect the debt whenever the estate sells the security.

2 **Unsecured creditors (*AIEDPO 1986*)**

➤ Debts of equal priority rank equally, and abate proportionately, if there are insufficient funds available.

B Solvent estates

1. **Property in the estate subject to any charge (*AEA 1925 s 35(1)*)**

    ➤ Mortgages, any charge imposed for unpaid IHT, or a debt in favour of a judgment creditor, is met by the property over which the charge is fixed.

    ➤ The will may override the statutory provisions by *either*:

    a) a direction to 'pay debts including any mortgage charge on Whiteacre out of residue', *or*

    b) expressing the gift to be 'free of mortgage'.

2. **Unsecured debts, funeral and testamentary expenses (*AEA 1925 s 34(1)*)**

    ➤ PRs first set aside a fund comprising undisposed of property from which they will later pay out pecuniary legacies. From this fund, they meet debts in the order dictated by the *AEA 1925 Sch I Part II*.

    ➤ Property passing under a will or intestacy bears the burden of debt equally. If there is no provision in the will, property which is undisposed of (ie: on a partial intestacy) is available first.

    ➤ The will may displace the statutory order by making:

    a) a gift of residue 'subject to' the payment of debts, *or*

    b) by charging property for this purpose and stating that property in a) and b) should not bear the liability.

IV Paying legacies

Transferring property to beneficiaries	
Property	**Method of transfer**
Personal chattels	An assent (written or oral) stating that the PRs have no further need of the items for the administration of the estate
National Savings certificates	Withdrawal or transfer forms
Shares	Stock transfer form; the grant will have to be produced
Premium bonds	These must be surrendered and the cash transferred to the beneficiary
Money in residuary estate	Cheque drawn on PRs' bank account
Land	A written assent signed by the PRs which names the person in whose favour it is made out (*AEA 1925 s 36(4)*). If the PRs are taking an indemnity covenant, the assent must be by deed. The assent should be endorsed on the original grant of representation; HM Land Registry has its own standard form of assent. *Either*: a) the PRs can register as proprietors, on producing the grant, and subsequently transfer the title to the beneficiary, *or* b) the PRs can supply the beneficiary with the assent and a certified copy of the grant so that he can apply for registration The Register is conclusive. Although it dispenses with the requirement for the grant to be endorsed, it is still good practice to obtain an endorsement

➤ The PRs should always obtain a valid receipt.

A Identifying the beneficiaries

1 **Class gifts**

   ➤ See p 147 for the rules governing the construction of these gifts.

2 *Wills Act 1837 s 33*

   ➤ Where a beneficiary dies a substitutional gift is implied in favour of the deceased beneficiary's children if the beneficiary was the testator's 'issue'.

3 **Children**

   ➤ References to 'children' are interpreted as follows (unless contrary intention is shown).

Statute	Effect	Protection of PRs
FLRA 1987 s 19(1)	For wills or codicils executed after 3 April 1988, a reference to a relationship is construed without regard to whether the relationship existed as a marriage/civil partnership Wills or codicils executed between 31 December 1969 and 4 April 1988 are construed similarly (*FLRA 1969 s 15*)	This offers PRs no protection The PRs should comply with the requirements of *TA 1925 s 27* (p 169)
ACA 2002 s 67	An adopted child is treated as the child of his adopted, rather than his natural parents An adopted child is deemed to have been born on the date of adoption Where more than one child is adopted on a day, then the actual order of their births dictates the order in which they are held to have been 'born' on the day of their adoption, but this maxim does not affect any reference to their ages (*s 69(2)*)	PRs are not under a duty to enquire into adoption. They are not liable if they distribute in ignorance of an adoption (*ACA 2002 s 72*) An adopted child may seek any property to which he is entitled from other beneficiaries
LA 1976 s 5(3)	A legitimated child is treated as a legitimate one *s 5(4)* duplicates *ACA 2002 s 69(2)*	*LA 1976 s 7*: this is a similar provision to the *ACA 2002 s 72*

B Paying different types of legacy

Specific legacies

▶ These gifts vest from death, so beneficiaries are entitled to income accruing from death.

▶ If the testator disposed of the property between making the will and dying, then the gift 'adeems' (ie: it fails). If the property's form has altered but it remains substantially the same (eg: a gift of shares in a company which has been taken over in return for shares in the company), the gift will not adeem.

▶ The beneficiary is responsible for costs incurred in preserving the asset between the death and transfer, unless the will states otherwise.

▶ The PRs supply *Form 185E* stating the gross income received; this enables a beneficiary to account to HMRC and meet whatever tax liability is owed as an individual.

▶ Where an asset is transferred directly to the legatee (rather than sold), the probate value serves as the 'base cost' at which the legatee is deemed to have acquired the asset (*TCGA 1992 s 62(4)*).

Pecuniary legacies

▶ Where the will is silent, the choice of which property to pay pecuniary legacies from is determined by different sets of rules, depending upon the circumstances.

  a) **The gift of residue is valid** (ie: there is no partial intestacy)

  The legacy is paid from personalty, unless one of 3 common law rules apply:

  i) the will specifies a fund of realty and personalty from which pecuniary legacies should be paid - both types of property bear the burden of gifts proportionately (*Roberts v. Walker* (1830) 1 R & My 752).

  ii) where a gift of realty does not distinguish realty from personalty, residuary realty can be used if personalty is insufficient (*Greville v. Brown* (1859) 7 HLC 689).

  iii) the testator leaves realty specifically for the payment of pecuniary legacies.

  b) **Partial intestacy and no express trust in the will**

  A trust arises under the *AEA 1925 s 33(1)*. Pecuniary legacies are paid from undisposed of property (*s 33(2)* requires that *Sch I Part I (i)-(ii)* of the Act should be followed).

  c) **Partial intestacy and an express trust in the will**

  The *AEA 1925 s 33* institutes a trust under which pecuniary legacies are paid from money realised on the sale of undisposed of property. However, under *s 33(7)* the statutory trust is supplanted by the express trust in the will. There is conflicting authority as to whether *either*:

  i) PRs should set aside a fund for the payment of pecuniary legacies in the order dictated by *AEA 1925 Sch II Part I (i)-(ii)* (*Re Midgley* [1955] Ch 576), *or*

  ii) the common law rules (above) apply (*Re Taylor's Estate* [1969] Ch 245).

▶ If there are insufficient funds available, pecuniary legacies abate proportionately.

▶ Pecuniary legacies are payable 1 year after the testator's death. PRs are not under a duty to distribute before this period is up (*AEA 1925 s 4*).

▶ Interest is payable in the following circumstances:

  a) when a pecuniary legacy is unpaid after a year, or after the passing of a named contingency, whichever occurs first, *or*

  b) if the legacy is in satisfaction of a debt which the testator owed, *or*

  c) the beneficiary is a child of the testator and no other fund exists for that child's maintenance, *or*

  d) the beneficiary is a minor and the testator's intention was to provide for the child's maintenance.

F Problems which can arise

    I   Obtaining a grant and interpreting the will
    II   A claim under the *I(PFD)A 1975*
    III Breach of duty by a PR
    IV A PR's death
    V   Failure of a gift

➤ There are 5 areas in which difficulties are likely to arise (this list is not exhaustive!).

I Obtaining a grant and interpreting the will

1 Someone objects to the issue of a grant (*NCPR r 44*)

➤ A caveat is lodged with the Probate Registry to prevent the issue of a grant.

2 A person entitled to take an oath fails to do so *or* fails to renounce

Citation to take or refuse a grant (*NCPR r 47*)

➤ When an executor has intermeddled, but not taken steps to acquire a grant within 6 months of the testator's death, then unless the executor can show good reason for his inaction, the citator can apply to court for an order allowing letters of administration to be issued under *NCPR r 20*.

➤ An applicant wishes to 'clear off' those with prior entitlement to a grant who have not applied for a grant.

3 A person entitled to a grant wishes to prove his right when another contests it

Citation to propound a will (*NCPR r 48*)

➤ To compel a named person with an interest in the estate (beneficiary or executor) to prove a will if they can.

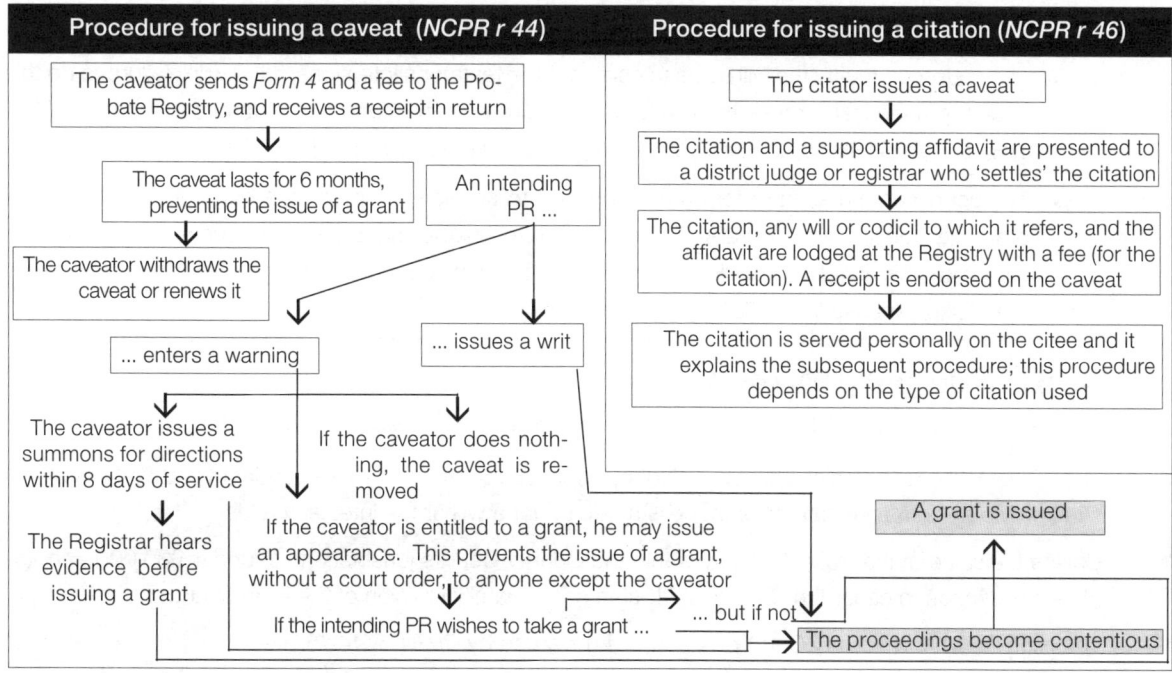

WILLS
Problems that can arise

4 The Registrar requires additional evidence before issuing the grant

Affidavit of due execution (NCPR r 16)

➤ This is necessary if *either* an attestation clause is not present *or* is corrupt, *or* there is some doubt about the execution due to uncertainty about the testator's capacity or intention.

➤ The affidavit is sworn by witnesses to the execution of the will.

Affidavit as to knowledge and approval (NCPR rr 13,16)

➤ This is necessary if the testator was blind, *or* illiterate, *or* frail, *or* there were suspicious circumstances.

➤ The affidavit is sworn by a witness, *or* anyone who went through the will with the testator and can give first-hand factual evidence.

Affidavit of plight and condition (NCPR rr 14,16)

➤ This is necessary if there are *either* alterations to the will after its execution, *or* a mark suggesting that other documents were originally attached to the will, *or* signs of an attempt to revoke the will.

➤ An affidavit is sworn by anyone with relevant first-hand factual knowledge.

Lost will (NCPR rr 15,16)

➤ Such a will is presumed to be destroyed with the intention to revoke it.

➤ If this presumption can be rebutted, or evidence can be produced to show *either* that the will existed after the testator's death *or* that a copy (or reconstruction) of it is accurate, then the Registrar may grant probate on the production of an affidavit testifying to these facts.

5 The validity of a codicil is doubted

➤ The executor(s) should commence a probate action under *NCPR r 45*.

6 The interpretation of the will is uncertain

➤ PRs may seek clarification from the court by issuing a claim form - usually this is done through an application to the Chancery Division of the High Court, but the County Court has jurisdiction for claims with a value up to £30,000.

◆ The admission of extrinsic evidence is permitted if the will is a) meaningless, *or* b) *prima facie* ambiguous, *or* c) ambiguous in the light of evidence (other than evidence of the testator's intention) (*AJA 1982 s 21*).

◆ The court can rectify the will so as to carry out the testator's intentions, if the will's failure to do this is due to a clerical error *or* the draftsman's failure to understand the testator's instructions (*AJA 1982 s 20, NCPR r 55, CPR r 57.12, Re Segelman (deceased)* [1995] 3 All ER 676, ChD).

◆ The court can make an order authorising PRs to act as instructed by a barrister who has been practising for at least 10 years. The barrister can resolve matters of construction which are *not* disputed. This absolves the PRs of liability and, since the court does not hear any argument, saves the estate expense (*AJA 1985 s 48*, see *CPR r 64*).

II A claim under the I(PFD)A 1975

➤ The *I(PFD)A 1975* allows close family (including a spouse or civil partner), dependants and co-habitees to seek provision from an estate when none is made under a will or the intestacy rules.

➤ Unless the value of the claim is clearly within the County Court's jurisdiction (ie: under £30,000), an application is made to either the Chancery Division or the Family Division of the High Court.

➤ The High Court and County Court procedure is governed by *CPR r 57.14-16*.

➤ The costs of pursuing litigation are considerable, and the defence will often send a 'Calderbank' letter to the claimant so that the claimant is liable for costs incurred after the letter.

III Breach of duty by a PR

➤ The standard of duty is that of 'utmost good faith', except for professional trustees when it is higher.
- Liability is personal and unlimited (*Kennewell v. Dye* [1949] Ch 517).
- A breach of duty occurs if a PR fails to preserve the value of estate assets, *or* to distribute as required by the will and statute, *or* uses the estate's assets for the wrong purposes (eg: self-enrichment).

➤ Unless it is excluded by the trust instrument, a trustee is under a duty of care when exercising powers conferred under *TA 2000 ss 3, 8, 11, 16-17, 34* and in certain other situations (*TA 2000 s 1, Sch 1*).

> The duty is to exercise such care and skill as is reasonable in the circumstances, having regard in particular to any special knowledge that he has (or holds himself out as having) and (if he acts in the course of a business or profession) any special knowledge or experience that it is reasonable to expect of such a person.

➤ Likely claimants include the following.

- **Missing beneficiaries**
    - The PRs should advertise to locate them, but if this fails they should seek a 'Benjamin' order from the court (*Re Benjamin* [1902] 1 Ch 723) (see *CPR r 64*). This shields the PRs from liability, but it does not prejudice the claimant's (or his PRs') right to pursue assets from other beneficiaries of the estate.

- **Creditors who are unknown to the PRs**
    - The PRs should protect themselves by:
        a) advertising in the *London Gazette,* and in a local newspaper in the vicinity of land the deceased owned, as well as placing a notice anywhere else which is appropriate (*TA 1925 s 27*).
            - An advertisement/notice must state a time period (of not less than 2 months from the date of the advertisement/notice) within which claimants may supply particulars of a claim; distribution should not begin until this period ends.
        b) searching HM Land Registry, the Central Land Charges Department and conducting local land searches to reveal any charges subsisting over land in the estate.
    - Creditors may pursue assets into the hands of the beneficiaries with a tracing action in equity.

- **Claimants under the *I(PFD)A 1975***
    - A PR should not distribute until 6 months after the grant of representation has been issued, thereafter there will be no personal liability under the *I(PFD)A 1975*, although the estate will be subject to any order which the court makes under its discretion to waive the limitation period.

- **Creditors who are unpaid after an 'unreasonable' delay**
    - PRs should pay pre-death debts with 'due diligence' (*Re Tankard* [1942] Ch 69).
    - PRs owe this duty to beneficiaries *and* creditors alike; any attempt to alter this duty by will is void.

- **Beneficiaries when debts are paid from the wrong property**
    - Where the interests of some beneficiaries are prejudiced, the doctrine of marshalling applies, so that their loss is made good from the rest of the estate.

- **Landlords**
    - Leaseholds (except statutory tenancies under the *Rent Acts*) vest in a PR in his 'representative' capacity, and *may* do so in a 'personal capacity' as a result of actual or constructive entry into possession (see table overleaf).

Liability	Release for PRs
In 'representative' capacity (*Re Bowes* **(1887) 37 Ch D128**)	
Under privity of estate: rent and breaches of covenant prior to death (to the extent that property is in their hands)	On the assignment, expiry or surrender of the lease
Under privity of contract: where the deceased was the original lessee Note: abolished for new leases granted on or after 1 January 1996 (*LT(C)A 1995 ss 1-5*)	a) PRs satisfy existing claims arising under the lease, *and* b) set aside money against any fixed or ascertained sums which the deceased had agreed in respect of the property, *and* c) assign it to a beneficiary or a purchaser (*TA 1925 s 26*)
In 'personal capacity' (*Re Owers, Public Trustee v. Death* [1941] Ch 389)	
Liable as assignees of the deceased's interest for: Covenants: liability is unlimited for any breach Rent: liability is limited to rent which the PRs actually receive, or would have done if they had acted with diligence	On the assignment, expiry or surrender of the lease, PRs can seek to protect themselves in one of 3 ways: a) taking out insurance, *or* b) seeking an indemnity from the beneficiaries, *or* c) creating an indemnity fund which is distributed to the beneficiaries once the liability has ended
Note: a landlord's remedies against beneficiaries are unaffected by any of this	

		Relieving PRs of liability
Either	a)	by the court if the PR 'acted honestly and reasonably and ought fairly to be excused' (*TA 1925 s 61*),
or	b)	in the form of an indemnity from a beneficiary's interest in the estate when the court is shown the written consent of a beneficiary who has been fully informed of the breach (*TA 1925 ss 62, 68(1)*),
or	c)	where the beneficiary (being *sui juris*) who has been fully informed of the breach of trust (known as '*devestavit*') consents to it (*Walker v. Symonds* (1818) 3 Swan 1 at 64).

IV A PR's death

➤ If a PR dies before a grant is issued, then his rights to the grant die with him.

➤ After a grant has been issued, one PR can administer the estate if the other PRs die: this is known as the chain of administration (*Flanders v. Clarke* (1747) 3 Atk 509).

➤ On the death of a sole surviving PR, the PR's executor steps into the deceased PR's shoes and shoulders all burdens and powers to administer the first testator's estate as well as the PR's estate (*AEA 1925 s 7*).

➤ Where a grant of probate or letters of administration are made to a deceased PR, and the chain of representation is broken, a grant *de bonis non administratis* is sought from the court in favour of whomever is entitled under *NCPR r 20* or *NCPR r 22* (Blackstone, *Commentaries* (14th ed), 506).

WILLS
Problems that can arise

V Failure of a gift

➤ A gift can fail through Ademption, Lapse, Abatement, or under *CPA 2004*.

1 Ademption

➤ As a will 'speaks from death', property given in the will may not still form part of the estate on death. If the substance of the gift, rather than its form, has altered then the gift fails.

2 Lapse

a) joint tenants: if a tenant predeceases the testator, the remaining tenant(s) take the gift in full - the gift does not lapse unless they all predecease the testator.

b) tenants in common: if one tenant predeceases the testator, the gift as a whole lapses.

c) class: remains valid *unless* all members of a class have predeceased the testator.

d) witness: this lapses *unless* the witness's signature merely supplemented those of 2 other valid witnesses.

e) divorced spouse/civil partner under a dissolved civil partnership:

this lapses unless the will shows a contrary intention (*WA 1837 ss 18A, 18C*).

3 Abatement

➤ Where the estate is not able to meet all the legacies, and there is no contrary intention in the will, general legacies abate in equal proportions (*Re Whitehead* [1913] 2 Ch 56).

➤ Demonstrative legacies do not abate with general legacies, unless the fund out of which the demonstrative legacies are to be paid is insufficient to pay them all (*Roberts v. Pocock* (1748) 4 Ves 150).

➤ If the estate is unable to meet all its debts, specific legacies abate amongst themselves, otherwise they do not abate with general legacies.

4 Gift to civil partner and overlapping gift to issue

➤ Unless a contrary intention is shown, if the terms by which property is devised or bequeathed to a civil partner would give a civil partner an absolute interest in that property, and the same instrument purports to give an interest to the testator's issue, the gift to the civil partner is presumed to be absolute (*CPA 2004 Sch4 para 5*).

Substitutional gifts

➤ A gift which adeems *or* lapses falls into residue, unless the will contains a valid gift over in favour of another beneficiary.

➤ *WA 1837 s 33* implies a substitutional gift to the testator's lineal descendants where the original gift was to the testator's children or remoter issue, and the intended donee predeceases the testator.

- There is no clear authority whether *WA 1837 s 33*:

    a) saves a contingent gift if the original donee has not satisfied the contingency before dying, *or*

    b) allows issue to take on satisfying the contingency specified for the original donee, *or*

    c) applies to class gifts 'to children living at my death'.

- A will should therefore always provide an express substitutional provision in case the named beneficiary predeceases the testator - this avoids uncertainty and ensures that the testator's wishes are followed.

CONVEYANCING

This chapter examines:

A	A chronological conveyance	174
B	Checking title and making searches	211
C	Variations to the standard contract	223
D	Leases	227
E	Security of tenure	233
F	Commonhold	239
G	Remedies	240

HM Land Registry plan colouring

➤ Red edging round a title.

➤ Green edging round land removed from the title.

➤ Blue shading over land subject to rights of way.

➤ Brown shading over land over which the registered title enjoys right of way.

➤ Green shading over areas of land within the title which do not form part of it.

It is not compulsory to adopt this scheme, but it is good practice to do so.

CONVEYANCING

A chronological conveyance

A   A chronological conveyance

The conveyance is divided into nine separate steps, outlined below.

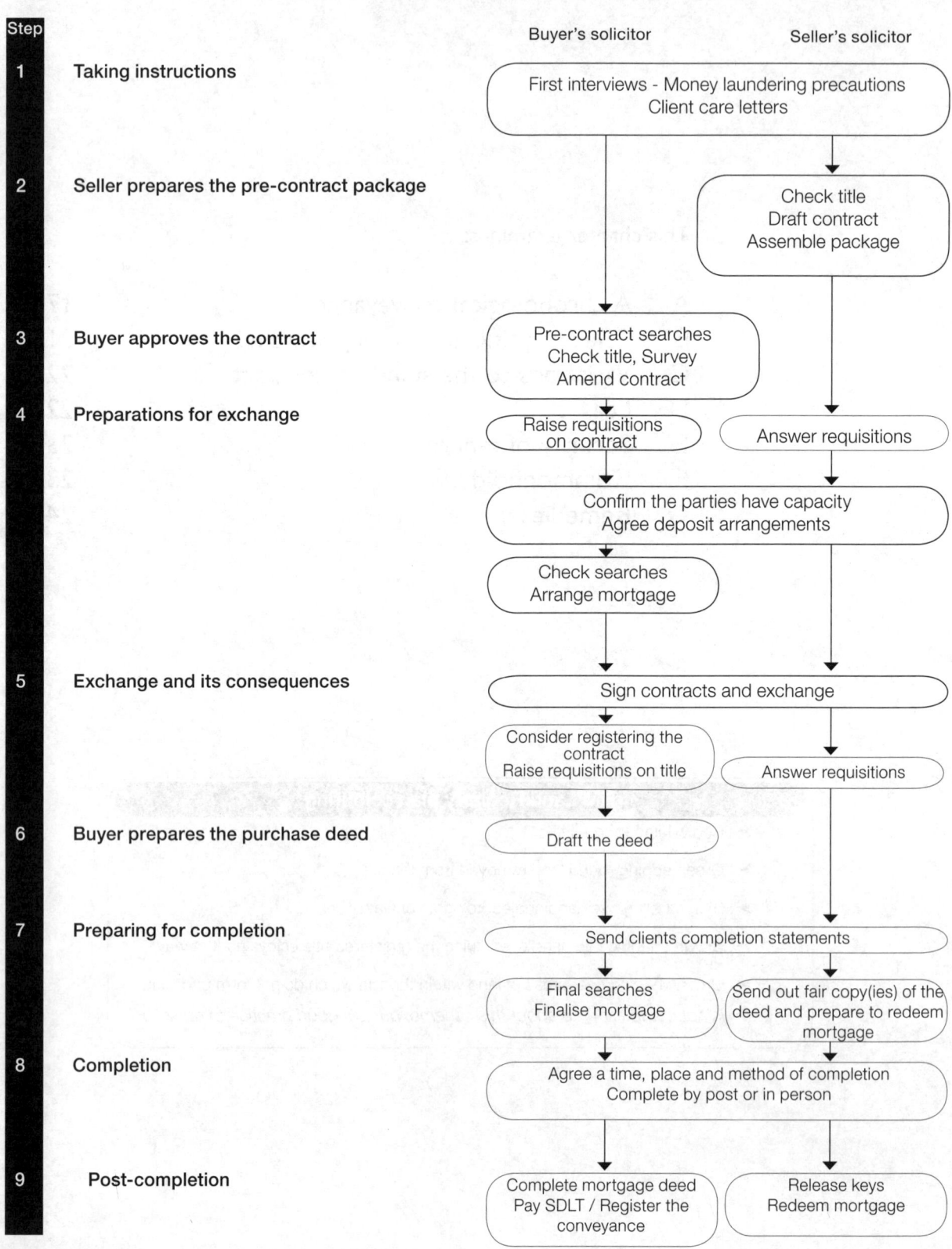

CONVEYANCING
A chronological conveyance

| Step 1 | Taking instructions |

      I   First interviews
      II   Post-interview formalities

I   First interviews

With the seller

Is there a conflict of interest? There are special provisions regarding this in *SPR rr 6-6A*

    Seller's name and address (and email): ....

    Seller's home and business telephone: ....

    Buyer's name and address: ....

    Estate agent's name and address: ....

    Buyer's solicitor's name, address, telephone, fax, DX: ....

    Property address: ....

Finance

➤ *Proceeds:*
- will these cover the costs of sale, pay off any mortgage and/or fund another purchase?
- where should money be paid (bank details, account number)? If the solicitor is to hold any client money comply with the *MLR* and *PCA 2002*.

➤ *Deposit*:
- has a preliminary deposit been paid? (Take a copy of the receipt for the file.)
- has a deposit been agreed?

- *Taxation*: will CGT be payable?
- *Mortgage*: will this need to be redeemed? (Note the name(s) and address(es) of lender(s).)
- *Solicitor's fees*: explain what these will be.

Property
- *Tenure*: freehold or leasehold? Will there be a full or limited title guarantee?
- *Deeds*: if a client does not hold them, obtain the address of whoever does (eg: building society).
- *Contents*: ask the client to fill out a fixtures and fittings form listing the property's contents.
- *Property*: are restrictive covenants breached? Have planning and use regulations been obeyed?
- *Residents:* are there any third parties with rights to occupy the property?

Transaction
- *Completion*: when convenient, synchronisation? (ie: is the seller coordinating a purchase?)
- *Terms*: have any particular terms been agreed?

With the buyer

As for the seller plus -

Finance
- *Money*: can the client afford the acquisition, including the associated costs (eg: SDLT, legal fees - estimate the cost of the searches, land registry fees, etc)?
- *Deposit*: will bridging finance be needed while an existing property is sold?
- *Mortgage*
  - Do not give advice outside *SFS(S)R 2001 r 3* unless regulated by the FSA.
  - Comply with *SIRC 1990* if the firm has a relationship with a mortgage provider.

Property
- *Intended use of the property*?
- *Survey*: the *caveat emptor* principle applies; the buyer chooses what sort of survey to have.
- *Location*: are plans, or special searches necessary?
- *Insurance:* how will the buyer protect himself from exchange to completion?

Transaction
- *Who is buying the property*: is advice about co-ownership needed?
  - For a joint tenancy the 'four unities' must be present - 'possession', 'interest', 'title' and 'time' (known as 'PITT'). If a joint tenant dies, the property passes to the survivor(s).
  - A tenancy in common arises if the 'four unities' are not present, if severance is implied or stated in a conveyance or transfer, or under an equitable presumption. Tenants' share(s) pass by will or under the intestacy rules.
- *Client's present residence*: will it be sold, and/or will notice have to be given to a landlord?

II   Post-interview formalities

- Write the client a letter complying with the *SCICCC 1999* summarising what was agreed at the meeting, what will happen next, what if anything the client needs to do, and the likely legal fees.
  - Ask the seller to fill in a *Seller's Property Information Form (prop 1)* which should ideally have been supplied at the interview, but may otherwise be enclosed with this letter.
- Fill out an attendance note.
- Write to the other party, explaining who the solicitor is acting for and how the solicitor can be contacted.
  - Explain whether the solicitor intends to use the Law Society's *Standard Terms and Conditions* and whether the solicitor wish to follow the Law Society's *Protocol*.
  - The Protocol should only be used if the other party is represented by a solicitor or a licensed conveyancer.
- Write to the estate agents to inform of the instruction to act and to ask for a copy of their particulars. (These provide information about the property which it is useful to have on file.)

| **Step 2** | **Seller propares the pre-contract package** |

      I   Check details of the seller's title
      II   Draft the contract
      III Assemble the pre-contract package
      IV Home Information Packs *[not yet in force]*

I Check details of the seller's title

➤ Find and trace the root of title (see pp 212-219).

Unregistered land	Registered land
➤ Obtain title deeds ♦ If a mortgagee holds the deeds as security, the mortgagee will usually release them in return for an undertaking from the solicitor that the mortgagee will be paid first out of any proceeds of sale	➤ Obtain an official copy of the Register

II Draft the contract

➤ All contracts take a similar form, and will generally include 3 sections:

   a) parties to the sale.

   b) conditions of the sale.

   c) memorandum of agreement.

➤ For the sake of convenience, the Law Society has produced Standard Terms and Conditions (4th ed., *October 2003*). These provide the model around which the following guide is based.

➤ When drafting a contract there are three layers of terms.

   ♦ The first layer is the open contract rules: these are terms which common law implies into contracts in the absence of any contrary intention between the parties.

   ♦ The second layer is the 'Standard Terms and Conditions' (*StC*): these form the backbone of the *StC*, and are found in small print on the inside pages of the Law Society's contract, they apply unless varied or excluded by the contract (*StC 1.1.4*).

   ♦ The third layer is the 'Special Conditions' (*SpC*): these override the *Standard Terms and Conditions*, and are found on the back page of the Law Society's contract.

➤ Check the accuracy of responses supplied by a seller against the title deeds in the solicitor's possession (a failure to do this could be a breach of *SPR r 1* as a failure to act in the client's best interests).

CONVEYANCING
A chronological conveyance

➤ A solicitor should:

a) be aware of the open contract rules, *and*

b) understand the effect of each Standard Term and Condition, *and*

c) if a client's needs have not been catered for, he should draft a Special Condition.

Complete the *Standard Terms and Conditions*

Date	Leave this blank on the draft; fill it in on the engrossed contract on exchange
Seller	Seller's full name and address
Buyer	Buyer's full name and address

Property
 	
Freehold /
Leasehold
	Delete 'Freehold' or 'Leasehold' as applicable
	
	Plan
	The contract should state whether a plan is:
	a) 'for identification purposes only' - the verbal description of the property prevails, *or*
	b) 'as more particularly delineated on the plan'. The plan prevails if doubt arises
	
	    Note that the Land Registry does not accept a plan 'for identification purposes only', and recommends a preferred scale of 1:1250-1:500 (urban property) and 1:2500 (rural property) (*Practice Guide 40*)
	    • Do not rely on the Land Registry plan - it is only a 'general boundary' unless fixed (*LRA 2002 s 60*) (for fixing boundaries, see *LRR 2003 rr 117-123*)
	
	♦ The seller is not usually obliged to make a statutory declaration (*StC 4.4.1*), but where the physical extent of the property is uncertain the buyer should insist that the seller does so
	
	A statutory declaration is usually paid for by:
	a) the seller if it is reasonable of the buyer to require one (*StC 4.4.2*), *or*
	b) the buyer in other circumstances
	Include any appurtenances (easements and rights from which the title benefits)

Title number / Root of title	*Unregistered land* : describe the root of title eg: 'the conveyance dated . . between . . (1) and ... (2)' *Registered land* : the title number on the Property Register
Specified Incumbrances	The seller should disclose: a) latent defects affecting the title to the property, *and* b) anything the seller does, or should, know about, *and* c) overriding interests in the property held by a third party, *and* d) the existence of any occupiers The seller should disclose fully, as *StC 4.2.1* prevents the buyer raising questions about incumbrances at a later date, provided they have been disclosed in the contract The seller need *not* disclose: a) his mortgage (*StC 3.1.2(d)*), *or* b) physical defects apparent on inspection (*StC 3.1.2(b)* puts the buyer on notice of these) NB: a property is sold subject to incumbrances specified in the contract and discoverable by inspection of the property before the contract (*StC 3.1.2*). A buyer accepts the property in the physical state it is in on exchange unless the seller is building or converting the property (*StC 3.2.1*).

CONVEYANCING
A chronological conveyance

Title guarantee (full / limited)	Delete as appropriate and/or qualify by a *SpC* if appropriate. If this is left blank, the seller gives full title guarantee (*StC 4.6.2*)
	
	The *LP(MP)A 1994* implies covenants into a contract governing the disposition of land (whether or not for valuable consideration). The covenants affirm that in the purchase deed the disposer:
	    1 has the right to dispose of the property (*s 2(1)*), *and*
	    2 will at his own cost give the title he purports to give (ie: title which is sufficient to satisfy the Chief Land Registrar) (*s 2(2)*), *and*
	
	a) a beneficial freeholder may give a <u>full title guarantee</u>
	    3 that the title is free of all charges and incumbrances and third party rights (*s 3(1)*)
	
	b) a trustee, fiduciary, PR or mortgagee (*s 12*) may give a <u>limited title guarantee</u>
	
	    4 that no right or charge over the property has been granted to a third party since the last disposition for value (*s 3(3)*)
	NB: a trustee appointed to overreach an equitable interest will generally not give any title guarantee
	
	c) a leaseholder (*s 4*) (in addition to 1-3, or 1,2 & 4) covenants that at the time of the disposition:
	    5 there is no breach of the tenant's obligations and nothing to render the lease liable to forfeiture, *and*
	    6 the lease is valid and subsisting
	
	d) a mortgagor covenants to perform all enforceable obligations under a rentcharge or lease (*s 5*)
	
	NB: these covenants may be modified by deleting *SpC 2* and drafting an appropriate *SpC*

Completion date	Under the open contract rules, this is in a 'reasonable time' *StC 6.1.1* specifies that completion will occur 20 working days after the contract date and that time is not of the essence unless a notice to complete is served If another date is envisaged fill that date in here
Contract rate	This is the rate of interest at which compensation is paid for delayed completion (*StC 7.3.2*) By default, the rate is 'The Law Society's interest rate from time to time in force' (*StC 1.1.1(e)*); this rate is currently 4% above Barclays base rate
Purchase price	Fill this in as agreed
Deposit	This is 10% of the total of the purchase price and the chattels price (*StC 2.2.1*) If the sum agreed differs, then fill in the agreed value here If the deposit is held as 'agent' for the seller (rather than stakeholder), then draft a *Special Condition* to this effect; this may, for example, happen where the seller is buying another property and wishes to use the deposit monies for the purchase
Chattels price (if separate)	Fill this in as agreed (details are found on the *Fixtures, Fittings and Contents Form*), or delete *SpC 3*
Balance	Add together the 'Purchase price' and the 'Chattels Price', then subtract the 'Deposit' SDLT may be payable on the sale if the consideration exceeds £125,000 (residential land) or £150,000 (non-residential or mixed land); the value of chattels is disregarded in working out how much (if any) SDLT is payable

Consider drafting *Special Conditions*:

Chattels	If the sale includes these, a *Fixtures, Fittings and Contents Form* should accompany the contract
	If chattels are not part of the sale, delete *SpC 3*

Vacant possession	Delete one of the alternative versions of *SpC 4*
	If the property is subject to leases or tenancies, then insert the details here

Liability on covenants	*StC 4.6.4* makes the buyer indemnify the seller against all future breaches of covenants. The buyer may seek a *SpC* that '*StC 4.6.4* shall not apply'
	The buyer's solicitor may try to include a *SpC* under which the seller indemnifies the buyer for any past breaches, *or* any which are current on the day of completion

Insurance	Common law passes risk to the buyer on exchange unless loss is due to the seller's lack of care
	StC 5.1.1 places risk with the seller until completion. Unfortunately, under this *StC*:
	a) the seller is under no obligation to insure the property during this time (*StC 5.1.3*), *and*
	b) the buyer may rescind if damage prevents the seller completing with the property in substantially the same state as on exchange (*StC 5.1.2(a)*)
	There are various possible solutions via *Special Conditions* to adress the lack of certainty this creates:
	a) oblige the seller to insure to completion, ensure that the terms of the policy protect the buyer's interest in the property (and that the buyer receives written notice that his interest is noted on the policy)
	b) cover the property under a block policy maintained by the solicitor
	c) take out a special policy (this is expensive and may lead to 'double insurance' and disputes between insurance companies over liability)
	d) seek agreement from a buyer or potential lender (eg: building society) to cover the risk
	NB: a lender often prefers it if the buyer to whom it will lend the purchase price takes the risk rather than leaving it up to the seller

Occupation by the buyer prior to completion	*StC 5.2* sets out terms under which, with the seller's consent, the buyer may occupy the property prior to completion.
	If these terms are inappropriate, an alternative *SpC* should be drafted

Void conditions	Conditions will be void that:
	♦ oblige a trustee to obtain consent from beneficiaries (*LPA s 42(1)*)
	♦ restrict the buyer's choice of solicitor (*LPA s 48*) - this is also a breach of *SPR r.1*
	♦ require the buyer to pay for the stamping of improperly stamped documents - this is the seller's responsibility (*SA 1891 ss 14(4), 117*)

Draft any other releases or documents which are necessary to accompany the contract.

➤ If a third party is in occupation that person may have an overriding interest or an interest under a trust of land; he or she should *either* be joined to the contract, *or* should sign a release:

> 'In consideration of the buyer entering this contract I, [..................]:
>
> a) [declare that I have no interest in or claim over the Property] / [give up any claim in or interest I may have over the Property];
>
> b) agree to the sale of the Property under this contract and will vacate the Property on or before completion of the contract; and
>
> c) will not register any rights over the Property, whether under the *FLA 1996* or otherwise, and I will ensure that any registrations made by me are removed before completion of the contract.'

♦ This should estop such a third party from entering a claim in equity.

• A child under the age of 18 should not have an equitable interest, assuming that it has not paid anything towards the cost of the property and occupies the property because its parents live there.

➤ Alternatively, appoint the third party as a trustee over the land and join them as such to the contract. This:

a) ensures any equitable interest the third party may have is overreached, *and*

b) binds the third party to vacate the property (*SpC 4*), *and*

c) implies a term into the contract that the third party will, prior to completion, remove the registration of that person's rights under the *FLA 1996*.

➤ *StC 9.3* provides that a buyer of a commonhold unit is aware of, and is taken to accept, the terms of the CCS and memorandum and articles of association of the commonhold association.

♦ A commonhold association may give notice (known as a 'commonhold unit information certificate'; *form 9*) to a new unit holder requiring it to pay debts owed to the association by a former unitholder in respect of a unit; such a sum must be paid within 14 days of the date on which the notice is given to the new unitholder (*CCS para 4.7.5*).

• If payment is not made within this time, interest runs (*CCS para 4.7.6*); when payment is made the association's right to enforce payment against the old unit holder is deemed to be assigned to the new unitholder (*CCS para 4.7.7*)

♦ To avoid such a situation arising, insert a *SpC* that any such debt will be paid prior to completion (evidenced in a manner reasonably satisfactory to the buyer, eg: a certified copy of a receipt from the commonhold association).

III   Assemble the pre-contract package

Unregistered land	Registered land
Certified copies of documents which must be included in the title: ◆ Evidence of devolution on death - death certificate, assent, grant of representation ◆ Evidence of any change of name of an estate owner - marriage certificate, deed poll, etc ◆ Discharge of any legal mortgages ◆ Pre-root documents specifying restrictive covenants ◆ Memoranda endorsed on documents of title, eg: sale of part, assent to a beneficiary, severance of a joint tenancy ◆ Power of attorney (under which a document within the chain of title has been executed) **Include an Index Map search (so the buyer can see that the land has not been registered)**	**LRA 2002 s 67:** a) Copy of Register entries b) Copy of the file plan ◆ Evidence or an abstract if registered title is inconclusive about anything ◆ A copy or an abstract of any document mentioned on the Register **StC 4.1.2** ➤ Requires an official copy (rather than a copy) of an individual register, a plan referred to in an individual register, and any document referred to in a register and kept by the registrar ➤ a) and b) may *not* be excluded by a *Special Condition*

➤ 2 copies of the draft contract
➤ Evidence of any discharged equitable interests
➤ Details of equitable interests which will be overreached in the transaction
➤ Expired leases if the tenant is still in possession
➤ Other documents referred to in the contract, or in the seller's possession which may prove helpful to the buyer:
  ◆ copies of any relevant planning permission
  ◆ NHBC certificates (if the property is a new building)
  ◆ copies of any relevant insurance certificates or guarantees (eg: relating to roofing or damp course work)
  ◆ any necessary consents (eg: building regulation consents)
  ◆ any plans
  ◆ *Seller's Property Information Form*
  ◆ 2 copies of a *Fixture, Fittings and Contents Form*
  ◆ if the property is a commonhold unit, copies of the commonhold community statement and the memorandum and articles of the commonhold association
  ◆ copies of any searches which the seller has made (these should not be relied on by the buyer, but they can provide the buyer with some comfort if a Bankruptcy search has been done against the seller (*Form K16*) showing that the seller is not subject to insolvency proceedings)
➤ Notification of the seller's target completion date(s)

IV Home Information Packs *[not yet in force]*

➤ *HA 2004 Part 5* (coming into force 1 June-2007) imposes a duty upon a 'responsible person':

a) to have in his possession, or under his control, a 'home information pack' (*HA 2004 s 155*), *and*

- A 'responsible person' is any person (the seller, and any estate agent acting for the seller) responsible for marketing residential property (*HA 2004 s 151*).

b) to provide a copy of a 'home information pack' to a potential buyer (*HA 2004 s 156*).

- A potential buyer who has made a request under *HA 2004 s 156* may be required:

  i) to pay a fee (not exceeding the reasonable cost of making and, if requested, sending a paper copy of the pack or document), *and*

  ii) to comply with written conditions relating to disclosure of that copy (*HA 2004 s 157*).

♦ These duties lie with an estate agent, rather than a seller, if an estate agent is acting for the seller and the seller is not taking (or has ceased to take) action which makes public that the property is on the market (*HA 2004 s 153*).

➤ This duty applies with respect to 'residential property' (premises in England and Wales consisting of a single dwelling-house, including any ancillary land (*HA 2004 s 148(1)*)), but not to:

♦ mixed commercial and residential property, *or*

♦ sales of tenanted properties (*HA 2004 s 160*), *or*

♦ leases of less than 21 years, *or*

♦ property excluded under *HIPR 2006 Part 5*.

➤ The contents of a home information pack are specified in the *HIPR 2006* - these include 'required' documents (listed in *r 8*) and 'authorised' documents (listed in *r 9*).

♦ A pack must include required pack documents, and may include authorised pack documents (*HIPR 2006 r 13*).

♦ Information advertising or marketing goods or services must not be included in a pack (*HIPR 2006 r 12*.)

➤ If a responsible person amends/obtains an updated version of a required document, he must include that amended/updated version (*HIPR 2006 r 18*)

♦ A responsible person may update an 'authorised' document (*HIPR 2006 r 20*) :

➤ The enforcement of duties imposed by *HA 2004 Part 5* is the responsibility of a local weights and measures authority, which may issue a penalty charge notice. Such a notice may require payment of an amount not exceeding £500 (*HA 2004 ss 167-168*, *Sch 8*).

♦ Breach of the duty to provide a copy of a home information pack, following a request from a potential buyer for a copy of a document which should be included in a pack, entitles that buyer to recover from the seller the cost of any reasonable fee incurred in obtaining a copy of that document (*HA 2004 s 170*).

Overview of 'required pack documents'

➤ The following are 'required pack documents' (*HIPR 2006 r 8*):

a) an index to the home information pack (complying with *HIPR 2006 Sch 2*), *and*

b) a sale statement (complying with *HIPR 2006 Sch 2*), *and*

c) evidence of title (eg: for registered land, an official copy of the register and the title plan)[§], *and*

d) a search of all parts of the appropriate land charges register, and search reports which comply with *HIPR 2006 Schs 8-9*[§], *and*

e) planning consents/building regulation certificates, *and*

f) seller's property information form, *and*

g) if the property is physically completed on or before the first point of marketing:

 i) a home condition report which complies with *HIPR 2006 Sch 5*, *and/or*

 ii) the terms of a new homes warranty which complies with *HIPR 2006 Sch 6* and an energy performance certificate,

 - If the property is not physically complete at that time, a document which complies with *HIPR 2006 Sch 7* must be included.

 i) any other home condition report which complies with *HIPR 2006 Sch 5* and was completed within 12 months preceeding the first point of marketing.

➤ For commonholds, required/authorised documents are set out in *HIPR 2006 Sch 3*.

➤ For leaseholds, the following are required documents (*HIPR 2006 Sch 4*):

a) a lease, *and*

b) regulations made by a landlord/management company, *and*

c) statements or summaries of service charges relating to the 36 months preceding the point of first marketing, *and*

d) the most recent requests for payment relating to the 12 months preceding the point of first marketing relating to service charges, ground rent, and insurance.

§ certain documents must be dated/obtained no earlier than 3 months before the date of first marketing (*HIPR r 14*).

Note: *In July 2006, the Government announced that the requirement to introduce home condition reports will not be compulsory when the legilsation comes into force on 1 June 2007.*

Step 3	Buyer approves the contract

      I   Make pre-contract searches
      II   Check the title documents supplied
      III Investigate each document
      IV Check the terms of any restrictive covenants
      V   Ensure there are no planning difficulties
      VI Commission a survey
      VII Check and amend the contract

I Make pre-contract searches

➤ For the searches necessary at this stage, see p 220.

II Check the title documents supplied

➤ The documents required are set out on pp 212-210.

➤ Questions to ask:
- is the root as described in the contract?
- is the chain unbroken since the root?
- are there any defects in title adverse to the buyer's interest?

III Investigate each document

A Registered land

➤ Check that the official copy of the register is correct and that priority periods have not expired, or are not about to expire.
- All land in England and Wales has been subject to compulsory registration from 1 December 1990.
- The *LRA 2002* allows Her Majesty to grant an estate in fee simple in absolute possession out of demesne land to Herself; such a grant is only treated as having been made if an application for registration is made. Certain other estates granted by Her Majesty must also be registered (*ss 79-85, LRR 2003 r 173*).
  - Land held by the Crown in demesne does not subsist as an estate in land and so, prior to the *LRA 2002*, could not be registered.

➤ Check that any plans are accurate.

B Unregistered land

➤ Start at the root, make written notes of omissions in the list of documents and of errors in the documents.

- Check
  - **Requirement of registration:** do an Index Map search (if not supplied by the seller) to ensure there has been no conveyance or sale since the area became subject to registration.
  - **Searches:** were these done against *all* previous owners under the correct names for the correct periods? Was completion for previous transfers within the priority period? Will completion be within the priority period? (If the answer to this question is 'no', the buyer should do a fresh search.)
  - **Incumbrances:** what are they? Is there an unbroken chain of indemnity for covenants?
  - **Easements and rights:** do they follow the title? Are there additions or subtractions?
  - **Description of property:** is this accurate? Are plans provided where necessary?
  - **Dates:** do these form an unbroken chain from the root?
  - **Parties:** check the identities of the parties to conveyances (eg: their names may have altered due to marriage or divorce; if so ask for documentary evidence to verify this).
  - **Receipt clause in a conveyance:** this is evidence that a seller's lien has been extinguished.
  - **Acknowledgement for the production of earlier deeds:** if needed, are the deeds present?
  - **Execution:** was this done by the correct parties in the correct form (ie: if positive covenants are present, did the buyers and the sellers both sign the conveyance)? Were there any assents by deed (this imports consideration without which an assentee is not bound)?
  - **Power of attorney:** if one was used, was it valid? A copy of the grant should be supplied.
  - **Endorsements on deeds:** if needed, are these present? Are there adverse memoranda?

➤ Examine documents included in the abstract of title.

- Deeds must be in the correct form:

BEFORE 31 JULY 1990
  - by an individual: signed, sealed, delivered as a deed. The seal must precede the signature. Delivery depends on intention; this is inferred from the signature and seal (*LPA s 73*).
  - by a company: sealed before a company secretary and a director (*LPA s 74*).

AFTER 31 JULY 1990

Clear on its face that it is a deed and delivered as a deed (*LP(MP)A 1989 s 1(2)(a)*):

  - by an individual: signed, signature witnessed and attested, or signed in his presence and at his command before 2 witnesses who attest the deed (*LP(MP)A 1989 s 1(3)*).
  - by a company: execution by affixing a seal, *or* by signature of a director and company secretary, or 2 directors if the document is expressed to be executed by the company. Execution and delivery are presumed if it is clear on its face that the document was intended as a deed (*CA s 36A(5)*).
  - by a LLP (formed under *LPA 2000*): as for a company, except signature is by 2 members.
- If a transaction is not a SDLT transaction (*FA 2003 Sch 19*) there should be a 'Particulars Delivered' stamp from HMRC on:
  a) freehold conveyances, *and*
  b) grants or assignments of leases of 7 years or more (*FA 1931 s 28*).
- If the instrument was chargeable to stamp duty (eg: executed prior to 1 December 2003), it should be duly stamped or certified to be exempt from duty.

IV Check the terms of any restrictive covenants

1. Inform the buyer that the covenant exists.
2. Find out whether it:
   a) affects the buyer's plans for the property, *or*
   b) has been breached in the past (eg: by building work), *or*
   c) adversely alters the property's value (a covenant preserving the character of the neighbourhood may actually enhance the value of a property, eg: if it was imposed by a developer and is rigorously enforced).

Validity
3. Does wording effectively annex the covenant to the land? If it does not, the covenant may be unenforceable.
4. If the covenant is post-1925, is it noted on the Charges Register, or as a Class D(ii) land charge?
   ➤ An unregistered covenant will be unenforceable.

Options if valid
5. If the covenant is valid, consider three options:
   a) Insurance: the insurance company will normally need:
      - a copy of the document imposing the covenant, or its exact wording, *and*
      - details of past breaches, and a copy of any planning permission for development, *and*
      - the date of the covenant's imposition, *and*
      - the date of the covenant's registration, *and*
      - a description of the nature of the neighbourhood, *and*
      - steps taken to trace whoever has the benefit of the covenant.
   b) Consent of the person with the benefit of the covenant to release/waive the covenant.
   c) An application to the Lands Tribunal to remove the covenant (*LPA s 24*): this is slow and expensive.

V Ensure there are no planning difficulties

Check ...

a) ...the date the property was originally built *and* the dates of subsequent additions or extensions.

b) ...that any alterations within the last 4 years *either* had planning permission *or* did not need it (and that any covenants in a lease have been complied with).

c) ..that any change of use over the last 10 years *either* did not need planning permission, *or* that it was granted (*and* that consent was granted by a landlord, if needed).

d) ...whether building regulation consent was gained *and* complied with for work done in the past year.

e) ...whether the property is a listed building *or* in a conservation area.

CONVEYANCING
A chronological conveyance

Planning permission

1. **A 'development' requiring permission (*TCPA 1990 s 55*) involves *either*:**

   a) 'building, engineering, mining, in, on, over or under the land', *or*

   b) a 'material change' in use, (ie: not within same use class under *TCP(UC)O 1987*), *or*

   c) an alteration of a listed building, or demolition in a conservation area (*P(LBCA)A 1990 s 74*).

2. **Limited permission to develop without permission is available (*TCP(GPD)O 1995*) for:**

   a) maintenance work.

   b) internal work not affecting the exterior.

   c) use within the curtilage of a building for a purpose incidental to dwelling in the building.

   d) change of use within a use class, *TCP(UC)O 1987*: A1, most shops; A2, providing financial or professional services to the public; B1, use as an office outside A2.

   e) development within a general development order, or under a local authority's *Article 4* direction.

3. **Applications for planning permission**

   ➤ An applicant need not own land, but must tell the owner (*TCPA 1990 s 66*); if a development order requires it, it will be necessary to advertise the application in the local press (*TCPA 1990 s 65*).

   ➤ There are two main types of permission.

   a) **Outline permission:** matters which are 'reserved' must be approved within 3 years.

   Work must usually start within 2 years from approval being granted for matters 'reserved' (*TCPA 1990 s 91*).

   b) **Full permission:** no matters 'reserved'; work must usually begin in 3 years (*TCPA 1990 s 92*).

   ➤ Listed building consent

   This is required for altering listed buildings. It should only be granted after considering 'the building or its setting or any features of architectural or historic interest' (*P(LBCA)A 1990 s 72*).

   ➤ Conservation area consent

   This is required to demolish a building in a conservation area. It should only be granted after considering 'preserving or enhancing the appearance of the area' (*P(LBCA)A 1990 s 66*).

4. **Penalties/enforcement**

   ➤ An enforcement notice may be served up to 4 years after a breach if there are unauthorised building operations, or an unauthorised change of use to a use as a single dwelling house. Otherwise, a notice may be served within 10 years of any other breach (*TCPA 1990 s 172*).

   ➤ The local authority may issue:

   a) a stop notice (*TCPA 1990 s 183*): where an enforcement notice has been served, this compels builders to stop work or face criminal penalties.

   b) a temporary stop notice (*TCPA 1990 ss 171E-H*): where it thinks there has been a breach of planning control and it is expedient to stop the activity immediately.

   c) a breach of condition notice (*TCPA 1990 s 187A*): to compel compliance with a condition.

   d) completion notice (*TCPA 1990 ss 94-96*): to compel the recipient to complete work.

   e) a repair notice (*P(LBCA)A 1990 ss 47-48*): to protect a listed building; may be a prelude to compulsory purchase.

   f) a building preservation notice (*P(LBCA)A 1990 s 3*): to prevent demolition or alteration.

VI   Commission a survey

➤ There are 3 common types of 'survey' which a buyer can commission:

   1   Valuation

   ✓ Cheap and fast.

   ✗ Very superficial, it only provides a guide as to whether a price appears fair in the present market.

   2   House buyer's report and valuation

   ✓ This is more thorough than a valuation.

   ✗ A surveyor's duty is owed primarily to the lender. (With very 'low' priced property there is a duty to the buyer as well (*Smith v. Eric S. Bush* [1990] 1 AC 831).)

   ✗ A lender is primarily concerned with ascertaining the property's resale value, so the survey will not give the buyer a clear idea of any major works which will need doing in the future.

   3   Full structural survey

   ✓ This is always relatively expensive.

   ✓ A full structural survey always provides the most detailed information.

   ✓ If the property is unusual (eg: has its own drains in a remote location), a buyer can request special checks.

   ✓ The surveyor owes the buyer a duty of care, and may be held liable in contract or tort.

   ◆ A survey is always advisable, but it should be considered particularly if:

   - the property's construction is unconventional, *or*
   - the property is in an unstable area, or is likely to be a source of structural problems (eg: mining area), *or*
   - the property is not detached, *or*
   - the property is of high value, *or*
   - the property is over 100 years old, *or*
   - a mortgage will provide only a small proportion (eg: under 75%) of the purchase price, *or*
   - alterations or extensions are planned, *or*
   - the property is not in good condition.

➤ Consider environmental liabilities and what action to take if contamination may be an issue.

   ◆ Compliance with a remediation notice issued by a local authority or the Environment Agency under *EPA 1990 Part IIA* may be prohibitively expensive; other relevant legislation includes *CL(E)R 2000*, *GR 1998* and the *PPC(EW)R 2000*. See also DETR *Guidance on Contaminated Land* (April 2000) and the Law Society's warning card issued in June 2001.

   ◆ If a person (a 'class A person') who causes or knowingly permits contamination cannot be identified, liability falls on an owner/occupier of land (including a mortgagee in possession) (a 'class B person') and complex exclusion provisions deal with the transfer of liability.

   - Make full enquiries, seek a specialist site investigation and consider where liability rests (under contract and the statutory exclusion provisions). It may be appropriate to require a seller to remedy contamination before completion, or to advise withdrawal from a transaction.

VII Check and amend the contract

Amending the contract

➤ Use red ink (and then green ink) to make amendments.

➤ Date alterations.

➤ Note on the contract 'Approved as drawn/amended on . . . [date].'

➤ Questions to ask
- Does the contract fulfill a client's instructions?
- Does it reflect what the buyer actually wants?
- Is it concise and unambiguous?
- Does it cater for the resolution of disputes?
- Does it describe the property accurately?
- Is a plan needed, and if so is one supplied to an adequate scale?
- Is the seller offering full title guarantee and if not, why not?
    - If the answer to this final question is 'no', it is for the buyer to make a commercial judgment of the extent of any liability, the risk involved in the circumstances, and the likely impact on the property's resale value.

Competition Act 1998

➤ Certain agreements relating to land are excluded from *CA 1998 Part I (Agreements affecting UK trade having the effect of preventing, restricting or distorting competition)* under the *CA 1998(LAER)O 2004*.
- *CA 1998 Part I* came into force on 1 March 2000.

➤ The exclusions embrace:
  a) a 'land agreement' which creates, alters, transfers, or terminates an interest in land, or an agreement to enter into such an agreement (*CA 1998(LAER)O 2004 r 4*), *and*
  b) obligations, or restrictions, which are ancillary to a land agreement imposed and accepted in the capacity of a holder of an interest in land (*CA 1998(LAER)O 2004 r 5*).

  Eg: positive or restrictive covenants as to user, or (in the case of a lease) covenants not to assign without obtaining a landlord's consent, to repair, or to insure.

➤ However the exclusions in the *CA 1998(LAER)O 2004* do not protect restrictions:
  a) to the terms of trading activity (eg: by reference to a type of product, brand, quantity, cost etc), *or*
  b) which relate to any trading relationship between landlord and tenant (eg: requiring the tenant to buy only from the landlord).

CONVEYANCING
A chronological conveyance

| Step 4 | Preparations for exchange |

  I   Precautions regarding the parties
  II Searches
  III Deposit
  IV Mortgage arrangements

I Precautions regarding the parties

1 Minors

➤ Provided that there is no restriction on the Register, the buyer may assume the seller is over 18.

➤ If land is held on trust *and* ...

  ... the trust instrument provides that a person should consent to any act of the trustees in relation to the land *and* that person is a minor, *then* ...

  ... a buyer is not prejudiced if this consent is not obtained.

  - Trustees of land are under a duty to obtain consent from the minor's parent, or whoever has parental responsibility for him or is his guardian (*TLATA 1996 s 10(3)*).

➤ A contract may be repudiated during a minority or in a reasonable time of majority (*MCA 1987*).

  ◆ A conveyance to a minor used to operate like a contract to convey (*SLA 1925 s 27(1)*), but from 1 January 1997 a conveyance has operated as a declaration of trust over land in favour of the minor (a contract under *SLA 1925 s 27* now also operates as a trust) (*TLATA 1996 Sch 1, para 1*).

2 Married couples/Civil partners

➤ If the seller is married/a civil partner, a spouse/civil partner may have 'home rights' (*FLA 1996 ss 30-31*); these may be registered already *but* they can be registered at any time before completion.

  ◆ A spouse/civil partner should either be:

  a) asked to execute a release before exchange, *or*

  b) appointed as a trustee and made party to the contract. This ensures:

  i)   any equitable interest the spouse/civil partner may have is overreached, *and*

  ii) binds the spouse/civil partner to vacate the property (*SpC 4*), *and*

  iii) implies a term into the contract that the spouse will remove any *FLA* notice prior to completion.

  ■ Such a trustee would not usually give any title guarantee.

  ◆ A right registered under the *FLA 1996* can be removed by submitting to the Registrar (assuming land is registered) (see further *Practice Guide 20*) *either*:

  - an application from the spouse/civil partner benefiting from it, *or*

  - an official copy of a court decree stating that the marriage/civil partnership has been terminated, *or*

  - an official copy of a court order ending the spouse/civil partner's home rights, *or*

  - a death certificate (*FLA 1996 Sch 4, paras 4(1)(a)-(c), 5(1)*).

➤ See also (3) overleaf for land held on trust for sale, or (after 1 January 1997) under a trust of land.

3   **Land held on trust**

➤ If land is held on trust, pay to all the trustees (being 2-4) or a trust corporation (*LPA ss 2, 27*).

- If there is only one trustee (not being a trust corporation), a second trustee should be appointed *either*:

    a)   before the contract is entered into, *or*

    b)   after the contract is entered into (so that the seller can fulfill the covenants as to title).

- A second trustee appointed to satisfy *LPA ss 2, 27* may not be prepared to give any covenant as to title, but the original owner who holds subject to the trust may give full or limited title guarantee.

➤ If a sole owner is named as the proprietor on the Register, comply with any restriction to take free of any equitable interest.

➤ There may be a restriction on the Register regarding a joint tenancy.

- On the death of a tenant the legal estate vests in the survivor(s), *either*:

    a)   execute a vesting assent in favour of a fully entitled survivor, *or*

    b)   insist on the appointment of another trustee and pay the purchase money to them both.

    - If a joint tenant murders his fellow tenant, the property does not pass on survivorship.

- If there is no restriction, assume that joint tenants hold absolutely; evidence of the deceased tenant's death (eg: death certificate) is needed (*LRR 2003 r 164*).

➤ From 1 January 1926, tenants in common and joint tenants held land under a trust for sale (under which they had a duty to sell land and a power to postpone sale). From 1 January 1997 land has been held by trustees under a trust of land (under which trustees have a power to sell land and a power to postpone sale).

- Trustees of land are under a duty to 'as far as is practicable, consult the beneficiaries of full age and beneficially entitled to an interest in possession in the land' (*TLATA 1996 s 11(1)*) (see box on next page).

- A buyer of unregistered land who is not put on notice is not prejudiced by any limitation of the trustees' power to convey land, or their failure to consult beneficiaries (*TLATA 1996 s 16(1)*).

    - A buyer who is on notice may take subject to the trust.

- A buyer of unregistered land is not (in any circumstances) prejudiced by any act of the trustees which contravenes any enactment or a rule of law or equity (*TLATA 1996 s 16(2)*).

- Trustees of unregistered land must, if the beneficiaries are absolutely entitled and of full age, execute a deed declaring that they are discharged from the trust. If they fail to do so, a court may order them to do so.

    - A buyer may rely on such a deed, provided he is not on notice that the trustees erred in making the conveyance to the beneficiaries (*TLATA 1996 s.16(4)-(5)*).

Overview of the powers and duties of trustees of land

➤ Trustees have power to sell land and power to postpone sale (*TLATA 1996 s 4*).

♦ This power can be expressly excluded or modified in the trust instrument or will (*TLATA 1996 s 8*).

> ➤ For trustees' power to buy a legal estate in land (leasehold or freehold) anywhere in the United Kingdom, see *TA 2000 s 8*.

➤ Trustees of land, when exercising 'any function' relating to the land subject to the trust must:

a) 'as far as practicable' consult beneficiaries who are of full age and beneficially entitled to an interest in possession, *and*

b) give effect to the beneficiaries' wishes, so far as is consistent with the general interest of the trust. If the beneficiaries dispute among themselves, the trustees should have regard to the wishes of the majority (by reference to the value of their combined interests under the trust) (*TLATA 1996 s 11(1)*).

• This does not apply either to trusts which expressly exclude this requirement *or* to will trusts which arose before 1 January 1997 (*TLATA 1996 s 11(2)*).

• This only applies to trusts created before 1 January 1997, if such of the settlor(s) who are still alive and of full capacity execute(s) a deed making an irrevocable election that it shall apply (*TLATA 1996 s 11(3)-(4)*).

➤ If the beneficiaries are of full age and absolutely entitled the trustees may, having obtained their consent, partition land, convey it to them or mortgage it to pay the beneficiaries 'equality money' (*TLATA 1996 s 7*).

♦ This power can be expressly excluded or modified in the trust instrument (*TLATA 1996 s 8*).

➤ If beneficiaries are of full age and absolutely entitled to an interest in possession, the trustees may delegate, by power of attorney, any of their functions as trustees which relate to the land (*TLATA 1996 s 9*).

➤ Trustees may not act so as to prevent *any* person occupying land from remaining in occupation, or so as to make it likely that *any* person might cease to occupy land, unless that person consents, or the trustees obtain a court order under *TLATA 1996 ss 14-15*.

➤ A beneficiary's interest under a trust is no longer subject to the 'doctrine of conversion' under which land given to a beneficiary under trust for sale was deemed to be a gift of the proceeds from the sale of the land, and a beneficiary of a trust of money to be invested in land had an interest in the land rather than the cash. Land is now be treated as land, and personal property as personal property (*TLATA 1996 s 3*).

♦ This does not apply to a will trust if the testator died before 1 January 1997 (*TLATA 1996 ss 3(2), 18(3)*), otherwise it applies to a trust irrespective of whether that trust arises or was created before or after that date (*TLATA 1996 s 3(3)*).

CONVEYANCING
A chronological conveyance

> ### The rights of beneficiaries under trusts of land
>
> ➤ A beneficiary of a trust of land, who is absolutely entitled to an interest in possession under the trust may occupy the land if occupation is among the purposes of the trust, or the trustees hold the land so that it is available for occupation, provided the land is not unsuitable for occupation by that beneficiary (*TLATA 1996 s 12*).
>
> ➤ If 2 or more beneficiaries are entitled to occupy land held on trust, trustees may not:
>
> - unreasonably exclude a beneficiary's right to occupy land, or restrict it with regard to:
>   - the purposes for which the land is held, *or*
>   - the settlor's intentions, *or*
>   - each beneficiary's circumstances, *but*
> - they may impose reasonable conditions on occupation, such as requiring a beneficiary to:
>   - pay outgoings or expenses in respect of the land, *or*
>   - assume any obligation in relation to the land or activities which take, or may take place on it (eg: comply with farming regulations, insure against a claim under the OLA 1984), *or*
>   - pay compensation to other beneficiaries whose entitlement to occupy the land has been restricted or excluded, *and*
>   - forgo another benefit under the trust to which the beneficiary would otherwise have been entitled (*TLATA 1996 s 13*).
>
> ➤ These provisions of *TLATA 1996* may *not* be excluded in the trust instrument and they apply to all trusts of land from 1 January 1997.

4 PRs

➤ PRs may become registered as proprietors of registered land by submitting the grant of probate (*LRR 2003 r 163*).

- **PR is registered:** the buyer should comply with any restriction on the Register.
- **PR is not registered:** the buyer should request a certified copy of a grant of probate and submit it with his application for registration.

➤ From 1 July 1995, one PR ceased to be able to bind the estate by contract. All the PRs who take a grant must be party to both the contract and the purchase deed (*LP(MP)A 1994 s 16*).

- Where there is a sole PR, the death certificate and the grant must be produced to show he acts alone.

➤ PRs do *not* need to seek consent from those interested in the administration of an estate before they sell land for the purposes of administration (*TLATA 1996 s 18*).

5 Companies (*LRR 2003 rr 181-185*)

➤ Lenders may insist that the Memorandum and Articles are checked to confirm that the company is acting within its powers, but a buyer should not be prejudiced if this is not done (*CA s 35A*).

➤ Limitations on the power to purchase may be contained in a restriction on the Register.

6 Charities (*LRR 2003 rr 176-180*)

➤ If there is no restriction, no precautions are needed. Otherwise check:

a) whether the transaction was authorised by statute or the deed governing the charity.

b) whether the charity has been granted an exemption certificate under the *Charities Act 1992*.

c) if there is no exemption certificate, whether consent has been gained. This needs evidence that:

- the trustees are satisfied that the deal is a good one, *and*
- the land was advertised for a period, and in the way a surveyor advised, *and*
- there is a written report from a qualified surveyor approving the sale, *and*
- prescribed words have been inserted stating that:
  - the charity is not exempt, *and*
  - the land is subject to *CA 1992 s 32*, *and*
  - the land is held on trust for the charity, *and*
  - the requirements of *s 32* have been complied with.

7 Mental impairment

➤ A contract or conveyance for value is binding unless one of the parties is unaware of the other's disability (*Hart v. O'Connor* [1985] 2 All ER 880), in which case it is voidable. A conveyance for no value involving someone of unsound mind is void.

➤ A receiver may deal with property with the court's consent (*MntHA 1983 s 99*); there will be no restriction on the Register unless the receiver is registered as the proprietor.

➤ If a trustee is mentally incapable of exercising his functions as a trustee, *and* ...

... all the beneficiaries are fully entitled *and* of full age, *and* ...

... nobody is willing and able to appoint a trustee to replace him under *TA 1925 s 36(1)*, then

... the beneficiaries may issue a written direction to the trustee's receiver, his attorney under an enduring power of attorney, or a person authorised under *MntHA 1983 Part VII*, requesting that person to appoint a replacement trustee (*TLATA 1996 s 20*).

◆ A buyer should ask to see a certified copy of any such direction together with the deed of appointment.

- Pre-contract enquiries should include a question as to whether a direction has been made and requisitions on title could include a request for confirmation that none of the beneficiaries withdrew the direction before it was complied with under *TLATA 1996 s 21(1)*.

Undue influence (non commercial surety) *(Royal Bank of Scotland v Etridge* [2001] UK HL 44)

➤ The client and the solicitor should meet face to face without the principal debtor present.
- The solicitor's duty is to his client alone and he is concerned only with his client's interests.
- The solicitor must be alive to any potential conflicts of interest and if these inhibit or may inhibit his advice he must not act or continue to act (if already acting).

➤ The solicitor should explain the purpose of his/her involvement.
- The lender will rely on a solicitor's involvement to counter suggestions of:
  a) lack of proper understanding of the transaction and its implications, *and*
  b) influence or pressure by the principal debtor.
- The solicitor must obtain the client's confirmation to act and advise on the legal and practical implications of the transaction.
- The solicitor should obtain from the lender any information that he may need.

➤ Advice should depend on the circumstances of each case; the minimum requirements include:
  a) explaining the documents and the consequences of signing them and ensuring that the client understands the worst case scenario such as the loss of a home and bankruptcy.
  b) explaining the seriousness of the risks involved.
     - The client should be told of:
       i) the purpose of the loan, its amount and principal terms, *and*
       ii) the possibility of the amount being increased, the terms being changed or a new facility being granted without notification, *and*
       iii) the amount of the client's liability (if it is unlimited the client must be made aware of that fact) and the client's means of meeting the liability should be considered.
     - The availability of other assets to meet repayments should be discussed as this enables the seriousness of the risk to be quantified.
  c) indicating that the client has a choice as to whether to proceed or not - the decision to agree or not agree is the client's alone.
     - Explanation of this choice may require a review of the client's current financial position including present indebtedness and current loan facilities.

➤ The client should be asked if he/she wishes to proceed.
- The client must indicate that he/she is content for the solicitor to confirm to the lender that the nature and effect of the documents have been explained.
- Instructions should be sought as to whether the terms of the documents should be negotiated.
  - The solicitor should consider with the client the need to:
    a) limit liability in terms of amount and/or time, *and*
    b) limit the lender's ability to change terms, amounts etc without the client's prior approval, *and*
    c) agree the order in which the lender will resort to available assets on enforcement to ensure that all other available assets are realised before resort is made to the client's assets.

Powers of an owner of registered land under *LRA 2002*

- *LRA 2002*, unlike the *LRA 1925*, specifies the powers which an owner of registered land enjoys.
- An owner of a registered estate has the power to (*LRA 2002 s 21(1)*):
    a) make a disposition of any kind permitted by the general law in relation to the registered estate, *and*
    b) to charge the estate at law with the payment of money.
- An owner of a registered charge has the power to (*LRA 2002 ss 21(2)-(3)*):
    a) make a disposition of any kind permitted by the general law in relation to that charge, other than:
        i) a transfer by way of mortgage, *or*
        ii) a sub-mortgage by sub-demise, *or*
        iii) a charge by way of legal mortgage, *and*
    b) charge at law with the payment of money indebtedness secured by a registered charge.
- A person who is the registered proprietor of a registered estate or charge, or entitled to be registered as proprietor of a registered estate or charge, may exercise an owner's powers (*LRA 2002 s 24*).
- A person's right to exercise an owner's powers is free from any limitation affecting the validity of a disposition, other than a limitation reflected by an entry on the register or imposed by, or under, the *LRA 2002* (*LRA 2002 s 26*).
    - Charge certificates have been abolished and the importance of land certificates reduced; the registered owner is presumed to have unrestricted powers of disposition in the absence of any register entry.

II Searches

- The buyer should check that these are all correct, and that exchange will occur before priority periods expire.

III Deposit

1 Where is the deposit coming from?

➤ Payment (unless sale is by auction) is by direct credit (a direct transfer of cleared funds to an account nominated by the seller's conveyancer and maintained by a clearing bank), or a cheque drawn on cleared funds from a solicitor's or licensed conveyancer's client account (*StC 2.2.3-2.2.4*).

- ◆ If a client account cheque is used the solicitor must be put in funds at least 5 working days in advance to ensure it clears (otherwise the *SARs 1998* may be breached).

➤ If payment is from a deposit account ensure that notice of withdrawal is given sufficiently early to avoid incurring an interest penalty *and* to make certain that the money is released for exchange.

➤ If bridging finance is required, arrange this in good time.

- ✓ A loan may qualify for tax relief as a 'charge on income'.
- ✗ A loan may be expensive.
- ✗ If the sale does not proceed liability must be discharged fast to prevent exorbitant interest payments.

2 How will the deposit be held?

➤ As agent for the seller

- ◆ This is the position under the general law unless the parties agree otherwise (or an auctioneer holds the deposit, in which case the auctioneer holds as stakeholder).
- ◆ *StC 2.2.5* permits a seller to use the deposit, or part of it, as a deposit on the purchase of a property in England or Wales as his residence, if the related purchase contract is entered into before completion (ie: of the contract for the seller's sale) and that related contract contains similar provisions to *StC 2.2.5-2.2.6*.
- ◆ A trustee is under a duty not to lose control of money held on trust, so if the seller is a trustee the seller's solicitor should hold the deposit as the seller's agent.

➤ As stakeholder (envisaged by *StC 2.2.6*)

- ◆ Unless the sellers are trustees *or* the seller wishes to use the deposit to buy another property (in accordance with *StC 2.2.5*), the seller's solicitor holds the deposit as stakeholder and is obliged to pay it to the seller on completion, together with accrued interest.

3 Where will the deposit be held?

➤ In a deposit account? This depends on whether interest penalties are imposed for short-term deposits and the feasibility of transferring money so it is available at need.

4 Interest on the deposit

➤ The solicitor must pay the client interest in accordance with *SAR 1998 r 24*.

➤ Estate agents must account to their client for interest over £500 (*EA(A)R 1981 r 7*).

➤ If money is held as stakeholder, interest should be paid to the buyer on completion (*StC 2.2.6*).

5 Troubleshooting

➤ Deposit insurance: an insurance policy is advisable if it is feared the seller may run off with the deposit.

➤ Buyer's lien: this attaches to the house for the amount of any deposit.

- ◆ The buyer can protect it with a notice (Registered land) or a C(iii) charge (Unregistered land).

➤ Estate agents must carry insurance against insolvency while holding a deposit (*EAA 1979 s 16*).

➤ If the cheque bounces this breaches a condition of the contract: the seller can treat the breach as repudiatory (*StC 2.2.2*), or allow the contract to continue. In either case he may sue for damages.

IV Mortgage arrangements

Types of mortgage			
Repayment		Endowment	Pension
Capital & Interest	Interest only	➤ The borrower makes repayments of interest only ➤ An insurance policy is taken out on the borrower's life when the mortgage is granted, and this repays the capital when it matures ✓ When the policy matures any surplus is paid to the borrower ✓ The insurance policy on the borrower's life gives the lender extra security on a borrower's death	➤ These are linked with pension arrangements ✓ May be tax efficient for the self-employed on high salaries
➤ The borrower makes monthly repayments of interest *and* capital	➤ The borrower makes monthly repayments of interest only ➤ The borrower is responsible for repaying capital before the end of the mortgage term. It is vital for a borrower to make arrangements to fund the capital, but if this is done this type of mortgage can be very flexible and simple		
✗ On the borrower's death the debt falls due from the estate; if the estate is insolvent and property prices fall, the lender is left with a bad debt. A mortgage repayment policy insures against this occurring (a lender often insists on the borrower taking out such a policy)		✗ If the policy does not cover the loan, the borrower must make good the shortfall ✗ The mortgage cannot be transferred unless the whole sum is repaid	

Interest rates can be, for a period or for the whole term of a mortgage, either:
- ➤ fixed - interest is payable at a set rate (eg: 6%), *or*
- ➤ capped - the interest rate may vary, but will not exceed the 'cap' (eg: will not exceed 8%, but unlike with a fixed rate the borrower will benefit if the rate is below the cap by paying interest at the lower rate), *or*
- ➤ variable - the interest 'floats', usually in line with the rate set by the Bank of England under the *BEA 1998*.

➤ Ensure that:
- ◆ if there is more than one borrower, both borrowers are named on the mortgage offer.
- ◆ none of the borrowers is subject to undue influence.
- ◆ if the mortgage is an 'investment' (ie: it is an endowment mortgage) or the firm is providing insurance mediation services, that the firm has the necessary authorisation to provide advice and that the *FSMA 2000* is complied with.
- ◆ the borrower is aware of the repayments and can afford them (even, if the mortgage carries interest at a variable rate, when interest rates rise).
- ◆ the borrower knows the overall cost of the mortgage (eg: the lender may insist the property is insured under its own block policy *and* that the borrower pays for this).
- ◆ the buyer has enough money in hand, after moving expenses, to proceed with the purchase.
- ◆ retentions for repair work are not such as to prevent the borrower meeting his financial obligations. If the lender retains some of the capital until specified repairs have been done, this may cause additional financing difficulties.
    - • The seller may allow the buyer access before completion to carry out work the lender requires. The lender will then release the whole of the loan to enable the buyer to complete.

- any conditions attached to the mortgage are not too onerous. Explain the effect of any conditions to the client, eg the terms of the mortgage may:
  - prohibit the borrower letting part of the property without the lender's consent, *and/or*
  - require the borrower to repair or alter the property (can the borrower afford to comply?), *and/or*
  - impose penalties for early redemption (this is common if the lender offers the borrower favourable terms as an inducement to select a particular mortgage, eg: a low rate of interest for an initial period), *and/or*
  - oblige the borrower to give a full title guarantee to the lender in the mortgage deed (This may present difficulties if the borrower does not receive full title guarantee from the seller).
- any guarantee premium (also known as a 'mortgage indemnity') which the lender demands is satisfactory. Is this sufficient to protect the borrower if house prices fall below the purchase price (known as the 'negative equity' trap)? Is the premium expensive?
  - If acting for the lender, note that the lender will only be able to recover the difference between the correct valuation and the negligent one (ie: not the fall in market values), *South Australia Asset Management Corporation v. York Montague Limited* [1996] 3 All ER 365, HL.
- there is no conflict if the lender instructs the buyer's solicitor. (Comply with *SPR r 6*).
  - If acting for a lender check whether the lender's instructions follow the Council of Mortgage Lenders' *Lenders Handbook for England and Wales*.
    - *Part 1* contains general instructions. *Part 2* comprises instructions for specific lenders (This is available via the internet, see www.cml.org.uk)
  - If a conflict of interest arises subsequently, the solicitor must cease acting, but he may not tell the other party the reason why as this would breach the duty of confidentiality.
- once a satisfactory offer has been made, the buyer accepts it within the time allowed.
- any arrangements with a mortgagee are coordinated with the rest of the transaction: with a repayment mortgage, mortgage insurance can be taken out to enable the mortgage policy to be redeemed if the borrower dies.
- the borrower is aware of, and takes out, appropriate insurance policies (lenders may insist on some/all of these):
  a) Endowment policy - suitable only for an endowment mortgage, covers the borrower's life.
  b) Mortgage indemnity policy - provides protection when the loan is for a high percentage (eg: 80% or more) of the purchase price.
  c) Mortgage repayment policy - pays off the mortgage if the borrower dies prior to redemption.
  d) Mortgage payment protection policy - will pay amounts due under the mortgage while the borrower is unemployed.
  e) Building insurance - offers cover if the building is subject to subsidence, fire, flooding, storm damage, etc. If part of a property (eg: a flat) is subject to a policy taken out by the landlord for the whole building, a lender may be satisfied with the landlord's policy if that policy meets its requirements.
    - Risk moves to the borrower in accordance with common law or the provisions of the contract.

| Step 5 | Exchange and its consequences |

 I   Exchange
 II Consequences of exchange

I Exchange

➤ The contract is signed.

- *Either* both parties sign one contract *or* they each sign identical copies (*LP(MP)A 1989 s 2*). For a contract to be binding under *s 2*, documents containing the terms of the contract must actually be exchanged (*Commission for the New Towns v. Cooper (Great Britain) Limited* [1995] 26 EG 129).
- The signatures need not be witnessed.
- A solicitor may sign, but should do so *either* under a power of attorney *or* with express written authority.
  - Failure to obtain the proper authority may be a breach of warranty of authority (*Suleman v. Shahisavari* [1989] 2 All ER 460).

➤ Do not exchange without a client's express written authority to do so.

➤ Exchange using either *Formula A, B, or C* (see box below) via:

- telephone (make a file note of the time of the exchange), *or*
- post/DX (*StC 2.1.1*): a contract is made when it (or the last copy, if more than one) is posted, *or*
- personally (usually at the office of the seller's solicitors), *or*
- fax (*StC 1.3.3*): for messages required under one of the Law Society's *Formulae* (ie: not to exchange the contract itself). A fax must be confirmed with hard copies as soon as possible.

Formula A	Formula B	Formula C
When one solicitor holds both contracts	When each solicitor holds their client's contract	For a 'chain' of transactions Each solicitor holds their client's contract and exchange is by telephone

➤ After exchange has taken place:

- make an attendance note.
- notify the insurer of the property (*StC 5.1* provides for the seller to bear the risk until completion).
- inform client/lender.
- comply with undertakings given under the exchange *Formula* and deal with the deposit in accordance with the contract and the *SARs*.
- if acting for the seller, write to any mortgagee asking for the confirmation of the amount required to redeem the mortgage on completion.

➤ consider registering the contract.

II Consequences of exchange

▶ Any subsequent variation to the contract which is agreed between the parties must comply with the *LP(MP)A 1989 s 2* (see previous page) (*McCausland and Another v. Duncan Lawrie Limited*, The Times, 18 June 1996, CA).

1 Consider whether to register the contract

▶ This is advisable if:

a) the seller's good faith is doubted, *or*

b) a dispute arises, *or*

c) there are more than 2 months between exchange and completion, *or*

d) the seller delays completion beyond the contractual date, *or*

e) the transaction is a sub-sale.

- Unregistered land: register the contract as a Class C(iv) land charge.

- Registered land: enter a notice on the Register as a minor interest in the land.

2 Death of a party

▶ PRs are bound to complete a contract which the deceased entered into. This can cause difficulties for the estate as the buyer's death may lead to a revocation of the mortgage offer.

3 Seller's bankruptcy

▶ The seller's trustee in bankruptcy may complete with a redrafted purchase deed (the bankrupt is not party to the deed), or the trustee may disclaim the contract.

4 Requisitions

▶ Requisitions may not be raised:

a) if the seller has provided the buyer with proof of title to the property and its ability to transfer it (or procure its transfer) before the contract was made, *or*

b) with respect to incumbrances specified in the contract or discoverable by inspection of the property before the contract (*StC 4.2.1*),

... *however* a buyer may raise requisitions in writing with respect to other matters within 6 working days of exchange, *or* when evidence of the seller's title is delivered to the buyer, whichever is later. The seller replies within 4 working days; the buyer then has 3 working days within which to make written observations on the seller's replies (*StC 4.3.1*).

▶ Under common law the buyer accepts the seller's title on delivery of the draft purchase deed to the seller. Often the draft deed is submitted with requisitions on title.

CONVEYANCING
A chronological conveyance

Step 6 — Buyer prepares the purchase deed

1 Procedure

- ➤ At least 12 working days before completion the buyer sends the seller a draft of the transfer: 2 copies, one of which is engrossed (*StC 4.3.2*).
- ➤ The seller's solicitor replies with any queries within 4 working days of the draft being delivered to him (*StC 4.3.2*).
- ➤ The buyer must deliver an engrossment to the seller at least 5 working days before completion (*StC 4.3.2*).
    - ◆ *Protocol 9.1*: the draft transfer and requisitions should be submitted as soon as possible after exchange, and within time limits set by the contract.

2 Form of the deed

- ➤ The transfer should comply with the *LPA s 52* as amended by the *LP(MP)A 1989 s 1*.
- ➤ Unregistered land: there is no prescribed form. *Form TR1* may be used.
- ➤ Registered land: use *Form TR1*.

3 Drafting

- ➤ The transfer should reflect the terms of the contract.
- ➤ Consideration: exclude chattels; a separate receipt for these is given to the buyer on completion.
    - ◆ VAT (if due) is included in the figure for consideration.

4 Parties

- ➤ All those whose consent to the transaction is necessary:
    - ◆ a receiver or liquidator.
    - ◆ a sub-purchaser on a sub-sale.
    - ◆ a lender with a charge over unregistered land may *either* join a conveyance *or* give the buyer a separate deed of release.
        - • A lender with a charge over registered land will not do this as it will release the land using *Form DS1* or a deed of release/receipt.

5 Signature

- ➤ The seller always signs the deed. The buyer signs the transfer if it contains a covenant or a declaration on his behalf.
- ➤ If an individual is incapable of signing, the transfer is read to him, and it can be signed on his behalf in the presence of 2 witnesses who attest his signature (*LP(MP)A 1989 s 1(2)(3)*).
- ➤ An attorney signs *either* 'O by his attorney P' *or* 'P as attorney on behalf of O'.
- ➤ A company may affix a seal in the presence of 2 directors, or a director and company secretary who sign the transfer. The seal is not essential, but the document must be a deed on its face (*CA s 36A*).

6 Plans

- ➤ Attach these to the transfer.
- ➤ HM Land Registry requires parties to sign the plan if it is to accept its inclusion.
    - ◆ Signing the plan is not compulsory for unregistered land, but it is advisable nonetheless.
    - ◆ If a company seals the transfer, it should seal the plan as well (this need not be witnessed).

7 **Witnesses** (where necessary)

➤ For evidential reasons an independent party is preferable. A witness cannot be a party to the deed (*Seal v. Claridge* (1881) 7 QBD 516).

➤ 2 witnesses are required if a signature is by proxy.

8 **Delivery**

➤ A transfer is usually held 'in escrow' (ie: conditional upon completion, signed but not dated).

➤ Delivery is presumed to be the date of execution unless the contrary is shown (*CA s 36A*).

➤ Receipt clause: this is sufficient discharge for the buyer (*LPA s 67*).

- A receipt clause authorises the buyer to pay consideration to the seller's solicitor (*LPA s 69*).
- A receipt is evidence, but not conclusive evidence, that the seller's lien over the property in respect of unpaid consideration is extinguished.

CONVEYANCING

A chronological conveyance

| Step 7 | Preparing for completion |

1   **Send the seller (and the buyer if necessary) a letter with an engrossed purchase deed**

➤ Explain:
- the purpose and contents of the purchase deed.
- any instructions for executing the deed and the date by which it should be returned to the solicitor.
- that the client should not date the purchase deed.

2   **Make final searches** (see p 221)

3   **Prepare and send completion statements to the clients**

➤ The seller's solicitor sends:
- the seller a statement of the sum due on completion, explaining how this was calculated, *and*
- the buyer 2 copies of the appropriate statement, together with any receipts if *either* the proceeds do not cover the price agreed *or* an apportionment is due (eg: in respect of a service charge), *or* for chattels.

➤ The buyer's solicitor sends the buyer a statement giving:
- the sum needed to complete, explaining how this was calculated, *and*
- a statement of the mortgage, mentioning how much will be advanced and retained, *and*
- the amount due in disbursements (eg: search fees, SDLT, etc), *and*
- the solicitor's costs (plus VAT).

4   **Finalise arrangements with the lender** (if acting for a lender)

➤ Buyer's solicitor ...
   ... sends the buyer's lender a report on the title and requests a cheque/telegraphic transfer to cover the advance. Ensure that the cheque is paid in to client account at least 5 days before completion.
   ... prepares an engrossment of the mortgage deed.
   ... checks that all outstanding requisitions and enquiries have been satisfactorily answered, and advises the client of any remaining difficulties.

➤ Seller's solicitor ...
   ... gives an undertaking to the seller's lender to secure redemption of the mortgage in so far as monies come into the solicitor's hands, and seeks authority to act as the agent of the seller's agent to redeem the mortgage just before completion.
   ... verifies that the completion statement is correct.
   ... prepares a form of discharge of the mortgage, and if acting for a seller's lender, checks its instructions as to completion.

5   **Settle arrangements for completion**

➤ If completion is by post consider using the *Law Society's Code for Completion by Post* and (in any event) make preparations appropriate to the method of completion chosen.
- In 'exceptional circumstances' (eg: the amount to redeem a seller's mortgage exceeds the minimum level of solicitor's indemnity insurance, *or* the lender is not a CML member), it is negligent for a buyer's solicitor to rely solely on an undertaking from the seller's solicitor to supply a *form DS1* following completion (*Patel v. Daybells* [2001] EWCA Civ 1229, CA).

Step 8 — Completion

➤ The contract and the purchase deed do *not* merge on completion (*StC 7.4*).
  ◆ This ensures that a claim in contract is preserved after completion.

1 Time

➤ Completion takes place on the twentieth working day after exchange (*StC 6.1*), subject to any *SpC*.
➤ If completion takes place after 2 pm, it is deemed to occur on the following working day in which case an apportionment in respect of incomings and outgoings is made, and the buyer is obliged to compensate the seller by paying interest at the contract rate (*StC 6.1.2, 6.3 and 7.3*).
  ◆ No apportionment is made, and no compensation is due, if the sale is with vacant possession and the buyer is ready, able and willing to complete (*StC 1.1.3*), but does not pay until after 2 pm because the seller has not vacated the property (*StC 6.1.3*).
  ◆ Late completion on a Friday afternoon involves the buyer paying 3 days' interest.

2 Place

➤ At the seller's conveyancer's office, or any place that conveyancer may reasonably specify (*StC 6.2.2*).

3 Money

➤ Money is paid by direct credit and, if appropriate, by an unconditional release of a deposit held by a stakeholder (*StC 6.7*).
  ◆ A 'direct credit' is a direct transfer of cleared funds to an account nominated by the seller's conveyancer and maintained by a clearing bank (*StC 1.1.1(g)*).

Usual methods of completion

Postal	Personal
The buyer's solicitor and the seller's solicitor agree, preferably in writing, whether to use the Law Society's *Code for Completion by Post*.	The buyer's solicitor:
	◆ brings the deed, other relevant documents (see below) and a banker's draft for the balance of the purchase price. (A cheque is not good enough as only cash or an equivalent to cash is permitted by *StC 6.7*)
The buyer's solicitor usually sends the balance of the completion monies to the seller's solicitor by telegraphic transfer early on the morning of completion	The seller's solicitor:
See next page for the *Code* (as revised with effect from 1 July 1998)	◆ checks and signs 2 copies of the schedule of deeds (and retains one, giving the other to the buyer)

In all cases:
- ◆ the seller obtains discharges for any mortgages, or gives an undertaking to discharge any mortgages.
- ◆ the buyer (on a personal completion) or the seller (on a postal completion) checks the purchase deed.
- ◆ the seller gives a receipt for chattels.

For unregistered land: documents of title are checked against the epitome of title which the seller has supplied.
- ◆ If the seller sells as a PR, or on a conveyance of part, endorse a memorandum on the grant of representation or original conveyance of the whole respectively.
- ◆ If the seller will retain any of the documents (eg: sale of part, or trust instrument (*LPA s 45(9)*)), the buyer's solicitor marks the abstract 'Examined against the originals at the office of .... on ...', and signs the abstract.
- ◆ If any of the documents of title are missing, the seller (or a fiduciary with custody of the relevant document) gives a written acknowledgement and undertaking, both of which are fulfilled at the seller's expense (*StC 4.6.5*).

CONVEYANCING
A chronological conveyance

Law Society's Code for Completion by Post

➤ A solicitor must expressly agree to adopt the *Code*, preferably in writing (*para 1*).

♦ Alterations must be agreed in advance and be in writing (*Preamble*).

1 Before completion

➤ The seller's solicitor specifies in writing to the buyer's solicitor the mortgages or charges which will be redeemed or discharged on or before completion to the extent that they relate to the property (*para 3*).

➤ The seller's solicitor undertakes:

   a) to have the seller's authority to receive the purchase money on completion, *and*

   b) on completion to have the authority of the proprietor of each mortgage or charge to receive the sum intended to repay it (*para 4(i)-(ii)*), *and*

   c) not to complete until he has the buyer's solicitor's instructions to do so (*para 4(iv)*).

   • The seller's solicitor undertakes that, notwithstanding a) and b), if he does not have the necessary authorities, he will advise the buyer's solicitor *either:*

      ▪ no later 4pm on the working day before the completion date that he does not have the authorities referred to in a) and b) above, *or*

      ▪ immediately if any authority is subsequently withdrawn (*para 4(iii)*).

➤ The buyer's solicitor sends the seller's solicitor instructions as to (*para 5*):
   i) documents to be examined and marked, *and*
   ii) memoranda to be endorsed, *and*
   iii) undertakings to be given, *and*
   iv) deeds and documents (eg: relating to rents, deposits, keys) to be sent after completion to the buyer ('*para 5(iv) documents*'), *and*
   v) any other relevant matters.

   • If no instructions are given the seller's solicitor is under no duty to examine, mark or endorse a document.

➤ The buyer's solicitor remits to the seller's solicitor the completion amount (notified in writing by the seller's solicitor, or else as stated on the contract), and these funds are held to the buyer's solicitor's order.

   ♦ If telegraphic transfer is used the seller's solicitor instructs the bank to telephone immediately on receipt.

➤ The seller's solicitor will notify the buyer's solicitor if at the time agreed for completion any of these requirements is outstanding.

2 Completion

➤ The seller's solicitor will complete (on receiving the completion monies, or later if so agreed with the buyer's solicitor) (*para 8*).

➤ The seller's solicitor undertakes when completing to comply with instructions as to the examination of documents etc under *para 5* and to redeem or discharge any mortgages specified in *para 3* which have not been redeemed or discharged (*para 9*).

➤ The seller's solicitor acts as the agent of the buyer's solicitor, without fee or disbursements (*para 2*).

3 After completion

➤ The seller's solicitor undertakes:

   a) to hold deeds and *para 5(iv)* documents referred to the buyer's solicitor's order, *and*

   b) as soon as possible, and in any event on the same day, to:

   i) confirm to the buyer's solicitor by telephone or fax that completion has occurred, *and*

   ii) to send written confirmation and (at the risk of the buyer's solicitor) the *para 5(iv)* documents by first class post or DX.

Step 9	Post-completion

1 **Seller's solicitor ...**

- ... instructs the estate agents to release the keys. Under *Protocol 11.3*, the solicitor should ensure the keys are released immediately and inform the buyer's solicitor when this has been done.
- ... deals with the proceeds of sale as instructed, and fulfils any undertakings (eg: to a mortgagee).
- ... redeems the mortgage and (once the mortgagee has redeemed the mortgage) sends the appropriate receipt to the buyer:
    - ♦ Registered land: obtain *Form DS1*.
    - ♦ Unregistered land: obtain a receipted mortgage deed.
- ... sends the client a letter, report and bill. This letter should make it clear that the client is responsible for informing the water authority, suppliers of gas, electricity, telephone services and the local Council (Council Tax) of the change in ownership (*Protocol 11.4*).

2 **Buyer's solicitor ...**

- ... completes the mortgage deed (eg: add date of completion).
- ... fulfils any undertaking to repay bridging finance (eg: from a mortgage advance).
- ... obtains an SDLT certificate from HMRC.
    - ♦ A SDLT certificate is obtained by submitting a land transaction return, a self assessment, and payment in respect of the SDLT payable to HMRC within 30 days of the effective date of the land transaction.
        - • There is no requirement to obtain a 'particulars delivered' ('PD') stamp if the transaction is an SDLT transaction (notifiable/chargeable to SDLT, or within *FA 2003 s 79*: *FA 2003 Sch 19*), otherwise a PD stamp should be obtained (*FA 1931 s 28*).
        - • If the consideration is contingent or uncertain and falls to be paid within 18 months after the effective date of the transaction, the purchaser can apply to defer payment of SDLT (*FA 2003 s 90*).
- ... applies to HM Land Registry to register the title and the mortgage, if appropriate (see next page).
    - ♦ An application may be made for 'prejudicial' information to be excluded (*LRR 2003 r 136*, *Form EX1*).
- ... if the buyer is a company/LLP, any fixed charge must be registered at Companies House within 21 days.
- ... discharges any entries which have been registered at HM Land Registry or the Central Land Charges Department to protect the contract.
- ... checks the official copy of the Register, the official copy of the plan (where a plan has been created or amended by the application), and the title information document received from HM Land Registry.
    - ♦ The title information document explains the reason for the issue of the official copy; it is provided for information purposes only.
- ... if the buyer has bought unregistered land from an attorney with a non-enduring power, or a power of attorney granted under *TLATA 1996 s 9*, he should advise the buyer to make a statutory declaration. If the buyer dies without doing so there will be a defect in the title where statute does not offer protection.
- ... if the property is a commonhold unit, give notice (on *form 10*) to the commonhold association within 14 days of the buyer becoming entitled to be registered as a proprietor of the unit (*CCS para 4.7.8*).

CONVEYANCING
A chronological conveyance

First registration

➤ If the 'requirement of registration' applies, the responsible estate owner (or his successor in title) must apply to be registered as proprietor of the registered estate (*LRA 2002 s 6(1)*).

The 'requirement of registration' (*LRA 2002 s 4*)

➤ The requirement of registration applies where there is:

a) a transfer (otherwise than by operation of law) of a qualifying estate for valuable or other consideration, by gift, or in pursuance of a court order, or by means of a vesting assent, *or*

- This does not include the assignment of a mortgage term or the assignment or surrender of a lease to the owner of the immediate reversion where the term merges on reversion.

b) the grant out of a qualifying estate in land for a term of years absolute of more than 7 years from the date of the grant, and for valuable consideration, by gift or in pursuance of a court order (but not a grant to a person as a mortgagee), *or*

c) the grant out of a qualifying estate in land for a term of years absolute to take effect in possession after the end of the period of 3 months beginning with the date of the grant, *or*

d) the creation of a 'protected first legal mortgage' of a qualifying estate, *or*

- A 'first legal mortgage' is a mortgage which on creation ranks in priority ahead of any other mortgages and takes effect as a mortgage to be protected by the deposit of documents relating to the mortgaged estate.

e) the grant of a lease under the 'right to buy' legislation (*HA 1985 Part 5*) out of an unregistered legal estate in land, *or*

f) a disposal by a landlord which leads to a tenant no longer being a secure tenant (*HA 1985 s 171A*) (including by means of the grant of lease out of an unregistered legal estate in land).

➤ A 'qualifying estate' is an unregistered legal estate which is a freehold estate in land, or a leasehold estate for a term which, at the time of the relevant event, has more than 7 years to run.

➤ The period for registration is 2 months beginning on the date the relevant event occurs (although the Registrar has discretion to extend this period) (*LRA 2002 s 6(4)-(5), LRR 2003 rr 21-38*).

- Send *Form FR1*, the correct fee, relevant documents and a list of documents (*Form DL1*).

- A caution against first registration may, in limited circumstances, be entered on the cautions register (*LRA 2002 ss 15-22, LRR 2003 rr 39-53, Practice Guide 3*, use *Form CT1*).

➤ If the requirement is not complied with the transfer, grant or creation becomes void as regards the legal estate (*LRA 2002 s 7(1)*).

- Title to the legal estate reverts to the transferor who holds on bare trust for the transferee, or (in the case of the grant of a lease or creation of a first protected mortgage) the grant or creation takes effect as a contract for valuable consideration to grant or create the relevant legal estate (*LRA 2002 s 7(2)*).

- The transferee, grantee or mortgagor is, on a retransfer, regrant or remortgage, liable to the other party for all proper costs of and incidental to retransfer, regrant or remortgage and is liable to indemnify such a person in respect of any other liability reasonably incurred by that person because of the failure to comply with the requirement of registration (*LRA 2002 s 8*).

➤ Where the requirement of registration does not apply, an unregistered legal estate in land, a rentcharge, a franchise or a profit à prendre may be registered by a person who such an estate is vested in or who is entitled to have such an estate vested in him (*LRA 2002 s 3*).

➤ An application may not be made under *LRA 2002 s 3* in respect of a lease unless that lease was granted for a term of which more than 7 years are unexpired and the right to possession under the lease is not discontinuous.

Registrable dispositions

➤ A disposition of a registered estate, or a registered charge, which is required to be completed by registration does not operate at law until the registration requirements are met (*LRA 2002 s 27(1)*).

- This applies to dispositions by operation of law, other than a transfer on death or bankruptcy of an individual, a transfer on dissolution of a body corporate, or the creation of a legal charge which is a local land charge (*LRA 2002 s 27(5)*).

- The registration requirements (*LRA 2002 Sch 2*) are satisfied by the registration on the register of the transferee, grantee, or chargee (or a successor in title) as proprietor of the relevant legal interest (*LRA 2002 s 27(4)*).

Dispositions which are required to be completed by registration

➤ In the case of a registered estate these are (*LRA 2002 s 27(3)*):

a) a transfer, *and*

b) where the registered estate is an estate in land, the grant of a lease of a term of years absolute:

   i) for a term of more than 7 years from the date of the grant, *or*

   ii) to take effect in possession after the end of the period of 3 months beginning with the date of the grant, *or*

   iii) under which the right to possession is discontinuous, *or*

   iv) in pursuance of the right to buy (under *HA 1985 Part 5*), *or*

   v) where a landlord makes a disposal which leads to a person ceasing to be a secured tenant under *HA 1985 s 171A*, *and*

c) where the registered estate is a franchise or manor, the grant of a lease, *and*

d) the express grant or reservation of an interest within *LPA 1925 s 1(2)(a)* (ie: an easement or profit à prendre), other than an interest capable of registration under the *CRA 1965*, *and*

e) the express grant or reservation of an interest within *LPA 1925 s 1(2)(b)/(e)* (ie: certain rentcharges or rights of entry exercisable over or annexed to a rentcharge), *and*

f) the grant of a legal charge.

➤ In the case of a registered charge these are (*LRA 2002 s 27(3)*):

a) a transfer, *and*

b) the grant of a subcharge.

➤ Send to HM Land Registry, an application (*Form AP1*), transfer (*Form TR1*) and fee, *plus* (as appropriate):

- a discharge of a registered charge (*Form DS1*) (or indicate an END has been sent).
- application to enter any relevant restriction (*Form RX1*) or notice (*Form AN1*).
- the new mortgage deed (and a certified copy).
- if the seller is a PR, a certified copy of the grant of representation.
- if the transfer was executed under a special power of attorney limited to the disposal the original power, *or* a certified copy of any other type of attorney.
- an SDLT certificate, if needed.
- a stamped addressed card for the District Registry to acknowledge the application.

CONVEYANCING
A chronological conveyance

HM Land Registry and E-lodgement

▶ Although e-conveyancing is not yet possible, HM Land Registry has launched the following electronic services which are intended to make conveyancing more efficient and quicker:

a) the electronic notification of discharge ('END') and electronic discharge ('ED'), *and*

b) the electronic lodgement service.

END and ED

▶ The END system is intended to reduce delays associated with arranging a discharge using a traditional paper-based system (see HM Land Registry, *Practice Guide 31, March 2003*).

- Lenders may participate in ENDs over a secure connection with the agreement of HM Land Registry.
- ENDs is unsuitable for discharge of part of the land - *Form DS3* must be used in such cases.

Steps

1 **A lender provides a borrower's solicitor with *Form END1*.**

2 **Instead of completing *Form DS1*, a borrower's solicitor completes a *Form END1*, pays off the charge and sends the lender the completed *Form END1*.**

3 **If the lender is satisfied that it has received the correct payment, having received the *Form END1* the lender transmits an END to HM Land Registry.**

▶ An END is an electronic communication of a title number, the date of the charge and the borrower's name.

4 *Either*:

▶ if no other party is involved: the borrower's solicitor sends *Form AP1* (which should refer to discharge by END, or simply END), *Form DS2* or *Form DS2E* and the charge certificate to HM Land Registry, *or*

▶ if another party is involved (eg: on sale): a revised form of undertaking should be agreed prior to completion. HM Land Registry suggest:

'In consideration of your today completing the purchase of [property] we (ie: the seller's solicitor) hereby undertake forthwith (1) to pay over [the lender] the money required to discharge the legal charge dated [date]; (2) to forward Form END1 to [the lender]; and (3) to forward to you a copy of the written confirmation or acknowledgment from the lender that an Electronic Notification of Discharge of the registered charge has been sent to HM Land Registry as soon as it is received by us'.

- A buyer's solicitor should consider split payments, seeking evidence of the seller's solicitor's authority, and whether there is sufficient insurance cover (*Patel v. Daybells*).

▶ The buyer's solicitor sends *Form AP1* (referring to discharge by END), *Form DS2* or *Form DS2E* to HM Land Registry as soon as possible (without waiting for confirmation that an END has been sent).

5 **HM Land Registry treat an END as authority to discharge.**

▶ A lender must either transmit an END or inform the solicitor seeking the discharge why an END cannot be transmitted within 21 working days of receiving the *Form END1*.

▶ ED, unlike END, cancels a charge electronically. It is currently being used by the Nationwide and Abbey National who took part in a pilot; the Land Registry plans to extend it to other lenders.

- For a suggested revised form of undertaking where ED is used, see the Law Society's website.

Electronic lodgement

▶ The following applications affecting the whole title to land can be lodged through the 'Land Registry Direct' service (HM Land Registry, *Public Information Leaflet 33*, January 2002):

- change of name (by marriage, or deed poll).
- death of joint proprietor.
- entry of joint proprietor restriction on severance of joint tenancy by notice
- change of address for service.
- change of property description.

B Checking title and making searches

  I Unregistered title
  II Registered title
  III Searches

I Unregistered title

A Freehold title

> **Root of title**
>
> A valid title has a 'root' which may be (*LPA s 44*):
>
> *either* a) a conveyance on sale, or legal mortgage at least 15 years old (this is preferable),
>
> *or* b) a voluntary assent or conveyance made after 1925,
>
> *and* it must be at the start of a chain which is uninterrupted up to the present day.
>
> It is not necessary to look behind the root except for (*LPA s 45*):
>
> ➤ an abstract of a power of attorney under which an abstracted document was executed, *or*
>
> ➤ earlier documents referred to in an abstract, *or*
>
> ➤ a plan referred to in the abstract, *or*
>
> ➤ any limitation or trust over any part of property in an abstracted document, or any document creating a trust, or any limitation relating to a document forming part of the epitome.
>
> *Do an index map search to check there is no caution against first registration/C(iv) land charge*

Documents capable of forming title

1 **Conveyance by trustees to themselves**

  ➤ This may be a breach of trust, and is voidable unless ...

   a) ... there is *either*:

    i) a pre-existing contract to purchase land or an option or right of pre-emption in favour of a trustee or PR, *or*

    ii) a PR is a beneficiary under a will or intestacy, *or*

   b) ... the consent of the beneficiaries was obtained and all were *sui juris*, *or*

   c) ... the conveyance was sanctioned by the trust instrument, *or*

   d) ... the conveyance was executed under a court order.

2 Conveyance by trustees of land

➤ Prior to 1 January 1997 when *TLATA 1996* came into force land was held by PRs, trustees, tenants in common and joint tenants under a trust for sale. Subsequently, such land has been held under a trust of land by trustees who have a power to postpone sale and a power to sell land (*TLATA 1996 s 4*).

➤ A buyer takes free of any interests under a trust if he pays to 2 or more trustees, or a trust corporation (*LPA ss 2, 27*). A conveyance by an individual trustee needs further investigation.

- Valid receipt is not given if money is paid or receipt given by 1 person acting *either*:
    a) as trustee and attorney for 1 or more trustees, *or*
    b) as attorney for 2 or more trustees (*TDA 1999 s 7*).

➤ From 1 January 1997, a buyer of unregistered land does not take free of the trust (even if he pays to 2 trustees) if he is put on notice of any limitation of the trustees' power to convey *or* of their failure to take proper account of the beneficiaries' interests (*TLATA 1996 s 16*).

➤ **Tenants in common**

If only one tenant survives, the buyer should ask to see the death certificate, the grant of representation and the assent in favour of the tenant's successor under the will or intestacy.

➤ **Joint tenants**

A buyer can assume severance has not occurred if (*LP(JT)A 1964 s 1*):

a) no memorandum of severance is endorsed on the conveyance under which the joint tenants bought the property, *and*

b) no bankruptcy proceedings are registered against either joint tenant, *and*

c) the conveyance *either*:
   i) contains a recital that the seller is solely and beneficially entitled, *or*
   ii) was executed pursuant to a contract for the sale of land dated before 1 July 1995, and the seller conveyed as 'beneficial owner'.

3 Conveyance by PRs

➤ If a grant is to 2 or more PRs, all must join the assent or conveyance.

➤ If only one PR survives, he can act alone.

- Check death certificates to ensure the other PRs were deceased at the time of the transfer.

➤ An assent passes the property to a beneficiary under a will. It should:

- be in writing, *and*
- be to the beneficiary named, *and*
- be signed by all the surviving PRs, *and*
- if covenants are contained, be by deed (*AEA 1925 s 36(4)*).

➤ An assentee (or buyer) should demand an endorsement on the grant of representation, otherwise the trustees may subsequently defeat the assent by making a statement under the *AEA 1925 s 36* so that a subsequent buyer for value takes in priority to the assentee.

- A donee is not protected by statute against trustees defeating the assent in this manner.

4 Voluntary dispositions below full market value

➤ These may be revocable under *IA 1986* (see also *I(No 2)A 1994* for the position of a buyer who gives value to a seller where the seller has acquired land for a disposition which was below market value).

5 Conveyance from an attorney

➤ The buyer's position depends on the type of power of attorney which the seller has: ...

- ... if the seller's attorney has a *security power*, the buyer takes a clean title if he has no actual knowledge that the power has been revoked (*PAA 1971 s 4*).

- ... if the seller's attorney has a *non-enduring power* the buyer takes a clean title if he acts in good faith without knowledge of revocation (death amounts to revocation) (*PAA 1971 s 4*).
    - Examples of a non-enduring power are:
        a) a general power (over all donor's assets).
        b) a special power (over specified assets).
        c) a trustee power (over assets held on trust).

  - A buyer acquiring land from a seller under a non-enduring power, or an unregistered enduring power, is protected if (*PAA 1971 s 5(4), EPAA 1985 s 9(4)*) either:

    a) the dealing between the attorney with the non-enduring power and the buyer occurred within 1 year of the power being granted, *or*

    b) the buyer makes a statutory declaration within 3 months of completion that he is ignorant of the revocation of the power (usually sent to the Land Registry with *Form AP1*).

        - A purchaser is protected if, within 3 months of the exercise of a trustee function, an attorney provides an 'appropriate statement' that at the time of exercise the donor had a beneficial interest in the property (*TDA 1999 s 2*).

- ... if the seller's attorney is a beneficiary of a trust and has a power of attorney granted by a trustee under *TLATA 1996 s 9(1)*, the buyer is protected if he deals in good faith, having no knowledge of the power's revocation (eg: by the beneficiary ceasing to be entitled to an interest in possession (*TLATA 1996 s 9(4)*), and swears a statutory declaration to this effect within 3 months of the completion of the purchase (*TLATA 1996 s 9(2)*).

- ... if the seller's attorney has an *enduring power* of attorney, check the Court of Protection to ensure that the power was correctly registered under *EPAA 1985 s 6*.
    - *MCA 2005 [not yet in force, and not expected to come into force until April 2007]* provides for the repeal of *EPAA 1985* and the replacement of an enduring power with a 'lasting power' of attorney.

➤ *TA 2000 s 11* enables a trustee to delegate delegable functions, see the 'Wills' Chapter.

- Delegation may be permitted by the trust instrument, by all the beneficiaries being *sui iuris*, or *TA 1925 s 25* which permits delegation of powers and discretions in relation to land, the capital proceeds of land or income arising from land (subject to any prohibition in the trust instrument).

➤ Powers granted before 1 October 1971 are governed by *LPA ss 126-128*.

6 Conveyance from a lender

➤ Legal mortgages: if the lender sold under a power of sale there will be no receipt on deed.

- For a building society mortgage receipted on or after 1 January 1987, valid receipt may be assumed if prescribed wording is present, signed by an authorised person (*BSA 1986, Sch 4 para 2(3)*) (the receipt need not name the person making the payment to redeem the mortgage).

- For a building society mortgage receipted before 1 January 1987, or for a bank mortgage, ensure the receipt names the holder of the legal and equitable title as the payer of the debt. Otherwise, the receipt operates to transfer the mortgage (*LPA s 115*); so if a PR or a trustee redeems a mortgage, the receipt should state that no transfer is intended.

    - If in doubt (or if the mortgage discharge post-dates the conveyance) make a land charge search against whoever bought from the borrower and ask for the title deeds from the lender/seller.

    - If a property is sold under a lender's power of sale, check that the power had arisen.

Documents retained by the seller

➤ If a seller has at any time retained documents of title (eg: the original conveyance on a sale of part, or a trust instrument on sale by trustees), a conveyance may include (*LPA s 64*):

a) an 'acknowledgement' entitling the buyer and any successor in title (but not a tenant paying rent) to demand whoever possesses the documents to produce them at the cost of the person making the request, *and*

b) an 'undertaking' giving the buyer and any successor in title (but not a tenant paying rent) a remedy in damages if the documents are mislaid, or perish due to fire or undue care.

Fiduciaries (eg: mortgagees, PRs, tenants for life, and trustees) are unlikely to have given an undertaking. If they have custody of documents, they may have given an acknowledgement.

Proving title

1 **Produce a sound root of title at least 15 years old**

➤ Include incumbrances not evidenced on the root, and which predate the root.

➤ A voluntary conveyance or assent will serve as a root provided it was made after 1925.

2 **Ensure that the root is sound**

➤ It should deal with *all* legal interests in the land.

➤ It should contain a recognisable description of the land.

➤ There are no elements which could cast doubt on the title.

3 **Produce an abstract, or an epitome of the title**

➤ List the documents comprising the root: these go to the buyer on completion (*StC 4.1.3, 4.6.5*).

If the root is not sound consider whether defective title indemnity insurance is affordable and offers adequate protection

B Leasehold title

Proving title			
	Grant (lease)	Grant (sub lease)	Assignment
Open contract rules	No title is given if the lease is under 15 years	*LPA s 44*: a head lease and title root (eg: all assignments) going back at least 15 years	*LPA s 44*: the lease itself and all assignments going back at least 15 years
	No entitlement under *LPA s 44(2)* to call for deduction of freehold title		
StC 8.2.4.	The seller provides everything necessary to give absolute title (ie: an epitome going back at least 15 years)		*StC 8.2.4* does not apply to assignments
Effect of a SpC?		To exclude *StC 8.2.4* if the head tenant never asked to see the freehold	To enable the buyer to check that the lease was validly granted *if* it was granted under 15 years ago (ie: right to call for head lease or evidence of reversionary title)

II Registered title

A The 'Register'

➤ The Register is conclusive as to the proprietor of a registered estate in land (*LRA 2002 s 58*).

1 Property Register *(LRR 2003 r 5)*

➤ Describes the property. The description does not exclude extraneous evidence from deeds, etc, unless the boundaries are 'fixed' by HM Land Registry at the proprietor's request.

➤ It gives details of:
- any mineral rights (*LRR 2003 rr 70-71*), *and*
- any rights from which the land benefits (*LRR 2003 rr 72-76*).

2 Proprietorship Register *(LRR 2003 r 8)*

➤ States, amongst other things, the class of title, the name of the proprietor, an address for service, indemnity covenants and positive covenants, and in the case of possessory title the name of the first registered proprietor (*LRR 2003 rr 64-65*).

3 Charges Register *(LRR 2003 r 9)*

➤ Charges (eg: mortgages): states, among other things, the date of the mortgage, the lender's name and an address for service on the lender.

Notices and restrictions

➤ A notice in respect of a registered estate or charge protects an interest (eg: a restrictive covenant) in registered land where an interest is intended to bind a person who acquires the land.

- No notice may be entered on the Register in respect of an excluded interest. An excluded interest is (*LRA 2002 s 33*):
    a) an interest under a trust of land, or a strict settlement under *SLA 1925*.
    b) a leasehold estate in land which is granted for a term of 3 years or less from the date of the grant and is not required to be registered.
    c) a restrictive covenant between lessor and lessee relating to demised premises.
    d) an interest capable of registration under *CRA 1965/CRA 2006*.
    e) an interest in, or rights attached to, any coal, or coal mine, or rights under *CIA 1994*.

- An agreed notice in respect of home rights, an inheritance tax charge, an *ANLA 1992* notice, variation of a lease under *LTA 1987*, a public right or customary right can be entered on application (*LRA 2002 s 35, LRR 2003 rr 80-82, Form AN1* although for home rights *Forms HR1/HR2* are used).

- The Registrar may unilaterally enter a notice (*LRA 2002 s 35, LRR 2003 r 89, Form 83*).

- The Registrar may also enter a notice in respect of unregistered interests (*LRA 2002 s 37, LRR 2003 r 89*).

➤ A restriction regulates the circumstances in which a disposition of a registered estate or charge may be the subject of an entry on the Register (*LRA 2002 s 40*).

- To enter a restriction submit *Form RX1* (*LRA 2002 s 43, LRR 2003 rr 91-100*) and, eg: on the right to deal with land of a sole proprietor (*Form A*), trustees (*Form B*), PRs (*Form C*), a limited company, or a charity, etc (see *LRR 2003 Sch 4*).

➤ For a bankruptcy notice see *LRR 2003 r 165*, and for a restriction see *LRR 2003 r 166*.

Overriding interests under *LRA 2002*

➤ On required registration (ie: first registration) the following are binding (*LRA 2002 Sch 1*):
- a leasehold estate in land granted for a term not exceeding 7 years (not subject to the requirement of first registration under *LRA 2002 s 4*).
- an interest belonging to a person in actual occupation (except for an interest under *SLA 1925*).
- a legal easement or profit à prendre.
- a customary right or a public right.
- a local land charge.
- an interest in any coal, or a coal mine, or rights of any person under *CIA 1994 ss 38, 49, 51*.
- certain rights to mines and minerals created before 1925.
- a franchise.*
- a manorial right.*
- a right to rent reserved to the Crown on the granting of a freehold estate.*
- a non-statutory right in respect of an embankment or sea/river wall.*
- a right to payment *in lieu* of a tithe.*

➤ On the making of a registrable disposition any right which would have been binding on first registration, *other than* (*LRA 2002 Sch 3*):
- a leasehold estate in land granted for a term not exceeding 7 years which is a registrable disposition.
- certain interests belonging to a person in actual occupation:
    i) under *SLA 1925, or*
    ii) the interest of a person of whom enquiry was made prior to the disposition who failed to disclose the right, *or*
    iii) an interest which belongs to a person whose occupation would not have been obvious on a careful inspection of the land at the time of the disposition and of which the person to whom the disposition is made does not have actual knowledge, *or*
    iv) a leasehold granted to take effect in possession after 3 months, which has not taken effect at the time of the disposition.
    - a legal easement or profit à prendre which is not registered under *CRA 1965 and*:
        i) is not within the actual knowledge of the person to whom the disposition is made, *and*
        ii) would not have been obvious on a reasonably careful inspection of the land.
- a PPP lease relating to transport in London (*LRA 2002 s 90*).

➤ *LRA 2002* preserves proprietary estoppel and mere equities (even if not noted on the Register) (*s 116*).

* These categories will cease to have effect at the end of the period of 10 years beginning on 13 October 2003 (*LRA 2002 s 117*).

NB: Transitional rules in *LRA 2002 Sch 12* govern the interaction of the new rules with the *LRA1925*.

Rectification of the Register and state indemnity under *LRA 2002*

➤ The Registrar may rectify the Register if it is erroneous (*LRA 2002 Sch 4 para 5*).

➤ A person who suffers loss by reason of, eg: rectification of the Register, a mistake the correction of which would involve rectification, a mistake in an official search, a mistake in an official copy or the loss or destruction of a document lodged at the Registry for inspection or safe custody, is entitled to be indemnified by the Registrar (*LRA 2002 Sch 8*).

B Freehold title

There are three classes of freehold title

1 **Absolute title (*LRA 2002 ss 9(2)-(3)*)**

   ➤ Absolute title is (despite its name) still subject to interests which are the subject of a Register entry, unregistered interests (within *LRA 2002 Sch 1*) and interests acquired under *LA 1980* of which the proprietor has notice (*LRA 2002 s 11(4)*).

2 **Possessory title (*LRA 2002 s 9(5)*)**

   ➤ This title is subject to adverse interests subsisting, or capable of subsisting, at the date of first (or subsequent) registration.

3 **Qualified title (*LRA 2002 s 9(4)*)**

   ➤ The State indemnity excludes a specified defect in the title.

   ◆ The Registrar may upgrade a title after 12 years or when he is satisfied a different class of title is merited (eg: possessory title can be upgraded to absolute title (*LRA 2002 ss 62-63, LRR 2003 rr 124-125*).

Proving title

LRA 2002 s 67

a) A copy of Register entries.

b) A copy of the filed plan.

   ➤ Evidence or abstract if the Register is inconclusive (for the fixing of boundaries, see *LRR 2003 rr 117-123*).

   ➤ Copy or abstract of any document mentioned on the Register (eg: a conveyance containing a restrictive covenant).

   ◆ Under *LRA 2002* a document kept by the Registrar referred to in the Register which is not an original is to be taken, as between the parties to a disposition, as correct and to contain all the material parts of the original document (*LRA 2002 s 120*).

   ◆ Note that a) and b) may *not* be excluded by a *Special Condition*.

StC 4.1.2

   ➤ Requires an official copy of items referred to in *LRR rr 134(1)(a)-(b),135(1)(a)* (ie: an individual register, a title plan referred to in an individual register, and any document referred to in the register of title and kept by the registrar).

➤ *LRA 2002 Part 8* provides for electronic conveyancing under which execution, communication to the Registrar and registration will take place simultaneously. When this is introduced under powers contained in *LRA 2002 s 93*, the Register will become conclusive as to as the priority of interests because creation and registration will take place at the same moment in time.

➤ Prior to the introduction of electronic conveyancing, the priority of any interest in registered land is determined by the date of creation (irrespective of whether the interest or disposition is registered) (*LRA 2002 s 28*), *unless* a disposition is made for valuable consideration in which case, on completion of that disposition, any preceding interest whose priority is not protected by registration is postponed to the registrable disposition (*LRA 2002 s 29*).

➤ Commonhold is a form of freehold title (*CLRA 2002 s 1*). Note, that if there is a transfer of a commonhold unit, there is also a transfer of an interest in a commonhold association. Consequently, a commonhold association should be notified; for a transfer by operation of law use *Form 12* (*CCS para 4.7.9*).

C Leasehold title

➤ In addition to absolute (*LRA 2002 s 10(2)*), qualified (*LRA 2002 s 10(5)*) and possessory title (*LRA 2002 s 10(6)*), there is a fourth class of leasehold title, 'good leasehold' title (*LRA 2002 s 10(3)*).

➤ The freehold reversion is unregistered, so the Registrar guarantees the lease only in so far as the grantor acted within his rights in granting the lease.

	Proving leasehold title		
	Grant (lease)	Grant (sub lease)	Assignment
Open contract rules	As the Register is a public document it is possible to apply for an official copy of the Register		Under *StC 4.1.2* the seller must supply an official copy of the Register rather than just a copy
		There is *no* right to see the head lease	
StC 8.2.4.	Imposes an obligation to apply for an official copy of the register *StC 4.1.2* applies so a copy of an official copy of the register is insufficient	Imposes an obligation on the seller to produce an official copy of the Register and a copy of the head lease	*StC 8.2.4* does not apply. Insert a SpC requiring the assignee to produce an official copy of the Register showing absolute title. If the lease only carries good leasehold title, insert a *SpC* requiring the assignor to deduce satisfactory superior title (ie: absolute reversionary title, or a good root of title at least 15 years before the grant of the lease)

III Searches

Checklist for making searches

1 Which searches are necessary? Is the form being used the correct one?

2 If a plan is needed, are 2 correctly coloured copies attached and is the scale sufficiently large?

3 Have any additional questions been correctly entered on the form (eg: *CON29* Part II)?

4 Is the correct fee included with the form (telephone first to confirm the rate)?

5 Are the addresses of the property and that for the answers to the search correct?

➤ Make a file note when the search request is dispatched.

➤ Check the file and chase up any late responses with the relevant authorities.

CONVEYANCING
Title and searches

Pre-contract searches			
Type of search	Information	Protection	Application
In all cases			
Enquiries of seller	The *Protocol* provides a standard form on which the seller lists fixtures, fittings and chattels included in the sale	The seller can refuse to answer questions. Misrepresentation is the buyer's only protection	*Form SPIF (+ FF & C)* There is a supplementary form for a tenant to fill in if a lease is being assigned
Local land charges	Information statute makes local authorities keep	Yes (*LLCA 1975 s.10*)	*Form LLC1*
Local authority	Information *not* required by statute: ➤ road schemes, *and* ➤ planning information, *and* ➤ smoke control orders, *and* ➤ imminent compulsory purchase orders	The authority, or water service company, is liable in negligence, subject to any exclusion clause on the search form	*Form CON29* Part I: for general queries Part II and additional enquiries: for specific matters, a charge is usually made for each item queried
Water service company	Water main and sewer records maintained by these companies under *WA 1989*		*Form CON29DW*
Coal search	Details of past, present and anticipated mineral extraction Check the Law Society's *Coal Mining Directory* for areas likely to be affected		*Form CON29M* is submitted to the surveyor at the Coal Authority's head office
Commons registration	A registered common, or rights of common may: a) restrict planning permission, *or* b) subject land to third party rights (eg: grazing)		*Form CR1*
Company search	a) The company exists, *and* b) it has power to buy or sell land, *and* c) it is not in receivership, administration or liquidation, *and* d) that the land is not subject to a charge	None	Companies House search
Unregistered land			
Index Map	➤ Cautions against first registration ➤ Pending applications for registration		*Form SIM*
Central Land Charges Department	Incumbrances existing over unregistered land: a) easements and covenants affecting the land b) mortgages c) estate contracts d) occupation rights under *FLA 1996*	15 working day priority period	*Form K15* Search the names of all past and present title holders since 1926 (if known) for the period of their ownership of the estate. Search against any owner who made a voluntary disposition in the last 5 years. Search through pre-1973 counties as well as present day ones.
Registered land			
Official copies of the Register	Details of title and incumbrances at HM Registry (*LRA 2002 s 72, LRR 2003 rr 147-160*)		*Form OS3* non-priority search *Form OS1*: priority search (all) *Form OS2*: priority search (part) *Form PRD1*: produce docs
Index Map	List of registered titles within the relevant area		*Form SIM*
Law Society Search Validation Insurance Scheme			
➤ For residential properties selling for up to £500,000 (a premium is payable to take advantage of the scheme) ➤ The scheme covers the difference between the original market price of the property and its value with the adverse entry			

CONVEYANCING
Title and searches

Pre-completion searches		
Type of search	Information	Application
Unregistered land		
Land Charges Department	See p 220	
Registered land		
HM Land Registry search	See p 220. There is a 30 business day priority period	*Form OS1* whole of property *Form OS2* part of property
Land Charges Department	Details of *unregistered freehold* if a lease has good leasehold title	*Form K15* search against landlord's name
If acting in particular circumstances		
With a company involved in the transaction	Use this to check that: a) the company is not in receivership, administration or liquidation, *and* b) that the land is not subject to a charge	Companies House search
For a lender	Bankruptcy search against the buyer	*Forms K15* and *K16*
	If making a priority search against the Register, do so in the lender's name so the buyer is protected. Note that the lender is not protected if the search is done in the buyer's name	*Form OS1* for whole property *Form OS2* for part of property 30 business day priority period
When a grant of probate (or a certified copy) are not available	Check that a grant has been issued to the party concerned and is still valid	Principal Probate Registry
When a party will complete using an enduring power of attorney	Check whether the power is registered, or whether registration is pending. a) If the power is registered *and* the grantor is still alive, the attorney may execute the deed b) If registration is pending, the attorney may only execute if the power falls within a limited category defined by *EPAA 1985*	Probate Registry *Form EP4*
If more than 3 months have passed since exchange	Repeat the Local Authority and Local Land Charges search	See p 221
If the contract is conditional on the results of subsequent searches		
House is under construction	Inspect the fabric to verify that it is satisfactory	Not applicable

Action if a pre-completion search shows an adverse entry

▶ Ascertain what the entry relates to.

▶ Contact the seller's solicitor and seek an undertaking that it will be removed prior to completion.

▶ If the search was at the Central Land Charges Department, apply for a copy of *Form 19* on which the entry was originally registered, to find out when (and by whom) it was registered.

▶ Keep client, lender and seller informed subject to the duty of confidentiality.

▶ Consider defective title indemnity insurance.

National Land Information Service ('NLIS')

➤ The NLIS allows certain searches to be carried out on the web.

◆ Data providers (eg: HM Land Registry) supply data to the NLIS hub and information is distributed from the NLIS hub by licensed channels (*www.transaction-online.co.uk*, *www.searchflow.co.uk*, and *www.tmproperty.co.uk*).

Searches

HM Land Registry and Land Charges Registry

➤ Home rights	*Form HR3*
➤ Official whole	*Form OS1*
➤ Index map search	*Form SIM*
➤ Official copies of the Register	
➤ Official copies of documents	
➤ Register view	
➤ Filed plan view	
➤ Daylist enquiry	
➤ ENDs enquiry	
➤ Computerised property description enquiry	
➤ Land charges search	*Form K15*
➤ Land charges bankruptcy	*Form K16*
➤ Land charges office copy	*Form K19*

Coal authority

➤ Coal mining search

Local authority

➤ Local land charges	*Form LLC1*
➤ Enquiries of a local authority	*Form Con 29*
➤ Common registration search	*Form CR21*

Water authority

➤ Water mains and sewers	*Form Con 29DW*

➤ Both the NLIS and HM Land Registry accept requests for an electronic (rather than paper) official copy of a register of title, title plan where the original is in electronic format; such an official copy is issued in 'pdf' format.

◆ A print from a 'pdf' will be accepted as an official copy, as will a forwarded 'pdf' file, provided in either case that the file has not been modified or corrupted.

◆ In determining whether an official copy is genuine, the HM Land Registry suggest asking: 'what does the document look like, and where did it come from?' (*Practice Guide 11, March 2004*).

C Variations to the standard contract

I	Conditional contracts
II	Sale of part
III	New buildings

I Conditional contracts

➤ The terms and conditions must be clear and certain.
- If planning permission is needed:
  - decide, if conditions are attached, what would entitle the buyer to rescind. In particular, consider whether the buyer may rescind if:
    - planning permission is not granted within a specified period, *or*
    - a planning application is never submitted.
  - settle who pays the fee for the application.
  - agree whether the application for planning permission should be for outline or for full consent, and the form of application.

➤ The contract should deal with all these issues and it must state unambiguously:
- the precise event on which the contract is conditional.
- by what time any conditions must be fulfilled.
- the exact terms on which the party with the benefit of the condition may rescind.

➤ Ensure there are no loopholes, except the single express condition enabling a party to rescind.

II Sale of part

The transaction proceeds as normal (see p 174 for 'step' chronology), with these differences.

Step 1: Taking instructions

➤ Obtain the consent of any lender with a charge over the land.
- Unregistered land: the lender executes a deed of release, or is joined to the conveyance.
- Registered land: the part to be sold is released from the mortgage by the lender completing *Form DS3,* to which a plan will be attached.

CONVEYANCING
Variations to the standard contract

Step 2: Seller prepares the pre-contract package

- There must be a scale plan, and a definition of the land sold and retained.
  - Registered land: use the title plan approved by HM Land Registry, or supply a plan which complies with the requirements of the *LRR 2003* (see further *Practice Guide 40*).
- Adapt the contract: draft any appropriate *Special Conditions*.

Protect the retained land from implied rights in favour of the plot disposed of	➤ Ensure that the sale does not include: any easement of way, light, or air which might interfere with, or restrict the free use of the retained land, for building or any other purpose ➤ The transfer to the buyer should expressly exclude any such rights
Impose new covenants	➤ These should be stated expressly ➤ Covenants which are negative in substance are advantageous as they will run with the land ➤ If covenants are to be enforceable against future owners they must be: a) expressly taken for the benefit of the retained land, *and* b) registered at HM Land Registry or the Central Land Charges Department
Grant any easements in favour of the plot over the retained land	➤ These may be needed to gain access to the plot, or connect services to it

Step 6: Buyer prepares the transfer

- Unregistered land: a professional drawn plan is advisable, though not essential.
  - Include in the transfer an acknowledgement that the seller has produced title deeds to the retained land and that they are in safe custody (*LPA s 64, StC 4.6.5*).
- Registered land: fill in the seller's title number on the purchase deed (*Form TP1*) and attach a title plan approved by HM Land Registry or a plan which complies with the guidelines in *Practice Guide 40*.
- If the land is a commonhold unit, the CCS must be updated using *form CM3* (*C(LR)R 2004 r 15*)

Step 7: Preparing for completion

- Registered land: make a pre-completion search on *Form OS2* attached to a plan.

Step 8: Completion

- Unregistered land
  - The buyer marks the abstract or epitome as examined against the original. The seller also does this under *Protocol 3.1*.
  - A memorandum of sale is endorsed on the seller's most recent title deed (*LPA s 200*).
  - The seller takes a note of any restrictive covenants which have been imposed, and keeps this with his documents of title.

Step 9: Post-Completion

- If the land is a commonhold unit, give notice (using *Form 11*) to the commonhold association of transfer of part of a unit within 14 days of the new owner becoming entitled to be registered a proprietor of that part of the unit (*CCS para 4.7.8*).
  - Use *Form CM3* to register the transfer at HM Land Registry (*C(LR)R 2004 r 15*).

CONVEYANCING
Variations to the standard contract

III New buildings

This is the same as for a freehold (see p 176 for 'step' chronology), with these additions:

Step 2: Seller prepares pre-contract package

- ➤ Special provisions apply when in relation to new home warranties (from 1 June 2007):
    - ◆ A warranty provider must undertake that it has conducted reasonable checks to ensure that the property is physically complete and is designed and finished to a reasonable standard (*HIPR 2006 Sch 6 para 9*).
        - • Eg: structural features will withstand normal residential wear for 60 years (if properly maintained) and meet all statutory requirements (eg: under *Building Act 1984* and *Building Regulations 2000*).
    - ◆ The warranty provider must undertake that it, or the developer, will put right, arrange to put right, or arrange financial compensation for any destruction of or damage to the property caused by defects:
        - a) of structural features which occur/are apparent within the first 10 years of the warranty period (*HIPR 2006 Sch 6 para 11*), *and*
        - b) other defects (eg: wiring, drains, gas, water, heating, ventilation, boilers (but not lifts), plaster, tiling, certain floor coverings, wall partitions, internal windows, doors, surface finishes, and fixtures which are apparent or occur within the first 2 years of the warranty period (*HIPR 2006 Sch 6 para 12*).
    - ◆ The warranty provider must also undertake to pay:
        - a) costs and expenses reaonably and necessarily incurred by those normally living at the property for removal/storage and alternative accomodation if the property becomes uninhabitable (*HIPR 2006 Sch 6 paras 13* and *18*), *and*
        - b) certain professional and other fees reasonably and necessarily incurred by a policy holder as a result of rectifying work (*HIPR 2006 Sch 6 paras 14* and *19*)).
    - ◆ If a property is newly built from foundations, the total liability may be limited to £500,000 (plus an annual increment) or the value of the property at the time it was completed (plus an annual increment) (*HIPR 2006 Sch 6 para 15*).
        - • There are separate limits for converted premises, and there may be an excess payable by a policy holder of no more than £1,000 (plus an annual increment) (*HIPR 2006 Sch 6 para 17*).
    - ◆ A new home warranty must be for at least 10 years (*HIPR 2006 Sch 6 para 6*).
        - • A liability under a home warranty must be covered by insurance (*HIPR 2006 Sch 6 para 3*).
- ➤ For the requirements when a home is not physically complete see *HIPR 2006 Sch 7.*

Step 3: Buyer approves the contract

- ➤ The contract is likely to be in a standard form which the developer wishes to use for the whole development. It may be that the seller is consequently reluctant to negotiate terms which differ from the standard model. Nonetheless, the buyer's solicitor must ensure that:
    - ◆ any restrictive covenants to which the land is subject do not unduly restrict the buyer's use of the property and any new covenants to be imposed in the transfer are not too onerous.
    - ◆ the seller undertakes to remedy any minor defects ('snagging') which emerge after completion within a specified time (and/or that the buyer is protected by an NHBC 'Buildermark' insurance policy).
    - ◆ the seller undertakes to leave the property in 'ship-shape and Bristol fashion' and will:
        - • landscape the development appropriately.
        - • hand the property over in a neat state and remove all builder's rubble.
        - • erect suitable boundary fences.

- extra payments for fixtures and fittings (jacuzzis, washing machines, etc) are quantified.
- a plan is supplied with the contract and is accurate.
- a 'long stop' completion date is incorporated in the contract. This should enable the buyer to rescind the contract if the work is unfinished after the time agreed. The seller may ask for completion to take place a certain number of days after work on the site is finished, in which case the buyer's solicitor should ensure that:
  - the period before completion is long enough for pre-completion searches and site inspections by the buyer and his lender.
  - the buyer has alternative accommodation while waiting for completion.
  - the buyer has access to bridging finance for this period of time, and that the buyer is given enough notice of the works being completed for the lender to put the buyer's solicitor in funds.

➤ If the seller offers a financing package, ensure that the buyer is properly (by a permitted third party, if appropriate) advised on whether it is suitable for his needs.

➤ The seller may offer comfort in the form of an NHBC 'Buildermark' insurance policy, or a similar product. A 'Buildermark' policy protects the buyer and his successors in title against structural defects for 10 years after completion. The buyer is insured against the builder's default, including its insolvency, for 2 years after completion.

- A lender may insist on such insurance cover.

➤ Examine a copy of any agreement between the developer and the highway authority under which the developer will put in roads and street lighting, and the authority will adopt them at a later stage (these agreements are authorised under *HA 1980 s 38*). Ensure the agreement is backed by an adequate bond, in case the developer becomes insolvent before completing its obligations.

- Similar considerations apply to drains and sewers, and agreements with the water authority under *WIA 1991 s 104*.
- Ensure there are appropriate easements (eg: to use roads) so that the buyer will have a right of access prior to adoption.
- Note that if the bond is inadequate the buyer may have to pay for the works to be carried out or for adoption.

Step 9: Post-completion

➤ Ensure the buyer receives the following documentation, and that it is kept with the title deeds:

- an NHBC pack (if appropriate). Return the tear-off form to the NHBC.
- a 'final certificate' from the local authority confirming that planning consent and building regulations have been complied with.

➤ Before 2 year cover under a 'Buildermark' policy against the builder's default runs out, advise the buyer to carry out a full structural survey to reveal any latent defects.

➤ If the property is a commonhold unit and no other units have yet been sold, the Register will indicate through a series of entries and restrictions on the Proprietorship Register that during a transitional period the rights and duties imposed by the CCS are not in force (as the title both to the common parts and every unit will be registered in the name of the original applicant for the land to be held as a commonhold).

- On the first unitholder becoming registered the CCS comes into force, the common parts are registered in the name of the commonhold association, and the entries on the Register relating to the transitional period will be removed.

D Leases

    I   Drafting a lease - outline points
    II   Management schemes
    III Procedure for granting a lease
    IV Procedure for assigning a lease
    V   Obtaining a landlord's consent to an assignment or transfer
    VI Procedure for assigning a lease over a commonhold unit
    VII Procedure for selling a reversion

I Drafting a lease - outline points

1 Definitions section

2 Grant

- The premium, ie: the sum which the tenant pays the landlord for the grant of the lease.
- The term, ie: how long the lease lasts for.
- Starting date, ie: when the term runs from; this need *not* be the date of completion as the landlord may wish a batch of leases to start on the same day irrespective of when he finds tenants so as to ensure that the reversion dates are the same.
- Ground rent: this is often paid on the quarter days.
- Rent review: basis of calculation/frequency.

> **Quarter days**
>
> Lady Day: 25 March
> Midsummer Day: 24 June
> Michaelmas: 29 September
> Christmas: 25 December

2 Easements and reservations

3 Common parts

- Identify these, provide for their maintenance and repair. This is usually done through a periodic service charge.

4 Tenant's covenants

- To pay rent, repair, not to make alterations or improvements, not to change user, or alienate the lease (eg: by subletting the property without the landlord's consent).

5 Landlord's covenants: to insure and keep common parts in repair

6 Insurance

- This can be achieved in several ways, but contributions to a block policy taken out by the landlord (or management company) ensure tenants are covered for the same risks.

7 Cesser of rent

- Lease may provide that a tenant may cease to pay rent if a building is burnt down, or on specified events.

8 Forfeiture clause

- This states in what circumstances the landlord may regain possession. A court order is needed for an occupied dwelling (*PEA 1977 s 2*). On breach of covenant, a notice is usually served under the *LPA s 146*.

Flats: common law presumptions

a) If the tenant is not responsible for something, then the landlord is presumed to be so.

b) External walls are included in the demise, even if the landlord is responsible for repairing them.

c) A flat includes the ceiling, at least to the underside of the floor joists to which the ceiling is attached.

d) If the ownership of a roof is not expressly reserved by the landlord, the top floor tenant can occupy or alter it (eg: build extra stories).

e) There is *no* presumption that internal boundary walls divide flats from each other or from common parts; therefore an accurate plan marking the extent of the flat, common parts and rights of way is essential.

II   Management schemes

These schemes govern how an estate is maintained; there are 3 types of scheme commonly used.

1   The landlord manages the estate either directly, or through an agent

- ✘ The landlord cannot walk away and wash his hands of day to day administration.
- ✘ Tenants are not given the freedom to organise things as they wish.
- ✘ Tenants do not have a contractual right to ensure their neighbours comply with their covenants. They rely on the landlord to police covenants which he has with each tenant.

2   Tenants covenant with each other by deed of covenant

- ✘ There is no co-ordination or general oversight - each tenant is on his own.
- ✘ Enforcement can be haphazard and difficult.

3   A management company is set up

- ✓ Enforcement by the company is practicable.
- ✓ The landlord is freed from the burden of administration.
- ✓ The landlord retains his investment in the reversion.
- ➤ There are 2 ways of setting up a private company (see the 'Business' Chapter): in both cases the landlord grants the lease and covenants to provide services. Then *either*:

    a) at a later date, the management company can join the lease and the landlord irrevocably instructs the tenant to pay the service charge to the company in consideration of the company undertaking the service obligations, *or*

    b) the landlord grants the company a concurrent lease of the block (effectively leasing the reversion). During the lease, the company becomes the tenant's landlord and provides the services specified in the lease', *or*

    c) transfer of reversion to a management company (only if the reversion has no real value).

III Procedure for granting a lease

This is the same as for a freehold conveyance (see p 174 for 'step' chronology), with these additions:

Step 2: Seller prepares the pre-contract package

➤ The landlord drafts the lease and the contract. He sends the buyer:

- proof of the freehold title (see pp 212, 216),
- if the lease is over a commonhold unit, a copy of the CCS and *Form 13* (notifying the tenant that it will be required to comply with the parts of the CCS which confer duties on him) (*CCS para 4.7.12*), *and*
- evidence that any lender with a charge over the land consents (if such consent is required as a term of the mortgage) to:
  a) the grant of the lease, *and*
  b) any alterations to the property, *and*
- a draft contract and a draft lease.
  - If the lease is a prescribed clause lease (*LRR 2003 r 58A*) granted on or after 19 June 2006, it must either begin with required wording (e.g. landlord's title number, parties, premium, term etc.) set out in *LRR 2003 Sch 1A*, or that wording must appear after any front sheet.

Liability on covenants

➤ For leases granted on or after 1 January 1996 (other than under an agreement entered into, or a court order made before that date *or* assignments made by operation of law after that date) the tenant is released from covenants on any subsequent assignment (*LT(C)A 1995 s 5*).

➤ The landlord can protect his position by inserting a covenant that the tenant shall:

a) secure adequate references from a future assignee and other requirements relating to financial standing.

b) enter into an 'authorised guarantee agreement' under which the tenant agrees to guarantee the performance of any covenants by the assignee until the assignee makes another assignment (or the tenancy is assigned by operation of law) (*LT(C)A 1995 s 16*).

Step 3: Buyer approves the contract

➤ The buyer checks the freehold title.

➤ The buyer should also discover whether the lease is sufficiently marketable and whether it will remain so if the buyer envisages assigning the term before the lease expires to secure a mortgage.

- Banks and building societies are reluctant to lend money for leases of under 60 years.

Step 6: Landlord prepares the 'deed'

➤ The landlord sends a fair copy to the buyer at least 5 working days before completion (*StC 8.2.5*).

- Note that a lease for less than 3 years does not need to be by deed (*LPA s 53*) (or in writing (*LPA ss 52(2)(d), 54(2)*)).

Step 9: Post-completion

➤ Any SDLT payable should be paid and an SDLT certificate sought for forwarding to HM Land Registry.

➤ If the lease is granted over a commonhold unit, notify (using *form 14*) the commonhold association within 14 days beginning on the date the tenancy is granted (*CCS para 4.17.15*).

IV Procedure for assigning a lease

This is the same as for a freehold conveyance (see p 176 for 'step' chronology), with these additions:

Step 2: Seller (ie: assignor) prepares the pre-contract package

➤ The seller should ensure that the contract contains an indemnity for the covenants.

- Prior to 1 January 1996 (at common law - but could be overridden by contract), *LPA s 77* provided for an indemnity where value was given for the estate in land.

- For leases granted on or after 1 January 1996 an indemnity is effectively provided for (*LT(C)A 1995, StC 4.6.4*).

➤ The seller sends the buyer (ie: the assignee):

Pre-contract package:
- the landlord's licence(s) permitting assignment (in the past and consent this time), *and*
- proof of leasehold title (unregistered title, see p 216; registered title, see p 221), *and*
- a copy of the original lease, *and*
- a *Seller's Leasehold Information Form* (*Prop 4*) ('SLIF') and a *Fixtures Fitting and Contents Form* (*Prop 6*) ('FFCF'), *and*
- a copy of the insurance policy, and a receipt for the last premium payment, *and*
- a copy of the receipt for the last payment of rent and the service charge, *and*
- a lender's consent to the assignment (if required under the terms of a loan subject to which the property is charged).

Step 4: Preparations for exchange

➤ As well as checking the lease, the SLIF/FFCF, the contract, the consents and the seller's title, the buyer must ensure:

- any references the landlord requires are prepared, *and*
- a surety is found (if required by the lease).

Step 6: Buyer prepares the purchase deed

➤ Registered land: use *Form TR1*.

➤ Unregistered land: add a covenant for title.

Step 7: Preparing for completion

➤ The seller should take the necessary steps to obtain the landlord's consent.

- The apportionment of rent or service charge should be checked (this is governed by *StC 6.3*). The buyer should ask to see service charge accounts for recent years.

Step 9: Post-completion

➤ SDLT is payable on the transfer or assignment of the lease.

➤ Send two copies of a notice of dealing to the landlord (and lender if appropriate) - the second copy to be receipted and returned.

V Obtaining a landlord's consent to an assignment or transfer

> ### Transfer of part - leases granted after 1 January 1996
>
> ➤ The general rule is that the tenant ceases to be liable for the covenants given by the tenant, or to be entitled to the benefits of covenants given by the landlord, in respect of the part of the premises which he assigns (*LT(C)A 1995 s 5(3)*).
>
> ➤ If the performance of a covenant is not attributable to the tenant or the assignee, the parties can agree to apportion liability (*LT(C)A 1995 s 9*) provided that within 4 weeks of the assignment the parties serve a notice on the landlord detailing the assignment, their agreement and their request that he should be bound by the apportionment.
>
> - If the landlord does not serve a notice objecting to the apportionment within 4 weeks of service on him, he is bound (if he does object, the parties may apply to the County Court for a declaration that it is reasonable for the apportionment to bind him) (*LT(C)A 1995 s 10*).
>   - A notice should comply with the *LT(C)A(N)R 1995*.

1 Qualified covenants (ie: where the landlord covenants not to unreasonably withhold consent)

➤ Consent may not be unreasonably withheld (*LTA 1927 s 19*).

- For leases granted on or after 1 January 1996 (except those granted under an agreement or court order dated before that date) ...

  ... over property which is *not* let as a private residence, ...

  - ... the landlord shall not be regarded as acting unreasonably if he refuses to grant consent, or agrees to grant it subject to conditions if the landlord cites a reason listed in an agreement with the tenant (eg: not to assign without securing for the landlord adequate references) (*LTA 1927 s 19A*).

➤ The landlord must respond within a 'reasonable' time, and must grant consent unless it is reasonable to withhold it (*International Drilling Fluids Ltd v. Louisville Investments (Uxbridge) Ltd* [1986] 1 EGLR 39).

- The landlord must send the tenant a notice giving any conditions attached to the consent or reasons for refusing it (*LTA 1988 s 1(3)*).

➤ The seller is responsible for seeking consent and using 'all reasonable efforts' to obtain it. If he fails, the buyer's remedy is rescission (*StC 8.3.2-3*).

➤ The landlord does not usually charge a premium, but he may ask the tenant to pay a reasonable administrative charge to cover his expenses.

➤ The licence is written, but it is not by deed unless it contains a covenant by the buyer (assignee).

- The landlord sends the seller a licence and retains a copy with his deeds of title.

2 Absolute covenants prohibiting assignment

➤ Although the lease prevents assignment, a tenant who wishes to assign can persuade the landlord to:

a) grant a deed of release from the covenant against assignment, *or*

b) vary the lease, *or*

c) give consent.

VI Procedure for assigning a lease over a commonhold unit

This is the same as for assigning any other lease, with these additions:

Step 2: Seller (ie: assignor) prepares the pre-contract package

➤ If the lease is over a commonhold unit, a copy of the CCS and *Form 15* (notifying the tenant that it will be required to comply with the parts of the CCS which confer duties on him) (*CCS para 4.7.16*).

Step 9: Post-completion

➤ If the lease is granted over a commonhold unit, notify (using *Form 14*) the commonhold association within 14 days beginning on the date the tenancy is granted (*CCS para 4.17.19*).

VII Procedure for assigning a reversion

This is the same as for a freehold conveyance (see p 174 for 'step' chronology), with these additions:

Step 2: Assignor (ie: landlord) prepares the pre-contract package

➤ The seller discloses the leases which have been granted over the property, together with details of the service charge accounts.

Steps 4 to 9: Assignor and assignee comply with the requirements of *LT(C)A 1995*

➤ The landlord may apply to be released from his covenants under the tenancy (*LT(C)A 1995 s.6(2)*), and a former landlord who immediately before the assignment was bound by a covenant under that tenancy may also apply for release (*LT(C)A 1995 s 7(2)*).

• The procedure involves service on the tenant of a notice, and an opposition procedure over 4 weeks from the date of service, similar to that set out in the box on p 231 (*LT(C)A 1995 s 8*).

➤ Any release of liability in respect of the landlord's covenants is accompanied by a loss of the benefit of the tenant's covenants.

➤ If the landlord only assigns the reversion in part and wishes to apportion liability in respect of non-attributable covenants which the landlord is obliged to perform, a procedure similar to that for tenants assigning part of the demised premises should be followed (*LT(C)A 1995 s 9(2)*).

• For this procedure, see the box on p 232. The only difference is that the application for the apportionment to become binding is served on the tenant(s) of the premises.

Gas safety

➤ A landlord (including a local authority, housing association, hostel owner, a private sector landlord, or landlord renting out a room or bedsit) who permits people to live in his property must ensure that there is maintained in a safe condition:

a) any relevant gas fitting, *and*

b) any flue,

... so as to prevent the risk of injury to any person in lawful occupation of the premises (*GS(IU)R 1998 r 36(2)*).

➤ A landlord may not delegate his duty to a tenant, must use a CORGI registered gas installer for the safety check and must leave a copy of that check with the tenant.

➤ Non-compliance is a criminal offence punishable, if the Health and Safety Executive take enforcement action under *HSWA 1974 s 37*, by imprisonment and/or an unlimited fine as well (if the landlord is a company) as disqualification for directors.

E Security of Tenure

There are 2 classes of tenancy which, on a new grant of a leasehold interest, may qualify for security of tenure by virtue of statute.

  I Residential tenancies
  II Commercial tenancies

I Residential tenancies

The main features of assured and assured shorthold tenancies

➤ The tenant has some security of tenure. When the fixed term expires, a statutory periodic tenancy automatically arises (*HA 1988 s 5(2)*). Unlike the situation for commercial property under *LTA 1954 Part II*, the tenant does not have to serve a notice to obtain a new tenancy.

➤ The statutory periodic tenancy may be ended by:

  a) a court order (*HA 1988 s 7*) (including a demotion order (*HA 1988 s 6A*)), or

  b) action taken by a tenant at common law to end the tenancy (surrender, etc) (*HA 1988 s 5(2)*).

➤ A landlord may regain possession of property let on an assured shorthold tenancy by serving a notice under *HA 1988 s 21*.

1 Is the tenancy an assured tenancy, or an assured shorthold tenancy?

Assured tenancy	Assured shorthold tenancy
Requirements (HA 1988 s 1(1)) ➤ dwelling house (includes a flat) ➤ let (ie: lease not a licence) ➤ as a separate dwelling (ie: at the time of the grant) ➤ to a tenant who is an individual (ie: not a company) and occupies the dwelling as its main or principal home Note: a dwelling has been held to be somewhere where 'all the major activities of life, particularly sleeping, cooking and feeding ...' take place (*Wright v. Howell* (1947) 92 Sol Jo26, CA)	➤ On or after 28 February 1997 the landlord serves a notice if an assured tenancy is *not* to be an assured shorthold (*HA 1988 s 19A*). ◆ A tenant who does not receive a notice under *s 19A* is entitled to request a written statement of the terms of the tenancy from the landlord (*HA 1988 s 20A*)

Exclusions from assured/ashured shortholds (outline)

➤ Lease granted, or contract to grant a lease, dated before 15 January 1989
➤ Student lettings
➤ Lettings to homeless persons under *HA 1985 Part II*
➤ Properties of a high rent or rateable value (eg: over £25,000 per annum if granted after 1 April 1990)
➤ Low rent properties (eg: under £1,000 per annum in the Greater London area if granted after 1 April 1990)
➤ Tenancies within the scope of the *LTA 1954 Part II*, or (in respect of assured shortholds) *HA 1988 Sch 2A*

2   **Are there special terms which statute implies into the lease, or another statutory regulation?**

➤ There are controls on the calculation and payment of service charges (*LTA 1985 ss 18-30*).

- Tenants and landlords may ask a leasehold valuation tribunal to assess whether a service charge is payable and the amount which is payable (*LTA 1985 s 27A*).
    - The tenant may challenge the landlord's choice of insurer or an excessive premium.
  - The right to apply to a tribunal under *HA 1996 s 83* does not apply if a tenant:
    a) agrees to or admits the service charge or insurance, *or*
    b) is a party to an arbitration agreement which covers the dispute.
- If a property is let as a 'dwelling', a landlord may not be able to re-enter the property or forfeit the lease for non-payment of a service charge, unless:
  - it is finally determined by (or on appeal from) a court or leasehold valuation tribunal, or by a tribunal under an arbitration agreement, that the amount of the service charge is payable by the tenant, *or*
  - the tenant admits that the service charge is payable (*HA 1996 s 81*).

➤ Certain assured tenancies are subject to rent control provisions (*HA 1988 s 22*).

➤ A licence, granted by a local authority, is needed for a 'house in multiple occupation' (*HA 2004 Part 2*).

- It is a criminal offence for a landlord not to obtain such a licence (*HA 2004 s 72*).

➤ For *all* new residential leases of under 7 years granted to a new tenant (eg: not a former tenant or one in possession at the time of a grant), statute implies covenants that the landlord will:
a) keep the exterior and structure in repair, *and*
b) ensure installations for heating, water and space and those supplying water, gas, electricity and sanitation are kept in repair and proper working order (*LTA 1985 ss 11-14*).

3   **Can the landlord regain possession?**

➤ The landlord commences proceedings by serving a notice on the tenant stating the ground(s) upon which he intends to take possession of the property (*HA 1988 s 8*). If *Ground 14A* (domestic violence) is relied on, the landlord's notice must meet additional requirements which are beyond the scope of this book (*HA 1988 s 8A*).

- The notice period depends upon which ground of *HA 1988 Sch 2* the landlord relies upon.

➤ In addition, if the tenancy is an assured shorthold, the landlord may regain possession at the end of the term by serving a notice under *s 21* of the *HA 1988* giving at least 2 months' clear notice of his intention to take possession.

- If the tenant has not vacated by the time the notice expires, the landlord can start posession proceedings.

4   **Does the tenant have the right to buy the freehold, or to a lease extension?**

➤ The tenant may have the right to buy the freehold, or extend the lease by up to 90 years if the term of the lease exceeds 21 years (*LRA 1967, LRHUDA 1993* as amended by *CHLRA 2002*).

➤ If, without 'reasonable excuse', a landlord fails to offer tenants first refusal on a disposal of his interest on or after 1 October 1996 he commits a criminal offence punishable by a fine of up to £5,000 (*HA 1996 Sch 6*).

- This applies if the premises contain 2 or more flats more than half of which are rented (*LTA 1987, Part I*).

CONVEYANCING
Security of tenure

Are there grounds for a cds for a court order for possession? (HA 1988 Sch 2)		
Assured tenancies		
Mandatory 1-8	Ground 1*:	a) at some time before the tenancy began the property was the landlord's principal home, *or* b) the landlord seeks possession for himself or his spouse as a principal home *and* the reversion was not acquired for money or money's worth
	Ground 2*:	a mortgagee under a pre-existing mortgage is exercising a power of sale
	Grounds 3-5*:	out of season holiday lettings, vacation lettings to students, lettings to ministers of religion
	Ground 6:	a) the landlord 'intends to demolish or reconstruct the whole or a substantial part of the dwelling, or carry out substantial building works ...', *and* b) the landlord did not acquire the reversion for money or money's worth, *and* c) possession is essential for the works (Varying the lease is unacceptable to the tenant or impractical)
	Ground 7:	death of a tenant. (A spouse's right to succession is unaffected by this ground (HA 1996 s 17))
	Ground 8:	rent arrears of 8 weeks if paid weekly, or 2 months if paid monthly, *when* notice is served *and* at the date of the hearing (plead Grounds 10 and 11 in the alternative) (amended by HA 1996 s 101)
		* The landlord must serve a notice stating that possession may be sought under the appropriate ground. This must be given 'not later than the beginning of the tenancy'
Discretionary 9-17	Ground 9:	the landlord offers 'suitable' alternative accommodation as defined in HA 1996 Sch 2 Part III
	Ground 10:	less than 3 months' rent is in arrears
	Ground 11:	persistent delay in paying rent
	Ground 12:	breach of tenancy clause which does not relate to rent
	Ground 13:	deterioration of the dwelling due to the tenant's neglect
	Ground 14:	the tenant or a person residing in or visiting the dwelling: a) is a nuisance or annoyance to anyone engaged in lawful activity in the vicinity, *or* b) is convicted for using the premises or allowing them to be used for illegal or immoral purposes, *or* c) commits an arrestable offence in the locality (see also *s 9A*)
	Ground 14A:	a) the occupiers are a married couple/CPs or living together as man and wife/CP, *and* b) one of the partners has left because of violence to themself or a child and is unlikely to return, *and* c) the landlord seeking possession is a 'registered social landlord' or a 'charitable housing trust' (inserted by HA 1996 s 148)
	Ground 15:	deterioration of furniture due to the tenant's conduct
	Ground 16:	the tenant's employment ends when the letting was a consequence of that employment
	Ground 17:	tenant's false statement, made knowingly or recklessly, induced the landlord to grant the lease (HA 1996 s 102)
Assured shorthold tenancies		

➤ The grounds are the same as those for assured tenancies

➤ In addition, a notice can be served under *s 21* of the *HA 1988* giving the tenant not less than 2 months' notice that the landlord requires possession of the dwelling

➤ If a landlord is a local housing authority, a housing action trust, or a registered social landlord it may apply to court for a secure tenancy to be terminated and replaced by a demoted tenancy if the tenant, or a person residing in, or visiting the dwelling has engaged in, or threatened to engage in, antisocial behaviour or the use of premises for unlawful purposes (*HA 1996 s 82A*).

♦ *HA 1996 ss 144A-P* offer a procedure to assist a landlord in regaining possession of a dwelling subject to a demoted tenancy.

CONVEYANCING
Security of tenure

II   Commercial tenancies

> **Commercial property leases - code of practice**
>
> ➤ This code of good practice (www.commercialleasecodeew.co.uk), endorsed by the Law Society and the British Property Federation, should be brought to the attention of landlords and tenants, especially if either are small businesses, before the grant of a lease.
>
> ➤ If the industry does not voluntarily implement the Code to make the market more transparent, the Government may legislate on the conduct of rent reviews and alternative dispute resolution.

➤ The *LTA 1954 Part II* provides some security of tenure to tenants of commercial property by extending the term indefinitely after the date on which it would otherwise determine at common law (*LTA 1954 s 24(1)*).

1   Does the *LTA 1954 Part II* apply to the tenancy?

➤ If a lease to which the Act would otherwise apply is to be granted, the parties may wish to consider contracting out of the *LTA 1954*.

➤ If the parties wish to contract out, then either:

a) a landlord must serve a warning notice at least 14 days before a tenant is committed to a lease, and the tenant must sign a simple declaration stating that this has been done, *or*

b) the parties can agree less than 14 days before a tenant is committed to a lease, and the tenant must sign a statutory declaration before a solicitor that the tenant has received and read a warning notice and accepts its consequences (*LTA 1954 s 38A, RR(BT)(EW)O 2003 Schs 1-2*).

> **Tenancies protected by the *LTA 1954 Part II***
>
> ➤ A tenancy is protected if it (*LTA 1954 s 23*):
>
> a) is a tenancy (ie: not a licence), *and*
>
> b) is of premises, *and*
>
> c) is occupied by the tenant, *and*
>
> d) is for the purposes of a business carried on by the tenant (or, by a company in which a tenant has a controlling interest, or if the tenant is a company a person with a controlling interest in the company) or for those and other purposes,
>
> ... provided that it is not excluded for any reason, eg:
>
> i) the tenancy is 'contracted out' under *LTA 1954 s 38A*, *or*
>
> ii) it is an agricultural holding (*LTA 1954 s 43(1)(a)*), *or*
>
> iii) it is granted by reason of employment (*LTA 1954 s 43(2)*), *or*
>
> iv) it is for a term certain not exceeding 6 months (*LTA 1954 s 43(3)*) (a tenancy at will is not for a 'term certain' and is therefore excluded).

2   If the *LTA 1954* applies, how can the landlord regain possession, or a new lease be granted under the *LTA 1954*?

➤ The *LTA 1954* operates a system of notices (simplified in certain respects and extended by the *RR(BT)(EW)O 2003*), which must be served correctly and at the appropriate times.

➤ A *s 25* notice is served by a landlord who either:

   a) wishes to regain possession, *or*

   b) is not opposing renewal.

> ◆ To be valid a *s 25* notice must be:
>
> • served not less than 6 months and not more than 1 year before the date of termination, *and*
>
> • given to the tenant, *and*
>
> • specify the date of termination, *and*
>
> • demand action of the tenant (eg: vacate the premises, or enter negotiations for a new tenancy), *and*
>
> • *either:*
>
>   a) *if the landlord wishes to regain possession*: explain on which of the statutory grounds (*s 30(1)(e)-(g)*) the landlord will oppose the grant of a new tenancy, eg:
>
>   i) a breach of the tenant's repairing obligations.
>
>   ii) persistent delay in paying rent.
>
>   iii) other substantial breaches.
>
>   iv) the landlord can provide suitable alternative accommodation.
>
>   v) the landlord needs possession for letting or disposing of the property as a whole.
>
>   vi) the landlord intends to demolish or reconstruct the property.
>
>   vii) the landlord intends to occupy the premises for his business or as his residence, *or*
>
>   b) *if the landlord is not opposing renewal*: contain proposals for the terms of a new lease.
>
> • be in the correct form set out in the *LTA 1954 Part II (Notices) Regulations 2004*.

➤ A *s 26* request is served by a tenant who wants a new tenancy.

> ◆ A *s 26* request must:
>
> • specify a date for the new tenancy to begin which is not more than 1 year and not less than 6 months after the date specified in the notice (which cannot be earlier than, apart from this legislation, the date the tenancy would have come to an end by effluxion of time or by a notice to quit given by the tenant), *and*
>
> • contain proposals for the new lease (the amount of detail depends on the tenant's negotiating tactics, eg: whether the tenant wishes to tell the landlord early on exactly what he wants), *and*
>
> • be in the form set out in the *LTA 1954 Part II (Notices) Regulations 2004*.

3 **Is the tenant entitled to any compensation on termination?**

➤ If the landlord terminates the tenancy under grounds in *s 30(1)(e)-(g)*, then generally the tenant will be entitled to compensation, or if a tenant has been induced not to apply for renewal by misrepresentation or concealment, or a tenant's application is withdrawn for these reasons (*s 37*).

➤ If the tenant has made improvements to the property, he may be entitled to compensation under *LTA 1927 Part I*.

CONVEYANCING
Security of tenure

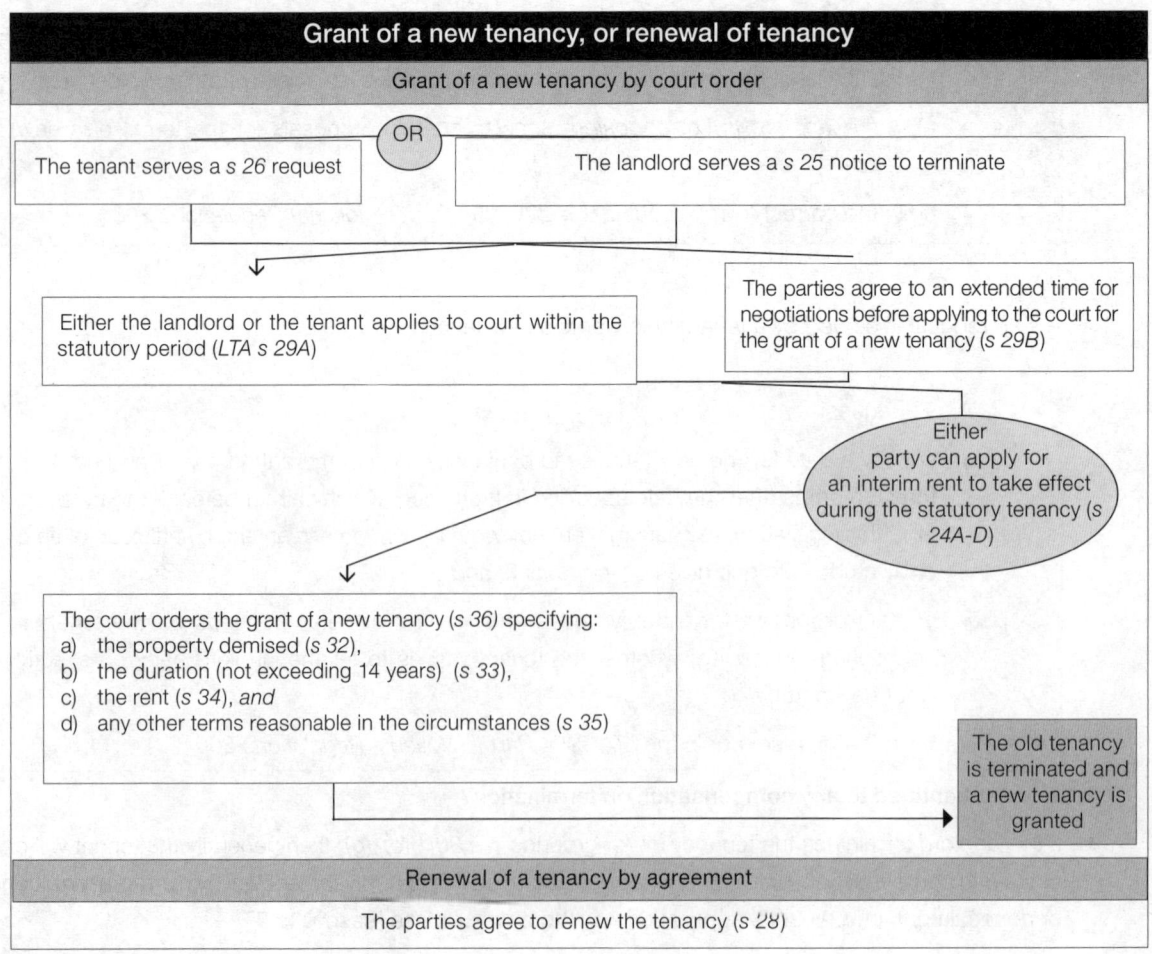

F Commonhold

➤ Commonhold is a new form of freehold tenure (*CLRA 2002 s 1*).

◆ An ownership interest in a commonhold property comprises both:

a) ownership of a 'unit' within a development, *and*

b) membership of a commonhold association ('CA'), a company limited by guarantee, which holds the common parts of a development and manages the development in accordance with a commonhold community statement ('CCS').

- A unit is defined in a CSS in accordance with *CR 2004 r 9* and does not include the structure and exterior (unless the unit is a self-contained building).

- A lease of a unit may not generally be granted for a term of more than 7 years (*CR 2004 r 11*).

➤ Commonhold is intended to offer a modern, transparent/flexible, and standardised alternative to leasehold.

◆ Eg: the CSS provides for the CA to insure (*CCS para 4.4*, *CLRA 2002 s 26(b)*) and repair/maintain (*CCS para 4.5*, *CLRA 2002 s 26(c)*) the common parts, and there are standard notifications (*CR 2004 Sch 4*) such as in respect of income a CA needs to raise by assessment (*Form 1*) and requesting payment of an assessment (*Form 2*).

◆ On registration of a commonhold development, any leasehold is extinguished (*CLRA 2002 s 9(3)(f)*).

➤ To register commonhold land:

Steps

1 Incorporate a CA at Companies House using the form of Memorandum and Articles set out in *CR 2004 Sch 1* and compliance with *CR 2004 rr 12-14*, *and*

2 Prepare a CCS in the form set out in *CR 2004 Sch 3* (*CR 2004 r 15*), and a plan of the development which is no larger than A0 size and is preferably 1/500 scale, based on an accurate survey (*HM Land Registry Practice Guide 60,* June 2004), *and*

3 Obtain the necessary consents (see *CLRA 2002 s 3* and *CR 2004 r 3*), broadly from those who have an interest in the property such as the registered proprietor of the freehold interest, or a chargee), *and*

4 Apply to HM Land Registry to register commonhold land using *Form CM1* (*C(LR) 2004 r 5*) plus:

a) a certified copy of the CA's certificate of incorporation, *and*

b) a certified copy of the CA's memorandum and articles of association, *and*

c) 2 certified copies of the CCS (future amendments must be made using *Form CM3*), *and*

d) the consents referred to in 'step 3' above in *form CON1* (*C(LR) 2004 r 7*),

e) a certificate given by the directors of the CA confirming that the memorandum & articles comply with *CR 2004*, the CCS satisfies the requirements of *CLRA 2002*, the land is not land which cannot become commonhold land (specified in *CLRA 2002 Sch 2*, eg: a flying freehold), the CA has not traded or incurred liability which has not been discharged, *and*

f) a statutory declaration from the applicant confirming that the required consents have been properly obtained, and giving details of any charge over part of a unit which is to be extinguished (*C(LR)R 2004 r 6*), *and*

g) if an application is with unitholders (eg: an existing freehold or leasehold is being converted to commonhold, rather than there being a new development) *Form COV 9* which contains a request that *CLRA 2002 s 9* applies and lists the units (giving for each the name and address of the proposed unit holder or joint unit holders).

G Remedies

  I   Notice to complete
  II Compensation for delayed completion
  III Contractual remedies

Vendor and purchaser application *(LPA s 49(1))*

➤ Under this section, either party may issue an application under *CPR 1998 Part 8* to resolve disputes connected with the transaction (but *not* one questioning the validity or existence of the contract itself).

➤ The court has summary jurisdiction to resolve such matters as:

a) the validity of a notice to complete.

b) whether the buyer is taking a clean title as promised in the contract.

c) whether a requisition on title is valid.

I Notice to complete

➤ Initially time is not of the essence (*StC 6.1*), unless the contract is conditional. It can be made of the essence if completion is delayed by serving a notice to complete.

➤ Time is 'of the essence' from the service of a notice to complete. Consequently, if completion does not occur when the notice specifies the party at fault commits a breach of contract.

- The innocent party may choose to terminate the contract after this breach and/or sue for damages.
- If the party who served the notice defaults, the recipient of the notice has a claim for breach. Consequently, a notice should only be served if you are sure you can complete.

1 At common law

➤ The notice must specify a 'reasonable' time for the new completion date.

➤ The party serving the notice must be ready, willing, and able to complete if the notice is to be valid.

2 *StC 6.8* displaces the common law rules

➤ The notice should state that it is served under this contractual provision.

➤ If a notice is served, the new completion date is set 10 clear days from the day of service.

➤ If the buyer has paid a deposit of under 10%, he must pay the full 10% on receipt of the notice.

➤ If the notice is ignored, the seller may rescind if he served the notice (*StC 7.5*), *or* the buyer may rescind if he served the notice (*StC 7.6*).

II Compensation for delayed completion

1. **Delay due to the seller's fault (at common law)**
   - The seller pays outgoings on the property during the period of delay.
   - The seller retains *whichever is less of*:
     a) the interest on the purchase price which the buyer pays at the general equitable rate, *or*
     b) the net income on the property.

2. **Delay due to the buyer's fault (at common law)**
   - The buyer pays outgoings on the property.
   - The buyer retains any income from the property.
   - The buyer pays the seller interest on the balance at the general equitable rate.

3. *StC 7.3* **(this overrides the common law regime)**
   - Whichever party causes the greater period of delay pays the other compensation at the contract rate.
   - The sum on which interest is paid depends on which party is liable to pay compensation.
     - The buyer's interest is calculated on the balance of the purchase price outstanding (ie: the deposit is deducted).
     - The seller's interest is calculated on the purchase price.
   - Interest runs for whichever is the shorter of:
     a) the time between the contractual completion date and actual completion, *or*
     b) the length of time during which the party liable to pay compensation was in default.

     NB: compensation under *StC 7.3* is deducted from any damages a court subsequently awards.

III Contractual remedies

Pre-completion	Post-completion
Action on the covenants for title	
For a list of the covenants implied by statute on, or after 1 July 1995, see p 182 Before 1 July 1995, *LPA s 76(1)* implied into conveyances or transfers of land for value covenants which depended on the seller's capacity (as 'beneficial owner', 'fiduciary' or 'settlor'), and whether the interest concerned was freehold or leasehold ➤ This action is *only* available *after* completion if the contract incorporates a non-merger clause similar to *StC 7.4*, otherwise the contract and the deed 'merge', removing the right to a remedy under the contract alone	
Rescission	

➤ This restores the parties to their original position
 ➤ The claimant may seek an indemnity in the contract for any loss incurred
 ➤ The claimant may seek damages if:
   a) hye is claiming rescission under *MA 1967 s 2(1)*, *or*
   b) rescission is due to the defendant's breach, *or*
   c) the claimant is seeking a declaration from the court that the defendant has committed a repudiatory breach of contract
 ➤ The claimant may *not* seek damages where obtaining rescission is the purpose of the action
 	
 The *StC* expressly reserve the right to rescind if:
 a) the seller makes a misrepresentation (an error of fact upon which the buyer relies in entering the contract) (*StC 7.1*), *or*
 b) the landlord does not grant a licence to assign (*StC 8.3*), *or*
 c) the condition of the property alters substantially before completion (*StC 5.1*)
 	
 StC 7.2 lists rights on rescission *under the contract*:
 a) documents are returned to the seller, *and*
 b) the buyer pays for cancelling any entry on the Register to protect the contract, and (unless recission results from a breach by the buyer) regains the deposit plus interest	

Damages for breach of contract	**Rectification**

➤ Calculated on the principle in *Hadley v. Baxendale* (1854) 9 Exch 341:
   ◆ all loss arising naturally from the breach which the parties could reasonably have foreseen on entering the contract would result from the breach
	➤ This is an equitable remedy: the document is altered to reflect the parties' original intentions
	
	 Either the parties agree,
	
	 or the court grants the remedy at its discretion if:
	
	   ◆ *both* parties were mistaken, *or*
	   ◆ *one* party was mistaken *and* the party 'in the know' was ...
	     a) aware of the error and so is estopped from resisting rectification, *or*
	     b) fraudulent, *or*
	   ◆ only one party is party to the document
	
	 Note:
	 if both rescission and rectification are available, the court may let the claimant choose (*Solle v. Butcher* [1950] 1 KB 671)

Specific performance	
➤ An equitable remedy in the court's discretion ➤ The court may award damages instead of granting specific performance (*SCA 1981 s 51*) ➤ The court may award damages as well as specific performance (*Johnson v. Agnew* [1979] 1 All ER 883)	
➤ For dispute resolution between a commonhold association and a unitholder see *para 4.11* of the *CCS*.	

BUSINESS

This chapter examines:

A	Partnerships (non-tax aspects)	244
B	Limited liability partnerships (non-tax aspects)	250
C	Private companies (non-tax aspects)	255
D	Public companies (non-tax aspects)	286
E	Converting businesses	289
F	Choice of business medium	290
G	Insolvency	292
H	Competition and trading	307
I	Commercial agreements	322
J	Employment	326

All taxation aspects are dealt with together in the 'Taxation' section of this book.

Companies Bill 2006

At the time of writing (August 2006), the Companies Bill 2006 is going through Parliament and is expected to have Royal Assent in October 2006.
The Bill amends and restates many of the provisions of CA 1985. The Bill also codifies certain provisions of case law. In some areas the Bill makes textual amendments to CA 1985 or other legislation. There are also numerous new provisions.

Right to establish a business (Treaty of Rome: Article 43)

➤ An EU citizen has a right to establish a business in any member state, provided that the requirements of national law regarding the running of that type of business are satisfied (ie: company, partnership, etc).

Right to provide services (Treaty of Rome: Article 49)

➤ There is a right for an EU citizen to provide services into any member state.

➤ *The proposed EU Services Directive aims to create a free market for the services sector.*

　　◆ *Its purpose is to remove the legal and administrative barriers that can hinder businesses from offering their services in another country, and to encourage cross-border competition.*

➤ *On 31 May 2006, the European Council reached agreement on the proposed Directive. The next stage will be the second reading in the European Parliament with the aim of adopting a final text during Finland's Presidency in the second half of 2006.*

A Partnerships

I	Formation of a partnership
II	A written agreement for a partnership
III	Obligations and liability of partners
IV	Dissolution of a partnership
V	After dissolution - distribution of assets
VI	Taxation: see 'Taxation' section

I   Formation of a partnership

➤ A partnership 'subsists between persons carrying on a *business in common* with a view to profit' (*PA s 1*) (our emphasis).

➤ A partnership can come into existence orally, *or* by an agreement, *or* through a course of conduct.

➤ There is no limit on the number of partners allowed (*RR(R20MLP)O 2002*).

➤ However the partnership comes into existence, the *Business Names Act 1985* should be complied with.

Business Names Act 1985		
Section		**Content**
1	➤	If the name is the partners' surnames, either alone or with their initials, forenames or an 's' to show that there is more than one partner with a given name, then no restrictions apply.
2-3	➤	Words listed in the *Company and Business Names Regulations 1981 (as amended)* (eg: names suggesting a connection with HM Government or the royal family or the words 'Chamber of Commerce') require the approval of the President of the Board of Trade.
4	➤	Unless a name approved under *s 1* is used, then the names of partners and the address for service of documents must appear both: a) on letters, orders, invoices, receipts and written demands for payment, *and* b) at the place of business to which suppliers and customers have access. These details must also be given to anyone who requests such information. If a firm has more than 20 partners, it is sufficient to give the address of the main place of business where the addresses and names can be found.
5	➤	Fines may be imposed for non-compliance with the *Act*, and a contract with a third party who is prejudiced by the infringement will be unenforceable.
7	➤	Breach of the *Act* is a crime.

II A written agreement for a partnership

➤ A written agreement is safest to effect a partnership. Various matters are highlighted below which the draftsman may wish to consider. References are to the *Partnership Act 1890*, unless otherwise stated, and the Act will apply if the partnership agreement is silent on a particular matter.

1. **Commencement date:** an objective test based on *s 1*. The date stated in the agreement is not conclusive.
2. **Name:** the firm's name (and its trading name if this is different). These must comply with *BNA 1985*.
3. **Financial input:** of each partner.
4. **Salaries:** if the agreement is silent, the partners will not be entitled to a salary (*s 24(6)*).
5. **Interest**
   ➤ Partners are entitled to interest at 5% on capital they advance in excess of their obligations under the terms of the partnership (*s 24(3)*).
   ➤ There is no entitlement to interest on capital until profits have been ascertained (*s 24(4)*).
6. **Capital profits or losses:** if the agreement is silent, these are shared equally (*s 24(1)*).
7. **Shares in profit derived from income:** if the agreement is silent, these are shared equally (*s 24(1)*).
8. **Drawings of money**
9. **Place and nature of business**
10. **Ownership of assets:** either i) by the partners privately, or ii) by partners on trust for all the partners.
11. **Work input**
    ➤ Full or part-time?
    ➤ Bar on the involvement of partners in other businesses during their membership of the partnership?
12. **Partners' roles**
    ➤ All the partners may manage the firm (*s 24(5)*), but this is inappropriate for 'sleeping' partners.
13. **Management**
    ➤ A simple majority prevails, unless otherwise stated (*s 24(8)*).
    ➤ Unanimity is required for i) changing the nature of the business (*s 24(8)*), ii) admitting new partners (*s 24(7)*), iii) changing the partnership agreement.
    ➤ If unanimity is required for anything else, put it in the contract.
14. **Duration of the partnership**
    ➤ i) At will, or ii) for a fixed term, or iii) for as long as a minimum of two partners remain.
    ➤ *PA s 26* provides that if no date is given, then if a notice of dissolution is given, it is effective immediately. To prevent this occurring inadvertently, a notice period should be specified.
15. **Death/bankruptcy/retirement:** if the agreement is silent, these dissolve a partnership (*s 33*).
16. **Expulsion of partners:** this is impossible without an express provision in the agreement (*s 25*).
17. **Paying for an outgoing partner's share.** Consider:
    ➤ either an *obligation* on (or an *option* for) the remaining partners to purchase the share.
    ➤ a method for valuing the share. Provide for professional valuation if the partners do not agree.
    ➤ a date on which payment falls due (a grace period allows those remaining to find new equity).
    ➤ whether an indemnity is included in the valuation.
18. **Restraint of trade on outgoing partners:** the clause must be 'reasonable' to be enforceable at common law (ie: with regard to time, geographical area, and whether the activity competes with the partnership).
19. **Income tax**
    ➤ An outgoing partner may be obliged to join the others in sending a tax election to HMRC.
    ➤ An outgoing partner should be indemnified against additional liability resulting from his election.
20. **Arbitration:** name an arbitrator in case of disputes between the partners (else recourse is to court).

III Obligations and liability of partners

A Generally

➤ Partners are bound to each other:

1 **in contract:** in accordance with the terms of the partnership agreement, *and*

2 **under the *PA ss 28-30* and a century of case-law as follows:**

- **Duty of utmost good faith:** partners are bound to each other by a set of duties that can collectively be called a duty of utmost good faith.

- Duty to render to each other true accounts and full information on all matters affecting the partnership (*s 28*).

- Duty to account for any benefit (eg: a transaction concerning the partnership made without the consent of the partnership) (*s 29*).

- Duty to account for the profits derived from any competing business (*s 30*).

➤ See also the effect of *C(ROTP)A 1999* on p 322.

B Firm's liability

Recovery from the firm
➤ The firm is a group of persons who were partners at the time the cause of action arose (*PA ss 9,17*).
➤ Recovery is possible from the partnership assets and also from partners personally.

➤ The firm may be liable:

1 **in tort:** for a partner's act or omission in the ordinary course of business, *or* an act with a partner's authority (*PA s 10*).

2 **in contract:** for agreements made by a partner with, or with the partners', 'actual' or 'ostensible' authority.

- **Actual authority:** this can be expressly *or* impliedly given in the partnership agreement, or it may arise from a factual situation or a decision of the partners.

- **Ostensible authority:** 4 conditions must be satisfied (*PA ss 5-8*):

  subjective test
  - a) the third party knows or believes he is dealing with a partner, *and*
  - b) the third party is unaware that the partner was not actually authorised, *and*

  objective test
  - c) the partner would usually be expected to be authorised to enter into such a transaction, *and*
  - d) the firm's type of business is consistent with the nature of the transaction.

C Personal liability of a partner

1 A partner to a third party

➤ A partner is personally liable in contract (if he or the firm are party to the contract) and in tort.
- Liability is without limit for debts incurred while a partner (*PA s 9*).
- Liability does *not* cease on leaving the firm for obligations incurred while a partner (*PA s 17*).

2 A partner to a partner

➤ A partner acting outside his authority can be liable to the other partners for breach of warranty of authority.

3 An ex-partner to a third party

➤ Any partner is liable for obligations incurred *after* his departure from the partnership if there is:

a) 'holding out' that the ex-partner is a partner (*PA s 14*) by:
  i) a representation (oral/written/conduct) *either* by the ex-partner, *or* with his knowledge, *and*
  ii) reliance on this representation by a third party,

or b) failure to notify of leaving the partnership (*PA s 36*).
- An ex-partner is liable *unless* notice of the change:
  i) is given to all who have dealt with the firm recently. This protects against claims from previous customers.
  ii) appears in the *London Gazette*. This protects against claims from future customers.

  Note: i) and ii) do not apply on death or bankruptcy, so an estate is not liable for a firm's subsequent acts.

4 A stranger to a third party

➤ A stranger will be liable for an obligation if he has been 'holding out' that he is a partner (*PA s 14*):
  i) by making a representation (oral/written/conduct) that he is a partner, *and*
  ii) a third party relies on this representation.

D Limitation of personal liability

1 By indemnity

a) No actual authority

Where a partner has acted without actual authority, the other partners are entitled to an indemnity for any loss they suffer as a result of the unauthorised act.

Note: i) an indemnity will only protect the other partners if the indemnifier is solvent.
  ii) the other partners will only be entitled to any indemnity if they act to mitigate their loss.

b) Outgoing partner indemnity

An outgoing partner may negotiate an indemnity from the remaining partners to protect himself.

2 By novation

➤ A 3-way agreement between a new partner, creditor and continuing partners by which the new partner takes on the outgoing partner's liability.

3 By suitable acts

➤ A leaving partner may try to limit liability by certain practical acts (see section 3b in C above).
- Eg: change the notepaper and the list of partners at the place of business, put suitable notices in relevant newspapers etc.

IV Dissolution of a partnership

➤ The partnership agreement will usually make provisions for when a partnership may be dissolved. Where it does not (or there is no partnership agreement), the following list of 9 defaults will apply.
- ◆ Always: '5' below will apply even if a partnership agreement caters for the other situations.
- ◆ Automatic termination: '1', '3' and '6' will terminate the partnership automatically.

➤ A partnership may be dissolved by ...

1. ... expiry
    ➤ A 'fixed term' partnership terminates at the end of its term (PA s 32(a)).
    ➤ A partnership intended to achieve a single undertaking ends when that undertaking is attained (PA s 32(b)).
    - ◆ If the partners continue acting in concert the agreement continues, but as a 'partnership at will'.

2. ... notice
    ➤ This is when any partner gives notice to the other(s) of his intention to dissolve the partnership.
    - ◆ Notice may be effective immediately, or after a specified period (PA s 32(c)).
    - ◆ Notice does not need to be written unless the partnership agreement is by deed (PA s 26(2)).

3. ... illegality
    ➤ When an event occurs that makes it unlawful to continue in partnership (eg: loss of a licence which is required for running the business) (PA s 34).

4. ... court order under PA s 35
    ➤ Regardless of what a partnership agreement may provide, the court has discretion to dissolve a partnership on one of the following grounds:

    Either when a partner, other than the partner applying to court ...

    - s 35(b) is rendered 'permanently' incapable of carrying out obligations under the agreement, *or*
    - s 35(c) engages in conduct prejudicial to the partnership's business, *or*
    - s 35(d) wilfully breaches the partnership agreement, or behaves in such a way that it is not reasonably practical for the other partners to continue the business.
    - s 35(e) Also, when the partnership can only be continued as a loss-making business, *or*
    - s 35(f) when the court regards dissolution as 'just and equitable'.

5. ... court order under *Mental Health Act 1983 s 96(1)(g)*
    ➤ This happens if a partner is a 'patient' (ie: mentally incapable of managing his affairs).

6. ... **death, bankruptcy** (PA s 33(1)), **retirement** (PA s 26) **or expulsion** (PA s 25) **of a partner**
    ➤ These events dissolve the partnership.

7. ... charging order
    ➤ If a partner's share in the partnership assets is subject to an order for payment of a private debt (PA s 23), a creditor can seek a court order for the asset's sale; when this sale takes place, a purchaser gains a share in the asset without becoming party to the partnership.
    ➤ When an order is made, the other partners may give notice of dissolution to prevent a third party purchaser gaining title to the asset (PA s 33(2)).

8. ... disposal
    ➤ A partner may insist on the sale of the business as a whole or in parts (PA s 39).

9. ... winding up
    ➤ Any partner, except a bankrupt, can apply to the court for the appointment of a receiver (PA s 38).

V   After dissolution - distribution of assets

➤ Partners all have continuing authority to act on behalf of the partnership after its dissolution (*PA s 38*).

➤ On dissolution, every partner has a right to insist that the partnership property is used to pay the firm's debts (*PA s 39*).

➤ If a dissolution occurs, the business may be sold:
  ◆ as a going concern, *or*
  ◆ by breaking up the business and selling off the assets.

➤ The assets (or proceeds from sale of the assets) are distributed in the following order (*PA s 44*):

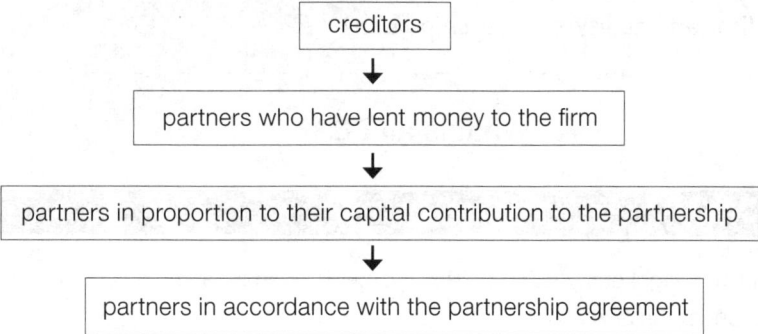

➤ When other partners continue the business, the outgoing partner is entitled to:
  a) interest at 5% on that partner's share of the assets, *or*
  b) whatever profit the court attributes to that partner's share of the partnership assets between the dissolution and the actual payment of his share (*PA s 42*).

➤ Where a partner dies, the entitlement under *s 42* to interest or ongoing profits is regarded as a debt owed to his estate from the date of his death (*PA s 43*).

VI   Taxation

➤ See the Taxation chapter: Income tax, CGT and IHT.

B Limited liability partnerships (LLPs)

  I   Formation of a LLP
  II A written agreement for a LLP
  III Obligations and liability of a LLP and its members
  IV Taxation - see 'Taxation' section

This section deals solely with an English law limited liability partnership (LLP) incorporated under the LPA 2000. It does not cover limited partnerships established under the Limited Partnerships Act 1907.

I Formation of a limited liability partnership (LLP)

A What is an LLP?

What is a LLP?

➤ A LLP is a new form of legal entity (*LPA 2000 s 1(1)*). It is a legal person in its own right as a body corporate formed under the *LPA 2000*.

  ◆ A LLP is a body corporate with unlimited capacity to act (eg: it can buy and sell property, sue and be sued and do anything which a natural person can do) (*LPA 2000 s 1(3)*).

➤ LLPs have been introduced with the broad intention of offering:

  a) limited liability to 'members' akin to that enjoyed by shareholders, *and*

  • In a partnership, partners have unlimited liability. For partnership debts and obligations this liability is joint; for loss or damage from a wrongful act or omission (in the ordinary course of a partnership's business or with the authority of the partners) of partners in a partnership, it is joint and several.

  b) the tax advantages of a partnership, as opposed to a company (ie: although the existence of the partnership may be important for computational purposes, a LLP or partnership is, unlike a company, transparent for tax purposes), *and*

  • See further the Taxation chapter.

  ▪ Note, in addition, that:

  ... the exemption from tax otherwise accorded to a pension funds and friendly societies, *and*

  ... the special treatment of the assets of an insurance company's long term insurance business

  ... do not apply if (and to the extent that) such an entity is a member of a property investment LLP whose business consists wholly or mainly of investing in land (*FA 2001 Sch 25*).

  c) limited public disclosure to protect a LLP's creditors.

B Formation of a LLP

Steps

1 2 or more persons associated for carrying on a lawful business with a view to profit subscribe their names to an incorporation document (*LPA 2000 s 2(1)(a)*).

2 Deliver to the Registrar (*LPA 2000 ss 2(1)(b)-(c)*) (*Form LLP2* suffices for both a) and b)):

a) the incorporation document (or an authenticated copy), *and*

Incorporation document
➤ The incorporation document must (*LPA 2000 s 2(2)*):   ◆ be in a form approved by the Registrar (or as near to such form as the circumstances allow), *and*   ◆ state the name of the LLP (which must comply with *LPA 2000 Sch 1 Pt 1*), *and*   ◆ state whether the LLP's registered office is to be situated in England and Wales, in Wales, or in Scotland, *and*   ◆ state the address of the registered office, *and*   ◆ state the name and address of each of the persons who are members of the LLP on incorporation, *and*   ◆ *either* specify which of those persons are to be designated members *or* state that every person who from time to time is a member of the LLP is a designated member.

b) a statement made by a solicitor engaged in the formation of the LLP or a subscriber to the incorporation document, that Step 1 has been complied with.

- It is an offence, punishable by a fine and/or imprisonment for up to 2 years to make this statement is a person knows it to be false or does not believe it to be true (*LPA 2000 ss 2(3)-(4)*).

3 The Registrar retains the incorporation document (or copy), registers it and issues a certificate that the LLP is incorporated with the name specified in the incorporation document (*LPA 2000 ss 3(1)-(3)*).

◆ The certificate is conclusive evidence that the requirements of *LPA 2000 s 2* have been complied with and that the LLP is incorporated (*LPA 2000 s 3(4)*).

II A written agreement for a LLP

➤ The mutual rights and duties of a LLP and its members may be governed by agreement between the members, or between the LLP and its members (*LPA 2000 s 5(1)(a)*).

◆ If there is no agreement *LLPR 2001* resolve matters by applying (with suitable modifications) law relating to partnerships (*LPA 2000 s 5(1)(b)*). Partnership law does not apply generally, but only in accordance with default provisions set out in *LLPR 2001 rr 7-8*.

> **Default provisions for agreement between members** (*LLPR 2001 rr 7-8*)
>
> ➤ All the members of a LLP are entitled to share equally in the capital and profits of the LLP (*r 7(1)*).
> ➤ The LLP must indemnify every member in respect of payments made and personal liabilities incurred by him in:
>   a) the ordinary and proper conduct of the LLP's business, *or*
>   b) or about anything necessarily done for the preservation of the business or property of the LLP (*r 7(2)*).
> ➤ Every member may take part in the management of the LLP (*r 7(3)*).
> ➤ No member is entitled to remuneration for acting in the LLP's business or management (*r 7(4)*).
> ➤ No person may be introduced as a member or voluntarily assign an interest in a LLP without the consent of all existing members (*r 7(5)*).
> ➤ Any difference arising as to ordinary matters connected with the LLP's business may be decided by a majority of the members, but no change may be made in the nature of the LLP's business without consent of all members (*r 7(6)*).
> ➤ The LLP's books and records are to be available for inspection at the LLP's registered office or at such other place as the members think fit and every member of the LLP may when he thinks fit have access to and inspect and copy any of them (*r 7(7)*).
> ➤ Each member shall render true accounts and full information of all things affecting the LLP to any member or his legal representative (*r 7(8)*).
> ➤ If a member, without the LLP's consent, carries on any business of the same nature as and competing with the LLP, he must account for and pay over to the LLP all profits made by him from that business (*r 7(9)*).
> ➤ Every member must account to the LLP for any benefit derived by him without the consent of the LLP from any transaction concerning the LLP, or from his use of the LLP's property, name or business connection (*r 7(10)*).
> ➤ No majority of the members can expel any member unless a power to do so has been conferred by express agreement between the members (*r 8*).

- An agreement made before a LLP's incorporation between the subscribers may obligate a LLP (ie: it is not necessary to novate an agreement between the partners after incorporation) (*LPA 2000 s 5(2)*).

➤ If a member:
- ceases to be member, *or*
- dies, *or*
- becomes bankrupt, *or*
- has his estate sequestrated or wound-up, *or*
- has granted a trust deed for the benefit of his creditors, *or*
- has assigned the whole or part of his share in a LLP (absolutely or by way of charge or security) ...
  - ... his PR/trustee in bankruptcy/liquidator/trustee/assignee may not interfere in the management or administration of any business or affairs of the LLP, but may receive from the LLP any amount to which the former member would have been entitled (*LPA 2000 s 7*).

➤ A LLP must ensure that where (*LPA 2000 s 9*):
  a) a person becomes or ceases to be a member (or a designated member) notice is delivered to the Registrar within 14 days, *and*
  b) there is a change in the name/address of a member, notice is delivered to the Registrar within 28 days.
  - The notice must be signed by a designated member of the LLP.
  - Non-compliance is an offence by the LLP and every designated member, punishable by a fine not exceeding level 5 on the standard scale (currently £5,000 (*CJA 1982 s 37*)).

III Obligations and liability of a LLP and its members

1 Obligations and liability of a LLP to third parties

➤ Every member is the agent of the LLP (*LPA 2000 s 6(1)*). But a LLP is not bound by anything done by a member dealing with a person if:

a) the member in fact has no authority to act for the LLP, *and*

b) the person knows that the member has no authority or does not know or believe the member to a member of the LLP.

- A former member of a LLP is regarded (in relation to any person dealing with the LLP) as still being a member of a LLP *unless*:
    i) the person has notice that the former member has ceased to be a member of the LLP, *or*
    ii) notice that the former member has ceased to be a member has been delivered to the Registrar.

➤ A LLP is liable to the same extent as a member if that member is liable to any person (other than another member of the LLP) as result of that member's wrongful act or omission in the course of the LLP's business or with its authority (*LPA 2000 s 6(4)*).

➤ A document signed by 2 members of a LLP and expressed to be executed by the LLP has the same effect as if executed under the LLP's common seal (*CA 1985 s.36A, LLPR 2001 Sch 2 Pt I*).

- A purchaser (in good faith for valuable consideration, including a lessee/mortgagee) may assume a document has been duly executed by a LLP if it purports to be signed by 2 members of the LLP.

2 Obligations of a LLP under *CA 1985* (as modified for LLPs by *LLPR 2001*)

➤ Certain *Companies Acts* obligations apply to LLPs (*LLPR 2001 Sch 1* applies *CA 1985 Part VII* to LLPs, and *Sch 2* applies the *CDDA 1986* and other provisions of the *CA 1985* to LLPs).

Eg: a LLP must: ...	CA 1985
... ensure the LLP's name appears outside its place of business	s 348
... ensure the LLP's place of registration, registered number and the address of its registered office appear on its on its correspondence	s 349
... keep accounting records	s 221
... prepare accounts (These are approved by the designated members and signed by designated members on behalf of the members)	ss 224-233
... deliver accounts and any auditor's report to every member of the LLP and holder of its debentures within 1 month of signature and in any event not later than 10 months after the end of the relevant accounting reference period ♦ The accounts must state the contributions of the partners to the LLP (*CA 1985 Schedules 4, 8, 8A*) ♦ Small and medium sized LLPs, like small companies, may submit less detailed accounts (*CA 1985 s 246, s 246A, s 247, Schedules 4, 8, 8A*)	s 238 s 241 s 244
... deliver accounts and auditor's report and annual returns to the Registrar of Companies	s 242, s 363
... register charges with the Registrar of Companies	s 399

3　Obligations and liability of members ...

Obligations and liability of members ...
... to the LLP
➤ Members owe a LLP a duty of good faith (akin to the fiduciary duty directors owe a company). 　◆ The DTI issued a consultation paper in February 2000 on the desirability of a statutory duty of good faith between partners. The DTI decided not to impose such a duty, but the default provisions in *LLPR 2001 r 7(9)-(10)* are intended to address this issue in a targeted way.
... to third parties
➤ The DTI took the view in a consultation paper issued in relation to the LLPs that the law is uncertain as to whether a third party who has suffered economic loss could successfully sue a member of the LLP. 　◆ *Williams v National Life Health Foods Ltd* [1998] 1 WLR 830 suggests that the courts would consider whether: 　　• the member assumed personal responsibility, *and* 　　• the third party relied on that assumption, *and* 　　• such reliance was reasonable.
... compliance with *CA 1985/IA 1986* (as modified for LLPs by *LLPR 2001*)
➤ A designated member may commit an offence if a LLP is in default of its statutory obligations, eg: if annual accounts are not filed with 28 days of the return date (*CA 1985 s 363*)). ➤ The designated members must appoint auditors, otherwise the members may do so at a meeting convened for that purpose (*CA 1985 ss 384-385*). ➤ A member may be liable for wrongful trading (*IA 1986 s 214*), or fraudulent trading (*CA 1985 s 458*). 　◆ The court may require a member to make a contribution if that member withdrew property within 2 years of the LLP being wound-up (*IA 1986 s 214A* as inserted by *LLPR 2001 Sch 3*).

IV　Taxation

➤ A LLP is essentially 'transparent', or 'look through', for tax purposes.

➤ See the Taxation chapter: Income tax and CGT. (For IHT see *IHTA 1984 s 267A*.)

C Private companies

References in this section apply to the Companies Act 1985, unless stated otherwise.

I	Establishment
II	Shareholders
III	Directors
IV	Finance
V	Taxation: see 'Corporation tax' section

> Note:
> *CA(EC)O 2000* permits documents/forms to be sent to and from the Registrar of Companies electronically

I Establishment

A Checks before establishing a company

➤ **Check 1:** search the index at Companies House to see if a desired name already exists.

➤ **Check 2:** do a trade mark search to see if the desired name already exists.

➤ **Check 3:** search local directories (eg: Yellow Pages, Thomson Local) to see if the desired name is already in use (to avoid passing off).

B Establishing a company

➤ There are 2 methods of establishing a company as a vehicle through which to run a business.

Method 1: from scratch

Step 1 Prepare:
1) Statutory books
2) *Form 10*
3) *Form 12*
4) Memorandum of Association
5) Articles of Association
6) Fee

File: items 2 to 6 with the Registrar of Companies.

Step 2 The Registrar incorporates the company if the documentation is in order (eg: the name does not need approval under *BNA 1985*). Incorporation occurs on the same day if submission is to the Central Registry (Cardiff) before 3 pm. Regional branches (London, Birmingham, Leeds, Edinburgh) also offer same day service.

Step 3 The Registrar issues the 'Certificate of Incorporation', bringing the company into existence as a legal person. Any pre-incorporation contract is voidable. The company can only participate in a pre-existing agreement through a contract of novation.

Method 2: buy a shelf company

➤ A shelf company has already been incorporated and 'sits on the shelf'.

➤ The existing directors of the shelf company resign and members complete a stock transfer form.

➤ It costs around £200 and it is fast and immediate. It is usual to change:
a) directors and secretary
b) shareholders
c) registered office
d) name
e) objects
f) articles
g) share capital.

➤ The purchased company comes with resignation letters from existing directors.

C Company documentation

1. **Statutory books** (These must be updated throughout the company's life.)
   a) Register of Members,
   b) Register of Directors,
   c) Register of Company Secretaries,
   d) Register of Directors' Interests,
   e) Register of Charges (this is necessary even if the company does not take out any loans),
   f) Minute Books for board and general meetings,
   g) Accounting records (only after incorporation), *and*
   h) Copies of directors' service contracts (only after incorporation).

2. *Form 10*
   ➤ This states the postal address of the company's registered office.
   ➤ It gives the details of the first directors and the company secretary who automatically take office on incorporation (see p 267 for an explanation of what details of the directors are required).
   ➤ It is signed by the subscribers to the memorandum, or by a solicitor on their behalf.

Later alteration of a company's registered office
The registered country must stay the same for this method:
First: the board passes a resolution ⟶ **Second:** file *Form 287*

3. *Form 12*
   ➤ This is a statutory declaration by a director, the company secretary, or a solicitor involved in the formation of the company that the *Companies Acts* have been complied with.
   ➤ It is sworn before a solicitor or commissioner for oaths.

4. **Memorandum of Association**
   ➤ The memorandum is printed and signed by at least one subscriber.
   ➤ It states the name, address, occupation of each subscriber, and the number of shares each will take on formation.
   ➤ It is dated and witnessed (one witness for both signatures is sufficient).
   ➤ It contains the following:

   a) Company name
      ◆ This must end with 'Limited' or 'Ltd' (*s 25*) *unless* the company is limited 'by guarantee' and conditions in *s 30* apply (limiting the company to humanitarian non-profit making activities).
      • A 'business name' is a trading name which a company may use in addition to the name under which it is incorporated. It need not end with 'Limited', but should comply with *BNA 1985* (see p 244):

As well as the business name...
...give the corporate name, and an address in the UK for serving documents:
a) on all letters, orders, invoices, etc, *and*
b) at all places of business to which customers have access, *and*
c) to any member of the public who requests this information.

- Existing company names are not permitted (*s 26*). A search of the Trademarks Index and Companies House will check if a name is in use (NB: no protection period after a search).
- An offensive name, or one suggesting a criminal offence, is also forbidden (*s 26*).
- The following require the President of the Board of Trade's written approval (*s 29*): a name suggesting connection with HM Government, the royal family, local authorities, any word /expression in regulations, or use of the words 'Chamber of Commerce' (*CBN(CC)A 1999*)).

Alteration of an existing company name

➤ A 'special resolution' alters the name (*s 28*). The change is advertised by the Registrar of Companies in the *London Gazette* (*s 711*); a third party is not fixed with notice until 15 days after the advertisement appears (*s 42*).

➤ The Registrar will issue a new certificate after payment of the fee.

➤ A change of name may become necessary if:

    a) the Registrar orders it because the name may harm or mislead the public (*s 32*), *or*

    b) a third party's injunction prevents its use (eg: for appropriating good will ('passing off')).

b) **Country in which the registered office is situated** (*s 2*)
- This cannot be altered.

c) **Limitation of members' liability** (*s 3*)
- This is frequently limited by 'share capital', unless stated otherwise.
- Alternatively, liability can be limited 'by guarantee', in which case the members are liable to the extent of the guarantee.

d) **Nominal capital**
- The maximum value of shares the company can issue. An ordinary shareholder resolution can alter this. (Such a resolution must be filed with the Registrar, see p 263.)

e) **Objects of the company** (*s 2*)
- The objects set out the purposes of the company and what it is allowed to do (ie: its powers).
- *CA 1989* permits a description as a 'general commercial company' which gives the company full freedom to do whatever it likes commercially, but it is unclear whether the company may perform actions which do not advance its business (eg: gifts to political parties or charity).
- Old-style objects clauses may have a *Bell Houses* formula. This is wording as follows:

The company is permitted to 'carry on any other trade or business whatsoever which can, in the opinion of the board ..., be advantageously carried on by the company in connection with, or ancillary to, any of the above businesses or the general business of the company' (*Bell Houses Ltd v City Properties Ltd* [1966] 2 QB 656).

- Old clauses may also end with an 'independent objects' clause. This is done to avoid restrictive case law which in some instances reads 'lesser' objects clauses as subordinate to a 'main' object (ie: as powers of the company rather than an object). An independent objects clause says that each object is an independent object.

Alteration of objects

➤ A special resolution alters the objects (*s 4*).

➤ Minority shareholders can appeal to court within 21 days (*s 5*).

5   **Articles of Association** (the 'constitution' governing a company's internal workings)

➤ This is a contract between the company and its members, governing members' rights in their capacity as members of the company (*s 14*).

➤ It is printed and signed by the subscribers to the memorandum, dated and witnessed.

➤ 'Table A' (see table below) is a model set of articles that will apply in the absence of other articles unless specifically excluded (*s 8*). However, it may need changes by including special articles, to:

- **empower directors to allot shares** (*s 80*).

- **empower directors to allot shares to whomever they wish:** lifting the statutory pre-emption rights of existing members to a pro rata allotment of newly issued shares (ie: in proportion to their existing holdings) without recourse to a general meeting (*s 89*).

- **enable directors to vote on issues in which they have a personal interest:** *Art 96* permits this in particular conditions; otherwise with a small company it can be difficult to achieve a quorum.

- **restrict members' right to transfer shares:** likely in a small family company where the members are anxious to retain control of membership. *Art 24* allows directors to refuse to transfer shares in certain limited circumstances.

- **prevent removal of directors: likely in small company.** If a director holds shares, a *Bushell v. Faith* clause is sensible as it multiplies his votes if a resolution proposes his removal. This provides some job security, but shareholders retain the right to remove directors by ordinary resolution (*s 303*).

Note: References in this chapter to Articles (Arts) assume Table A applies.

➤ Articles can be altered by a special resolution if the change is *bona fide* and in the best interests of the company as a whole (*s 9*).

Summary of Table A

Articles	Subject matter	Articles	Subject matter
Shares		72	Delegation of directors' powers
2-5	Share capital	73-80	Directors' appointment and retirement
6-7	Share certificates	81	Directors' disqualification and removal
8-11	Lien over shares	82	Directors' remuneration
12-22	Calls on shares and their forfeiture	83	Directors' expenses
23-28	Transfer of shares	84-86	Directors' appointments and interests
29-31	Transmission of shares	87	Directors' gratuities and pensions
32-34	Alteration of share capital	88-98	Directors' proceedings
35	Purchase of own shares	**General**	
Meetings		99	Secretary
36-37	General meetings	100	Minutes
38-39	Notice of general meetings	101	Company seal
40-53	Proceedings at general meetings	102-108	Dividends
54-63	Members' votes at general meetings	109	Accounts
Directors		110	Capitalisation of profits
64	Number of directors	111-116	Notices
65-69	Alternate directors	117	Winding up
70-71	Directors' powers	118	Indemnity

BUSINESS

Private companies

First board meeting

Consideration may be given to the following:

1. Electing a chairman / managing director / any directors with special responsibility.
2. Approving the cost of formation: the company can reimburse the subscribers by a novation contract.
3. Adopting a business name.
4. Opening a bank account.
5. Ordering stationery complying with the requirements in *s 349*, to state:
   a) the company name, its place of registration and registered number (*s 351*), *and*
   b) the address of its registered office (*s 351*), *and*
   c) *either* the names of *all* its directors *or* none of their names (s 305).
   - If a business name is used, the company's name and an address in Great Britain for the service of documents must be given.
   - The information given in a) and b) demanded by *s 351* for stationery should also be displayed at any place where the company conducts business (*s 348*).
6. VAT registration with HMRC.
7. PAYE and National Insurance obligations: contact the local tax office.
8. Insurance.
   - Ensure all the company's assets and necessary insurance policies are in its own name.
9. Appointing an auditor.
10. By default, the accounting reference date is fixed by statute as the last day of the month of incorporation (*s 224(3)*). This may be changed later by submitting *Form 225*.
11. Adopting a company seal (*s 350*).
12. Awarding directors' service contracts.
    - If the contract is for over 5 years, the board must resolve to seek shareholders' approval.
13. Allotting shares.
14. Whether to call a general meeting to obtain authority from shareholders to:
    - award directors service contracts of longer than 5 years.
    - allot shares (ordinary resolution *s.80)*. Ensure that any pre-emption rights (*s 89*) do not restrict this.
    - adopt an elective regime, see box at the base of this page.
15. Issuing debentures.

Elective resolutions

➤ These simplify the management of private companies by:
   a) giving the directors authority for any specified or indefinite period to allot shares (rather than being limited to 5 years) (*s 80A*).
   b) dispensing with the obligation to lay accounts and reports before an AGM (*s 252*).
   c) dispensing with the need to call AGMs automatically (but a member can still insist on one being called) (*s 366A*).
   d) reducing consent required to hold an EGM at short notice from 95% to a minimum of 90% (*s 369(4)* and *s 378(3)*).
   e) dispensing with the annual reappointment of auditors (*s 386*).

➤ These must be passed unanimously.

➤ Revocation of any of these is by ordinary resolution (*s 379A*).

II Shareholders

A Joining a company (ie: becoming a member)

➤ The original subscribers to the memorandum are members automatically, regardless of whether they are entered on the Register of Members.

➤ Anyone can become a member of a company if he buys shares in that company.

- However, the directors must agree to write a person into the Register of Members, otherwise there are consequences which are listed below.

Register of Members

➤ This must state: the name, address and the number of shares held by each member, plus consideration for the shares, and the dates on which the shareholder's membership of the company begins and ceases (s 352).

➤ The details of new members must be entered within 2 months of acquisition, however they acquire their shares. Directors cannot refuse to enter a name unless the articles permit this - wrongful refusal can be overcome by applying to a court for rectification of the register.

➤ Between acquisition and registration, the prospective member is beneficially entitled to the shares. Dividends and voting rights of the existing registered member must be 'used' at the acquirer's direction.

➤ If a company has only one member, the register must state when this state of affairs begins and ends (otherwise there is a fine for the company and the responsible officer, plus a daily default fine).

➤ The court can order the register to be rectified if *either*:

   a) a name is 'without sufficient cause' entered incorrectly, or there is 'default ... or unnecessary delay' in entering a member's details (s.359), *or*

   b) it is 'just and equitable' to do so (*Burns v Siemens Brothers Dynamo Works Ltd* [1919] 1 Ch 225).

B Shareholders' rights

➤ Obligations between shareholders and the company (or any combination of them) are governed by the memorandum and articles (s 14).

➤ For a summary of shareholders' rights, see the chart overleaf.

➤ If Table A is effective, shareholders may *not* reverse management decisions made by the board (*Art 75*).

➤ **Voting:** a shareholder can generally vote as he sees fit *unless*:

   a) individually, or together with other directors, he holds 50% or more of the shares: this prevents his voting to permit an abuse of power in his capacity as a director, *or*

   b) a majority shareholder ignores 'equitable considerations'. The court may overrule a special resolution passed which disregards these 'equitable considerations' (*Clemens v Clemens Brothers Ltd* [1976] 2 All ER 268).

➤ All members have a right to attend and vote at an Annual General Meeting ('AGM') of the company.

➤ All members have a right to attend and speak at a general meeting called at any other time - an Extraordinary General Meeting ('EGM').

BUSINESS

Private companies

All shareholders' rights		
Rights	**Notes**	**Statute**
Restrain an *ultra vires* act	Only before the act is done (after the company is bound). Remedy is an injunction	s 35(2)
To a share certificate	Within 2 months of allotment/lodgement of share transfer. *Prima facie* evidence of title	s 185
To a copy of annual accounts at a general meeting and right to be sent a copy	Applies even if an elective resolution dispensing with an AGM is in force. In certain instances, a summary financial statement may be sent instead of full accounts	s 240 C(SFS)R 1995
To have a say in removing or appointing a director		s 303
Name on Register of Members	Unless subject to a special article	s 352
To a dividend (if declared)	May not increase the sum recommended by directors, but may decrease it	Arts 102-8
To an AGM	This applies even if an elective resolution dispensing with the need to call an AGM is in force. Ultimately, a member may apply to the DTI which may convene a meeting for the purposes of which that member alone will represent a quorum (CA s 367)	s 366 s 366A
To prevent an AGM being held on short notice		s 369
To receive notice of general meetings		s 370
To attend and vote at general meetings		s 370
Ask a court to call an EGM	If a members' boycott prevents a quorum, a court can reduce the quorum required to 1	s 371
To prevent the adoption of the elective regime		s 379A
To block a written resolution		s 381A
Inspect AGM/EGM minutes	Available at the registered office for consultation	s 383
Not to be unfairly prejudiced	Prejudice to rights as a member may be past, present, or future	s 459
Have a company wound up	Available if 'just and equitable' and the member has a 'tangible interest'. Not available if it prejudices someone unfairly.	IA1986 s 122(g)
Members with a minimum of 5% of the voting rights		
Place item on the agenda for an AGM	Written request to a company 6 weeks before an AGM with money to cover the company's expenses. (This may be refunded at the meeting.) If directors call an AGM within the 6 weeks, adequate notice is deemed to have been given	s 376
Circulate written statement	Written requisition deposited with company at least 1 week before a GM	s 376
Members with a minimum of 10% of the voting rights		
Call an EGM	May *not* be excluded by articles. Members deposit at the registered office a written requisition which is signed by them all and states the reason for calling the meeting. If within 21 days, the directors do not call a meeting, to be held within 28 days of notice being sent out (ie: the maximum delay is 7 weeks from request), then members can call a meeting within 3 months and recover the cost from the company, which may deduct it from the directors' fees. Where members call the meeting they have an implied right to set the agenda (s 368(3))	s 368
	This section, like *s 368*, allows members to call an EGM, but it differs in 3 respects: a) it applies to members with 10% or more of the *issued* (not the *paid up*) shares, *and* b) it permits the members themselves to summon the meeting, *and* c) it may be excluded by the articles	s 370
Prevent an EGM being held on short notice (unless an elective resolution is in force, in which case they can only do this with *greater than 10%* of the voting rights)		s 369(3)(b)
Demand a poll vote		s 373 Art 46

BUSINESS
Private companies

Shareholders' agreement

> This binds members in matters beyond the scope of the articles and is used in practice to impose extra obligations on those concerned.
> - It is a private document, and unlike the articles is not open to public inspection.
> - It cannot be altered without the *unanimous* consent of all those who are party to it.
> - It cannot override obligations under the articles or statute.
> - It provides a remedy in breach of contract - via an injunction or damages.
> - Possible uses include:
>   - to arrange for the sale of the business as a going concern to the company when a company is initially set up,
>   - Eg: setting out the allotment of shares or the grant of debentures,
>   - agreeing to appoint a particular managing director, chairman, director etc,
>   - joining a director, who is not a shareholder, to the agreement to enhance his job security by obliging the other signatories not to vote for his dismissal,
>   - agreeing to grant a particular member a services contract,
>   - binding the signatories to pursue a particular management policy - such matters are usually left to the board by the articles, and an agreement gives shareholders a direct influence on how the company is managed,
>   - agreeing to change the name of the company or to have some policy regarding this,
>   - pre-emption rights, where enshrining this in the articles would be too public an act,
>   - to allow a member to leave the company by obliging the other signatories to purchase the shares.

Methods to control the Board

> The shareholders may specifically want to control the board and may use the following methods:
> - increasing the number required for a quorum at a GM,
> - appointing proxies when a shareholder is not at a GM,
> - preserving the balance of power (eg: by inserting special articles restricting the transfer of shares),
> - specifying in a shareholders' agreement a valuation and buy-out mechanism,
> - replacing or amending the statutory pre-emption rights,
> - inserting a restrictive objects clause in the memorandum,
> - amending *Art 70* (Table A) to limit the powers of the board,
> - amending *Art 72* (Table A) (concerning delegation of board powers).

C Safeguards for shareholders

➤ Members have a cause of action in contract to enforce rights as members of the company (*s 14*).
- Relevant rights include rights to:
  a) a share of surplus capital on winding up.
  b) a lawfully declared dividend.
  c) vote at meetings.
- The liability of shareholders is limited to the amount invested in their shares.

  Note: a company can use *s 14* to compel members to fulfil contractual obligations (eg: pay for shares).

1 Shareholders' common law actions

➤ General rule: members cannot sue in the company's name (*Foss v Harbottle* (1843) 2 Hare 461).

➤ There are 4 exceptions to this rule (not dealt with in this book). If a member *does* succeed in bringing an action under these exceptions:
- the action is 'derivative' as the claimant is pursuing a right which belongs to the company itself. *The company* is the claimant. If successful, *the company* is granted a remedy, not the member.
  - There is a preliminary hearing to see whether the facts fall within one of the relevant exceptions. If so, this is followed by the main hearing, to determine liability.

2 Shareholders' statutory actions: 'unfair prejudice' (*s 459*)

➤ The member's rights as a shareholder include rights under statute, the memorandum, the articles and any shareholders' agreement.

➤ Whether or not there is unfair prejudice is an objective test, so prejudice is viewed from the perspective of the 'reasonable bystander' (*Re R A Noble & Sons (Clothing) Ltd* [1983] BCLC 273).
- A shareholder cannot ordinarily complain of unfairness unless there has been a breach of the terms by which he had agreed that the company would be run (but this is tempered by equitable considerations). *s 459* depends on 2 features (*O'Neill v Phillips* [1999] 1 WLR 1092):
  - the way in which a company is run is regulated by rules to which the shareholders agree, *and*
  - this 'contract' is treated by equity as a contract of good faith.

➤ The court can make 'any order it thinks fit' (*s 461(1)*) and a non-exhaustive list of powers is given (*s 461(2)*). These include:
- authorising a member to bring a civil action in a company's name.
- restraining a company from an act, or compelling it to act so as to avoid the 'unfair prejudice'.
- providing for a member's shares to be purchased by other members or a company at a fair price.

➤ An action brought under *s 459* is not derivative, as the claimant is suing in his own right. Consequently, *the claimant* will receive a remedy if his plea is successful.

3 Petition to wind up the company (only if 'just and equitable') (not covered in detail here)

Will the courts intervene?

➤ There is conflicting authority as to whether the courts will now intervene wherever it is equitable if there is no precedent for them to do so (*Heyting v Dupont* [1964] 2 All ER 273, *Prudential Assurance Co v Newman Industries Ltd (No 2)* [1982] Ch 204).

➤ Previous cases where the courts have granted a minority shareholder a remedy include where:
- the company acted illegally.
- the company passed an ordinary resolution when a special or extraordinary resolution is needed.
- the majority shareholders 'defrauded' a minority member (*Clemens v Clemens Bros* [1976] 2 All ER 268).

D Shareholders' meetings

Extraordinary General Meetings ('EGMs')	Annual General Meetings ('AGMs')
➤ If Table A is applicable, then the board may call these at any time (*Art 37*), and in certain circumstances shareholders may do so (see p 261)	➤ No AGM need be held in the calendar year of incorporation or the following year, provided one is held within 18 months of incorporation (*s 366*) ➤ An AGM is called once every calendar year; the maximum gap between convening AGMs is 15 months (*s 366*) ➤ If an elective resolution is in force, then the need to call an AGM may be dispensed with (*s 366A*)

➤ There are **5** requirements for a meeting, discussed below:
  1) a valid notice of the meeting must be sent out.
  2) the correct form of resolution must be proposed.
  3) the meeting must be quorate.
  4) the correct formalities must be observed at the meeting itself.
  5) the voting must be correctly carried out.

1 Notice of the meeting (*s 369, Art 38*)

If by post: add 2 days to these numbers because a notice is deemed to be given 48 hours after it was posted (Art 115).

Meeting	Notice	Short notice	
AGM	21 clear days	If *all* the shareholders agree	An elective resolution is effective if less than 21 days notice is given, if all entitled to attend and vote at a meeting agree (*s 379A(2A)*)
EGM (generally, but see the box below)	14 clear days	If a majority holding 95% of the voting capital agrees NB: An elective resolution can reduce this to 90%	
EGM where: a) there are special or elective resolutions proposed, *or* b) there is a resolution to appoint a director, *or* c) (according to some interpretations of *s 379*, which is ambiguous), there is a resolution to remove a director (see p 268)	21 clear days		
		Invalid notice (the time given or the contents of the notice are incorrect)	
		General rule: in Table A, any resolution passed will be invalid (*Art 111*) *unless* the error in the notice is accidental (*Art 34*)	

a) Contents of the notice

➤ Name of company, date, time and place of meeting.

➤ State whether the meeting is an AGM or an EGM.

➤ The exact wording of special *or* extraordinary resolutions *or* resolutions requiring special notice.

➤ Ordinary resolutions *must* be given in sufficient detail for members to decide whether to attend.

➤ A proxy notice *must* be included (*s 372(3)*).

➤ Accidental errors may not invalidate the notice (see 'Invalid notice' in table above).

b) Recipients and service

➤ Notice is sent in writing to all members, directors, the auditor and all persons entitled to a share in consequence of death or bankruptcy of a member (*Art 38*), provided that:
  i) the member has a registered address in the UK (*Art 112*).
  ii) a PR or trustee in bankruptcy informs the company of their address, otherwise service is sufficient at the member's registered address (*Art 116*).

➤ Notice may be served personally, else it is deemed to be served 48 hours after posting (*Art 115*).

2 Resolutions to be proposed

➤ An ordinary resolution (more than 50%) is sufficient unless statute or the articles require otherwise. (For written resolutions, see below; for elective resolutions, see p 259.)

Note: directors (or members with minimum 5% voting rights) may, at the company's expense, prepare a statement for circulation before the meeting.

Resolution	Type of meeting	Majority needed
Special	AGM or EGM	75% of those present and voting NB: more than 25% blocks these
Extraordinary	AGM or EGM	
Ordinary	AGM or EGM	More than 50% of those present and voting NB: 50% blocks these - this is 'negative control'
Elective	AGM or EGM	Unanimous consent of all who are entitled to vote

Shareholders' written resolutions (s 381A)

- ➤ A less cumbersome alternative to holding a general meeting.
- ➤ Where statute requires documents such as a director's service contract to be open to inspection, copies must be sent to members with the resolution.
- ➤ Written resolutions must be signed by *all* the members entitled to attend and vote at a general meeting, or on their behalf.
- ➤ The resolution is passed on the signature of the final member (s 381A(3)).
    - ◆ The resolution must be sent to the auditors for checking at the time, or before the resolution is supplied to a member for signature (s 381B).
    - ◆ If a director/the secretary does not ensure that this is done, the party responsible will be liable for a fine (s 381B(2)) *unless*:
        - ● it is not practical to comply, *or*
        - ● he believed on reasonable grounds either that the copy had been sent or that the auditors had otherwise been informed of its contents.
    - ◆ If the resolution is not shown to the auditor, this does not affect the validity of the resolution (s 381B(4)).
- ➤ This procedure may *not* be used (according to *Sch 15A*) to dismiss *either*:
    - ◆ a director (s 303), *or*
    - ◆ an auditor (s 390).
- ➤ Records and filing are as for a normal resolution at a GM.

After a shareholders' resolution has been passed (s 380)

1. Resolutions should be filed with the Registrar at Companies House within 15 days if they are:
    - ◆ special,
    - ◆ extraordinary,
    - ◆ ordinary, but only those that increase the authorised share capital, give or revoke s 80 authority to allot shares, or revoke an elective resolution,
    - ◆ elective,
    - ◆ written.
2. Write up the minutes.
3. The board must meet and resolve to carry out any act which the shareholders have authorised *if* they wish to use this authority, but they are not compelled to do so.

3   **Quorum**

➤ The necessary quorum is 2, unless the company has 1 member (*s 370*).

➤ The articles can increase the minimum required (*s 370*).

➤ A member present through a third party proxy counts, provided the proxy is not a member in his own right as well.

➤ A quorum must be maintained throughout the meeting, else resolutions passed are invalid (*Art 41*).

4   **Formalities at the meeting (proxies, minutes, sole members, chairman)**

➤ The rights of proxies must be respected:

- a company may not require the deposit of a proxy more than 48 hours notice before a meeting (*s 372(5)*).
- a proxy may speak at the meeting (*s 372*).

➤ Minutes of the meeting should be kept (*s 382*).

➤ A sole member must provide the company with written notice of his resolution, otherwise although its validity is unaffected, he will be liable for a fine (*s 382B*).

➤ A chairman runs the meeting. He is usually the same individual as the chairman in a board meeting.

5   **Voting**

➤ Voting is *either* on a show of hands *or* by poll.

- On a show of hands: one vote per person, proxies are not counted.
  - This usually happens unless a poll vote is called.
- A poll vote: one vote for each share, proxies count.
  - A poll vote can be demanded by (*Art 46*) *either*:

    a) the chairman, *or*

    b) two members or proxies, *or*

    c) members or proxies with 10% or more of the total voting rights or paid up capital.
  - The *CA 1985* provides a safeguard that articles may *not* be altered so as to raise the threshold above a top limit of *either* at most ...

    a) ... 5 members, *or*

    b) ... members with more than 10% of the total voting rights or paid up capital

    ... having the ability to request a poll (*s 373*).

➤ The chairman has a casting vote that can be used if votes are tied (*Art 50*). It cannot be used to create a tie.

➤ If votes are equal, the negative view takes priority and a resolution is defeated (unless a chairman's casting vote is used).

III Directors

A Appointment

➤ The first directors are named on *Form 10,* and they take office on incorporation.

➤ Thereafter they are appointed by the board's resolution confirmed by ordinary resolution, or directly by ordinary resolution (*Arts 38, 76-79*).

- ◆ Each prospective director must sign a consent, *Form 288a*, which is filed at Companies House.

➤ A director will need to possess 'qualification shares' to join the board if a special article requires this.

➤ The director's name, address, occupation, and nationality must be entered on the Register of Directors.

➤ If necessary, the Register of Directors' Interests is also updated.

> **Confidentiality of directors' residential addresses**
>
> ➤ *CJPA 2001 s 45* inserts new sections into *CA 1985* (*ss 723B-723F*) to provide for a confidentiality order to be made regarding residential addresses if there is a serious risk of violence or intimidation.

1 Number of directors

➤ There must be at least 2 directors (*Art 64*), but this can be altered by a special article.

2 Shadow director

➤ A shadow director is any person (ie: even a legal person such as a company) who instructs the board or a governing majority of it and they are accustomed to follow that person's directions (*s 741* and *Re Unisoft Group Ltd (No 2)* [1994] BCC 766). This excludes a professional advisor.

3 Alternate director

➤ A director may appoint a fellow director as an alternate director, but the board must approve the appointment of a non-board member (*Art 65*).

➤ An alternate director is treated like the other directors and is given notice of board meetings (*Art.66*).

4 Remuneration of non-executive directors

➤ This is set by a general meeting (*Art 82*).

5 Service contracts

➤ When the board is about to discuss a director's contract, the director must declare his personal interest (*s 317*) (see p 270).

➤ The director concerned may not either vote *or* count in a quorum for this particular matter (*Arts 94-96*).

- ◆ In a small company, a special resolution could reduce the quorum in this instance, or an ordinary resolution could be used to the same end.

➤ Members must consent by ordinary resolution for contracts over 5 years, otherwise the fixed-term clause is void and the agreement becomes terminable at 'reasonable notice' (*s 319*).

- ◆ The contract must be available for inspection for 15 days before the members' meeting and at the meeting itself.

➤ All contracts with more than 1 year to run, and with a notice period of more than 1 year, must be permanently available for inspection by members at the registered office, the place where the Register of Members is kept, or the company's principal place of business *(s 318)*.

B Loss of office

1 Events on loss of office

➤ A director may, depending on his contract, simultaneously lose any executive office.
- He may claim for wrongful or unfair dismissal, or redundancy.
- He may be entitled to compensation under his contract.

➤ The board and officers:
- file *Form 288b* at Companies House, *and*
- delete the director's name from the Register of Directors and amend the Register of Directors' Interests, *and*
- remove the director's service contract from the registered office.

2 Automatic removal

a) *Articles 73-80*

➤ The directors (except the managing director) retire by rotation.

➤ All directors retire at the first AGM, but are automatically reappointed unless members pass a resolution to the contrary.

➤ Thereafter 1 in 3 directors must retire and be put forward for re-election. They must take turns to comprise this third. Those who retire are automatically re-elected unless members pass a resolution to the contrary.

➤ In a small company where membership and directorship go hand in hand, a special article can remove the requirement to retire every 3 years.

b) *Companies Act 1985 s 303:* removal by members

Steps	
1	The members have the right to remove a director at any time by ordinary resolution.
2	Members contemplating seeking the dismissal of a director should check the director's service contract to ascertain what compensation may be due under it.
3	A member gives 'special notice', leaving a formal notice at the registered office at least 28 days before a general meeting. (If one is called in this period (ie: less than 28 days after this special notice), then notice is deemed to have been given) (*s 379*)
4	On receipt of the 'special notice', the company should immediately inform the director concerned (*s 304(1)*).
5	If the board does not call a meeting the member can *either*: i) if he owns at least 5% of the shares, request an AGM and put a resolution on the agenda, *or* ii) if he owns at least 10% of the shares, summon an EGM. ♦ Due to ambiguous drafting in *s 379*, it is better to give 21 days' notice of the meeting (although depending on the clause's construction 14 days may be sufficient).
6	The director can make a written representation to members and circulate a statement to them, as well as speak at the meeting (even if he is not a member).
7	If there is a *Bushell v Faith* clause (see next page) in the articles and the resolution concerns a director's employment, his votes will increase in proportion to the size of his shareholding. ♦ Where the director has enough shares to defeat an ordinary resolution removing him from the board, consider passing a special resolution to remove this article.

3   **Disqualification**

   a) *Article 81*

   ➤ This article lists 5 circumstances in which a director will cease to be entitled to hold office:

   a) the director ceases to be a director because of the *CA 1985* or otherwise by law.

   b) the director is declared bankrupt.

   c) the director becomes mentally ill.

   d) the director resigns.

   e) the director is absent from board meetings for more than 6 months without the board's permission, and the board resolves that he should cease to sit on the board.

   b) *Company Directors' Disqualification Act 1986*

   ➤ Disqualification may last from 2 to 15 years, depending on the director's previous conduct and the nature of the offence (*CDDA 1986* and *Re Sevenoaks Stationers (Retail) Ltd* [1991] Ch 164).

   ➤ Disqualification is imposed for:

   ◆ general misconduct in relation to the company, *or*

   ◆ a criminal offence, *or*

   ◆ persistent default over filing with the Registrar of Companies, *or*

   ◆ fraudulent trading, *or*

   ◆ for a company which has gone insolvent, and the director's conduct during the insolvency makes him unfit to hold office.

4   **Protecting a director's position**

   ➤ To protect his position, a director might try to:

   ◆ insert a *Bushell v Faith* clause in the articles. Where the director is also a shareholder, this multiplies the director's voting power at a general meeting at which his dismissal is on the agenda.

   ◆ pass a special article restricting the transfer of shares.

   ◆ replace the statutory pre-emption rights under *s 89* with a special article covering shares issued for any consideration.

   ◆ hold 25% of the voting shares for some, or over 50% to control the board's composition.

   ◆ hold a debenture which is conditional on the lender remaining a director.

   ◆ ensure damages are due under a service contract if the director is removed.

   ◆ remove the chairman's casting vote (especially if there are only 2 directors on the board).

   ◆ set the necessary quorum at a higher number than 2.

   ◆ replace *Arts 94-95* with a special article permitting directors to contribute to a quorum and to vote on resolutions which concern themselves.

   ◆ ensure the appointment of an alternate director to represent an absent director at board meetings.

C Directors' duties and restrictions

> **Duty to declare personal interests**
>
> ➤ Whenever the board is about to discuss a matter in which the director is personally interested, he must make a formal declaration of his interest (*s 317*). **Failure to do so is a criminal offence.**

1 **Fiduciary duty**

  a) A general duty of good faith owed to the company

   ➤ Power must be used for the benefit of the company *and* for the reason it was conferred.

   ➤ A breach entitles the company to seek losses or an account of profits from a director.

   Note: the articles, or service contract, may impose extra obligations.

  b) Not to make a secret profit

   ➤ If a conflict of interest arises, a director must *either*:

   i) fully disclose relevant facts and obtain the members' resolution to sanction it (impossible if the director is a majority shareholder, as this endorses a fraud on the minority), *or*

   ii) account to the company for any profits which accrue from the secondary venture.

   ➤ *Art 85* permits personal interests if disclosed to the board and the director is not defrauding.

  c) Not to exceed power under articles or abuse powers

   ➤ The director should not use powers for a purpose other than that for which they were given.

   ➤ An ordinary resolution can absolve a director of liability for a particular act, so long as there is no fraud on the minority.

  d) Duty to disclose information

   ➤ Service contracts: right for shareholders to inspect, unless under 12 months (see p 267).

2 **Duty of skill and care**

   ➤ Skill is a subjective test - ie: the competence reasonably expected of someone with a particular director's knowledge and experience.

   ➤ Care is an objective test - ie: the care a reasonable person would exercise on his own behalf.

   ➤ Unless extra duties are owed under a service contract, a director only owes a duty to attend board meetings and vote when he reasonably can.

3 **Major duties related to company records**

   Some of the following duties are a criminal offence if not complied with.

  a) Annual accounts

   ➤ The directors of every company must prepare accounts for the company for each of its financial years (*s 226*) which contain a Profit & Loss account and balance sheet (*s 226A*).

   ◆ The balance sheet must be signed by a director on behalf of the board (*s 233*).

   ◆ The accounts must be laid before the company in general meeting and sent to the Registrar within 10 months of the accounting reference date (*s 241, s 242, s 244*).

   ➤ The accounts must contain a statement that there is no relevant audit information of which the auditors are unaware and that the director has taken all steps to make himself aware of such information (and a director commits a criminal offence if the statement is false) (*s 234ZA*).

   ➤ Accounts may be less detailed for small/medium companies (*ss 246, 246A, 247, Sch 4, 8, 8A*).

   ◆ An Auditor's report may not be necessary for certain companies (see p 273).

b) **Director's report** (*s 234, s 234ZZA, s 234ZZB*)
- ➤ The directors must submit a directors' report for each financial year which must contain:
  - ◆ the names of the persons who, at any time during the financial year, were directors, *and*
  - ◆ the principal activities of the company in the course of the year, *and*
  - ◆ the amount (if any) that the directors recommend should be paid by way of dividend, *and*
  - ◆ a business review being a fair review of the business of the company and a description of the principal risks and uncertainties facing the company.
- ➤ The directors' report must be laid before the company and sent to the Registrar within 10 months of the accounting reference date (*s 241, s 244*).

c) **Annual return** (*ss 363, 364, 364A*)
- ➤ Duty to submit this to the Registrar within 28 days of the 'return date'.
  - ◆ The 'return date' is 1 year after incorporation, and thereafter 1 year after the last return.
- ➤ This shows amongst other things, the address of the registered office, principal business activities, details of directors and the company secretary, certain details about shares.

d) **Register of Directors** (*s 288*)
- ➤ Contains name, address, business occupation, date of birth, nationality, other directorships.

e) **Register of Directors' Interests in the company** (*s 325*)
- ➤ Number of shares and debentures held by directors, their spouses and children under 18.
- ➤ Information must be given within 5 days of joining the board or gaining the interest.
- ➤ Company secretary updates it.

4 **Duty to consider the interests of employees** (*s 309*)
- ➤ Directors must consider employees' interests and balance these against members' interests.
- ➤ Employees do not have the right to enforce this.

5 **Duty to comply with rules on stationery** (*s 305*)
- ➤ All directors' names must appear, or none of them.

6 **Statutory restrictions**

The following topics have statutory restrictions where directors are concerned:

a) **Gratuitous compensation** (*s 312*)
- ➤ A 'golden handshake' must have prior approval of members by ordinary resolution (*s 312*).
- ➤ Redundancy rights, compensation for unfair dismissal and breach of contract are unaffected.

b) **Service contracts** (*s 319*)
- ➤ These may not exceed 5 years, unless approved by members' ordinary resolution (see p 267).

c) **Substantial property transactions** (*s 320*)
- ➤ Directors' transactions with the company are forbidden if an asset is of 'requisite value':
  - a) over £100,000, *or*
  - b) between £2,000 and £100,000 *and* representing more than 10% of the company's net assets as shown in the latest accounts (or if no accounts, 10% of paid up share capital).
- ➤ BUT the transaction is permitted if members authorise it, by passing an ordinary resolution.
  - ◆ If members' approval is not gained, the contract is voidable. Any director who authorised it must indemnify the company for any loss, and account to it for any profit.

d) **Contract with a sole member who is a director** (*s 322B*)

➤ The contract must be written, or the terms should be set out in a memorandum, or in the minutes of the first board meeting after the contract is made.

➤ The company and defaulting officers are liable to be fined if this is not done.

e) **Restriction on loans to directors** (*s 330*)

➤ These are forbidden, unless the amount concerned is very small.

➤ *s 330* does not make it a criminal offence to make such loans. It is often ignored in practice.

➤ *s 330* gives the company redress (for profit or losses accruing to the company due to the transaction) against a director who receives the loan and against directors who authorised it.

D Board meetings

Board meetings
➤ A board meeting may be called by *any* director at *any* time (*Art 88*).
➤ Notice must be 'reasonable' and given to every director who is in the country. (Oral notice is sufficient.)   ◆ What is 'reasonable' depends on the issue to be discussed and the make-up of the board.   • In practice 'reasonable' is very often taken to be 7 days.

1 Votes

➤ One per director.

➤ Resolutions are passed by a simple majority.

➤ *Art.88* gives the chairman a casting vote, but a special resolution may remove this, in which case the negative view takes precedence and a resolution is defeated.

➤ Personal interests may stop a director voting (*Art 94*). A *s 317* declaration must be made to avoid criminal liability.

◆ Even a single director at a board meeting of one must make this declaration and note it in the minutes: *Neptune (Vehicle Washing Equipment) Ltd v Fitzgerald* [1995] 3 All ER 811, Ch D.

➤ *Art.94* permits voting if the director is buying shares in the company or lending it money, otherwise it forbids him to vote if he has an interest, *unless* it comes within the 4 exceptions listed in *Art 94*.

➤ The board has powers of management (*Art 70*).

◆ In a deadlock, the Board should summon a general meeting.

2 Quorum

➤ 2 constitute a quorum, unless directors themselves or a special article dictate otherwise (*Art 89*).

➤ A director with a personal interest does not qualify as part of a quorum (*Art 95*).

3 Minutes

➤ Minutes must be kept of every board meeting (*Art 100, s 382(1)*).

4 Written resolutions

➤ Written resolutions avoid the need for a meeting, but consent must be unanimous (*Art 93*).

◆ Under *Art 94,* a written resolution cannot be used if there is a director who cannot vote. However, this restriction is often ignored in practice.

E Company officers

1 Chairman

- The board elects a chairman and may remove the chairman at any time (*Art 91*).
- The chairman has a casting vote, but this is revocable by special article (*Art 88*).
- The casting vote can be used if directors' votes are tied, but it may *not* be used to create a tie.
- The chairman resolves disputes over whether a board meeting is quorate, and over voting rights.

2 Managing director

- The managing director is entrusted with the company's daily administration, but the board may alter or withdraw a managing director's powers at any time (*Art 72*).
- The managing director is a member of the board, but he does not need to retire by rotation at every third AGM as the other directors do (*Art 84*).

3 Company secretary

- It is compulsory to have a company secretary (*s 283*).
- The first secretary is named on *Form 10*.
- Subsequent secretaries are appointed by the board (*Art 99*).
- The board sets the terms of the appointment (*Art 99*).
- The secretary has ostensible authority (and probably actual authority) to act in administrative matters (*Panorama v Fidelis* [1971] 2 QB 711). This includes keeping the statutory books.
- The board can remove the secretary at any time. Compensation depends on the terms of employment (*Art 99*).

4 Auditor

The need for an auditor in a small company (*s 246, s 247 and s 249A*)				
Balance sheet	Over £2.8 million	Any	£2.8 million or less	Shareholders holding at least 10% of shares can insist on an audit
Turnover	Any	Greater than £5.6 million	£5.6 million or less	
Need for an auditor?	✓	✓	✗	

- Directors appoint an auditor before the first AGM.
    - The auditor must be a certified or chartered accountant who is independent of the company.
- At the end of the first AGM, the auditor's office ends. The members decide who will act as auditor until the next AGM (*s 384*).
- Under the elective regime, the auditor is appointed within 28 days of the annual accounts being sent to members - he is deemed to be returned to office (*s 385A*).
- Members can remove the auditor at any time by an ordinary resolution at a general meeting (*s 391*). The procedure is the same as for the removal of a director (see p 268).
- The auditor may resign by sending a written notice to the company's registered office (*s 392*). This notice must state whether there are suspicious circumstances. This prevents an auditor abandoning members to a fraud (*s 394*).

F Liability

1 **Generally**

A director is *not* personally liable, *except* if he ...

> *s 727*: a court may excuse a director either wholly or partly from liability if it is fair to do so

- ➤ ... gives a personal guarantee.
    - ◆ This will occur in a small company where the banks insist on a personal guarantee to back loans.
- ➤ ... acts while disqualified by court order.
    - ◆ He will be liable for all debts the company incurs during this period.
- ➤ ... trades 'fraudulently' (*IA s 213*) (see p 305).
    - ◆ This means the director is knowingly party to fraudulent trading.
    - ◆ An action under this section is only possible during liquidation when the liquidator may petition the court for the director to contribute to the company's assets.
- ➤ ... trades 'wrongfully' (*IA s 214*) (see p 305).
    - ◆ The director knows or ought to know that the company's insolvency is likely, *and*
    - ◆ The director fails to act to minimise the loss of creditors, *and*
    - ◆ The director may be required to contribute to the company's assets during liquidation.
- ➤ ... breaches a warranty of authority.
    - ◆ The director purports to act for the company, but acts *ultra vires*.
    - ◆ If the director has ostensible authority, the company is bound.
- ➤ ... delegates wrongfully.
    - ◆ A director delegates a function(s) to employees whom he should have known to be incompetent.
- ➤ ... breaches a fiduciary/statutory duty (see pp 270-271).

2 *Ultra vires* **acts (ie: acts outside the objects clause of the company's memorandum)**

a) Company acts *ultra vires* (*s 35*)

- ➤ The company is bound provided its agent had actual or ostensible authority to act (see p 323).
- ➤ The directors are liable for a breach of duty.
- ➤ Members can ratify a breach and indemnify directors by passing special resolutions.

b) Agent acts *ultra vires*, but within the company's power (*s 35A*)

- ➤ Board of directors: power to bind the company (and to authorise others to do so) is unfettered.
    - ◆ Provided a third party acts in good faith the company will be bound.
    - ◆ Members can ratify the directors' acts with an ordinary resolution.

c) Agent (eg: unauthorised director or company secretary)

- ➤ If the agent has 'ostensible' authority the company is bound.
- ➤ Members can ratify the act with an ordinary resolution.

Note:

- ➤ Although Companies House is a public register, third parties are not fixed with constructive notice of a company's constitution (*s 35B*).
- ➤ Members can seek an injunction to prevent an *ultra vires* act being committed (*s 35(2)*).
- ➤ Notwithstanding personal liability, an agent or director will not be subject to a penalty unless the company actually incurs a loss due to their actions.

BUSINESS
Private companies

Party	Act	Actual authority?	Apparent authority?	Company bound?	Can board ratify?	Director liable?
Board	*intra vires*	✓	✓ (Board always has this)	✓ (ss 35, 35A and 35B)	Ratification by the Board if within the Board's power else ratification by an appropriate resolution at a GM (unless a fraud on the minority)	✗
Board	*ultra vires*	✗ (always for UV)	✓ (Board always has this)	✓ (ss 35, 35A and 35B)	A special resolution is needed to ratify a UV act (effectively changing the objects clause)	✓
Single Director	*intra vires*	✓	✓ (must be if Board has actual authority)	✓	Ratification by the Board if within the Board's power else ratification by an appropriate resolution at a GM (unless a fraud on the minority)	✗
Single Director	*intra vires*	✗	✓	✓	Ratification by the Board if within the Board's power else ratification by an appropriate resolution at a GM (unless a fraud on the minority)	✓
Single Director	*intra vires*		✗	✗ No because it is not an act done with the authority of the Board ss 35, 35A, 35B do not apply	Ratification by the Board if within the Board's power else ratification by an appropriate resolution at a GM (unless a fraud on the minority)	✓
Single Director	*ultra vires*	✗ (always for UV)	✓	✓	A special resolution is needed to ratify a UV act (effectively changing the objects clause)	✓
Single Director	*ultra vires*		✗	✗ No because it is not an act done with the authority of the Board ss 35, 35A, 35B do not apply	A special resolution is needed to ratify a UV act (effectively changing the objects clause)	✓
Unauthorised agent	*intra vires* or *ultra vires*	✗	✗	✗	✗	Not applicable

IV = *intra vires*
UV = *ultra vires*

Instructions for use of this box:
Read it from left to right

- grey areas indicate a choice that has to be made depending on circumstances
- non-grey areas indicate consequences that automatically flow from whatever is on the left

IV Finance

➤ This section examines 2 methods by which companies raise money: by loans and by shares.

A Debentures

➤ Directors and a lender take the following steps to grant a debenture:

Steps	
1	Check whether the company has authority to borrow (this applies to the directors).
2	Make searches (this applies to the lender).
3	Agree the type of the security.
4	Agree the terms of the debenture.
5	Follow the procedure for granting the debenture.
6	Register the debenture.
7	Comprehend the lender's remedies.
8	Redeem the debenture.

These steps are expanded below

1 Check whether the company has authority to borrow (this applies to the directors)

➤ A company may not borrow money unless it has the power under its memorandum or articles to do so.

- A 'general trading company' has implied authority, but the large City institutions prefer there to be actual authority in the articles.

➤ The directors should check they have power in the memorandum/articles to borrow.

- *Art 70* gives directors the power to borrow.

2 Make searches (this applies to the lender)

➤ The lender should make a search of the Charges Register at Companies House which lists the date on which any charge was created, the amount of the security, the property subject to the charge and the holder of the charge.

- If these particulars are given incorrectly on the Register, then registration is void against an administrator, liquidator or purchaser for value.

➤ The lender should also check at Companies House to ensure that:

- the directors have power to borrow - he should inspect the memorandum and articles.
  - Although this is sensible, it is not *necessary* as *s 35* says that the company has power ostensibly and a third party does not need to check whether it *actually* has such power.
- the directors have been properly appointed - he should inspect *Form 10* and *Form 288a* which will confirm the authorisation of particular individuals to act on the company's behalf.
- the property is not already subject to a prior charge on the Charges Register.

  Note: the lender should ask the holder of a floating charge for a 'letter of non-crystallisation', stating that the charge has not crystallised.

➤ The lender should search HM Land Registry and the Land Charges Department. Both keep records of charges over land. A 'purchaser' for value is only fixed with notice of charges which appear on *these* registers, irrespective of whether the charge is also registered at Companies House.

3   **Agree the type of security**

   a) **A fixed charge** is a charge over specified property. It prevents the company disposing of that asset without the debenture holder's agreement.

   b) **A floating charge** hangs over a class of property. The company may dispose of the property in the class without the debenture holder's agreement. If an event specified in the debenture occurs, the charge 'crystallises' and the property in the class becomes 'fixed'. At this point the rules for a fixed charge apply. Examples of when a charge may crystallise include when:

   - a winding up petition is presented to a court (*s 463*), *or*
   - there is a members' resolution to voluntarily wind up the company (*s 463*), *or*
   - an administration order is made against the company, *or*
   - any other event specified in the debenture occurs.

   c) **A personal guarantee** may be required from the directors, in which case they will be personally liable if the company defaults.

   - The director concerned must make a *s 317* declaration at the board meeting when the loan is discussed (see p 270).

4   **Agree the terms of the debenture**

   ➤ **Repayment date:** on a fixed date *or* on the occurrence of a specified event.

   ➤ **Interest:** when payable and how the rate will be calculated.

   ➤ **Conditions:** if the charge is a floating one, the lender will impose a condition preventing the subsequent creation of a fixed charge over the property as this would take priority over the floating charge on liquidation.

   - The company is responsible for registering this prohibition.

   ➤ **Power to appoint a receiver and an administrative receiver:** to be exercised if the company defaults on interest or capital repayments.

   - **A receiver** has power to sell assets (and it is usual to have power to appoint one for a fixed charge).
     - A receiver should be expressly empowered to:
       - sell assets, *and*
       - manage the company, *and*
       - take legal proceedings in its name.
   - **An administrative receiver** has management powers (and it is usual to have power to appoint one for a floating charge).

   ➤ **Any other powers:** eg: power to sell the security, power to run the business, etc.

5   **Follow the procedure for granting the debenture**

   ➤ The board resolves to grant the debenture.

   ➤ 2 directors sign the debenture.

BUSINESS
Private companies

6. **Register the debenture as a charge** (ss 395-397)

    (NB: The Companies Act 1989 imposes a new regime for registration, but this is not yet in force and the government has indicated it will not be brought into force. Below are the present rules still in force.)

    ➤ Register the charge at Companies House and pay the fee.
    - If appropriate, register it also with HM Land Registry or the Land Charges Department.

    ➤ It is the company's duty to register the charge, but anyone interested in it may do so.
    - The security of an *un*registered charge is void against:
        - an administrator,
        - a liquidator,
        - a creditor of the company - the creditor ranks as an unsecured creditor,
        - a person who has registered a proprietary right or interest in the property subject to the charge.
    - A second charge which is registered, takes precedence over a first unregistered charge.

    ➤ The debenture should be registered at Companies House within 21 days (s 395).
    - The *Companies Act 1985* requires the registration of 'prescribed particulars' of the charge and the instrument of the charge at Companies House.

    ➤ Late registration
    - Either seek leave of the court for late registration (s 404) or take out a fresh charge.

    ➤ Incorrect registration
    - Corrupted register entries do not offer protection so the lender should check a copy of the entry.
    - Errors can be corrected (s 404). Although alterations are not retrospective, the court can order that the alteration should be valid if it does not prejudice a third party.

7. **Comprehend the lender's remedies**

    ➤ If remedies are required, then appoint an administrative receiver.
    - An administrative receiver should notify the following of his appointment: the company, creditors and the Registrar (IA s 46).

8. **Redeem the debenture**

    ➤ The company sends a memorandum of discharge, usually *Form 403*, to the Registrar (s 403).
    ➤ The lender endorses a receipt for repayment on the debenture.

B Shares

1. **Share capital**

Money from sale of shares
➤ The company can use the money raised from the sale of shares as it sees fit.
➤ If the company receives money for the shares above the nominal value, the extra consideration is paid into a share premium account (s 130).
➤ If the company receives money for the shares below the nominal value, the shareholder must pay the company a sum equal to the discount in the shares plus interest (s 100).

a) **Types of shares**

➤ **Fully paid:** the shareholder has paid the company the share's nominal value.

➤ **Partly paid:** the shareholder has paid the company only part of the share's nominal value.
- If the company goes into liquidation, the shareholder will have to pay creditors whatever sum remains unpaid.
- Redeemable shares cannot be partly paid (Art 3).

BUSINESS
Private companies

b) Issue of new shares (allotment)

Steps

1 A board meeting resolves to issue shares.

2 A general meeting is called to obtain shareholders' approval if:

a) the authorised share capital needs to be increased. This can be done provided:
- the articles permit it (*Art 32* does), *and*
- the members pass an ordinary resolution.

b) the directors lack valid authority to allot shares under *s 80*. This authority can be granted either:
- by an ordinary resolution (this must be filed with the Registrar). This lasts for a maximum of 5 years unless an elective resolution is in force, see p 259.
- by the articles (although an ordinary - *not a special* - resolution can revoke this).

c) the directors wish to suspend pre-emption rights under *CA s 89*.

CA s 89
➤ The company must offer existing shareholders the shares on a pro rata basis for 21 days. After 21 days, any shares not allotted can be taken by third parties (but not on terms more favourable than those offered to shareholders).

- The directors will want to disapply *s 89* rights where:
  - the consideration is wholly in cash, *or*
  - the directors do not intend to offer existing members the chance to take up their pro rata entitlement (*either* because members are unlikely to do so, *or* because the directors wish to broaden the company's membership), *or*
  - the directors do not wish to keep the share offer open for 21 days.

  Note: *s 89* authority is only valid provided that the *s 80* authority in force when the *s 89* authority was granted is still valid.

Suspending pre-emption rights: 3 methods	
1	Insert a special article.
2	Pass a special resolution. A written circular (which is usually sent out with a notice of a GM) to shareholders before the meeting must explain: a) the reason for suspending *s 89* pre-emption rights, b) the consideration for the shares, c) a justification for the value of the consideration being asked for the shares.
3	Use a written resolution: the circular is the same as that for passing a special resolution.

3 File with the Registrar the memorandum if this has been amended, *Form 123* (increase of share capital), any special resolutions and any ordinary resolutions that increase the authorised share capital, or that give or revoke *s 80* authority to allot shares.

4 The board resolves to issue shares. Any offer for those shares must come from a prospective shareholder, and must *not* be offered by the company to the public.

5 Payment need not be in cash, but if the consideration takes any other form, the written contract and *Form 88(2)* are filed with the Registrar.
- Where the contract is oral, *Form 88(3)* is used.

6 The board resolves to seal share certificates.

2 Acquisition and transmission of shares

a) Transfer of shares

Step 1 The donor or vendor completes and signs a stock transfer form.

- ➤ If the shares are partly paid, the transferee also signs the form.
- ➤ Stamp duty/SDRT may be payable - see 'Taxation'.

Step 2 The transferee sends the stock transfer form to the company.

Step 3 The company amends the Register of Members and issues a certificate in the transferee's name within 2 months (s 183).

- ➤ Directors can refuse to transfer the shares if they are empowered to do so by a special article.
    - ◆ Table A (*Art 24*) does *not* permit this if the shares are fully paid.
    - ◆ The directors may refuse under *Art 24* if *either*:
        a) the shares are partly paid and the directors do not approve of the transferee, *or*
        b) the company has a lien over them, *or*
        c) there is a procedural irregularity such as:
            - the transfer is not lodged at the registered office with the share certificate, *or*
            - the transfer relates to more than one class of share, *or*
            - the transfer is in favour of more than 4 transferees.
    - ◆ The directors must act in good faith and decide within a reasonable time (under 2 months) (s 183).
    - ◆ If the directors refuse, and they are acting *ultra vires, or* the transferee shows they are acting in bad faith, the court will order the register to be rectified.
    - ◆ If the directors validly refuse to transfer shares, this does not entitle the transferee to seek damages or rescission of the contract to purchase the shares. In such a case:
        - the transferor remains the legal owner of the shares and holds them on trust for the transferee.
        - the transferor receives notice of general meetings, and he may both vote and receive dividends, but he must act as the transferee instructs.

Step 4 If the transferee is a director:

- ➤ he must inform the company in writing within 5 days (s 324), and the Register of Directors' Interests is amended (s 325).

Step 5 The company records the transfer on the annual return.

b) Transmission of shares

- ➤ Transmission of shares occurs when a member dies.
- ➤ Shares vest automatically in PRs or trustees in bankruptcy by operation of law. However, although the PRs or trustees control the beneficial interest, they are not members of the company and so cannot vote or receive dividends. They can either:
    i) elect for registration as members in their own right, *or*
    ii) nominate a transferee (ie: transfer the shares to a beneficiary or creditor who can then apply for registration as a member).

BUSINESS
Private companies

3 **Reducing share capital - 3 methods**

    a) Reduce share capital (ss 135-137)

- This requires a special resolution and the court's consent.
- The company can:
  - cancel further liability on partly paid shares, *or*
  - repay to members surplus capital without reducing the capital available to repay creditors, *or*
  - reduce the value of the shares in line with capital losses. (This does not prejudice creditors as it merely represents an admission of losses that have been incurred.)

    b) Buy back its own ordinary shares which have been issued (s 162)

- Repurchased shares are effectively cancelled.
- It is only possible to buy back ordinary shares if:
  - the articles permit it (*Art 35* does), *and*
  - the members pass a special resolution to do so (the shares affected carry no voting rights), *and*
  - the company has money available which will be from one of the following sources:
    - i) distributable profits ('in reserves') (s 168), *or*
    - ii) an issue of shares (s 171), *or*
    - iii) capital (s 173), but only if:
      - there is no other possible source of finance, *and*
      - shareholders pass a second special resolution approving the use of capital (the shares affected carry no voting rights), *and*
      - creditors are notified, *and*
      - the directors make a statutory declaration of the company's solvency for the next year.

      NB: *Art 35* in *Table A* specifically permits it (subject of course to the above), *and*
  - the contract is available at the registered office for 15 days before a general meeting and 10 years after it (s 169(4)), and is at the general meeting itself (s 164).

[Conditions for buy-back of shares]

- *Form 169* is sent to the Registrar. It states the number of shares bought and the nominal value of the shares.
- Note:
  - a) if the directors make the statutory declaration erroneously, they may be personally liable together with the purchaser of the shares to compensate the company's creditors.
  - b) a vendor shareholder cannot vote at the meeting.

    c) Issue redeemable shares (s 159)

- The company can buy back this type of share if:
  - i) the shares are fully paid up, *and*
  - ii) it has already issued non-redeemable shares.
- *Art 3* permits the issue of redeemable shares, but a special article must set out terms on which the shares are redeemable, eg: whether at the company's or a shareholder's behest.
- The members pass a special resolution to amend the articles, to state the terms and manner of the issue. *(NB: s 159A is not yet in force, but will require all companies to state the terms and manner of such an issue in the articles.)*
- The members can approve an issue of redeemable shares by ordinary resolution.

> ### Note on taxation (TA 1988 ss 219-224)
>
> ➤ Money received by an individual from the company is usually classified as a dividend or distribution subject to income tax as savings and investment income (*IT(TOI)A 2005 Part 4*).
>
> ➤ However, on a redemption, repayment or purchase of shares by a company, an individual is treated as having made a disposal for capital gains tax purposes rather than having received income if:
>
>   a) the owner of the shares is domiciled, resident and ordinarily resident in the UK during the year of assessment in which the transaction occurs (*TA 1988 s 220(1)*), *and*
>
>   b) has possessed the shares for 5 years (*TA 1988 s 220(5)*), *and*
>
>   c) the sale 'substantially' reduces his holding or that of his associates (partners, close relatives, etc) (*TA 1988 s 222(1), s 224*),
>
>   ... *and the transaction was either:*
>
>   'wholly or mainly for the purposes of benefiting a trade carried on by the company' and not ' to enable the owner of the share to participate in a company's profits without receiving a dividend or for the avoidance of tax' (*TA 1988 s 219(1)(a)*),
>
>   *or*
>
>   i) the money received is applied to pay IHT within 2 years of death, *and*
>
>   ii) the IHT arises on death, *and*
>
>   iii) undue hardship would arise if the company did not repurchase the shares (*TA 1988 ss 219(1)(b)-(2)*).

4 **Prohibition on financial assistance for purchasing shares** (*s 151*)

➤ A company is prohibited from helping a third party to buy its shares.

- It is a criminal offence incurring imprisonment of up to 2 years and/or a fine.
- Such transactions are void and unenforceable.

➤ Such 'financial assistance' is defined by a list given in *s 152(1)*.

➤ A whole set of exceptions is listed in *s 153*, but many exceptions have been cut back due to recent case law. However, although a company is restricted by *s 151*, it *can* give financial assistance if it goes through the 'whitewash procedure' (*ss 155-158*). It can do this if:

a) the articles permit it, *and*

b) the directors make a statutory declaration that the company is solvent and will remain so over the next year, *and*

c) the members consent by special resolution (within 1 week of the statutory declaration), *and*

d) the auditor confirms the directors' statutory declaration.

Note: if the borrower is a director then a loan is forbidden by *s 330*. The *CA 1985* does not impose a criminal penalty, but it imposes an obligation on the directors who authorise the loan to indemnify the company for any resulting loss (see p 272).

➤ The House of Lords considered *s 151* in considerable detail in *Brady v Brady* [1989] AC 755, but a pragmatic approach is to be found in a judgment of Hoffmann J in *Charterhouse Investment Trust Ltd v Tempest Diesels Ltd* [1986] BCLC 1, where he emphasises that the 'commercial realities of each transaction' should be examined to determine if financial assistance is being given.

5 Dividends

➤ The directors consider the payment of a 'final' dividend after the accounts have been completed, and recommend it to a general meeting. The accounts for the calculation of a final 'dividend' must be the last set for the financial year, prepared in accordance with *s 226* (ie: audited, put before the members, filed with the Registrar, etc).

➤ At any time during an accounting period, the directors can decide to declare an 'interim' dividend if this appears 'justifiable by the profits of the company available for distribution' (*Art 103*). For the payment of an 'interim' dividend, the company can prepare 'interim' accounts.

➤ Dividends can only be paid if there are 'profits available' (*s 263*).
  - There are 'profits available' if the undistributed trading profit which has accumulated during the past year and previous years exceeds the total amount of debts which have fallen due over the past year and previous years.
  - In addition to the normal accountancy rules which are applied in working out the extent of profits and losses, there are some statutory rules (*s 263*):
    - capitalised profit (ie: profit used to repay bonus shares or buy back shares) *is not* treated as profit.
    - loss written off against a reduction of share capital *is not* treated as a loss.
    - a provision against anticipated losses (ie: the reduction in the value of wasting assets) *is* treated as a loss (*s 275*).

➤ A general meeting votes upon whether to accept the directors' recommendation; it may not vote for a higher dividend than the directors propose (*Art 102*).

➤ Members can sue the company for unpaid 'final' dividends as a debt which is owed to them from the date when the dividend was declared. There is no debt action for unpaid 'interim' dividends as members may not expect these as of right until the money is actually paid to them.

➤ Members knowingly in receipt of dividends paid when there are insufficient 'profits available' must refund the money to the company (*s 277*).
  - Directors are personally liable for breach of duty if any such sums are unrecovered after the company has paid a dividend without sufficient 'available profits'.

C Comparison of shareholding and debenture holding

	Shareholder	Debenture holder
Management control	✓ The investor may attend GMs and vote to influence how the company is run	✗ The lender usually has no right to vote at meetings
Income	✗ Dividends cannot be paid unless the company makes a profit	✓ The amount of interest and its payment dates are guaranteed. If insufficient profits are available, interest will have to be paid out of capital
Security	✗ The capital will not be repaid unless the company buys back its own shares or issue redeemable shares ✗ The value of the capital may fluctuate ✓ The capital may go up (or down!) ✗ Capital is not returned if the company is insolvent on winding up	✓ The capital will be repaid on a predetermined date *or* when the debenture holder demands it ✓ The capital sum will normally remain set at the amount of the loan ✗ The capital sum will not appreciate ✓ Capital will be recovered on insolvency if the debenture is secured
Investment's marketability	✗ The articles may restrict the transfer of shares	✓ The debenture can be sold to anyone
Tax	✗ Dividends are not tax deductible	✓ Interest on the loan may be deductible as a debit on a 'loan relationship' (see p 105)

Summary of company procedure

Transaction	Authority	Resolution	Internal procedures	External procedures
Appoint directors for at least 5 years	s 319	Ordinary	The contract is kept at the registered office for 15 days before the meeting and at the meeting itself	
Allot shares (if this power is not in the articles)	s 80	Ordinary		File resolution. Within 1 month of allotment, file Form 88(2) and the contract if consideration is in kind, or Form 88(3) if the contract is oral
Remove statutory pre-emption rights	s 95	Special		File resolution
Introduce elective regime	ss 379A-380	Elective		File resolution
Cancel elective regime	s 379A	Ordinary		File resolution
Change company name	s 28	Special	Alter memorandum	File amended memorandum and resolution
Select business name		Board resolution	Alter stationery as appropriate	
Increase nominal share capital	s 121	Ordinary		File resolution, Form 123 and amended memorandum
Change objects	s 4	Special		File amended memorandum and resolution
Change articles	s 9	Special		File amended articles and resolution
Remove a director	s 303	Ordinary	Complainant gives the board special notice 28 days before an EGM. The board gives a copy of this notice to the director. The board should resolve to call an EGM with 21 days' notice (arguably 14 is sufficient). A director can make a written representation which the board circulates to members. Alter the Register of Directors and the Register of Directors' Interests	File Form 288b
Remove an auditor	s 391	Ordinary	Special notice procedure as for the removal of a director	Give the Registrar notice within 14 days of the resolution
Alter minimum directors from 2	Art 64	Special		File resolution
Fix salary of non-executive director	Art 82	Ordinary		File resolution
Relax quorum requirement for a director voting on own service contract	Art 97	Alter articles by special resolution. Or temporarily relax rules under the Art.96 ordinary resolution		File resolution if it is a special resolution
Reduce share capital	ss 135-137	Special		File resolution. Obtain the court's consent
Sanction a 'substantial property transaction'	s 320	Ordinary	After the transaction it may be necessary to alter the Register of Directors' Interests	

BUSINESS
Private companies

Transaction	Authority	Resolution	Internal procedures	External procedures
Gratuitous payment to a director	s 312	Ordinary		
Retirement by rotation		No resolution. This is automatic (Art 76)		
Repurchase ordinary shares	s 162	Special	Update Register of Members, Register of Directors' Interests	Form 169 (stating number of shares and nominal value)
Financial assistance to buy shares	s 155	Special	Statutory declaration of solvency by the directors, confirmed by the auditor	File resolution and statutory declaration
Approve dividend	Art 102	Ordinary		
Absolve liability for *ultra vires* act		Special		File resolution
Grant indemnity for *ultra vires* act		Special		File resolution
Absolve liability for exceeding actual authority		Ordinary		
Issue of a debenture		Board resolution	The board resolves to take out the loan and to affix the company seal. 2 directors, *or* 1 director and the company secretary sign the agreement. Update Register of Charges	Register with Form 395 at Companies House within 21 days. Charges over land should be registered with the Land Charges Department or HM Land Registry
Redemption of a debenture		Board resolution	Lender endorses receipt on the debenture. Update Register of Charges	File statutory declaration and memorandum of satisfaction (Form 403) that the debt has been repaid
Voluntary winding up - company is insolvent	IA s 84 / IA s 378	Extraordinary	see p 303	File the extraordinary resolution
Winding up - company is solvent	IA s 84	Special	see p 303	File the special resolution
Approve voluntary arrangement	Insolvency Rules	Ordinary (members) 75% by value (unsecured creditors)	see p 301	
Move registered office		Board resolution		File Form 287

Note:
a) the table on the previous page and the table on this page assume that Table A is in force and has not been amended
b) every members' resolution which is passed concerning the company's management will need a separate board resolution if it is to be executed
c) written resolutions are an acceptable alternative to members' resolutions passed at meetings in all cases *except* those listed on p 265
d) a complete list of which resolutions are to be filed can be found in s 380

D   Public companies

    I   UK PLCs
    II   European Public Limited Liability Companies (SEs)

I   UK PLCs

Advantages and extra stringencies associated with UK plcs

Pros
- ✓ Shares and debentures may be offered to the public. (There is a criminal penalty for a private company which does this (*s 81*).)
- ✓ Prestige.
- ✓ A public company may hold treasury shares (which it can use to stabilise its share price) (*s 162 - s162D*).
- ✓ The company may apply for listing of its securities if it has traded for at least 3 years and at least 25% of its shares are held by the public (cf. the Listing Rules.)

Cons
- ✗ Costs of changing name on memorandum and stationery.
- ✗ The rules of the City Code on Takeovers and Mergers will apply which obliges anyone who alone, or in concert with others, acquires 30% of the shares to make a bid for all the shares.
- ✗ Non-cash consideration for shares must be independently valued within 6 months (*ss 44, 103*).
- ✗ There is no elective regime.
- ✗ The prohibition on loans to directors (and associates) extends to quasi-loans & credit transactions (*ss 330-331*).
- ✗ Criminal penalties: loans to directors (*s 342*), giving unlawful financial assistance (*s 151*).
- ✗ There is an absolute bar on financial assistance to buy shares (*s 151*).
- ✗ The company must call an EGM if 'net assets' fall to 50% or less of the share capital (*s 142*).
- ✗ The company needs a special resolution, or article to disable statutory pre-emption rights (*s 95*). (A private company may do this in its memorandum or articles (*s 91*).)
- ✗ Dividend rules are stricter. A plc may only make a distribution when distributable profits equal accumulated realised profits less accumulated realised losses, plus the excess of unrealised losses over unrealised profits.
- ✗ A plc may not redeem or purchase shares from capital (*s 171*).
- ✗ 7 months to lay AGM accounts after accounting period ends (private companies have 10) (*s 244*).
- ✗ Written resolutions may not be used.
- ✗ Minimum of 2 directors (*s 282*).
- ✗ Directors may not be appointed over 70. They must leave office at the AGM after their 70th birthday, unless members agree otherwise (*s 293*).
- ✗ The directors' report and accounts must contain far more detail.
- ✗ For listed companies: the Combined Code on Corporate Governance must be complied with.

➤ Admission to listing is the responsibility of the FSA and admission to trading is the responsibility of the London Stock Exchange. However, a condition of admission to each is a listing with the other.

Conversion to a plc

Requirements

1. Issued share capital is a minimum of £50,000.
2. At least 25% (£12,500) of the share capital is fully paid to the nominal value and the whole of any premium (*s 45*).
3. The memorandum must state that the company is a public limited company and the name must include 'plc'.

Procedure

Steps

1. Special resolutions to (a) re-register as a plc, *and* (b) alter the memorandum, adding 'plc' to the company's name.
2. Apply for registration as a plc.
3. Adopt a new memorandum and articles suitable for a public company.
4. Send to the Registrar (*s 43*):
   ◆ a printed copy of the new memorandum and articles,
   ◆ a copy of the latest balance sheet,
   ◆ an auditor's report that the company's net assets are not less than its capital balance sheet,
   ◆ a statutory declaration made by a company secretary or director that the net asset value in the auditor's report is accurate and that the requirements of the *Companies Acts* have been complied with.
5. The Registrar issues a certificate of incorporation as a plc.

II European Public Limited Liability Companies (SEs)

➤ On 8 October 2001, the European Council created a legal form of European Company known as the Societas Europaea (SE) which became law throughout the EU on 8 October 2004.

   ◆ This was over 30 years after negotiations for the creation of a European company were initiated!

➤ Sources of law:

   ◆ At the EU level: Euro Regulation 2157/2001 and Directive 2001/86/EC.

   ◆ At the UK level: implemented by *EPLLCR 2004*.

➤ Objectives of an SE:

   ◆ to create a European company with its own legislative framework which allows companies incorporated in different Member States to merge or form a holding company or joint subsidiary, while avoiding the legal and practical constraints arising from the existence of multiple legal systems, *and*

   ◆ to involve employees in the SE and recognise their place and role in the company.

   • This does not mean participation in day-to-day decisions (which are a matter for the management) but participation in the supervision and strategic development of the company.

   • Several models of participation are possible:

      a) a model in which the employees form part of the supervisory or administrative board, *or*

      b) a model in which the employees are represented by a separate body, *or*

      c) other models to be agreed between the management or administrative boards of the founder companies and the employees or their representatives in those companies (levels of information and consultation being the same as in (b).

   • Employees' representatives must be provided with financial and material resources and other facilities to enable them to perform their duties properly.

- **Formation:** there are 4 ways of forming an SE:
  - merger (available only to public limited companies from different Member States), *or*
  - formation of a holding company (available to public and private limited companies with their registered offices in different Member States or having subsidiaries or branches in Member States other than that of their registered office), *or*
  - formation of a joint subsidiary, *or*
  - conversion of a public limited company previously formed under national law.
- **Registration (and liquidation):** must be disclosed for information purposes in the Official Journal of the European Communities. Every SE must be registered in the State where it has its registered office, in a register designated by the law of that State.
- **Registered office:** must be where the SE has its central administration (ie: its true centre of operations).
  - The SE can easily transfer its registered office within the EU.
- **Minimum capital:** 120,000 euros (unless the registered office is in a Member State where national law requires a larger capital for companies exercising certain types of activity).
- **Annual accounts:** the SE must draw up annual accounts comprising the balance sheet, the profit & loss account (and notes to accounts), and an annual report giving a fair view of the company's business and of its position (consolidated accounts may also be required).
- **Tax:** the SE is treated the same as any other multinational (ie: it is subject to the tax regime of the national legislation applicable to the company and its subsidiaries). SEs are subject to taxes and charges in all Member States where their administrative centres are situated. NB: SE tax status is not perfect because there is no tax harmonisation at the European level (for UK tax rules, see *FA(No2) 2005 Part 4*).
- **Company rules:** must provide for general meeting of shareholders and for either a management board and a supervisory board (2 tier system) or an administrative board (1 tier system).
  - 2 tier system: management by a management board whose members have power to represent the company in dealings with third parties and in legal proceedings. They are appointed and removed by the supervisory board. No person may be a member of both the management board and the supervisory board of the same company at the same time.
  - 1 tier system: management is by an administrative board whose members have the power to represent the company in dealings with third parties and in legal proceedings. Powers of management may be delegated to one or more of its members.
- The following require authorisation of the supervisory board or the deliberation of the administrative board:
  - any investment project requiring an amount more than the percentage of subscribed capital, *and*
  - the setting-up, acquisition, disposal or closing down of undertakings, businesses or parts of businesses where the purchase price or disposal proceeds account for more than the percentage of subscribed capital, *and*
  - the raising or granting of loans, the issue of debt securities and the assumption of liabilities of a third party or suretyship for a third party where the total money value in each case is more than the percentage of subscribed capital, *and*
  - the conclusion of supply and performance contracts where the total turnover provided for is more than the percentage of turnover for the previous financial year.
    - The percentage is to be determined by the Statutes of the SE but may not be less than 5% nor more than 25%.

BUSINESS
Converting businesses

E Converting businesses

> ▨ A shaded box indicates that a point also applies to a LLP incorporated under the *LPA 2000*

Converting sole trader to partnership	Converting a partnership to a company/LLP
Formalities	
▨ Draw up a partnership agreement ➤ Decide on the ownership of capital assets, which can be: ♦ leased or licensed to the firm ♦ owned by the partners jointly - this requires a transfer or conveyance ♦ held on trust by a partner for all the partners ➤ Comply with *BNA 1985*	➤ Purchase or ▨ create a company/LLP ➤ Observe the formalities for board and shareholder meetings ▨ Draw up a contract for sale of the business: ♦ listing the assets being sold, consideration and method of payment ♦ stating the company's acceptance of the seller's title to assets ♦ recording the company's acceptance of stock in its current condition ♦ apportioning the value of assets ♦ providing an indemnity from the company in respect of business liabilities. ➤ Comply with *BNA 1985*, and *CA ss 25-30* (see p 244 and pp 256-257)
Income tax	
	➤ The seller may incur a 'balancing charge' on the sale of capital assets (*CAA 2001 s 61/IT(TOI)A 2005 s 242*). If the ex-partners are controlling shareholders, then they and the company and partners may elect for the company to inherit the business's writing down allowance (there are 2 years in which to make this election) (*CAA 2001 s 266*) If this election is made, no 'balancing charge' is deemed to arise on the discontinuance of trade by the partnership (*CAA 2001 s 267(2)*) ➤ Unrelieved trading losses can be carried forward and offset against any salary or dividends paid by the company to the vendor, as long as shares in the company provided most of the consideration for the sale (*TA 1988 s 386*)
Capital taxation	
▨ A sole trader going into partnership may be disposing of chargeable assets. Consider: ♦ annual exemption ♦ hold-over relief on a *gift* ♦ taper relief	➤ Insofar as shares are consideration for the transfer of assets, gains can be 'rolled-over' into shares on condition that all the business's assets (except cash) are sold to the company and that the shares issued by the company qualify for the Enterprise Investment Scheme (*TCGA 1992 ss 150-150C, Sch 5B*). This has disadvantages: ♦ any subsequent gain may be liable to double taxation ♦ assets transferred to the company are available to creditors if it becomes insolvent, and so might not be recoverable
SDLT	
➤ SDLT is less likely to be applicable as title to assets may not be transferred	➤ SDLT may be due on an instrument transferring or agreeing to transfer an interest in UK land, see pp 133-136 ▨ ♦ There is an exemption for a transfer to a LLP within 1 year of incorporation (*FA 2003 s 65*)
VAT	
➤ If the company is not registered *before the sale*, the seller must charge VAT unless the business is transferred as a going concern (*VATA s 49*)	
Employees	
Transfer of Undertakings (Protection of Employment) Regulations 2006 ➤ When the business is taken over, the employees retain all the rights they enjoyed previously	

BUSINESS
Choice of business medium

F   Choice of business medium

> **Note on shaded boxes in this chapter**
> A shaded box on this page indicates that a point applies to a LLP incorporated under the *LPA 2000*
> A shaded box on the next page indicates that a point applies to a partner in a LLP (also under the *LPA 2000*)

➤ The choice of business medium determines how a business is financed and run.

➤ Issues that concern clients include:
   - the different liabilities assumed by sole traders or partners (as opposed to shareholders).
   - the amount of statutory control over the business.
   - how easily profits may be extracted from the business.
   - working out what tax is payable by the business and what tax is payable by the individuals involved (although this depends on whether they are sole traders, directors or shareholders.)

➤ As a general rule:
   - Partnerships are better initially when profits are low (because of lower running costs and start-up relief).
   - Companies are usually better initially when profits are expected to be higher.

	Sole trader or partnership	Company
	General matters	
Personal liability for debts	✘ Unlimited liability ✘ A partner and a sole trader are personally liable for debts the business incurs Note: A novation agreement or an indemnity only protects if the guarantor is solvent NB: Under the self assessment regime, partners are in most cases no longer jointly and severally liable for income tax	✓ Limited liability ✓ Members are only liable to the extent of the fully paid up value of the shares ➤ Directors are not personally liable *unless* they: • give a personal guarantee • breach their fiduciary duty to the company • trade wrongfully or fraudulently (*IA 1986 ss 213-214*) • breach certain statutory administrative requirements • sign a document giving an incorrect company name
Finance	✘ Can only create fixed charges ✘ A new partner is liable for future debts	✓ Can create a qualifying floating charge ✓ A new investor in shares only incurs limited liability
Management	✓ Flexibility: the business can be organised as the participants wish ✘ All partners have apparent authority to bind the firm	✓ Management is largely divorced from capital investment ✓ Shareholders have no authority to act for the company
Status		✓ Often seen by clients as more substantial and 'solid'
Setting-up and initial cost	✓ Theoretically free as acting in a certain way is enough to start a partnership ✘ For a partnership, an agreement ought to be drawn up, so in practice this is not a viable 'short-cut'	✘ Many statutory requirements must be fulfilled: • the formalities at start-up, *and* • the ongoing formalities
Statutory control	✓ This is minimal	✘ The inconvenience of maintaining the required registers, minutes, annual returns, etc ✘ The expense of professional advice to ensure compliance with statutory requirements ✘ Restrictions on certain activities: • purchase and redemption of its own shares • paying dividends solely out of 'available' profit as defined by *CA 1985 s 263*
Publicity	✓ Need reveal only the partners' names and their addresses for the service of documents	✘ Information filed at Companies House is open to public inspection. This includes annual accounts but for a 'small company' a profit & loss account does not have to be filed, and smaller companies do not need audits (see p 273)

BUSINESS
Choice of business medium

Sole trader or partnership	Company	Director
Income tax / National insurance contributions		
✓ Expenses are more generous: anything 'wholly and exclusively for the purposes of the trade'		✓ Expenses: 'wholly, exclusively and necessarily in the performance of an employee's duties'
£0-£2,150 at 10% £2,150 - £33,300 at 22% £33,300+ at 40% ✗ Profit £33,300+ at 40% not 23.75%-32.75%	£0 - £300,000 at 19% £300,001- £1,500,000 at 32.75% £1,500,000+ at 30% The above assumes that profits are retained in the company so that the non-corporate distribution rate does not apply ✓ Reinvestment is easier if profit is taxed in the 19% band	£0-£2,150 at 10% £2,150 - £33,300 at 22% £33,300+ at 40%
✓ Start-up relief over first 4 years ✓ Losses can be set against an individual's income or gains from other sources	Check whether *IT(EP)A 2003 ss 49-56* apply (see p 86)	
✗ A sole trader/partner pays Class 4 contributions related to profit and Class 2 contributions at a flat rate ✓ Neither Class 4 or 2 qualify for tax relief, but the overall burden is less ✗ Benefits are poorer than for employees	✓ A company may claim tax relief on secondary national insurance contributions	✗ No tax relief on national insurance contributions ✓ Benefits are more generous than for a self-employed person
✓ Interest on a loan to buy into a partnership/LLP may be set against income tax as a 'charge on income' (*TA 1988 s 362*)	✓ Interest on a loan to buy shares may be a 'charge on income' (see p 86)	

Sole trader or partner	Director/Shareholder	Company
Capital gains tax		**Corporation tax**
	✓ Annual exemption and taper relief	✗
✓ Roll-over relief on replacement of 'qualifying assets'	✓ Roll-over relief on replacement of 'qualifying assets' *if* the company is a personal trading company	✓
✓ Hold-over relief on a gift of business assets	✓ Hold-over relief on a disposal of assets used by the company (other than shares) not at arm's length provided the company is a personal trading company	✗
Double taxation		
✓ A trader or partner only pays CGT once	✗ Company: pays corporation tax on gains (subject to reliefs or the substantial shareholding exemption). Shareholder: pays CGT on corresponding rises in share value ✓ This can be alleviated or prevented if a company distributes capital profit ✗ An asset-owning shareholder who licenses/leases them to the company is only taxed once	
Inheritance tax		
✓ Business property relief ✓ Instalment option: always available on business assets	✗ Business property relief is not always available, see p 102 ✗ The instalment option is only available if *either* the transfer concerns a controlling holding *or* other conditions exist	Generally not applicable (unless a close company, etc)

G Insolvency

All references in this section are to the Insolvency Act 1986, unless stated otherwise.

A general outline only is presented below.

  I   Personal insolvency
  II   Partnership insolvency
  III LLP insolvency
  IV   Corporate insolvency
  V   A note on statutory demands
  VI   Cross-border EU insolvency

I Personal insolvency

A Voluntary arrangement

✓ Avoids stigma and disability of bankruptcy.	✗ The supervisor of the voluntary arrangement does *not* have power to set aside transactions.
✓ Cheaper and quicker.	
✓ Creditors retain the option of petitioning the court if a debtor defaults.	✗ Creditors may not get paid in full.

➤ This is commonly referred to as an 'IVA' (ie: individual voluntary arrangement).

➤ The debtor may choose to apply for a moratorium (called an 'interim order'). In return, the debtor agrees to a voluntary repayment plan (*s 252*).

   ◆ During the period of this interim order:
      • no bankruptcy petition relating to the debtor may be presented or proceeded with, *and*
      • no landlord or other person to whom rent is payable may exercise any right of forfeiture by peaceable re-entry in relation to premises let to the debtor in respect of a failure by the debtor to comply with any term or condition of his tenancy of such premises, except with the leave of the court, *and*
      • no other proceedings, and no execution or other legal process, may be commenced or continued and no distress may be levied against the debtor or his property except with the leave of the court.

➤ A resolution for a voluntary arrangement must be passed by a majority of at least 75% (by value) of the creditors present in person or by proxy. The resolution binds every unsecured creditor (but if an unsecured creditor did not have notice of the meeting, he may apply to the court for relief) (*s 262*).

➤ A debtor may enter a voluntary arrangement at any time before a bankruptcy petition by the debtor is pending (*s 253(5)*).

➤ A voluntary arrangement may take the form of a 'composition', ie: the creditor and debtor agree the payment of a lesser sum in full satisfaction of the claim. Alternatively, it can take the form of a 'scheme of arrangement' which can be on any terms acceptable to the parties (eg: sale of assets, etc).

BUSINESS
Insolvency

Steps	
1	The debtor appoints a qualified person such an insolvency practitioner known as a 'nominee' to investigate his finances (*s 253*).
2	The debtor prepares a proposal for the intended nominee setting out (*IR 1986 r 5.3*):
	i) the terms of the IVA (this is what is actually known as the 'proposal'), *and*
	ii) a short explanation why, in his opinion, a voluntary arrangement is desirable, *and*
	iii) reasons why the creditors may be expected to concur with such an arrangement.
3	The proposal is sent to the intended nominee, who then decides whether to act as nominee (*IR 1986 r 5.4*).
4	If the debtor has not already delivered a statement of affairs to the nominee, then shortly after sending the proposal, the debtor must send to the nominee a statement of affairs containing particulars of his creditors, debts, other liabilities, assets and other information as may be prescribed (*IR 1986 r 5.5*).
5	The debtor may choose to apply for an interim order (the moratorium described above). This usually lasts for 14 days but can be extended (*ss 255(6), 256(4)*).
6	The nominee prepares a report on the proposal to the court including whether a creditor's meeting should be held (and giving the nominee's opinion on whether the proposal has a reasonable prospect of being approved and implemented (*s 256(1)*).
7	The court considers whether, based on the nominee's recommendation, a creditors' meeting is necessary to obtain their approval (*s 258*).
	◆ **If an interim order has been made:** If a meeting is necessary, then during the period of the interim order, creditors can examine the proposed voluntary arrangement.
	◆ **An interim order has not been made or applied for:** If a meeting is necessary, then creditors can examine the proposed voluntary arrangement (*IA ss 256A-258*).
	◆ more than 75% (by value) of creditors at the meeting must agree to the IVA (*IR 1986 r 5.23*).
8	Provided that consent is obtained, a bankruptcy order is avoided, and the nominee is appointed as the debtor's 'supervisor' to ensure the IVA is carried out in accordance with its terms (*s 263*).

False representations by the debtor (*s 262A*)

➤ The debtor commits an offence if, for the purpose of obtaining the approval of creditors to a proposal, he makes any false representation or fraudulently does, or omits to do, anything.

➤ This applies even if the proposal is not approved.

➤ This offence carries a penalty of imprisonment or a fine, or both.

Fast-track procedure (*s 263A*)

➤ The debtor can use a fast-track procedure to make an IVA if:
  ◆ the debtor is an undischarged bankrupt (ie: this is a post bankruptcy IVA), *and*
  ◆ the official receiver is specified in the proposal as the nominee in relation to the voluntary arrangement, *and*
  ◆ no interim order has been made.

BUSINESS
Insolvency

B Bankruptcy

Steps

1 A petition is made to a court with insolvency jurisdiction, by any of the following:

a) **Creditor (1)** (*s 267*) ...

   i) ... who is owed £750 or more, *and*

   ii) the debt is for a liquidated sum payable now, or at a certain future time, and is unsecured, *and*

   iii) the debtor is unable to pay or has no reasonable prospect of doing so.

   ◆ The evidence for this is:
   - 1) there is evidence of the debtor's failure to comply with a statutory demand within 3 weeks, *and*
   - 2) there is no outstanding application to set aside a statutory demand.

   or • the debtor has failed to satisfy execution of a judgment debt.

b) **Creditor (2)** ... who is bound by a voluntary arrangement where the debtor has not complied with the arrangement, or the debtor has entered the scheme giving misleading information.

c) **Debtor** ... with a statement of affairs showing that he is unable to pay his debts (*s 272*).

2 A bankruptcy order is made at a court hearing (at least 14 days must elapse between service of the petition and the hearing), or the court may appoint an insolvency practitioner to investigate the possibility of an IVA. A bankruptcy order will be entered into the public register of bankruptcy orders.

3 The courts appoints an official receiver (*s 287*) until the bankrupt's estate vests in the trustee in bankruptcy.

◆ If a creditor began the action, the debtor has 21 days to submit a statement of affairs (*s 288*).

4 A creditors' meeting is held at the official receiver's discretion *or* if 25% of creditors (by value) request it (*s 294*).

5 A trustee in bankruptcy is appointed by the creditors at the meeting, *or* if no meeting is called or no appointment is made by creditors, the official receiver will act as the trustee in bankruptcy (*s 293*).

6 The bankrupt's property vests in the trustee (see chart opposite '*Property vesting in the trustee*') (*s 306*).

7 The function of the trustee is to get in, realise, and distribute the bankrupt's estate to satisfy the creditors (see chart opposite for '*Trustee's powers to gather assets*').

8 A bankrupt is discharged from bankruptcy at the end of the period of **1 year** beginning with the date on which the bankruptcy commences (*s 279*).

◆ However, the court may extend this if the bankrupt has failed or is failing to comply with an obligation in the relevant legislation.

◆ The one year discharge period may be reduced if the Official Receiver files a notice stating that further investigation into the bankrupt's conduct and affairs is unnecessary, or has been concluded.

9 When the bankruptcy order is discharged, the discharge (*s 281*):

◆ releases the bankrupt from all the bankruptcy debts, but has no effect on the functions (so far as they remain to be carried out) of the trustee of his estate,

◆ does not affect the right of any secured creditor of the bankrupt to enforce his security for the payment of a debt from which the bankrupt is released,

◆ does not release the bankrupt from any bankruptcy debt which he incurred connected with fraud,

◆ does not usually release the bankrupt from any liability to pay damages for negligence, nuisance or breach of a statutory, contractual or other duty or damages for personal injuries to any person,

◆ does not release any person other than the bankrupt from any liability.

Property vesting in the trustee in bankruptcy

Property retained by the bankrupt	Property vesting in the trustee
➤ Any right which is purely personal, rather than proprietary ➤ Tools of a trade, vehicle (s 283(2)) ➤ Bankrupt's and family's furniture, bedding and clothing (s 283(2)) Note: the above might be replaced by functional cheaper versions ➤ Trust property eg: trust property held for a minor	➤ All other property Note: If the debtor only partly owns his house, the trustee in bankruptcy will need an order for sale from the court (LPA 1925 s 30) Note: Where the debtor's property is an interest in a dwelling-house which at the date of the bankruptcy was the sole or principal residence of the bankrupt, the bankrupt's spouse or a former spouse of the bankrupt, then at the end of the period of 3 years (beginning with the date of the bankruptcy) that interest ceases to be comprised in the debtor's estate and vests in the debtor (without conveyance, assignment or transfer). However, this does not apply if during that 3 year period, the trustee realises that interest, applies for an order for sale of that dwelling-house or applies for an order for possession of the dwelling-house (s 283A). ♦ If the house if of low value (defined in secondary legislation) the trustee will not be granted an order for sale of the property (s 313A).

➤ Initially the bankrupt can usually continue to occupy the family home *if either:* (ss 336-338)
   a) a spouse has a right of occupation under the *MHA/FLA*, or
   b) the bankrupt is living with minors and therefore has a right of occupation under the *MHA/FLA*
➤ During the first year a possession order is unlikely to be granted as the needs of the children are paramount
➤ After 1 year, an order for possession will probably be granted as the creditors' interests now become paramount

Trustee's powers to gather assets

Transaction	Time of transaction	Defence	Effect
At an undervalue (ss 339, 341)	With an unconnected person ➤ Within 5 years prior to bankruptcy, *and* the debtor is insolvent at the time or became so as a result of the transaction		All such property is 'reclaimed' under a court order by the trustee, and distributed to the creditors
	With an associate ➤ Within 2 years prior to bankruptcy	a) The debtor was not insolvent at the time, *or* b) the debtor did not become insolvent as a result of the transaction	
To create a preference (ss 340-341)	With an unconnected person ➤ Within 6 months prior to bankruptcy, *and* the debtor was insolvent at the time or became so because of the transaction, *and* the debtor intended to prefer, *and* the creditor was thus put in a better position	The debtor did not intend to prefer, or pressure was exerted to prefer	
	With an 'associate': ➤ Within 2 years prior to bankruptcy, *and* the debtor was insolvent at the time or became so due to this transaction (presumed), *and* the creditor was put in a better position as a result (presumed)	a) The debtor was not insolvent at the time, *or* b) the debtor did not become insolvent as a result of the transaction The debtor did not intend to prefer, or pressure was exerted to prefer	
At an undervalue to defraud creditors (s 423)	No time limit		

➤ 'Onerous' contracts or property - if an interested third party serves notice, a trustee must disclaim the contract or property within 28 days, otherwise he loses this right to disclaim and will be deemed to have adopted any contract (ss 315-316)
   ♦ Third parties who lose from a disclaimed contract claim loss from the bankrupt's estate
➤ Any disposition made between the day of presentation of the petition and the vesting of the bankrupt's estate in the trustee is void unless the court consents (s 284)

A trustee is *not* entitled to pursue:
➤ sale proceeds from a fully enforced judgment order obtained before the bankruptcy order was made (s 346)
➤ goods which, before a bankruptcy order was made, a landlord has distrained for up to 6 months arrears of rent (s 347)

Disabilities (ie: things the bankrupt may not do)
➤ **BROs:** *IA 1986 s 281A* and *Sch 4A* set out the rules for bankruptcy restrictions orders (BROs) which impose restrictions on bankrupts who abuse the system or whose conduct has been dishonest or otherwise culpable, either before or after bankruptcy. BROs run for 2 to 15 years.
➤ It is a criminal offence to take credit above £250 without disclosing the bankruptcy or to trade under a non-bankrupt name without disclosing the bankrupt name (*s 360*).
➤ A bankrupt may not retain membership of a partnership (the consequences of becoming a bankrupt while a partner) depend on the partnership agreement.
➤ A bankrupt may not retain directorships (*Art 81* of Table A and *CDDA 1986 s 11*).

Order of distribution

Order ↓

1. **Secured creditors:** they realise their security and account to the trustee for any surplus. If the security is not sufficient to discharge the whole debt, they are treated as unsecured creditors for the balance
2. **Bankruptcy expenses and costs**
3. **Preferential debts:** these rank equally and abate equally (*ss 328, 386, Schedule 6*)
   - Employee wages owed for the final 4 months prior to the bankruptcy order (subject to an individual maximum)
   - Holiday pay which is owed to employees
4. **Unsecured creditors:** these rank equally and abate equally
5. **Postponed creditors** (eg: loan between spouses)

Any surplus after paying these 5 sets of creditors goes to the bankrupt

False representations by the bankrupt (*s 356*)

➤ The bankrupt is guilty of an offence if he makes any material omission in statements about his affairs.

➤ The bankrupt is guilty of an offence if:

- knowing or believing that a false debt has been proved by any person under the bankruptcy, he fails to inform the trustee as soon as practicable, *or*
- he attempts to account for any part of his property by fictitious losses or expenses, *or*
- at any meeting of his creditors in the 12 months before petition or (whether or not at such a meeting) at any time in the initial period, he did anything which would have been an offence under the bullet above if the bankruptcy order had been made before he did it, *or*
- he has made a false representation or fraud to obtain the consent of any creditors to an agreement with reference to his affairs or to his bankruptcy.

II Partnership insolvency

Insolvent Partnerships Order 1994, IA 1986

➤ The parts of the *IA* regarding company voluntary arrangements and administration apply to partnerships.

➤ The partnership is treated as an unregistered company even though a partnership is not a legal person in its own right. There are different treatments for creditors' and members' winding up petitions.

➤ The law of bankruptcy does not apply to the firm but individual partners may be subject to bankruptcy orders, whereupon the official receiver becomes trustee.

➤ A modified form of moratorium applies to partnerships with similar criteria to small companies, see p 301.

III LLP insolvency

➤ The *IA 1986* applies to a LLP broadly as it does to a company incorporated under *CA 1985*.

- *LLPR 2001 r 5* and *Sch 3* apply the *IA 1986* (with appropriate modifications) to LLPs.

IV Corporate insolvency

A Alternatives to liquidation

➤ There are 3 alternatives:

1. The company is declared defunct.
2. The company goes into administration (or very rarely an administrative receiver is appointed).
3. A voluntary arrangement is made.

1 The company is declared defunct (*CA ss 652-653*)

➤ The company ceases trading.

➤ The Registrar of Companies can act on his own initiative to strike off the company.

➤ The Registrar must advertise his intention to strike off the company.

➤ For up to 20 years, a prejudiced member or creditor may apply for the company to be restored.

➤ The liability of every director, managing officer and member of the company continues, and may be enforced as if the company had not been dissolved (*s 652(6)(a)*).

2 The company goes into administration (or very rarely an administrative receiver is appointed).

Paragraph numbers in this sub-section refer to paragraphs in IA 1986 Sch B1, unless otherwise stated.

A note on debentures and administrative receivers

➤ Until recently, most debentures allowed a debenture holder to appoint an administrative receiver in the event he was not paid sums owed under the debenture, provided the holder had security (floating charge or a fixed and floating charge) over substantially the whole of the assets of the company.

➤ *IA 1986* (by *EA 2002*) now prohibits appointing an administrative receiver except in very limited circumstances (eg: if there is a capital market arrangement). Administrators are now appointed in situations that would have been handled by an administrative receiver.

a) Nature of administration

➤ Whether or not appointed by the court, an administrator is an officer of the court (as well as an agent of the company) and can only be appointed if qualified to act as an insolvency practitioner.

➤ An administrator may not be appointed if the company is already in administration.

➤ A company cannot go into administration if:

◆ a resolution for voluntary winding-up has been passed (*para 8(1)(a)*), or

◆ a winding-up order has been made (subject to an application by the liquidator or a floating charge holder) (*para 8(1)(b)*).

b) Purpose of administration

➤ The administrator is required, where he thinks it is reasonably practicable, to carry out his functions **with the objective of rescuing the company as a going concern**. Where that is not reasonably practicable or that objective would not provide the best result for the company's creditors as a whole, the administrator may substitute another purpose of:

a) achieving a better result for the company's creditors as a whole than would be likely if the company were wound up (without first being in administration), or

b) realising property in order to make a distribution to one or more secured or preferential creditors.

➤ An administrator must have regard to the interests of all creditors.

c) **Appointment of administrator**

➤ Administrators can be appointed by court order or by holders of floating charges and companies or their directors **without a court hearing** (*paras 14-34*).

i. **Appointment by court** (*paras 10-13*)

➤ A company or its directors, or one or more creditors of a company (which could include a floating charge holder) can apply to court for an administration order.

➤ The court may only make an order if it is satisfied that the company is, or is likely to become, unable to pay debts and that an order is reasonably likely to achieve an objective/the purpose of administration.

➤ Once an administration application has been made, the applicant must notify anyone who has appointed, or can appoint, either an administrative receiver or an administrator (*para 12(2)*). The application for administration cannot be withdrawn without the permission of the court (*para 12(3)*).

➤ On hearing an administration application, the court may either make the order, dismiss the application or make any other appropriate order (*para 13*).

ii. **Appointment by the holder of a floating charge** (*paras 14-21*)

➤ Floating charge holders can appoint an administrator of their choosing, provided that :

- the floating charge on which the appointment relies is enforceable, *and*
- the floating charge holder has given notice to the holder of any superior floating charge, *and*
- the company is not in liquidation, *and*
- neither an administrative receiver nor administrator is already in office.

➤ Before the administrator takes office, the floating charge holder must file a notice of appointment with the court identifying the administrator and including a statement of consent from the administrator. He must also attach a statutory declaration by the floating charge holder stating that he has a qualifying floating charge over the whole or substantially the whole of the company's property and that this is or was enforceable on the date of the appointment.

iii. **Appointment by company or directors** (*paras 22-34*)

➤ A company or its directors can only appoint an administrator if :

- the company has not been in administration (instigated by the company or directors) nor subject to a moratorium in respect of a failed CVA in the previous 12 months, *and*
- the company is or is likely to become unable to pay its debts, *and*
- there is no outstanding winding-up petition/application for administration, *and*
- the company is not in liquidation, *and*
- there is no administrator or administrative receiver in office.

➤ A 'notice of intention to appoint' must identify the proposed administrator (*para 26(3)*).

➤ Once the 'notice of intention to appoint' is sent to the floating charge holder and filed at court, an interim moratorium commences (*para 44(2)*).

➤ During the notice period, a floating charge holder entitled to appoint an administrator may either agree to the proposed appointment or appoint their choice of administrator (*para 14*).

- The company or directors must give floating charge holders at least 5 business days' notice in writing of their intention to appoint an administrator in this way (*para 26*).
- The 'notice of intention to appoint' must also be filed with the court and accompanied by a statutory declaration, stating that the application meets the relevant criteria.

- If the floating charge holder consents to the company's/directors' nominee or does not respond to the notice within 5 business days, the company/directors must make the appointment no more than 10 business days after filing their 'notice of intention to appoint' (*para 28(2)*). If out of time, the interim moratorium ceases to have effect and an administrator cannot be appointed.
➤ If there is no floating charge holder, the company/directors file the 'notice of appointment' at court together with a statutory declaration stating that the application meets the relevant criteria.
➤ A 'notice of appointment' must attach a statement from the administrator: a) consenting to act and b) stating that the purpose of administration is reasonably likely to be achieved. After this, the administrator is automatically appointed and takes office once the 'notice of appointment' and attached documents are filed at court. The company or directors then notify the administrator of their appointment.
➤ If, for whatever reason, the administrator's appointment is discovered to be invalid, the court may order the person who made the appointment to indemnify the administrator against liability (*para 34*).

d) **Effects of the administration**
➤ Any outstanding winding-up petitions are dismissed (unless the administration is because a floating charge holder has appointed an administrator, when any winding-up petition is suspended) (*para 40*).
➤ If an administrative receiver (AR) is in office, the court dismisses an administration application unless the AR's appointee or the court thinks the appointee's security may be set aside (*para 39*).
➤ An AR (and a receiver if asked by the administrator) must vacate office (*para 41*).
➤ Once in administration (ie: an administration order is made or administrator appointed), a moratorium starts from the filing date of the administration application/notice of intention to appoint. Then:
- no resolution cannot be passed, or order made, to wind up the company (*paras 42 and 43*).
- no steps can be taken by creditors to enforce their rights without the consent of the administrator or the permission of the court (*para 43*).
- every business document issued by the company or the administrator must identify the administrator and state that the affairs, business and property are being managed by him (*para 45*).

e) **Functions of the administrator**
➤ On appointment, an administrator must take custody or control of all company property (*para 67*).
➤ The administrator may do anything necessary or expedient for the management of the affairs, business and property of the company (including removing or appointing a director (*paras 59, 61*).
➤ The administrator may make a distribution:
- to secured creditors and preferential creditors without permission of the court (*para 65*).
- to unsecured creditors with the permission of the court (*para 66*).
- if he thinks that the payment is likely to assist in achieving the purpose of administration (*para 66*).
➤ The administrator may dispose of property subject to a floating charge (as created), as if the property were unencumbered, without the consent of the floating charge holder. However, the floating charge holder has first call on the proceeds of sale (*para 70*).
➤ The court may give the administrator power to override the rights of the holder of a fixed security over the company's property and power to dispose of the property in question as if it were owned by the company. However, the holder of the fixed security has first call on the proceeds of sale (*para 71*).

f) **Procedure**

Steps

1 The administrator is appointed and sends notice of the appointment (*paras 45-48*):
- to the company and its creditors as soon as is reasonably practicable
- to the Registrar of Companies within 7 days of the appointment.

2 By notice, the administrator requires a representative of the company to give a statement of affairs within 11 days of the notice being received. This statement must be verified by a statement of truth and give details of the company's property, debts and liabilities, and the details of each creditor and their security.

3 As soon as reasonably practicable (and in any event within 8 weeks of the administration starting) the administrator must make proposals to achieve the purpose of administration. He sends them to:
- the Registrar of Companies,
- the company's creditors (with an invitation to an initial creditors' meeting, which must be held as soon as reasonably practicable and in any event, within 10 weeks of the administration commencing), *and*
- every member of the company (by publishing a notice).

(If the administrator does not consider that it is reasonably practicable to rescue the company and/or achieve a better result for the creditors than on a winding-up, his statement must state why (*para 49*).)

4 The administrator presents the proposals at the initial creditors' meeting.
- If the administrator thinks that the company can be rescued as a going concern, he puts the proposal to the creditors who decide whether to accept an arrangement (eg: a CVA), reject the proposals or, if the administrator himself consents, amend the proposals.
- If company rescue is not reasonably practicable or would not get the best outcome for creditors, the administrator explains why. He puts a proposal to the creditors to achieve a better result for the company's creditors as a whole. The creditors vote on whether to accept, modify or reject the proposal.
- The administrator does not call a meeting of the creditors where it is thought there will be no funds available from the insolvent estate for unsecured creditors or where the administrator thinks there are funds to pay all creditors in full. However, within a set period, such a meeting may be requisitioned by creditors whose debts amount to at least 10% of the total debts of the company (*para 52*).

5 The administrator's statement of proposals may not include (*para 73*):
- any proposal that affects the right of a secured creditor to enforce his security without his consent, *or*
- any action resulting in a preferential debt being paid other than in a priority to a non-preferential debt.

6 Only a creditors' meeting may modify the administrator's proposals (*para 54*).
- The administrator cannot subsequently make any substantial revisions to the proposals without first obtaining the agreement of the creditors.

7 After the conclusion of the initial creditors' meeting (and any subsequent meeting), the administrator reports any decision taken to the court and the Registrar of Companies.

8 If the creditors fail to approve the proposals, the court may provide that the administrator's appointment shall cease, adjourn the hearing conditionally or unconditionally, make an interim order, make an order on a suspended petition for winding up or any other appropriate order (*para 55*).

Note: All time periods in Steps 3 and 4 can be extended with the permission of the court or with the consent of the creditors.

BUSINESS
Insolvency

3 **A voluntary arrangement is made** (*ss 1-7*) ie: a company voluntary arrangement ('CVA')

Aim: for the company to agree on a binding plan to repay debts so the company can survive.

Steps

1. If it is a 'small company', it may apply for a moratorium on actions against it (*Sch A1*).

2. The directors draft a proposal for a composition or scheme of arrangement.

3. An authorised person (eg: an insolvency practitioner), called a 'nominee', reports to the court, stating whether in his opinion the proposal has a reasonable prospect of being approved/implemented and whether meetings of shareholders and creditors should be held to consider the proposal. Unless the court directs otherwise, meetings of shareholders and creditors are held.

   - Consent must be obtained from more than 50% of the members who are present and voting, and more than 75% (by value) of the unsecured creditors who are present and voting.

   - However, a decision by the creditor's meeting to approve the CVA prevails over a member's meeting to reject the CVA, subject to a right by a member to challenge this in court (*s 4A*).

4. If approved, this approval is reported to the court.

5. The 'nominee' now becomes the 'supervisor' and carries out the CVA.

➤ Consequences:

- A CVA binds every creditor who had notice of, and was entitled to attend and vote at the meeting.
- It is *not* binding on secured creditors unless they agree to be bound by the arrangement.
- If the company defaults, creditors or members can petition to have the company wound up.

CVA 'small' company moratorium (*IA 1986 Sch A1*)

➤ A 'small company' may apply for a moratorium by filing certain documents with the court.

- A small company has at least 2 of 3 conditions applicable to it in the year ending with the date of filing, or in the financial year of the company which ended last before that date (*CA s 247*):

   a) turnover is not more than £5.6 million,

   b) the balance sheet total is not more than £2.8 million,

   c) there are not more than 50 employees.

- A small company cannot apply for a moratorium if:

   - the company is in administration, *or*
   - the company is being wound up, *or*
   - there is an administrative receiver of the company, *or*
   - a voluntary arrangement has effect in relation to the company, *or*
   - there is a provisional liquidator of the company, *or*
   - a moratorium has been in force for the company at any time during the period of 12 months ending with the date of filing, *and*

      i) no voluntary arrangement had effect at the time when the moratorium came to an end, *or*

      ii) a voluntary arrangement in force at any time in that period came to an end prematurely, *or*

   - an administrator held office during 1 year before the filing date, *or*

CVA 'small' company moratorium (IA 1986 Sch A1) (cont.)

- it is a holding company of a group which does not qualify as a small/medium-sized group, *or*
- on the filing date, it is a party to a capital market arrangement (where under the issue of a capital market investment a party has incurred a debt of at least £10 million), *or*
- it is a project company for a public-private partnership project, and includes step-in rights, *or*
- on the date of filing, it has incurred a liability under an agreement of £10 million or more.

➤ **The moratorium starts** when certain documents are filed with the court.

➤ **The moratorium ends** at the earlier of 28 days after it begins or at the end of the day on when the CVA meetings are first held (or, if the meetings are held on different days, the later of those days). A meeting to establish a CVA may extend the moratorium for a further 2 months from the CVA meeting.

➤ While the moratorium is in force:

- no petition may be presented for the winding up of the company, *and*
- no meeting of the company may be held except with the nominee's consent or leave of the court and subject (where the court gives leave) to such terms as the court may impose, *and*
- no resolution may be passed or order made for the winding up of the company, *and*
- no petition for an administration order in relation to the company may be presented, *and*
- no administrative receiver of the company may be appointed, *and*
- no administration application may be made or administrator appointed, *and*
- no landlord may exercise any right of forfeiture by peaceable re-entry for premises let to the company (if the company has failed to comply with any term or condition of its tenancy of such premises), except with the leave of the court, *and*
- nothing else may be done to enforce security over the company's property, or to repossess goods in its possession under any hire purchase agreement, except with the leave of the court, *and*
- no other proceedings or execution or other legal process may be started or continued, and no distress may be levied, against the company or its property except with the leave of the court, and
- there are special rules relating to an uncrystallised floating charge (not dealt with here), *and*
- security granted by the company may only be enforced if, at the time it was granted, there were reasonable grounds for believing that it would benefit the company, *and*
- business correspondence must carry a statement of the nominee's name and that the moratorium is in force (but if not done transactions are still enforceable by third parties), *and*
- the company may not obtain credit of £250 or more from a person who has not been informed that a moratorium is in force, *and*
- there are several other restrictions on what the company may do during this time.

B Liquidation

1 Voluntary liquidation

Sometimes a company may be wound up following criteria laid down in the articles (eg: to enable the shareholders to extract their capital). Otherwise it may be wound up after a special resolution has been passed, or after an extraordinary resolution has been passed due to its perceived liabilities.

Steps

1. The directors prepare a statement of affairs.

2. Either (a) or (b) will apply below depending on whether the company is solvent or insolvent.

    a) The company is *solvent*. This is known as a members' voluntary liquidation since the members will control the winding up of the company.

    The directors make a statutory declaration that the company will be able to pay its debts, including interest, within a period not exceeding 1 year (and this must be done within 5 weeks prior to passing a resolution to wind up the company) (*s 89*). They summon a general meeting (*s 89*) at which the members may:

    i) pass a special resolution to wind up the company (s 84), and advertise the fact in the London Gazette within 14 days of the resolution being passed (s 85), and

    ii) pass an ordinary resolution to appoint a liquidator (s 91).

    or:

    b) The company is *insolvent*. This is known as a creditors' voluntary liquidation. It is not a remedy available to creditors, but rather it is a procedure supervised by creditors.

    The members pass an extraordinary resolution to wind up the company (*s 84, CA s 378*), and the resolution is advertised in the *London Gazette* (*s 85*). Separate meetings are held for creditors and members to appoint a liquidator - generally all meetings are held on the same day.

    ◆ The creditors should meet within 14 days of the members' general meeting (s 98), where they are shown a statement of affairs by the directors (s 99).

    ◆ The creditors may appoint a liquidator.

    ◆ The creditors' choice of liquidator takes priority over that of the members (s 100).

3. The liquidator advertises his appointment and notifies the Registrar of Companies (*s 109*).

4. The liquidator has the same powers and duties as for a compulsory insolvency (see p 305).

5. After the company's assets have been distributed, the liquidator makes final reports prior to dissolution to a meeting of members (members' voluntary winding up)(*s 94*), *or* to meetings of members and creditors (creditors' voluntary liquidation)(*s 106*).

6. The liquidator sends the final return to the Registrar of Companies (*ss 94(3),106(3)*).

7. The Registrar dissolves the company 3 months after receiving the liquidator's final return (*s 201*).

BUSINESS
Insolvency

2 **Compulsory liquidation** (for unsecured creditors. Secured creditors usually have more specific remedies, eg: appointing an administrative receiver or receiver)

Steps

1. A creditor *or* the company petitions the Chancery Division of the High Court on one of 7 statutory grounds (*ss 122 (a)-(g)*) (eg: the company is unable to pay its debts).
   - The company is *presumed* to be unable to pay its debts if:
     - a statutory demand has been served by a creditor (minimum debt of £750) and is outstanding for 3 weeks, *or*
     - execution has been issued for an unsatisfied judgment debt.
   - If this presumption does not arise, insolvency must be shown to the court by taking into account actual, prospective and contingent liabilities.

2. The court has discretion to grant a winding up order (*s 125*).

3. The court appoints an official receiver. He is the liquidator until another is appointed (*s 136*). He:
   - takes the board's powers and is obliged to alter the company's notepaper so that the insolvency is apparent to third parties (*s 188*).
   - advertises his appointment in the *London Gazette* and the local paper.
   - notifies the Registrar of Companies and the company itself of his appointment.

4. The directors present a statement of affairs to the official receiver (or liquidator) within 14 days of the order. He reports to the court on the reasons and causes for the failure, and generally the position, dealings, etc, of the company, and any suspicious circumstances (*ss 131-132*).

5. The receiver calls separate members' and creditors' meetings, and may nominate an alternative liquidator to the official receiver (*s 136(5)*).
   - The official receiver *must* call a creditors' meeting if 25% (by value) request it (*s 136(5)*).
   - The creditors' nomination as liquidator takes priority.

6. The liquidator takes the board's powers and collects in all property of the company (see '*Liquidator's powers to recover assets*' on the next page) (Powers are listed in IA 1986 Sch 4).

7. The liquidator distributes assets (see below for the '*Order of distribution*').

8. After distribution, the liquidator notifies the Registrar of Companies, who dissolves the company 3 months later (*s 202*).

9. The liquidator makes a final report to the creditors' and the members' meetings (*s 146*).

Distribution	Order of distribution
➤ Property does NOT vest in the liquidator (as he is the company's agent), but he is under a duty to take it all into his possession. ➤ Legal proceedings against the company cannot proceed without leave of court. Leave will be refused, for example, if it gives a creditor a chance to 'promote' himself from an unsecured position.	1 Liquidator's expenses incurred during the winding up ↓ 2 Preferential creditors (s 175) ↓ 3 Floating chargees (in order of charge registration) ↓ 4 Ordinary unsecured creditors ↓ 5 Members of the Company **BUT see the caveat on the left:**

CAVEAT

➤ Where a floating charge relates to a company which has gone into liquidation/ is in administration, the liquidator/administrator must make some of the company's net property (maximum £600,000) available for the satisfaction of unsecured debts in preference to the proprietor of a floating charge (*IA 1986 s 176A*), *unless*
- the company's net property is less than £10,000, *or*
- the liquidator/administrator thinks that the cost of making a distribution to unsecured creditors would be disproportionate to the benefits, *or*
- the court orders otherwise.

➤ The amount of net property to be made available for unsecured debts is 50% of the first £10,000 of net property and 20% of net property in excess of £10,000 (*IA(PP)O 2003*).

BUSINESS
Insolvency

Liquidator's (and administrator's for ss 238, 239, 423) powers to recover assets

Transaction	Requirements	Defence	Effect
At an undervalue (s 238)	Within 2 years prior to the insolvency + the company was insolvent at the time or became so as a result of this transaction (presumed if with a connected person)	A bad bargain was: ➤ in good faith ➤ on reasonable grounds ➤ for genuine commercial reasons	He can set aside the transaction. (It is actually more complicated than this, but it holds true in general terms)
To create a preference (s 239)	Within 6 months prior to the onset of insolvency + the company was insolvent at the time or became so as a result of this transaction + voluntary act + desire to prefer + creditor put in a better position as a result		
	Within 2 years prior to the onset of insolvency for a transaction with a 'connected person' + insolvent at the time or became so as a result of this transaction + voluntary act + creditor put in a better position as a result	Pressure was exerted on the company (no desire to prefer)	
At an undervalue to defraud creditors (s 423)	An attempt to put assets beyond the reach of the person making, or who at some time, may make a claim, or otherwise prejudicing the interests of such a person	None	
Fraudulent trading (s 213)* Criminal offence CA s 458	➤ A positive act ➤ The business has been carried on with intent to defraud creditors or for a fraudulent purpose	No such intention	The court will require an offender to contribute to the company's assets insofar as it thinks it proper in the circumstances
Wrongful trading (s 214)*	➤ A director knew, or ought to have concluded that there was no reasonable prospect of the company avoiding insolvency; and ➤ did not take every step he ought to have taken to minimise loss to creditors	On becoming aware, he took every step that a reasonably diligent person would have, to minimise loss to creditors	

* The liquidator alone can seek an order under these sections

Charges

Fixed charge: is void against the liquidator if unregistered (or registered after 21 days of creation of charge) (CA s 395)

Floating charge: is void against the liquidator if:
- unregistered (or registered after 21 days of creation of the charge) (CA s 395), or
- (except to the extent of the value of consideration provided to the company in money or money's worth at the same time, or after the creation of the charge):
  - (if in favour of a connected person) the charge was created within 2 years of liquidation, or
  - (if in favour of an unconnected person):
    i) the charge was created within 1 year of liquidation, and
    ii) the charge was created at a time when the company was insolvent or became insolvent as a result (IA s 245).

A liquidator may not pursue sale proceeds of a fully enforced judgment order obtained before the bankruptcy order. If the order is not fully enforced, the sheriff will transfer any seized goods to the liquidator (s 183)

A liquidator may set aside 'onerous contracts', or disclaim 'onerous property', provided he replies to any inquiry by an interested third party within 28 days (s 178). 'Onerous' means that it is a drain on the company's assets or cash flow

V A note on statutory demands

- A statutory demand is a powerful creditor weapon because it obviates the need for court proceedings.
    - A debtor's failure to comply for 3 weeks can become the basis of a bankruptcy/insolvency petition.
- It is not a court document so the creditor must serve it and prove service.
- *IR 1986 (r 6)* set out the detailed requirements.

VI Cross-border EU insolvency

- EC *Regulation 1346/2000* has direct effect. In the UK it is implemented by *I(A)R 2002*, amending *IR 1986*.
    - It is intended to improve the efficiency and effectiveness of insolvency proceedings with an EU cross-border element without harmonisation. It sets out a framework for the different EU insolvency systems.
- There are 2 types of insolvency proceedings:
    - Main proceedings
        - These can be opened in the member state where the debtor has its 'centre of main interests'. There is no complete definition of this expression but for a company there is a rebuttable presumption that this is the place of the registered office. However, the Regulation provides that the centre of main interests should correspond to the place where the debtor conducts the administration of his interests on a regular basis and is therefore ascertainable by third parties.
        - The legal effects of main proceedings must be recognised in all other member states and the officeholder appointed in the main proceedings must be recognised, and will be able to exercise his powers, in other member states without the need for a further court order.
    - Secondary (or ancillary) proceedings
        - These can be opened by either the officeholder in the main proceedings, or any person or authority authorised to do so in the member state in which the application is made, in any territory where the debtor possesses an 'establishment'.
        - Secondary proceedings are limited in scope to assets in the member state where they are opened. In limited cases, such proceedings may be opened before main proceedings - they are then called 'territorial proceedings', eg: if local creditors request it or where main proceedings cannot be opened under the law of the member state where the debtor has his main centre of interest.
- UK insolvency proceedings that will be recognised:
    - **Main proceedings** (*Annex A*): In the UK: winding up by or subject to the supervision of the court, creditors' voluntary winding up (with confirmation by the court), administration, voluntary arrangements under the insolvency legislation and bankruptcy.
    - **Secondary proceedings** (*Annex B*): In the UK: winding up by or subject to the supervision of the court, creditors' voluntary winding up (with confirmation by the court) and bankruptcy.
    - NB: Receivership and administrative receivership are not listed as a main or secondary proceeding for the UK as they are considered a self-help remedy for the secured creditor.
- **Choice of law:** The general rule is that the law of the member state in which proceedings are opened will generally determine all the effects of those proceedings including the conditions for opening the proceedings, their conduct and closure. There are exceptions to this, eg: rights in rem and set-off rights.

H Competition and trading

I	Merger control law	IV	Enforcement of competition law
II	EU competition law	V	Free movement of goods
III	UK competition law	VI	Sale of goods / supply of services

I Merger control law

A European merger control

➤ *Merger Control Regulation 139/2004* came into force on 1 May 2004 and provides for a system of merger control for mergers with a 'Community dimension'. The Commission has sole jurisdiction for this.

- ◆ 'Community dimension' is assessed by minimum bounds for worldwide turnover, Community-wide turnover, and in some cases, national turnover (*Article 1*).
- ◆ Purely national mergers are excluded but may be subject to national legislation.

➤ The Commission must evaluate such concentrations to see if they are compatible with the common market (*Article 2*).

➤ **Notification:** Concentrations with a Community dimension must be notified to the Commission prior to their implementation and following the conclusion of the agreement, the announcement of the public bid, or the acquisition of a controlling interest (*Article 4*).

- ◆ Notification may also be made where the undertakings concerned demonstrate to the Commission a Community dimension and a good faith intention to conclude an agreement or, in the case of a public bid, where they have publicly announced an intention to make such a bid.

➤ **Publication:** The Commission must publish the notification, the names of the undertakings concerned, their country of origin, the nature of the concentration and the economic sectors involved (*Article 4*).

➤ **Decision:** The Commission must examine the notification as soon as it is received and publish a decision within 25 working days as set out below (*Articles 6* and *10(1)*).

- ◆ Where it finds that the concentration notified is not within scope, it publishes a decision saying so.
- ◆ Where it finds that the concentration notified, although within scope, does not raise serious doubts as to its compatibility with the common market and it decides not to oppose it, it publishes a decision saying that it is compatible with the common market.
  - • An indication that a concentration will not impede competition is if the market share of the undertakings does not exceed 25 % either in the common market or in a substantial part of it (*Recital 32*).
- ◆ Where it finds that the concentration notified falls within scope and raises serious doubts as to its compatibility with the common market, it may initiate negotiation with the parties who have a chance to modify the proposal or agree to conditions. These negotiations are closed by a decision as above.

➤ The implementation of concentrations should be suspended until a final decision of the Commission has been taken but it is possible to derogate from this suspension on rare occasions (*Recital 34*).

➤ In certain circumstances, the Commission can refer a case to a relevant Member State (*Article 9*).

➤ The Commission has wide powers to request information and to mount inspections (and ask Member States to help) (*Articles 11-13*) and to impose fines and penalties (*Articles 14-15*).

B UK Merger control

➤ *EA 2002 Pt 3* reforms the UK's regime for merger control. It replaces the previous merger control regime (except control of newspaper mergers). The main provisions about mergers provide for:

- final decisions to be taken by the Office of Fair Trading (OFT) and Competition Commission (CC).
- a new test of whether a merger will result in a substantial lessening of competition.
- discretion for the competition authorities to clear a merger or allow it to proceed with less stringent competition remedies in circumstances where, notwithstanding an expected substantial lessening of competition, they expect it to result in defined types of customer benefit.
- the Secretary of State may decide mergers which raise defined public interest considerations.
- a two-stage approach to merger control.
    - The OFT will carry out the first stage investigation to decide whether a CC reference is required.
    - The CC will carry out the second stage, in-depth investigation where necessary.
- a system of voluntary rather than compulsory pre-notification of mergers.
- statutory maximum timetables for competition authorities to reach final decisions for both first and second stage investigations.
- a UK-based turnover test to determine whether a merger is subject to merger control procedures.

➤ The European Commission has sole jurisdiction for mergers with a 'Community dimension' (see previous page).

➤ *EA 2002 ss 71-95* sets out the enforcement powers of the OFT, CC and Secretary of State before, during and after a merger reference.

➤ Enforcement takes two forms: undertakings and orders.

- Undertakings are given voluntarily by one or more of the parties to a merger. Once accepted by the relevant authority, these become legally binding and enforceable in the courts.
- Orders are made by the authorities and prohibit the parties specified in the order from doing something or specify that they must take certain action.

➤ Before and during a reference, undertakings and orders seek to prevent any action being taken that might prejudice the eventual outcome of the merger inquiry.

II EU competition law

Article 81: restriction or distortion of competition

➤ This article prohibits agreements, decisions and concerted practices ...
- ... between undertakings or associations of undertakings ...
- ... which have as their object *or* effect ...
- ... prevention, restriction or distortion of competition within the EU.

➤ Such agreements are void. However, *Article 81(2)* permits severance of an offending term if national law permits this.
- English law does permit this.

Avoiding infringement of *Article 81*

➤ **Agencies** (guidelines to *Regulation 2790/1999*, see p 324.) There is no infringement if:
- the principal and agent are pursuing the same economic interest, *and*
- the agent does not take the financial risk, and does not act independently of the principal.

➤ **Agreements between parents and subsidiaries**
- These are *usually* treated as one 'undertaking', and therefore are not caught by *Article 81*.

➤ **Agreements of 'minor importance' (which are not 'black-listed' agreements)**
- Agreements under this Commission Notice (*2001/C 368/07 - Dec 2001*) do not infringe *Article 81*.

  Ie: where the parties' combined share of the relevant market does not exceed 10% (for horizontal agreements) or 15% (for vertical agreements) of the total market in the agreement area.
- The Notice also contains guidelines for national courts.
- The Commission is not bound by the Notice, but compliance with it will avoid heavy fines.

➤ **Block exemptions**
- These allow parties to certain types of agreement to include anti-competitive/*Article 81* infringing provisions in their agreements. However, they will be permitted, if the agreement is drafted strictly in accordance with a block exemption. Block exemptions list forbidden 'black' clauses (eg: export bans) which must be avoided and permitted 'white' clauses (eg: certain territorial restrictions).
- Examples of block exemptions are:
  - *Regulation 2790/1999* - vertical agreements (see also p 324)
  - *Regulation 2658/2000* - specialisation agreements ⎫ horizontal
  - *Regulation 2659/2000* - research and development agreements ⎭ agreements
  - *Regulation 772/2004* - new technology transfer

➤ **Notification to the Commission:** this protects against fines in respect of the period from the date of notification until the Commission's 'first adverse reaction' (ie: possibly before its final ruling).
- The Commission then has 3 options:

  a) **Negative clearance:** a declaration that *Article 81* is not infringed.

  b) **Individual exemption:** granted under *Article 81(3)* if the agreement can be justified because it will 'contribute to the improvement of production or distribution of goods, or to promoting technical or economic progress, while allowing consumers a fair share of the resulting benefit'. An exemption binds the Commission, but few are granted and the process is lengthy.

  c) **Comfort letter:** a non-binding reassurance that *either Article 81* is not infringed, *or* a block exemption covers the agreement, *or* the Commission is closing its files for the moment.

> **Article 82: abuse of a dominant position**
>
> ➤ This article prohibits abuse by one or more undertakings of a dominant position ...
>   - ... within the EU or a substantial part of it ...
>   - ... which may affect trade between member states.
> ➤ A market share of 40% or more is a good indication that an undertaking is dominant in a market.
>   - Markets can be defined widely or narrowly (eg: passenger aircraft or commuter aircraft).
>   - A market is evaluated:
>   - geographically, *and*
>   - by product market.
>   - The test is 'what other product, if any, can be substituted for the product in question, given the nature of it, its price and its intended use?' (*United Brands v Comm.* [1978] ECR 207).

> **Avoiding infringement of *Article 82***
>
> ➤ If dominant in the market, an undertaking should not abuse its position.
> ➤ The European Commission ('Commission') can grant negative clearance. This is a declaration that an agreement does not contravene *Article 82*.
>   - This is the only option open to an undertaking to avoid infringement.

III   UK competition law

A   The Office of Fair Trading (OFT)

➤ The OFT has the function of (*EA 2002 ss 6-8*):
  - making the public aware of the ways in which competition may benefit consumers in, and the economy of, the United Kingdom; and
  - giving information or advice in respect of matters relating to any of its functions to the public.
  - making proposals or giving other information or advice on matters relating to any of its functions to any Minister of the Crown or other public authority
  - promoting good practice in the carrying out of activities which may affect the economic interests of consumers in the United Kingdom.

➤ The OFT is the enforcing body under the *CA 1998*.
  - Appeals from the OFT are to the Competition Commission.

B   Common law restraint of trade doctrine

➤ The restraint of trade doctrine prevents restrictive covenants being enforceable *unless*:
  - they are reasonably limited as to time, space and scope, *and*
  - they are reasonably necessary in the context of the whole agreement.

C   Competition Act 1998

➤ *CA 1998 s 60:* UK competition authorities must ensure there is no inconsistency with European competition law and must have regard to any statement/decision of the EC Commission.

CA 1998: The Chapter I prohibition

➤ This is modelled on the European *Article 81* regime but certain EU principles are not relevant eg: EU market principles and objectives.

➤ The Chapter I prohibition prohibits agreements, decisions and concerted practices between undertakings or associations of undertakings which have as their object *or* effect prevention, restriction or distortion of competition within the UK.

➤ Such agreements are void (but offending terms may be severed).

➤ Some agreements are not caught, eg: mergers, land agreements etc.

Avoiding infringement of the Chapter I prohibition

➤ **Outside scope:** Generally, the OFT says there is no 'appreciable effect' if the parties' combined share of the relevant market is not greater then 25%.
- A market share of less than 25% will have 'appreciable effect' if the agreement fixes prices, sets minimum resale prices or is part of a network of agreements that have a cumulative effect.

➤ **"Small agreements":** There is limited immunity for 'small agreements' (ie: all agreements between undertakings where their combined applicable turnover does not exceed £20 million) (*CA(SACMS)R*).

➤ **Exemptions:** 2 types:
- **Block exemptions** made by the OFT, which must be an agreement that (*CA 1998 ss 6, 9*):
  - contributes to:
    - improving production or distribution, *or*
    - promoting technical or economic progress,

    while allowing consumers a fair share of the resulting benefit, *and*
  - does not:
    - impose on the undertakings concerned restrictions which are not indispensable to the attainment of those objectives, *or*
    - afford the undertakings concerned the possibility of eliminating competition in respect of a substantial part of the products in
- **EU exemptions or decision** (ie: EU block exemptions/decision, p 309) (*CA 1998 ss 10-11*).

➤ **Notification to the EC Commission** (see p 309): this gives immunity from fines in *CA 1998* but infringements may still be investigated by OFT.

CA 1998: The Chapter II prohibition

➤ This is based on *Article 82* but certain EU principles are irrelevant eg: EU market principles/objectives.

➤ The Chapter II prohibition provides that any conduct on the part of one or more undertakings which amounts to the abuse of a dominant position in a market is prohibited if it may affect trade within the UK.
- A market share of 40% or more is a good indication that an undertaking is dominant in that market.
  - Markets can be defined widely or narrowly (eg: passenger aircraft or commuter aircraft).
  - A market is evaluated:
    - geographically, *and*
    - by product market.

Avoiding infringement of the Chapter II prohibition

➤ If dominant in the market, an undertaking should not abuse its position.

➤ **Minor conduct:** There is limited immunity from penalty for conduct of minor significance (ie: conduct by an undertaking whose applicable turnover does not exceed £50 million) (*CA(SACMS)R*).

IV Enforcement of competition law

Enforcement of EU competition law (Regulation 1/2003)

Art		
2	**Burden of proof:** In national or Community proceedings, the burden of proof is on the party alleging infringement. An undertaking claiming an *Article 81(3)* exemption bears the burden of proof of it.
3	**Relationship of national/EC law:** There must be simultaneous enforcement of national and EC in the competition law area but Member States may have national law which is stricter than EC law.
5/6	**National powers:** National competition authorities and courts have power to apply *Articles 81 & 82*.
7	**Finding infringement:** Where the Commission finds infringement, it may require undertakings concerned to end the infringement. It may impose on them any behavioural (this is preferred) or structural remedies which are proportionate to the infringement and necessary to end the infringement.
8	**Interim measures:** In urgent cases (ie: risk of serious and irreparable damage to competition), the Commission may order interim measures, on the basis of a prima facie finding of infringement.
9	**Commitments:** The Commission may accept a commitment from an undertaking to meet the Commission's concerns instead of making a finding of an infringement.
11	**Cooperation:** The Commission and the competition authorities of the Member States apply the EC competition rules in close cooperation (including by exchanging information)
13	**Suspension/termination of proceedings:** Where competition authorities of 2 or more Member States act against the same agreement, any of them may suspend the proceedings or reject the complaint on the grounds that another is dealing with it. The Commission may also reject a complaint on the ground that a competition authority of a Member State is dealing with the case and vice versa.
16	**Uniformity of legal application:** National courts cannot rule on agreements, decisions or practices so as to be inconsistent with a decision adopted or contemplated by the Commission.
17-19	**Investigations:** Where circumstances suggest that competition may be restricted/distorted within the EC, the Commission may conduct an inquiry into a particular sector of the economy or into particular types of agreement across various sectors. In that inquiry, the Commission may request undertakings concerned to supply information, carry out inspections and interview any person who consents to be interviewed to collect information relating to the subject matter of the investigation.
20-21	**Inspection:** The Commission has wide powers of inspection, including powers to: ♦ enter premises, land and means of transport of undertakings (and also the homes of directors and staff if there is reasonable possibility that important evidence is actually kept there), *and* ♦ examine books and records related to the business, irrespective of the medium of storage, *and* ♦ take or obtain in any form copies of or extracts from such books or records, *and* ♦ seal business premises, books or records during and to the extent necessary for inspection, *and* ♦ ask any representative or member of staff for explanations on facts or documents relating to the subject-matter and purpose of the inspection and to record the answers.
22	**Member State investigations:** Member State competition authorities may in their own territory carry out any inspection under national law on behalf of the competition authority of another Member State.
23	**Penalties imposable by the Commission:** An undertaking may be fined a maximum percentage of its total turnover in the preceding business year as follows: ♦ For intentionally or negligently giving incorrect/misleading information: maximum 1%. ♦ For infringing *Article 81/82*: maximum 10%.

> The Commission applies a publicly-declared fining policy within these limits (last updated June 2006). In fixing the fine, regard is had to the gravity and duration of any infringement

Enforcement of competition law by the OFT in the UK (*CA 1998 s 25*)

➤ The OFT may conduct an investigation if there are reasonable grounds for suspecting that:
  - there is an agreement which:
    - may affect trade within the United Kingdom, *and*
    - has as its object or effect the prevention, restriction or distortion of competition within the UK, *or*
  - there is an agreement which:
    - may affect trade between Member States, *and*
    - has as its object or effect the prevention, restriction or distortion of competition within the EU, *or*
  - the Chapter II prohibition has been infringed, *or*
  - the prohibition in Article 82 has been infringed, *or*
  - at some time in the past, there was an agreement which at that time:
    - may have affected trade within the UK, *and*
    - had as its object or effect the prevention, restriction or distortion of competition within the UK, *or*
  - at some time in the past, there was an agreement which at that time:
    - may have affected trade between Member States, *and*
    - had as its object or effect the prevention, restriction or distortion of competition within EU.

➤ The OFT has sweeping powers of investigation and enforcement similar to those of the European Commission (see previous page) but also backed by criminal sanction (*CA 1998 s 26*).

➤ The OFT must make a decision as to whether infringement of EU or UK Competition law has occurred. It can also accept commitments from persons to take certain action so as to avoid a finding of infringement (*CA 1998 ss 31-31E*).

➤ The OFT has power to give such directions as it sees fit to end any infringement (enforced by courts).
  - The OFT can also give interim measures directions, pending the completion of an investigation.

➤ Fines imposed by the OFT for infringements of competition law may be up to 10% of an undertaking's turnover during the preceding year (*CA 1998 s 36* and *CA(DTP)O 2000*).
  - For infringments of the Chapter I prohibition only, there is immunity for 'small' agreements and for infringments of the Chapter II prohibition only, there is immunity for 'conduct of minor significance', but not, in either case if the agreement or conduct is in respect of price fixing (*CA 1998 ss 39-40*).
  - The amount of the fine depends on the seriousness of the abuse, the party's position in the market, the size of the offender, and any mitigating factors such as co-operation with the OFT.
  - An undertaking may appeal against the OFT's ruling to the Competition Commission.

➤ If there is any overlap between European penalties and those which the OFT seeks to impose, the OFT must take the European penalties into account so there is no 'double jeopardy'.

➤ *EA 2002 ss 188-202* provide for criminal offences for individuals who dishonestly engage in cartel agreements. These operate alongside (but are narrower than) the existing regime that imposes civil sanctions on undertakings that breach the competition provisions of *CA 1998*.

V Free movement of goods

Treaty of Rome: *Articles 28 and 29*

➤ *Articles 28* and *29* prohibit quantitative restrictions on imports and exports and all measures having equivalent effect.

- 'Equivalent effect' means 'all trading rules enacted by member states that are capable of hindering, directly, or indirectly, actually or potentially, intra-community trade' (*Procureur du Roi v Dassonville* [1974] ECR 837).

- The measure must have some discriminatory effect (ie: putting imports at a disadvantage (*Re Keck and Mithouard* (Joined Cases C-267/91 and C-268/91) [1993] ECR I-6097; [1995] 1 CEC 298).
    - Before *Keck* it had been held that some marketing provisions had infringed *Article 28*. *Keck* seems to say that rules about selling arrangements/marketing probably do not come within *Article 28* and so it is not clear how the courts will treat such rules now.

- *Article 28* applies not only to the official laws of the state, but also when the state acts through another undertaking or 'bodies established or approved by an official authority' (*Re Peter Vriend* [1980] ECR 327, *Commission v Ireland* [1982] ECR 4005).

- The effect can be indirect and need not be the main purpose of the legislation (*Torfaen Borough Council v. B & Q plc* [1989] ECR 765) (one of the Sunday trading cases), and it includes bureaucratic procedures (*Rewe-Zentralfinanz GmbH v Landwirtschafiskammer* [1975] ECR 843).

- Discrimination against national goods is allowed since *Article 28* is not meant to give a level playing-field, but rather to avoid discrimination against imports (*Nederlandse Bakkerij Stichting v Edah BV* [1986] ECR 3359).

Two classes of exception to *Article 28*

1 Rule of reason (if both domestic and imported products are affected)

➤ National legislation for 'fiscal supervision, the protection of public health, the fairness of commercial transactions and the defence of the consumer' (*Rewe-Zentral AG v Bundesmonopolverwaltung fur Branntwein (Re Cassis de Dijon)* [1979] ECR 649), and the protection of the environment (*Commission v Denmark* [1989] CMLR 619) will not infringe *Article 28*.

➤ The 'rule of reason' test. Is the restriction ...
   a) ... justifiable under EU law, *and* ...
   b) ... in proportion to its declared aim? (ie: is the effect 'direct, indirect or merely speculative' and does it 'impede the marketing of imported products more than the marketing of national products' (*Stoke-on-Trent City Council v B & Q plc* [1993] 1 All ER 481))?

2 *Article 30*

➤ Certain laws will escape the prohibition of *Articles 28* and *29*. Such laws must be:

- to uphold public morality in a state (*R v Henn & R v Darby* [1979] ECR 3795 (pornography import)), *or*
- on grounds of public policy, *or*
- to maintain public security (internal and external), *or*
- to protect public health, *or*
- to protect national treasures, *or*
- to protect intellectual property rights

BUT such laws must not *either*:
a) constitute a means of arbitrary discrimination, *or*
b) be a disguised restriction on trade between member states.

VI Sale of goods / supply of services

A Terms implied by statute and regulation (generally)

➤ Terms may be implied by the 3 statutes listed in the following table where a contract for sale or supply of goods and/or services (*SGA s 55*) is silent as to certain matters.

➤ Other legislation also mandates certain rules in contracts (eg: *LPCD(I)A 1998* and *CP(DS)R 2000*).

Term	*SGA 1979* amended by *SSGA 1994/5*	*SGSA 1982* amended by *SSGA1994*			*SG(IT)A 1973*	When a term is implied into a contract *and* a few details as to the nature of the term
	Contract for sale of goods	Contract for hire	Contract for transfer of goods / Contract for work + materials	Contract for services	Contract for hire purchase	
Description	s 13	s 8	s 3		s 9	Goods/services must correspond with description (if sold by description)
Satisfactory quality	s 14(2) s 14(2A)	s 9(2) s 9(3)	s 4(2) s 4(3)		s 10(2)	Implied when dealing in the course of seller's business. Not applicable to: a) defects shown to the customer, *or* b) defects which the customer's examination ought to have revealed
Fitness for purpose	s 14(3)	s 9(4) s 9(5)	s 4(4) s 4(5) s 4(6)		s 10(3)	On a consumer sale, seller is liable for public statements made by the seller or producer regarding the subject of the sale
Title	s 12	s 7 (Possession)	s 2		s 8	Always implied
Price	s 8					See p 316
Payment	s 10					See p 316
Ownership	ss 16-18					See p 316
Risk	s 20					See p 317
Delivery	s 29					See p 317
Sample	s 15	s 10	s 5		s 11	Always implied on a sale by sample
Reasonable care and skill				s 13		Implied when dealing in the course of the seller's business
Within reasonable time				s 14		Implied when dealing in the course of the seller's business. Not applicable if the time is fixed by contract, or is left to be agreed in the manner set out in the contract, *or* is determined by a course of dealing between the parties
Reasonable charge				s 15		Always implied. Not applicable if charge is fixed by contract, or is left to be agreed in the manner set out in the contract, *or* is determined by a course of dealing between the parties

B Sale of Goods Act 1979

➤ When a sale of goods contract is formed, sometimes not all terms that are supposed to be included, are in fact included. The following defaults only apply where the contract does not make provision.

Sale of Goods Act 1979

s	Area	Content
		Formation of the contract
2	Definition	A contract for sale of goods is a contract by which the seller (S) transfers or agrees to transfer the property in goods to the buyer (B) for a money consideration, called the price
8	Price	Where price is not agreed, or determined by fact, B must pay a reasonable price
10	Time of payment	Not of the essence Note: other stipulations as to time depend on the terms of the contract
15	Sale by sample	2 implied terms: ♦ the bulk corresponds with the sample in quality ♦ the goods are free from any defect not apparent on a reasonable examination of the sample
		Effect of the contract
16 17 18	Ownership	Ownership passes when the parties intend it to pass ♦ If the parties do not express an intention as to when ownership passes, the time it does pass depends on the type of contract:

Rule	Type of contract	Ownership passes
1	Unconditional contract for specific goods in a deliverable state	When the contract is made
2	Contract for specific goods to be put into a deliverable state	When they are in a deliverable state and B is told of this
3	Contract for specific goods where something must be done to ascertain the price	When the price is set and B is told what it is
4	Goods on approval for sale and return	When *either*: ♦ B indicates his acceptance of the goods to S, *or* ♦ B's conduct implies that he accepts the sale transaction *or* ♦ B retains the goods beyond a reasonable period (or agreed time) without rejecting them
5	Unascertained goods	When goods are available and unconditionally appropriated to the contract (ie: ascertained)

Specific goods: 'goods identified and agreed on at the time the contract of sale is made' (*SGA s 61(1)*)

s	Area	Content

19	Reservation of title
	
	Note: the importance of retention of title clauses is manifest on insolvency; their purpose is either to recover goods when a business becomes insolvent, or failing that, to put the debtor in a strong position in negotiations with the receiver
		♦ S may reserve title to 'specific goods' or those 'appropriated to the contract' by a 'retention of title clause'
		♦ There are 3 types of these clauses, known collectively (and confusingly!) as '*Romalpa*' clauses.
		  a) Retention of title clause: title is reserved until payment is received
		  b) 'All moneys clause': title does not pass until *all* moneys owing to S, whether under this contract or any other contract, are paid
		  c) A true '*Romalpa*' clause: title is retained in the goods, and S is permitted to trace the purchase price into the hands of a third party to whom the goods are sold
		  • a) and b) are generally upheld by the courts
		  • c) succeeded on particular facts once when a fiduciary relationship was found between S and B (*Aluminium Industrie v Romalpa Aluminium Ltd* [1976] 2 All ER 552). Attempts to copy it have failed and the Courts construe c) as an unregistered (ie: void) charge
		♦ To stand a chance of being effective (ie: to stand a chance of being construed as more than just a charge that is void and being construed instead as a right to repossession) a clause should:
		  • reserve full *legal* title to the goods (equitable and/or beneficial title are insufficient), *and*
		  • entitle the seller to enter the buyer's property to inspect and repossess the goods, *and*
		  • oblige the buyer to store the goods separately, or label them, so they can be identified as being appropriated to the contract

Sale of Goods Act 1979 (cont.)

s	Area	Content
Effect of the contract (cont.)		

s	Area	Content
20	Risk	◆ Goods are at the risk of S unless property is transferred to B ◆ If property has been transferred to B, goods are at B's risk whether delivery has been made or not ◆ If goods are delayed due the fault of one party, the goods are at the risk of the party at fault NB: On a consumer sale, goods are at S's risk until delivered to the consumer
20A	Undivided shares in bulk	When goods within a bulk become identified *and* the price has been paid for the goods in the bulk, *then* ◆ property in undivided share is transferred to B, *and* ◆ B becomes an owner in common of the bulk
21	Capacity to pass property	One cannot give what one does not have - *nemo dat quod non habet*. (Exceptions include factors, S in possession after sale, and motor vehicles (*HPA 1964 s 27(5)(a)*)
Performance of the contract		
27 28	Duties	S must deliver the goods and B must accept and pay for the goods Delivery and payment are concurrent (ie: cash on delivery)
29 31	Delivery	**Place of delivery:** S's place of business (or if not, his residence) Note: if goods are specific goods and they are known to be at another place, delivery is at that other place Note: delivery to an independent carrier is counted as delivery to B **Delivery time:** S must send the goods within a reasonable time and at a reasonable hour
30	Wrong quantity delivered	**Smaller quantity than expected:** B may reject all the goods (unless he is not a consumer and the shortfall is only slight) B may accept all the goods. If so, he must pay for them at the contract rate **Larger quantity than expected:** B may accept the right quantity and reject the excess B may reject the whole (unless he is not a consumer and the excess is only slight) B may accept all the goods. If so, he must pay for them at the contract rate
31 34 35 35A 36	Acceptance ?	**B accepts the goods by:** ◆ intimating to S that he accepts, *or* ◆ after the goods have been delivered, acting in a manner inconsistent with the ownership of S **B rejects the goods:** ◆ B has a right to reject the goods if he has not had a reasonable opportunity to examine the goods (this cannot be waived if B is a consumer) ◆ B has a right to reject part of the goods ◆ B is not bound to return rejected goods ◆ B does not have to accept the goods if they unexpectedly arrive in instalments
41 42 44 45	Unpaid seller	An unpaid seller, if he has received no payment, or tender of payment may: ◆ have a lien on the goods or part of them for the price, *or* ◆ (if B is insolvent) stop the goods in transport, *or* ◆ (if the goods are perishable and S informs B he has not been paid) re-sell the goods
Remedies		
48A 49 50 15A	Things go wrong	**Remedies for S** ◆ **Property has passed and S has received no payment** - S sues for the price ◆ **Property has passed and payment time has passed without payment** - S sues for the price ◆ **B wrongfully refuses to accept the goods** - S sues for damages and losses 'directly and naturally' flowing from B's breach of contract **Remedies for B** ◆ **S does not deliver** - B sues for damages and losses 'directly and naturally' flowing from S's breach of contract ◆ **S breaches a warranty** - B sues for damages NB: if S breaches ss 13-15 (see p 315) and B is a non-consumer, and the breach is slight, this may be treated as a breach of warranty NB: if B is a consumer and goods do not conform to contract at time of delivery, B may require S to repair or replace the goods (unless impossible or disproportionate, in which case B can require a reduction in the purchase price or a rescission of the contract). A defect discovered within 6 months after delivery is presumed to have been there at the time of delivery unless shown otherwise by S

C Other statutory rules and regulations

Consumer guarantees

➤ Under *SSGCR 2002 r 15*, if goods are sold to a consumer with a consumer guarantee, the consumer guarantee takes effect at the time the goods are delivered as a contractual obligation owed by the guarantor under the conditions set out in the guarantee statement and the associated advertising.

➤ A guarantee must be in plain intelligible language and state duration, territorial scope and name and address of the guarantor.

Late Payment of Commercial Debts (Interest) Act 1998

➤ *LPCD(I)A 1998* gives a creditor a statutory right to claim interest on debts paid late (*s 1*) in contracts for the sale/hire of goods/services where purchaser and supplier both act in the course of business.

- 'Business' includes professions and government departments or local/public authorities.
- Exempt contracts include consumer credit agreements, mortgages, charges or security (*s 2*).

➤ Interest starts to accrue on (*s 4*): *either* the day after the contractual date for payment,

or if none, 30 days from the later of:
- delivery of the invoice for payment, *or*
- delivery/performance of the relevant goods/services.

- The interest rate is 8% above the official dealing rate in force on 30 June (for interest starting between 1 July-31 December) or 31 December (for interest starting between 1 January-30 June).
- There are slightly different rules for advance payments (not dealt with here).

➤ Once interest starts to accrue, the supplier is entitled to a fixed sum (in addition to the statutory interest on the debt) which is specified in *s 5A(2)*.

➤ Contracting-out of *LPCD(I)A 1998* before the debt is created is not permitted unless there is a substantial contractual remedy for late payment in the contract (*s 8*).

Consumer Protection (Distance Selling) Regulations 2000

Reg

➤ There are many types of distance sales, including those made over the Internet. *CP(DS)R 2000* implements (most of) Euro Directive 97/7/EC on the protection of consumers in relation to distance contracts.

- *FS(DM)R 2004* implements Euro Directive 2002/65/EC on the distance marketing of consumer financial services (ie: services of a banking, credit, insurance, personal pension, investment or payment nature which the FSA/OFT do not regulate under their existing regulatory structures). For these things, It contains similar provisions to *CP(DS)R 2000*.

4 ➤ *CP(DS)R 2000* applies to contracts for goods or services to be supplied to a consumer where the contract is made exclusively by means of distance communication (ie: any means used without the simultaneous physical presence of the consumer and the supplier.

5 - *CP(DS)R 2000* do not apply to 'excepted contracts' ie: contracts:
   - for the sale an interest in land except for a rental agreement, *or*
   - relating to financial services, *or*
   - concluded by means of an automated vending machine or automated commercial premises, *or*
   - concluded with a telecommunications operator through a public pay-phone, *or*
   - concluded at an auction.

6 - Most of *CP(DS)R 2000* do not apply to contracts for the supply of groceries by regular delivery or contracts for the provision of accommodation, transport, catering or leisure services.

19 ➤ The contract must be performed within 30 days, subject to agreement between the parties. If the supplier cannot supply the goods/services ordered, he may offer substitutes if set conditions are met.

26-27 ➤ The OFT must consider complaints about a breach of *CP(DS)R 2000*.

Consumer Protection (Distance Selling) Regulations 2000 (continued)

Reg 7
- In good time **prior to the conclusion of the contract** the supplier must:
  - provide to the consumer the following information in a clear and comprehensible manner:
    - the supplier's identity and, if the contract requires advance payment, the supplier's address, *and*
    - a description of the main characteristics of the goods or services, *and*
    - the price of the goods or services including all taxes and delivery costs where appropriate, *and*
    - the arrangements for payment, delivery or performance, *and*
    - the existence of a right of cancellation (except in the exceptional cases - see below), *and*
    - the cost of using the means of distance communication, if not at the basic rate, *and*
    - the period for which the offer or the price remains valid, *and*
    - where appropriate, the minimum duration of the contract, in the case of contracts for the supply of goods or services to be performed permanently or recurrently.
  - inform the consumer if he proposes that, if the goods/services ordered by the consumer are unavailable, he will provide substitutes of equivalent quality and price, *and*
  - inform the consumer that the cost of returning any such substitute goods to the supplier in the event of cancellation by the consumer will be met by the supplier.

8
- The supplier must confirm in writing, or on other durable medium available and accessible to the consumer, most of the information already given **and** some additional information, eg:
  - conditions and procedures relating to the cancellation rights, including:
    - where the consumer must return the goods for a cancellation, notification of that fact, *and*
    - information as to whether the consumer or supplier is responsible for the cost of return if the consumer cancels the contract, *and*
    - in a services contract, information of how the right to cancel may be affected by the consumer agreeing to performance of the services starting before the end of the cooling-off period.
  - information on after-sales services/guarantees), *and*
  - conditions for exercising any contractual right to cancel, where the contract is of an unspecified duration or a duration exceeding 1 year.

10-12
- There must be a 'cooling off period' so the consumer can cancel the contract by giving notice of cancellation. The effect of this notice is that the contract is treated as if it had not been made.
  - If the supplier gives the specified information on time, the cooling-off period is 7 working days from: i) (for services) the day after the date of the contract, *or* ii) (for goods) the day after the date of delivery.
  - If the supplier fails to supply the required information, the cooling-off period is extended by 3 months (but if the performance of a services contract has begun with the consumer's agreement before the expiry of the cooling-off period and the supplier has not supplied information, different rules apply).
  - If the supplier complies with the information requirement later than he should have done but within 3 months, the cooling-off begins from the date he provided the information.

13
- There is no cancellation right (unless the parties agree) if the contract is for the supply of:
  - services, if performance of the contract has begun with the consumer's agreement either before the end of the cancellation period or after the supplier has supplied information (see above), *or*
  - goods/services where price depends on financial market fluctuations outside the supplier's control, *or*
  - goods made to the consumer's specifications or clearly personalised or which by reason of their nature cannot be returned or are liable to deteriorate or expire rapidly, *or*
  - audio or video recordings or computer software if they are unsealed by the consumer, *or*
  - newspapers, periodicals or magazines, *or*
  - gaming, betting or lottery services.

14
- If the consumer cancels, the consumer must be reimbursed within a maximum of 30 days.

15
- If the consumer cancels the contract, a related credit agreement is automatically cancelled.

17
- On cancellation, the consumer must restore goods to the supplier if he collects them, but meanwhile the consumer must take reasonable care of them. The consumer does not have to return goods but if he breaches a requirement under the contract, he must pay the supplier's recovery costs.

21
- If the consumer's payment card is used fraudulently, he may cancel the payment. If the payment has already been made, he is entitled to a re-credit or to have all sums returned by the card issuer.

D Exclusion clauses

➤ A clause which successfully excludes or limits liability must have overcome certain hurdles:

1 Common law rules

➤ **Incorporation:** the clause must be properly incorporated into the contract (ie: reasonable steps must be taken to draw the term to the promisee's attention).

➤ **Construction:** the clause must cover the breach which occurs.

➤ **Particular common law rules:** the *'contra proferentem'* rule - any ambiguity in a term of the contract is interpreted against the party attempting to rely on the exclusion.

2 Some statutory/regulatory rules - background

➤ Certain rules cannot be contracted out of. For example, the *CP(DS)R 2000*, the Unfair Contract Terms Act (*'UCTA'*) and the *Unfair Terms in Consumer Contracts Regulations 1999* (*'UTCC'*).

➤ *CP(DS)R 2000* has been dealt with on the previous 2 pages.

➤ *UCTA* has been in English law since 1977. *UTCC* on the other hand, is a relatively recent development and is based on a European directive.

- There are 3 problems with having these 2 sources of legislation:

    a) There is a degree of overlap because:
    - *UCTA* covers exclusion and limitation of liability clauses in business and consumer contracts.
    - *UTCC* covers unfair terms in consumer contracts which have not been individually negotiated.
        - An 'unfair term' is a term which is contrary to the requirement of good faith and causes a significant imbalance in the parties' rights/obligations to the detriment of the consumer.
    b) Key concepts such as 'consumer' are defined differently in both pieces of legislation.
    c) The list of contracts exempted from each legislative regime is different and must be checked.

UCTA and *UTCC*

➤ Where there is a **consumer contract** containing an **unfair exemption clause**, there is an overlap between the *UCTA* and *UTCC* and both must be checked against the contract.

- The procedure is as follows:

Steps	
1	Check definitions in *UCTA*
2	Check *UCTA* (see box overleaf)
3	Tighten the contract to comply with *UCTA*
4	Check definitions in *UTCC*
5	Check *UTCC* (if a consumer contract) (see box overleaf)
6	Tighten the contract to comply with *UTCC*

➤ *UCTA* does not apply to International Supply Agreements (*UCTA 1977 s 26*).

Step 2: *Unfair Contract Terms Act 1977*: contents

	Attempted exclusion	Effect
s 2	a) The common law duty of care, *or* b) liability under the *Occupiers Liability Act 1957*	Void for death *or* personal injury Valid for other loss if the clause satisfies the requirement of reasonableness'
s 3	General exclusion of liability NB: This section is only applicable if one party 'deals as a consumer' and/or uses the other's standard written terms ➤ Covers 2 parties dealing in business ➤ Not applicable to implied terms	Entitles the promisor to offer performance of the contract 'substantially different from that which was reasonably expected of him', subject to the 'requirement of reasonableness'
s 6	*SGA* or *SG(IT)A* implied terms: ◆ Description, satisfactory quality, fitness for purpose, sample	Exclusion is void against purchaser 'dealing as a consumer', but otherwise it is valid if it satisfies the 'requirement of reasonableness'
	◆ Title	Always void
s 7	Where possession or ownership of goods passes under a contract which is not a sale of goods or hire purchase contract, ◆ any term is implied by law, *or* ◆ s 2 of the *SGSA* (Title), *or* ◆ right to transfer goods	◆ Exclusion is void if a party is dealing as a consumer, otherwise a clause is valid subject to satisfying the 'requirement of reasonableness' ◆ s 2 *SGSA* (Title) is not excludable ◆ Subject to 'reasonableness'

Requirement of reasonableness (*s 11*) is ...

'... a fair and reasonable [term] ... having regard to the circumstances which were, or ought reasonably to have been, known to or in the contemplation of the parties when the contract was made'

➤ Although the guidelines exist in *Schedule 2* to define reasonableness, they are only obligatory for *ss 6-7*. Nevertheless, the courts frequently use them in other cases too. They include:
   ◆ the customer's knowledge
   ◆ the bargaining position of the parties
   ◆ whether the contract involved the customer making a special order

Step 5: *Unfair Terms in Consumer Contracts Regulations 1999*: contents

Section	Breakdown of the section
r 3	Interpretation clause. Includes the definition of: ◆ seller/supplier (any natural/legal person acting for purposes relating to his trade, business or profession), ◆ consumer (any natural person acting for purposes outside his trade, business or profession - different to *UCTA*)
r 4	Regulations apply to unfair terms in contracts between a seller/supplier and a consumer *but* subject matter of the contract and price are not tested for fairness (*r 6(2)*)
r 5	Key concept of an 'unfair term' which is a term 'contrary to . . . good faith [which] causes a significant imbalance in . . . rights . . . to the detriment of the consumer'
r 6	To see if a term is unfair, it must be looked at in context at the time it was made
r 7	Terms must be in plain, intelligible language; if not, the term will be construed in the consumer's favour
r 8	Unfair terms do not bind a consumer.
r 10-15	The OFT considers any complaints made and has various powers
Schedule 2	Examples of unfair terms

➤ The OFT has published a bulletin covering the following topics:
   ◆ the most common unfair terms in consumer contracts
      eg: • entire agreement clauses
          • penalty clauses
          • variation of price clauses
   ◆ terms that have been successfully excluded after OFT intervention
      eg: • 'The Council accepts no liability for loss or damage to cars parked in this car park ... howsoever caused.'

1 Commercial agreements

    I   Third party rights in contracts
    II   Agency agreements
    III Distribution agreements
    IV Choosing the right type of agreement
         (Agency, Distribution, Franchise or Licence?)

I Third party rights in contracts

➤ Under C(ROTP)A 1999, if a contract is made with the purpose of conferring a benefit on a third party, under certain circumstances that person has a right to sue for breach of contract.

II Agency agreements

A 3 types of agency

3 types of agency		
Classical sales agency	P authorises A to enter into contracts with C on behalf of P	Note: in this chapter P=Principal A=Agent C=Customer
Marketing agency	P authorises A to introduce customers (C) to P	
Note: a del credere agent guarantees C's performance for an additional commission		

B Legislative rules

Commercial Agents (Council Directive) Regulations 1993	
Affects all commercial agents operating in the UK after 1 January 1994	Regulation
◆ oblige the principal and the agent to exchange certain information	3-4
◆ govern the amount of commission paid to an agent and the method of payment	6-12

◆ provide for compensation to be paid to the agent on termination especially where:
  a) the agent has been deprived of commission which proper performance of his duties would have procured for him, while the principal retains substantial benefits linked to the agent's activities, *or*
  b) the agent has been unable to amortise the costs and expenses that he had incurred in the performance of the contract on the principal's advice
◆ give the parties a choice between an indemnity or compensatory arrangement on termination
  • Where no preference is expressed, the agent will be entitled to compensation (*rr 17-18*)
  • The right to damages, as well as an indemnity (linked to the fruits of the agent's efforts), is preserved
	13-19

◆ renders any attempt to restrain an agent's trade after termination void, unless it:
  a) is contained in a written agreement
  b) defines a geographical area where the agency operates *or* the area in which customers are situated
  c) ceases no more than 2 years after termination
	20

Note: a) agencies in other EU member states may be governed by a version of the *Regulations* enacted in accordance with that state's laws. Complicated questions of jurisdiction and applicable law determine which courts (UK or foreign) will enforce which set of legislation (UK, local state or EU directive) b) certain classes of agent, such as unpaid agents, insolvency practitioners and those whose 'activities as agents are considered to be secondary' are excluded from the *Regulations*	

C The law of agency: basic principles

➤ An agency agreement can be oral or written, express or implied.

1 Authority

➤ **Actual authority:** this can be given expressly *or* impliedly.

➤ **Ostensible authority.** Four conditions must be satisfied (*PA ss 5-8*):

subjective test
- a) C knows or believes he is dealing with A, *and*
- b) C is unaware that 'A' is not actually authorised, *and*

objective test
- c) 'A' would usually be expected to be authorised to enter into such a transaction, *and*
- d) P's type of business is consistent with the nature of the transaction.

2 Liability

➤ **When A is authorised to act**
- ♦ P is liable for A's acts.
- ♦ A is not liable unless the contrary is agreed, expressly or implicitly, by A and P or A and C.

➤ **When A is *un*authorised to act**
- ♦ Generally, P is not liable to C for A's acts.
- ♦ If A has ostensible authority, but has exceeded his actual authority, P will be liable and A may be liable to P and C for breach of warranty of authority.

3 Ratification of A's acts

➤ P can 'ratify' (ie: agree to be bound by) a contract by an unauthorised A if:

a) C could identify P when the contract was agreed, *and*

b) P has contractual capacity at the date of the contract and the date of ratification, *and*

c) the act is capable of ratification (ie: not illegal), *and*

d) ratification occurs within a reasonable time.

4 Non-disclosure of agency

➤ If A does not disclose his agency, P can always intervene *unless:*

a) the contract between A and C, expressly or impliedly excludes an agency, *or*

b) C wished to contract with A, *or*

c) the 'personality' of the parties is central to the contract.

5 Termination

➤ The agency agreement can be terminated by *either* A *or* P at any time subject to the contract.

➤ If P who is a debtor gives a creditor authority to act as an agent, then while the debt remains outstanding, the agency is irrevocable (*Greer v Downs Supply Co* [1927] 2 KB 28).

➤ The contract is terminated by the death or mental incapacity of A or P, but A is protected if he acts in ignorance of P's incapacity (*PAA 1971 s 5(1)*).

6 Payment

➤ Payment to A by C does not discharge a debt owed to P by C unless *either* A has authority (actual or apparent) to receive the payment, *or* P is undisclosed.

➤ Payment by P to A does not discharge a debt owing to C unless C misleads P into thinking that the money is to reimburse A for money already paid to C.

III Distribution agreements

A Types of distribution agreement

➤ Distribution agreements with anti-competitive provisions may infringe European/UK competition law. Eg:

1. **Exclusive distribution** - distributor alone may distribute supplier's goods in a particular territory, but supplier may still make passive sales in the territory.
2. **Sole distribution** - as in 1, but supplier can actively sell within the 'exclusive territory'.
3. **Selective distribution** - supplier attempts to retain control over the sales that his distributor makes.
4. **Exclusive purchasing** - distributor promises to buy goods from a sole supplier for an 'exclusive territory'.

B Relevant law

➤ See pp 307-313 for relevant law and possible ways to avoid infringement.

black clauses
white clauses

Block exemption covering vertical agreements (*Regulation 2790/1999*)

➤ Vertical agreements are agreements or concerted practices entered into by 2 or more undertakings each of which operates at a different level of the supply or production chain, which relate to the conditions under which a party may purchase, see or resell certain goods or services, and which contain restrictions within the scope of *Article 81(1)*.

➤ The exemption only applies if the market share held by the supplier does not exceed 30 % of the relevant market on which it sells the contract goods or services.

➤ If a vertical agreement contains exclusive supply obligations, the exemption only applies if the market share held by the buyer does not exceed 30 % of the relevant market on which it purchases the contract goods or services.

➤ The exemption does not apply to vertical agreements which, directly or indirectly, in isolation or in combination with other factors under the control of the parties, have as their object a restriction on:

- the buyer's ability to determine its sale price (even though the supplier may impose a maximum sale price or recommend a sale price, provided that it does not amount to a fixed or minimum sale price due to pressure), *or*
- active or passive sales to end users by members of a selective distribution system operating at the retail level of trade, without prejudice to the possibility of prohibiting a member of the system from operating out of an unauthorised place of establishment, *or*
- cross-supplies between distributors within a selective distribution system, including between distributors operating at different level of trade, *or*
- limitation, agreed between a supplier of components and a buyer who incorporates those components, which limits the supplier to selling the components as spare parts to end-users or to repairers or other service providers not entrusted by the buyer with the repair or servicing of its goods, *or*
- the territory into which the buyer may sell the contract goods or services.

NB: the following restrictions *are* allowed - restrictions on:

- active sales into the exclusive territory or to an exclusive customer group reserved to the supplier or allocated by the supplier to another buyer, where such a restriction does not limit sales by the customers of the buyer.
- sales to end users by a buyer operating at the wholesale level of trade.
- sales to unauthorised distributors by the members of a selective distribution system.
- the buyer's ability to sell components, supplied for the purposes of incorporation, to customers who would use them to manufacture the same type of goods as those produced by the supplier.

➤ The exemption does not apply to the following direct or indirect obligations contained in vertical agreements:

- an obligation which is indefinite or exceeds 5 years. A non-compete obligation which is tacitly renewable beyond 5 years is deemed to have been concluded for an indefinite duration. However, there are slightly different rules for where contract goods or services are sold by the buyer from premises and land owned by the supplier or leased by the supplier from third parties, *or*
- an obligation forbidding members of a selective distribution system from selling brands of competing suppliers, *or*
- an obligation forbidding the buyer, after termination of the agreement, from manufacturing, purchasing, selling or reselling goods or services, unless such an obligation:
  - relates to goods or services which compete with the contract goods or services, *and*
  - is limited to the premises and land from which the buyer has operated during the contract period, *and*
  - is indispensable to protect know-how transferred by the supplier to the buyer, and provided that the duration of such non-compete obligation is limited to a period of 1 year after termination of the agreement (this obligation is without prejudice to the possibility of imposing a restriction which is unlimited in time on the use and disclosure of know-how which has not entered the public domain).

IV Choosing the right type of agreement

	Agency agreement	Distribution agreement
Supervision	This depends on the type of agency: **classical sales agency:** requires more supervision over the agreement **marketing agency:** requires less supervision over the agreement ✗	There is no need for day to day supervision, and the principal specifies any detailed requirements in the agreement. These are preferable if the principal wishes to deal in a new geographical market with minimum expense and inconvenience ✓
Goods	Suitable for goods which are ordered on a 'one-off' basis to a customer's individual specification	Suitable for standard ranges of goods which do not require specialist after-sales support
Prices	➤ The supplier sells directly to the retailer ➤ The supplier controls the price ➤ The agent takes commission ✓	➤ The supplier sells to the distributor who marks up the resale price ➤ The supplier can 'recommend', but cannot control the price as *Article 81* and *CA 1998* prohibit price-fixing ✗
Risk	P takes the risk, A gets the commission ✗	The distributor takes the risk ✓
Marketing	The supplier retains tight control over marketing ✓	The supplier has less say; the distributor has more freedom of action ✗
Enforcing contracts	This is difficult as the supplier sells to many customers ✗	This is straightforward as there is only one buyer - the distributor ✓
Liability	This depends on the type of agency: **classical sales agency:** the principal is directly liable in contract to customers **marketing agency:** the agent has no actual authority to act on the principal's behalf ✗	The principal is only liable in contract to the distributor The principal may be liable to consumers under the *CPA 1987* or *GPSR 1994* ✓
Protection of a territory	As a principal and agent are separate undertakings, the agent can be given an 'exclusive territory' ✓	**Passive sales** cannot be banned (*either* those by a distributor outside his territory, *or* by a supplier within the territory) **Active sales** by either party in contravention of an 'exclusive territory' can usually be banned ✗
Article 81 problems	Usually non-applicable as principal and agent are counted as one undertaking ✓	This can be a problem, unless use is made of a block exemption ✗
Taxation	An overseas business trading through an agency in the UK may be subject to corporation tax	This depends on the agreement's wording, and the extent of the principal's presence in the UK
Compensation	The agent may seek compensation for termination under *CA(CD)R 1993* ✗	The only remedies are those usually available in contract and tort ✓

✓ advantage ✗ disadvantage

Franchise

➤ These are suitable vehicles for exploiting a 'business format' (eg: Pizza Hut).
  ◆ The franchisor can control closely many aspects of the product, and thus protect and foster his goodwill without incurring the capital costs of expanding in new markets
  ◆ The franchisee also benefits from the accumulated goodwill. He contributes his own capital. His freedom to innovate is rather limited by the franchise

Licence

➤ These enable the exploitation of intellectual property rights by permitting a third party to use a process, or manufacture a product
  ◆ The licensor is spared the difficulties and capital investment involved in manufacture
  ◆ A licence (possibly combined with a distribution agreement) may be vital where national laws insist that products are manufactured within a given area

J Employment

Businesses should be aware of 'free movement', 'residence' and 'equal treatment' rights' in EU member states as well as UK employment legislation. Also, with the state reducing its retirement provisions, advice on 'pensions in the UK' is also vital.

- I   Free movement and residence: principles (EU law)
- II Residence rights and equal treatment (EU law)
- III UK employment legislation: statutory rights
- IV Pensions in the UK

I   Free movement and residence: principles (EU law)

Treaty of Rome: Article 39

- This article prohibits discrimination based on nationality between workers of member states, for employment, or remuneration and other conditions of work and employment.
  - *Article 39* extends to the right to move freely in search of employment.
  - Recipients of services have a right to seek services from another member state (*Article 49* and *Luisi v Ministero del Tesoro* [1984] ECR 377). This embraces the right to vocational training at no extra fee due to nationality (*Gravier v City of Liege* [1985] ECR 593).

Derogation and exclusions

- *Article 39(3)* allows a member state to refuse to comply with the rights set out in *Article 39* on the grounds of public policy, public security or public health.
- Member States may restrict the freedom of movement and residence of Union citizens and their family members, irrespective of nationality, on grounds of public policy, public security or public health. These grounds must not be invoked to serve economic ends (*Directive 2004/38, Article 27*).
- *Article 39(4)* excludes jobs in the public service 'involving the exercise of official authority and functions relating to safeguarding the general interests of the state' (*Commission v Belgium* [1980] ECR 3881).

Family (*Directive 2004/38, Articles 18, 23*)

- Irrespective of nationality, family members of a worker/self-employed person who reside with him in a host Member State have the right of permanent residence there, if the worker/self-employed person has acquired himself the right of permanent residence (*Directive 2004/38, Article 18*).
- Irrespective of nationality, family members of a Union citizen who have the right of residence or the right of permanent residence in a Member State are entitled to take up employment or self-employment there (*Directive 2004/38, Article 23*).

II Residence rights and equal treatment (EU law)

1 Temporary residence

➤ Union citizens have the right of residence in another Member State for a period of up to 3 months without any conditions (but must hold a valid identity card/passport) (*Directive 2004/38, Article 6*).

- This also applies to family members in possession of a valid passport who are not nationals of a Member State accompanying or joining the Union citizen.

➤ Union citizens have the right of residence in another Member State for more than 3 months if they (*Directive 2004/38, Article 7*):

a) are workers or self-employed persons in the host Member State, *or*

b) have sufficient resources for themselves and their family members not to become a burden on the social assistance system of the host Member State during their period of residence and have comprehensive sickness insurance cover in the host Member State, *or*

c) are enrolled at an establishment, accredited or financed by the host Member State, to study (including vocational training) *and* have comprehensive sickness insurance cover in the host Member State and assure the relevant national authority that they have sufficient resources for themselves and their family members not to become a burden on the social assistance system of the host Member State during their period of residence, *or*

d) are family members accompanying or joining a Union citizen who satisfies one of (a)-(c) above.

➤ The residence right includes family members who are not nationals of a Member State, accompanying or joining the Union citizen, provided that the Union citizen satisfies one of (a)-(c) above.

2 Permanent residence

➤ Union citizens who have resided legally for a continuous period of 5 years in the host Member State have an unconditional right of permanent residence there (*Directive 2004/38, Article 16*).

- The right is lost only through absence from the host state for greater than 2 consecutive years.

- This also applies to family members who are not nationals of a Member State and have legally resided with the Union citizen in the host Member State for a continuous period of 5 years.

➤ Union citizens have an unconditional right of permanent residence before a continuous period of 5 years in the host Member State if they are (*Directive 2004/38, Article 17*):

- workers or self-employed people who, at the time they stop working, have reached the age laid down by the law of that Member State for entitlement to an old age pension or workers who cease paid employment to take early retirement, provided that they have been working in that Member State for at least the preceding 12 months and have resided there continuously for more than 3 years (or the age of 60 if the law of the host Member State does not grant the right to an old age pension to certain categories of self-employed persons), *or*

- workers or self-employed persons who have resided continuously in the host Member State for more than 2 years and stop working there as a result of permanent incapacity to work, *or*

- workers or self-employed persons who, after 3 years of continuous employment and residence in the host Member State, work in an employed or self-employed capacity in another Member State, while retaining their place of residence in the host Member State, to which they return, as a rule, each day or at least once a week.

3   **Equal treatment**

➤ Subject to other EU law, Union citizens residing on the basis of *Directive 2004/38* must enjoy equal treatment with nationals of the host Member State. This extends to family members who are not nationals of a Member State and who have the right of residence/permanent residence (*Directive 2004/38, Article 24*).

- Eg: There must be no discrimination against citizens of other member states for employment, dismissal, social and taxation status, training, and union membership (*Regulation 1612/68, Article 2*).

- However, the host Member State is not obliged to give social assistance during the first 3 months of residence nor (prior to acquisition of a right of permanent residence) to grant maintenance aid for studies for student grants/loans to persons other than workers, self-employed persons, persons who retain such status and members of their families.

➤ **Mutual recognition of qualifications:** A diploma after 3 years' higher professional education or training is accepted in all Member States. If national criteria differ substantially, one can submit to an aptitude test *or* an 'adaptation' period of up to 3 years (*Directive 89/48*). Many qualifications are also mutually recognised (*Directive 2005/36/EC*).

- Eg: *Directive 77/249* facilitates the effective excercise by lawyers of the freedom to provide services.

III   UK employment legislation: statutory rights

a)   *Employment Rights Act 1996 s 1*

➤ The employer must provide the employee with a written statement, within 2 months of employment commencing, stating certain particulars:

Statement of employment	
• the name of the employer • the name of the employee • the date that employment began • the period of 'continuous employment' for statutory purposes • pay and how the pay is timed • the hours of work • holiday time (and any holiday pay) • sickness time (and any sickness pay) • pensions	• notice periods • job title • place of work • expected length of employment • any collective agreements • certain details if the employee must work outside the UK for more than 1 month • disciplinary procedures • complaints procedures

b)   *Employment Relations Act 1999*

➤ Contains greater employee rights (eg: unfair dismissal compensation capped at £52,600 and the inability to contract out of unfair dismissal on expiry of a fixed term contract).

➤ Contains greater family-friendly provisions (eg: extended maternity leave).

➤ Contains rights to 13 weeks parental unpaid leave after 1 years' continuous service; 2 weeks' paid paternity leave (at £100 per week) for those with 26 weeks' service; paid adoption leave; reasonable time off for domestic incidents)

➤ Contains greater collective rights (eg: trade union recognition for collective bargaining; prohibition on blacklisting of trade unionists for recruitment).

➤ In principle, part time workers cannot be treated less favourably than full-time workers of the same employer under the same employment contract (*PTWDR*).

c) **_Employment Act 2002_ and various regulations containing details**
   - ➤ This provides increased rights for maternity leave, paternity leave and adoption leave.
   - ➤ This provides new rights relating to flexible working and fixed term employees.
   - ➤ This also provides for amendments to tribunal rules and dispute resolution procedures.

d) **_Human Rights Act 1998_** (and see p 34)
   - ➤ HRA's impact is likely to be felt most in relation to Art.8 (right to family and private life) and Art.14 (right not to be discriminated against). Workers in the public sector may rely on the HRA directly. Workers in the private sector may rely on the HRA indirectly, in support of other employment law claims.

e) **_Equal Pay Act 1970_**
   - ➤ An employer must provide equal pay for men and women employed to do the same/comparable work.

f) **_Sex Discrimination Act 1975, Sex Discrimination Act 1986, Race Relations Act 1976, Disability Discrimination Act 1995, Equality Act 2006_ and various employment regulations (including from 1 October 2006, the _Employment Equality (Age) Regulations 2006_)**
   - ➤ An employer must not discriminate directly or indirectly on grounds of sex, race, marital status, religion, belief, sexual orientation or ethnic or national origin. Harassment is also banned in many areas.
   - ➤ It is unlawful (unless justified) to discriminate against disabled employees or potential employees, whether in recruitment, working conditions or promotion prospects. There is also a duty to take reasonable steps to prevent a disabled person being disadvantaged by the employer's working arrangements or physical features of the work premises.
   - ➤ _EE(A)R 2006_ prohibit age discrimination in employment and vocational training. They apply to all individuals in work or seeking work or access to training, to all employers and to all providers of vocational training (including further and higher education institutions) and vocational guidance. The regulations include a number of exemptions (eg: in relation to retirement and service related benefits) and provide for other differences if they can be objectively justified.

g) **_Health and Safety at Work Act 1974_ (and the common law duty to take reasonable care for the health and safety of the employee at work)**
   - ➤ The employer has a duty to provide the employee with a safe place of work, safe equipment and to provide a Health and Safety policy. Breach leads to criminal prosecution.
   - ➤ The employee can sue for damages for breach of common law duty _and_ breach of statutory duty.

h) **_Data Protection Act 1998_**
   - ➤ This imposes obligations on a processor of 'personal data' to process in accordance with 8 principles. It has very strict conditions about 'sensitive' data and also restricts transfer of data outside the EEA.

i) **_Transfer of Undertakings (Protection of Employment) Regulations 2006_**
   - ➤ These regulations apply when a business is transferred as a 'going concern'.
     - ◆ The contract of employment of any employee employed by the seller of a business immediately before the transfer is not ended by the transfer.
     - ◆ The employer's liability and obligations under the contract are transferred to the seller.

j) **_Collective Redundancies and Transfer of Undertakings (Protection of Employment) Amendment) Regulations 1995 and 1999_**
   - ➤ All business transfers and certain redundancies oblige an employer to consult with employees either through a trade union or elected employee representatives.

k) *Trade Union and Labour Relations (Consolidation) Act 1992*
➤ This provides the statutory framework for trade union membership and recognition.

l) *Asylum and Immigration Act 1996 s 8* (to be replaced by *Immigration, Asylum and Nationality Act 2006 s 21* when it is brought into force)
➤ It is a criminal offence for an employer to employ a person who either has not been granted leave to remain in the UK or whose leave is not 'valid and subsisting'.
◆ A statutory defence exists for employers who check that their employees are permitted to work in the UK. This can be done by checking documents listed in the legislation and held by individuals.

m) *Working Time Regulations 1998*
➤ These set limits on average weekly working hours and set minimum rest periods and holidays.

n) *Transitional Information and Consultation of Employees Regulations 1999*
➤ These regulations establish European Works Councils and a procedure to inform and consult with employees in EU-scale enterprises.

Some rights before and on being made redundant

➤ **Wrongful dismissal: Notice rights** (*ERA 1996 ss 86-93*)
  ◆ This means **the employer has failed to give the employee the necessary period of notice**.
  ◆ The employee can claim damages.
  ◆ The contract will normally stipulate the correct notice period that should have been given.
    • There is a statutory minimum period of notice.

➤ **Unfair dismissal** (*ERA 1996 ss 94-134*)
  ◆ This means **the employer has dismissed the employee for an unfair reason (after a minimum of 1 year's continuous service)**.
  ◆ To determine if the reason for dismissal is fair the employer must show: **a)** the reason *and* **b)** that the reason falls within a defined list in *s 98(2)* or is substantial enough so as to justify dismissal *and* **c)** that he acted reasonably (*s 98*). *Sections 99-104* contains reasons that do not justify dismissal eg: pregnancy.
  ◆ The employee can claim:
    • reinstatement, *or*
    • re-engagement in the service of the employer, *or*
    • compensation according to a statutory formula.

➤ **Redundancy** (*ERA 1996 ss 135-181*)
  ◆ This means that if the employee is made redundant after 2 years of qualifying service he is entitled to a redundancy payment calculated by a statutory formula.

Employment-related factors to consider when starting a business

- the number of employees and the responsibility for them
- the terms of any contracts of employment
- employment legislation (see the previous and this page)
- health and safety legislation
- insurance legislation
  - This includes statutory duties to obtain and display a certificate of insurance in respect of employees and accidents
  - This may include motor insurance
- allowing employees time off to perform statutory duties including:
  - public duties (eg: jury service or acting as a magistrate)
  - trade union duties
- the need to provide personnel services (sometimes called human resources) for employees
- the need to deal with payroll and the implementation of PAYE machinery

IV Pensions in the UK

Pension reform

➤ New pensions rules, introduced by *FA 2004 Part 4,* came into force on 6 April 2006.

➤ The new rules introduce a univeral system which operates by reference to:

    a) a lifetime allowance on the amount of pensions savings that can benefit from tax relief (£1.5 million in 2006 rising to £1.8 million in 2010), *and*

        • Benefit rights under defined benefit schemes are valued by being multiplied by 20.

    b) an annual allowance of up to 100% of earnings subject to a cap. In 2006/07 the cap is £215,000 in 2006, and it will rise to £255,000 in 2010.

        • The contribution of a non-taxpayer is imited to £2,808 (with tax relief, the gross contribution which such a person may make in a tax year is, therefore, £3,600).

➤ If an individual makes a contribution to a pension scheme, that individual will be entitled to tax relief:

    a) **non-tax payer/basic rate** taxpayer is entitled to tax relief at the rate of 22% (which the scheme provider claims from HMRC), *and*

    b) a **higher rate** taxpayer is entitled to tax relief at the rate of 40%; the pension scheme provider claims 22% from HMRC, and the individual claims 18% from HMRC when submitting his/her tax return.

➤ Contributions cannot be carried back, or carried forward, to a year other than the year of payment.

➤ If an employer makes a contribution to a pension scheme, that contribution:

    a) should be deductible by the employer for tax purposes, *and*

    b) is not treated as taxable income for the employee.

➤ Neither capital gains tax, nor income tax, are payable in respect of assets within a pension fund.

➤ If the lifetime allowance is exceeded a tax charge will arise equal to 25% of the excess funds over the lifetime allowance (if such excess is taken as a lump sum the rate of the tax charge is 55%).

➤ The general retirement age, and hence the age at which a pension can be drawn, will rise from 50 to 55 by 2010 (save in cases of ill health).

➤ A pension scheme may pay out a tax free lump sum equal to the lower of:

    a) 25% of the value of an individual's pension rights, *and*

    b) 25% of the individual's lifetime allowance.

➤ A pension scheme can provide income for an individual by means of income withdrawal. Income withdrawal can be:

    a) 'unsecured' prior to age 75, *then*

    b) 'secured' via an an annuity purchased no later than 75.

        • An annuity must generally be purchased before the age of 75, unless the individual establishes an 'alternatively secured pension' (On death it may, subject to an IHT charge, be possible to pass by will the benefit of any surplus arising under an alternatively secured pension).

CIVIL LITIGATION

This chapter examines:

Note: use this chart as a 'map' to sections 'B' to 'I'

A	First steps	334
	● Overview of proceedings	340
B	Court matters applicable throughout litigation	341
C	Starting proceedings	355
D	Defendant's options	365
E	Claimant's options	370
F	Applications for court orders	371
G	Interim remedies	381
H	Offers to settle / payments into court	385
I	Allocation (and automatic transfer)	392
J	Small claims track	394
K	Fast track	397
L	Multi track	399
M	Disclosure and inspection	401
N	Evidence	406
O	Trial preparations	411
P	The trial	415
Q	Costs	417
R	Enforcing judgments	423
S	Appeals	430

The tracks: J, K, L

Rules of the court

➤ Rules of court procedure are governed by the **Civil Procedure Rules (CPR)** (exceptions are in *r 2.1*).

- Definitions of terms in the *CPR* are listed in *r 2.3* and also in a glossary at the back.
- Each *Part* contains rules - notation is as follows: eg: *Part 7 r 7.2(2)* refers to rule 7.2(2) in *Part 7*.
- Each *Part* is supplemented by practice directions - we use notation as follows: *eg: PD7: 8.2* refers to paragraph 8.2 in the Practice Direction that supplements *Part 7*.

➤ For some purposes, some of the old rules that existed prior to the CPR are retained.

- For the High Court, these are the Rules of the Supreme Court (*RSC*) now in *Schedule 1* to the *CPR*.
- For the county courts, these are the County Court Rules (*CCR*) now in *Schedule 2* to the *CPR*.

CIVIL LITIGATION
First steps

A First steps

Is the claim viable?			
CONTRACT	**TORT**		**LATENT DAMAGE**
	NEGLIGENCE	**PERSONAL INJURY**	
1 Is the defendant worthy of attention?			
Is the defendant i) traceable and ii) solvent?			
2 How strong is the claimant's case?			
Does the evidence i) show all the elements required in law, *and* ii) prove these elements on the balance of probabilities?			
3 Has the limitation period expired? (*LA 1980*)			

6 years from the breach of contract (*s 5*)	6 years from when the damage occurs (*s 2*)	3 years from (*s 11*):
		a) the date of the accident, *or*
		b) the date of knowledge that (*s 14*):
		  i) the injury is significant enough for proceedings +
		  ii) an injury is due to the defendant's fault +
		  iii) the defendant's identity becomes known
			Either:
			a) 6 years from the date on which the cause of action accrues (*s 14A*), *or*
			b) (if later than a)), 3 years from the date that a claimant could start proceedings because a claimant now has:
			  i) the knowledge* required for bringing an action, *and*
			  ii) a right to bring such an action (ie: recovery from a defendant seems realistic)
			
			(**NB**: it must not be more than 15 years from the date of the breach)
			
			*Knowledge means knowledge of the facts such that an action may be brought eg: the identity of the defendant and that the damage was due to the defendant's fault, etc

For death and personal injury, the court has discretion to override the limitation period (*s 33*)			
4 What damages are available?			

Generally
Loss which flows naturally from the breach
 	
Loss which was within the reasonable contemplation of the parties at the time the contract was made
 	
There is a duty on the claimant to mitigate loss
 	
Debt claims
If the action is a claim for debt, the one claiming the sum outstanding does not have the duty to mitigate his loss, which applies to all other types of damages
	Direct loss and consequential loss which is a reasonably foreseeable consequence of the negligence
	
	Note: It is doubtful whether pure economic loss can be recovered
		a) **Special damages:** liquidated claims for actual financial loss up to the date of the trial
		b) **General damages:** unliquidated, compensating for:
		  i) past and future non-financial loss, *and*
		  ii) future financial loss
		c) *SS(RB)A 1997*: if the claimant receives state benefits:
		  i) the defendant obtains a certificate of recoverable benefits from the Department of Social Security (DSS) Compensation Recovery Unit (CRU)
		  ii) the defendant is obliged to pay to the CRU the *full* amount of certain benefits listed which have been paid to the injured person
		  iii) where part of the compensation payment itself from the defendant to the claimant is in respect of a particular kind of loss, (loss of earnings, cost of care, loss of mobility) and benefits have been paid to the claimant for this kind of loss, the defendant may deduct the relevant benefits from the compensation payment (ie: the claimant is paid damages net, less the sum due to the DSS which the defendant forwards to the CRU within 14 days of the claimant receiving compensation)
		NB: No deductions are possible for pain and suffering ie: the victim keeps all the damages for pain and suffering.
		d) *DA 1996 (CPR rr 41.4 - 41.10)*: a court awarding damages for future pecuniary loss may, on its own, order that damages are wholly or partly to be as periodical payments. For other personal injury damages, a court may only order that damages are to take the form of periodical payments if the parties consent. But a court may not make an order for periodical payments unless satisfied that the continuity of payment under the order is reasonably secure	

5 Does the claim carry interest?			

Interest is given from:
a) the date when the action arose to judgment *or*
b) date of payment (if sooner) *either*
  i) at the contract rate, *or*
  ii) at a court's discretion (unlikely to exceed the judgment debt rate)
Debt claims
High Court: 8% from final judgment date
County Court: see rules on p 425
	At the Court's discretion	Judgment for a sum ...
		a) ...over £200: a court must award interest (but will not do if it has a special reason (*SCA1981 s 35A*)
		b) ...£200 or less: at the court's discretion
		
		The rate is usually:
		i) 0% for future loss of earnings
		ii) 2% from the service of the claim form to the trial, for pain, suffering and loss of amenity
		iii) half the court's average Special Account average rate from the accident to the start of trial for 'special damages'
			At the Court's discretion

6 What other remedies are possible?			
Eg: possession orders, injunctions, etc.			

CIVIL LITIGATION
First steps

A Consider 10 alternatives to issuing proceedings

1 Negotiation

➤ This is always better than litigation and should normally be conducted 'without prejudice'.

2 Alternative dispute resolution (ADR)

➤ It is the duty of a solicitor to put the possibility of ADR to the client.

- See also the Pre-action Protocol Practice Direction provisions and effect on costs (p 338).
- 'All members of the legal profession should now routinely consider with their clients whether their disputes are suitable for ADR.' (per Dyson LJ in *Halsey v Milton Keynes NHS Trust* [2004] EWCA 576).
- There are many types of ADR, eg: mediation, neutral evaluation, expert determination, etc.

➤ In mediation, a third party mediates and the mediation may or may not be binding.

- If no binding agreement is reached, then arbitration or litigation is possible later.

➤ ADR is usually quicker, cheaper and less destructive of the parties' relationship than litigation.

3 Motor Insurers' Bureau ('MIB') (see www.mib.org.uk)

➤ The MIB was established in 1946 and administers a guarantee fund through 2 agreements between the MIB and the government. There 2 schemes are updated periodically:

Victims of *uninsured* drivers (agreement of 13 August 1999)	Victims of *untraced* drivers (agreement of 14 February 2003)
Commence proceedings ↓ Give notice in writing to MIB of the date of Claim Form service by the first to occur of: a) 7 days after: • the date when the Claimant receives notice from Court that service of the Claim Form or other originating process has occurred, *or* • the date when the Claimant receives notice from the Defendant that service of the Claim Form has occurred, *or* • the date of personal service, *or* b) 14 days after: • the date when service is deemed to have occurred according to the CPR. ↓ Give copies of relevant documents to MIB within 14 days of starting proceedings ↓ If 7 days after final judgment against the Defendant driver the claim is not satisfied, the MIB will meet the claim together with costs ↓ Judgment must be assigned to the MIB so it may try and recover from the insured driver	The death or injury must not have been caused deliberately by the untraced driver ↓ Give notice to the police within: **14 days** of the accident for death and bodily injury, *and* **5 days** of the accident for property damage or, in either case, as soon as reasonably possible ↓ Notify the MIB by letter within: **3 years** of the accident for death/bodily injury claims **9 months** of the accident for property damage claims ↓ The MIB itself investigates the merit of the claim (Negligence *must* be proved) ↓ The MIB will cover death, bodily injury, damage to property and there is no need to prove these costs. (Note: the MIB will award the same heads of damages that a court would)
	Appeals against the amount of damages is by arbitration
	An accelerated process may be available allowing the Claimant and MIB to reach a compromise (with no full investigation). If there is a disagreement, a full investigation is carried out.
The first £300 of property damage (and any property damage over £250,000) is not covered	
• The MIB pays to the CRU money owed to NHS trusts and hospitals (*RT(NC)A 1999*).	

There are other 7 day limit dates to notify various documents too

4 Statutory demand: see p 306.

CIVIL LITIGATION
First steps

5 **Insurance (motor accidents)**

➤ The decision how to claim depends on the type of insurance policy concerned:

a) **Compulsory risks** (required by *RTA 1988*). Such insurance covers ...

- ... death or injury to any other person, *and*
- ... property damage up to £250,000, excluding damage to the insured vehicle and its contents, *and*
- ... the cost of emergency hospital treatment.

b) **Third party, fire and theft.** Such insurance additionally covers...

- ... the insured against these risks.

c) **Comprehensive.** Such insurance additionally covers...

- ... damage to the insured's vehicle and limited compensation for a driver's injuries.

➤ Claims against the insured's own insurance (*only* if the policy is 'comprehensive').

- A 'no-claims' bonus may be lost, increasing the premium payable on the policy in the future.
- The insured may have to pay an 'excess' as a contribution to damages.
- The insurance company may insist that the insured lends their name to any legal proceedings.
- If the other party has 'comprehensive' insurance, the companies may agree between themselves to cover the costs of their own insured - the claimant has no control over the settlement they reach. This is called 'knock for knock'.
- The claimant may also choose to proceed against the other party or their insurer's for any *un*insured losses, eg: the amount of the excess *or* loss of any discount given by a no claims bonus.

➤ Claims against the other party's insurance.

- Provided the claimant serves a notice on the defendant's insurers within 7 days of commencing proceedings, he can recover damages from them, even if they are entitled to avoid *or* cancel the policy (*ss 151-152 RTA 1988*).

➤ Insurance is not necessarily an alternative to proceedings in the courts because of subrogation of rights - the insurer may still bring the action, leading to litigation.

6 **Criminal Injuries Compensation Authority**

➤ The Criminal Injuries Compensation Authority was set up in 1964 to award, *ex gratia*, compensation to the victims of crime. Awards are normally small but in some severe cases may be substantial.

➤ There is a fixed scale of awards (see *CICA 1995*). The absolute maximum it may award is £500,000.

7 **Criminal compensation order** (*PCC(S)A 2000 ss 130-134*)

➤ This is available for personal injury losses or damage following a criminal offence (other than loss due to accident arising out of there being a personal motor vehicle on a road). Compensation may be payable for damage which is not covered by the MIB.

- Magistrates' Court: fine up to £5,000 for each offence.
- Crown Court: fine unlimited, taking account of the defendant's means.

8 **Arbitration under *Arbitration Act 1996***

➤ This may or may not be cheaper and faster than litigation depending on the circumstances. Procedures is governed by *Arbitration Act 1996* (not covered here). It is binding, with appeal to the courts.

9   **Trade schemes**
    ➤ These are operated by various trade and professional bodies and include Royal Institute of Chartered Surveyors (RICS) and the Association of British Travel Agents (ABTA).

10 **Application in a foreign jurisdiction** - (*CJJA 1982 & PIL(MP)A 1995*) NB: See also p 423.
    ➤ A person domiciled in the UK, or a company based in the UK, may sue in the UK.
    ➤ A UK claimant may sue abroad if:
    ◆ for contractual claims: *either* the defendant is domiciled abroad, *or* the cause of action arose abroad, *or* a foreign law or jurisdiction is stipulated in the contract.
    ◆ for tortious claims: *either* the tort occurred abroad, *or* the damage was suffered abroad.
    NB: Consider the costs and remedies, and the likelihood of enforcement in foreign jurisdictions.

B   How will the client finance the action?

➤ The client may be eligible for LSC funded help. If not, the solicitor should:

a) explain that the client is responsible for all the solicitor's costs and that if the case is lost he may have to pay the other side's costs. Even if the client is successful, costs are at the court's discretion and will not be awarded to the client automatically, the client will have to meet any shortfall, *and*

b) ask the client for a 'payment on account' to finance preparatory work, expert's reports, etc.

➤ A CFA should also be considered where appropriate.

C   Is there a relevant pre-action protocol?

➤ Pre-action protocols are intended to improve pre-action contact between the parties, to ease exchange of information between the parties and to allow both sides to more fully investigate a claim at an earlier stage. All this is to encourage early settlement.

➤ The extent to which a party has (or has not) complied with any relevant pre-action protocol, is one of the factors a Court will consider when making orders as to costs (see p 417) and sanctions (see pp 344-345) and giving directions to manage proceedings (see pp 398 and 400).

➤ There are currently 8 pre-action protocols for:
    ◆ personal injury claims (if likely to be allocated to the fast track)
    ◆ resolution of clinical disputes
    ◆ construction and engineering disputes
    ◆ defamation
    ◆ professional negligence
    ◆ judicial review
    ◆ disease and illness claims
    ◆ housing disrepair cases

➤ There is also a pre-action protocol PD *which contains some rules of general application in all cases.*

    ◆ Eg: 'In cases not covered by any approved protocol, the Court will expect the parties, in accordance with the overriding objective and ... [other] matters ... to act reasonably in exchanging information and documents relevant to the claim and ... in trying to avoid the necessity for the start of proceedings.'

    ◆ Eg: 'Where a person enters into a funding arrangement ... he should inform other potential parties to the claim that he has done so' (and failure to do so means he cannot recover any additional liability).

    ◆ Eg: If non-compliance has led to proceedings which might otherwise not have needed to be started or to costs that might otherwise not have been incurred, a court may order the party at fault:
        • to pay all or a part of costs of the proceedings of the other party or parties
        • to pay costs on an indemnity basis
        • (if a claimant) to be deprived of interest and/or award interest at a lower rate
        • (if a defendant) to award interest at a higher rate (not exceeding 10% above base rate).

CIVIL LITIGATION
First steps

Pre-action protocol PD

- Parties to a potential dispute should follow a reasonable procedure ... which is intended to avoid litigation ... It should normally include:
  - the claimant writing to give details of the claim,
  - the defendant acknowledging the claim letter promptly,
  - the defendant giving within a reasonable time a detailed written response,
  - the parties conducting genuine and reasonable negotiations with a view to settling the claim economically and without court proceedings.

- The claimant's letter should:
  - give sufficient concise details to enable the recipient to understand and investigate the claim without extensive further information,
  - enclose copies of the essential documents which the claimant relies on,
  - ask for a prompt acknowledgement of the letter, followed by a full written response within a reasonable stated period. (For many claims, a normal reasonable period is 1 month),
  - state if court proceedings will be issued if the full response is not received within the stated period,
  - identify and ask for copies of any essential documents which the claimant wishes to see,
  - state (if this is so) that the claimant wishes to enter into mediation or another ADR method,
  - draw attention to the court's powers to impose sanctions for failure to comply with this practice direction and, if the recipient is likely to be unrepresented, enclose a copy of this PD.

- The defendant should acknowledge the claimant's letter in writing within 21 days of receiving it, stating when the defendant will give a full written response. If the time for this is longer than the period stated by the claimant, the defendant should give reasons why a longer period is needed.

- The defendant's full written response should as appropriate:
  - accept the claim in whole or in part and make proposals for settlement (and if accepted in part only, the response should make clear which part is accepted and which part is not accepted), *or*
  - state that the claim is not accepted.

- If the defendant does not accept the claim or part of it, the response should:
  - give detailed reasons why the claim is not accepted, identifying which of the claimant's contentions are accepted and which are in dispute,
  - enclose copies of the essential documents which the defendant relies on,
  - enclose copies of documents asked for by the claimant, or explain why they are not enclosed,
  - identify and ask for copies of further essential documents which the defendant wishes to see,
  - state whether the defendant is prepared to enter into mediation or other ADR.

- **The parties should consider whether some form of ADR procedure is more suitable than litigation, and if so, try to agree which form to adopt.**
  - **If this is not done, then the Court must have regard to this when determining costs.**
  - Both parties may be required by the Court to provide evidence that alternative means of resolving their dispute were considered. The Courts take the view that litigation should be a last resort, and that claims should not be issued prematurely when a settlement is still actively being explored.

- **However, no party can or should be forced to mediate or enter into another form of ADR.**

- Documents disclosed by either party in accordance with this practice direction may not be used for any purpose other than resolving the dispute, unless the other party agrees.

CIVIL LITIGATION
First steps

After the first client meeting

1 Write to the client confirming instructions (giving information required by *SCICCC 1999*, see pp 12-13).

2 Consider possibilities for settlement. Discuss possible approaches with the client to avoid litigation.

3 Take some general statements from the client and witnesses to get a 'feel' for the case.

4 Make a site visit, if relevant, as soon as possible and take appropriate photographs, etc.

5 Consider whether experts may be needed and prepare possible names (see p 414).

6 Research any relevant law.

7 **Road traffic accident cases only**
- Write to the Chief Superintendent requesting a copy of the police accident report.
- Obtain a certificate of conviction from the court (if appropriate).
- Serve a *s 151/s 152* notice on the defendant's insurers before issuing proceedings or within 7 days after issuing proceedings.

8 **Personal injury cases only:**
- Comply with the relevant pre-action protocol. Prepare the calendar with appropriate reminders.
- Write to the client's employer for details of gross and net salary over the 26 weeks prior to the accident, the employee's prospects and details of the employment contract.
- Write to the Inland Revenue to claim a tax rebate (if appropriate).
- Notify the Compensation Recovery Unit within 14 days of receiving a letter before action.

9 Send a letter before action to the defendant stating:
   a) for whom the solicitors are acting, *and*
   b) the factual circumstances by which the claim has arisen, *and*
   c) the action the solicitors are preparing to take, *and*
   d) brief details of any loss, injury or damage.
- The letter should demand either settlement *or* a response within 7 to 14 days, failing which proceedings will be issued. The letter should warn that any claim will include interest and costs.

10 Negotiate or propose some other means of reaching a settlement (eg: ADR or *Part 36* - see p 385)
- Before proceedings are issued the solicitor has no implied authority to settle.
- After proceedings have been issued the solicitor has implied authority to settle; however, the client's express authority should always be sought (ideally in writing).
- Negotiations should normally be conducted 'without prejudice' so that nothing in the negotiations will be admissible in court.

11 Consider drawing up formal 'Instructions to Counsel' and arranging a conference (see p 412).

12 Consider forcing the potential defendant or a third party to give information by applying for an order for pre-action disclosure (see p 402)
- ask the defendant to co-operate by letter. This should save the claimant costs.
- An order can be made against *anyone* who holds property central to the case.
- An order might permit: photography, detention and custody, inspection, testing, and sampling.

CIVIL LITIGATION
First steps

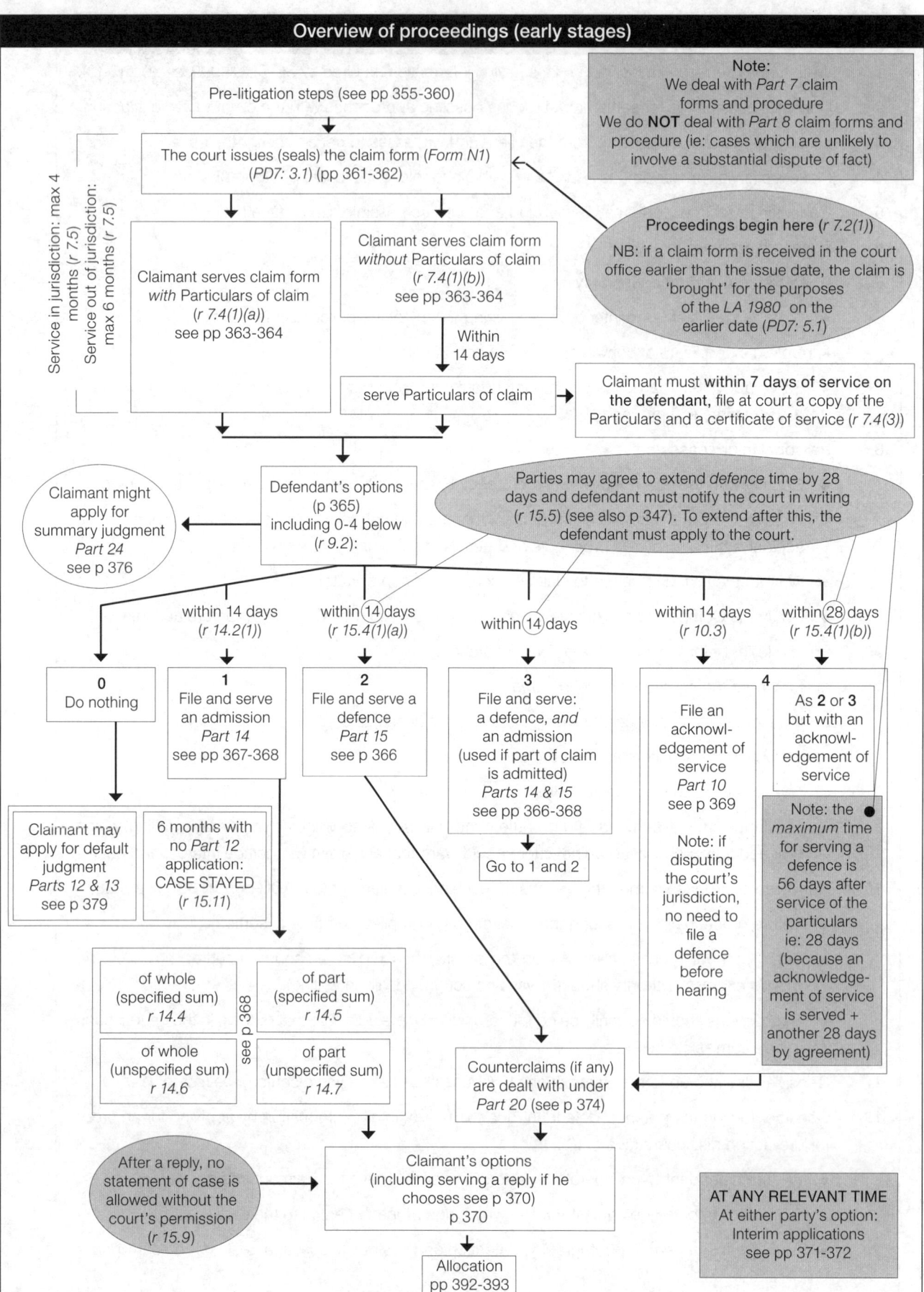

B Court matters applicable throughout litigation

      I   General powers of the court
      II   Provisions as to time
      III Documents for court
      IV Statements of case
      V   Statements of truth
      VI Service of documents

I General powers of the court

A The court's overriding objective

The court's overriding objective in applying the *CPR* (r 1)

➤ The *CPR* are a new procedural code with the overriding objective of enabling the court to deal with cases justly.

- 'justly' means:
    a) ensuring that the parties are on an equal footing, *and*
    b) saving expense, *and*
    c) dealing with the case in ways which are proportionate:
        i) to the amount of money involved, *and*
        ii) to the importance of the case, *and*
        iii) to the complexity of the issues, *and*
        iv) to the financial position of each party, *and*
    d) ensuring that a case is dealt with expeditiously and fairly, *and*
    e) allotting to a case an appropriate share of the court's resources, while taking into account the need to allot resources to other cases.

➤ The court must seek to give effect to the overriding objective when it:
- exercises any power given to it by the *CPR*, or
- interprets any rule.

➤ The parties are required to help the court to further the overriding objective.

➤ The court must further the overriding objective by actively managing cases.

Decisions under pre-*CPR* cases

➤ Decisions under pre-CPR rules will not be followed, even on identical wording (*Biguzzi v Rank Leisure* [1999] 1 WLR 1926). However, thought processes underlying decisions under pre-CPR rules will not be thrown out (*UCB Corporate Services v Halifax (SW) Ltd* [1999] CPLR 691) and in practice **are** often followed.

B Case management powers

The court's general powers of case management (r 3.1)

➤ The court has these additional general powers of management (unless a rule provides otherwise):
- to extend or shorten the time for compliance with any rule, practice direction or court order (even if an application for extension is made after the time for compliance has expired),
- to adjourn or bring forward a hearing,
- to require a party or a party's legal representative to attend the court,
- to hold a hearing and receive evidence by telephone or by using any other method of direct oral communication,
- to direct that part of any proceedings (eg: a counterclaim) be dealt with as separate proceedings,
- to stay the whole or part of any proceedings or judgment either generally or until a specified date or event,
- to consolidate proceedings,
- to try 2 or more claims on the same occasion,
- to direct a separate trial of any issue,
- to decide the order in which issues are to be tried,
- to exclude an issue from consideration,
- to dismiss or give judgment on a claim after a decision on a preliminary issue,
- to order any party to file and serve an estimate of costs,
- to take any other step or make any other order for the purpose of managing the case and furthering the overriding objective.

➤ When the court makes an order, it may:

a) make it subject to conditions, including a condition to pay a sum of money into court, *and/or*

b) specify the consequence of failure to comply with the order or a condition.

➤ A power of the court under the *CPR* to make an order includes a power to vary or revoke the order.

The court's powers to make an order of its own initiative (r 3.3)

➤ Except where a rule or some other enactment provides otherwise, the court may exercise its powers on an application or of its own initiative (*Part 23*).
- Where the court proposes to make an order of its own initiative it *may* (but does not have to) give any person likely to be affected an opportunity to make representations.
  - If it does so it must set the time by and the manner in which the representations must be made.
  - It must give each party likely to be affected by the order at least 3 days' notice of the hearing.

➤ A party affected by the order may apply to have it set aside, varied or stayed. Such an application:

a) must be made within such period as may be specified by the court, *or*

b) if the court does not specify a period, must be made not more than 7 days after the date on which the order was served on the party making the application.

➤ If the court of its own initiative strikes out a statement of case or dismisses an application, and it considers that the claim or application is totally without merit:

a) the court's order must record that fact; *and*

b) the court must at the same time consider whether it is appropriate to make a civil restraint order.

C Power to strike out a statement of case (r 3.4)

	Striking out a statement of case	
Grounds (r 3.4(2))	**1** A statement of case (or part of a statement of case) discloses no reasonable grounds for bringing or defending a claim (r 3.4(2)(a)), or Eg: the particulars of claim set out no facts indicating what the claim is about, or are incoherent and make no sense, or do not disclose no legally recognisable claim against the defendant (PD3.4: 1.4) Eg: a defence consists of a bare denial, sets out no coherent statement of facts, or those facts (being coherent) would not even if true amount in law to a defence (PD3.4: 1.6) or **2** A statement of case (or part of a statement of case) is an abuse of the court's process or is otherwise likely to obstruct the just disposal of proceedings (r 3.4(2)(b)), or Eg: a claim is vexatious, scurrilous, or obviously ill-founded (PD3.4: 1.5). or **3** There has been a failure to comply with a rule, practice direction or court order (r 3.4(2)(c))	
Procedure (if court acts of its own volition on grounds set out in r 3.4(2(a)(-(b)))	Striking out a claim (PD3.4: 2)	Striking out a defence (PD3.4: 3)
	➤ A court officer must issue a claim form, but before returning the form to the claimant or taking any step to serve it on the defendant, the officer may consult a judge if the officer believes that there may be grounds for the claim to be struck out. ➤ The judge may make an order of his own initiative to ensure that the claim is disposed of or proceeds in a way which accords with the rules: this includes an order that: ♦ the claim be stayed until further order, or ♦ the claim form be retained by the court and not served until the stay is lifted, or ♦ no application by the claimant to lift the stay be heard unless the claimant files other documents (eg: a witness statement).	➤ A court officer may consult a judge if the officer believes that there may be grounds for the defence to be struck out. ➤ The judge may either: ♦ make an order of his own initiative (eg: striking out the defence or extending the time for the defendant to file a defence), or ♦ make an order under for further information r 18.1 (see p 378)
	➤ A court may exercise its powers under r 3.4(2) at any time of its own volition ➤ If a judge acts of his own volition, he may decide to hold a hearing before making an order	
Order to strike out	➤ The court may make any consequential order it considers appropriate (r 3.4(3)) ➤ If a claimant's statement of case (or part of it) is struck out, and ... the claimant has been ordered to pay costs to the defendant, and ... before the claimant pays those costs, he starts another claim against that defendant arising out of facts which are substantially the same as those relating to the struck out claim, ... the court may on the defendant's application stay the second claim until the costs of the struck out claim have been met (r 3.4(4)).	If the court strikes out a claimant's statement of case and it considers that the claim is totally without merit: a) the court's order must record that fact; and b) the court must at the same time consider whether it is appropriate to make a civil restraint order.
Judgment without trial after striking out (r 3.5)	➤ If a party's statement of case (or part of its statement of case) is struck out as a term of a court order and that party does not comply with that order, then ... Either... ... if the order relates to the whole statement of case, a party may obtain costs by filing a request for judgment *provided that* if the party wishing to obtain judgment is the claimant, the claim is for: • a specified amount of money, and/or • an amount of money to be decided by the court, and/or • delivery up of certain goods where the claim form gives the defendant the alternative of paying their value OR ... a party must make an application under *Part 23* (see p 371) if he wishes to obtain judgment. ➤ A party may apply within 14 days after receiving a judgment under r 3.5 to have that judgment set aside (r 3.6(1)-(2)). ➤ The court must set aside judgment if the right to enter judgment had not arisen at the time when judgment was entered (r 3.6(3). ➤ If an application to set aside is made for any other reason, r 3.9 applies (r 3.6(4))	

D Sanctions: powers and procedure

➤ Where a party has failed to comply with a rule, *PD* or court order, any sanction for failure to comply has effect unless the party in default applies for and obtains relief from the sanction (*r 3.8(1)*).

➤ Where the sanction is the payment of costs, the party in default may only obtain relief by appealing against the order for costs (*r 3.8(2)*).

Sanctions for non-payment of certain fees (*r 3.7, 3.7A, PD3B*)

➤ A court fee is usually payable by a claimant:
- a) ◆ on filing the allocation questionnaire, *or*
  - ◆ if a claimant is not required to file an allocation questionnaire,

and b) ◆ on filing the pre-trial checklist, *or*
  - ◆ if a claimant is not required to file a pre-trial checklist.

➤ A court fee may be payable by a counterclaimant in respect of a counterclaim.

➤ If the fee is not paid (or no exemption has been applied for), the court will serve a notice on the claimant/counterclaimant specifying the date by which the claimant/counterclaimant must pay.

➤ After the notice, if the claimant/counterclaimant does not pay the fee (or make an application for an exemption from or remission of the fee) by the date specified in the notice:
- ◆ the claim/counterclaim is automatically struck out without further order of the court (and the court sends the other party a notice of this), *and*
- ◆ a claimant (only) is liable for the defendant's costs (unless the court orders otherwise), *and*
- ◆ any interim injunction which the court granted may cease to have effect 14 days after the date on which the claim is struck out (see *r 25.11*).

Sanctions for non-compliance with case management directions (*PD28: 5, PD29: 7*)

➤ Where a party has failed to comply with a case management direction, any other party may apply for an order to enforce compliance or for a sanction to be imposed or both of these.

➤ A party applying for such an order must not delay and must first warn the other side of his intention.

➤ The court may take any such delay into account when it decides whether to make an order imposing a sanction or whether to grant relief from a sanction imposed by the rules or any *PD*.
- ◆ Postponement of a trial is a last resort and will be for the shortest time possible. The court may require a party *and* his legal representative to attend where such an order is sought. Other than in exceptional circumstances, the court will not allow failure to comply with directions to lead to postponement. The court will assess steps each party should take to prepare for trial, directs those steps be taken in the shortest possible time and impose a sanction for non-compliance.
- ◆ The court will not postpone any other hearing without a very good reason, and the failure of a party to comply on time with directions previously given will not be treated as a good reason.

Civil restraint orders (*r 3.11, PD3C, r 2.3*)

➤ If a party issues 2 claims/makes 2 applications totally without merit, the court may make **a limited civil restraint order** (ie: stopping him from making further applications in current proceedings, *or*

➤ If a party persistently issues claims or makes applications totally without merit, the court may make **an extended civil restraint order** (ie: stopping him from issuing certain claims or making certain applications in specified courts), *or*

➤ If a party issues claims or makes applications in spite of an extended civil restraint order, the court may make **a general civil restraint order** (ie: stopping him from issuing any claim or making any application in specified courts).

Obtaining relief from sanctions (r 3.9)

➤ On an application for relief from sanctions (which must be supported by evidence) the court will consider all the circumstances including:
- the interests of the administration of justice,
- whether the application for relief has been made promptly,
- whether the failure to comply was intentional,
- whether there is a good explanation for the failure,
- how much a party in default has complied with other rules, *PD*s, court orders, pre-action protocols,
- whether the failure to comply was caused by the party or his legal representative,
- whether the trial date or the likely trial date can still be met if relief is granted,
- the effect which the failure to comply had on each party,
- the effect which the granting of relief would have on each party.

II Provisions as to time

Provisions as to time (rr 2.8-2.11)

➤ **days:** time expressed in the *CPR* as a number of days means clear days.
  - 'clear days' do not include:
    a) the day on which the period begins, *and*
    b) (if the end of the period is set by reference to an event), the day on which that event occurs.
  - Where the specified period is 5 days or less *and includes* a Saturday or Sunday; *or* a Bank Holiday, Xmas Day or Good Friday; then that day does not count.

➤ **month:** 'month' in any judgment, order, direction or other document, means a calendar month.

➤ **time limits (1):** Where the court gives a judgment, order or direction with a time limit, the last date for compliance must, wherever practicable:
  - be expressed as a calendar date, *and*
  - include the time of day by which the act must be done.

➤ **time limits (2):** Where the date by which an act must be done is inserted in any document, the date must, wherever practicable, be expressed as a calendar date.

Time limits may be varied by the parties (r 2.11)

➤ Unless the court orders otherwise, any time limits specified by the *CPR* or by the court for a person to do any act may be varied by the written agreement of the parties.
  - Exceptions are:
    - any sanctions imposed have effect unless defaulting party obtains relief, *or*
    - when the *CPR* specifies the sanctions for failure to comply with a fixed time (r 3.8(3)), *or*
    - variation of the times in a case management timetable for fast track and multi-track, *or*
    - time limits for an appeal to the Court of Appeal (see p 430).

III   Documents for court

Documents for court (r 5.2, 5.3)

➤ A document should be legible, duly authorised and must not be unsatisfactory for a similar reason.
➤ If a document must be signed, it may be manual, printed by computer or another mechanical means.
➤ Every document prepared by a party for filing or use at the court:

must be (PD5: 2.2):
- (unless impracticable) on A4 paper of durable quality having a margin not less than 3.5 cm wide, *and*
- fully legible and should normally be typed, *and*
- where possible, bound securely so as not to hamper filing or otherwise each page should be endorsed with the case number, *and*
- so that pages have consecutive numbering, *and*
- divided into numbered paragraphs, *and*
- such that all numbers, including dates, are expressed as figures, *and*
- give in the margin the reference of each document mentioned that has already been filed.

may be filed at court by fax (in which case a hard copy must not be sent) (PD5: 5.3) **BUT**:
- Faxes should not be used to send letters or documents of a routine or non-urgent nature.
- If a fax is sent after 4pm, it is treated as filed the next day that the court office is open.
- The following documents may *not* be faxed unless there is an unavoidable emergency:
  - documents that attract a fee (and the nature of the emergency must be explained in the fax together with an undertaking to make payment), *or*
  - a *Part 36* payment notice (and the nature of the emergency must be explained in the fax together with an undertaking to make payment), *or*
  - a document relating to a hearing less than 2 hours ahead, *or*
  - trial bundles or skeleton arguments.

Electronic communication and filing of documents (r 5.5, PD5B)

➤ Definitions:
- A court or court office which has published an email address for the filing of documents on the Court Service website www.courtservice.gov.uk is a **'specified court'**.
- A document listed on the Court Service website as a document that may be sent to or filed in a specified court by email is a **'specified document'**.

➤ Rules:
- A party to a claim in a specified court may send a specified document to the court by email.
  - But a party must not use email to take any step in a claim for which a fee is payable.
- The email message must contain the name, telephone number and email address of the sender and should be in plain text or rich text format rather than HTML.
- Correspondence and documents may be sent as text in the email body or as attachments, except for documents required to be in a practice form (which must be sent as attachments).
  - Note: Court forms may be downloaded from the Court Service website.
  - Attachments must be sent in a format supported by the software used by the specified court to which it is sent. The format or formats which may be used in sending attachments to a particular specified court are listed on the Court Service website.
  - The length of attachments and total size of email must not exceed the maximum which a particular specified court has indicated that it can accept on the Court Service website.
- Where proceedings have been commenced, the subject line of the email must contain:
  - the case number, *and*
  - the parties' names (abbreviated if necessary), *and*
  - the date and time of any hearing to which the email relates.

CIVIL LITIGATION
Throughout litigation

Online forms service (PD5B: 6)

➤ Some courts run an 'online forms service' which is a service available at www.courtservice.gov.uk. The service contains certain documents which a user may complete online and then submit electronically to a specified court.

➤ A party to a claim in a specified court may send a specified document to the court using the online forms service.

➤ A party may use the online forms service to take a step in a claim for which a fee is payable.

- The fee must be paid, using the facilities available at the online forms service, before the application, or other document attracting a fee, is forwarded to the specified court.

➤ The online forms service assists a user in completing a document accurately but the user is responsible for ensuring that the rules and practice directions relating to the document have been complied with.

➤ Transmission by the service does not guarantee that the document will be accepted by the court.

General rules about filing of documents electronically (PD5B: 8)

➤ Where a party files a document electronically, he must not send a hard copy of that document to the court.

➤ A document is not filed until the transmission is received by the court, whatever time it is shown to have been sent.

- The time of receipt of a transmission will be recorded electronically on the transmission as it is received.

- If a transmission is received after 4pm, the transmission is treated as received and any document attached to the transmission is treated as filed, on the next day the court office is open.

➤ The court will normally reply by email where the response is to a message transmitted electronically *and* the sender has provided an e-mail address.

➤ Parties are advised *not* to transmit electronically any correspondence or documents of a confidential or sensitive nature, as security cannot be guaranteed.

➤ If a document transmitted electronically requires urgent attention, the sender should contact the court by telephone.

Statement of truth in documents filed electronically (PD5B: 9)

➤ Where a party wants to file a document electronically with a statement of truth, that party should retain the document with the original signature and file with the court a version of the document satisfying 1 of the following:

- the name of the person who has signed the statement of truth is typed underneath the statement, *or*

- the person who has signed the statement of truth has applied a facsimile of his signature to the statement in the document by mechanical means, *or*

- the document that is filed is a scanned version of the document containing the original signature to the statement of truth.

IV Statements of case

A Statements of case generally

Statements of case

➤ Statements of case are documents that each party produces, containing formal statements of case.
- Statements of case focus the parties and the court on the pertinent issues.

➤ A subsequent statement of case must not contradict or be inconsistent with an earlier one
- eg: a reply to a defence must not bring in a new claim. Where new matters arise, the appropriate course may be to seek the court's permission to amend the statement of case (*PD16: 9.2*).

➤ Time limits for service are often (and usually) extended by agreement between parties (see p 345).

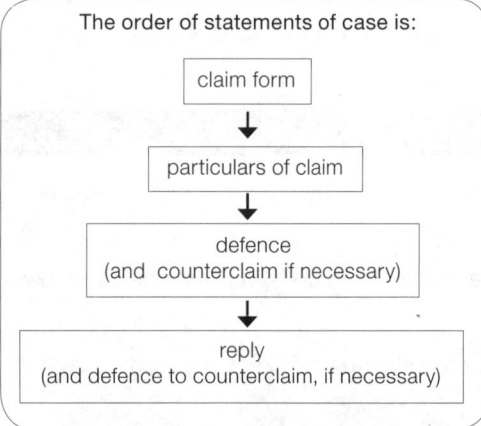

The order of statements of case is:

claim form → particulars of claim → defence (and counterclaim if necessary) → reply (and defence to counterclaim, if necessary)

Every statement of case must be headed with the title of the proceedings stating (*PD7: 4.1*):
- the claim number of the proceedings
- the court or Division in which they are proceeding
- the full name of each party
- his status in the proceedings (ie: claimant/defendant)

Where there is more than 1 claimant and/or more than 1 defendant, the parties should be described in the title as follows (*PD7: 4.2*):

(1) AB
(2) CD
(3) EF
   Claimants
(1) GH
(2) IJ
(3) KL
   Defendants

Drafting tip
- A typical claim is structured using the formulation: DUTY → BREACH → LOSS

Clinical negligence practice tip
- The words 'clinical negligence' should appear at the top of every statement of case (*PD16: 9.3*).

6 practice rules for statements of case

1. State all material facts
2. State facts relevant to the action
3. State facts, not evidence
    - One exception to this rule is criminal convictions (see p 363)
4. Refer to any point of law on which the claim/defence is based (*PD16: 13.3*)
5. Give the name of any witness a party proposes to call (*PD16: 13.3*)
6. Attach to or serve with the statement of case a copy of any document which is necessary to the claim/defence (including any expert's report) (*PD14: 16.3*)
7. If exceptionally a statement of case exceeds 25 pages (excluding schedules) an appropriate short summary must also be filed and served (*PD16: 1.4*).

B Amendments to statements of case

➤ Amendments generally take effect retrospectively from the date of the original document.

➤ Limited amendments only are allowed (see box below) if:
- the limitation period has expired, or
- parties are to be amended.

➤ In practice, amendments are often agreed (subject to costs). However, a party applying for an amendment will usually be responsible for the costs of and arising from the amendment.

If a party has amended his statement of case where permission of the court was not required, the court may disallow the amendment (r 17.2)

What to do when amending

➤ Any amended statement of case (and its court copy) must be endorsed as follows (PD17: 2.1):
- *where the court's permission is required:*
  'Amended [Particulars of Claim *or other*] by Order of [Master .....][District Judge .... *or other*] dated......'
- *where the court's permission is not required:*
  'Amended [Particulars of Claim *or as may be*] under CPR [rule 17.1(1) or (2)(a)] dated...........' (see box below).
➤ The statement of case in its amended form need not show the original text, but the court may direct that the amendments should be shown *either* (PD17: 2.2):
- by coloured amendments, either manuscript or computer generated, *or*
- by use of a numerical code in a monochrome computer generated document.
➤ Where colour is used, the text to be deleted should be struck through in colour and any text replacing it should be inserted or underlined in the same colour (PD17: 2.3).
- The order of colours for successive amendments is: red, green, violet and yellow (PD17: 2.4).
➤ All amendments must carry a statement of truth (see p 351).

Amending before service

- A statement of case may be amended any time before service of it on any other party (r 17(1)).
- Procedure (PD17: 1):

  Steps
  1. Usually the court will hold a hearing unless the parties agree otherwise between themselves.
  2. When making an application to amend a statement of case, the applicant should file with the Court: a) the application notice *and* b) a copy of the statement of case with proposed amendments.
  3. Where permission to amend is given, the applicant, within 14 days of the date of the order (or other period directed by the court), must file with the court the amended statement of case.
  4. If the substance of the statement of case is changed by reason of the amendment, the statement of case should be re-verified by a statement of truth.
  5. The amender should serve a copy of the order and the amended statement of case on every party to the proceedings, unless the court orders otherwise.

Amending after service

- After service, a party may amend a statement of case only:
  - (r 17.1(2)(a)): with written consent of all other parties, *or*
  - (r 17.1(2)(b)): with the permission of the court (but subject to substitution of parties and limitation rules below).
- The court may give consequential directions (r 17.3).

NB: if changing the parties use the procedure steps on the next page instead

Amending after limitation expiry

➤ After a limitation period has expired, the only amendment a court may allow is one (r 17.4):
- whose effect is to add/substitute a new claim, *but only if* the new claim arises out of the same (or substantially the same) facts as a claim in respect of which the party applying for permission has already claimed a remedy, *or*
- to correct a mistake as to the name of a party, *but only if* the mistake was genuine and not one which would cause reasonable doubt as to the identity of the party in question, *or*
- to alter the capacity in which a party claims if the new capacity is one which that party had when the action started or has since acquired.

➤ The court may add/substitute a party only if (r 19.5(2)):
- the relevant limitation period was current when the proceedings were started, *and*
- a) the new party is to be substituted for a party who was named in the claim form in mistake for the new party, *or*
  - b) the claim cannot properly be carried on by or against the original party unless the new party is added or substituted as claimant or defendant, *or*
  - c) the original party has died or is under a bankruptcy order and his interest/liability has passed to the new party

Note: For personal injuries, the court may add/substitute a party where it directs that (r 19.4) *LA 1980 s 11/s 12* does not apply to the claim by/against the new party or the issue of whether those sections apply shall be determined at trial.

CIVIL LITIGATION
Throughout litigation

Adding or substituting a party (after service)

The court may (r 19.2):

- **Add** a party if:
  a) it is desirable to add the new party so that the court can resolve all the matters in dispute in the proceedings, *or*
  b) there is an issue involving the new party and an existing party which is connected to the matters in dispute in the proceedings, and it is desirable to add the new party so that the court can resolve that issue

- **Substitute** a party if:
  a) the existing party's interest or liability has passed to the new party, *and*
  b) it is desirable to substitute the new party so that the court can resolve the matters in dispute

  Note: To substitute a party, an application may be made without notice (r 19.4)

Procedure for adding/substituting parties (r 19.4):

Steps

1* An application for permission to amend may be made by:
   a) an existing party, *or*
   b) a person who wishes to become a party.

2 If adding/substituting *the claimant*, the applicant files:
   a) the application notice, *and*
   b) the proposed amended claim form and particulars of claim, *and*
   c) the signed, written consent of the new claimant to be added/substituted, *and*
      Note: if this consent is not filed, the order and the addition/substitution of the new party as claimant, will not take effect until the signed, written consent of the new claimant is filed.
   d) evidence setting out the proposed new party's interest in or connection with the claim (PD19:1.3).
      - Substitution only: evidence must also show the stage the proceedings have reached and what change has occurred to cause the transfer of interest or liability (PD19: 5.2).

3a **Addition only:** the application notice is filed under *r 23.3* and served under *r 23.4* (PD19: 1.4) (see pp 371-372).

3b **Substitution only:** the application notice is filed under *r 23.3* (PD19: 1.4) (see p 371).

4* The hearing is held (if appropriate).

5* An order giving permission to amend will, unless the court orders otherwise, be drawn up (PD19: 1.5).

6* The order must be served on:
   a) all parties to the proceedings, *and*
   b) any other person affected by the order.
   It will be served by the court unless the parties wish to serve it or the court orders them to do so (PD19: 1.5)

7* The court may give consequential directions about:
   a) filing and serving the claim form on any new defendant, *and/or*
   b) serving relevant documents on the new party, *and/or*
   c) the management of the proceedings.

8a If adding/substituting *a claimant*, the court may direct (PD19: 3):
   a) a copy of the order to be served on every party and any other person affected by the order, *and/or*
   b) copies of the statements of case + any documents referred to in those to be served on the new party, *and/or*
   c) the applicant must file, within 14 days an amended claim form and particulars of claim.

8b If adding/substituting *a defendant*, the court may direct (PD19: 3):
   a) the claimant to file with the court, within 14 days (or as ordered), an amended claim form and particulars of claim for the court file, *and/or*
   b) a copy of the order to be served on all parties to the proceedings and any other person affected by it, *and/or*
   c) the amended claim form + particulars of claim, forms for admitting, defending, acknowledging the claim + statements of case + any other documents referred to in those, must be served on the new defendant, *and/or*
   d) unless the court orders otherwise, the amended claim form + particulars of claim must be served on defendants.
   Note: A new defendant does not become a party until the amended claim form has been served on him.

Removing a party (after service)

The Court may (r 19.2):

- Delete a party if: it is not desirable for that person to be a party

Procedure: the steps in the table above with a '*' apply here, with the following amendments (PD19: 4):

Steps

2 Replace steps 2 and 3 above with: the claimant must file with the court an amended claim form and particulars of claim.

8 Replace step 8 above with: a copy of the order must be served on every party and on any other person affected by the order.

CIVIL LITIGATION
Throughout litigation

V Statements of truth (Part 22)

- **In the following documents:** The following documents must be verified by a statement of truth:
  - all statements of case (claim form, particulars of claim, defence, counterclaim reply etc.), *and*
    - if a statement of case is amended, the amendments must be verified by a statement of truth.
  - a response providing further information, *and*
  - witness statements (including expert's reports), *and*
  - application notices if an applicant wishes to rely on matters set out in it as evidence, *and*
  - certificates of service, *and*
  - application notices for a third party debt order (*r 72.3*), a hardship payment order (*r 72.7*) or a charging order (*r 73.3*) (see pp 427-428).

  Note: A statement of truth not contained in the document it verifies, must clearly identify that document.

- **What it is:** a statement that the party putting forward the document (or in a witness statement, the maker of the witness statement) (or in a certificate of service, the signor of the certificate) believes that the facts stated in the document are true.
  - **Litigation friends:** If a party is conducting proceedings with a litigation friend, the statement of truth is a statement that the litigation friend believes the facts stated in the document being verified are true.

- **Who signs it:** (see p 347 for electronic document filing rules). The statement of truth must be signed by:
  - in the case of a statement of case, a response or an application, the party or litigation friend, *or* the solicitor on behalf of the party or litigation friend, *or*
  - in the case of a witness statement, the maker of the statement.

  Note 1: Signature by a registered company - signature must be by a person holding a senior position in the company/corporation who must state the office/position he holds. A senior position means a director, the treasurer, secretary, chief executive, manager or other officer of the company/corporation.

  Note 2: Signature by partnership - signature must be by any of the partners, or a person having the control or management of the partnership business.

  Note 3: Signature by solicitor - if a party has a solicitor, the solicitor may sign but the statement refers to the *client's belief*, not his own. The solicitor must sign his own name, *not* that of his firm. He must state the capacity in which he signs and the name of his firm where appropriate. The court takes it to mean:
  - that the client on whose behalf he has signed had authorised him to do so, *and*
  - that before signing he explained to the client that in signing the statement of truth he would be confirming the client's belief that the facts stated in the document were true, *and*
  - that before signing he informed the client of the possible consequences if it should subsequently appear that the client did not have an honest belief in the truth of those facts (see below).

- **No statement of truth:** a statement of case is effective unless struck out, *but* a party cannot rely on it as evidence of any matters in it (and for a witness statement, the court may direct that it is not admissible).

- **Penalty for false statement:** contempt of court proceedings may be brought against the signor (*r 32.14*).

Form of the Statement of Truth (PD22)

- **For a statement of case**, a response, an application notice or a notice of objections:
  '[I believe][the (claimant etc.) believes] that the facts stated in this [name document being verified] are true.'
- **For a witness statement:** 'I believe that the facts stated in this witness statement are true.'
- If the statement of truth is contained in a separate document, that document must be headed with the title of the proceedings and claim number. The document being verified should be identified as follows:
  - claim form: 'the claim form issued on [date]'
  - particulars of claim: 'the particulars of claim issued on [date]'
  - statement of case: 'the [defence or as may be] served on the [name of party] on [date]'
  - application notice: 'the application notice issued on [date] for [set out the remedy sought]'
  - witness statement: 'the witness statement filed on [date] or served on [party] on [date]'

VI Service of documents (in the jurisdiction only)

A Address for service (subject to 'alternative' service below)

➤ An address for service must include a full postcode, unless the court orders otherwise (r 6.5(2)).

➤ A party must give an address for service which is (r 6.5(3)):

a) the address of his residence or place of business, or

b) the business address of his solicitor

➤ If party has a solicitor:

- **if it is not the claim form:** the address is the business address of the solicitor (r 6.5(5)).

- **if it is the claim form:** the address is the business address of the solicitor if the solicitor is authorised to accept service (r 6.13) or as below:

➤ If party has no solicitor (or he is not authorised to accept service) a document should be served as follows (r 6.5(6)):

Address for service if address not given and no solicitor	
Nature of party to be served	Place of service
Individual	◆ usual or last known residence
Proprietor of a business	◆ usual or last known residence, or ◆ place of business or last known place of business
Individual suing/being sued in the firm name	◆ usual or last known residence, or ◆ principal or last known place of business of the firm
Company registered in England and Wales	◆ principal office of the company, or ◆ any place of business of the company within the jurisdiction which has a real connection with the claim

'Alternative' service

➤ The court may make an order permitting service by an alternative method if a normal service method cannot be used (r 6.8).

- An application for this:

a) may be made without notice, and

b) must be supported by evidence.

- The evidence required is (PD6: 9.1):
  - the reason for seeking an order for an alternative method of service, and
  - what steps have been taken to serve by other permitted means.

➤ Such an order must specify the method of service and the date when the document will be deemed to be served.

B Service of documents on children and patients

➤ There are special rules for service on children/patients (we list no detail here) (r 6.6). Very generally:

- Service on a child is through a parent, guardian or person with whom the child lives, and

- Service on a patient is on the MHA 1983 authorised person or if none, the person with whom the defendant resides or in whose care he is, ...

... BUT once a litigation friend is appointed, service is on the litigation friend.

CIVIL LITIGATION
Throughout litigation

C Who will serve the document and how?

➤ The court will serve a document which it has issued or prepared *unless* (r 6.3):

Party service
- a) a rule provides that a party must serve the document in question, *or*
- b) the party on whose behalf the document is to be served notifies the court that he will serve it himself,
- c) a *PD* provides otherwise, *or*
- d) the court orders otherwise, *or*
- e) the court has failed to serve and has sent a notice of non-service to the party on whose behalf the document is to be served.

➤ Where the court serves a document, it may decide which of the methods of service it will use (r 6.3(2)).

- The method will normally be by first class post (*PD6: 8.1*).

- Where the court serves a claim form, delivers a defence or notifies a claimant that the defendant has filed an acknowledgment of service, the court also serves/delivers a copy of any filed notice of funding provided it was filed at the same time as the other document being delivered/served and copies were provided for service (*PD6: 8.3*).

- Where a document to be served by the court is served by post and it is returned to the court, the court must notify the party who requested service stating that the document was returned (r 6.11).

- Where the court bailiff is to serve a document and the bailiff is unable to serve it, the court must notifiy the party who requested service (r 6.11A).

➤ **Filing:** Where a party prepares a document which is to be served by the court, that party must file a copy for the court, and for each party to be served (r 6.3(3)).

Extra rules for service of a claim form (r 6.13-6.14)

➤ **Claim form served by the court:**
- Where a claim form is to be served by the court, the claim form must include the defendant's address for service (and if the defendant's solicitor is authorised to accept service, the defendant's address for service may be the business address of the defendant's solicitor), *and*
- the court must send the claimant a notice which includes the deemed date of service.

➤ **Claim form served by the claimant:**
- claimant must file a certificate of service within 7 days of service of the claim form, *and*
- he may not obtain judgment in default unless he has filed the certificate of service.

Service on companies and partnerships

Service on a company (r 6.4(4), PD6: 6.1 - 6.2)	Service on a partnership (r 6.4(5), PD6: 4.1, 4.2)

➤ A document is served by:
• **leaving a document at or posting it to an authorised place** (*CA 1985 s 725*) (r 6.2(2)), *or*
• **leaving it with a person holding a senior position within the company or corporation**
  • a senior position is:
    1) for a registered company: a director, the treasurer, secretary, chief executive, manager or other officer of the company or corporation.
    2) for a non-registered company: a director, the treasurer, secretary, chief executive, manager or other officer of the company or corporation, the mayor, chairman, president, town clerk or similar officer of the corporation.
	➤ A document is served personally on a partnership where partners are being sued in the name of their firm by leaving it with:
	• **a partner**, *or*
	• a person who, at the time of service, has the control or management of the partnership business at its principal place of business.
	➤ A claim form or particulars of claim which are served by leaving them with a person at the principal or last known place of business of the partnership, must *at the same time,* serve a notice specifying whether that person is being served:
	1) as a partner, *or*
	2) as a person having control or management of the partnership business, *or*
	3) as both.

CIVIL LITIGATION
Throughout litigation

Types of service and when service takes effect

NB: The rules below apply unless the text later specifies otherwise (r 6.1)

Method of service (r 6.2)	When service takes effect (r 6.7)	Rules about the method of service	

Personal (This method may not be used on the Crown)	When delivered but if served after 5pm on a business day or at the weekend or a bank holiday, then the next business day	➤ A document may be served personally (r 6.4), but
		♦ *must* be served on a solicitor if:
		  a) he is authorised to accept service, *and*
		  b) has notified the party serving the document in writing that he is authorised
			Note for whole box: See the provisions about time on p 345

Delivery to a permitted address	Day after it was delivered to or left at the permitted address		
First class post	Second day after posting	➤ This method of service and the rules that govern it also apply to an alternative service which provides for delivery on the next working day	
Leaving at a DX	Second day following day it is left	➤ A document can only be sent by DX if (PD6: 2.1, 2.2): ♦ a) the other party's address for service includes a DX number, *or* b) the other party's writing paper (or that of his legal representative) has a DX number, *and* ♦ the other party (or his legal representative) has not indicated in writing that they are unwilling to accept service by DX	

Fax sent before 4 pm on a business day	Same day	➤ (Subject to *PD6: 3.3* below) A document can be served by fax and other electronic communication can used if (PD6: 3.1-3.4):
		♦ **the party who is to be served (or his legal representative) has previously expressly indicated in writing to the party serving:**
		  i) that he is willing to accept service by electronic means, *and*
		  ii) the fax number, e-mail address or electronic identification to which it should be sent.	

Fax sent after 4 pm on a business day, *or* Fax sent on a non-business day	Next business day	Note: The following is written indication for the above purpose: i) a fax number is set out on the writing paper of the legal representative of the party who is to be served, *or* ii) a fax number, e-mail address or electronic identification is set out on a statement of case or a response to a claim filed with the court.	
Other means of electronic communication	Second day after the day on which it is transmitted	♦ A party seeking to serve a document by electronic means should first seek to clarify with the party who is to be served whether there are any limitations on the recipient's agreement to accept service by such means (including the format in which documents are to be sent and the maximum size of attachments that may be received) (PD 6: 3.2). ♦ An address for service given by a party must be within the jurisdiction. Any fax number must be at the address for service. Where an e-mail address or electronic identification is given with an address for service, the e-mail address or electronic identification will be deemed to be at the address for service (PD 6: 3.3). ♦ Where a document is served by electronic means, the party serving the document need not also send a hard copy by post or DX (PD 6: 3.4).	

Certificate of service (r 6.10)

➤ Where a rule, PD or order requires a certificate of service, the certificate must state certain details which depend on the service method (eg: for fax service, the date & time of transmission).

C Starting proceedings

I	Identifying the parties (and some extra procedural points that result)	IV	Initial documents needed to file with the claim form
II	Selecting the court	V	The claim form
III	Hearings	VI	Particulars of claim

I Identifying the parties (and some extra procedural points that result)

1 Joint claimants (r 19.3)

➤ Where a claimant claims a remedy to which someone else is jointly entitled, all persons jointly entitled must be parties unless the court orders otherwise.

♦ If any person does not agree to be a claimant, he must be made a defendant, unless the court orders otherwise.

2 Joining possible claims

➤ A claimant may use a single claim form to start all claims which can be conveniently disposed of in the same proceedings (r 7.3). A claimant does not need leave of the court for this.

3 If claimant/defendant is trading under another name

4 If claimant/defendant is suing/being sued in a representative capacity   see p 361

5 If claimant/defendant is a firm

6 If claimant/defendant is a company registered in England & Wales: see pp 353 and 361

7 If claimant/defendant is a partnership: see p 353

➤ Suing partners in the firm name:

    ✓ makes service easier, *but*

    ✗ leave is needed for enforcing judgment against the individual partners' own assets.

> See also *Sch 1 r 81* (to be re-enacted as *PD:7 5A, 5B and 5C* from 2 October 2006)

8 Claimant or defendant is a patient within *MHA 1983* (Part 21 and PD21)

➤ A patient must bring or defend proceedings by a litigation friend (*r 21.2(1), PD21: 1.2*) (see p 356).

➤ The patient is referred to in the title as 'X (by Y his litigation friend)' (*PD21: 1.3*).

➤ If the patient has no litigation friend (*r 21.3(2)*):

♦ prior to service of claim form, no applications are allowed without the court's permission, *and*

♦ during proceedings, no steps are allowed without the court's permission *except*: issuing and serving the claim form and applying for appointment of a litigation friend.

➤ If a party becomes a patient during proceedings, no party may take any step in the proceedings without the permission of the court until the patient has a litigation friend (*r 21.3(3)*).

➤ When a party ceases to be a patient, the litigation friend's appointment continues until it is ended by a court order (*r 21.9*).

9 Insurers

➤ In a road traffic accident case, if insurers are involved, the claimant must send a *s 151/152 RTA 1988* notice to the defendant's insurers within 7 days of issuing proceedings. This enables the defendant's insurers to defend the claim, and for the claimant to claim against them if he wins.

CIVIL LITIGATION
Starting proceedings

10 Claimant or defendant is a child (ie: under 18 - a minor) *(Part 21 and PD21)*

➤ A child must bring or defend proceedings by a litigation friend *unless* the court has made an order permitting the child to do so on his own behalf (*r 21.2(2), PD21: 1.4*).

➤ Where the child (*PD21: 1.5*):

- has a litigation friend, the child is referred to in the title as 'X (a child by Y his litigation friend)', *or*
- conducts proceedings on his own behalf, the child is referred to in the title as 'X (a child)'.

➤ If the child has no litigation friend, and the court has not ordered an exemption (*r 21.3(2)*):

- prior to service of the claim form, no applications are allowed without the court's permission, *and*
- during proceedings, no steps are allowed without the court's permission except: issuing and serving the claim form and applying for appointment of a litigation friend.

➤ The litigation friend is personally liable for costs, but is usually indemnified for these by the child.

➤ When a child (who is not a patient) reaches 18, a litigation friend's appointment ceases (*r 21.9*). The child may adopt or repudiate proceedings on coming of age during the proceedings.

➤ No settlement, compromise or payment and no acceptance of money paid into court is valid, without the approval of the court. Any money won by the child will be dealt with by direction of the court but will usually be paid into court and invested until the child is 18 (although sums may be drawn and paid earlier to the child for his immediate needs) (*r 21.10-21.11*).

A litigation friend *(Part 21, PD: 21)*

➤ **Duties:** a litigation friend must:
- fairly and competently conduct proceedings on behalf of the child or patient, *and*
- have no interest adverse to that of the child or patient, *and*
- where the child or patient is a claimant, undertake to pay any costs which the child or patient may be ordered to pay in relation to the proceedings (subject to any right he may have to be repaid from the assets of the child or patient).

➤ **What to file (1):** to become a litigation friend *without a court order* the potential litigation friend must (*PD21: 2.3*):
- (for a patient with *MHA* authorisation) file an official copy of the order/other document which constitutes the authorisation under *MHA 1983*, *or*
- (for a child or a patient without *MHA* authorisation) file a certificate of suitability stating:
    a) that he consents to act, *and*
    b) that he knows or believes that the [claimant] [defendant] is a [child][patient], *and*
    c) (for a patient only) the grounds of his belief and if his belief is based upon medical opinion attaching any relevant document to the certificate, *and*
    d) that he can fairly and competently conduct proceedings on behalf of the child or patient and has no interest adverse to that of the child or patient, *and*
    e) where a claimant, an undertaking to pay any costs which the child or patient may be ordered to pay in relation to the proceedings, subject to any right he may have to be repaid from the assets of the child or patient, *and*
    f) which he has signed in verification of its contents.

➤ **What to file (2):** the litigation friend must serve a certificate of suitability (*PD21: 2.4, 2.4A*):
- for a child (who is not a patient), on one of the child's parents/guardians or none, on the person with whom the child resides or in whose care the child is, *and*
- for a patient, on the person authorised under *MHA 1983* to conduct proceedings on behalf of the patient or if none, on the person with whom the patient resides/in whose care the patient is (NB: 'c' in the above list can be ignored).

➤ **When to serve/file** (*r 21.5*):
- for claimant: serve authorisation or certificate of suitability with a certificate of service (see p 354) when the claim form is issued.
- for defendant: file authorisation or certificate of suitability with a certificate of service (see p 354) at the time when first taking a step in the proceedings on behalf of the defendant.

➤ **Who to serve:** the litigation friend must serve on every person on whom the claim form should be served (*r 21.5*).

CIVIL LITIGATION
Starting proceedings

II Selecting the court

A Courts generally

High Court	County Courts
There is 1 High Court divided into: **Chancery Division** (includes: ♦ Patent Court ♦ Companies Court) Used for: landlord and tenant disputes, trusts, contentious probate, partnership actions, intellectual property actions and actions requesting equitable remedies **Family Division** **Queens Bench Division** (includes: ♦ Commercial Court ♦ Admiralty Court) Used for: claiming damages in contract actions and tort actions	There are *many* county courts ♦ The Central London County Court Business List is sometimes used for certain high value business/commercial transactions ♦ The Central London Civil Trial Centre is at the Central London County Court. More complex County Court cases are heard here, especially those expected to last for more than 1 day. Cases may be referred here by any London County Court

B Where to *start* a claim (PD7: 2)

➤ In general (*and subject to the rest of the rules in this section*), any action which both the High Court and the county courts have jurisdiction to deal with may be started in either the High Court or a county court.

♦ Note: in calculating the *value* of a claim in this section see the large grey box on p 362.

♦ The jurisdiction of the High Court and the county courts is as follows:

The jurisdiction of the courts at commencement of a claim (CCA 1984, HCCCJO 1991)	
Jurisdiction of the High Court	Jurisdiction of the county courts
Tort claims over £15,000 (Note overlap with county courts)	Tort claims up to £50,000 (*CCA 1984 s 15*)
Contract claims over £15,000 (Note overlap with county courts)	Contract claims up to £50,000 (*CCA 1984 s 15*)
Personal injury claims worth £50,000 or more	Personal injury claims worth under £50,000 (*SI 1991/724*)
Libel (unless the parties agree otherwise)	Equitable interests and land charges disputes where the property has a value of £30,000 or less (*CCA 1984 s 23*)
Slander (unless the parties agree otherwise)	Note: A claim may be started using Money Claim Online if the only remedy claimed is a specified amount of moneyless than £100,000 (excluding any interest or costs claimed) and the claimant is not a child or patient or funded by the LSC. The claim must be against a 1 defendant or 2 defendants if the claim is for a single amount against each of them (*PD7E*).
Search orders (authorises a party to search for documents or property at their opponent's premises)	
Freezing injunctions (to freeze assets)	
Judicial review	

➤ **Claims of damages or a specified sum: the £15,000 rule**

♦ worth more than £15,000 *may* be commenced in the High Court or the county courts (up to £50,000).

♦ worth £15,000 or less *must* be commenced in the county courts.

➤ **Personal injury action: the £50,000 rule**

♦ worth £50,000 or more - *must* be commenced in the High Court

♦ worth less than £50,000 - *must* be commenced in the county courts.

➤ **Claimant's belief:** the High Court (and not a county court) should hear a case if (subject to the above) a claimant believes the following factors are of a sufficiently high level:

Claimant's factors		
1	**Financial value of the claim and the amount in dispute**	
2	**Complexity:**	of facts, legal issues, remedies or procedures involved
3	**Importance of the outcome:**	to the public in general

C Transfer of a claim after the claim has been started (Part 30)

➤ A claim will usually proceed in the court in which it was commenced.

➤ However, in certain cases the claim can be transferred to a different court. This happens if a court does not have jurisdiction (see the table on the previous page) or if the following rules apply:

1   **County Court transfer to another County Court** (r 30.2(1)-(3))

➤ A county court may order proceedings before that court, or any part of them (eg: a counterclaim) to be transferred to another county court if it is satisfied that:

a) an order should be made having regard to the 'transfer criteria' (see box on p 359), or

b) the following proceedings could be more conveniently or fairly taken in that other county court:

application is made to the court where the claim is proceeding

♦ the detailed assessment of costs, or

♦ the enforcement of a judgment or order, or

c) proceedings have been started in the wrong county court in which case the Court may order they:

♦ be transferred to the county court in which they ought to have been started, or

♦ continue in the county court in which they have been started, or

♦ be struck out.

d) the rules for 'Automatic Transfers' apply (claim is for a specified amount, was commenced in a court which is not the defendant's home court, has not otherwise been transferred to another defendant's home court under an application to set aside or vary default judgment and the defendant is an individual), see p 392 for detail.

2   **High Court transfer within itself** (r 30.2(4)-(6))

➤ The High Court may, having regard to the 'transfer criteria' (see box overleaf), order proceedings in the Royal Courts of Justice (RCJ) or a district registry (DR), or any part of such proceedings (eg: a counterclaim) to be transferred:

♦ from the RCJ to a DR, or

♦ from a DR to the RCJ, or

♦ from a DR to another DR.

> An application for an order must, if the claim is proceeding in a DR, be made to that DR

➤ A DR may order proceedings before it for detailed assessment of costs to be transferred to another DR if it is satisfied that the proceedings could be more conveniently or fairly taken in that other DR.

3   **High Court transfer to a County Court**

➤ **Discretionary transfer:** the High Court can transfer whatever it wants to a county court (CCA 1984 s 40).

♦ This might occur in the following types of cases:

a) cases that *could* only be started in the High Court, eg: slander, libel.

b) cases that *should* never have started in the High Court *must* be moved to a county court (CCA 1984 s 40), eg: a personal injury action worth less than £50,000.

c) cases that can be heard in either court.

➤ **Automatic transfer:** there will be automatic transfer to a county court unless a 'statement of value' showing the action is worth at least £15,000 (or a statement saying why the action ought to be heard in the High Court) is delivered at the appropriate time.

4 General power of High Court to transfer to a county court and a county court to High Court

➤ Generally, the High Court has power to transfer cases to a county court and a county court has power to transfer cases to the High Court (*CCA 1984 ss 40-42*). It must take account of the 'transfer criteria' (*r 30.3*).

Transfer criteria (*r 30.3*)

➤ The following are matters which the court must have regard to when considering whether to make a transfer order:

- the financial value of the claim and the amount in dispute, if different, *and*
- whether it would be more convenient or fair for hearings (including the trial) to be held in some other court, *and*
- the availability of a judge specialising in the type of claim in question, *and*
- whether the facts, legal issues, remedies or procedures involved are simple or complex, *and*
- the importance of the outcome of the claim to the public in general, *and*
- the facilities available at the court where the claim is being dealt with and whether they may be inadequate because of any disabilities of a party or potential witness, *and*
- whether the making of a declaration of incompatibility under *HRA 1998 s 4* has arisen or may arise, *and*
- High Court Factors - ie: factors that might include a court more to having a case heard in the High Court (*PD29: 2.6*):
    - professional negligence claims.
    - Fatal Accident Act claims.
    - fraud or undue influence claims.
    - defamation claims.
    - claims for malicious prosecution or false imprisonment.
    - claims against the police.
    - contentious probate claims.

Transfer procedure (*r 30.4*)

➤ Where the Court orders proceedings to be transferred, the court from which they are to be transferred must give notice of the transfer to all the parties.

Application to set aside a transfer order (*PD30: 6*)

➤ Where a party may apply to set aside an order for transfer the application should be made to the Court which made the order.

➤ Such application should be made in accordance with *Part 23*, see p 371.

Competition law claims (*r 30.8*)

➤ Where there is a competition claim under *CA 1998 Part I* or *Articles 81/82*, a special transfer procedure applies.

III Hearings

	Hearings - miscellaneous provisions (Part 39)
In public (r 39.1) Note: see also telephone hearings p 373	➤ A hearing is in public, *unless* ◆ publicity would defeat the object of the hearing, *or* ◆ the hearing involves matters relating to national security, *or* ◆ confidential information is involved and publicity would damage that confidentiality, *or* ◆ privacy is necessary to protect the interests of a child or patient, *or* ◆ it is the hearing of an application made without notice and a public hearing would be unjust to the respondent, *or* ◆ the hearing involves uncontentious matters arising in the administration of trusts or a deceased person's estate, *or* ◆ the court considers a private hearing necessary in the interests of justice. ➤ The court may order the identity of a party or witness not be disclosed if this is necessary to protect the interests of that party or witness.

Failure to attend trial
(r 39.3)
	➤ The court may proceed in a party's absence, *but*
	◆ if no party attends, the court may strike out the whole of the proceedings.
	◆ if the claimant does not attend, the court may strike out the claim and any defence to a counterclaim.
	◆ if the defendant does not attend, it may strike out the defence and/or counterclaim (r 39.3(1)).
	➤ If a court strikes out proceedings (or any part of proceedings) under r 39.3 it may subsequently them (r 39.3(2)).
	➤ A party who does not attend and has a order or judgment made against it under r 39.3 may apply for that order or judgement to be set aside (r 39.3(3)).
	◆ An application for proceedings to be restored or an order/judgment to be set aside must be supported by evidence (r 39.3(4))
	◆ The court may only grant an application to restore proceedings or set aside an order/judgment if the applicant:
	  a) acted promptly when he found out that the claim had been struck out or the order/judgment set aside, *and*
	  b) had a good reason for not attending the trial, *and*
	  c) has a reasonable prospect of success at trial (r 39.3(5)).

Timetable for trial (r 39.4)	➤ When the court sets a timetable for a trial under: ◆ r 28.6 (Fast track) (see p 397), *or* ◆ r 29 (Multi track) (see p 399) ... ... it will do so in consultation with the parties.
Trial bundles (r 39.5)	➤ A claimant must file a trial bundle containing documents required by any relevant practice direction and any court order, unless the court orders otherwise. ➤ The trial bundle must be filed not more than 7 days and not less than 3 days before the start of the trial (see p 411).
Representation at trial of companies/ corporations (r 39.6)	➤ An employee may represent a company or corporation at trial if that employee has been authorised by the company or corporation to appear at trial on its behalf and the court gives permission.

IV Initial documents needed to file with the claim form

➤ Documents to file with the claim form include:
- the particulars of claim (if not on the claim form or if not being served after the claim form), *and*
- for a legally assisted claimant, a notice of funding + any amendments (*PD:Costs 19*), *and*
- the relevant defence / admission / acknowledgment of service forms, *and*
- the fee, *and*
- any relevant litigation friend documents (see p 356).

V The claim form (*Part 7*)

A General

▶ Proceedings are started when the court issues a claim form at the request of the claimant (*r 7.2(1)*).

◆ A claim form is issued on the date entered on the form by the court (*r 7.2(2)*).

▶ Drafting the claim form must be done on *Form N1* (*PD7: 3.1*).

▶ There are 2 other ways of starting claims. These are where there is:

◆ no substantial dispute of fact. *Part 8* procedures apply and *Form N208* (*PD7: 3.1*) is used as the claims form. *Part 8* proceedings are not dealt with in this book.

◆ a specialist jurisdiction (known as a 'list') (eg: the Commercial Court) (not dealt with in this book).

B Procedure for the claimant's solicitors to issue the claim form

Steps

1. Prepare at least 3 copies of the claim form and all documents accompanying it (see steps 4 and 5 below); one for the claimant, one for each defendant and one for the court.

2. Sign the copies.

3. Prepare the 'Response Pack' consisting of: 1) the correct admissions form; 2) the correct defence form *and* ; 3) the acknowledgement of service form.

4. If the claimant is legally funded, prepare the notification of legal funding and copies (*PD:Costs 19*).

5. If the claimant is a child or a patient, prepare the litigation friend documents (see p 356).

6. Prepare the court fee - cheques are payable to 'HM Paymaster General'.

7. Take, or send (include the SAE if so), the claim form and response pack and any of the above documents to the court, together with the court fee.

8. The court will issue a claim number, seal the documents and issue the claim form.

9. Once issued the claim form can be served within 4 months (within the jurisdiction) (see p 342).

Filling in the parties on the claim form	
Party	Wording on claim form
Individual	▶ Insert all known forenames and surname, whether Mr, Mrs, Miss, Ms or Other (eg: Dr) and residential address (**including** postcode and telephone number) ▶ Where the defendant is a proprietor of a business, a partner in a firm or an individual sued in the name of a club or other unincorporated association, the address for service should be the usual or last known place of residence **or** principal place of business of the company, firm or club or other unincorporated association
Child (ie: under 18) *or* patient under *MHA 1983*	▶ See pp 355-356 for correct form in title and procedure
Trading under another name	▶ Insert the words: 'trading as' and the trading name, eg: 'Mr X trading as X's dairies'
Suing or being sued in a representative capacity	▶ State the capacity, eg: 'Mr X as the representative of Ms Y (deceased)'
A firm	▶ Insert the firm name followed by 'a firm', eg: 'X - a firm' ▶ Insert an address for service which is either a partner's residential address or the principal or last known place of business
A company registered in England and Wales	▶ Insert the company name and an address which is either the company's registered office or any place of business that has a real, or the most, connection with the claim eg: the shop where goods were brought ▶ Verify the company's details with a company search

CIVIL LITIGATION
Starting proceedings

VI Particulars of claim

➤ Particulars of claim form the main statement of case that sets out the claimant's case.

➤ Particulars of claim must (*r 7.4*):

   a) be contained in the claim form, *or*

   b) be served with, but separate to, the claim form, *or*

   c) be served on the defendant within 14 days after service of the claim form (provided it is still within the time that the claim form could be served - ie: within 4 months after its date of issue - see p 340).

   - If the particulars of claim are not included in or have not been served with the claim form, the claim form must also contain a statement that particulars of claim will follow (*PD7: 6.1, PD16: 3.3*).

   ◆ If practicable, the particulars of claim should be set out in the claim form (*PD16: 3.1*).

➤ Where the claimant serves particulars of claim at a different time to the claim form, he must, within 7 days of service on the defendant, file a copy of the particulars with the court, together with a certificate of service (see p 340) (*r 7.4(3)*).

➤ When particulars of claim are served on a defendant, whether they are contained in the claim form, served with it or served subsequently, they must be accompanied by (*r 7.8(1)*):

   a) a form for defending the claim, *and*

   b) a form for admitting the claim, *and*

   c) a form for acknowledging service.

Compulsory matters (*PD16: 8.1, 8.2*)

➤ The claimant must set out specifically the following matters where he wishes to rely on them in support of his claim

   - any allegation of fraud
   - the fact of any illegality
   - details of any misrepresentation
   - details of all breaches of trust
   - notice or knowledge of a fact
   - details of unsoundness of mind or undue influence
   - details of wilful default
   - any facts relating to mitigation of loss or damage
   - **Conviction:** a claimant who wants to rely on evidence under *s 11 CEA 1968* of a conviction must include:
     - a statement that he wants to rely on a conviction under *s 11 CEA 1968*, *and*
     - the type of conviction, finding or adjudication and its date, *and*
     - the court which made the conviction, finding or adjudication, *and*
     - the issue in the claim to which it relates.
   - **Certain special types of damages:** a claimant seeking aggravated damages, exemplary damages or provisional damages must include a statement to that effect and the grounds for claiming them

Interest (*r 16.4*)

➤ A claimant seeking interest must state the following:

   a) a statement to that he is seeking interest, *and*

   b) a statement that:

      i) that he is seeking interest under the terms of a contract, *or*

      ii) that he is seeking interest under an enactment (state which), ★ *or*

      iii) that he is seeking interest on some other basis (state which) (eg: see p 334), *and*

   c) (if the claim is for a specified amount of money), he must state:

      i) the percentage rate at which interest is claimed, ★ *and*

      ii) the date from which it is claimed, *and*

      iii) the date to which it is calculated (must not be later than the date the claim form is issued), *and*

      iv) the total amount of interest claimed to the date of calculation, *and*

      v) the daily rate at which interest accrues after that date

(High Court interest is sought under *SCA 1981 s 35A*)

(County Court interest is sought under *CCA 1984 s 69*)

(For debt actions, interest may have been set by an agreement - if not then the rate is set by statutory instrument (now 8%) (see p 425))

CIVIL LITIGATION
Starting proceedings

Drafting the particulars of claim (r 7.4, PD7A: 6, r 16.4, PD16: 3-9)

Particulars of claim which are served separately from the claim form must contain (PD16: 3.8):
- the name of the court in which the claim is proceeding, *and*
- the claim number, *and*
- the title of the proceedings, *and*
- the claimant's address for service.

Give a concise statement of the facts on which the claimant relies (r 16.4)
- It is good practice to set this out as numbered paragraphs
- Examples of typical facts (in addition to the compulsory matters) to include are set out below:

Breach of contract	Problem with goods	Personal injury
◆ whether contract is oral or written	◆ price of the goods	◆ date and place of the accident
◆ date of + parties to the contract	◆ date the goods were sold	◆ names of those involved
◆ purpose of the agreement	◆ particulars of goods	◆ allegation of negligence
◆ consideration (unless under seal)	◆ date delivery was due	◆ (with 'particulars of negligence')
◆ the term breached		

Compulsory matters which must specifically be stated if relied on (PD16: 8.1):

Breach of contract claims (PD16: 7)	Personal injury claims (PD16: 4)
Written agreement: ◆ attach or serve a copy of the contract/documents constituting the agreement (Note: the original(s) should be available at the hearing) ◆ attach any general conditions of sale incorporated in the contract (but where any of the above are bulky, attach or serve only the relevant parts of the contract/documents). **Oral agreement:** ◆ set out the contractual words used and state by whom, to whom, when and where they were spoken **Agreement by conduct:** ◆ specify the conduct relied on and state by whom, when and where the acts constituting the conduct were done	◆ state the claimant's date of birth ◆ state brief details of the claimant's personal injuries ◆ attach a schedule of details of any past and future expenses and losses which he claims ◆ (if relying on evidence of a medical practitioner) attach or serve a report from a medical practitioner about the personal injuries which he alleges in his claim ◆ (if a provisional damages claim), add a statement: 1) that he is seeking an award of provisional damages under either *SCA 1981 s 32A* or *CCA 1984 s 51*, *and* 2) that there is a chance that at some future time the claimant will develop some serious disease or suffer some serious deterioration in his physical or mental condition, *and* 3) specifying the disease or type of deterioration in respect of which an application may be made at a future date. (see p 384 (*Part 41*) for more details)

Fatal accident claims (PD16: 5)	Others claims (PD16: 6, r.19.5A)
◆ state that the claim is brought under the *FAA 1976* ◆ state the dependents on whose behalf the claim is made ◆ state the date of birth of each dependent ◆ state details of the nature of the dependency claim Note: A fatal accident claim may include a claim for damages for bereavement. The claimant may also bring a claim under the *LR(MP)A 1934* on behalf of the estate of the deceased	For: ◆ Hire purchase claims ◆ Wrongful interference with goods certain details must be included (not listed here)

A claimant who wishes to rely on certain matters must specifically state them
(see 'Compulsory matters' box on the facing face)

A claimant who seeks interest must state he is seeking interest and add
certain details (r 16.4) (see 'Interest' box on the facing page)

Add the prayer for relief headed 'AND THE CLAIMANT CLAIMS:'
Specify exactly what the claimant wants the court to order

Add a statement of truth (see p 351) (PD16: 3.4)
'[I][the claimant] believe[s] that the facts stated in these particulars of claim are true.'

Drafting tip
- A typical claim is structured using the formulation:

  DUTY
  ↓
  BREACH
  ↓
  LOSS

D Defendant's options

1	Draft a full or partial defence and/or counterclaim (*Part 20*)	p 366
2	Make an admission of all or part of the claim	p 367
3	Acknowledge service (delaying the time for service of a defence)	p 369
4	Dispute the court's jurisdiction	p 369
5	Strike out a statement of case (may also be made with 8 below)	p 343
6	Transfer the claim to a different court	p 358 / p 369
7	Join a third party to the claim or make an additional claim (*Part 20*)	p 374-375
8	Seek summary judgment	p 376
9	Set aside a default judgment	p 377
10	Find out further information about the claim	p 378
11	Seek security for costs	p 384
12	Seek a consent order	p 380
13	Seek an interim remedy of the type listed on p 383	p 381

> Including:
> - an interim injunction
> - an interim declaration
> - an order for the detention, custody or preservation of property or inspection or taking of a sample or carrying out of an experiment on or with property, *and* authorising a person to enter land in the possession of a party to carry out that order.
> - a 'freezing injunction
> - a 'search order'.
> - an order for disclosure of documents or inspection of property
> - an order for an interim payment made under *r.25.6* (see p 383).

14	Make (or accept on a counterclaim) a *Part 36* offer or payment or other type of settlement	p 385-391
15	Require the claimant to admit facts or part of the case	p 406
16	Require the claimant to prove the authenticity of a document	p 406

Claiming additional liability if legally funded (*PD:Costs 19*)

Note: A party who will claim an additional liability under a funding arrangement must give other parties information about this (eg: in the defence, acknowledgement etc.), but there is no need to specify the amount of additional liability separately nor to state how it is calculated until it is assessed.

CIVIL LITIGATION
Defendant's options

I Defence and counterclaim

A The defence

> *Times for filing/serving are set out on p 340*

➤ A defence is the statement of case setting out the defence to the claimant's particulars of claim.

➤ **Dealing with the claimant's allegations:** In his defence, the defendant must state (*r 16.5*):

- which allegations he admits, *and*
- which allegations he is unable to admit or deny, but which he requires the claimant to prove, *and*
- which of the allegations in the particulars of claim he denies.
    - He must state his reasons for denying any allegation, *and*
    - if he is putting forward a different version of events, he must state his own version.

➤ **Failing to deal with an allegation:** If the defendant is silent as to an allegation (*r 16.5*):

a) if the claim includes a money claim, it is deemed that he requires any allegation relating to the amount of money claimed be proved by the claimant *unless* the defendant expressly admits the allegation.

b) if he has set out in his defence *the nature of his case in relation to the issue to which that allegation is relevant*, it is counted as if he requires that allegation to be proved.

c) if a and b above do not apply, it is counted *as if admits that allegation*.

> *See p 343 Ground 1 for consequences of a bare denial*

➤ **Disputing the statement of value in the statement of claim:** the defendant must state why he disputes it *and* (if he can), give his own statement of the value of the claim (*r 16.5*).

➤ **Representative capacity** (*r 16.5*): if a defendant acts in a representative capacity, he must state what it is.

➤ **Address for service** (*r 16.5*): the defendant must give an address for service *unless* he has filed an acknowledgment of service under *Part 10* (see p 369).

➤ **Statement of truth:** the defence must be verified by a statement of truth (see p 351) (*PD16: 11, Part 22*).

- The wording is: '[I believe][the defendant believes] that the facts stated in the defence are true.'

➤ **A defence of set-off** (*r 16.6*): where a defendant contends he is entitled to money from the claimant *and* relies on this as a defence to the whole or part of the claim, the contention may be included in the defence and set off against the claim, whether or not it is also an additional claim under *Part 20* (see pp 374-375).

Compulsory matters to insert in the defence (*PD16: 12, 13.1*)

The defendant must set out specifically the following matters where he wishes to rely on them in support of his claim:

- **Limitation defence:** the defendant must give details of the expiry of any relevant limitation period he has relied on

- **Personal injuries claim:**
    - where claimant attached a medical report about his alleged injuries, defendant should:
      a) state in the defence whether, concerning the matters in the medical report, he:
        - agrees with those matters, *or*
        - disputes those matters (giving his reasons), *or*
        - neither agrees nor disputes but has no knowledge of those matters, *and*
      b) if he has obtained his own medical report on which he intends to rely, attach his own medical report to his defence.
    - where claimant included a schedule of past and future expenses and losses, defendant should include in, or attach to, his defence a counter-schedule stating which items he:
        - agrees, *or*
        - disputes (supplying alternative figures where appropriate), *or*
        - neither agrees nor disputes but has no knowledge of

---

B The counterclaim

➤ Where a defendant serves a counterclaim (i.e. an additional claim - see pp 374-375) the defence and counterclaim should normally form one document with counterclaim following on from the defence.

II Admissions

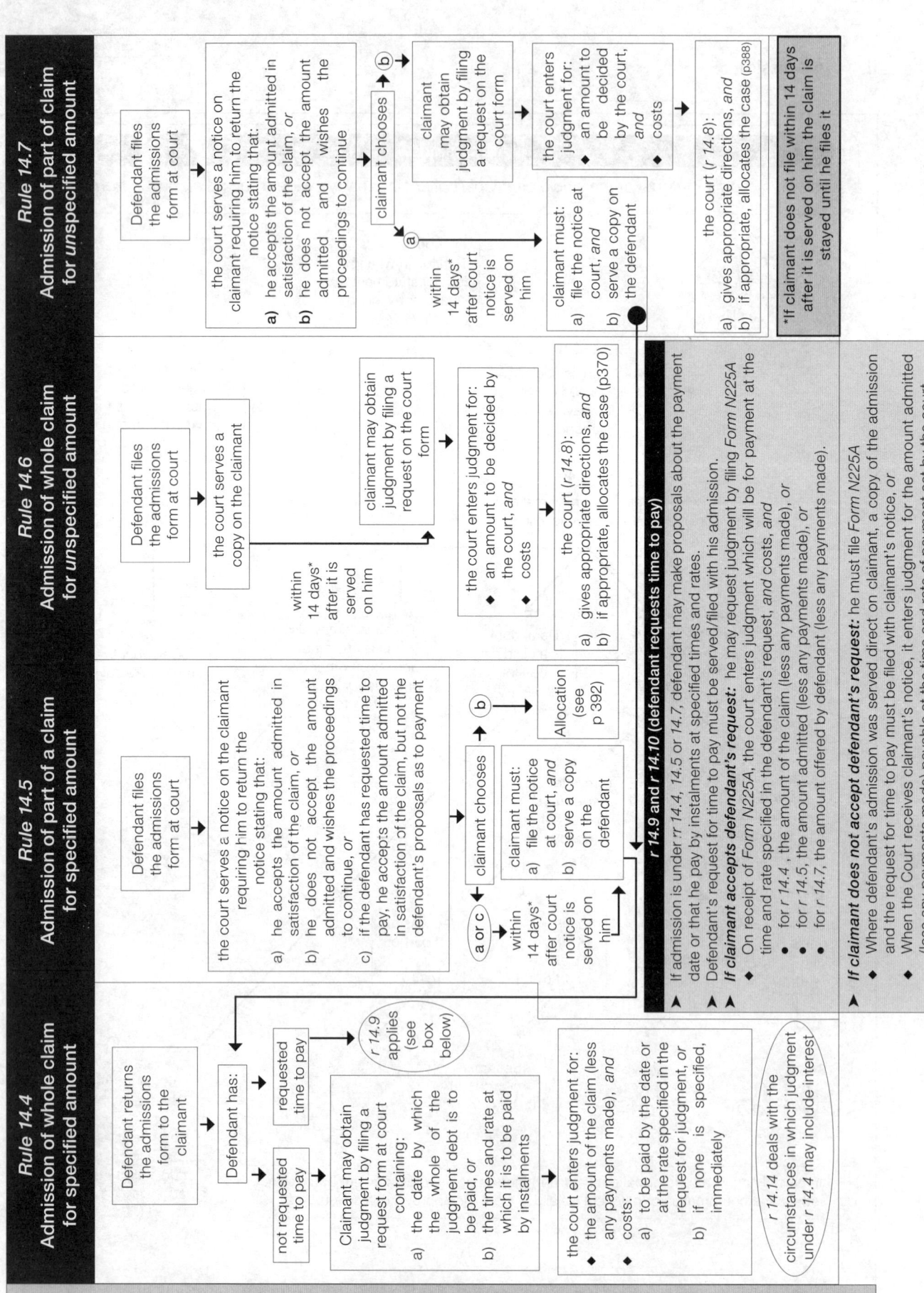

III Acknowledgement of service (Part 10)

➤ A defendant must file an acknowledgment of service (*Form N9*) if:
  - he is unable to file a defence within the period specified (see p 340 and below), *or*
  - he wishes to dispute the court's jurisdiction (see below).

  Note: A defendant who files an acknowledgment of service does not, by doing so, lose any right that he may have to dispute the court's jurisdiction (see below) (*r 11(3)*).

➤ **Period:** The general rule is that the period for filing an acknowledgment of service is:
  - where the defendant is served with a claim form which states that particulars of claim are to follow, 14 days after service of the particulars of claim, *and*
  - in any other case, 14 days after service of the claim form.

➤ The claimant may obtain default judgment (see p 377) if:
  - a defendant fails to file an acknowledgment of service within the period specified above, *and*
  - does not within that period file a defence (see p 366) or serve or file an admission (see pp 367-368).

➤ On receipt of an acknowledgment of service, the court must notify the claimant in writing.

➤ An acknowledgment of service must be signed by the defendant or his solicitor and include the defendant's address for service, or if represented by a solicitor, his solicitor's address.

IV Disputing the court's jurisdiction (Part 11)

➤ A defendant may apply to the court for an order declaring that the court has no such jurisdiction or should not exercise any jurisdiction which it may have, if he:
  - disputes the court's jurisdiction to try the claim, *or*
  - argues that the court should not exercise its jurisdiction.

➤ A defendant making such an application *must* first file an acknowledgment of service (see above).

➤ **Period:** An application must be made within 14 days after filing an acknowledgment of service (and must be supported by evidence).
  - The defendant accepts that the court has jurisdiction to try the claim if he:
    - files an acknowledgment of service, *and*
    - does not make such an application within 14 days after filing an acknowledgment of service.

➤ **Court makes a declaration:** that it has no jurisdiction/will not exercise its jurisdiction and may also:
  - set aside the claim form, *and/or*
  - set aside service of the claim form, *and/or*
  - discharge any order made before the claim was commenced or served, *and/or*
  - stay the proceedings.

➤ **Court does not make a declaration, then:**
  - the acknowledgment of service ceases to have effect, *and*
  - the defendant may file a further acknowledgment of service within 14 days or such other period as the court may direct, *and*
    - If the defendant does file a further acknowledgment of service, he is treated as having accepted that the court has jurisdiction to try the claim.
  - the court must give directions for filing and service of the defence in a *Part 7* claim (or filing of evidence in a *Part 8* claim) if a further acknowledgment of service is filed.

Note: Where a defendant disputes the court's jurisdiction he must file written evidence but he need not in a *Part 7* claim file a defence before the application hearing (or in a *Part 8* claim file any other written evidence).

CIVIL LITIGATION

Claimant's options

E Claimant's options

1	Obtain judgment after the defendant admits all or part of the claim	p 379
2	Reply to a counterclaim made by the defendant	p 370
3	Strike out a statement of case (may also be made with 6 below)	p 343
4	Transfer the claim to a different court	p 358
5	Join a third party to the claim or make an additional claim (*Part 20*)	p 374-p 375
6	Seek summary judgment	p 376
7	Seek a default judgment	p 377
8	Find out further information about a defendant's case	p 378
9	Seek a consent order	p 380
10	Seek an interim remedy of the type listed on pp 381-384	p 381

Including:
- an interim injunction
- an interim declaration
- an order for the detention, custody or preservation of property or inspection or taking of a sample or carrying out of an experiment on or with property, *and* authorising a person to enter land in a party's possession to carry out the order.
- a 'freezing injunction
- a 'search order'
- an order for disclosure of documents or inspection of property
- an order for an interim payment made under *r 25.6* (see p 383).

11	Accept (or make on a counterclaim) a *Part 36* offer/payment/other settlement	p 385-391
12	Seek a discontinuance of the action	p 379
13	Require the defendant to admit facts or part of the case	p 406
14	Require the defendant to prove the authenticity of a document	p 406

Claiming additional liability if legally funded (*PD:Costs 19*)

Note: A party who will claim an additional liability under a funding arrangement must give other parties information about this (eg: in the claim form etc.), but there is no need to specify the amount of additional liability separately nor to state how it is calculated until it is assessed.

Reply and defence to counterclaim (*r 15.8, r 16.7, PD15: 3.2A*)

➤ If a claimant files a reply to the defence, he must (*r 15.8*):
- file his reply when he files his allocation questionnaire, *and*
- serve his reply on the other parties at the same time as he files it.

➤ A statement of truth is required (see p 351).

➤ A claimant filing a reply to a defence who fails to deal with a matter raised in the defence, is taken to require that matter to be proved (*r 16.7*).

➤ A claimant who does not file a reply to the defence is not taken to admit matters raised in it (*r 16.7*).

> If the allocation questionnaire filing date is later than the defence to counterclaim filing date, the court normally orders the defence to counterclaim to be filed by the same date as the reply. If the court does not order this, the reply and defence to counterclaim may form separate documents

F Applications for court orders (Part 23)

I   Generally
II Making an application
III The applications
IV Consent orders
V   Declaratory judgments

I Generally

> - An 'application notice' is a document in which an applicant states his intention to seek a court order (*r 23.1*).
> - An applicant must file an application notice *unless*:
>   a) a rule or *PD* permit otherwise, *or*
>   b) the court dispenses with the requirement for an application notice (*r 23.3*).

- An application should be made as soon as it is apparent that it is necessary or desirable (*PD23: 2.7*).
- Whenever possible, an application should be made so that it can be considered at any other hearing (eg: case management conference, allocation or listing hearing) for which a date has already been fixed or is about to be fixed (*PD23: 2.8*).
    - If a date for a hearing has been fixed and a party does not have sufficient time to serve an application notice, he must inform the other parties and the court (in writing) as soon as possible of the nature of the application and the reason for it (*PD23: 2.10*) (unless circumstances require secrecy (*PD 23: 4.2*)).
        - The party wishing to make the application should make the application orally at the hearing.
    - At the hearing, the court may wish to review the conduct of the case and give any necessary case management directions (*PD23: 2.9*).
        - The parties must be ready to assist the court and answer questions the court asks for this purpose.

II Making an application

A Which court?

Which court?
> An application must be made to the court in which the claim was started (*r 23.2*) unless:
• a claim has not been started → ... the court in which the claim is most likely to be started (except when there is good reason otherwise)
• the claim has been transferred to another court → ... the court to which the claim has been transferred
• the parties have been notified of a fixed date for trial → ... the court where the trial is to take place
• proceedings to enforce judgement have begun → ... any court which is dealing with the enforcement of the judgement (unless a practice direction provides otherwise)

B The application notice: contents, form and procedure

	Application notice: contents, form and procedure
Contents and Form	➤ An application notice must state the order an applicant seeks and (briefly) why the applicant seeks the order (*r 23.6*). ➤ An application notice must be signed and include (*PD 23: 2.1*): ◆ the title of the claim, *and* ◆ the reference number of the claim, *and* ◆ the full name of the applicant, *and* ◆ where the applicant is not already a party, the address for service, *and* ◆ a request for a hearing or a request that the application be dealt with without a hearing. ➤ An application notice must be verified by a statement of truth (*Part 22*) if the applicant wishes to rely on matters set out in the application as evidence.

Procedure	**Steps**
	1 The applicant files the application notice at court.
	2 A copy of the application notice must be served on each respondent (unless a rule, *PD* or court order provide otherwise) (*r 23.4*).
	A copy an application notice must be served as soon as practicable after the notice is filed and (unless a rule or *PD* specify otherwise) must be served at least 3 days before the court is to deal with the application (*r 23.7(1)*).
	◆ If an application notice is served and the period of notice is shorter, the court may direct that sufficient notice has been given (*r 23.7(4)*).
	3a Hearing requested: on receipt of the application notice the court notifies the applicant of the time and the date for the hearing (*PD 23: 2.1*).
	3b Request for no-hearing: as the Master or District Judge determines, the court *either*:
	◆ if the application **is suitable** for consideration without a hearing, informs the applicant and the respondent and gives directions for the filing of evidence, *or*
	◆ if the application **is not suitable** for consideration without a hearing, notifies the applicant and the respondent of the time and date for the hearing and may give directions as to the filing of evidence (*PD 23: 2.3-2.5*).
	
	• The court may deal with the application without a hearing if *either* (*r 23.8*):
	  ▪ the parties agree to the terms of the order sought, *or*
	  ▪ the parties agree that the court dispose of the application without a hearing, *or*
	  NB: the parties should inform the court in writing and each party should confirm that all evidence and other material on which that party relies has been disclosed to the other parties to the application (*PD23: 11.1*).
	  ▪ the court does not consider that a hearing would be appropriate.
	
	➤ If the court is to serve a copy of the application notice, the applicant must file a copy of any written evidence in support when he files the notice itself (*r 23.2(7)*).
	➤ An application notice must be served with:
	◆ a copy of any written evidence in support (unless that evidence has already been filed or served on the respondent) (*r 23.7(5)*), *and*
	◆ a copy of any draft order which the applicant has attached to the application, *and*
	◆ a statement of costs at least 24 hours before any interim hearing (*PD:Costs 13.5*).
	➤ Costs of interim hearings are routinely assessed at the conclusion of the hearing by summary assessment, see p 420.

Applications totally without merit (*r 23.12, r 3.11, PD3C*)
➤ If the court dismisses an application and it considers that the application is totally without merit, the court order must record that and the court must consider whether it is appropriate to make a civil restraint order (see p 344).

CIVIL LITIGATION
Applications for court orders

C Applications made without service of an application notice

➤ A court may dispose of an application without notice only (*PD 23: 3*):
- where there is exceptional urgency, *or*
- where the overriding objective is best furthered by doing so, *or*
- by consent of all the parties, *or*
- with the court's permission, *or*
- where the date for a hearing has been fixed and there is not sufficient time to serve a notice (*PD23: 2.10*), *or*
- where a court order, rule, or *PD* permits.

➤ If the court makes an order (granting or dismissing the application) a copy of the application notice and any evidence in support must be served ...

...on any party or person against whom the order was made and against whom the order was sought ...

...*unless* the court orders otherwise (*r 23.9(2)*).

➤ An order granted with respect to an application made without notice must contain a statement of the right to have the order set aside or varied (*r 23.9(3)*).

➤ A person who was not served with a copy of an application notice may apply to have the order set aside or varied (*r 23.10(1)*).
- This application to set aside or vary must be made within 7 days after the date on which the order was served on the person who wishes to make that application for set aside/variation (*r 23.10(2)*).

Telephone hearings (*PD23: 6.1, 6.1A, 6.2-6.5*)

➤ The court may order an application (or part of an application) to be dealt with by telephone hearing only if all the parties have consented and no party is acting in person; if a court so orders it will allocate a time and give any directions necessary for the telephone hearing.

➤ No representative of a party may attend the judge in person without the other party's agreement.

➤ If a telephone application is sought, the application notice should indicate this. If it does not indicate this, a request for a telephone hearing should be made as early as possible.

➤ The following directions will apply to telephone hearings, subject to any direction to the contrary:
- The applicant's legal representative must arrange the telephone conference for the precise time fixed by the court (giving the operator the telephone numbers of all those participating and the sequence in which they are to be called). *[The telecom provider must be on an approved court list [not yet in force but will be from 2 October 2006].*
- The sequence in which the participant's are to be called is:
  a) the applicant's legal representative and (if on a different number) his counsel, *then*
  b) the legal representative (and counsel) of all the other parties, *then*
  c) the judge.
- Each speaker must remain on the line after being called by the operator (the call may be 2 or 3 minutes before the time fixed for the application).
- When the judge has been connected the applicant's legal representative introduces the parties in the usual way.
- The judge may require a party to use a handphone if the use of a speakerphone causes the judge or any party difficulty in hearing what is said.
- The telephone charges debited to the account of the party initiating the call are treated as part of the costs of the application.

CIVIL LITIGATION
Applications for court orders

III The applications

A Making an additional claim (including a counterclaim) (Part 20)

Purpose: Additional claims are made under *Part 20*. It applies to (*r 20.2*):

- a **counterclaim** by a defendant against the claimant or against the claimant and some other person, *and/or*
- an **additional claim** by a defendant against any person (whether or not already a party) for contribution or indemnity or some other remedy, *and/or*
- where an additional claim has been made against a person who is not already a party, any additional claim made by that person against any other person (whether or not already a party).

	Counterclaims		Contribution/Indemnity against a party (*r 20.6*)	Other (*r 20.7*)
	Against claimant (*r 20.4*)	Other (*r 20.5*)		
Procedure for making an additional claim	Defendant files particulars of the counterclaim. If the counterclaim is filed with the defence, court's permission is not needed. If the counterclaim is not filed with defence, the court's permission is needed	Defendant applies to court for an order that the person be added as an additional party. The application is without notice (unless the court orders otherwise). When making the order, the court will give case management directions	A defendant who has filed an acknowledgement of service or defence, files a notice containing a statement of the nature and grounds of his additional claim for contribution/indemnity and serves it on the party. The court's permission is needed unless he files and serves it with his defence or, if his claim is against a party added to the claim later, within 28 days after that party files his defence.	A defendant does not need the court's permission to make an additional claim if that claim is issued before or at the same time as he files his defence (otherwise the court's permission is needed). An additional claim is made when the court issues the appropriate claim form. Particulars of an additional claim must be contained in or served with the claim form

Application for the court's permission to issue a counterclaim or other additional claim	➤ An application must be supported by evidence stating (*PD20: 2*):
	  ◆ the stage which the action has reached (including, where possible, a timetable of the action to date; if delay is a factor in the application, an explanation should be given), *and*
	  ◆ the nature of the additional claim or details of the question/issue which needs to be decided, *and*
	  ◆ a summary of the facts on which the additional claim is based, *and*
	  ◆ the name and address of any proposed additional party.

	Counterclaims against an existing party only (*r 20.8(1)(a)*)	Contribution/Indemnity (*r 20.8(2)*)	Other (*r 20.8(1)(b)*)
Service of an additional claim (*r 20.8*)	On every other party when a copy of the defence is served	Not applicable	On the person against whom it is made within 14 days after the date on which the additional claim is issued by the court

> ➤ If the additional claim form is served on a non-party it must be accompanied by (*r 20.12(1)*):
>   ◆ a form for defending the claim, *and*
>   ◆ a form for admitting the claim, *and*
>   ◆ a form for acknowledging service, *and*
>   ◆ a copy of every statement of case which has been served in the proceedings and such other documents as the court may direct.
> ➤ A person who is not already a party to the proceedings on whom an additional claim is served becomes a party on service of the additional claim (*r 20.10(1)*).
> ➤ A copy of the additional claim form must be served on every existing party (*r 20.12(2)*).

CIVIL LITIGATION
Applications for court orders

(A continued...) Making an additional claim (including a counterclaim (Part 20)

Should an additional claim be a separate claim?	➤ When considering whether to permit an additional claim to be made, to dismiss an additional claim or to require an additional claim to be dealt with separately, the court may have regard to (r 20.9(1)-(2)): ◆ the connections between the additional claim and the claim made by the claimant against the defendant, and ◆ whether the additional claimant seeks substantially the same remedy as some other party seeks from him, and ◆ whether the additional claimant wants the court to decide any question connected with the subject matter of proceedings: i) between existing parties, but also between existing parties and a person not already a party, or ii) against an existing party in a different capacity to that in which that existing party is already a party to the proceedings.
General application of CPRs	➤ The *CPRs* generally apply to additional claims as to any other claim, *except* that (r 20.3): **All claims** ◆ the general rules applicable to time limits for serving a claim form (see p 340) do not apply (see previous page for the rules which do apply)(r 20.3(2)). ◆ the claim need not include a statement of value (which would otherwise be needed under r 16.3(5)) to commence a claim in the High Court, see p 362 (r 20.3(2)). ◆ The preliminary stage of case management, at allocation (see p 392), does not apply (r 20.3(2)). **For counterclaims** ◆ Part 14 (Admissions) applies (see pp 367-368) (r 20.3(4)). ◆ Part 12 (Default judgment) applies (see p 377) (r 20.3(3)). **Additional claims other than counterclaims** ◆ rr 14.3-14.14 (Admissions - see pp 367-368) do not apply (r 20.3(4)). ◆ Part 12 (Default judgment - see p 377) does not apply (r 20.3(3)). ➤ If the additional claim is not a counterclaim or claim for contribution/indemnity, and the party against whom the additional claim is made fails to file an acknowledgment of service or defence in respect of the additional claim then (r 20.11): a) the party against whom the additional claim is made is deemed to admit the additional claim and is bound by any judgment in the main proceedings so far as that judgment is relevant to any matter arising in the additional claim, and b) if default judgment is given against the additional claimant, the additional claimant may obtain judgment in respect of the additional claim by filing a request in the relevant practice form. NB: The court's permission is needed to enter judgment under 'b' if the additional claimant has not satisfied the default judgment against him *or* wishes to obtain judgment for any remedy other than a contribution or indemnity (r 20.11(3)). ◆ An application for the court's permission may be made without notice, unless the court directs otherwise (r 20.11(4)). ◆ A court may at any time set aside or vary a judgment under 'b'.
Case management (r 20.13, PD20: 5)	➤ Where a defence to an additional claim is filed, the court considers the conduct of the case and gives appropriate directions (r 20.13(1)). ◆ Where the defendant to an additional claim files a defence (other than to a counterclaim), the court arranges a hearing to consider case management of the additional claim. This will normally be at the same time as a case management hearing for the original claim and any other additional claims. The court arranges a hearing and gives notice of the hearing to each party likely to be affected by any order made at the hearing (PD20: 5.1-5.2). ➤ At the hearing, the court may (PD20: 5.3): ◆ treat the hearing as a summary judgment hearing. ◆ order the dismissal of the additional claim. ◆ give directions as to how a claim or issue set out in or arising from the additional claim should be dealt with. ◆ give directions as to the extent to which the additional defendant will take part in the trial of the claim and will be bound by any judgment or decision in the action. • When giving directions, the court must ensure as far as practicable the claims are managed together (r 20.13(2)).

CIVIL LITIGATION
Applications for court orders

B Summary judgment (Part 24)

Purpose: the claimant or defendant seeks judgment quickly and cheaply without the expense and delay of a trial

Grounds (r 24.2)

A **claimant** has no real prospect of succeeding on the claim or an issue

A **defendant** has no real prospect of successfully defending the claim or issue

+ There is no other compelling reason why the cause or issue should be disposed of at trial

Procedure (r 24.4)

➤ A claimant may not apply until the defendant has filed an acknowledgement of service or a defence *unless* the court gives permission or a *PD* provides otherwise (eg: the claimant seeks an order for specific performance *(PD24: 7.1(b))*.

➤ An application must *(PD24:2(3))*:

a) identify concisely any point of law or provision in a document on which the applicant relies, *and/or*

b) state that it is made because the applicant believes that on the evidence the respondent has no real prospect of succeeding on the claim or issues, or of successfully defending the claim or issue

+ The applicant knows of no other reason why the disposal of the claim or issue should await trial

- If the application relies on written evidence but does not contain that written evidence, the application should identify that evidence *(PD24: 2(4))*.
- The application should draw the respondent's attention to *r.24.5(1)* governing evidence *(PD24: 2(4))*.

➤ If a claimant applies before a defence has been filed, the defendant need not file a defence before the hearing.

➤ The parties will have at least 14 days notice of the date fixed for the hearing and the issues which it is proposed that the court will decide.

Where a claimant has not complied with a relevant pre-action protocol, an action for summary judgment will not normally be entertained before the defence has been filed or the time for doing so has expired *(PD24:2(6))*

Evidence (r 24.5)

Hearing fixed as a result of an application by a party		Hearing fixed by the court of its own volition	
Respondent (r 24.5(1))	Applicant (r 24.5(2))	Any party (r 24.5(3)(a))	Any party in reply (r 24.5(3)(b))
At least 7* days before the hearing file written evidence and serve copies on the other parties to the application ...	At least 3 days before the hearing file written evidence and serve copies on the respondent ...	At least 7* days (unless the court orders otherwise) before the hearing file written evidence and serve copies on the other parties to the application ...	At least 3 days (unless the court orders otherwise) before the hearing file written evidence and serve copies on the respondent ...

... unless evidence has already been filed or served on the appropriate party *(r 24.5(4))*

* 4 days before the hearing if an order for specific performance is sought *(PD24: 7.3)*.

Possible orders (r 24.6)

➤ The orders which the court (usually a Master or a District Judge) may make include *(PD24: 3(1), 5.1)*:

a) judgment on the claim.

b) striking out or dismissal of the claim.

c) dismissal of the application.

d) a conditional order.

- Eg: an order requiring a party to pay money into court or take a specified step *and* providing for that party's claim to be dismissed or statement of claim struck out if he does not comply *(PD 24: 5.2)*.
- Made if it appears possible but improbable that a claim/defence will succeed *(PD 24: 4)*.

➤ If the application is not dismissed or an order is not made disposing of the claim, the court will give case management directions *(PD24: 10)*.

Summary judgment is **not** available against a defendant in proceedings *(r 24.3)*:

◆ for possession of residential premises against a tenant, or mortgagor or a person holding over after the tenancy ends, *or*

◆ for an admiralty claim *in rem*.

CIVIL LITIGATION
Applications for court orders

C Default judgment (Parts 12 and 13)

Purpose:	The claimant wants to obtain judgment when the defendant (rr 12.1-12.2): a) has failed to file an acknowledgement of service, *or* b) has failed to file a defence ... *but* not for a claim under *CCA 1974*, under the *Part 8* procedure, *or* where a rule or *PD* provides that a claimant may not obtain default judgment (eg: *PD12: 1.2-1.3*) *or* for non-counterclaim additional claims (r 20.3(3)).

Grounds	➤ The claim has been properly served and (r 12.3(1)-(2)):
	a) the defendant has not filed an acknowledgment of service or a defence and the time limit has expired, *or*
	    ◆ A certificate of service on the court file is sufficient evidence that particulars of claim have been served on the defendant (PD12: 4.1)
	b) an acknowledgment of service has been filed but a defence has not been filed and the time limit has expired, *or*
	c) in a counterclaim made under *r 20.4* (see p 374) a defence has not been filed and the time limit has expired...
	... *provided that* it is not the case that (r 12.3(3)):
	    ◆ the defendant has applied for summary judgment and that application has not been disposed of, *or*
	    ◆ the defendant has applied to have the claimant's statement of claim struck out under *r 3.4* (see p 343), and that application has not been disposed of, *or*
	    ◆ the defendant has satisfied the whole claim (including costs), *or*
	    ◆ it is a money claim and the defendant has filed or served on the claimant an admission of liability to pay all the money claimed with a request for time to pay.

Procedure	➤ The claimant **files a request** on the relevant practice form if the claim is for (r 12.4(1)):
	a) a specified amount of money, *and/or*
	b) an amount of money to be decided by the court, *and/or*
	c) delivery of goods (if the claim form gives the defendant the alternative of paying their value).
	The request may specify the date by which the debt is to be paid, or the time/rate for instalments (r 12.5(1)) and interest (r 12.6(1))
	➤ The claimant **makes an application** under *Part 23* (see p 371) if the claim (r 12.4(2)):
	    ◆ includes a claim for any remedy other than those set out in a) to c) above, *or*
	    ◆ the claimant seeks a judgment for costs (which are not fixed costs - see p 419) only (r 12.9), *or*
	    ◆ is against a child, a patient, a claim in tort by one spouse/civil partner against the other (r 12.10(a)), *or*
	    ◆ is against a defendant who has not filed an acknowledgement of service *and* is a State, diplomat, immune under the *IOA 1968* or *IOA 1981*, *or* has been served out of the jurisdiction (without leave), *or* is domiciled in Scotland, Northern Ireland or a territory to which the Brussels or Lugano Conventions apply *or* is a Member State of the EU (except Denmark) (r 12.10(b)).
	NB: If the defendant is an individual, the claimant must provide the defendant's date of birth (if known) in Part C of the application notice (r 12.4(2)).

Judgment (on a request)	➤ If a claim is for a specified sum of money, the judgment is for the amount of the claim (less any payments made) and costs (r 12.5(2)): a) to be paid by the date or at the rate specified in the request, *or* b) if no date/rate are specified, immediately. ➤ If a claim is for an unspecified amount of money, judgment is for an amount to be decided by the court and costs (r 12.5(3)). ➤ If a claim is for the delivery of goods the judgment requires the defendant to deliver the goods (or if he does not) to pay the amount decided by the court and costs (r 12.5(4)). ◆ If judgment is for an amount decided by the court, it gives directions and may allocate the case (r 12.7).

Setting aside a judgment in default

Grounds	➤ The court **must** set aside judgment if (r 13.2): a) any of the conditions for obtaining that judgment were not satisfied, *or* b) the whole of the claim was satisfied before judgment was entered. ➤ The court **may** set aside judgment if (r 13.3): a) the defendant has a real prospect of successfully defending the claim, *or* b) there is some other good reason why the judgment should be set aside or varied or the defendant should be allowed to defend the claim

CIVIL LITIGATION
Applications for court orders

D Further information (Part 18)

Purpose: to clarify any matter which is in dispute in proceedings or provide additional information with regard to such a matter - even if the matter is not contained in or referred to in the statement of case

Format of request	➤ A written request specifying the clarification or information sought, stating the time by which a response must be served (the time for response must be 'reasonable' (*PD18: 1.1*)).
	➤ The request:
	   ◆ must be concise and strictly confined to matters 'reasonably necessary and proportionate' (*PD18: 1.2*), *and*
	   ◆ should take the form of a single comprehensive document, not be piecemeal (*PD18: 1.3*), *and*
	   ◆ should be a separate document *unless* it is brief *and* the reply is likely to be brief, in which case it may in the form of a letter (*PD 18:1.4*), *and*
	   ◆ should (*PD 18:1.6(a)*):
	      ● be headed with name of the court, the title and number of the claim, *and*
	      ● in the heading state it is a request under *Part 18*, identify both parties, use separate numbered paragraphs for each request, *and*
	      ● identify each document and the paragraph/words to which a request relates.
	➤ If convenient, numbered paragraphs should appear on the left of the page so that a response may appear on the right (if the request is in this form any extra copy should be served for use by the respondent) (*PD18: 1.6(2)*).
	
	Service of the Request (*PD 18: 1.7*)
	➤ Subject to the general court provisions as to use of email (see pp 346-347), a Request should be served by email if reasonably practicable.

Format of reply	➤ In writing, dated, signed by the respondent or his legal representative (*PD18: 2.1*).
	➤ A point by point reply to the request.
	➤ For each point, repeat the request verbatim and provide a reply (unless the format suggested in *PD18: 1.6(2)* is used (see above)).
	➤ A response must be verified by a statement of truth (*PD18: 3*) (see p 351).
	➤ The person making a reply must file it at court and serve it on the other parties.
	
	➤ If a party objects to complying with a request or is unable to do so within the time stated in that request, that party must (*PD18: 4*):
	   ◆ promptly inform the party making the request, *and*
	   ◆ give reasons (eg: disproportionate expense), *and*
	   ◆ give a date by which he expects to be able to comply.

Court application	➤ An application under *Part 23* (see p 371), with (*PD18: 5*):
	   ◆ the text of the order sought, *and*
	   ◆ a description of the response, if any ... *plus* ...
	   ◆ costs if sought (*PD18: 5.8*).
	➤ If a party has not responded to a request served on him and at least 14 days have passed since the request was served and the time stated in it for a response has expired (*PD18: 5.5*):
	   ◆ the applicant need not serve a copy of the application notice on the party to whom the request was made, *and*
	   ◆ the court may deal with the application without a hearing ... *otherwise* ...
	      ... the application notice and any order made must be served on all other parties to the claim (*PD18: 5.6-5.7*).

CIVIL LITIGATION

Applications for court orders

E   Judgment on admissions

Purpose: to reduce/avoid the expense of a trial by resolving agreed issues beforehand

Time	➤ If a claim form states that particulars of claim will follow, 14 days after the service of those particulars *otherwise* 14 days after service of the claim form (*r 14.2*) (see p 340).

Procedure	➤ A party gives written notice that it admits the whole or part of another party's case (*r 14.1(1)-(2)*).
	 ➤ The claimant may enter judgment (*r 14.1(4)*) (see p 367-368).
	
	 If the claim relates to a specified amount of money, or an unspecified amount of money (*rr 14.4-14.7*):
	 Steps
	 1. The defendant files the relevant *Practice Form* with the court.
	 2. The court serves a notice on the claimant, requiring him to return the notice.
	 3. Within 14 days the claimant must file the notice and serve a copy on the defendant (otherwise proceedings are stayed until the notice is filed).
	
	 ➤ A defendant may request time to pay (*rr 14.9-14.13, PD 14: 5-6*).
	 ◆ A claimant will not accept a defendant's proposals for payment must file a notice in set form.
	 ◆ The court determines the time and rate of payment.
	 • If the amount outstanding is less than £50,000 a court officer may make this determination (there is no hearing).
	 • A judge may make this determination at a hearing. If a judge holds a hearing:
	 ▪ the court gives each party at least 7 days' notice of the hearing, *and*
	 ▪ where the claim was not started at the defendant's home court or subsequently transferred there, it will transferred there if:
	   a) the claim is for a specified amount of money, *and*
	   b) the defendant is an individual, *and*
	   c) the claim was not started in a specialist list.
	 • If a court officer makes the determination, or a judge does so without a hearing, either party may apply for a redetermination within 14 days of service of the determination on the applicant.

F   Discontinuance (Part 38)

Purpose: Discontinuance halts the action.

The defendant is entitled to costs (other than in respect of claims allocated to the small claims track) to the date notice of discontinuance is served on him for the part of the proceedings that are discontinued (*r 38.6*)

Claimant's right to discontinue	➤ The claimant may discontinue without seeking leave. But if the court has granted an interim injunction or any party has given an undertaking to the court the claimant must obtain the court's permission (*r 38.2(2)(a)*). ➤ If the claimant has received an interim payment *either* the defendant must consent in writing *or* the court gives permission (*r 38.2(2)(b)*). ➤ If there is more than one claimant, *either* every other claimant must consent in writing *or* the court gives permission (*r 38.2(2)(c)*).
Claimant	a) File a notice of discontinuance (*r 38.3(1)(a)*): ◆ stating that a copy has been served on every other party (*r 38.3(2)*). ◆ (if the consent of another party is needed), attaching a copy of that consent (*r 38.3(3)*). ◆ (if there is more than 1 defendant), stating against which defendant the claim is discontinued (*r 38.3(4)*). b) Serve a copy of the notice on every party to the proceedings (*r 38.3(1)(b)*).
Defendant	➤ May apply to have a notice of discontinuance set aside (*r 38.4(1)*). ➤ An application may not be made more than 28 days after the date on which the notice was served on that defendant (*r 38.4(2)*).

	1) The permission of the court is need for the claimant to subsequently make a claim against the same defendant if (*r 38.7*):
	   a) the claimant discontinued the claim after the defendant filed a defence, *and*
	   b) the new claim arises out of facts which are the same, or substantially the same, as those out of which the original claim arose.
	 2) If proceedings are only partly discontinued *and* the claimant fails to pay costs under *r 38.6* within 21 days of the date on which the parties agreed costs *or* the court ordered the costs to be paid, the court may stay the rest of the proceedings until the costs are paid (*r 38.8*).

IV Consent orders

Consent orders (and judgments) (r 40.6)

Purpose: To obtain a court order without a hearing, thus saving time and costs.

➤ A consent order (or judgment) is drawn up in the terms agreed, expressed as being 'By Consent', and signed by the legal representative acting for each of the parties to whom the order relates, or by a litigant in person (r 40.6(7)).

➤ A consent order (or judgment) may be drawn up and sealed by a court officer if (r 40.6(2)):

a) none of the parties is a litigant in person, *and*

b) the court's approval is not required by the *CPR*, a *PD* or any enactment, *and*

c) either (r 40.6(3)):

   i) the order (or judgment) is for:
      - payment of an amount of money (including damages or the value of goods to be decided by the court).
      - delivery up of goods with or without the option of paying the value of the goods or the agreed value.

   ii) the order is for:
      - dismissal of any proceedings (wholly or in part).
      - stay of proceedings (the terms agreed may be recorded in a schedule to the order, or elsewhere).
      - stay of enforcement (unconditionally, or on condition that money due is paid by instalments specified in the consent order).
      - setting aside of a default judgment (*Part 13*) which has not been satisfied.
      - payment out of money which has been paid into court.
      - discharge from liability of any party.
      - payment, assessment or waiver of costs, or such other provision for costs as may be agreed.

   NB: see p 423 for the drawing up and filing of judgments and orders - those rules apply to judgments and orders entered and sealed by a court officer (r 40.6(4)).

➤ If a court officer may not draw up and seal a consent order (or judgment), any party may apply for an order (or judgment) in the terms agreed (r 40.6(5)).

   ◆ The court may deal with the application without a hearing (r 40.6(6)).

Form of consent order (PD40B: 3.4)

➤ A consent judgment or order must:
   ◆ be drawn up in the terms agreed, *and*
   ◆ bear on it the words 'By Consent', *and*
   ◆ be signed by:
      - solicitors or counsel acting for each of the parties to the order, *or*
      - where a party is a litigant in person, the litigant.

A special type of consent order (known as a Tomlin order)

➤ Purpose: To stay the action by consent of both parties on terms set out in a schedule to a court order.

➤ Procedure: Both parties submit a consent order. The agreement terms are set out in a schedule to the order.

   ◆ If enforcement is necessary, an application can be made to court for specific performance or an injunction.

➤ Any payment to be made under an order is *not* treated as being paid under a judgment, so statutory interest is not available as it is on judgments under *JA 1838 s 17*.

V Declaratory judgments

➤ The court may make binding declarations whether or not any other remedy is claimed (r 40.20).

G Interim remedies (*Parts 25 and 41*)

I *Part 25* interim remedies generally
II Making an application for a *Part 25* interim remedy
III An application for further damages under *Part 41*

I *Part 25* interim remedies generally

➤ An order may be made at any time (including before proceedings are started and after judgment) (*r 25.2(1)*).

  ◆ Before a claim is made, a court will only grant an interim remedy if the matter is urgent *or* it is desirable to do so in the interests of justice (*r 25.2(2)(b)*).

➤ If a court grants an interim remedy before a claim commences, it should give directions that a claim be commenced (unless it is an order for disclosure or inspection before start of a claim) (*r 25.2(3)-(4)*).

➤ A defendant may not apply for an interim order before he has filed an acknowledgment of service or a defence (*r 25.2(2)(c)*), unless he has the court's permission.

Types of *Part 25* interim remedies (*r 25.1*)

a) an interim injunction (prohibiting a person from doing, or requiring a person to do, something).
b) an interim declaration.
c) an order for the:
   i) detention, custody or preservation of property, *and/or*
   ii) inspection of property, *and/or*
   iii) taking of a sample of property, *and/or*
   iv) carrying out of an experiment on or with property, *and/or*
   v) sale of property which is perishable or which it is desirable to sell quickly, *and/or*
   vi) payment of income from property until the claim is decided, *and*
d) an order authorising a person to enter land to carry out an order under (c)(i) to (vi) above.
e) an order to deliver up goods (under *Torts (Interference with Goods) Act 1977*).
f) an order (known as a 'freezing injunction'), restraining a party from:
g) removing from the jurisdiction assets located here, *or*
h) dealing with any assets (irrespective of whether the assets are located in the jurisdiction ...
i) directing a party to provide information about assets which are, or may be, the subject of an injunction under (f) above.
j) an order requiring a party to admit another party to premises to preserve evidence etc. made under *CPA 1997 s 7* (known as a 'search order').
i) an order for disclosure of documents or inspection of property before a claim has been made under *SCA 1981 s 33* or *CCA 1984 s 52*.
j) an order for disclosure of documents or inspection of property against a non-party made under *SCA 1981 s 34* or *CCA 1984 s 53*.
k) an order for an interim payment made under *r 25.6* (see p 383).
l) an order for a specified fund to be paid into court or secured, in cases of dispute over rights to it.
m) an order permitting a party seeking to recover personal property, to pay money into court pending the outcome of proceedings and directing that, if he does, the property shall be given to him.
n) an order directing a party to prepare and file accounts relating to a dispute.
o) an order directing any account to be taken or inquiry to be made by the court.
p) an order under *Art 9* of Directive 2004/48 on the enforcement of intellectual property rights (ie: an order in intellectual property proceedings making the continuation of an alleged infringement subject to the lodging of guarantees).

II Making an application for a *Part 25* interim remedy

➤ A court may grant an interim remedy on an application made without notice, if it appears that there are good reasons for not giving notice (*r 25.3(1)*).

➤ An application must be supported by evidence, unless the court orders otherwise (*r 25.3(2)*).

- If notice has not been given, evidence in support of the application must state reasons why notice has not been given.

➤ The general rules relating to applications in *Part 23* apply (see pp 371-373).

A Injunctions

1 Jurisdiction

➤ The judge with jurisdiction to conduct the trial has the power to grant an injunction (*PD25: 1.3*).

- However, in the High Court, Masters and District Judges may grant injunctions (*PD25: 1.2*):

  a) by consent (a Master or District Judge may, with consent, vary or discharge an order granted by any judge (*PD25: 1.4*)), *and*

  b) in connection with a charging order and the appointment of a receiver, *and*

  c) in aid of execution of judgments.

➤ A High Court judge, or any other judge duly authorised, may grant 'search orders' and 'freezing injunctions' (*PD25: 1.1*).

2 Making an application

➤ The application notice must state the order sought *and* the date, time and place of hearing (*PD25: 2.1*).

- For court service, the applicant must file sufficient copies for the court and each respondent (*PD25: 2.3*).

- A draft order should be filed, plus a disk containing the draft in a format specified in the *PD* (*PD25: 2.4*).

➤ The application notice and evidence must be served as soon as practicable after issue (*PD25: 2.2*) and in any event not later than 3 days before the hearing.

3 Evidence

➤ Evidence must generally be set out (*PD 25: 3.2*):

  a) in a witness statement, *or*

  b) a statement of case (if it is verified by a statement of truth), *or*

  c) the application itself (if it is verified by a statement of truth).

➤ However, an application for a 'freezing injunction'/'search order' must be supported by affidavit.

➤ In either case, all material facts of which the court should be aware should be set out (including, if appropriate, why notice is not given) (*PD25: 3.3-3.4*).

4 Urgent applications without notice

➤ These are usually dealt with at a hearing, but in cases of 'extreme urgency' may (where the applicant is acting by counsel or solicitors) be by telephone (*PD25: 4*).

CIVIL LITIGATION
Interim remedies

B Interim payments

Note: **Purpose:** The claimant wants an advance from the defendant against a debt or damages.
a) Before applying to court, it is wise to negotiate with an insurance company for a voluntary payment.
b) If resolving the case takes longer than expected, the claimant can make additional applications.

Conditions	➤ The court is satisfied that *either* (r 25.7(1)):
	a) the defendant has admitted liability to pay damages or a sum of money to the claimant, *or*
	b) the claimant has obtained judgment for damages or a sum of money (not costs) to be assessed, *or*
	c) the claimant would obtain judgment for a substantial amount of money (not costs) at trial (whether or not the defendant is the only defendant or one of a number of defendants to the claim), *or*
	d) the claimant is seeking an order for possession of land *and* the court is satisfied that, if the case went to trial, the defendant would be liable (even if the claim for possession fails) to pay the claimant a sum for the use and occupation of the land while the claim is pending, *or*
	e) in a claim with 2 or more defendants and the order is sought against any one or more, that:
	    ◆ if the claim went to trial, the claimant would obtain judgment for a substantial amount of money (not costs) against at least one defendant (but the court cannot determine which), *and*
	    ◆ all the defendants are either:
	        • a defendant that is insured in respect of the claim, *or*
	        • a defendant whose liability will be met by an insurer under *RTA 1988 s 151* or an insurer acting under the MIB Agreement (or the MIB where it is acting itself), *or*
	        • a defendant that is a public body.

Amount	➤ A 'reasonable proportion of the damages' which 'the court considers just' taking account of (r 25.7(4)-(5)): a) the sum likely to be recovered by the claimant, *and* b) any contributory negligence, *and* c) any counterclaim or set-off on which the defendant is likely to rely.
Legal help	➤ Interim payments are paid directly to the claimant ie: are *not* subject to a statutory charge (see pp 16-18)
Time	➤ The time for acknowledging service has expired (ie: 14 days after service of claim) (r 25.6(1))
Applicant	➤ A copy of the application notice must be served at least 14 days before a hearing and be supported by evidence (r 25.6(3)) which deals with (PD25 (Interim Payments): 2.1): a) the sum of money sought by way of interim payment, *and* b) the items or matters in respect of which interim payment is sought, *and* c) the sum of money for which final judgment is likely to be given, *and* d) the reasons for believing the conditions set out in r 25.7 (see above) are satisfied, *and if appropriate* e) any other relevant matters (eg: why the plaintiff needs the money), *and* f) states, in a personal injury action, details of special damages and past and future loss, *and* g) in a claim under the *FAA 1976*, details of the persons on whose behalf the claim is made. ➤ A medical report or statement of special damages should be exhibited (PD25 (Interim Payments): 2.2).

Respondent/ Applicant	➤ The respondent may serve written evidence in reply.
	    ◆ The respondent must file the evidence and serve copies on every other party to the application at least 7 days before the hearing (r 25.6(4)).
	    ◆ If the order is not by consent and the defendant is liable to pay recoverable benefits to the Secretary of State under the *SS(RB)A 1997*, the defendant should obtain a certificate of recoverable benefits (and this certificate should be filed at the hearing of the application) (PD25 (Interim Payments): 4).
	➤ An applicant wishing to rely on written evidence in reply must file written evidence and serve a copy on the respondent at least 3 days before the hearing (r 25.6(5)).

Consequences	1) The secrecy rule applies after this order - ie: the trial judge is not told about it until liability and quantum are resolved, unless the defendant agrees (r 25.9). 2) A preamble to a final judgment should set out the amounts and dates of any interim payment(s). Any final judgment is reduced by the amount of any interim payment(s) (PD25 (Interim Payments): 5). 3) The court may order the claimant to repay the defendant (with interest) any surplus if the final award exceeds the interim payment (r 25.8).

CIVIL LITIGATION
Interim remedies

C Security for costs (rr 25.12 - 25.15)	
	Purpose: to order the claimant (or another person) to give security (in any form the court may direct) for the costs incurred by the defendant in the action or in other proceedings
Procedure	Application supported by written evidence.
Grounds	◆ The court is satisfied that, having regard to all the circumstances of the case, it is just to make an order, *and* ◆ a) The claimant is resident outside the jurisdiction but not resident in a Brussels contracting state (ie: under the Brussels Convention, a Lugano contracting state (ie: under the Lugano Convention) or a state under *EC Regulation 44/2001* on jurisdiction, *or* b) the claimant is a company or other body and there is reason to believe that it will be unable to pay the defendant's costs if ordered to do so, *or* c) the claimant has changed his address since the claim was commenced with a view to evading the consequences of litigation, *or* d) the claimant failed to give his address in the claim form, or gave an incorrect address in that form, *or* e) the claimant is acting as a nominal claimant and there is reason to believe that he will be unable to pay the defendant's costs if ordered to do so, *or* f) the claimant has taken steps in relation to his assets that would make it difficult to enforce an order for costs against him.
	An LSC funded claimant Where a legally funded client who has Cost Protection (see p 422) is required to give security for costs, the amount of that security shall not exceed the amount (if any) which is a reasonable one having regard for all the circumstance's (including the client's financial resources and his conduct). (CLS(C)R 2000 r 6)

III An application for further damages under *Part 41*

Provisional damages in personal injury claims (r 41.1-41.3)	
Purpose:	In a personal injury claim, a claimant may want provisional damages assuming his health will not deteriorate
Grounds	a) The particulars of claim include a claim for provisional damages, *and* b) the court is satisfied that the injured person will not develop disease or suffer deterioration *and* the injured person is entitled to apply for further damages at a future date if he develops the disease or suffers the deterioration.
Order (r 41.2)	◆ The order for provisional damages must specify (each) disease or (each) type of deterioration for which an application may be made at a future date and the period within which each application may be made (a claimant may subsequently make more than 1 application to extend this time).
Claimant applying for further damages (r 41.3)	◆ Only 1 more application is allowed for each disease/deterioration set out in the special damages award. ◆ The claimant must give at least 28 days notice to the defendant of his intent to apply for further damages. • If the claimant knows that the defendant is insured and the identity of the insurers, the claimant must also give 28 days written notice to the insurers. ◆ Within 21 days after the end of the 28 day period, the claimant must apply for directions.

H Offers to settle/payments into court (*Parts 36-37*)

I   General caveat as to *Part 36* consequences
II Form and content of a *Part 36* offer/payment notice
III Making a *Part 36* offer/payment
IV Accepting a *Part 36* offer/payment
V   Consequences

> **Calderbank offer: costs control**
>
> ➤ This is used where a payment into court is not suitable to resolve a claim (*Calderbank v Calderbank* [1975] All ER 333).
>
> ➤ The defendant makes a written offer 'without prejudice save as to costs'.
>
> ◆ If the offer is not accepted, the offer letter remains secret from the trial judge until liability and quantum are resolved.
>
> ◆ If the damages offered in the letter are not exceeded by the judgment, then the judge may ask the claimant to pay both sides' costs from the date of the offer.

I General caveat as to *Part 36* consequences

➤ Nothing in *Part 36* prevents a party making an offer to settle in any way he chooses (*r 36.1(2)*).

◆ An offer not made in accordance with *Part 36,* (eg: a Calderank offer) only has the consequences set out in Section V below if the court so orders.

➤ Offers to settle and payments made into court in accordance with *Part 36* have the consequences set out in Section V below.

➤ While a claim is on the small claims track, an offer to settle or a payment into court in accordance with *Part 36* do not have the consequences set out in Section V below unless the court so orders (*r 36.2(5)*).

II Form and content of a *Part 36* offer/payment notice

➤ A defendant's offer to settle a money claim will only have the consequences set out in *Part 36* if it made by way of a *Part 36* payment (*r 36.3(1)*).

◆ If a payment-out of court to a claimant following a *Part 36* offer or a *Part 36* payment would be a compensation payment within *SS(RB)A 1997*, a defendant to a money claim may make an offer which shall have the consequences set out in Section V below **even if that defendant does not make a *Part 36* payment** if:

a) at the time the offer is made the offeror has applied for, but not received, a certificate of recoverable benefits, *and*

b) the offeror makes a *Part 36* payment not more than 7 days after the offeror receives the certificate (*r 36.23(2)*).

➤ If a claim includes a money claim and a non-money claim, and a defendant wants to settle the whole claim (with *Part 36* consequences) but to pay money for the money part of the claim and make a non-money offer for the non-money part of the claim, that defendant must (*r 36.4*):

a) make a *Part 36* payment in respect of the money claim, *and*

b) make a *Part 36* offer in relation to the non-money claim.

CIVIL LITIGATION
Offers to settle/payments into court

A *Part 36* Offer (*r 36.5*)	A *Part 36* Payment notice (*r 36.6*)
➤ **May:** ♦ relate to the whole claim, or any part of the claim, or any issue which arises out of the claim (*r 36.5(2)*). ♦ be made by reference to an interim payment (*r 36.5(5)*). ♦ if made by a defendant, be limited to liability up to a specified proportion (*r 36.5(4)*). ➤ **Must** be in writing (*r 36.5(1)*) and give the additional information set out below, *and* ♦ **if made not less than 21 days before trial**, be expressed to remain open for 21 days from the date on which it is made and provide that it may only be accepted after 21 days if the parties agree liability for costs or the court gives permission (*r 36.5(6)*) ♦ **if made less than 21 days before trial**, state that acceptance requires agreement by the parties as to costs or the court's permission (*r 36.5(7)*)	➤ **Must** give the additional information set out below, *and* ♦ state the amount of the payment (*r 36.6(2)(a)*). ♦ if the claim includes a claim for provisional damages, the notice must state whether the defendant is offering to agree to the making of an award for provisional damages. If the defendant offers to accept such an award, the notice must state (*r 36.7(3)(a)-(c)*): a) that the defendant pays the sum on the assumption that the injured person will not develop disease or suffer disease or suffer deterioration specified in the notice, *and* b) the offer is subject to the condition that the claimant must make any claim for further damages within a limited period (the period must be states). ♦ if the defendant wishes to settle a claim which includes both a claim for money and a non-money claim (*r 36.4(3)*): a) identify the document containing the terms of the *Part 36* offer, *and* b) state that notice of acceptance of the payment will be treated as acceptance also of the *Part 36* offer. ♦ if money is recoverable under *SS(RB)A 1997* as a compensation payment state (*r 36.23*): a) the amount of gross compensation, *and* b) the name and amount of any benefit by which the gross amount is reduced in accordance with *SS(RB)A 1997 s 8, Sch 2*, *and* c) that the sum paid in is the net amount after benefit deduction. **A Part 36 Payment must be accompanied by a Part 36 Payment notice**

Additional information for inclusion in an offer or payment notice

➤ An offer and a payment notice must both:
♦ state whether the offer/payment relates to the whole of the claim, or to part of it, or to an issue which arises in the claim (and which part or issue) (*rr 36.5(3)(a)), 36.6(2)(b)*).
♦ state whether the offer/payment takes into account any counterclaim (*rr 36.5(3)(b)), 36.6(2)(c)*).
♦ if the offer/payment is expressed not to include interest, state whether interest is offered/included and if so, the amount offered/included, the rate(s) offered/included and the period(s) for which it is offered/included (*rr 36.5(3)(c), 36.6(2)(e), 36.22(2)*).
• Unless an offer/payment notice indicates otherwise the offer/payment is treated as including interest until the last date on which it could be accepted without needing the court's permission (*r 36.22(1)-(2)*).

Part 36 and personal injury claims which include claims for future pecuniary loss (*r 36.2A*)

➤ If a claim for damages for personal injury is (or includes) a claim for future pecuniary loss, a Part 36 offer (*r 36.2A(4)-(5)*):
♦ **may** contain an offer to pay (or an offer to accept):
• the whole or part of the damages for future pecuniary loss in the form of:
■ either a lump sum or periodical payments, *or*
■ both a lump sum and periodical payments, *or*
• the whole or part of any other damages in the form of a lump sum,
♦ **must** state the amount of any offer to pay the whole or part of any damages in the form of a lump sum,
♦ **may** state what part of the offer relates to damages for future pecuniary loss to be accepted in lump sum form,
♦ **may** state, where part of the offer relates to other damages to be accepted in the form of a lump sum, what amounts are attributable to those other damages,
♦ **must** state what part of the offer relates to damages for future pecuniary loss to be paid or accepted in the form of periodical payments and must specify:
• the amount and duration of the periodical payments, *and*
• the amount of any payments for substantial capital purchases and when they are to be made, *and*
• that each amount is to vary by reference to the retail prices index (or to some other named index, or that it is not to vary by reference to any index),
♦ **must** state either that any damages which take the form of periodical payments will be funded in a way which ensures that the continuity of payment is reasonably secure in accordance with *DA 1996 s 2(4)* or how such damages are to be paid and how the continuity of their payment is to be secured.
➤ If the Part 36 offer offers to pay damages as both a lump sum and periodical payments, the claimant may only give notice of acceptance of the offer as a whole (*r 36.2A(7)*).

CIVIL LITIGATION
Offers to settle/payments into court

III Making a *Part 36* offer/payment

1 Generally

➤ A *Part 36* offer or a *Part 36* payment may be made at any time after proceedings have started (*r 36.2(4)*); a *Part 36* payment may not be until proceedings have started (*r 36.3(2)*).

  ◆ Serve the Part 36 payment notice on the offeree. File at the court: a copy of the payment notice and a certificate of service confirming service on the offeree. Send to the Court Funds Office: the payment, usually a cheque made payable to the Accountant General of the Supreme Court, a sealed copy of the claim form and Court Funds Office *Form 100 (PD 36:4.1)*.

➤ A defendant may choose to treat the whole or part of the sum paid into court as a *Part 36* payment if *either* (*r 37.2(1)-(2)*):

  a) the court makes an order subject to conditions (including that a sum of money be paid into court) and specifies the consequence of failure to comply with the order or condition (*r 3.1(3)* see p 341 et seq.), *or*

  b) the court orders a party to pay a sum into court as that party has failed without good reason to comply with a rule, PD or pre-action protocol (*r 3.1(5)*, see p 341 et seq.), *then ...*

    ◆ If a defendant chooses to treat it so, he must file a *Part 36* payment notice (*r 37.2(3)*).

➤ The offeror must serve the *Part 36* payment notice on the offeree and file a certificate of service of the notice (*r 36.6(3)*).

➤ A party making a payment into court under a court order must serve notice of the payment on every other party and file a certificate of service of the notice (*r 37.1(1)*).

2 Timing an offer/payment

➤ A *Part 36* offer is made when received by the offeree (*r 36.8(1)*).

  ◆ An improvement of a *Part 36* offer is effective when received by the offeree (*r 36.8(3)*).

  ◆ If a *Part 36* offer is withdrawn it will not have the consequences which a *Part 36* offer otherwise has (*r 36.5(8)*).

➤ A *Part 36* payment is made when written notice of the payment into court is served on the offeree (*r 36.8(2)*).

  ◆ An increase in a *Part 36* payment is effective when notice of the increase is served on the offeree (*r 36.8(4)*).

  ◆ A Part 36 payment may only be withdrawn or reduced with the court's permission (*r 36.6(5)*).

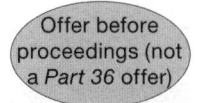

➤ An offer to settle made before the commencement of proceedings (and which is therefore **not** a *Part 36* offer) is made when received by the offeree (*r 36.10(5)*) (see further Section V below).

3 Clarifying an offer/payment

➤ Within 7 days of a *Part 36* offer or a *Part 36* payment being made, the offeree may ask for clarification (*r 36.9(1)*).

  ◆ An offeror has 7 days from receipt of a request for clarification to provide that clarification (*r 36.9(2)*).

    • If clarification is not provided within this time then (assuming the trial has not started) the offeree may apply for an order that the offeror provide the requested clarification (*r 36.9(2)*).

IV   Accepting a Part 36 offer/Part 36 payment

A   Generally

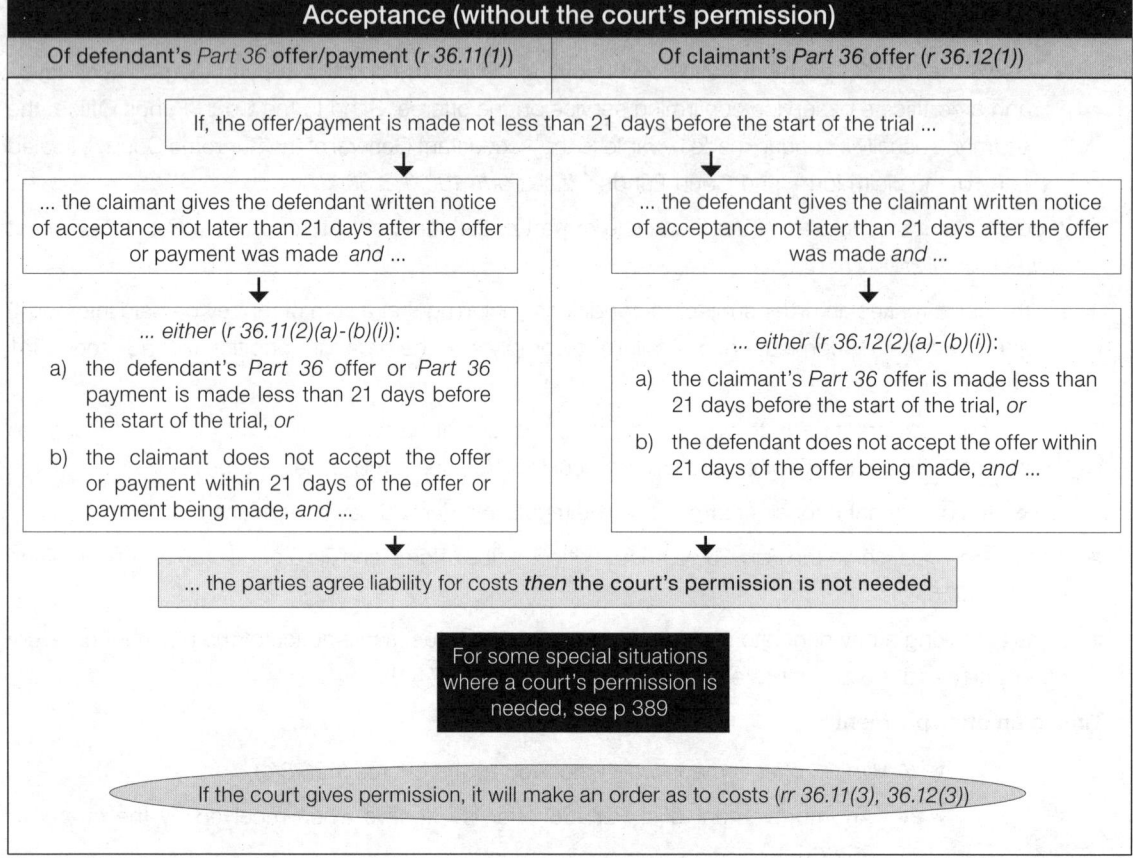

➤ **Time of accepting an offer/payment:** a *Part 36* offer or a *Part 36* payment is accepted when notice of acceptance is received by the offeror (*r 36.8(5)*).

- Where an offer is made to settle the whole of a claim which comprises a money claim and a non-money claim, acceptance of the *Part 36* payment is treated as acceptance of the *Part 36* offer relating to the non-money claim (*r 36.4(4)*).

- If the claim includes a claim for provisional damages a claimant must, within 7 days of accepting a *Part 36* payment, apply to the court for an order for an award of provisional damages under *Part 41* r 41.2 (*r 36.7(5)*).

  • Money paid into court may not be paid out until this *Part 41* application is disposed of (*r 36.7(6)*).

Applications relating to funds in court (*PD37: 6.1, 6.2*)

➤ Subject to the bullet point below, any application relating to money or securities which have been paid into court (except an application for payment out of the money or securities) must be made by an application without notice (but the court may direct notice to be served on any person).

➤ Where money paid into court is accepted by or on behalf of a child or patient, *r 21.11(1)(b)* provides that the money must be dealt with in accordance with court directions and not otherwise.

B Special situations

1   **Claim made by or on behalf of/against a child or patient** (*r 36.18*)

➤ Permission of the court is required to accept a *Part 36* offer or a *Part 36* payment.

➤ A court order is required for the payment out of a sum in court.

- If the court gives a claimant permission after a trial has started, the order deals with the whole costs of proceedings.

2   ***Part 36*** **offer or** ***Part 36*** **payment made by some, but not all, defendants** (*r 36.17*)

➤ A claimant must apply to court for:

- an order permitting a payment out in respect of any sum held in court, *and*
- such order as to costs as the court considers appropriate, *unless either:*

    a) **defendants are sued jointly or in the alternative,** in which case the claimant need not seek the permission of the court (ie: *r 36.11(1)*, see top left of the box on p 388), where:

    - the claimant discontinues against those defendants who have not made the offer/payment, *and*
    - those defendants give written consent to the acceptance of the offer/payment, *or*

    b) **a claimant alleges that the defendants have a several liability,** in which case the claimant may accept the offer/payment in accordance with (*r 36.11(1)*) (see top left of the box on p 388) and continue his claim against the other defendants if he is entitled to do so.

3   **Offer to settle made before proceedings commence** (*r 36.10(4)*)

➤ An offeree needs permission of the court to accept such an offer (or an associated payment) once proceedings have begun (*r 36.17*).

V Consequences

A Offer to settle made before proceedings commence

➤ When making any order as to costs the court will consider any offer made before proceedings, if that offer (*r 36.10(2)-(3)*):

a) is expressed to be open for at least 21 days after the date on which it is made, *and*

b) if made by the defendant in the proceedings, includes an offer to pay the costs of the offeree up to the date 21 days after the date it was made, *and*

c) if the offeror is a defendant to a money claim:

   i) the offeror makes a *Part 36* payment within 14 days of service of the claim form, *and*

   ii) the amount of that *Part 36* payment is not less than the amount offered before proceedings began.

B Prior to judgment

Costs

1. **Permission of the court not needed to accept *Part 36* offer or *Part 36* payment - costs**
   - ➤ **Defendant accepts claimant's offer:** claimant entitled to costs up to the date on which the defendant serves notice of acceptance (*r 36.14*).
   - ➤ **Claimant accepts defendant's offer or payment:** claimant entitled to costs up to the date of serving notice of acceptance (unless the court orders otherwise) (*r 36.13(1)*).
     - ◆ If a *Part 36* offer or *Part 36* payment relates to only part of a claim and when the claimant serves notice of acceptance the claimant abandons the remainder of the claim, the claimant is entitled to costs up to the date of serving the notice of acceptance (unless the court orders otherwise) (*r 36.13(2)*).
     - ◆ If the *Part 36* offer or *Part 36* payment states that a defendant's counterclaim has been taken into account in the offer/payment, the claimant's costs include any costs attributable to the counterclaim (*r 36.13(3)*).
     - ◆ Costs under *r.36.13* are payable on a standard basis (see p 417), if not agreed (*r 36.13(4)*).

2. **Permission of the court needed to accept *Part 36* offer or *Part 36* payment - costs**
   - ➤ Costs are as the court orders.

3. **Effect of acceptance**
   - ➤ The claim is stayed (*r 36.15(1)*).
     - ◆ If the court's approval is needed the stay does not take effect until approval is given (*r 36.15(4)*). If approval is not needed the stay takes effect on acceptance.
   - ➤ If the acceptance of a *Part 36* offer relates to **the whole claim** the stay is upon the terms of the offer and either party may apply to enforce those terms (*r 36.15(2)*).
   - ➤ If a *Part 36* offer or a *Part 36* payment relate to **part of the claim,** the claim is stayed as to that part and the court decides costs (unless the parties have done so) (*r 36.15(3)*).
   - ➤ Where a *Part 36* offer has been made and a party alleges that another party has not offered the terms and the party making the allegation may claim a remedy for breach of contract by apply to court without the need to start new proceedings (unless the court orders otherwise) (*r 36.15(6)*).

   > ➤ Where a *Part 36* payment is accepted, the claimant obtains payment by making a request for payment in the practice form (*r 36.16*).
   >   - ◆ If a payment to a claimant is a compensation payment (as defined in *SS(RB)A 1997 s 1*), the court may treat the money paid into court as being reduced by any sum equivalent to any recoverable benefits paid to the claimant since the date of the payment into court and may direct payment out accordingly (*r 36.23(5)*).

C At trial

1. **The judge**
    - ➤ The judge is generally not told that a *Part 36* payment has been made until all questions of liability and the amount of money to be awarded have been decided (*r 36.19(2)*).
        - ◆ Circumstances where the judge may be told include where (*r 36.19(3)*):
            - the proceedings have been stayed following the acceptance of a *Part 36* offer/payment.
            - liability has been determined (before any assessment of the money claimed) and the fact that a *Part 36* payment has (or has not) been made may be relevant to costs in respect of the liability issue.

2. **Claimant does not do better than a *Part 36* offer (ie: judgment is not more advantageous than the terms of the offer) or a *Part 36* payment**
    - ➤ Claimant pays the defendant's costs incurred after the latest date when the offer/payment could have been accepted without needing the court's permission (unless the court considers this unjust) (*r 36.20(2)*).
        - ◆ Where a payment to a claimant is a compensation payment (as defined in *SS(RB)A 1997 s 1*), that claimant fails to better a *Part 36* payment if he fails to obtain judgment for more than the gross sum specified in the payment notice (*r 36.23(4)*).

3. **Claimant does better than a *Part 36* offer (ie: judgment is more advantageous than the terms of the offer)**
    - ➤ The court may (unless it considers it unjust to do so (*r 36.21(4)*)) award the claimant:
        a) **interest** for some or all of the period starting with the latest date on which the defendant could have accepted the offer without needing the court's permission (*r 36.21(2)*).
            - Interest may not exceed a rate 10% above the base rate set by the Bank of England which is used as the basis for other banks' lending rates.
            - The court may not award interest on interest.
        b) **costs on an indemnity basis** (see p 417) from the latest date when the defendant could have accepted the offer without needing the court's permission and interest on those costs not exceeding 10% above the base rate set by the Bank of England as the basis for other banks' lending rates (*r 36.21(3)*).
    - ➤ In considering whether it would be unjust to make the orders referred to in a) and b) above, the court takes into account all the circumstances including the (*r 36.21(5)*):
        - ◆ terms of any *Part 36* offer.
        - ◆ stage in proceedings when any *Part 36* offer/payment was made.
        - ◆ information available to the parties at the time any *Part 36* offer/payment was made.
        - ◆ parties' conduct with regard to giving or refusing to give information to enable a *Part 36* offer/payment to be evaluated.

> Where a claim includes a claim under the *Fatal Accidents Act 1976* and the *Law Reform (Miscellaneous Provisions) Act 1934* the court has power to apportion money paid into court between the different claims (*r 37.4*)

CIVIL LITIGATION
Allocation

1 Allocation (and automatic transfer) (*Part 26*)

On the sooner of (*r 26.3(2)*):
all defendants have filed their defences
or
the period for filing the last defence has expired (see p 340)

↓

the court serves the allocation questionnaire on each party (*r 26.3(1)*) unless:
a) there is admission of part of a specified sum (*r 14.5*) (see pp 367-368), *or*
b) the defence is 'the debt has already been paid' (*r 15.10*), *or*
c) the court has said there is no need for an allocation questionnaire

Note:
The date for filing the allocation questionnaire cannot be varied by agreement between the parties (*r 26.3(6A)*)

Where the claim:
(*rr 26.2(1), 26.2(3), 26.3(3)*)
a) is for a specified amount, *and*
b) was commenced in a court which is not the defendant's home court, *and*
c) has not otherwise been transferred to another defendant's home court under an application to set aside or vary default judgment, *and*
d) the defendant is an individual

the date for filing is specified in the allocation questionnaire (*r 26.3(1)*) (NB: this must be at least 14 days after the date it is deemed to be served by the court) (*r 26.3(6)*)

file:
- allocation questionnaire
- the fee, see p 344
- estimate of costs in set form* (*PD: Costs 6*)
- if the claimant has a reply, file the reply (*r 15.8*)

*do not need to include additional liability arrangements (see p 422)

Possible (Pre-) Allocation Hearing (see box overleaf)

Failure to file (*PD26: 2.5*)
a) no party files within time:
  - file is referred to a judge for directions,
  - the judge usually orders that, unless an allocation questionnaire is filed within 3 days from service of that order, the claim and any counterclaim will be struck out.
b) not all parties (but at least 1 does) file:
  - court may allocate the claim to a track if it has enough information to do so, *or*
  - court may order that an allocation hearing is listed and that all/any parties must attend

↓

... then the claim is transferred to the home court of the first defendant to file a defence

Note: Where a claimant notifies the court under *r 15.10* or *r 14.5* (see above) that he wishes the proceedings to continue, the court transfers the proceedings to the defendant's home court when it receives that notification. If proceedings are *not* automatically transferred the court serves an allocation questionnaire on each party at this time (*rr 26.2(4), 26.3(4)*)

When (*r 26.5*):
- every defendant has filed an allocation questionnaire, *or*
- the period for filing the allocation questionnaires has expired, *or*
- any stay has expired (see 'stay' box overleaf)

Court allocates the case to a track
(see 'Allocation Factors' box overleaf)
(and it may also hold an 'allocation hearing' see box overleaf (*r 26.5(4)*):
Note: parties may all consent to a different track

Multi track (*r 26.6(6)*)
The normal track for any claim for which the small claims track or the fast track is not the normal track

Small claims track (*r 26.6(1)-(3)*)
for any claim which has a financial value of not more than £5,000 BUT if the claim is for personal injuries or residential premises, this is only the normal track if:
a) personal injuries:
  - the financial value of the claim is not more than £5,000, *and*
  - the financial value of any claim for damages for personal injuries is not more than £1,000
b) includes a claim by a tenant of residential premises against his landlord:
  - the tenant is seeking an order requiring the landlord to carry out repairs or other work to the premises (whether or not the tenant is also seeking some other remedy), *and*
  - the cost of the repairs or other work to the premises is estimated to be not more than £1,000, *and*
  - the financial value of any other claim for damages is not more than £1,000

Fast track (*r 26.6(4)-(5)*)
for any claim:
a) where small claims track is not the normal track, *and*
b) the financial value is not more than £15,000, *and*
c) the court considers that the trial is likely to last for no longer than 1 day, *and*
d) oral expert evidence at trial will be limited to:
  - 1 expert per party in relation to any expert field, *and*
  - expert evidence in 2 expert fields

Note: The court, in particular, takes account of limits on disclosure, the extent of expert evidence and whether the trial is likely to last more than 1 day

The court serves on each party (*r 26.9*):
- notice of allocation on every party
- a copy of the allocation questionnaires filed by the other parties
- a copy of any further information provided by another party about his case (whether by order or not)

Allocation Factors (rr 26.7-26.8)

➤ When deciding the track for a claim, the court shall have regard to:
- the financial value, if any, of the claim.
  - The court may direct the claimant to justify the amount.
  - The amount should disregard:
    - any amount not in dispute, *and*
      - ❶ Note: an amount for which the defendant does not admit liability is in dispute.
      - ❷ Note: a part amount for which judgment has been entered (eg: summary judgment) is not in dispute.
      - ❸ Note: a part amount claimed as a distinct item which the defendant admits he is liable for is not in dispute.
      - ❹ Note: a sum offered and accepted in satisfaction of any item which is part of the claim is not in dispute.
      - Note: Therefore, if there is a claim above £5,000 and the defendant makes, before allocation, an admission that reduces the amount in dispute to a figure below £5,000, the small claims track is the normal track. As to recovery of pre-allocation costs, the claimant can, before allocation, apply for judgment with costs on the amount of the claim that has been admitted.
    - any claim for interest, *and*
    - costs, *and*
    - any contributory negligence.
  - Where 2 or more claimants have started a claim (using 1 claim form) against the same defendant and each claimant's claim is separate from the other claimants, the court considers the financial value of each separately.
- the nature of the remedy sought.
- the likely complexity of the facts, law or evidence.
- the number of parties or likely parties.
- the value of any counterclaim or other additional claim (see p 374) and the complexity of any matters relating to it.
  - If there is more than 1 money claim (eg: where there is an additional *Part 20* claim) the court will not generally aggregate the claims but generally regards the largest of them as determining the financial value of the claims.
- the amount of oral evidence which may be required.
- the importance of the claim to persons who are not parties to the proceedings.
- the views expressed by the parties (including any other information the parties may provide).
- the circumstances of the parties.

Stay (r 26.4, PD26: 3)

➤ When filling in the allocation questionnaire, a party may request the proceedings be stayed while all try to settle.
➤ The court stays proceedings (in whole or in part) for 1 month (or other specified period it considers appropriate) if:
- all parties request a stay, *or*
- the court, on its own, considers that such a stay would be appropriate.

➤ The parties may apply to extend any stay. (This may be by letter to the court.)
- The extension is generally for no more than 4 weeks unless clear reasons are given to justify a longer time.

➤ After a stay, the claimant must tell the court if a settlement has been reached.
➤ **No settlement:** If the claimant does not tell the court by the end of the period of the stay that a settlement has been reached, the court gives such directions as it considers appropriate.
➤ **Settlement:** Where the whole proceedings are settled during a stay, any of the following are treated as an application for the stay to be lifted:
  a) an application for a consent order (in any form) to give effect to the settlement, *or*
  b) an application for the approval of a settlement where a party is a person under a disability, *or*
  c) giving notice of acceptance of money paid into court in satisfaction of the claim or applying for money in court to be paid out.

Allocation Hearings or Pre-Allocation Hearings (PD26: 2.4, 5, 6)

➤ When there is *any* type of hearing or a special allocation hearing, the court may at any time before allocation:
- dispense with the need for allocation questionnaires, hold an allocation hearing, make an order for allocation and give directions for case management, *or*
- fix a date for allocation questionnaires to be filed and give other directions.

➤ Where the court orders a *special* allocation hearing, it gives the parties at least 7 days notice and brief reasons.
➤ A legal representative at an allocation hearing should be the person responsible for the case and *must* be familiar with the case and able to provide the court with information it is likely to need to take decisions about allocation and case management. He must also have sufficient authority to deal with any issues that arise.
➤ The court may also deal with summary disposal of issues at any pre-allocation hearing (eg: summary judgment).

The duty of consultation (PD26: 2.3)

➤ The parties should consult each other and co-operate in completing the allocation questionnaires.
➤ They should try to agree the case management directions which they will invite the court to make.
- The process of consultation must not delay the filing of the allocation questionnaires.

CIVIL LITIGATION
Small claims track

J Small claims track (*Part 27*)

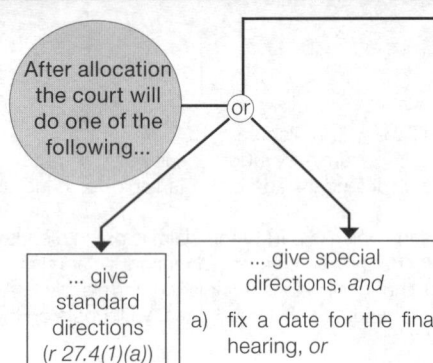

After allocation the court will do one of the following...

... give standard directions (r 27.4(1)(a))

... give special directions, and
a) fix a date for the final hearing, *or*
b) direct the court to consider further special directions no later than 28 days after the date the special directions were given (r 27.4(1)(b)-(c))

... fix a date for a preliminary hearing:
a) ♦ if the court considers special directions are needed to ensure a fair hearing, *and*
 ♦ it appears necessary for a party to attend court to ensure he understands what he must do to comply with special directions, *or*
b) to enable the court to dispose of the claim as a party has no real prospect of success at a final hearing, *or*
c) to enable the court to strike out a statement of case, or part of a statement of case, as that struck out wording discloses no reasonable grounds for bringing or defending the claim (rr 27.4(1)(d), 27.6(1))

... give notice that the court proposes to deal with the claim without a hearing and invite the parties to notify the court by a specified date if they agree (r 27.4(1)(e))

The court gives the parties at least 21 days' notice of the date fixed for the final hearing (unless the parties agree to accept less notice), and informs them of the time allowed for the final hearing (r 27.4(2))

Standard Directions (*PD27: App. B*)

1. Each party must deliver to every other party and to the court office copies of all documents on which he intends to rely at the hearing no later than [   ] [14 days before the hearing]. (These should include the letter making the claim and the reply.)
2. The original documents must be brought to the hearing.
3. [Notice of hearing date and time allowed.]
4. The parties are encouraged to contact each other with a view to trying to settle the case or narrow the issues. However the court must be informed immediately if the case is settled by agreement before the hearing date.
5. No party may rely at the hearing on any report from an expert unless express permission has been granted by the court beforehand. Anyone wishing to rely on an expert must write to the court immediately on receipt of this Order and seek permission, giving an explanation why the assistance of an expert is necessary.

Sample Special Directions (*PD27: App. C*)

♦ The [ ] must clarify his case. He must do this by delivering to the court office and to the [ ] no later than [ ] [a list of [ ]] [details of [ ]]
♦ The [ ] must allow the [ ] to inspect by appointment within [ ] days of receiving a request to do so.
♦ The hearing will not take place at the court but at [ ].
♦ The [ ] must bring to court at the hearing the [ ].
♦ Signed statements setting out the evidence of all witnesses on whom each party intends to rely must be prepared and copies included in the documents mentioned in paragraph 1. This includes the evidence of the parties themselves and of any other witness, whether or not he is going to come to court to give evidence.
♦ The court may decide not to take into account a document [or video] or the evidence of a witness if these directions have not been complied with.
♦ If he does not [do so] [ ] his [Claim][Defence] [and Counterclaim] will be struck out and (specify consequence).
♦ It appears to the court that expert evidence is necessary on the issue of [ ] and that that evidence should be given by a single expert to be instructed by the parties jointly. If the parties cannot agree about who to choose and what arrangements to make about paying his fee, either party MUST apply to the court for further directions. The evidence is to be given in the form of a written report. Either party may ask the expert questions and must then send copies of the questions and replies to the other party and to the court. Oral expert evidence may be allowed in exceptional circumstances but only after a further order of the court. Attention is drawn to the limit of £200 on expert's fees that may be recovered.
♦ If either party intends to show a video as evidence he must:
 a) contact the court at once to make arrangements for him to do so, because the court may not have the necessary equipment, and
 b) provide the other party with a copy of the video or the opportunity to see it at least [ ] days before the hearing.

CIVIL LITIGATION
Small claims track

1 **Conduct of a hearing**
- ➤ The court may, if all the parties agree, deal with the claim without a hearing (*r 27.10*).
- ➤ The court may adopt any method of proceeding at a hearing that it considers fair (*r 27.8(1)*).
    - ◆ Hearings are informal (*r 27.8(2)*).
- ➤ Strict rules of evidence do not apply (*r 27.8(3)*).
    - ◆ The court need not take evidence on oath (*r 27.8(4)*).
    - ◆ The court may limit cross-examination (*r 27.8(5)*).
        - • Eg: a judge may (*PD27: 4.3*):
            - ▪ ask questions of any witness before allowing another person to do so, *or*
            - ▪ refuse to allow cross-examination of any witness until all the witnesses have given evidence-in-chief, *or*
            - ▪ limit cross-examination of a witness to a fixed time/subject/issue.
- ➤ The court must give reasons for its decision (*r 27.8(6)*, see also *PD27: 5.1-5.5* and box below).
- ➤ The hearing will generally be conducted in public (*PD27: 4.1(1)*).

Recording of the hearing and reasons for the judgment (*PD27: 5.1-5.5*)

- ➤ A hearing that takes place at the court will be tape recorded by the court.
- ➤ A party may obtain a transcript of such a recording on payment of the proper transcriber's charges.
- ➤ The judge may give reasons for his judgment as briefly and simply as the nature of the case allows. He will normally do so orally at the hearing, but he may give them later at a hearing either orally or in writting.
- ➤ Where the judge decides the case without a hearing (or a party who has given appropriate notice does not attend the hearing) the judge will prepare a note of his reasons and the court will send a copy to each party.

---

2 **Representation**
- ➤ A case may be presented by a party, a lawyer or a lay representative (*PD27: 3.2(1)*).
    - ◆ A 'lay representative' is a person other than a barrister, a solicitor or a legal executive employed by a solicitor (*PD27: 3.1(2)*)
- ➤ A lay representative may not exercise his right of audience (*LR(RA)O 1999, PD27: 3.2(2)*):
    a) if his client does not attend the hearing, *or*
    b) at any stage after judgment, *or*
    c) on an appeal brought against any decision made by the district judge in the proceedings.
        - • The court has a general discretion to hear anybody, even in circumstances excluded by the *LR(RA)O 1999* (*PD 27:3.3(3)*).
- ➤ A corporate party may be represented by any of its officers or employees (*PD27: 3.2(4)*).

3 **Experts**
- ➤ An expert may not give evidence at a hearing without the court's permission (*r 27.5*).

4 Non-attendance

Party does not attend *and*:
i) gives the court and the other party written notice (an '**Excuse Notice**'), at least 7 days before the hearing that he will not attend, *and*
ii) has served on the other party at least 7 days before the hearing date any other documents which he has filed with the court, *and*
iii) in the Excuse Notice requests the court to decide the claim in his absence

↓

The court will take into account that party's statement of case and any other documents that party has filed with the court and served (*r 27.9(1)*)

Claimant does not attend the hearing *and* no Excuse Notice is given

↓

The court may strike out the claim (*r 27.9(2)*)

Defendant does not attend the hearing *or* give an Excuse Notice *and* the claimant attends or gives an Excuse Notice

↓

The court may decide the claim on the basis of the claimant's evidence alone (*r 27.9(3)*)

If neither party attends, or gives notice, the court may strike out the claim and any defence or counterclaim (*r 27.9(4)*)

The court has a general power to adjourn a hearing, eg: a party wishes to attend but cannot do so for a good reason (*PD27: 6.2*)

Setting aside judgment and rehearing under *Part 27*

➤ A party may apply for an order setting aside judgment and for the claim to be reheard if (*r 27.11(1)*):

a) he was not present or represented at the hearing of the claim, *and*

b) did not give an Excuse Notice.

Procedure	➤ Party applies not more than 14 days after the day on which notice of the judgement was served on him (*r 27.11(2)*).
Grounds	➤ The court may grant the application only if the applicant (*r 27.11(3)*): a) had a good reason for not: i) attending, *or* ii) being represented, *or* iii) giving an Excuse Notice, *and* b) has reasonable prospect of success at the hearing.
Order	➤ The court fixes a new hearing for the claim. ➤ The new hearing may take place immediately after the hearing of the application and may be dealt with by the same judge.

Appeals under the small claims track

➤ An appeal from a decision of a small claims track court is made under *Part 52* as for other appeals (see p 430).

➤ However, for a small claims track appeal, unlike for other appeals:

◆ the appellant only needs to file the following documents (and no other documents are required) (*PD52: 5.8*):

- a sealed copy of the order being appealed, *and*
- the order giving or refusing permission to appeal (and the reasons), *and*
- a record of the reasons of the judgement of the lower court but only:
  - to enable the court to decide if permission should be granted to appeal, *or*
  - if permission has been granted, to enable it to decide the appeal.

◆ the respondent may provide a skeleton argument, but is not required to do so (*PD52: 7.7A*).

/ CIVIL LITIGATION
Fast Track

K Fast Track

Allocation to the fast track
↓

Case management 1
The court gives directions including (rr 28.2(2), 28.3(1)-(2)):
- a) fixing the trial date, *or*
  b) fixing a period (not exceeding 3 weeks) within which the trial is to take place, *and/or*
- a) disclosure of documents, *and/or*
  b) service of witness statements, *and/or*
  c) expert evidence.
- disclosure (standard - see pp 401-403, non-standard or none).

↓

Notice of allocation
The court sends this to the parties and it includes:
- the trial date or trial period (r 28.2(3)), and
- date for filing the pre-trial checklist.

↓

Pre-trial checklist
(r 28.5(1))
No later than 2 weeks before the date specified in the notice of allocation for the return of the completed checklist (or in any later direction of the court) the court sends the parties a pre-trial checklist (listing questionnaire) (unless it considers one is not needed)

↓

DATE (given in allocation notice (see above) for parties to file:
- the pre-trial checklist (and usually the fee, see p 344).
- costs estimate (PD28: 6.1).

↓

Exchange
The parties are encouraged to exchange copies of the pre-trial checklists before they are filed to avoid the court being given conflicting or incomplete information (PD28: 6.1).

↓

Case management 2
The court:
As soon as practicable after the date specified for filing a completed pre-trial checklist the court will:
- gives appropriate directions and further steps to be taken for the trial, including a trial timetable,
- fix the date for the trial (or, confirms it if one has been given).

↓

Notice of Trial
The court gives the parties notice of trial.

↓

Trial
(see p 415)

standard period between giving of directions and trial is not more than 30 weeks (r 28.2(4))

Minimum 2 weeks

date specified for filing a pre-trial checklist is not more than 8 weeks before the trial date or the beginning of the trial period (r 28.5(2))

Minimum 3 weeks (r 28.6(2))

Note Items in bold also apply to multi-track

Fast Track case management
(ie: Directions hearings at allocation/listing hearings)
(r 28.5(3)-(4), PD28: 2, 6)

➤ Case management is generally given at 2 stages in the case:
  - at allocation to the fast track, *and*
  - on filing a pre-trial checklist.
➤ It is usual not to hold a hearing for directions as the parties are expected to cooperate in directions.
➤ The Court will hold a hearing to give directions when it is 'necessary or desirable'.
➤ If this is because of the default of a party (or his legal representative) it usually involves a sanction (see p 344).
➤ The Court may give directions at any hearing on the application of a party or on its own initiative.
➤ When any hearing has been fixed it is the duty of the parties to consider what directions the court should be asked to give and to make any application that may be appropriate to be dealt with at that hearing.
➤ When the Court fixes a hearing to give directions it will give the parties at least 3 days notice of the hearing.

Problems with the pre-trial checklist

➤ The court may give directions (including fixing a hearing) if:
  a) a party files a completed pre-trial checklist but another party does not, *or*
  b) a party has failed to give all the information requested by the pre-trial checklist, *or*
  c) the court considers it is necessary to enable it to decide what directions to give to complete preparation of the case for trial.
➤ Where the court holds a hearing the date must be as early as possible and the parties are given at least 3 days' notice of the date.
➤ **No party files:** if no party files a completed pre-trial checklist by the specified date, the court orders that unless it is filed within 7 days from service of that order, the claim/defence/counterclaim will be struck out without further court order.
➤ **A party files:** where a party files a pre-trial checklist but another party does not do so, the court normally gives listing directions, fixing/confirming the trial date and provide for steps to be taken to prepare the case for trial.

CIVIL LITIGATION
Fast Track

Directions on allocation (PD28: 3-4)

➤ The court's first concern is to ensure that issues between parties are identified and necessary evidence is prepared + disclosed. If in doubt about directions, the court holds a hearing (listed as promptly as possible).

➤ The court may have regard to any document filed with an allocation questionnaire containing further information *provided* that the document states either that its contents have been agreed with every other party or that it has been served on every other party and when it was served.

Agreed directions	No agreed directions
The court may approve these if:	The court's general approach is:
◆ the parties have filed these, *and*	● to give directions for the filing and service of any further information required to clarify either party's case,
◆ the court considers that they are suitable, *and*	
◆ they set out a timetable (referring to calendar dates) for steps to prepare the case, *and*	● to direct standard disclosure (see pp 401-403) between the parties,
◆ they include a date or a trial period (which must not be longer than 3 weeks) when it is proposed that the trial will take place (where the latest proposed date for the trial or the end of the trial period is not later than 30 weeks from the date of the directions order), *and*	● to direct the simultaneous exchange of witness statements,
	● to give directions for a single joint expert unless there is good reason not to do so,
◆ they include provisions about disclosure of documents, *and*	● if no directions for a single expert are given:
• these may limit disclosure to standard disclosure between all parties or to less than that, *and/or*	• to direct simultaneous exchange of experts' reports
• these may direct that disclosure take place by supply of copy documents without a list (but it must in that case either direct that the parties must serve a disclosure statement with the copies or record that they have agreed to disclose in that way without such a statement)	• (if experts' reports are not agreed) to direct a discussion between experts and preparation of a report.
◆ they include provision about both factual and expert evidence (eg: none is required), *and*	**Note:** If the court does not approve agreed directions but gives directions itself without a hearing, it takes the parties' proposed directions into account in deciding on directions
◆ they contain other appropriate provisions.	

➤ Typical timetable: (periods from notice of allocation)
  ◆ Disclosure — 4 weeks
  ◆ Exchange of witness statements — 10 weeks
  ◆ Exchange of experts' reports — 14 weeks
  ◆ Sending of pre-trial checklists by the Court — 20 weeks
  ◆ Filing of completed pre-trial checklists — 22 weeks
  ◆ Hearing — 30 weeks

If the court thinks that some/all steps in the timetable are unnecessary it may omit them - eg: if pre-action protocols have been complied with or other steps have already been taken

➤ Varying the Court's directions - the procedure is outside this book but is set out in *r 28.4* and *PD28*:

Directions on listing (PD28: 7)

➤ The court must confirm or fix the trial date, specify the place of trial and give a time estimate.
  ◆ The trial date must be fixed and the case listed on the footing that the hearing will end on the same calendar day as that on which it commenced.

➤ The parties should seek to agree directions (see practice box above) and may file the proposed order. (The court may make an order in those terms or it may make a different order.)
  ◆ Agreed directions should include provisions about evidence (including expert evidence, see p 414), a trial timetable and time estimate, preparation of a trial bundle, other matters needed to prepare the case for trial.

➤ Varying the Court's directions - the procedure is outside this book but is set out in *r 28.4* and *PD28: 4*.

Fast track standard directions (PD28: Appendix)

➤ Standard Directions are listed in the Appendix to *PD28* but include provisions on:
  ◆ FURTHER STATEMENTS OF CASE
  ◆ REQUESTS FOR FURTHER INFORMATION
  ◆ DISCLOSURE OF DOCUMENTS
  ◆ WITNESSES OF FACT
  ◆ QUESTIONS TO EXPERTS
  ◆ REQUESTS FOR INFORMATION ETC.
  ◆ DOCUMENTS TO BE FILED WITH PRE-TRIAL CHECKLIST
  ◆ DATES FOR FILING PRE-TRIAL CHECKLIST AND THE TRIAL
  ◆ DIRECTIONS FOLLOWING FILING OF PRE-TRIAL CHECKLIST

CIVIL LITIGATION
Multi-Track

L Multi-Track

Allocation to the multi-track
↓

Case management 1
The court (r 29.2(1)-(2)):
- a) gives directions for the management of the case and sets a timetable for the steps to be taken between the giving of directions and the trial, *or*
  b) fixes:
  i) a case management conference, *and/or*
  ii) a pre-trial review.
- gives any other directions relating to case management.
- fixes the trial date or period in which the trial is to take place.

↓

Notice of allocation
The court sends this to the parties and it includes (r 29.2(23)):
- the trial date or trial period, *and*
- date for filing the pre-trial checklist.

↓

Pre-trial checklist
(r 29.6(1) and (4))
No later than 14 days before the date specified in the notice of allocation for the return of the completed checklist (or in any later direction of the court) the court sends the parties a pre-trial checklist (listing questionnaire) (unless it considers one is not needed)

↓ *(Minimum 14 days)*

DATE (given in allocation notice (see above)) for parties to file:
- the pre-trial checklist (and usually the fee, see p 344).
- costs estimate (PD29: 8.1).

↓

Exchange
The parties are encouraged to exchange copies of the pre-trial checklists before they are filed to avoid the court being given conflicting or incomplete information (PD29: 8.1(5))

→ **Pre-trial review**
The Court *may* (but does not have to) decide to:
- hold a pre-trial review, *or*
- cancel a previously fixed pre-trial review.
If so, it serves a notice of its decision at least 7 days before the date fixed for the hearing/cancelled hearing

(date specified for filing a pre-trial checklist is not more than 8 weeks before the trial date or the beginning of the trial period (PD29: 8.1(3))

↓

Case management 2
The court (r 29.8, PD29: 8.1(6)):
As soon as practicable after:
- a) each party has filed a completed pre-trial checklist, *or*
- b) the court has held a listing hearing, *or*
- c) the court has held a pre-trial review,
the court will:
- set a trial timetable (*unless* one has already been fixed, or the court considers that it would be inappropriate to do so),
- fix or confirm the date for the trial or the week within which the trial is to begin.

→ **Notice of Trial**
The Court gives the parties notice of the trial timetable and the date or trial period

↓

Trial (see p 415)

Multi-Track case management
(ie: Directions hearings)
(r 29.3, 29.6, PD29: 3, 5, 8)

➤ Any time after the claim has been allocated the court may fix:
- a case management conference, *or*
- a pre-trial review.

Note: at such hearings, if a party is legally represented, that representative must be familiar with the case and have authority to deal with any issues that are likely to arise.

➤ A party must apply to court if he wishes to vary any dates fixed for:
- a case management conference
- a pre-trial review
- return of a pre-trial checklist
- the trial
- the trial period.

Note: Any date set by the court or the *CPR* for doing any act may not be varied by the parties if it makes it necessary to vary any of these dates.

➤ The court may give directions without a hearing.

➤ Whether or not the court has fixed a trial date or period, it may either:
- give directions for certain steps to be taken and fix a date for a case management conference or a pre-trial review to take place after they have been taken, *or*
- fix a date for a case management conference.

➤ Items in bold in the case management box for 'Fast Track' apply here.

➤ If the court fixes a hearing to give directions it gives the parties at least 3 days' notice of the hearing unless a pre-trial review (see chart left).

➤ Where a party applies for a direction not included in a set case management timetable he must do so as soon as possible so as to minimise the need to change the timetable.

Problems with the pre-trial checklist

➤ Items in bold in this section under 'Fast Track' apply here too.

➤ Where the court holds a hearing the date must be as early as possible and the parties are given at least 3 days' notice of the date (unless a pre-trial review - see left).

➤ A party files: where a party files a pre-trial checklist but another party does not do so, the court will fix a hearing. Whether or not the defaulting party attends the hearing, the court will normally fix or confirm the trial date and make other orders about the steps to be taken to prepare the case for trial.

CIVIL LITIGATION
Multi-Track

Directions on allocation (PD29: 4)

➤ The court tailors directions to the needs of the case and the steps which the parties have already taken to prepare the case of which it is aware. In particular it will have regard to the extent to which any pre-action protocol has or (as the case may be) has not been complied with.

➤ The court's first concern is to ensure that issues between parties are identified and necessary evidence is prepared + disclosed. If in doubt about directions, the court holds a hearing (listed as promptly as possible).

➤ The court may have regard to any document filed with an allocation questionnaire containing further information *provided* that the document states either that its contents have been agreed with every other party or that it has been served on every other party and when it was served.

Agreed directions	No agreed directions

The court may approve these if:
◆ the parties have filed these, *and*
◆ the court considers they are suitable, *and*
◆ they set out a timetable (referring to calendar dates) for steps to prepare the case, *and*
◆ they include a date/trial period (which must not be later than reasonably necessary), *and*
◆ they include provisions about disclosure of documents, *and*
  • these may limit disclosure to standard disclosure between all parties or to less than that, *and/or*
  • these may direct that disclosure take place by supply of copy documents without a list (but it must in that case either direct that the parties must serve a disclosure statement with the copies or record that they have agreed to disclose in that way without such a statement)
◆ they include provision about both factual and expert evidence (eg: none is required), *and*
◆ they contain other appropriate provisions.
	The court's general approach is:
	◆ to give directions for the filing and service of any further information required to clarify either party's case,
	◆ to direct standard disclosure (see pp 401-403),
	◆ to direct the simultaneous exchange of witness statements,
	◆ to give directions for a single joint expert unless there is good reason not to do so,
	◆ if no directions for a single expert are given:
	  • to direct simultaneous exchange of experts' reports
	  • (if experts' reports are not agreed) to direct a discussion between experts and preparation of a report
	NB: if expert evidence is required on issues of liability and amount of damages, the court may direct that the exchange of reports that relate to liability are exchanged simultaneously and those relating to amount of damages are exchanged sequentially.
	◆ to list a case management conference after the date for compliance with directions,
	◆ to specify a trial period.
	Note: If the court does not approve agreed directions but gives directions itself without a case management conference, it takes any proposed directions into account in deciding on directions.

➤ **Varying the Court's directions** - the procedure is outside this book but is set out in *PD29: 6*.

Directions on listing (PD29: 9)

➤ The court must fix the trial date or week, give a time estimate and fix the place of trial.

➤ The parties should seek to agree directions and may file the proposed order. (The court may make an order in those terms or it may make a different order.)
  ◆ Agreed directions should include provisions about evidence (especially expert evidence - see p 414), a trial timetable and time estimate, preparation of a trial bundle, other matters for preparation for trial.

➤ **Varying the Court's directions** - the procedure is outside the scope of this book but is set out in *PD29: 6*.

What happens at a case management conference? (PD29: 5)

➤ A review of the steps taken in the preparation of the case (especially compliance with any directions).

➤ The court gives directions about steps to progress of the claim in accordance with the overriding objective.

➤ The court records agreements reached between parties about issues + conduct of the claim.

➤ Topics usually considered include:
  ◆ whether the claimant has made his claim clearly (especially any amount he is claiming),
  ◆ whether any amendments are required to the claim, a statement of case or any other document,
  ◆ what disclosure of documents (if any) and factual evidence is necessary,
  ◆ what expert evidence is reasonably required and how and when it should be obtained and disclosed,
  ◆ what arrangements should be made to clarify, obtain further information or put questions to experts,
  ◆ whether it is just and saves costs to order a split trial or the trial of one or more preliminary issues.

➤ The court will not at this stage give permission to use expert evidence unless it can identify each expert by name or field in its order and say whether his evidence is to be given orally or by the use of his report.
  ◆ A party who obtains expert evidence before obtaining a direction about it does so at his own risk as to costs, *except* where he obtained the evidence in compliance with a pre-action protocol.

➤ The parties and their legal advisers should:
  ◆ ensure that all documents that the court is likely to ask to see are brought to the hearing,
  ◆ consider whether the parties should attend,
  ◆ consider whether a case summary will be useful (containing a brief chronology of the claim, the issues of fact which are agreed or in dispute and the evidence needed to decide them, maximum 500 words and prepared by the claimant and agreed with the other parties if possible) , *and*
  ◆ consider what orders each wishes to be made and give notice of them to the other parties.

M Disclosure and Inspection (Part 31)

I   Generally
II   Disclosure
III   Inspection

I   Generally

- 'Disclosure' is a statement by a party that a document exists or has existed (*r 31.2*).
- The duty to disclose is limited to a document which is or has been in a party's control (*r 31.8*), ie:
   a) it is or was in his physical possession, *or*
   b) he has or has had a right to possession of it, *or*
   c) he has or has had a right to inspect or take copies of it.

> **Documents and copies**
>
> - A 'document' is anything in which information of any description is recorded (*r 31.4*).
>   - A 'copy' is anything onto which information recorded in a document has been copied (by whatever means, whether directly or indirectly) (*r 31.4*).
>   - A copy which contains a modification, obliteration or other marking or feature on which a party intends to rely or which adversely affects his case or another party's case or supports another party's case is a separate document (*r 31.9*).
>   - A party need not disclose more than one copy of a document (*r 31.9*).

- Any duty of disclosure continues until the proceedings are concluded (*r 31.11(1)*).
   - If a document comes to a party's notice during proceedings, he must immediately notify every other party (*r 31.11(2)*).
   - Disclosure and/or inspection may take place in stages if the parties agree or the court so directs (*r 31.13*).
- A party may not rely on any document which he fails to disclose or to which he does not permit inspection, unless the court gives permission for him to rely on it (*r 31.21*).

> **Claim to withhold disclosure or inspection** (*r 31.19*)
>
> - A person may apply, without notice (and supported by evidence), for an order permitting him to withhold disclosure of a document on the ground that disclosure would damage the public interest.

CIVIL LITIGATION
Disclosure and Inspection

Order for specific disclosure or inspection (r 31.12)

➤ A court may make an order for specific disclosure or inspection (r 31.12(1)).

Discovery	Inspection
➤ An order that a party must (r 31.12(2)): • disclose documents or classes of documents specified in the order, and/or • carry out a search to the extent specified in the order, and/or • disclose any documents located as a result of that search.	➤ An order that a party must permit inspection of a document (or class of documents) which that party disclosed, being a document which: • adversely affects his own case, or • adversely affects another party's case, or • supports another party's case ... ... but is a document which that party considered would be disproportionate to the issues in the case to permit inspection (r 31.12(3)).

II Disclosure

	Before proceedings / By a person not party to proceedings	
	Before proceedings	**By a non party**
Application (supported by evidence)	Under *SCA 1981 s 33* or *CCA 1984 s 52* (Sch 2 r 16)	Under *SCA 1981 s 34* or *CCA 1984 s 53* (Sch 2 r 17)

Grounds	a) the respondent is likely to be party to subsequent proceedings, *and*
	b) the applicant is likely to be a party to those proceedings, *and*
	c) if proceedings had started the respondent's duty of standard disclosure would extend to the documents, *and*
	d) disclosure before the start of proceedings is desirable to:
	   i) dispose fairly of the anticipated proceedings, *or*
	   ii) assist in resolving the dispute without proceedings, *or*
	   iii) save costs.
		a) the documents are likely to support the case of the applicant or adversely affect the case of another party, *and*
		b) disclosure is necessary to *either*:
		   i) dispose fairly of the proceedings, *or*
		   ii) save costs.

Order	◆ Must ...
	  • specify the documents or classes of documents for disclosure, *and*
	  • require the respondent to specify those document which are no longer in his control or in respect of which he claims a right or duty to withhold inspection.
	◆ May ...
	  • require the respondent to indicate what has happened to documents which he no longer controls, *and*
	  • specify the time and place for disclosure and inspection.	

➤ 'Standard disclosure' requires a party to disclose only the documents (r 31.6):
- on which he relies, *and*
- which adversely affect his own case or another party's case or support another party's case, *and*
- which he is required to disclose by a *PD*.

➤ Standard disclosure is normal (*PD31: 1.1*) and is ordered unless the court directs otherwise (*r 31.5(1)*).
- The court may dispense with or limit standard disclosure (*r 31.5(2)*).
- The parties may agree in writing to dispense with or limit standard disclosure (in which case the agreement should be lodged with the court (*PD31: 1.4*))(*r 31.5(3)*).

Duty of search (*r 31.7*)

➤ For standard disclosure a party has a duty to make a reasonable search for documents which (*r 31.7(1)*):
- adversely affect his own case or another party's case or support another party's case, *or*
- he is required to disclose by a *PD*.

➤ 'Reasonableness' in ascertained by reference to a number of factors, include (*r 31.7(2)*):
- the number of the documents,
- the nature and complexity of the proceedings,
- the ease and expense of retrieval of any particular document,
- the significance of any document which is likely to be located as a result of the search.

Procedure for standard disclosure (*r 31.10*)

Parties

➤ Each party must make and serve on every other party a list in practice *Form N265* (*r 31.2, PD31: 3.1*).
- The parties may agree in writing to disclose documents without making a list and to disclose without making a disclosing statement (*r 31.8*).

List

➤ The list must:
- identify the documents in a convenient order and manner as concisely as possible (*r.31.10(3)*)
  - Usually this means: listed in date order, numbered consecutively, and concisely described. A large number of documents in a particular category may be listed as such (*PD 31: 3.2*)
- indicate documents for which a right or duty to withhold inspection is claimed *and* those documents which are no longer in that party's control (*plus* what has happened to those documents) (*r 31.10(4)*).
- include a disclosure statement which (*r 31.10(4)-(5)*):
  - sets out the extent of the search, *and*
    - The statement should state that the belief of the disclosing party that the extent of the search is reasonable in all the circumstances.
    - Attention should be drawn to limitations adopted for proportionality reasons and reasons should be given (eg: expense, difficulty, marginal relevance) (*r 31.7(3)*), PD 31: 4.2)
  - certifies that the party making the disclosure understands the duty to disclose, *and*
  - certifies that the best of that party's knowledge he has carried out the duty to disclose.
- if the person making the statement is a company, firm, association or other organisation (*r 31.10(7)*):
  - identify the person making the statement (name, address, position or the basis on which he makes the statement (*PD 31: 4.3*)), *and*
  - explain why that person is considered the appropriate person to the make the statement.

Electronic disclosure (*PD31: 2A*)

➤ A 'document' includes electronic documents such as email, other electronic communications, word-processed documents and databases.
- It also includes documents stored on servers and back-up systems, electronic documents that have been 'deleted' and metadata.

➤ Before the first Case Management Conference, the parties should discuss issues that may arise regarding searches for, and preservation of, electronic documents.
- This may involve providing information about categories of electronic documents within each party's control, the computer systems, electronic devices and media on which any relevant documents may be held, the storage systems maintained by the parties and document retention policies.

➤ Parties should co-operate early regarding the format of electronic copy documents on inspection.

➤ Having electronic documents affects the extent of the reasonable search required for standard disclosure. Some factors that may be relevant in deciding the reasonableness of a search are:
- The number of documents involved.
- The nature and complexity of the proceedings.
- The ease and expense of retrieval of any particular document.
- The significance of any document likely to be located during the search.

➤ It may be reasonable to search some or all of the parties' electronic storage systems.
- Search might be keyword (agreed as far as possible between the parties) or other means.

➤ In the case of any difficulty or disagreement, the matter should be referred to a judge for directions at the earliest practical date, if possible at the first Case Management Conference.

III Inspection

➤ When a document has been disclosed to a party, that party has the right to inspect that document *unless* (*r 31.3*):

   a) the document is no longer in the possession of the party who disclosed it, *or*

   b) the party disclosing the document has a right or duty to withhold inspection, *or*

   c) the party disclosing the document ...

   ... (which adversely affects his own case or another party's case or supports another party's case) ...

   ... considers that it would be disproportionate to issues to permit inspection and he stated in his disclosure statement that inspection of the document would not be permitted as to do so would be disproportionate.

➤ A party may inspect a document mentioned in (*r 31.14*):
- a statement of case, a witness statement or a witness summary, *or*
- an affidavit, *or*
- an expert's report (although material instructions on the basis of which the report was prepared need only be available for inspection if the court so orders having reasonable grounds for believing that the statement of instructions is inaccurate or incomplete) if the expert's report has not been previously disclosed in proceedings and provided that that party gets a court order first.

CIVIL LITIGATION
Disclosure and Inspection

Inspection of witness statements ... or not

➤ A witness statement which stands as evidence in chief is open to inspection during the course of the trial unless the court otherwise directs (r 32.13(1)).

➤ However, a party may apply for a direction that a witness statement should not be open for inspection (r 32.13(2)).

Grounds for the court's refusing inspection	➤ The court is satisfied that the statement (or words or passages in the statement) should not be open to inspection due to (r 32.13(3)-(4)): a) the interests of justice, or b) the public interest, or c) the nature of any expert medical advice in the statement, or d) the nature of any confidential information in the statement, or e) the need to protect the interests of any child or patient.

➤ A party must give written notice of a wish to inspect a document. The party who disclosed the document must permit inspection not more than 7 days after receipt of this notice (r 31.15).

◆ A party may request a copy and if that party also undertakes to pay reasonable copying costs, the party who made the disclosure must supply a copy not more than 7 days after receiving the request.

➤ If a party accidentally allows inspection of a privileged document, the party who inspected it may use it, or its contents, only with the permission of the court (r 31.20).

Privilege

➤ Some documents are recognised by law as 'privileged', they must be disclosed *but* do not have to be available for inspection. The following categories of documents are privileged:

legal professional privilege

1 **Solicitor-client correspondence**, for the purpose of legal advice.

2 **Solicitor-third party correspondence**, if created after litigation is commenced, *or* if created with a view to starting litigation or to obtain evidence or advice.

3 **Client-third party correspondence**, if the primary purpose at the time of creation was to see if legal advice should be obtained for existing or contemplated litigation.

4 **'Without prejudice' evidence of negotiations** (unless as evidence of a settlement which was reached where the dispute is whether any settlement was reached at all!).

5 **Public policy material**, eg: defence, NSPCC, social work and probation records.

6 **Material incriminating a party to the proceedings** (in UK criminal or penal proceedings).

➤ Secondary evidence of a privileged document is admissible, unless prevented by an injunction (but see 'Professional ethics' in the 'Conduct' section).

➤ Privilege belongs to the client, so the solicitor may not waive it without the client's authority.

Privilege: restrictions on categories 1 to 3 above

➤ The Court of Appeal in *Three Rivers District Council v Bank of England (Disclosure) (No 3)* [2003] EWCA Civ 474 restricts the scope of legal professional privilege:

◆ Legal advice privilege will only apply to advice given in relation to a client's legal rights and obligations. However, what amounts to legal rights and obligations is less clear.

◆ Legal advice privilege can no longer be assumed despite the existence of a solicitor's retainer. Not all correspondence between client and solicitor will automatically qualify for the protection of legal advice privilege.

N Evidence

I	Generally	IV	Expert evidence
II	Witnesses (Statements, summaries)	V	Hearsay
III	Opinion	VI	Notarial acts and instruments

I Generally

➤ The court has a general power to control evidence by giving directions as to (*r 32.1*):
- the issues which require evidence, *and*
- the nature of the evidence which the court requires to decide those issues, *and*
- the way in which evidence is to be placed before the court ...

... even if this involves excluding evidence which would be otherwise admissible (*r 32.2*).

- Any fact which needs to be proved by the evidence of a witness is usually proved *either* at trial (by the witnesses' oral evidence given in public) *or* at any other hearing by evidence in writing (*r 32.3*).
  - At a **hearing other than trial**, a party may rely on his statement of case or his application notice provided that the statement or application notice are verified by a statement of truth (*r 32.6*).
- The court may allow a witness to give evidence through a video link or by other means (*r 32.3*).

➤ Contempt of court proceedings may be brought (by the Attorney General, or with the court's permission) against a person who makes, or causes to be made, a false statement in a document verified by a statement of truth without an honest belief in the statement's truth (*r 32.14*).

Notice to admit or produce documents (*r 32.19*)
◆ A party is deemed to admit the authenticity of a document disclosed to him under *Part 31* (see pp 401-405) unless he serves notice that the wishes the document to be proved at trial.
◆ A notice must be served by the latest date for serving witness statements or within 7 days of disclosure of the document - whichever is later.

Notice to admit facts (*r 32.18*)	
◆ A party may serve notice on another party requiring him to admit facts, or part of the case, specified in the notice	
Service	◆ No later than 21 days before the trial.
Admission	◆ The admission may be used against the party making it only in the proceedings in which the notice to admit is served and only by the party who served the notice.
	◆ The court may allow a party to amend or withdraw an admission on such terms as it thinks fit.

II   Witnesses (Statements, summaries)

➤ A witness statement is a written statement signed by a person; it contains the evidence which that person would be allowed to give orally (*r 32.4(1)*).

- The court (*r 32.4(2)-(3)*):
  - **will order** a party to serve on the other parties any witness statement on which that party intends to rely on in relation to any issues of fact to be decided at trial, *and*
    - At trial where a witness is called to give oral evidence, a witness statement will stand as a witnesses' evidence in chief unless the court orders otherwise (*r 32.5(2)*).
    - If a witness statement (or summary) is not served within the time limit specified by the court, the witness may not be called to give oral evidence unless the court gives permission (*r 32.10*).
    - If a party who has served a witness statement does not call the witness to give evidence at trial or put the witness statement in as hearsay evidence, any other party may put the witness statement in as hearsay evidence (*r 32.5(5)*).
  - **may direct** the sequence in which statements are served and whether statements are to be filed.
- A witness statement must comply with the relevant *PD* (*r 32.8*).
  - If a statement does not comply with *Part 32* or *PD32*, the court may refuse to admit it as evidence and may refuse to allow costs arising from its preparation) (*PD32: 25.1*).

Witness statements

➤ A witness statement must (*PD32: 17-20*):
- be headed with the name and number of the proceedings and the Court or Division.
- state at the top right hand corner of the first page:
  - the party on whose behalf it is made, *and*
  - the initials and surname of the witness, *and*
  - the number of the statement in relation to that witness, *and*
  - the identifying initials and number of each exhibit referred to, *and*
  - the date the statement was made.
- if practicable, be in the witnesses' own words.
- be expressed in the first person.
- state the full name of the witness, the witnesses' place of residence (or if he is making the statement in a professional or business capacity - the address at which he works, his position and the name of his firm/employer).
- the witness' occupation (or if the witness has none, his description).
- whether the witness is a party to the proceedings or is the employee of such a party.
- indicate which statements are from the witnesses' own knowledge and which are from his information and belief (and any source for such information and belief).
- be verified by a statement of truth: 'I believe that the facts stated in this witness statement are true' (see p 351).

➤ Any exhibit should be verified and identified by the witness.

➤ If a party is required to serve a witness statement for use at trial but cannot obtain a witness statement, that party may apply to court for permission to serve a witness summary instead of the statement (*r 32.9(1)*).

- The application is an application without notice.

- A 'witness summary' is a summary of the evidence (if known) which would be included in a witness statement or (if the evidence is not known) matters about which the party serving the summary wishes to question the witness (*r 32.9(2)*).

Plans, photographs, models, etc (*r 33.5*)

➤ Where evidence (eg: a plan, a photograph, business records which may be given in evidence under *CEA 1995 s 9*, or a model) is **not**:

   a) contained in a witness statement, affidavit or an expert's report, *or*

   b) to be given orally at trial, *or*

   c) evidence in respect of which a hearsay notice must be given under *r 32.2*, ...

   ... that evidence may only be receivable if the party intending to rely on the evidence gives notice to the other parties (unless the court orders otherwise).

- Where evidence is to be given as evidence of a fact, notice must be given not later than the last day for serving witness statements, *unless either*

   • the evidence forms part of expert evidence, in which case notice is given when the expert's report is served on the other party, *or*

   • there is not to be a witness statement *or* the evidence is solely to disprove an allegation made in a witness statement, in which case notice is at least 21 days before the hearing the evidence is to be put.

- If evidence is produced for a reason other than as evidence of fact or expert evidence, the party intending to rely on it must give at notice at least 21 days before the hearing.

➤ A party must give other parties every opportunity to inspect the evidence and agree its admission without further proof.

III Opinion

➤ A witness may only testify as to matters observed by him and may not give his *opinion* about those matters.

➤ Opinion 'evidence' is inadmissible unless it is:

   1. **expert opinion** (*CEA 1972 s 3(1)*).

      - This is opinion on any relevant matter on which the expert is qualified to give expert evidence.

   2. **perception** (*CEA 1972 s 3(2)*).

      - The witness conveys relevant facts personally perceived by him. The reason for this relaxation is that it is not always possible to separate facts from inferences.

IV Expert evidence

➤ See p 414.

V Hearsay

Hearsay: a statutory meaning

➤ Hearsay is 'a statement made by someone *other* than the person *now* giving evidence, intended to prove the truth of the matter stated' whether first hand hearsay (ie: reported directly from a source) or multiple hearsay (coming from a source *via* intermediaries).

Hearsay: a plain English meaning (!)

➤ Hearsay is an assertion, other than one made by a person while giving oral evidence in the proceedings, if the assertion is used to prove the truth of what it asserts.

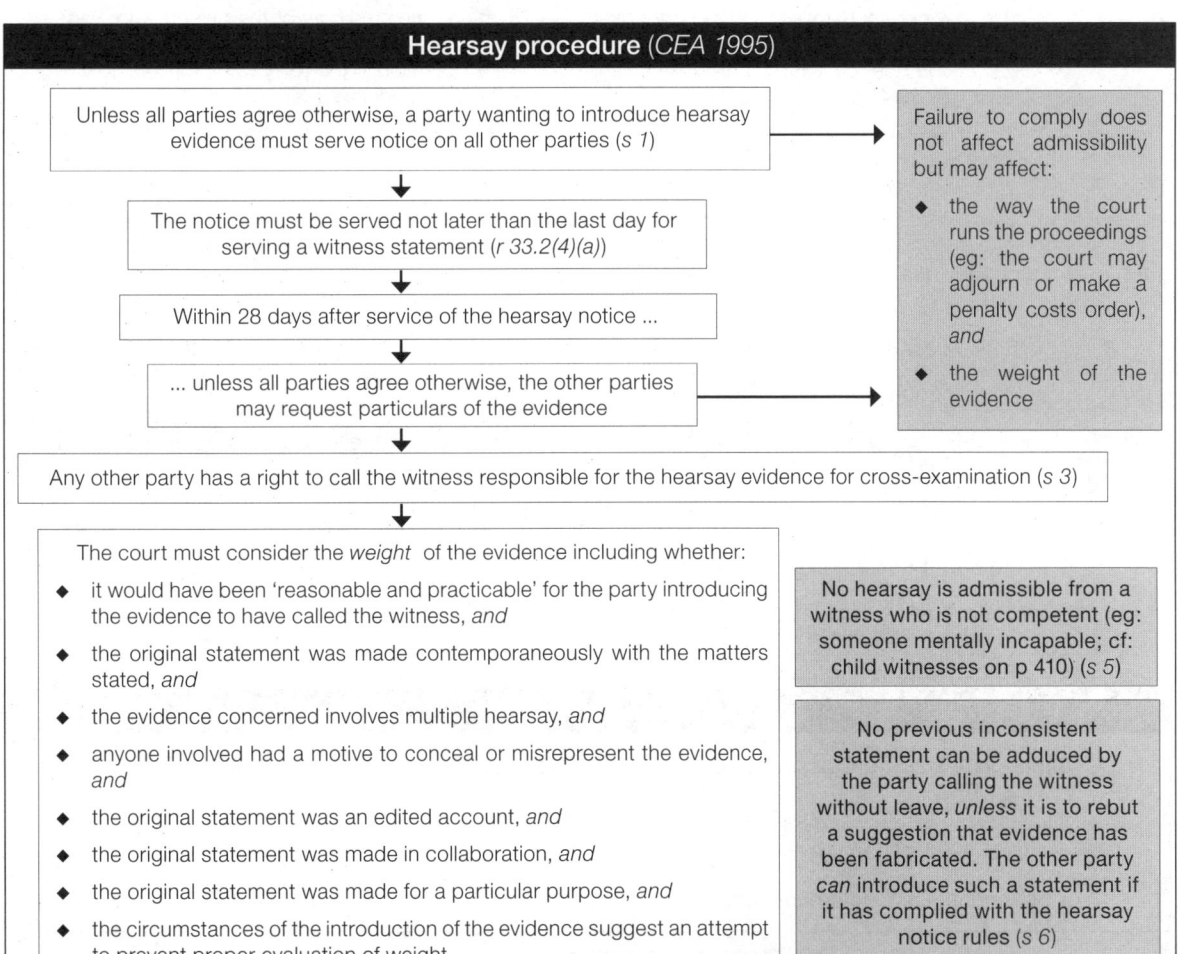

Hearsay procedure (*CEA 1995*)

Unless all parties agree otherwise, a party wanting to introduce hearsay evidence must serve notice on all other parties (*s 1*)

↓

The notice must be served not later than the last day for serving a witness statement (*r 33.2(4)(a)*)

↓

Within 28 days after service of the hearsay notice ...

↓

... unless all parties agree otherwise, the other parties may request particulars of the evidence

↓

Any other party has a right to call the witness responsible for the hearsay evidence for cross-examination (*s 3*)

↓

The court must consider the *weight* of the evidence including whether:
- it would have been 'reasonable and practicable' for the party introducing the evidence to have called the witness, *and*
- the original statement was made contemporaneously with the matters stated, *and*
- the evidence concerned involves multiple hearsay, *and*
- anyone involved had a motive to conceal or misrepresent the evidence, *and*
- the original statement was an edited account, *and*
- the original statement was made in collaboration, *and*
- the original statement was made for a particular purpose, *and*
- the circumstances of the introduction of the evidence suggest an attempt to prevent proper evaluation of weight.

Failure to comply does not affect admissibility but may affect:
- the way the court runs the proceedings (eg: the court may adjourn or make a penalty costs order), *and*
- the weight of the evidence

No hearsay is admissible from a witness who is not competent (eg: someone mentally incapable; cf: child witnesses on p 410) (*s 5*)

No previous inconsistent statement can be adduced by the party calling the witness without leave, *unless* it is to rebut a suggestion that evidence has been fabricated. The other party *can* introduce such a statement if it has complied with the hearsay notice rules (*s 6*)

Published works

➤ Published works and records are admissible as evidence of the facts contained (*CEA 1995 s 7*).

Contents of a hearsay notice

➤ A hearsay notice must state:

   a) identify the hearsay evidence (*r 33.2(3)(a)*), *and*

   b) state that the party serving the notice will rely on the hearsay evidence at trial (*r 33.2(3)(b)*), *and*

   c) if the witness is not being called to give evidence, gives the reason why the witness will not be called (*r 33.2(3)(c)*).

   - If the witness is not being called to give evidence, the party intending to rely on the hearsay evidence must, when he serves the witness statement inform the other parties that the witness is not being called to give evidence and give the reason why the witness is not being called (*r 33.2(3)(c)*).

   - If the hearsay is in a document, the party proposing to rely on the hearsay evidence must supply a copy to any party who requests a copy (*r 32.2(4)(b)*).

Cross-examination	Credibility
➤ Any other party may apply to the court for permission to call the maker of statement to be cross-examined on the contents of the statement (*r 33.4(1)*). ◆ An application must be made not more than 14 days after the day on which the notice is served on the applicant (*r 33.4(2)*).	➤ If any other party wishes to call evidence to attach the credibility of the person who made the statement, that party must give notice of this intention to the party who proposes to give hearsay evidence (*r 33.5(1)*). ◆ Notice must be given not more than 14 days after the day on which the hearsay notice was served on the party who wishes to dispute credibility (*r 33.5(2)*).

➤ 1 notice may deal with more than 1 witness.

➤ The duty to give a notice of intention to rely on hearsay evidence does not apply (*r 33.3*):

   a) to evidence at hearings other than trials, *or*

   b) an affidavit or a witness statement which is to be used at trial but which does not contain hearsay evidence, *or*

   c) to a statement which a party to a probate action wishes to put in evidence and which is alleged to have been made by the person whose estate is the subject of the proceedings, *or*

   d) where a *PD* excludes the requirement to give such a notice.

Business records

➤ Although hearsay, business records are admissible in evidence (*CEA 1995 s 9(1)*).

   ◆ To be accepted as a business record, a document must be certified by an officer of the business (*CEA 1995 s 9(2)*).

   ◆ Computerised statements are also *prima facie* admissible as hearsay (*CEA 1995 ss 1-2*).

VI   Notarial acts and instruments

➤ A notarial act or instrument may be received in evidence without further proof as duly authenticated unless the contrary is proved (*r 32.20*).

O Trial preparations

    I   Making up the trial bundle
    II   Should counsel be instructed?
    III Ensuring attendance of witnesses or taking depositions
    IV   Expert evidence

I Making up the trial bundle (r 39.5, PD39: 3)

Steps

1. Check through the court's case management directions to see where the trial will be.

2. Check whether any relevant hearings are needed to 'flesh out' existing directions (eg: listing hearings, case management conferences, pre-trial review).

3. The court will consult the parties when it sets a timetable for a trial under (r 39.4):
    - r 28.6 (fast track - fixing/confirming the trial date and giving directions), *or*
    - r 29.8 (multi-track - setting a trial timetable and fixing/confirming the trial date or week).

4. The contents of the trial bundle should be agreed where possible.

5. **Not more than 7 days and not less than 3 days before the start of the trial**, the claimant's solicitor files the trial bundle containing copies of (NB: originals should be available at trial):
    - the claim form and all statements of case,
    - a case summary and/or chronology where appropriate,
    - requests for further information and responses to the requests,
    - any notices of intention to rely on evidence (eg: photographs) (see p 408) which are *not*:
        - contained in a witness statement, affidavit or experts report, *or*
        - being given orally at trial, *or*
        - hearsay evidence,
    - all witness statements being relied on as evidence,
    - any witness summaries,
    - any medical reports and responses to them,
    - any experts' reports and responses to them,
    - any order giving directions as to the conduct of the trial,
    - any notices of intention to use hearsay evidence (see p 410),
    - any other necessary documents.

    > **Trial bundles** should be paginated and indexed with a description of each document. If the total number of pages is more than 100, place numbered dividers between groups of documents. The bundle should be contained in a ring binder or lever arch file. Where there is more than 1 bundle, each should be distinguishable (eg: by different colours or letters). If there are numerous bundles, a core bundle should be prepared containing the core documents essential to the proceedings, with references to supplementary documents in the other bundles

6. The parties should also agree where possible that:
    - documents contained in the bundle are authentic even if not disclosed, *and*
    - documents in the bundle may be treated as evidence of facts stated within even if a hearsay notice has not been served (see p 410).

7. Where it is not possible to agree the contents of the bundle, a summary of the points on which the parties are unable to agree should be included.

8. The party filing the trial bundle should supply identical bundles to all the parties to the proceedings and for the use of the witnesses.

    NB: a reading list together with an estimated length of reading time and an estimated length of the hearing signed by all advocates is also required to be lodged.

II Should counsel be instructed?

Steps
1. A brief: usually needed if a barrister is instructed
2. A conference may be necessary
3. The barrister's fee

1 A brief: usually needed if a barrister is instructed

➤ A brief is the traditional presentation of the case to the barrister who will appear at the hearing.

➤ The brief should include:
- the heading of the action, *and*
- a list of enclosures being forwarded to counsel (eg: client's statement, witness statements, pleadings, any LSC funding certificate, experts' reports, *relevant* correspondence, pleadings, setting down bundle, trial bundle, counsel's earlier advice, etc).

➤ It should then:
- identify the client.
- set out *both* sides of the case.
- indicate the solicitor's view, and draw attention to where advice is specifically needed.
- formally request counsel to carry out the task required.

➤ The back sheet should be endorsed with:
- the title of the action.
- a definition of what the instructions are.
- counsel's name and that of his chambers.
- the solicitor's firm's name, address and reference.
- if relevant, the LSC funding reference number.

Note: the third person is traditionally used in writing to counsel.

2 A conference may be necessary

➤ This is useful if the facts are complex, or if counsel wishes to assess a client as a witness, or to fully comprehend and assess his injuries.
- The solicitor should arrange this with the counsel's clerk if it is thought necessary.

➤ A written opinion may be specifically requested.
- Costs will not be allowed unless the court decides the need for the conference was reasonable.

3 The barrister's fee

➤ If LSC funding covers it, the LSC will pay the fee.

➤ A solicitor negotiates the fee on behalf of a private client. The solicitor is liable to counsel for the fee, so a solicitor should ensure that he has been put in funds by a client before the barrister is instructed.
- The appearance fee is payable once the brief is delivered, but it is usually waived or reduced if the action settles before the hearing.
- The fee covers 1 day, unless otherwise agreed. A 'refresher' is due on subsequent days.

CIVIL LITIGATION
Trial preparations

III Ensuring attendance of witnesses or taking depositions (Part 34)

➤ The solicitor must check the availability of witnesses.

➤ Sometimes witnesses may not attend court voluntarily and it is necessary to compel them to do so by a witness summons.

- **Expert witnesses:** may prefer to be summonsed as the obligation helps break appointments.
- **Police officers:** *must* be summonsed, as they will not otherwise give evidence in a civil matter.

Witness summons (rr 34.2-34.7, PD34: 1, 3)

Purpose:	A witness summons is a document issued by the court requiring a witness to: ◆ attend court to give evidence, *and/or* ◆ produce documents to the court
Time	➤ General rule: must be served **at least 7 days** before the date on which the witness is required to attend. ◆ A court may change this time limit.

Procedure for issue	**Steps**
	1. A witness summons must be in the specified form.
	2. There must be a separate witness summons for each witness.
	3. Obtain the court's permission to issue the summons if summons is to be issued:
	   a) less than 7 days before the date of the trial, *or*
	   b) for a witness to attend court to give evidence or to produce documents on any date except the date fixed for the trial, *or*
	   c) for a witness to attend court to give evidence or to produce documents at any hearing except the trial.
	4. Issue the summons - 2 copies of the witness summons should be filed with the court for sealing.
	◆ 1 copy will be kept on the court file.
	Note: A witness summons is issued on the date entered on the summons by the court.

Procedure for service	**Steps**
	1. A witness summons will be served by the court *unless* the issuing party indicates in writing, at the time of issue, that he will serve it himself.
	2. Prepare the 'witness sum' to pay the witness for travelling expenses and loss of time as follows:
	◆ the witness's expenses for travelling to court and returning to his home or place of work, *and*
	◆ a sum for time during which earnings or benefit are lost (or a lesser sum it may be proved the witness will lose by attending court.
	3. Decide who is to serve the witness summons (see below).
	4a **Self-service:** 1 Notify the court in writing that self-service will be the method of service
	                      2 Serve the witness summons and offer the witness the 'witness sum' at the time.
	4b **Service by the court:** 1 Deposit, in the court office, the 'witness sum'
	                                2 The court will serve the witness summons

Depositions (rr 34.8-34.11)

➤ At times, a party may wish to apply for a witness to be examined *before* a hearing or trial.

- Such a witness is called a 'deponent' and his evidence is called a 'deposition'.
  - The examination is usually conducted as if the witness were giving evidence at a trial.

➤ A deposition may be given in evidence at a hearing or trial *unless* the court orders otherwise.

- However, the court *may* require a deponent to attend the hearing and give evidence orally.

➤ If deposition evidence is to be used, notice must be served at least 21 days before the hearing/trial.

➤ If a deposition is used at trial, it is treated as a witness statement for the purposes of prior inspection.

IV Expert evidence (*Part 35*)

➤ **Needed?** Expert evidence is restricted to what is reasonably required to resolve the proceedings (*r 35.1*).
   ◆ If a claim is on the fast track, the court will not direct an expert to attend a hearing unless it is necessary in the interests of justice (*r 35.2(2)*).

➤ **Duty:** An expert has an overriding duty to help the court on the matters within his expertise (*r 35.3*).

➤ **Permission:** No party may call an expert or use an expert's report without the court's permission (*r 35.4(1)*).
   ◆ To apply for permission a party must (*rr 35.4(2), 35.13*):
      • identify the field in which he wishes to rely on expert evidence, *and*
      • identify, where practicable, the expert in that field on whose evidence he wishes to rely, *and*
      • disclose the evidence to the other parties.
   ◆ The court may limit the amount of the expert's fees and expenses that the party who wishes to rely on the expert may recover from any other party (*r 35.4(4)*).

➤ **The report:** Expert evidence must be given in a written report unless the court directs otherwise (*r 35.5(1)*).

➤ **Questions:** A party may ask an expert written questions about his report.
   ◆ The answers become part of the report.
   ◆ Unless the court orders otherwise, or the parties agree, questions:
      • may be put once only, *and*
      • must be put within 28 days of service of the expert's report (and be copied to solicitors), *and*
      • must be for the purpose only of clarification of the report.
   ◆ Not answering means the evidence may be disregarded and have costs penalties.
   ◆ The party instructing the expert must pay the fees for the questions (*PD35: 5.3*).

➤ **Joint experts:** Where 2 or more parties each wish to submit expert evidence the court may direct that the evidence on that issue is given by 1 joint expert only (*r 35.7*).
   ◆ Each instructing party must give a copy of its instructions to the other party (*r 35.8*).
   ◆ The court has a wide discretion to make orders as to the expert's role and his fees (*r 35.8*).
   ◆ The instructing parties are usually jointly and severally liable for the expert's fees and expenses (*r 35.8*).

➤ **Court's discretion:** The court has a wide discretion with regard to experts. It may eg: direct that the experts discuss certain matters between themselves, prepare statements of (non-binding) agreed and non-agreed issues, give the expert directions (particularly if the expert requests them), etc.

➤ **Instructions to an expert:** are not privileged against disclosure but the court will not order disclosure of a specific document or allow cross-examination of the expert in court, *unless* it thinks there are reasonable grounds to consider the instructions were inaccurate or incomplete. If the court thinks so, it will allow the cross-examination where it appears to be in the interests of justice to do so (*r 35.10(4), PD35: 4*).

Content of the expert's report (*r 35.10, PD35*)

➤ The experts report should be addressed to the court and must contain:
   ◆ the substance of all material instructions (written *or* oral), on the basis of which the report was written,
   ◆ details of the expert's qualifications,
   ◆ details of any literature or other material on which the expert has relied in making the report,
   ◆ details of who carried out any test or experiment which the expert has used for the report and whether or not the test or experiment has been carried out under the expert's supervision,
   ◆ the qualifications of the person who carried out any such test or experiment,
   ◆ (if there is a range of opinion on matters in the report), a summary of it, and reasons for his own opinion,
   ◆ a summary of the conclusions reached,
   ◆ At the end: a statement that the expert understands his duty to the court and has complied with it,
   ◆ A statement of truth (see p 351): ' I believe that the facts I have stated in this report are true and that the opinions I have expressed are correct.'

P The trial

Steps

1 ### The claimant's side makes the opening speech
- ➤ This involves taking the judge through the statements of case and introducing agreed exhibits.
- ➤ The judge may dispense with this (particularly in fast track cases - *PD28: 8.2*).

2 ### The claimant gives evidence
- ➤ This is done by oral examination, but examination-in-chief is conducted by using the witness statement exchanged previously, unless the court decides otherwise.
- ➤ The sequence of questioning is:
    - ◆ examination-in-chief by the claimant's side,
    - ◆ cross-examination by the defendant's side,
    - ◆ re-examination (on points arising from the cross-examination) by the claimant's side.
- ➤ The defendant's case must be put to the claimant during cross-examination.
- ➤ Each side should check the admissibility rules (see p 406 et seq).

3 ### The claimant's side presents evidence
- ➤ This is done by oral examination of the witnesses.
- ➤ The sequence of questioning is:
    - ◆ examination-in-chief by the claimant's side. (This is conducted by using the witness statements exchanged previously, unless the court decides otherwise.)
    - ◆ cross-examination by the defendant's side,
    - ◆ re-examination (on points arising from the cross-examination) by the claimant's side.
- ➤ The defendant's case must be put to the witness.
- ➤ Each side should check the admissibility rules (see p 406 et seq).
- ➤ If a witness gives consistently unfavourable or adverse answers to the surprise of the claimant, the claimant's side should ask the judge to declare the witness hostile.
    - ◆ If the judge does so, previously inconsistent statements can be put to the witness (see CEA 1995 s 6 and the law on hearsay p 409).

4 ### The defendant's side makes its opening speech
- ➤ The defendant's side may make an opening speech.
- ➤ The judge may dispense with this (particularly in fast track cases - *PD28: 8.2*).

CIVIL LITIGATION
The trial

cont. 5 — **The defendant gives evidence**

- This is done by oral examination, but examination-in-chief is conducted by using the witness statement exchanged previously, unless the court decides otherwise.
- The sequence of questioning is:
  - examination-in-chief by the defendant's side,
  - cross-examination by the claimant's side,
  - re-examination (on points arising from the cross-examination) by the defendant's side.
- The claimant's case should be put to the defendant.
- Each side should check the admissibility rules (see p 406 et seq).

6 — **The defendant's side presents the evidence**

- This is done by oral examination of the witnesses.
- The sequence of questioning is:
  - examination-in-chief by the defendant's side. (This is conducted by using the witness statements exchanged previously, unless the court decides otherwise.)
  - cross-examination by the claimant's side,
  - re-examination (on points arising from the cross-examination) by the defendant's side.
- The claimant's case must be put to the witness.
- Each side should check the admissibility rules (see p 406 et seq).
- If a witness gives consistently unfavourable or adverse answers to the surprise of the defendant, the defendant's side should ask the judge to declare the witness hostile.
  - If the judge does so, previously inconsistent statements can be put to the witness (CEA 1995 s 6 and see the law on hearsay p 409).

7 — **The defendant's side's closing speech**

- The defendant may make a closing speech.

8 — **The claimant's side's closing speech**

- The claimant may make a closing speech.

9 — **Judgment is given and any necessary orders are made**

Are leading questions allowed?	
Examination-in-chief	✗ (except to obtain a denial of the other party's case)
Cross examination	✓
Re-examination	✗ (except to obtain a denial of the other party's case)

Q Costs

I	Basis on which costs are awarded	V	Assessment
II	Duty to notify client of costs orders	VI	Costs in special cases
III	Costs orders and the court's discretion	VII	Assessment of costs of an LSC funded client
IV	Costs at trial		

I Basis on which costs are awarded

▶ Costs awarded are a *reasonable* amount in respect of all costs *reasonably* incurred (*r 44.4(1)*).

▶ There are 2 bases on which a Court may assess and award costs (the choice is up to the judge)(*r 44.4(2)*):

  1 **Standard basis (most usual)** (*r 44.4(2)*)

   ◆ The costs must also be proportionate to the matters in issue.

   ◆ Doubts over what is 'reasonable' or 'proportionate' are resolved in favour of the paying party.

  2 **Indemnity basis (rare)** (*r 44.4(3)*)

   ◆ Doubts over what is 'reasonable' are resolved in favour of the receiving party.

II Duty to notify client of costs orders

▶ Where a party has a solicitor and the party is not present when the order is made, the party's solicitor must notify his client in writing of the costs order *and* why the order was made (*r 44.2*).

  ◆ This notification must be no later than 7 days after the solicitor receives notice of the order (*r 44.2*).

III Costs orders and the court's discretion

▶ The court may make an order about costs at any stage in a case (*PD:Costs 8.3(1)*).

▶ The court has discretion as to (*r 44.3(1)*):

  ◆ whether costs are payable by one party to another, *and*

  ◆ the amount of those costs, *and*

  ◆ when costs are to be paid.

> Costs may also be agreed between the parties

> The court may at any stage in a case order any party to file an estimate of costs and to serve copies on all other parties

▶ If the court makes a costs order (*except* an order for fixed costs) it may either (*r 44.7*):

  ◆ make a summary assessment of the costs (see p 420), *or*

  ◆ order detailed assessment of the costs by a costs officer (see p 421).

▶ **General rule:** the unsuccessful party is ordered to pay the costs of the successful party (*r 44.3(2)*).

▶ **Not using the general rule:** in deciding what order (if any) to make about costs, a court has regard to all the circumstances, including (*r 44.3(4) - 44.3(5)*):

  ◆ the conduct of all the parties before (especially the extent of any compliance with any pre-action protocol) and during the proceedings, *and*

  ◆ whether it was reasonable for a party to raise, pursue or contest a particular allegation or issue, *and*

  ◆ whether a claimant who has wholly or partly succeeded in his claim, exaggerated his claim, *and*

  ◆ whether a party has succeeded on part of his case, even if he has not been wholly successful, *and*

  ◆ any payment into court (or admissible offer to settle) made by a party which is drawn to the court's attention (whether or not made in accordance with *Part 36* (see also pp 385-391)).

CIVIL LITIGATION
Costs

If the court decides (or does not) to make an order about costs ... (r 44.3, PD:Costs 8.5)

➤ **General rule:** the unsuccessful party is ordered to pay the costs of the successful party.
  ♦ If the factors on the previous page apply, the court may use its discretion to make one of several possible orders, including the following:

Order	Effect	Usual reasoning of court
costs *or* costs in any event	The 'winner' in the costs order is entitled to costs for the relevant part of the proceedings, whatever other costs orders are made in the proceedings	The loser's conduct is unreasonable *or* costs relate to a collateral issue
costs in the case *or* costs in the application	The 'winner' in the costs order, at the end of the proceedings, is entitled to costs for the relevant part of the proceedings	Costs are preliminary to trial and conduct of both parties is reasonable
costs reserved	The decision about costs is deferred to a later occasion. If no later order is made the costs will be costs in the case	It is not yet possible to make a decision on the reasonableness of either party's conduct
Claimant's/ Defendant's costs in the case/	♦ If the 'winner' in the costs order is awarded costs at the end of the proceedings, he is entitled to his costs for the relevant part of the proceedings ♦ If any other party is awarded costs at the end of the proceedings, the party in whose favour the final costs order is made is not liable to pay the costs of any other party for the relevant part of the proceedings	Named party's conduct is only considered reasonable if he succeeds later at trial. The loser's conduct is unreasonable
costs thrown away	Where, eg: a judgment or order is set aside, the 'winner' in the costs order is entitled to the costs which have been incurred as a consequence. This includes the costs of: ♦ preparing for + attending any hearing where the judgment/order which has been set aside was made, ♦ preparing for + attending any hearing to set aside the judgment or order in question, ♦ preparing for + attending any hearing at which the court orders an adjournment, ♦ any steps taken to enforce a judgment or order which was later set aside.	The loser's conduct is unreasonable *or* costs relate to a collateral issue
costs of and caused by	Where, eg: a costs order is made on an application to amend a statement of case, the 'winner' in the costs order is entitled to costs of preparing for + attending the hearing and costs of any consequential amendments to his documents	The loser's conduct (which may be reasonable) causes the other party to incur consequential costs
costs here and below	The 'winner' in the costs order is entitled to his costs in respect of the proceedings in the court making the order and also (generally) to costs of the proceedings in any lower court	The 'winner' was correct in having the hearing in a higher court during the proceedings
no order as to costs (r 44.13) or each party pays its own costs	Each party is to bear his own costs of the relevant part of the proceedings, whatever costs order the court makes at the end of the proceedings	Merits (or lack of merits) of both sides are equal
Costs forthwith	The 'winner' in the costs order, is entitled to costs and to have these assessed immediately.	Costs are unusually heavy or loser's conduct is unreasonable and the court wishes to express disapproval

Where the court makes an order or direction on an application without notice and its order does not mention costs, it will be deemed to include an order for applicant's costs in the case (r 44.13(1A))

Possible costs orders (r 44.3(6)-(8))

♦ pay a proportion of another party's costs
♦ pay a stated amount in respect of another party's costs
♦ pay costs from or until a certain date only
♦ pay costs incurred before proceedings have begun
♦ pay costs relating to particular steps taken in the proceedings
♦ pay costs relating only to a distinct part of the proceedings
♦ pay interest on costs from or until a certain date, including a date before judgment

Where the court has ordered a party to pay costs, it may order an amount to be paid on account before the costs are assessed

CIVIL LITIGATION
Costs

> **Factors the court takes into account in deciding the amount of costs** (r 44.5)
> - the conduct of all the parties, including in particular:
>   - conduct before and proceedings, *and*
>   - the efforts made, if any, before and during the proceedings in order to try to resolve the dispute.
> - the amount or value of any money or property involved.
> - the importance of the matter to all the parties.
> - the complexity of the matter or the difficulty/novelty of questions raised.
> - the skill, effort, specialised knowledge and responsibility involved.
> - the time spent on the case.
> - the place and circumstances of the work.

IV Costs at trial

A Which type of costs rules apply for costs at trial?

B Fixed costs (*Part 45*)

➤ The amount of fixed costs (solicitors charges) claimable are (*Part 45, Section I*):

- fixed commencement costs by reference to Table 1 in *Part 45* (NB: the amount claimed in the claim form - or the value of goods claimed if specified - is used to determine the band in Table 1 that applies to the claim). The bands in Table 1 are:
  - i) >£25 to £500, ii) >£500 to £1,000, iii) >£1,000 to £5,000 or the only claim is for delivery of goods and no value is specified on the claim form, *or* iv) the value of the claim is >£5,000, *and*
- certain additional costs for certain types of service of documents, *and*
- fixed costs on judgment entry *but* only if the claimant has claimed fixed commencement costs on the claim form *and* if he is given judgment for certain types of claim (set out in Table 3 in *Part 45*), *and*
- certain miscellaneous fixed costs (set out in Table 4 in *Part 45*).

➤ *Part 45, Section II* sets out costs for costs-only proceedings, or proceedings for approval of a settlement/compromise for or against a child or patient, where: i) the dispute arises from a road traffic accident, *or* ii) the agreed damages include personal injury and/or property damages, *or* iii) the total value of the agreed damages does not exceed £10,000, *or* iv) if a claim had been issued for the amount of agreed damages, the small claims track would not have been the normal track.

➤ *Part 45, Sections III, and IV* set out the percentage increase allowed under a CFA which provides for a success fee where the dispute: i) arises from a road traffic accident or ii) is between an employee and his employer arising from a bodily injury sustained by the employee. *Section V* provides for fixed recovery success fees in employer liability disease claims.

C Fast track trial costs (Part 46)

➤ **General rule:** this applies *only* where, *at the date of the trial*, the claim is allocated to the fast track. Costs are awarded for an advocate who prepares for/appears at the trial, based on value of the claim as follows:

'Value of claim'	Up to £3,000	£3,000 to £10,000	More than £10,000
Costs	£350	£500	£750

NB: Sometimes the court may vary the amounts payable under the general rule

➤ The court may also apportion costs to reflect the respective degrees of success on the issues at trial.

1 **Claim is only for the payment of money and claimant gets costs:** 'value of claim' = total amount of the judgment excluding interest, costs and any reduction made for contributory negligence.

2 **Claim is only for the payment of money and defendant gets costs:** 'value of claim' = the amount specified in the claim form (excluding interest and costs), *or*, if no amount is specified, the maximum amount the claimant reasonably expected to recover (see the statement of value in the claim form), *or* more than £10,000, if the claim form says the claimant cannot reasonably say how much this is.

3 **Claim is only for a remedy other than the payment of money:** 'value of claim' = more than £3,000 but not more than £10,000, unless the court orders otherwise.

4 **Claim includes a claim for payment of money and for a remedy other than the payment of money:** 'value of claim' = the highest of the values under 1, 2 and 3 above.

Note on counterclaims: If a defendant counterclaim has a higher value than the claim and the claimant succeeds at trial on both the claim *and* counterclaim, 'value of claim' = the value of the defendant's counterclaim.

➤ There are certain special rules where an advocate acts for more than 1 claimant/defendant.

Note on 'additional liability': the court may also make an award in respect of 'additional liability' (*r 46.3(2A)*).

V Assessment

➤ Where the court does not order fixed costs (or no fixed costs are provided for) the amount of costs payable will be assessed by the court. This will be by summary or detailed assessment (*r 44.7*).

   ◆ A costs order is decided by a detailed assessment unless the order says otherwise (*PD:Costs 12.2*).

➤ **General rule:** detailed assessment of costs of any proceedings (or any part) should not take place until the conclusion of the proceedings, but the court *may* order them to be assessed immediately (*r 47.1*).

➤ **The 2 types of assessment are summary assessment and detailed assessment:**

1 **Summary assessment**

➤ **General rule:** Whenever a court makes an order about costs which does not provide for fixed costs to be paid the court should consider whether to make a summary assessment of costs (*PD:Costs 13.1*). Usually, the court makes a summary assessment (unless there is good reason not to (*PD:Costs13.2*)):

   a) at the end of a fast track trial, when the order will deal with the costs of the whole claim, *or*

   b) at the end of any other hearing which has lasted not more than 1 day, when the order will deal with the costs of the application or matter to which the hearing related.

   NB: the general rule is that there is no summary assessment if the court has ordered 'costs in the case'.

➤ **Written statement** (*PD:Costs 13.5*): Each party claiming costs drafts a written costs statement (excluding any additional liability) showing in a schedule: hours claimed, hourly rates, fee earner grade, amount + nature of disbursements (except counsel's fee for appearing at the hearing), solicitor's costs for attending/appearing at the hearing, counsel's fees for the hearing, and VAT - all signed by the party/his solicitor.

➤ **Serving the statement** (*PD:Costs 13.5(4)*): As soon as possible (and in any event not less than 24 hours before the hearing) the statement must be filed and copies served on any party who might pay those costs.

➤ **The hearing:** The court specifies the amount payable separately as base costs and as additional liability (for solicitor's charges, disbursements and allowable VAT) and amounts awarded as Fast Track Trial Costs.

CIVIL LITIGATION
Costs

2 Detailed assessment

Steps

1 **Drafting the bill** - Receiving party drafts a bill of costs - include (*PD:Costs 4.1-4.4, 4.9, 4.13*):
- title page containing the full title of the proceedings and the name of the party whose bill it is,
- a description of the document giving the right to assessment and certain background information,
- items of costs claimed under the certain headings,
- summary showing the total costs claimed on each page of the bill,
- schedules of time spent on non-routine attendances,
- certain certificates (eg: LSC certificate and any other relevant certificates).

Note 1: Each item claimed in the bill of costs must be consecutively numbered.

Note 2: The bill of costs must not contain claims for costs or court fees relating solely to the detailed assessment proceedings other than costs claimed for preparing and checking the bill.

2 **Serving the bill** - Receiving party serves the bill of costs, notice of commencement and various other documents (*rr 47.6-47.8, PD:Costs 32*)
- This must be done within 3 months of the date of judgment, direction, order, award, right to costs arose (for *Part 36*) etc., otherwise the party may be penalised for the delay.

3 **Disputing the bill?** - (*rr 47.9, 47.13, 47.14, PD:Costs 40*)
- Paying party (and any other party) may dispute the bill - this must be done by serving points of dispute within 21 days after the date of service of the notice of commencement, on the receiving party and every other party. The parties may agree to vary this period (*PD:Costs 35.1*).
- Within 21 days after service of the points of dispute, the receiving party may serve a reply.
- Within 3 months of the expiry of the period for starting detailed assessment proceedings, the receiving party must file a request for a detailed hearing. This must be accompanied by a copy/copies of:
  - the notice of commencement; the bill of costs; the document giving the right to detailed assessment; the points of dispute (annotated to show agreed/disputed items and their value); replies served; costs orders made by the court; fee notes + other written evidence served on the paying party; if there is a dispute about the receiving party's liability to pay costs to his solicitors, any written information/letter provided by the solicitor explaining calculation of charges; a statement signed by the receiving party/his solicitor giving contact details of the receiving + paying party and other persons who have served points of dispute and giving a time estimate for the hearing.
- Not less than 7 days before the hearing and not more than 14 days before (*PD:Costs 40.11-12*), the receiving party must file with the court papers supporting the bill: ie: instructions + briefs to counsel (in chronological order); all advices, opinions, drafts in response; reports + opinions of medical and other experts; correspondence files and attendance notes; papers relevant to additional liability.
- The detailed assessment hearing is held.

4 **Default costs certificate** - an order to pay the costs to which it relates (*rr 47.11-47.12*)
- The receiving party may file a request for a default costs certificate if he has not been served with any points of dispute or if the 21 days in '3' above has expired.

5 **Interim costs certificate** (*r 47.15*)
- The court may at any time after the receiving party has filed a request for a detailed assessment hearing, issue an interim costs certificate for such sum as it considers appropriate.

6 **Final costs certificate** (*r 47.16*)
- When a completed bill is filed (which must be within 14 days after the end of the detailed assessment hearing) the court will issue a final costs certificate and serve it on the parties. It will include an order to pay the costs to which it relates, unless the court orders otherwise.

7 **Appeal** - there are limited rights to appeal (*rr 47.20-47.23*) (see p 430).

VI Costs in special cases

➤ For solicitor and own client costs, see 'Bills' (see p 24).

➤ For costs pursuant to a contract, costs payable to non-parties, trustees/PRs, children, patients or litigants in person or costs due to pre-claim disclosure, there are special rules (not dealt with here) (*Part 48*).

VII Assessment of costs of an LSC funded client (r 47.17, PD44: 21,22)

➤ **Summary Assessment:**

- The court must not make a summary assessment of the costs of a receiving party who is an LSC funded client (*PD:Costs13.9*).

- The court may make a summary assessment of costs payable by an LSC funded client (*PD:Costs13.10*).

The LSC funded client is the... (r 47.17, PD:Costs 21, CLS(CP)R 2000)

...winner	...loser

The costs of the winner's solicitor:
• there may be a detailed assessment hearing for the winner's 'solicitor and own client costs'
Other Inter partes costs:
• there may be an order for other inter partes costs to be decided by assessment if not agreed:
  • If there is a detailed assessment, a bill of costs may be at 2 rates:
    i) at the prescribed rate (payable by the LSC), *and*
    ii) at a 'private individual's rate' (paid by the other side)
	The costs of the loser's solicitor:
	• the loser's solicitor can claim these costs by filing an LSC schedule for the prescribed rates (and following the '**Summary Assessment**' procedure above if appropriate)
	Other Inter partes costs:

Is Costs Protection available?

- Yes → The LSC pays the costs of the winner up to the Cost Protection cap. The LSC funded client must pay any costs (after assessment if necessary) after the benefit of the Cost Protection cap
- No → The LSC funded client must pay the costs (after assessment if necessary)

Usually, money recoverable through recovery of inter partes costs will pay for the costs of the winner's solicitor. However the LSC may keep: • any *inter partes* costs awarded in favour of the winner, *and* • any contributions made by the legally helped party, *and* • **the statutory charge** (ie: the LSC has the first call on any damages won).	Before the LSC can be ordered to pay the whole or any part of the costs incurred by a non-LSC party: • proceedings must be finally decided in favour of the non-funded party, *and* • unless there is good reason for a delay, the non-funded party must provide written notice of intention to seek an order against the LSC within 3 months of the costs order, *and* • the court must be satisfied that it is 'just and equitable' in the circumstances that costs should be made out of public funds, *and* • (in a court of first instance), the proceedings must have been instituted by the LSC funded client and the non-funded party is an individual and will suffer financial hardship unless the order is made

The LSC keeps any contribution paid by the losing LSC funded client

➤ Generally, 'Costs Protection' is available to an LSC funded client but not in respect of **Help at Court** or **Legal Help**
  - In the case of Legal Help, if he later receives Legal Representation/General Family Help/Help with Mediation for the same dispute (but not any of these three in family proceedings), then costs protection does apply.

➤ Costs Protection is given by *AJA 1999 s 11*: '[that] costs cannot exceed the amount it is reasonable for [an LSC funded client] to pay having regard to all the circumstances including the financial resources of all the parties to the proceedings and their conduct in connection with the dispute to which the proceedings relate.'

Additional Liability (r 44.3A) (see also pp 22-23)

➤ Additional liability is:
  - a percentage increase in solicitor's charges, *or*
  - the litigation insurance premium.

➤ Additional liability is assessed (either by summary assessment or detailed assessment) at the end of proceedings (or part of proceedings) to which the funding arrangement relates.

R Enforcing judgments

I	Judgment and orders	IV	Interest on judgment debts
II	Reciprocal enforcement	V	Methods of enforcement (extracting
III	Investigating the debtor's means		a judgment debt from a debtor)

I Judgment and orders (Part 40)

1 Form

➤ Every judgment/order must bear: the date on which it is given/made and the court seal (r 40.2(2)).

2 Drawing-up and filing

> **Exception:** Judgments/orders in the QBD at the RCJ are drawn up by the parties (unless it is an order by the court on its own initiative or unless the court otherwise orders) (r 40.3(4)).

➤ By the court unless *either*:

  a) the court orders or permits a party to draw it up *or* dispenses with the need to draw it up, *or*

  b) the order is a consent order (r 40.3(1)).

  ◆ If a party draws up an order, that party must file it no later than 7 days after the date on which the order is ordered or permitted to be drawn up so that the court can seal it. *If he does not do so in this period,* any other party may draw it up and file it (r 40.3(3)).

3 Service and effect

➤ If a party draws up a judgment/order and the court is to serve it, that party must file a copy to be retained by the court *plus* sufficient copies for service on himself and on the other parties. When the court has sealed the judgment/order it serves a copy on each party (r 40.4(1)).

➤ An order which is not made at trial must (unless the court orders otherwise) be served on the applicant, the respondent any other person who the court orders to be served (eg: where a party is acting by a solicitor the party in addition to the solicitor) (r 40.4(2), 40.5).

➤ A judgment/order takes effect from the day it is given/made, or any date the court specifies (r 40.7).

4 Set aside and correction

➤ Any person (even if not a party) directly affected may apply for set aside or variation (r 40.9).

➤ The court may correct accidental errors; a party may apply for correction without notice (r 40.12).

5 Compliance

➤ A party must comply with a judgment/order for the payment of amount of money (including costs) within 14 days of the date of the judgment/order *unless* a) the judgment/order specifies otherwise, b) the *CPR* specify otherwise (eg: *Part 12* (default judgment) and *Part 14* (judgment on admissions)), or c) the court has stayed the proceedings or judgment (r 40.11)).

II Reciprocal enforcement (Part 74)

➤ **Enforcing a foreign judgment in England and Wales:** Judgments from EU states (*EC Reg 44/2001* for EU States (see also *Part 74*), Brussels + Lugano Conventions for Denmark), and certain other countries (*AJA 1920, FJ(ER)A 1933*) may be registered in English courts and enforced (*CJJO 2001 and CJJ(AICS)O 2001*).

➤ **Enforcing an English judgment outside the jurisdiction:** English judgments may be registered and enforced elsewhere in the UK (eg: Jersey), in EU member states and in certain other European countries (*CJJA 1982*). There is also provision for reciprocal enforcement of some other foreign judgments (*AJA 1920, FJ(ER)A 1933*). *EC Reg 44/2001* is also relevant (see above).

  ◆ If a country is not covered, fresh proceedings should be started there.

CIVIL LITIGATION
Enforcing judgments

III Investigating the debtor's means

Investigating and tracing a debtor

Step 1: Use an enquiry agent
- ◆ This is to investigate and trace a debtor (set a cost ceiling to limit the expense).
- ✓ This is relatively fast and may unearth more than an oral examination will.
- ✗ It is more expensive than an oral examination.

Step 2: Seek an order to obtain information from judgment debtors (*Part 71*)
- ◆ This is an examination of the means of a debtor while he is under oath.

Procedure for oral examinations

Part 71 contains rules which provide for a judgment debtor to be required to attend court to provide information, for the purpose of enabling a judgment creditor to enforce a judgment or order against him.

Preparing to apply for the Order
- ➤ A judgment creditor may apply for an order requiring:
    - ◆ a judgment debtor, or if a company, an officer of that company, to provide information about:
        - • the judgment debtor's means, *or*
        - • any other matter about which information is needed to enforce a judgment or order.
- ➤ An application must be issued in the court which made the judgment or order but if the proceedings have since been transferred to a different court, it must be issued in that court.

↓

Application
- ➤ The applicant (judgment creditor) prepares an application (which may be without notice) which must state:
    - ◆ the name and address of the debtor,
    - ◆ which judgment or order the judgment creditor is seeking to enforce,
    - ◆ the amount presently owed (if the application is to enforce a judgment or order for money),
    - ◆ if the debtor is a company, the name, address and position of the officer to be ordered to attend court,
    - ◆ whether the applicant wishes the questioning to be conducted before a judge (and giving reasons),
    - ◆ which documents are to be produced, *and*
    - ◆ which matters the applicant wishes the judgment debtor (or officer of the judgment debtor) to be questioned about (if the application is to enforce a judgment or order which is not for money).

↓

Consideration of the application
- ➤ A court officer considers the application without a hearing, *but*:
    - ◆ may, when appropriate, refer it to a judge, *and*
    - ◆ will refer it to a judge, if the applicant requests questioning before a judge.

→ **Issue of the order**
- ➤ The court issues an order specifying:
    - ◆ compulsory attendance, usually at the county court for the district where the debtor resides, at a specified time,
    - ◆ when attending, the obligation to produce at court documents described in the order,
    - ◆ the obligation to answer on oath such questions as the court may require, *and*
    - ◆ a notice warning of imprisonment for contempt of court in the event of non-compliance.

Service of the order
- ➤ Not less than 14 days before the hearing, the applicant (or someone on his behalf) must serve the order personally on the person ordered to attend unless:
    - ◆ the court orders otherwise, *or*
    - ◆ these are county court proceedings and the applicant is an individual litigant in person, when the order will be served by the court bailiff.
- ➤ If the order is to be served by the applicant, he must inform the court not less than 7 days before the date of the hearing if he has been unable to serve it.

← (from Issue of the order)

Travelling expenses
A person ordered to attend may, within 7 days of being served with the order, ask the applicant to pay him a sum reasonably sufficient to cover his travelling expenses to and from court.

↓

Filing the affidavit
- ➤ The applicant must file an affidavit by the person who served the order (unless it was served by the court) giving details of how and when it was served, stating:
    - ◆ that the person ordered to attend court has not requested payment of his travelling expenses, *or*
    - ◆ that the applicant has paid a sum in accordance with such a request, *and*
    - ◆ in any event, stating how much of the judgment debt remains unpaid.
- ➤ The applicant must either file the affidavit not less than 2 days before the hearing or produce it at the hearing.

The hearing
The court officer examines the debtor who is on oath. If the hearing is before a judge, the creditor examines the debtor. The evidence is tape recorded.
The creditor may request a costs order.

Note: The debtor may offer to pay by instalments and the creditor can decide whether to accept or not.

Note: Failure to attend or answer, results in an order by a High Court/circuit judge for committal to prison ('suspended' when issued for the first time).

CIVIL LITIGATION
Enforcing judgments

IV Interest on judgment debts (*Judgment Act 1838 s 17*)

➤ Interest (under *JA 1838 s.17* or *CCA 1984 s 74*) runs from the date a judgment is given *unless* the *CPR* or a *PD* provide differently or the court orders otherwise (*r 40.8*).

High Court: Interest on judgment debts

➤ **High Court:** all judgment debts currently carry interest at 8% (see p 334) from the date the judgment is entered until final payment, regardless of whether the sum represents damages or costs.

➤ Where a county court judgment is being enforced in the High Court, the judgment is treated as one of the High Court for enforcement purposes.

County Courts: Interest on judgment debts

➤ **County Court:** (*County Court (Interest on Judgment Debts) Order 1991*) (as amended)

A Judgments over £5,000

a) all judgments over £5,000 carry interest at 8% from the date judgment is entered until final payment.

b) when enforcement proceedings begin, interest ceases to run *unless* the proceedings produce no payment.
- If anything at all is recovered, then the balance of the debt becomes interest-free.

c) An application to enforce interest must be made. This must be done with a certificate setting out:
- the amount of interest claimed, *and*
- the sum on which the interest is claimed, *and*
- the dates to and from which interest has accrued, *and*
- the rate of interest.

NB: If a judgment before trial leaves quantum to be assessed, interest runs from the date of final judgment (*Thomas v Bunn* [1991] 1 AC 362).

NB: Interest does *not* accrue on instalments (or judgment for deferred sums), until the instalment falls due.

B Judgments £5,000 and under

a) If a debt is a qualifying debt under the *LPCD(I) 1998*, it will attract interest under *LPCD(I) 1998* at the specified rate (see pp 318 and 334).

CIVIL LITIGATION
Enforcing judgments

V Methods of enforcement (*Part 70*)

➤ A judgment creditor wishing to enforce a High Court judgment or order in a county court must apply to the High Court for an order transferring the proceedings to that county court.

➤ If a judgment or order is given or made in favour of or against a person who is not a party to proceedings, it may be enforced by or against that person by the same methods as if he were a party.

Methods of enforcement	Assets available	Costs
1 Writ of fieri facias or warrant of execution	Goods and chattels	See p 419 for costs of enforcing judgments
2 Third party debt order	Money held on the debtor's behalf by others	
3 Charging order, stop notice or stop order	Land/Securities	
4 Attachment of earnings order	Earnings	
5 Appointment of a receiver	Various	
6 Bankruptcy or winding up	Various	

1 Writ of fieri facias or warrant of execution
(*HCCJO 1991 Art 8, HCCJ(A)O 1996, Sch 1 r 46, r 47, Sch 2 r 26*)

	High Court	County Court
What judgments are enforceable and where?	High Court judgments County Court judgments if £600 or over	County Court judgments under £5,000 (unless proceedings are under *CCA 1984*)
	◆ If a debt is payable by instalments, the claim form can be issued for an instalment or the whole amount	
Procedure	The creditor completes: a) 2 copies of the writ of *fieri facias*, *and* b) a *praecipe* for a writ of *fieri facias* He sends these to the court office together with the judgment and assessment notice (if costs are involved) NB: If enforcing a county court judgment, the creditor completes a combined certificate of judgment and request for writ of *fieri facias* too	The creditor completes a form of request for a warrant of execution. He files it at the court with a fee
Execution	The court seals the claim form, returns one copy to the creditor who forwards it to the under-sheriff for the county where the debtor resides or carries on his business. The under-sheriff sends it to an officer for execution	The bailiff for the district where the debtor resides or carries on business executes the warrant
	It may not be executed on Sunday, Good Friday or Xmas Day.	

The creditor should tell the officer about all seizable items of which he knows, eg: the type and registration number of a car. The relevant court officer seizes the goods and auctions them off to pay the debt and expenses

Items exempt from seizure (*Law of Distress (Amendment) Act 1888 s 4, AJA 1956 s 37*)

- Goods on hire or hire-purchase
- Tools, books, vehicles and items necessary for the debtor's personal use in his job or business. A vehicle will be seized unless the debtor satisfies the officer that no reasonable alternative transport is possible and that mobility is essential
- Clothing, bedding, furniture, provisions and household equipment for the basic domestic needs of the debtor and his family. Microwaves (when a conventional oven is present), stereos, TVs and videos are *not* regarded as being vital for domestic survival!

Methods of seizure

- The following are forbidden for the court officer: a) forcible entry to premises, *or* b) taking goods from the debtor's person.
- 'Walking possession' is a method by which the sheriff/other enforcement officer or bailiff agrees not to remove items if the debtor agrees not to dispose of them or permit them to be moved. (This gives the debtor an extra chance to meet the claim, or oppose seizure.)
- The debtor may apply for suspension of execution. If he succeeds, the writ of *fieri facias* is suspended conditionally on payment by specified instalments.

CIVIL LITIGATION
Enforcing judgments

2 Third party debt orders (Part 72)	
Purpose and Conditions	➤ *Part 21* contains rules which provide for a judgment creditor to obtain an order for the payment to him of money which a third party who is within the jurisdiction owes to the judgment debtor. ➤ The debt *must* belong to the judgment debtor solely and beneficially. ➤ The third party must be within the jurisdiction of UK courts.

Procedure outline	➤ The creditor makes an application for an interim third party debt order.
	➤ If granted, the creditor needs to ask the court for a final third party debt order.
	➤ Each application for a third party debt order:
	  ◆ may be made without notice, *and*
	  ◆ must be issued in the court which made the judgment/order being enforced but if the proceedings have since been transferred to a different court, it must be issued in that court.

Application for a third party debt order	➤ The application notice must contain the following information:
	  ◆ the name and address of the judgment debtor,
	  ◆ details of the judgment or order sought to be enforced,
	  ◆ the amount of money remaining due under the judgment or order,
	  ◆ if the debt is payable by instalments, the amounts which are due and remain unpaid,
	  ◆ the name and address of the third party,
	  ◆ if the third party is a bank or building society:
	    • its name and branch address where the debtor's account is believed to be held, *and*
	    • the account number or, if not known, the fact it is not known,
	  ◆ confirmation that to the best of the judgment creditor's knowledge or belief the third party:
	    • is within the jurisdiction, *and*
	    • owes money to or holds money to the credit of the judgment debtor,
	  ◆ if the judgment creditor knows or believes that any person other than the judgment debtor has any claim to the money owed by the third party:
	    • his name and (if known) his address, *and*
	    • such information as is known to the judgment creditor about his claim,
	  ◆ details of other applications for third party debt orders by the creditor for the same debt,
	  ◆ the sources/grounds of the creditor's knowledge/belief for the 3 preceding ◆ points, *and*
	  ◆ **verification by a statement of truth.**
	➤ The application will initially be dealt with by a judge without a hearing.

Consideration of the application for interim third party debt order	➤ The judge may make an interim third party debt order:
	  ◆ fixing a hearing to consider whether to make a final third party debt order, *and*
	  ◆ directing that until that hearing the third party must not make any payment which reduces the amount he owes the judgment debtor to less than the amount specified in the order.
	➤ An interim third party debt order will specify the amount which the third party must retain.
	➤ An interim third party debt order becomes binding on a third party when it is served on him.
	➤ The hearing date must not be less than 28 days after the interim third party debt order is made.

Service of interim third party debt order	➤ Copies of the interim order, the application notice and supporting documents must be served:
	  ◆ on the third party, not less than 21 days before the date fixed for the hearing, *and*
	  ◆ on the judgment debtor not less than:
	    • 7 days after a copy has been served on the third party, *and*
	    • 7 days before the date fixed for the hearing.
	➤ If the judgment creditor serves the order, he must either file a certificate of service not less than 2 days before the hearing, *or* produce a certificate of service at the hearing.

Obligations of third parties served with interim order	➤ A bank/building society must search to identify all accounts held with it by the judgment debtor and must disclose relevant details to the court and the creditor within 7 days of being served. ➤ A non-bank/building society must notify the court and the creditor in writing within 7 days of being served, if he claims not to owe any money or to owe less than amounts specified.

The hearing for the final order	➤ The court may:
	  ◆ make a final third party debt order,
	  ◆ discharge the interim third party debt order and dismiss the application,
	  ◆ decide any issues in dispute, *or*
	  ◆ direct a trial of any such issues, and if necessary give directions.
	➤ The court may, on an application by a debtor opposing the application, transfer it to the court for the district where the judgment debtor resides/carries on business, or to another court.
	➤ There is provision for an individual debtor to ask for a hardship payment order if the debtor or his family are suffering hardship in meeting ordinary living expenses.
	➤ There is provision for the debtor or the third party to object to the issue of a final third party debt order by filing written evidence of the grounds of objection at least 3 days before the hearing.
	➤ A final third party debt order is enforceable as an order to pay money.
	➤ If the creditor is awarded costs he shall, unless the court otherwise directs, retain those costs out of the money recovered and the costs are deemed to be paid first out of the money he recovers.

3 Charging orders over land or securities (Charging Orders Act 1979, Part 73)

Charging orders against a judgment debtor's interest in assets

Practical matters	➤ If seeking charges against land: do an index map search to discover if the land is registered. ➤ Search for prior incumbrances and give written notice of the order to prior chargees.
Which judgments are enforceable?	**In the High Court:** High Court judgments for over £5,000 / County Court judgments for over £5,000 **In a County Court:** All High Court judgments / All County Court judgments

Procedure outline	➤ The creditor makes an application for a charging order.
	➤ The application:
	  ◆ may be made without notice, *and*
	  ◆ must be issued in the court which made the judgment/order being enforced but if the proceedings have since been transferred to a different court, it must be issued in that court. But:
	    • If the application is made under a council tax regulations, it must be issued in the county court for the district in which the relevant dwelling is situated.
	    • If the application is for a charging order over an interest in a fund in court, it must be issued in the court in which the claim relating to that fund is or was proceeding.
	    • The enforceability limits above will always override.

Application for a charging order	➤ The application notice must contain the following information:
	  ◆ the name and address of the judgment debtor,
	  ◆ details of the judgment or order sought to be enforced,
	  ◆ the amount of money remaining due under the judgment or order,
	  ◆ if the debt is payable by instalments, the amounts which are due and remain unpaid,
	  ◆ if the creditor knows of any other creditors of the debtor, their names and (if known) addresses,
	  ◆ identification of the asset or assets which it is intended to charge,
	  ◆ details of the judgment debtor's interest in the asset
	  ◆ the names and addresses of people who must be served (see below), *and*
	  ◆ **verification by a statement of truth.**
	➤ The application will initially be dealt with by a judge without a hearing.

Consideration of the application	➤ The judge may make an interim charging order:
	  ◆ imposing a charge over the debtor's interest in the asset to which the application relates, *and*
	  ◆ fixing a hearing to consider whether to make a final charging order.

Service of the interim charging order	➤ Copies of the interim order, the application notice and supporting documents must be served not less than 21 days before the date fixed for the hearing on:
	  ◆ the judgment debtor;
	  ◆ such other creditors as the court directs;
	  ◆ if the order relates to an interest under a trust, on such of the trustees as the court directs;
	  ◆ if the interest charged is in securities other than securities held in court, then generally, the keeper of the register,
	  ◆ if the interest charged is in funds in court, the Accountant General at the Court Funds Office.
	➤ If the judgment creditor serves the order, he must either file a certificate of service not less than 2 days before the hearing, *or* produce a certificate of service at the hearing.

The hearing for the final	➤ The court may:
	  ◆ make a final charging order confirming that the charge imposed by the interim charging order shall continue, with or without modification,
	  ◆ discharge the interim charging order and dismiss the application,
	  ◆ decide any issues in dispute, *or*
	  ◆ direct a trial of any such issues, and if necessary give directions.
	➤ There is provision for the debtor or the third party to object to the issue of a final charging order by filing written evidence of the grounds of objection at least 7 days before the hearing.
	➤ If the court makes a final charging order which charges securities other than securities held in court, the order will include a stop notice unless the court otherwise orders.
	➤ Any order must be served on everyone on whom the interim charging order was served.
	➤ The court may, on an application by a debtor opposing the application, transfer it to the court for the district where the judgment debtor resides/carries on business, or to another court.

Getting the money	➤ By sale of the property. This is achieved by applying to a court with jurisdiction with a *Part 8* claim form, a copy of the charging order and written evidence. ➤ Where property is owned by more than one person, sale cannot be ordered. However, the creditor may instead be entitled to apply for an order for sale under *TLATA 1996 s 14*.

Stops orders and stop notices against a judgement debtor's interest in assets

➤ A 'stop order' is an order of the High Court not to take, in relation to funds in court or securities specified in the order, certain steps listed in *Charging Orders Act 1979 s 5(5)*. A 'stop notice' is similar but the steps cannot be taken without first giving notice to the person who obtained the notice.

CIVIL LITIGATION

Enforcing judgments

4	Attachment of earnings order *(Attachment of Earnings Act 1971, Sch 2 r 27)*
	County Court only - High Court proceedings are transferred to the County Court
Conditions	The debtor is employed (not self-employed or unemployed). The sum due exceeds £50
Application	File an application form ↓ The court informs the debtor of the application and asks him to: ♦ pay the sum due, *or* ♦ file a statement of means form

If the debtor replies	**Steps**
	1. The court makes a diary entry when the form is returned.
	2. The court then fixes repayment according to the following 2 guidelines:
	   a) 'normal deduction rate' (this is the amount of money to be deducted), *and*
	   b) 'protected earnings rate' (this is an amount the debtor must be left with - a 'safety net' for the debtor).
	3. The order is served on the debtor and the employer and a copy sent to the creditor. The service is as follows:
	
	    ┌───┐
	    │ The order is served by the court sending it by first class post to the debtor *unless* the creditor requests personal service, in which case, it is served by the judgment creditor delivering the order to the debtor personally │
	    └───┘
	    ↓
	    ┌───┐
	    │ When the order is served by the court, it is deemed served on the seventh day after the date on which the order was sent to the debtor │
	    └───┘
	    ↓
	    Where an order is sent by the court and it is returned undelivered the court sends notice of non-service to the judgment creditor together with a notice saying he may request bailiff service. A bailiff serves by:
	    ♦ inserting the order, enclosed in an envelope addressed to the debtor through the debtor's letter box, *or*
	    ♦ delivering the order to some person (apparently not less than 16 years old) at the debtor's address, *or*
	    ♦ delivering the order to the debtor personally
	
	4. The employer must forward to the court:
	   a) the deduction, *and*
	   b) up to £1 for himself for administrative expenses on each deduction under the order (*AtEA 1971 s 7*).
	5. If either party object or court staff consider that the statement has insufficient information, a judge hears the matter, but meanwhile the employer complies with the order unless varied.
	6. If the debtor tells the court he un/self-employed, the application is dismissed.

If the debtor *does not* reply	**Steps** **1.** The court automatically issues an order to produce a statement of means. **2.** The bailiff serves this personally on the debtor. (If the creditor provides the employer's name and address, the court may ask the employer for a statement of earnings). **3.** If the debtor does not respond at all, the court automatically issues a 'notice to show cause' which the bailiff serves. **4.** Failure to attend a subsequent hearing before a district judge will ultimately lead to committal to prison.

5	Appointment of a receiver *(Sch 1 rr 30 and 51)* (not dealt with here)

6	Bankruptcy (individual) or winding up (company)
Steps **1** **2**	If no execution has so far been levied, issue a statutory demand. If execution has been levied but is unsatisfied, see the procedures for bankruptcy/winding up on p 292 et seq

S Appeals

A very simplified table of possible Appeal Courts (AJA(DA)O 2000, Part 52)			
Appeal from:	**Appeal to:**	**Leave needed?**	**Powers on Appeal**
a District Judge of a county court (r 52.1, PD52: 2A.1)	Circuit Judge of a county court	Yes unless the appeal is against: ◆ a committal order, *or* ◆ a refusal to grant habeas corpus, *or* ◆ certain actions under CA 1989 (r 52.3)	The appeal court has all the powers of the lower court (r 52.10) eg: to affirm, set aside, vary an order or judgment eg: to refer any claim or issue for determination by the lower court eg: to order a new trial/hearing eg: to make an order for interest payment eg: to make a costs order **BUT** the appeal is limited to a review of the decision of the lower court unless it is in the interests of justice to hold a rehearing (r 52.11) Note: for extra provisions on small claims track appeals, see p 396
a Master, a District Judge of the High Court, a Circuit Judge (r 52.1, PD52: 2A.1)	High Court Judge	To obtain leave, an application must be made to: a) the lower court at the hearing at which the decision was made, *or* b) the appeal court **Permission may be granted if:** ◆ the court considers the appeal would have a real prospect of success, *or* ◆ there is some other compelling reason	
High Court Judge (r 52.1, PD52: 2A.1) A final decision on a *Part 7* claim allocated to the multi-track (PD52: 2A.1, 2A.2)	Court of Appeal (SCA 1981 ss 15-18)		
Court of Appeal	House of Lords	Yes to the Court of Appeal if refused, apply to the House of Lords	
High Court under the *AJA 1969 s 12* 'leap-frog' procedure ('Civil Appeals' PD March 2000)			
Court of Appeal (Sch 1 r 114)	European Court of Justice	Yes Any reference is up to the national court	The court can make a ruling on any matter in the Treaty of Rome 1957
High Court (Sch 1 r 114 and *Civil Appeals' PD March 2000*)			
Crown Court			
Costs an authorised costs officer on a detailed assessment (but not if LSC funded) (rr 47.20-47.23)	**Costs** a costs judge or a District Judge of the High Court	No	**Costs** power to rehear proceedings and make any order/directions appropriate

➤ An appeal is allowed if:

  ◆ a decision of a lower court was:

    • wrong, *or*

    • unjust because of a serious procedural or other irregularity in the proceedings of the lower court.

Note: Judicial review as an 'appeal' against decisions is not dealt with in this table. It is covered by *Part 54*	Note: References to the European Court of Human Rights are not dealt with in this table	Note: Certain specialised jurisdictions (eg: insolvency) are not dealt with in this table

CRIMINAL LITIGATION

This chapter examines:

		Overview of the criminal process	432
	A	Criminal investigations	433
	B	Arrest and interview	434
	C	Court matters applicable generally	451
	D	Remand and bail	454
either way	E	Mode of trial/Allocation on an 'either way' offence	460
summary	F	Preparations for summary trial	464
	G	Summary trial	465
either way / indictable	H	Sending for trial and committal	467
indictable	I	Preparations for Crown Court hearings and trial	474
	J	Crown Court hearings and trial	475
	K	Sentencing powers	478
	L	Sentencing procedure and mitigation	491
	M	Appeals	493
	N	Disclosure	495
	O	Evidence at trial	497
	P	Forthcoming changes	512

Note: The law as set out in this section of the *Legal Practice Companion*:
- applies to adults only unless the text specifically indicates otherwise, *and*
- does not cover the special rules on terrorism, sexual offences, fraud and drugs, unless the text specifically indicates otherwise.

CRIMINAL LITIGATION
Overview of the criminal process

CRIMINAL LITIGATION
Criminal investigations

A Criminal investigations

➤ A code of practice applies for criminal investigations conducted by police officers (*CPIA 1996 s 23(1)*).

➤ The code provides that there are different functions to be performed by (*para 3.1*):

- the investigator,
- the officer in charge of an investigation,
- the disclosure officer.

Duty to retain material

➤ The investigator has a duty to retain material obtained in a criminal investigation which may be relevant to the investigation (*para 5.1*).

Time to retain material

➤ All material which may be relevant to an investigation must be retained until a decision is taken whether to institute proceedings against a person for an offence (*para 5.7*).

➤ If a criminal investigation results in proceedings being instituted, all material which may be relevant must be retained at least until (*paras 5.8-5.10*):

- the prosecutor decides not to proceed with the case, *or*
- the accused is acquitted, *or*
- the accused is convicted.
    - If the accused is convicted the material must be retained until the later of:
        - the convicted person is released from custody, *or*
        - 6 months from the date of conviction, *or*
        - if an appeal is in progress, the time that the appeal is determined, *or*
        - if the Criminal Cases Review Commission (see p 494) is considering an application:
            - the time it decides not to refer the case to the Court of Appeal,
            - the time that the appeal is determined.

Preparation of schedules (*para 6.6 and 7.1*)

➤ The following schedules must be prepared and given to the prosecutor if:

- the accused is charged, *and*
    a) the offence is triable only on indictment, *or*
    b) the offence is triable summarily *and* the accused is considered likely to plead not guilty, *or*
    c) the offence is triable either way *and*
        i) it is considered that the offence is likely to be tried on indictment, *or*
        ii) it is considered that the accused is likely to plead not guilty at a summary trial.
    NB: If, in (b) or (c)(ii), it is considered that the accused will plead guilty, and contrary to this, he pleads not guilty, then a schedule must be prepared as soon as practicable (*para 6.8*).

➤ Material which may be relevant to an investigation, which the disclosure officer believes will *not* form part of the prosecution case must be listed on a schedule (*para 6.2*).

Non-sensitive material (*para 6.3*)	Sensitive material (*para 6.4*)
Material which the disclosure officer does not believe is sensitive must be listed on a schedule of non-sensitive material	Material which is believed to be sensitive must be: ♦ listed on a schedule of sensitive material, *or* ♦ (in exceptional circumstances) revealed to the prosecution.

B Arrest and interview

References in this section are to PACE, unless otherwise stated. References to 'Code' are to the PACE Codes of Practice, which do not have statutory force, but with which the police must sometimes comply (eg: s 39(1)).

I	Dealing with crime without arrest	VIII	Charge
II	Powers of arrest	IX	Samples in police detention
III	Voluntary attendance	X	Other rights at a police station
IV	Detention before charge	XI	Detention after charge: 1 of 3 alternatives
V	Interview		
VI	Inferences from silence	XII	What happens next
VII	Identification		

The 8 *PACE* codes of practice

Code A: for the exercise by police officers of statutory powers of stop and search, *and* for the requirement of police officers and police staff to record public encounters

Code B: for searches of premises by police officers and the seizure of property found by police officers on persons or premises.

Code C: for detention, treatment and questioning of persons by police officers

Code D: for identification of persons by police officers

Code E: on audio recording interviews with suspects

Code F: on visual recording with sound of interviews with suspects

Code G: for the statutory power of arrest by police officers

Code H: on the treatment of persons in connection with *Terrorism Act 2000 s 41* and *Sch 8*

I Dealing with crime without arrest

Penalty notices (*CJPA 2001 s 2 as amended by ABA 2003 s 87*)

➤ Police may issue penalty notices on the spot/at a police station to offenders over 16 for certain disorder offences. However, if a police officer believes the courts are more appropriate, all usual powers (eg: arrest) are available. A penalty notice is notice of the opportunity to discharge any liability to conviction by paying a fixed penalty. There is no criminal conviction or admission of guilt associated with payment of the penalty, but the alleged offender may opt for trial by a court - risking conviction. Failure to pay the penalty/opt for trial can lead to a fine of 1.5 times the penalty amount.

Young person's reprimand (*CDA 1988 ss 65-66*)

➤ A young person may be reprimanded or warned (if this has not happened before) under certain circumstances instead of being arrested. He may be referred to a youth offending team.

Conditional cautions (*CJA 2003 ss 22-27*)

➤ A 'conditional caution' for an offence is half way between a simple caution and a full charge.

➤ It is a caution which has conditions attached to it with which the offender must comply. It can be given if 5 requirements are satisfied: a) there is evidence against the offender, b) that a 'relevant prosecutor' (defined in *s 27*) considers that the evidence would be sufficient to charge him and that a conditional caution should be given, c) the offender admits the offence, d) the offender has been made aware of what the caution (and failure to comply) would mean, e) that he signs a document containing details of the offence, the admission, the offender's consent to the caution, and the conditions imposed.

➤ If the offender fails without reasonable excuse to satisfy the conditions attached to the conditional caution he may be prosecuted for the original offence.

II Powers of arrest

A Powers to arrest

1 **Arrest powers for a constable for ANY OFFENCE**

> ➤ *PACE s 24* and *Code G* deal with statutory powers of police to arrest persons suspected of involvement in a criminal offence (*G: 1.1*).
>
> ➤ The right to liberty is a key principle of *HRA 1998*. Arrest is an obvious and significant interference with that right (*G: 1.2*).
>
> ➤ Arrest must be fully justified and officers exercising the power should consider if the necessary objectives can be met by other, less intrusive means (*G: 1.3*).
>
> ➤ Arrest must never be used simply because it can be used. Absence of justification for exercising the powers of arrest may lead to challenges should the case proceed to court. When the power of arrest is exercised it is essential that it is exercised in a nondiscriminatory and proportionate manner (*G: 1.3*).
>
> ➤ If *PACE s 24* and *Code G* are not observed, both the arrest and the conduct of any subsequent investigation may be open to question (*G: 1.4*).
>
> ➤ A lawful arrest requires 2 elements (*G: 2.1*):
>
> **Element 1:** A person's involvement or suspected involvement or attempted involvement in the commission of a criminal offence, *and*
>
> **Element 2:** reasonable grounds for believing that the person's arrest is necessary.
>
> ➤ Arresting officers must inform a person arrested that they have been arrested, even if this fact is obvious, and of the relevant circumstances of the arrest in relation to both elements and to inform the custody officer of these on arrival at the police station (*G: 2.2*).

Element 1: Involvement in the commission of an offence

➤ **Involvement in the commission of an offence:** A constable may arrest without warrant in relation to any offence (*s 24(1)-(6)* and *G: 2.3*) (except for one exception, not dealt with here). A constable may arrest anyone:

  ◆ who is about to commit an offence or is in the act of committing an offence (*s 24(1)*), or

  ◆ whom the officer has reasonable grounds for suspecting is about to commit an offence or to be committing an offence (*s 24(1)*), or

  ◆ whom the officer has reasonable grounds to suspect of being guilty of an offence which he has reasonable grounds for suspecting has been committed (*s 24(2)*), or

  ◆ anyone who is guilty of an offence which has been committed or anyone whom the officer has reasonable grounds for suspecting to be guilty of that offence (*s 24(3)*).

➤ In considering the individual circumstances, the constable must take into account the situation of the victim, the nature of the offence, the circumstances of the suspect and the needs of the investigative process (*G: 2.8*).

Element 2: Necessity

➤ The power of arrest is only exercisable if the constable has reasonable grounds for believing that it is *necessary* to arrest the person (G: 2.4) based on the following exhaustive criteria ((s 24(4)-(6)) and G: 2.9).

a) to enable the name of the person in question to be ascertained (in the case where the constable does not know, and cannot readily ascertain, the person's name, or has reasonable grounds for doubting whether a name given by the person as his name is his real name), *or*

b) correspondingly as regards the person's address, *or*
   - An address is a satisfactory address for service of summons if the person will be at it for a sufficiently long period for it to be possible to serve him or her with a summons; or, that some other person at that address specified by the person will accept service of the summons on their behalf (G: 2.9).

c) to prevent the person in question:
   i) causing physical injury to himself or any other person, *or*
   ii) suffering physical injury, *or*
   iii) causing loss or damage to property, *or*
   iv) committing an offence against public decency (only applies where members of the public going about their normal business cannot reasonably be expected to avoid the person in question), *or*
   v) causing an unlawful obstruction of the highway, *or*

d) to protect a child or other vulnerable person from the person in question, *or*

e) to allow the prompt and effective investigation of the offence or of the conduct of the person in question, *or*
   - Eg (*G: 2.9*): Where there are reasonable grounds to believe that the person:
     - has made false statements, *or*
     - has made statements which cannot be readily verified, *or*
     - has presented false evidence, *or*
     - may steal or destroy evidence, *or*
     - may make contact with co-suspects or conspirators, *or*
     - may intimidate or threaten or make contact with witnesses, *or*
     - where it is necessary to obtain evidence by questioning.
   - Eg (*G: 2.9*): When considering arrest in connection with an indictable offence, there is a need to:
     - enter and search any premises occupied or controlled by a person, *or*
     - search the person, *or*
     - prevent contact with others, *or*
     - take fingerprints, footwear impressions, samples or photographs of the suspect
   - Eg (*G: 2.9*): ensuring compliance with statutory drug testing requirements.

f) to prevent any prosecution for the offence from being hindered by the disappearance of the person in question.

2 Arrest powers for non-constables for ANY OFFENCE

subject to

➤ A person other than a constable may arrest without a warrant (*s 24A*):
- anyone who is in the act of committing an indictable offence, *or*
- anyone whom he has reasonable grounds for suspecting to be committing an indictable offence.

➤ Where an indictable offence has been committed, a person other than a constable may arrest without a warrant:
- anyone who is guilty of the offence;
- anyone whom he has reasonable grounds for suspecting to be guilty of it.

➤ The powers of summary arrest above are exercisable only if:
- the person making the arrest has reasonable grounds for believing that for any of the reasons below it is necessary to arrest the person in question, *and*
- it appears to the person making the arrest that it is not reasonably practicable for a constable to make it instead.

Reasons for arrest (*s 24A(4)*)

➤ To prevent the person in question:
- causing physical injury to himself or any other person, *or*
- suffering physical injury, *or*
- causing loss of or damage to property, *or*
- making off before a constable can assume responsibility for him.

➤ This does not apply to the offence of racial or religious hatred under *POA 1986 ss 17–29N* (ie: Parts 3 and 3A) (*s 24A(5)*).

B Rules immediately following arrest

Records of arrest (*Code G: 4*)

➤ The arresting officer is required to record in his pocket book or by other methods used for recording information (*G: 4.1*):
- the nature and circumstances of the offence leading to the arrest, *and*
- the reason or reasons why arrest was necessary, *and*
- the giving of the caution, *and*
- anything said by the person at the time of arrest.

➤ The record must be made at the time of the arrest unless impracticable to do (*G: 4.2*).
- If not made at that time, the record should then be completed as soon as possible thereafter.

➤ On arrival at a police station, the custody officer must open the custody record. The information given by the arresting officer on the circumstances and reason or reasons for arrest must be recorded as part of the custody record. Alternatively, a copy of the record made by the officer (under *G: 4.1* must be attached as part of the custody record (*G: 4.3*).

CRIMINAL LITIGATION
Arrest and interview

1 **Arrest away from a police station**

➤ There are 3 options:
   a) take the arrested person to the police station, *or*
   b) release the arrested person without bail, *or*
   c) release the arrested person on bail (see box below).

➤ If a person is arrested at a place other than at a police station, that person should be taken to the police station as soon as practicable (*s 30(1A)*).

- A person arrested by a constable at any place other than a police station *must* be released without bail if before that person reaches a police station, a constable is satisfied that there are no grounds for keeping him under arrest or releasing him on bail under *s 30A* (*s 30(7)-(7A)*).
- A constable who releases a person in this way must record the fact that he has done so as soon as practicable after the release (*s 30(8)-(9)*).

➤ However, nothing written above prevents a constable delaying taking a person to a police station or releasing him on bail if the presence of the person at a place (other than a police station) is necessary in order to carry out such investigations as it is reasonable to carry out immediately (*s 30(10)-(10A)*).

- Where there is any such delay, the reasons must be recorded when the person first arrives at the police station or (as the case may be) is released on bail (*s 30(11)*).

Arrest away from a police station: release of the arrested person on bail (ss 30A, 30B, 30C, 30D)

➤ If a person is arrested at a place other than at a police station, a constable may release such a person on bail at any time before he arrives at a police station.

➤ A person released on bail in this way must be required to attend a police station.
- No other requirement may be imposed on the person as a condition of bail.

➤ The constable must give that person a notice in writing before he is released stating:
- the offence for which he was arrested,
- the ground on which he was arrested,
- that he is required to attend a police station (it *may* also specify the police station which he is required to attend and the time when he is required to attend).
  - If the notice does not include this last item, the person must subsequently be given a further notice in writing which contains that information.

➤ Nothing prevents the re-arrest without a warrant of a person released on bail in this way if new evidence justifying a further arrest has come to light since his release.

➤ Failure to attend a police station at a specified time means a constable may arrest that person without a warrant.

2 **Arrest at a police station (or away from a police station and person then taken there)**

➤ The custody officer (at least a sergeant) must decide to:

   a) charge the suspect immediately (*s 37(7)(d)*), *or*

   b) release the suspect (whether on bail or not) without charge (*s 37(7)(b)-(c)*), *or*

   c) detain the suspect before charge (see Section IV below), *or*

   d) release the suspect on bail and without charge to allow the DPP to decide whether to charge the suspect with an offence or not or whether to give a caution or not (*s 37(7)(a)* and *s 37A-37D*).

Note: A suspect is treated as arrested if he returns to a police station to answer to bail.

CRIMINAL LITIGATION
Arrest and interview

Cautions: wording

➤ Wording: *'You do not have to say anything. But it may harm your defence if you do not mention when questioned something which you later rely on in court. Anything you do say may be given in evidence.'* (*C:10.5*, see pp 442-443).

➤ When a requirement to caution arises at a time when the restriction on drawing adverse inferences from silence applies, the wording is: *'You do not have to say anything, but anything you do say may be given in evidence.'* (*C: Annex C: 2*, see pp 442-443)

➤ A caution *must* be given:
   a) on, or just before, arrest (*C:10.4*), *and*
   b) on a custody officer authorising detention (it must be given in a written form) (*C:3.2*), *and*
   c) before an interview (*C:10.1*), *and*
   d) following a break in questioning (*C:10.8*), *and*
   e) when charging a detained person (*C:16.2*).

Table of various offences

Offence	Type	Magistrates' maximum penalty	Crown court maximum penalty
		cf: Mandatory and racially aggravated sentences p 479	
Theft (*TA 1968 s 7*)	Either way	6 months [to be 12 months when CJA 2003 s 282 is in force] £5,000 fine (*MCA 1980 s 32, CJA 1982 s 37*) This is the General Magistrates' Sentencing Power ('GMSP')	7 years Unlimited fine (*CJA 2003 s 163*)
Burglary (*TA 1968 s 9*)	Either way		10 (14* years if a dwelling) Unlimited fine (*CJA 2003 s 163*)
	Indictment*		
Fear or provocation of violence (*POA 1986 s 4*)	Summary		Not applicable
Actual bodily harm (*OAPA 1861 s 47*)	Either way		5 years Unlimited fine (*CJA 2003 s 163*)
Robbery (*TA 1968 s 8*)	Indictment	Not applicable	Life Unlimited fine (*CJA 2003 s 163*)
Careless driving (*RTA 1988 s 3*) (*RTOA 1988 Sch 2*)	Summary	£2,500 fine Endorsement of licence: obligatory Disqualification: discretionary, else endorse 3-9 points Disqualification until a re-test is discretionary	Not applicable
Dangerous driving (*RTA 1988 s 2*) (*RTOA 1988 Sch 2*)	Either way	GMSP	2 years, unlimited fine
		Disqualification: obligatory Endorsement of offence on licence: obligatory with 3-11 points A re-test before requalifying is obligatory	
Taking a conveyance (*TA 1968 s 12*) (*RTOA 1988 Sch 2*)	Summary	GMSP Disqualification: discretionary	Not applicable
Aggravated vehicle taking (*TA 1968 s 12A*) (*RTOA 1988 Sch 2*)	Either way	GMSP	2 years (14 years if death results) Unlimited fine (*CJA 2003 s 163*)
	Summary if aggravating feature is that damage is worth £5,000 or less	*and* Endorsement on licence is obligatory: endorse 3-11 points Disqualification: obligatory	

CRIMINAL LITIGATION
Arrest and interview

III Voluntary attendance

➤ An individual attending voluntarily at a police station may leave at will (s 29).

➤ If prevented from leaving, he must be informed that he is under arrest (s 29).

IV Detention before charge

➤ A person at a police station to answer to bail is treated as under arrest for the relevant offence (s 34(7)).

➤ **Following arrest**
   ◆ Detention is permitted if the custody officer has reasonable grounds to believe *either* (s 37(2)):
      a) that there is insufficient evidence to charge the suspect and detention is necessary to obtain that evidence by questioning, *or*
      b) it is necessary to secure or preserve evidence, or to obtain it by questioning.

➤ The police should interview the suspect as soon as possible and decide immediately after an interview whether a charge will be brought - if no charge is brought, release should be immediate (s 34(2), s 41(7)).

Detention timetable (before charge)							
		c = custody officer i = at least an inspector			s = at least a superintendent m = magistrate		
Monday 1.00 pm		Arrival at the police station. Detention clock begins to run (s 41(2)(a)(i))		Tuesday 1.00 pm cont.	24 hour offset cont.	b) it is an indictable offence, *and* c) the investigation is being conducted diligently and expeditiously NB: This new authorisation is only possible if it is: i) before 24 hours from when the detention clock began to run (s 42(4)), *and* ii) after the second review	s
Monday 1.10 pm		Detention is 'authorised' (when no warrant) by the custody officer under the grounds in s 37(2)	c				
Monday 7.10 pm	+6 hours offset	Latest time for first review of detention. Detention may continue if the original grounds are still valid (s 40(3)) NB: The suspect or his solicitor may make representations	i	Wednesday 1.00 am	36 hour offset	The superintendent's authority expires. Charge or release *unless* a magistrate grants warrant of further detention (s 43) (NB only for an indictable offence)	m
Tuesday 4.10 am	+9 hour offset	Latest time for second review; thereafter reviews at 9 hourly intervals (s 40(3))	i	Thursday 1.00 pm	72 hour offset	The magistrate's warrant expires. Charge or release *unless* a magistrate grants extension of warrant of further detention (s 44)	m
Tuesday 1.00 pm	24 hour offset	Charge, or release (on bail or not) (s 41(7)) *unless* a superintendent has reasonable grounds to believe: a) grounds in s 37(2) still exist, *and*	s	Friday 1.00 pm	96 hour offset	Charge or release (s 44 (3)(b)) **MAXIMUM LIMIT**	

Black background offsets are based from time detention was authorised and are cumulative offsets
White background offsets are based from time of arrival at police station and are absolute offsets

Safeguards on interview at a police station

- **Rest:** for a continuous period of 8 hours in 24 hours, preferably at night (C:12.2).
- **Drink or drugs:** no questioning if the suspect is unable to grasp the significance of questions due to drink or drugs, *unless* the superintendent or an officer of higher rank authorises it for the protection of people or property (C:11.18).
- **Interview room:** heated, lighted, ventilated; chair for the defendant to sit on (C:12.4, 12.6).
- **Breaks:** at recognised meal times, refreshments every 2 hours (C:12.8).
- **Identification:** a policeman must identify himself and anyone else present before interview (C:12.7).
- **Juveniles (under 17):** accompanied by an 'appropriate' adult (a parent/guardian or social worker) for certain situations (C:1.7, 11.15).
- **Mentally disordered:** accompanied by an 'appropriate' adult (a relative/other responsible person or a special social worker) for certain situations (C:1.7, 11.15).

V Interview

➤ An interview is the questioning of a person regarding their involvement or suspected involvement in a criminal offence or offences (for which a caution would need to be given under *C:10.1*) (*C:11.1A*).

➤ After arrest, an interview should not be held until the suspect reaches the police station *unless* delay would endanger persons or evidence, alert others, or cause serious loss or damage to property (*C:11.1*).

➤ Prior to the commencement or recommencement of an interview, the suspect must be reminded that he has a right to free legal advice and that the interview can be delayed for this (*C:11.2*), see p 449.

➤ At the start of an interview at a police station, any significant statement/silence made before a suspect's arrival must be put to him. He must be asked if he would like to confirm, deny, or add anything (*C:11.4*).

➤ No oppression may be used by police during questioning (*C:11.5*).

➤ Any interview before charge (or for which a suspect has not been informed he may be prosecuted) must cease when the officer in charge of the investigation (*C:11.6*):
- is satisfied all relevant questions about the offence have been put to the suspect, *and*
- has taken account of any other available evidence, *and*
- (or for a detained suspect the custody officer) reasonably believes there is sufficient evidence to provide a realistic prospect of conviction for that offence if the person was prosecuted for it.

➤ A record must be made during an interview (or as soon as practicable after it) (*C:11.7-11.14*).

➤ Interviewing is forbidden after the suspect has been charged, *unless* it is necessary to (*C:16.5*):
- minimise harm to a person or the public, *or*
- clarify ambiguity in an answer or statement, *or*
- enable the defendant to comment on new information unearthed since he was charged.

➤ See interviews and other legal rights (p 449) and advice on the qualified right to silence (pp 442-443).

Recording an interview	
Audio recording of interview (*Code E*)	**Non-taped interview**

➤ Compulsory *unless* the offence is a purely summary offence (*E:3.1(a)*)
• A master recording and a working copy are made (*E:2.2*)
• The master recording is sealed, and signed by the suspect and the interviewing officer (*E:2*)
• The defence may access the working copy
• A written summary is sent to the defence who may agree that it is admissible as evidence
  • If the defence objects, a full transcript is made and the seal on the master recording is broken in court
	➤ Summary offences only
	• An accurate written record must be made (*C:11.7*)
	• The record must be made during the interview or as soon as practicable after it (*C:11.7-11.8*)
	• An interviewee must read and sign the record (*C:11.11*). Refusals to do so must be recorded. Note: *C:11E* says that if the suspect agrees, the words are 'I agree that this is a correct record of what was said' and he signs his signature
	• The interview record will be served on the defence
	  • If the defence agrees, the record is admissible
	  • If the defence objects, oral evidence is admissible and the officer may refresh his memory from contemporaneous notes

Visual recording of interview (*Code F*)	**Outside the context of an interview**
➤ *PACE s 60A* allows visual recording of interviews but there is no statutory requirement to visually record interviews. • The rules are the same as for audio interviews • Each party must be present if the seal on the master recording is broken (*F:6.4*).	➤ Comments made by the suspect should be (*C:11.13*): • recorded in writing and signed by the officer concerned, *and* • shown to the suspect, who must have an opportunity to read, time and sign them. A refusal to sign should be recorded
Written statement under caution	
This is a prepared statement by the suspect setting out his version of events. It may also be a confession. The rules and the form are set out in *Annex D to Code C*	

VI Inferences from silence

➤ The *CJPO 1994* cuts down on a suspect's/accused's right to remain silent. The rules are now as follows:

	s 34		s 36	s 37

Situation	a) Before being charged, *and*
	b) while being questioned under caution by a constable, *and*
	c) the constable is trying to discover whether, or by whom, an offence has been committed
		On a suspect being charged or officially informed he may be prosecuted for an offence	a) On being arrested, *and*
			b) with an object, substance or mark:
			  i) on his person, *or*
			  ii) in or on his clothing or footwear, *or*
			  iii) in his possession, *or*
			  iv) in any place in which he is, at the time of his arrest, *and*
			c) the constable reasonably believes that the object, substance or mark has something to do with the suspect participating in a specified offence, *and*
			d) the constable informs the suspect of his suspicions and asks him to account for the object, substance or mark
				a) On being arrested, *and*
				b) the suspect is at a place where a constable reasonably believes that the person's presence may be to do with participation in an offence, *and*
				c) the constable reasonably believes that the suspect's presence has something to do with the suspect participating in a specified offence, *and*
				d) the constable informs the suspect of his suspicions and asks him to account for his

Consequences apply if:	a) Suspect fails to mention a fact he might reasonably be expected to mention, *and* b) he later relies on that fact in his defence		Suspect fails or refuses to provide an explanation	Suspect fails or refuses to provide an explanation
Consequences	The court or magistrates can 'draw such inferences as appear proper' from the silence as applied to: 1 a submission of 'no case to answer' in a trial (see p 466 and p 475) 2 determining the guilt or innocence of a defendant at trial NB: Such inferences do not decide the matter alone, there must be other factors too (*CJPO 1994 s 38*)			

ss 34, 36 and 37 will most often apply only to interviews in police stations (because of the general rule prohibiting interviews outside police stations). The usual interview safeguards for police station interviews will, of course, still apply

Practical advice on silence in light of case law

➤ If advising a suspect to stay silent, one should record the reason to avoid 'adverse inferences' at trial (see p 511).
➤ It is wrong to advise clients to answer only some questions but not others, as the *whole* interview will be admissible and the silences will be hard to explain.
➤ The idea that 'an inference can never strengthen the prosecution case but only weaken a defence case once it has been found there is a case to answer' has been eroded by case law:
  ◆ If the defence makes a submission of no case to answer, the prosecution may still respond that the defence has relied on facts not mentioned on an earlier occasion (*R v Hart & R v McLean* [1998] CLY 1056). This is significant in:
    • cases where a client has had a 'no comment' interview and then answered questions in a second interview or had several no comment interviews but later hands in a prepared statement when charged. If a solicitor believes there is no case to answer, he should advise the client to stay silent throughout. (Although it might be sensible to make a prepared statement, this should be kept in the solicitor's papers for use only if the judge dismisses the defence submission that there is no case to answer).
    • identification cases where there is going to be a case to answer at any stage because it is critical to raise any alibi at the first possible opportunity and at a time when the police can still check the alibi without the suspect being able to brief the alibi witness (see *R v Taylor* 1999 Crim LR 77).
  ◆ Solicitors and clients should not give reasons for a client staying silent unless they are content for the prosecution to inspect the solicitor's notes of the private consultation which preceded that interview, because the giving of reasons waives legal privilege (*R v Condron* [1997] 1 WLR 827 and *R v Bowden* [1999] 2 Cr App R 176). This is significant since *CPIA 1996 s 66* has been in force because a witness summons may now be made against defence solicitors requiring their attendance with their notes at the trial.

CRIMINAL LITIGATION
Arrest and interview

Principles from *R v Cowan; Gayle; Ricciardi* [1995] 3 WLR 818 CA

➤ In normal circumstances, the burden of proof of proving the silence and inferences from it, is on the prosecution.

➤ The defendant's entitlement to remain silent is his right and choice.

➤ An inference from a failure to answer questions cannot on its own prove guilt (*CJPO 1994 s 38(3)*)

➤ A tribunal of fact (eg: the trial court) must first have established a case to answer before drawing a *s 34* inference.

➤ A tribunal of fact (eg: the trial court) might draw an adverse inference, if despite:

   ◆ any evidence relied on to explain the silence, *or*

   ◆ the absence of any evidence to explain the silence ...

... the tribunal concluded that silence could only sensibly be attributed to:

   ◆ the defendant having no answer, *or*

   ◆ the defendant has no answer that would stand up to interrogation.

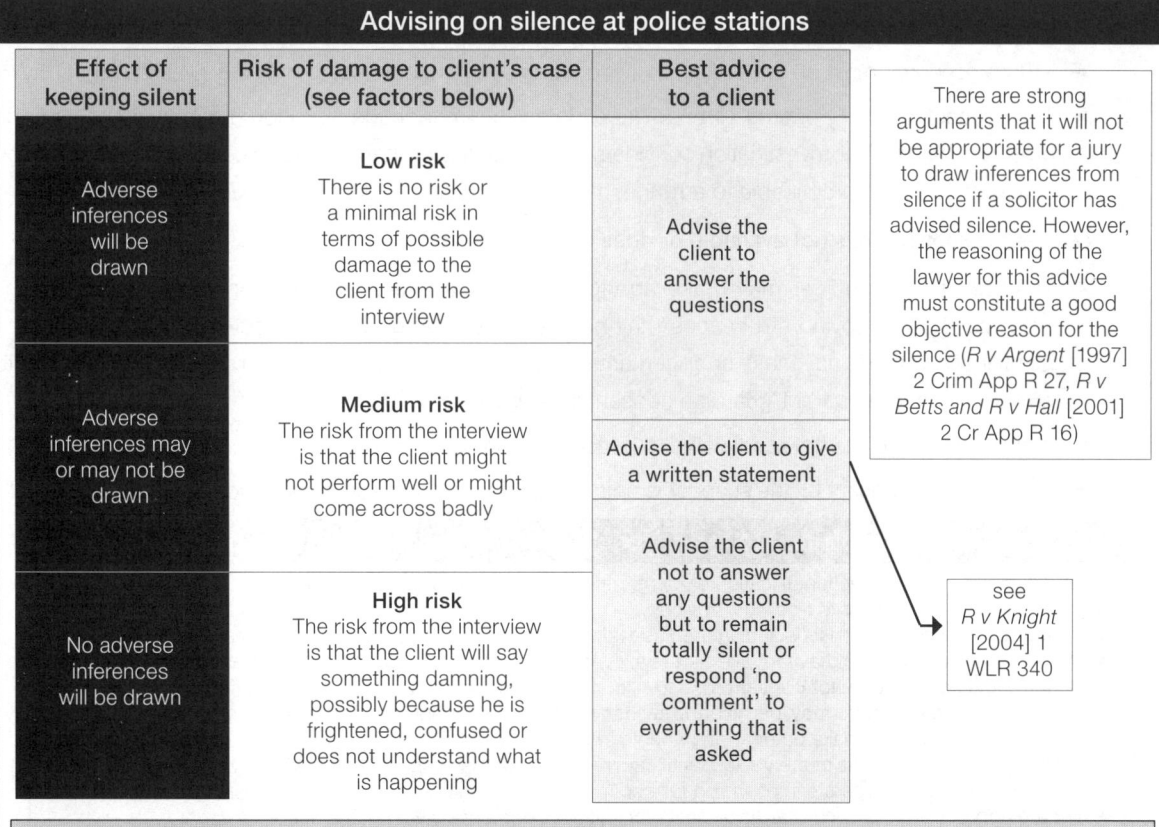

Factors to consider in evaluating risk

- whether an early explanation will avoid the suspect being charged at all
- the evidence the police already have - if this is overwhelming, a confession may be advisable to help later in mitigation
- the capacity of a suspect to handle the stresses of an interview (eg: maturity, age and psychological ability to handle the interview)
- the gravity of the offence
- whether the suspect has any prior experience of either questioning or custody

VII Identification

➤ There are identification issues if there is disputed identification evidence (see Disputed identification (Turnbull guidelines) and the warning at trial, p 502).

➤ There are 6 methods of identification (methods B to D are listed in *D:3.4 to 3.10*):

A	Court identification.	**D**	Group identification (*Annex C to Code D*).
B	Video identification (*Annex A to Code D*).	**E**	Showing of photographs (*Annex E to Code D*).
C	Identification parade (*Annex B to Code D*).	**F**	Confrontation (*Annex D to Code D*).

1 Suspect is not known by police

➤ A witness may be taken to a particular place to try to identify a person they have seen. Although the variables (eg: number, age, sex, race of people) and manner of identification cannot be controlled, the safeguards applicable to methods B to D should be followed as far as practicable (*D:3.2*).

➤ A witness must not be shown photographs, computerised or artist's composite likenesses or 'E-fit' images if the identity of the suspect is known to the police and the suspect is available to take part in a video id, an id parade or a group id. If the suspect's identity is not known, the showing of such images to a witness must be done in accordance with *Annex E* rules (not dealt with here) (*D:3.3*).

2 Suspect is known (ie: enough information to justify arrest), available and consents to B to D

➤ All id procedures must performed by an inspector or above unconnected with the investigation (*D:3.11*).

➤ The suspect is initially offered either a video identification or an identification parade (*D:3.14*) or if the officer in charge of the investigation considers more satisfactory than those choices and the identification officer considers it practicable to arrange, he is offered a group identification (*D:3.16*).

3 Suspect is known but is not available or does not consent to B to D

➤ The identification officer may make arrangements for a video identification (using still images if necessary). Any moving/still images may be used and may be obtained covertly. Alternatively, the identification officer may make arrangements for a group identification. (These rules also be applied to juveniles where the parent/guardian consent is refused) (*D: 3.21*).

➤ If methods B to E are not practicable, the identification officer may arrange a confrontation (*D: 3.23*).

➤ Any refusal of consent by the suspect is noted and **this may be used in evidence against him at trial**.

Matters to be explained to the suspect before methods B, C & D above (*D: 3.17*)

- the purposes of the video identification or identification parade or group identification,
- the suspect's entitlement to free legal advice,
- the procedures for holding it (including the suspect's right to have a solicitor or friend present),
- that the suspect does not have to take part in a video identification, id parade or group identification,
- that **if the suspect does not consent** to, and take part in, a video identification, identification parade or group identification, **the refusal may be given in evidence** in a subsequent trial and police may proceed covertly without his consent or make other arrangements to test whether a witness can identify the suspect,
- whether, for the purposes of the video identification, images of the suspect have previously been obtained and if so, that he may co-operate in providing further images for use in place of those previously taken,
- where appropriate, the special arrangements for juveniles or mentally vulnerable people,
- that if the suspect should significantly alter his appearance between being offered an identification procedure and any attempt to hold an identification procedure, this may be given in evidence if the case comes to trial, and the identification officer may then consider other forms of identification,
- that a video or photograph may be taken of the suspect when they attend for any identification procedure,
- whether the witness has been shown photographs, a computerised or artist's composite likeness or similar likeness or picture by the police during the investigation before the identity of the suspect became known,
- that if the suspect changes his appearance before a identification parade it may not be practicable to arrange one on the day in question or subsequently and, because of the change of appearance, the identification officer may then consider alternative methods of identification,
- that the suspect or his solicitor will be provided with details of the description of the suspect as first given by any witnesses who are to attend the video identification, id parade, group identification or confrontation.

A Court identification

- ➤ Used as a last resort (its evidential value is limited as the witness is 'identifying' a man in the dock).
- ➤ The witness is asked whether he recognises the prisoner in the dock.
- ➤ Consent is *not* required.

B Video identification (*Code D: Annex A*)

- ➤ A witness is shown moving images of a known suspect, together with similar images of others who resemble the suspect.
- ➤ The set of images must include at least 8 others *in addition* to the suspect who so far as possible resemble the suspect in age, general appearance and position in life (*D:2 Annex A*).
- ➤ If the suspect has an unusual physical feature (eg: facial scar, tattoo, etc.) hairstyle or hair colour which does not appear on the images of the other people that are available to be used, steps may be taken to conceal the location of the feature on the images of the suspect and the other people *or* to replicate that feature on the images of the other people (*D:2A Annex A*).
- ➤ All subjects are filmed in the same position, doing similar things, under identical conditions unless: (i) the identification officer reasonably believes it is not practicable due to a suspect's refusal to cooperate *and* (ii) the different conditions would not point a witness to an individual image (*D:3 Annex A*).
- ➤ Each person is identified by number (*D:5 Annex A*).
- ➤ The suspect or his lawyer are shown the sequence first to see if they object (*D:7 Annex A*).
- ➤ The witness must *not* be told if another witness has made an identification or communicate with any other witness (*D:10 Annex A*).
- ➤ Only 1 witness views the set of images at any one time and is told the person they saw earlier may or may not be in the sequence of images to follow (*D:11 Annex A*).
- ➤ Once the witness has seen the sequence and has indicated he does not want to view it again, he is asked to identify by number anyone he saw on a previous occasion (*D:12 Annex A*).

C Identification parade (*Code D: Annex B*)

- ➤ A suspect must be given a reasonable opportunity to have a solicitor or friend present (*D:1 Annex B*).
- ➤ An id parade may happen in a normal room or a room with a screen permitting witnesses to see the id parade without being seen. The procedures for the composition and conduct of the id parade are the same in both cases, but an id parade with a screen may take place only when the suspect's solicitor, friend or appropriate adult is present or the id parade is recorded on video (*D:2 Annex B*).
- ➤ Before the id parade takes place the suspect or his solicitor must be provided with details of the first description of the suspect by any witnesses who are to attend the id parade. Where a broadcast or publication is made, the suspect or their solicitor should also be allowed to view any material released to the media by the police to recognise or trace the suspect, provided it is practicable to do so and would not unreasonably delay the investigation (*D:3 Annex B*).
- ➤ 8 persons *in addition* to the suspect take part who so far as possible resemble the suspect in age, height, general appearance and position in life (*D:9 Annex B*).
- ➤ Where the suspect has an unusual physical feature, eg: a facial scar or tattoo which cannot be replicated on other members of the id parade, steps may be taken to conceal the location of that feature on the suspect and the other members of the identification parade if the suspect and their solicitor or appropriate adult agree, eg: by use of a plaster or a hat (*D:10 Annex B*).
- ➤ When the suspect is brought to the place where the id parade is to be held, the suspect or his lawyer are asked whether they have any objection to the arrangements for the id parade or to any of the other participants in it and to state the reasons for the objection (*D:12 Annex B*).
- ➤ The suspect may select his own position in the line, but may not otherwise interfere with the order of the people forming the line. Where there is more than one witness the suspect must be told, after each witness has left the room, that they can if they wish change position in the line. Each position in the line must be clearly numbered, whether by means of a numeral laid on the floor in front of each identification parade member or by other means (*D:13 Annex B*).
- ➤ The witness must *not* be told if another witness has made an identification or communicate with any other witness (*D:14 to 16 Annex B*).
- ➤ When the identification officer or civilian support staff is satisfied that the witness has properly looked at each member of the id parade, they ask the witness whether the person they saw on an earlier relevant occasion is on the identification parade and, if so, to indicate the number of the person concerned (*D:17 Annex B*).
- ➤ If the witness wishes to hear any identification parade member speak, adopt any specified posture or see an identification parade member move, the witness must first be asked whether he can identify any person(s) on the identification parade on the basis of appearance only. When the request is to hear members of the identification parade speak, the witness must be reminded that the participants in the identification parade have been chosen on the basis of physical appearance only. Members of the identification parade may then be asked to comply with the witness's request to hear them speak, to see them move or to adopt any specified posture (*D:18 Annex B*).
- ➤ A video recording must normally be taken of the identification parade. Where that is impracticable a colour photograph must be taken. A copy of the video recording or photograph shall be supplied on request to the suspect or his solicitor within a reasonable time (*D:23 Annex B*).

CRIMINAL LITIGATION
Arrest and interview

D Group identification (Code D: Annex C)

- Group identifications may take place either with the suspect's consent or covertly without his consent (*D:2 Annex C*).
- The location of the group identification is a matter for the identification officer, although he may take into account any representations made by the suspect, appropriate adult, his solicitor or friend (*D:3 Annex C*).
- The place where the group identification is held should be one where other people are either passing by or waiting around informally, in groups such that the suspect is able to join them and be capable of being seen by the witness at the same time as others in the group. Eg: people leaving an escalator, pedestrians walking through a shopping centre, passengers on railway and bus stations, waiting in queues or groups (*D:4 Annex C*).
- If the group identification is to be held covertly, the choice of locations are limited by the places where the suspect can be found and the number of other people present at that time. In these cases suitable locations might be along regular routes travelled by the suspect, including buses or trains or public places frequented by the suspect (*D:5 Annex C*).
- Although the number, age, sex, race and general description and style of clothing of other people present at the location cannot be controlled by the identification officer, in selecting the location the officer must consider the general appearance and numbers of people likely to be present (*D:6 Annex C*).
- Immediately after a group identification procedure has taken place a colour photograph or a video should be taken of the general scene, where this is practicable, so as to give a general impression of the scene and the number of people present. Alternatively, if it is practicable, the group identification may be video recorded (*D:8 Annex C*).
- An identification carried out remains a group identification notwithstanding that at the time of being seen by the witness the suspect was on his or her own rather than in a group (*D:10 Annex C*).
- A suspect must be given a reasonable opportunity to have a solicitor or friend present (*D:13 Annex C*).
- The witness must *not* be told if another witness has made an identification or communicate with any other witness (*D:14 to 17 Annex C*).
- Witnesses must be brought to the place where they are to observe the group one at a time. Immediately before the witness is asked to look at the group the person conducting the procedure must tell the witness that the person they saw may or may not be in the group and that if they cannot make a positive identification they should say so. The witness must then be asked to observe the group in which the suspect is to appear (*D:18 Annex C*).
- There are special rules for moving groups (*D:19-24 Annex C*) and stationery groups (*D:25-29 Annex C*).
- If the suspect unreasonably delays joining the group, or having joined the group, deliberately conceals himself from the sight of the witness, this may be treated as a refusal to co-operate in a group identification (*D:30 Annex C*).
- If the witness identifies a person other than the suspect that person should be informed what has happened and asked if they are prepared to give their name and address (*D:31 Annex C*).
- When finished, the suspect must be asked if he wants to comment on the conduct of the procedure (*D:32 Annex C*).
- If identification is carried out covertly, a suspect has no right to have a solicitor, appropriate adult or friend present. Also any number of suspects may be identified at the same time (*D:35-36 Annex C*).

E Showing of photographs (Code D: Annex E)

- An officer of the rank of sergeant or above is responsible for supervising and directing the showing of not less than twelve photographs at a time, which shall, as far as possible, all be of a similar type. The actual showing may be done by a constable or civilian support staff (*D:1 and 4 Annex E*).
- The supervising officer confirms that the first description of the suspect given by the witness has been recorded before the witness is shown the photographs (*D:2 Annex E*).

F Confrontation (Code D: Annex D)

- A witness is confronted with the suspect and asked if it is the correct person.
- Before the confrontation takes place the witness must be told that the person they saw may or may not be the person they are to confront and that if he or she is not that person then the witness should say so (*D:1 Annex D*).
- Before the confrontation takes place the suspect or their solicitor must be provided with details of the first description of the suspect given by any witness who is to attend the confrontation. Where a broadcast or publication is made, the suspect or his solicitor must be allowed to view any material released by police to the media (to recognise or trace the suspect) provided that it is practicable to do so and would not unreasonably delay the investigation (*D:2 Annex D*).
- Force may not be used to make the face of the suspect visible to the witness (*D:3 Annex D*).
- Confrontation must take place in the presence of the suspect's solicitor, interpreter or friend unless this would cause unreasonable delay (*D:4 Annex D*).
- The suspect is confronted independently by each witness, who is asked "Is this the person?". If a witness identifies the person but cannot confirm it, he is asked how sure he is that the person is the same as earlier (*D:5 Annex D*).
- The confrontation normally takes place in the police station, either in a normal room or in one equipped with a screen permitting a witness to see the suspect without being seen. A room equipped with a screen may be used only when the suspect's solicitor, friend or appropriate adult is present or the confrontation is recorded on video (*D:6 Annex D*).
- After the procedure each witness shall be asked whether they have seen any broadcast or published films or photographs or any descriptions of suspects relating to the offence and their reply is recorded (*D:7 Annex D*).

VIII Charge

➤ When the officer in charge of the investigation reasonably believes there is sufficient evidence to provide a realistic prospect of the detainee's conviction they must without delay inform the custody officer who will be responsible for considering whether the detainee should be charged (*C:16.1*).

IX Samples in police detention

1 Intimate samples in police detention (*s 62*)

➤ Intimate samples are (*s 65*): Blood, semen, urine, pubic hair, dental impressions or a swab taken from any part of a person's genitals or from a person's body orifice other than the mouth.

➤ An intimate sample may b¬e taken from a person in police detention only if:
- a police officer of at least the rank of inspector authorises it to be taken, *and*
- consent is given.
  - Refusal of consent without good reason means that the jury may draw such inference as they like (*s 62(10)*).

(Note: Different rules apply for testing for Class A drugs (*s 63B*).)

➤ **Grounds for authorisation:** An officer may only give such an authorisation if he has reasonable grounds:
- for suspecting the involvement of the person from whom the sample is to be taken in a recordable offence, *and*
  - A recordable offence is defined in *NPR(RO)R 2000*.
- for believing that the sample will tend to confirm or disprove his involvement.

➤ **Authorisation:** may be given orally (confirmed in writing as soon as practicable) or in writing.

➤ **Consent:** must be given in writing.

➤ **Who may take the sample:**
- Urine may be taken by anyone.
- A dental impression may be taken only by a registered dentist.
- For any other form of intimate sample, it may be taken only by a registered medical practitioner or a registered health care professional.

Safeguards for samples

➤ Once authorisation has been given and it is proposed that a sample will be taken, an officer must inform the person from whom the sample is to be taken of the giving of the authorisation and the grounds for giving it (including the nature of the offence in which it is suspected that the person from whom the sample is to be taken has been involved).

➤ Once a sample has been taken from a person, the following must be recorded in the custody record as soon as practicable after the sample is taken:
- the authorisation by virtue of which it was taken, *and*
- the grounds for giving the authorisation, *and*
- the fact that the appropriate consent was given.

2   **Non-intimate samples in police detention** (*s 63*)

➤ Non-intimate samples are (*s 65*): Nails, non-pubic hair, a swab taken from any part of a person's body other than a part from which a swab taken would be an intimate sample, saliva, skin impression.

➤ Consent in writing must be given, *unless* 1 of 4 reasons applies:

1. ◆ The person is in police detention because of his arrest for a recordable offence, *and*
   ◆ the person has not had a non-intimate sample of the same type and from the same part of the body taken in the course of the investigation of the offence by the police, or he has had such a sample taken but it proved insufficient, *or*

2. ◆ The person is being held in custody by the police on the authority of a court, *and*
   ◆ an officer of at least the rank of inspector authorises it to be taken without the appropriate consent, *or*
   • Grounds for authorisation are the same as for intimate samples

3. ◆ The person has been charged with a recordable offence or informed that he will be reported for such an offence, *and*
   ◆ either he has not had a non-intimate sample taken from him in the course of the investigation of the offence by the police or he has had a non-intimate sample taken from him but either it was not suitable for the same means of analysis or, though suitable, the sample proved insufficient, *or*

4. The person has been convicted of a recordable offence.

➤ The 'Safeguards for samples' box (see previous page) also applies to non-intimate samples.

➤ The power to take a non-intimate sample without consent is exercisable by any constable.

3   **Other powers** (*ss 54A, 61, 64A, 60AA, 61A*)

➤ There are powers to take fingerprints usually with consent only (but with many exceptions when they can be taken with no consent); powers to take photographs, powers to remove disguises, powers to take impressions of footwear.

A solicitor's role at the police station - a solicitor should ...
➤ ... go prepared and take: ◆ *PACE, Codes of Practice*, the Law Society's *Guide to the Conduct of a Solicitor at a Police Station*, copies of the relevant LSC funding application forms.   ◆ a letter (on headed paper) to be handed to the suspect explaining the solicitor's offer to advise the suspect if he requests it.   ◆ a standard proforma for taking instructions, pen and paper.   ◆ cigarettes (tobacco!), as many people request these.
➤ ... keep account of passing time with reference to the time limits for detention.
➤ ... attend any interview at which the client is questioned.
➤ ... listen to his client, and offer advice calmly; his role is to advise.
➤ ... ask for the investigating officer; seek details of why a client is detained and evidence against him.
➤ ... ask, as soon as he arrives at the police station, to see the custody record (the police must agree under C:2.4) and ask to speak to the custody officer.
➤ ... take a contemporaneous note of all that occurs. The solicitor may later be a witness!
➤ If a relative/friend requested the solicitor, the suspect must decide whether to see the solicitor.

X Other rights at a police station

Right to legal advice

➤ All detainees must be informed that they may at any time consult and communicate privately with a solicitor, whether in person, in writing or by telephone, and that free independent legal advice is available from the duty solicitor (*C: 6.1*).

On arrest (*PACE s 58*)

➤ This is a right which a suspect has on arrival at the police station, and subsequently whenever he requests it.

➤ Legal advice from a *particular* solicitor can be delayed for up to 36 hours from the time detention was originally authorised if:

   a) the investigation concerns an indictable offence, *and*
   b) a superintendent, or a higher officer, authorises the delay, *and*
   c) there are reasonable grounds for believing that this will prevent interference with evidence or people *or* alert others still at large *or* hinder the recovery of property.

➤ If legal advice from a particular solicitor is delayed on the basis of the reasons above, access to another solicitor must be offered (*Code C, Annex B, Paragraph 3*).

➤ The defendant must be told of an attempt by a solicitor (on the solicitor's arrival) to contact him (*Code C:6.15*).

At interview

➤ A person who has requested legal advice may not be interviewed (or continue to be interviewed) unless he has received that legal advice, unless *either* (*C:6.6*):

   a) legal advice is barred under *PACE s 58* (see above) *or:*
   b) a superintendent, or a higher officer has reasonable grounds for believing that *either:*
      i) delay will lead to interference with or harm to evidence, harm to persons or property, alert others or hinder the recovery of property, *or*
      ii) the solicitor has been contacted and agreed to attend but waiting for his arrival will cause unreasonable delay to the investigation (*C:6.6*), *or*
   c) an inspector authorises an interview *and* the nominated solicitor cannot be contacted or will not attend, *and* the defendant refuses the duty solicitor (*C:6.6*), *or*
   d) an inspector authorises an interview *and* the defendant changes his mind about wanting legal advice and agrees in writing or on the record of the interview (eg: video, tape, etc.) (*C:6.6*).

➤ The solicitor may intervene during the interview (*C:6D*):
   ◆ to clarify or challenge improper questions or the manner in which they are put.
   ◆ to advise the client not to reply.
   ◆ to give further legal advice.

➤ The interviewer may not exclude a solicitor from the interview unless his conduct is such that an interviewer is unable properly to put questions to the suspect and an officer of at least superintendent rank is first consulted and he first speaks to the solicitor (unless a superintendent is unavailable, in which case an inspector not connected to the investigations must do this) (*C:6.10*).

Reminders of the right to legal advice

➤ There is a right to be reminded of the right to legal advice (*C: 6.5, Annex B*):
   ◆ when first brought to the police station (or if attending voluntarily)
   ◆ before the start or recommencement of an interview at a police station.
   ◆ before a review of detention.
   ◆ after a charge if:
      • a police officer wants to draw a suspect's attention to the written or oral statement of another person, *or*
      • if further questions are to be put to a suspect about the offence.
   ◆ before an identification parade or a request for an intimate body sample.

Right to have someone informed of arrival at the police station

➤ The right can be delayed for up to 36 hours if (*C: 6.5, Annex B*):

   a) the investigation concerns an indictable offence, *and*
   b) an inspector, or higher officer, authorises it, *and*
   c) there are reasonable grounds for believing that this will prevent interference with evidence or people, alert others still at large, or hinder the recovery of property.

XI Detention after charge: 1 of 3 alternatives

1. **The custody officer *must* release the accused unconditionally (unusual) or on police bail (s 38).**
    - ➤ Police bail might be conditional upon the accused attending court on a particular date, etc. (*PACE 1984 s 47*) (This is the most usual and likely occurrence out of the options on this page.)
    - ➤ Conditions may be set if necessary (*BA 1976 s 3A*):
        i) to ensure that the accused surrenders to custody, *and/or*
        ii) to ensure that the accused does not commit an offence while on bail, *and/or*
        iii) to ensure that the accused does not interfere with a witness or obstruct justice, *and/or*
        iv) for the accused's own protection or, if he is a child/young person, for his own welfare/interests.
        NB: The police have a power of arrest if a suspect fails to answer to police bail (*s 46A*).

or 2. **The custody officer *must* keep the accused in police detention if (*CJPO 1994 s 25*):**
    - ➤ ... the suspect is charged with, and has previously been convicted of: murder, attempted murder, manslaughter (and has been given a custodial sentence), rape or attempted rape.
        ◆ He must then be brought before a magistrate as soon as possible (*s 46(1)*).

or 3. **The custody officer *may* keep the accused in police detention if (*s 38(1)*):**
    a) his name or address is unascertainable or doubtful, *or*
    b) detention is necessary because he has reasonable grounds to believe the suspect will fail to appear at court to answer to bail, *or*
    c) (if arrested for an imprisonable offence), detention is necessary to prevent commission of an offence, *or*
    d) (if arrested for a non-imprisonable offence), detention is necessary to protect anyone else from physical injury or damage to property, *or*
    e) detention is necessary to prevent interference with the administration of justice or investigations, *or*
    f) detention is necessary for the suspect's own protection, *or*
    g) in a case where a sample may be taken under *s63B*, he has reasonable grounds for believing detention is necessary to enable the taking of a Class A drugs sample.
    - ➤ He must then be brought before a magistrate as soon as possible (*s 46(1)*).

Note: 'imprisonable offence' is defined in the *Schedule* to the *BA 1976*.

XII What happens next

What happens post charge (per offence type)	

➤ **Summary offences**
◆ The police must 'lay an information' at a Magistrates' Court within 6 months of the commission of the offence (*MCA 1980 ss18,127*).
◆ An 'information' may only concern one offence, otherwise it is void for duplicity (*CrPR r 7.3(1)*).
◆ When an 'information' is laid, the court issues a summons directing the defendant when to appear.
	➤ Dangerous or careless driving (*RTOA 1988 s 1*)
	◆ If there is no accident as a result of these offences, there can be no conviction for these offences, unless as a preliminary:
	  a) the defendant is warned at the time of the offence that a prosecution is possible, *or*
	  b) a summons is served on the defendant within 14 days, *or*
	  c) within 14 days, a notice of intended prosecution is served on the registered keeper (at the time of the offence) of the vehicle.

➤ **Indictable offences (including 'either way' offences)** ◆ An indictment must be drawn up. ◆ It should be drawn up within 28 days of committal (or, if sent for trial, within 28 days of copies of documents containing the evidence being served), but this time can be extended (*I(P)R 1971 r 5*).	➤ Summary offence linked with indictable or 'either way' offence: see 'Mode of trial'/Allocation, p 460.

C Court matters applicable generally

    I   The overriding objective
    II   Criminal case management
    III Variations to orders and time
    IV Hearings

I   The overriding objective

Rules of the court

- Rules of court practice and procedure are governed by the **Criminal Procedure Rules** (*CrPR*).
    - Definitions of terms in the *CrPR* are listed in *r 2.2* and also in a glossary at the back.
    - Each *Part* contains rules - notation is as follows: eg: *r 7.2(2)* refers to rule 7.2(2) in *Part 7*.
- The *CrPR* are new and are a first step in the creation of a new, consolidated criminal procedural code.
    - *Parts 4 to 78* are a consolidation of the existing rules of court, which are for the time being re-enacted without any substantial changes as part of the *CrPR*.
- There is a Consolidated Criminal Practice Direction which can be found at: http://www.dca.gov.uk/criminal/procrules_fin/contents/practice_direction/pd_consolidated.htm .

The court's overriding objective in applying the *CrPR* (r 1)

- The *CrPR* are a new code with the overriding objective that criminal cases be dealt with justly, ie:
    a) acquitting the innocent and convicting the guilty, *and*
    b) dealing with the prosecution and the defence fairly, *and*
    c) recognising the rights of a defendant, particularly those under *ECHR Art 6*, *and*
    d) respecting interests of witnesses, victims and jurors and keeping all informed of progress, *and*
    e) dealing with the case efficiently and expeditiously, *and*
    f) ensuring that appropriate information is available when bail and sentence are considered, *and*
    g) dealing with the case in ways that take into account the gravity of the offence alleged, the complexity of what is in issue, the severity of the consequences for the defendant and others affected and the needs of other cases.
- The court must further the overriding objective in particular when:
    - exercising any power given to it by legislation (including these *CrPR*), *and*
    - applying any practice direction, *and*
    - interpreting any rule or practice direction.
- Each participant, in the conduct of each case, must:
    - prepare and conduct the case in accordance with the overriding objective, *and*
    - comply with these *CrPR*, practice directions and directions made by the court, *and*
    - at once inform the court and all parties of any significant failure by anyone to take any procedural step required by the *CrPR*.

II Criminal case management

The court's general powers of case management (rr 3.2, 3.3, 3.5)

➤ The court must further the overriding objective by actively managing the case (and giving any appropriate direction as soon as possible), including:
- early identification of the real issues and the needs of witnesses, *and*
- achieving certainty as to what must be done, by whom, and when, in particular by the early setting of a timetable for the progress of the case, *and*
- monitoring the progress of the case and compliance with directions (see box below), *and*
- ensuring that evidence, disputed or not, is presented in the shortest and clearest way, *and*
- discouraging delay, dealing with as many aspects of the case as possible on the same occasion, and avoiding unnecessary hearings, *and*
- encouraging the participants to co-operate in the progression of the case, *and*
- making use of technology.

➤ Each party must actively assist the court in fulfilling its duty to actively manage a case (and applying for a direction if needed to further the overriding objective).

➤ The court may give any direction and take any step actively to manage a case unless that direction or step would be inconsistent with legislation. In particular, the court may:
- nominate a judge, magistrate, justices' clerk or justices' clerk's assistant to manage the case, *and*
- give a direction on its own initiative or on application by a party, *and*
- ask or allow a party to propose a direction, *and*
- for the purpose of giving directions, receive applications/representations by letter, telephone and any other means of electronic communication (and conduct a hearing by such means), *and*
- give a direction without a hearing, *and*
- fix, postpone, bring forward, extend or cancel a hearing, *and*
- shorten or extend (even after it has expired) a time limit fixed by a direction, *and*
- require that issues in the case be determined separately, and decide in what order, *and*
- specify the consequences of failing to comply with a direction.

Case progression officers (r 3.4)

➤ At the start of the case each party must nominate an individual responsible for progressing that case and tell other parties and the court who he is and how to contact him.

➤ In doing so, the court must nominate a court officer (called a 'case progression officer') responsible for progressing the case and make sure the parties know who he is and how to contact him.

➤ The case progression officer must:
- monitor compliance with directions, *and*
- ensure that the court is kept informed of events that may affect the progress of that case, *and*
- ensure that he can be contacted promptly about the case during ordinary business hours, *and*
- act promptly and reasonably in response to communications about the case, *and*
- if he will be unavailable, appoint a substitute to fulfil his duties.

III Variations to orders and time

Varying a court direction (r 3.6)

➤ A party may apply to vary a direction if:
- the court gave it without a hearing, *or*
- the court gave it at a hearing in his absence, *or*
- circumstances have changed.

➤ A party who applies to vary a direction must:
- apply as soon as practicable after he becomes aware of the grounds for doing so, *and*
- give as much notice to the other parties as the nature and urgency of his application permits.

Varying a time limit (r 3.7)

➤ The parties may agree to vary a time limit fixed by a direction, but only if:
a) the variation will not affect the date of any hearing that has been fixed or significantly affect the progress of the case in any other way, *and*
b) the court has not prohibited variation by agreement, *and*
c) the court's case progression officer is promptly informed.

➤ The court's case progression officer must refer the agreement to the court if he doubts anything in (a) above is satisfied.

IV Hearings

Rules as to hearings (r 3.8)

➤ At every hearing, if a case cannot be concluded there and then the court must give directions so that it can be concluded at the next hearing or as soon as possible after that.

➤ At every hearing the court must, where relevant:
- if the defendant is absent, decide whether to proceed nonetheless, *and*
- take the defendant's plea (unless already done) or if no plea can be taken then find out whether the defendant is likely to plead guilty or not guilty, *and*
- set, follow or revise a timetable for the progress of the case, which may include a timetable for any hearing - including the trial or (in the Crown Court) the appeal, *and*
- in giving directions, ensure continuity in relation to the court and to the parties' representatives where that is appropriate and practicable, *and*
- where a direction has not been complied with, find out why, identify who was responsible, and take appropriate action.

/ CRIMINAL LITIGATION
Remand and bail

D Remand and bail

I   Remand generally: in custody or on bail ?
II Bail

I   Remand generally: in custody or on bail ?

➤ Remand is considered at every adjournment. It is to ensure the defendant will appear at the next hearing.

➤ The defendant has a right to bail. It is for the prosecution to show why this should not be granted.

Remand ...	
... in custody	... on bail
Remand before conviction or sending for trial/committal for trial (MCA 1980 s 128)	
➤ Remand for a maximum of 8 days at a time. ◆ This can be extended for another 8 days at a time if another hearing approves it. ➤ However, custody can be extended for 8 days at a time *without the defendant being present*, if: ◆ the defendant consents, *and* ◆ a solicitor is acting, *and* ◆ there have not been more than 3 consecutive remand hearings in the defendant's absence. ➤ A court can remand a defendant in custody for up to 28 days (MCA 1980 s 128A) if: ◆ it has previously remanded him in custody for the same offence, *and* ◆ he is in court, *and* ◆ it can set a date for the next stage of proceedings to occur, so he can be remanded until then. ➤ For a summary offence, the maximum time limit for an adult to be in custody from his first appearance until the start of the summary trial is 56 days (PO(CTL)R 1987 r 4A). ➤ For an either way/indictable offence, the maximum time limits for an adult for cumulative detention are (PO(CTL)R 1987 r 5, POA 1985 ss 22, 22B): ◆ for up to 56 days in a Magistrates' Court before a summary trial. ◆ for up to 70 days before committal proceedings. ◆ for up to 112 days in the Crown Court between committal for trial and the start of the trial. ◆ for up to 182 days in the Crown Court between sending for trial and the start of the trial (less any period in custody). • Solicitors should mark the Crown Court file with the period so as to make an application for bail when the period has expired. Bail must then be given. • If the time limits expire, the proceedings are stayed. Certain types of proceedings can be reinstituted afresh within 3 months. NB: The defence should *not* warn the prosecution when the time limits are about to expire. NB: A court may extend a limit if the prosecution has acted with all due diligence and expedition *and* there is good and sufficient cause.	➤ The maximum time limit is unlimited (!) with the defendant's consent.
Remand after committal (MCA 1980 s 6(3))	
➤ Remand until the case is heard (this can take months), subject to the limits above. *This will be replaced by similar provisions regarding sending for trial when CJA 2003, s 41 and Schedule 3 are brought into force abolishing committal.*	➤ Remand on conditions set by the court until the case is heard.
Remand after conviction, until the next hearing (most probably sentencing) (MCA 1980 s 10(3))	
➤ Magistrates' Courts may remand in custody for up to 3 weeks. ➤ The Crown Court may remand until the next hearing, whenever that is.	➤ Magistrates' Courts can remand for up to 4 weeks. ➤ The Crown Court may remand until the next hearing.

II Bail

A Right to bail (BA 1976 s 4)

➤ There is a *right* to bail for:

  a) defendants before conviction, *and*

  b) defendants after conviction during an adjournment for reports, *and*

  c) offenders before magistrates for breaching a requirement of a community order.

➤ BUT there is *no* right to bail for:

  a) a defendant before the Crown Court awaiting sentence, *or*

  b) a defendant before the Crown Court awaiting appeal against conviction or sentence, *or*

  c) someone with a previous conviction for murder, attempted murder, manslaughter, rape or attempted rape and who is now charged with any one of these *unless* the Court/constable (as applicable) finds there to be 'exceptional circumstances' (BA 1976 s 4(8), CJPO 1994 s 25).

B Procedure for bail hearings

Steps

1. The prosecution objects to bail.
2. The defence applies for bail.
3. Evidence is called (rules of evidence do not apply - *Re Moles* [1981] Crim LR 170).
4. The court decides on remand in custody or on bail.
5. The court must give a note stating whether or not bail will be granted, together with reasons why and a list of any conditions it imposes and reasons for those conditions.

Duty to hear further applications (MCA 1980 ss 10,18 and SCA 1981 s 81)	
Magistrates' Court	**Crown Court**
◆ There is a duty on the court to hear further applications for bail if a defendant is still in custody and the right to bail still applies • On a first re-hearing the court hears any argument of fact or law • On subsequent hearings, the court can only hear new arguments	◆ There is a duty on the court to hear further applications for bail if a defendant is still in custody and the right to bail still applies • On a first re-hearing the court hears any argument of fact or law • On subsequent hearings, the court can only hear new arguments ◆ There is a duty to hear further applications from those in custody: • prior to trial, sentence and appeals *and* • when a Magistrates' Court has refused bail after adjournment *and* a certificate of full argument is presented to court ▪ Whenever the case has *not* been sent to the Crown Court for trial, sentence or appeal, a certificate of full argument is required from the Magistrates' Court before a bail hearing is possible
Hearing before a High Court judge in chambers (a last resort if neither of the above courts grant bail) (CJA 1967 s 22)	
✘ No CDS legal funding is available - this is a civil matter	✘ As a matter of practice, no court will grant bail later if the judge in the High Court refuses it

C Refusing bail

➤ In several circumstances, the court may refuse bail and sometimes the court must refuse bail.

- The rules are different as to whether the offence in question is imprisonable or not.

1 Imprisonable offences

➤ The court may refuse bail if any of the following grounds apply (*BA 1976 Schedule I Part I*):

- The court is satisfied that substantial grounds exist to believe that a defendant would (*para 2*):
    - fail to surrender to custody, *and/or*
    - commit another offence (see also the 'Factors' box on the next page), *and/or*
    - interfere with witnesses or obstruct the course of justice.
- The offence is indictable/either way and the defendant was on bail at the time of the offence (*para 2A*). *[This will abolished when the alternative para 2A (see box) is brought into force.]*
- The court is satisfied that the defendant should be kept in custody for his own protection or, if he is a child or young person, for his own welfare (*para 3*).
- The defendant is in custody pursuant to a court sentence (*para 4*).
- The court is satisfied that it has not been practicable to obtain sufficient information for the purpose of taking a bail decision due to lack of time since proceedings started (*para 5*).
- The defendant was arrested for absconding or breaking the bail conditions set for *this* offence (*para 6*). *[This will abolished when the alternative para 6 (see box) is brought into force.]*
- There is an adjournment for enquiries/reports for which the defendant needs to be in custody.

CJA 2003 s 14(1) [not yet in force] replacement of para 2A

➤ *Para 2A will say that bail must be refused if the defendant is over 18 and it appears to the court that he was on bail in criminal proceedings on the date of the offence*

- *unless the court is satisfied that there is no significant risk of the defendant committing an offence while on bail (whether subject to conditions or not).*

CJA 2003 s 15(1) [not yet in force] replacement of para 6

➤ *Para 6 will say that bail must be refused if the defendant is over 18 and it appears to the court that, having been released on bail in or in connection with the offence, he failed to surrender to custody*

- *unless the court is satisfied that there is no significant risk that, if released on bail (whether subject to conditions or not), he would fail to surrender to custody.*

Refusal of bail and Class A drugs (*CJA 2003 s 19*)

➤ Unless the court is satisfied that there is no significant risk of a defendant committing an offence while on bail, bail must be refused if the defendant is an adult *and*:

- the defendant has been charged with an imprisonable offence, *and*:
- there is drug test evidence that the person has a specified Class A drug in his body, *and*
- either the offence is a drugs offence associated with a specified Class A drug or the court is satisfied that there are substantial grounds for believing that the misuse of a specified Class A drug caused or contributed to that offence or provided its motivation, *and*
- the person does not agree to undergo an assessment as to his dependency upon or propensity to misuse specified Class A drugs or, has undergone such an assessment but does not agree to participate in any relevant follow-up offered.

CRIMINAL LITIGATION
Remand and bail

2   **Non-imprisonable offences**

➤ The court may refuse bail if any of the following grounds apply (*BA 1976 Schedule I Part II*):

- It appears to the court that, having been previously granted bail, the defendant failed to surrender to custody and the court believes, in view of that failure, that the defendant, if released on bail (whether subject to conditions or not) would fail to surrender to custody (*para 2*).

- The court is satisfied that the defendant should be kept in custody for his own protection or, if he is a child or young person, for his own welfare (*para 3*).

- The defendant is in custody pursuant to a court sentence (*para 4*).

- The defendant, having been released on bail, has been arrested for absconding and the court is satisfied that there are substantial grounds for believing that if released on bail (whether subject to conditions or not) he would fail to surrender to custody, commit an offence on bail or interfere with witnesses or otherwise obstruct justice (*para 5*).

Factors in considering the above sets of grounds

➤ Strictly speaking, the court only has to consider the factors below in relation to the grounds under *BA 1976 Schedule I Part I*, paras 2 and 6 (ie: two of the grounds listed for refusing an imprisonable offence).

- However, in practice these factors apply to all the grounds.

➤ Factors (*BA 1976 Schedule I Part I, para 9*):

- the nature and seriousness of the offence or default (and the probable method of dealing with the defendant for it),

- the character, antecedents, associations and community ties of the defendant,

- the defendant's record as respects the fulfilment of his obligations under previous grants of bail in criminal proceedings,

- (except in the case of a defendant whose case is adjourned for inquiries or a report), the strength of the evidence of his having committed the offence or having defaulted (*para 9*),

- any other relevant factors.

➤ When a court decides whether it is satisfied that there are substantial grounds for believing that the defendant, if released on bail (subject to conditions or not), would commit an offence while on bail (part of the first ground for refusing bail for an imprisonable offence), the court must give particular weight to the fact that the defendant was on bail in criminal proceedings on the date of the offence, *provided that* the defendant is under 18 and it appears to the court that he was on bail in criminal proceedings on the date of the offence (*BA 1976 Schedule I Part I, para 9AA*).

Drugs (*BA 1976 s 4(9)*)

➤ In taking any decisions under 1 or 2 above, the court must consider any misuse of controlled drugs.

Prosecution appeals about the grant of bail

➤ If new evidence comes to light after bail has been granted by a Magistrates' Court for an either way or indictable offence, the prosecution can ask the court to reconsider the decision to grant bail (*BA 1976 s 5B*).

➤ Where a Magistrates' Court grants bail to a person charged with, or convicted of, an imprisonable offence, the prosecution may appeal the granting of bail to the Crown Court (*B(A)A 1993 s 1(1), CJA 2003 s 18*).

D Bail conditions (BA 1976 s 3)

➤ The court may impose conditions:

- to ensure that the defendant surrenders to custody, *and/or*
- to ensure that the defendant does not commit an offence while on bail, *and/or*
- to ensure that the defendant does not interfere with a witness, or obstruct the course of justice in relation to himself or another, *and/or*
- for the defendant's own protection or, if he is a child/young person, for his own welfare/interests, *and/or*
- to ensure that the defendant makes himself available for enquiries to be made to assist the court in dealing with him for the offence, *and/or*
- to ensure that the defendant (before the time for him to surrender to custody ie: his next appearance in Court) attends an interview with an authorised legal advisor.

Conditions which a court *may* set	
Condition	Rules
surety	◆ The sum depends on a surety's wealth, character, previous convictions, or his proximity to the defendant. ◆ The surety pays the money to the court if the defendant defaults on his bail conditions - no money is paid to the court on bail being granted.
security	◆ The defendant surrenders his money, chattels, passport, etc.
reporting	◆ Reporting to the police station at specified intervals.
curfew	◆ Compulsory attendance between certain times at a certain place.
residence	◆ Residence, for example, in a bail hostel. ◆ (If so, the defendant may also be required to comply with bail hostel rules (BA 1976 s 3(6ZA).)
non-communication with a prosecution witness	◆ This may involve alternative accommodation for the defendant (possibly in a bail hostel) if a prosecution witness is a relative living in the same house.
electronic monitoring	◆ only if someone is at least 12 years old (and certain statutory conditions are fulfilled) (BA 1976 s 3(6ZAA) by CJPA 2001 s 131).

Conditions which a court *must* set

➤ If the defendant is accused of murder, the court must set as a condition that he be medically examined (unless previous reports of his medical condition are satisfactory) (BA 1976 s 6A).

Appeal against certain bail conditions (CJA 2003 s 16)

➤ A right of appeal to the Crown Court exists against imposition by magistrates of certain bail conditions relating to residence, provision of a surety or a security, curfew, electronic monitoring or contact.

➤ Breach of a bail condition entitles the police to arrest the defendant - the breach is not an offence, but it may provide a ground on which bail can be withdrawn (BA 1976 s 7).

- The defendant must be produced before a properly constituted court within 24 hours of arrest (excluding Sundays, Good Friday and Christmas Day - *R v Glen Parva Young Offender Institution ex p G* [1998] QB 877).

E Surrender and absconding

1 Surrender

➤ A defendant granted bail must surrender at the time and place appointed (*BA 1976 s 6*).

➤ Failure to surrender is an offence unless there is a 'reasonable' cause.

- The defendant has the burden of proof in showing a 'reasonable' cause (*BA 1976 ss 6(2), 6(3)*).
    - A failure to give to a person granted bail in criminal proceedings a copy of the record of the decision shall not constitute a reasonable cause for that person's failure to surrender to custody (*BA 1976 s 6(4)*).
- The court may issue a warrant for the defendant's arrest (*BA 1976 s 7(1)-(2)*).

2 Absconding

➤ An offence of failing to surrender (ie: absconding) is punishable either on summary conviction or as if it were a criminal contempt of court (*BA 1976 s 6(5)*).

➤ Where a magistrates' court convicts a person of an offence of absconding, the court may send him in custody or on bail to the Crown Court for sentence (*BA 1976 s 6(6)*):

- if it thinks that the circumstances of the offence are such that greater punishment should be inflicted for that offence than the court has power to inflict, *or*
- in a case where it sends that person for trial to the Crown Court for another offence, that it would be appropriate for him to be dealt with for the absconding offence by the court before which he is tried for the other offence.

➤ Penalties (*BA 1976 s 6(7)*):

- **Magistrates** may impose a fine of up to £5,000 and a sentence of up to 3 months.
- The Crown Court may impose an unlimited fine and a sentence of up to 1 year.

➤ Time limits (*BA 1976 s 6(10)-(12)*):

- Where a person has been released on bail granted by a constable, a magistrates' court cannot try that person for absconding unless:
    - an information is laid for the absconding offence within 6 months from the time of its commission, *or*
    - an information is laid for the absconding offence no later than 3 months from the time of the occurrence of the first of the following events below to occur after the commission of the relevant offence:
        - the person surrenders to custody at the appointed place, *or*
        - the person is arrested, or attends at a police station, in connection with the absconding offence or the offence for which he was granted bail, *or*
        - the person appears or is brought before a court in connection with the absconding offence or the offence for which he was granted bail.

CRITICAL LITIGATION
Mode of trial

E Mode of trial/Allocation on an 'either way' offence

➤ This page shows the law as it stands before *CJA 2003 s 41* and *Schedule 3* is brought into force.

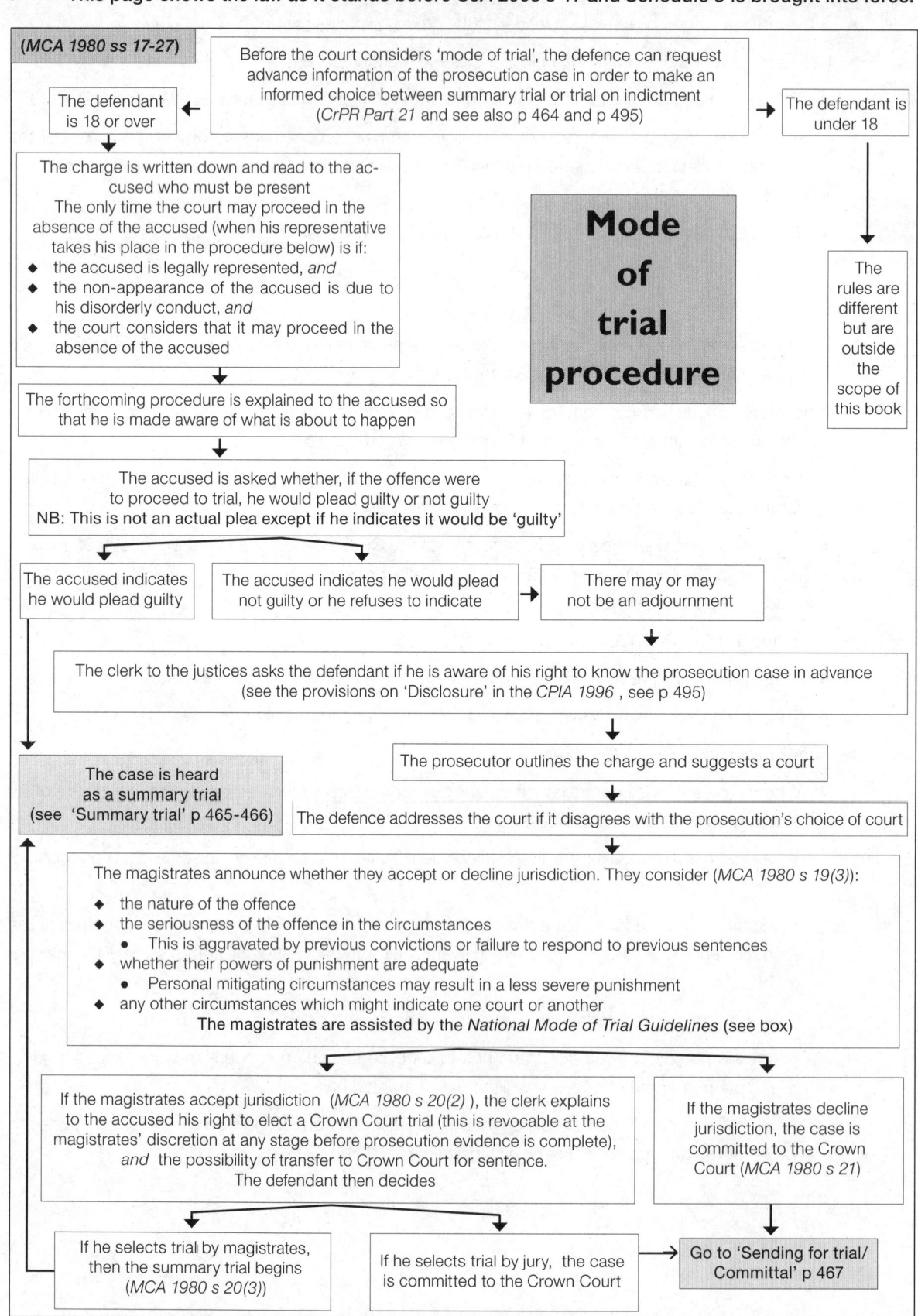

460

CRIMINAL LITIGATION
Mode of trial

▶ *This page shows the law as it will stand after CJA 2003 s 41 and Schedule 3 are brought into force [not yet in force].*

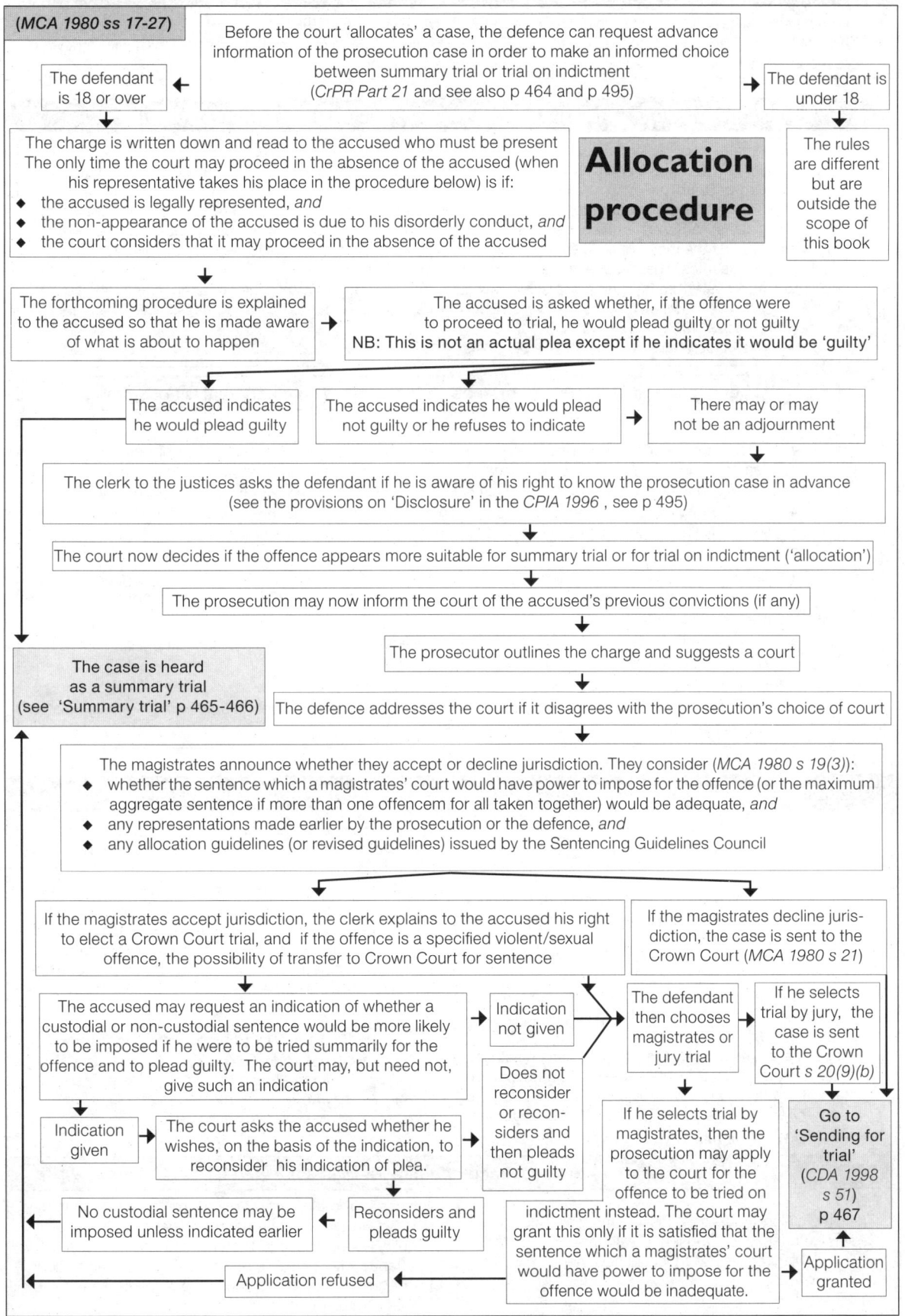

CRIMINAL LITIGATION
Mode of trial

Defendant elects summary trial and subsequently changes his mind before all the prosecution evidence has been heard

- The magistrates have discretion to refer the case to the Crown Court (*MCA 1980 s 25*).
- This will be repealed when *CJA 2003 s 41* and *Schedule 3* is brought into force. It will be replaced with a new prosecution right to challenge as per the chart on the preceding page.

National Mode of Trial Guidelines *(to be replaced by Allocation Guidelines)*

a) Magistrates should assume that the prosecution version of the facts is correct.
b) If there is a complex question of law or fact, then magistrates should consider transferring the matter to the Crown Court.
c) If more than one defendant is charged, each may select a different court regardless of the choice of the other(s). Advance indication for preference for a particular court by one defendant in such a case is irrelevant at the mode of trial hearing stage - *R v Ipswich Justices ex parte Callaghan* 159 JP 748.
d) The magistrates must assume there will be a summary trial unless:
  - magistrates' sentencing powers will be insufficient (although they may later change their minds about whatever decision they reach (*R v Flax Bourton Magistrates' Court, ex parte Commissioners of Customs & Excise* (1996) 160 JP 481), *or*
  - one of the aggravating factors below exists.

List of aggravating factors, per offence, that suggest a summary trial is *not* suitable

1 Burglary
- Dwelling: daytime - house occupied, night-time - house usually occupied, series of offences, soiling, damage, vandalism, professional hallmarks, high value of unrecovered property (greater than £10,000). NB: Violence or the threat of it means it *must* be sent to the Crown Court (*MCA 1980 Sch I para 28(c)*)
- Non-dwelling: fear or violence caused to anyone lawfully on the premises, professional hallmarks, substantial vandalism, high value of unrecovered property (greater than £10,000)

2 Theft
- Breach of trust by one in authority, committed or disguised in a sophisticated manner, organised gang, vulnerable victim, high value of unrecovered property (greater than £10,000), racist connection

3 Violence and assault
- Weapon likely to cause serious injury, more than minor injury by kicking or head-butting, serious violence to a victim whose work brings him in contact with the public

4 Dangerous driving
- Defendant on alcohol/drugs, grossly excessive speed, racing, prolonged course of such driving, related offences, significant damage or injury sustained

Summary offences linked to indictable offences which may be tried in the Crown Court

CJA 1988 s 40(1): Defendant accused of...	CJA 1988 s 41(1): Defendant accused of an offence which is...
... common assault, taking a conveyance, driving whilst disqualified, certain types of criminal damage, assaulting a prison custody officer or a secure training centre custody officer *and* a) i) the summary offence is based on the same facts or evidence as the indictable offence, *or* ii) the summary offence is of a similar character to the indictable offence with which the defendant is also charged, *and* b) facts/evidence relating to the offence were disclosed "to examining justices in the presence of the person charged" [to be changed to: "by material served on the person charged" when CJA 2003 s 41 is brought into force [not yet in force].]	a) punishable with imprisonment or involves obligatory or discretionary disqualification from driving, *and* b) it appears to the court that the summary offence arises out of circumstances which are the same as, or connected with, those giving rise to the offence that is triable 'either way' *CJA 1988 s 41(1) and its consequences will be repealed when CJA 2003 s 41 is brought into force because the existing rules will be subsumed into the new rules for sending for trial [not yet in force]*

Subsequent procedure for trial

The Crown Court must treat the summary offence as an indictable offence, but must deal with the offender as a Magistrates' Court would have done	Evidence for the summary offence is not heard at committal. In the Crown Court the procedure depends on the plea: a) guilty plea: the court sentences for the summary offence with the same powers as a Magistrates' Court b) not-guilty plea: the summary offence is sent to the magistrates for trial

Advice to a client about selecting a court for trial

➤ There are several factors to consider which include the following:

1. **Previous conviction?**

   ✘ Magistrates' Court: magistrates may be seen as case-hardened, and may already be familiar with a police officer or with the defendant.

   ✓ Crown Court: conviction is thought by some to be less likely in a Crown Court where juries can be seen as sympathetic.

   Note: There is no objective proof to support either of these contentions.

2. **If there is a question of admissibility of evidence ...**

   ✘ Magistrates' Court: magistrates decide matters of fact and law (ie: when giving a verdict, magistrates must attempt to 'forget' evidence which they have heard before holding it to be inadmissible).

   ✓ Crown Court: a Crown Court judge rules on the law, the jury decides matters of fact (ie: the jury is sent out while the judge decides evidential matters, so the jurors never hear evidence unless it is admissible).

3. **Questions of cost**

   ✓ Magistrates' Court: costs will be lower.

   ✘ Crown Court: costs will be higher.

4. **Questions of stress**

   ✓ Magistrates' Court: less publicity means less stress.

   ✘ Crown Court: more publicity means more stress.

5. **Is the defendant in custody?**

   ✓ Magistrates' Court: delay before trial is shorter (usually about 1 month).

   ✘ Crown Court: delay before trial is longer (about 6 months).

6. **Sentence**

   ✓ Magistrates' Court: sentences are less severe than in the Crown Court (but the defendant may be referred to the Crown Court for sentencing for certain crimes).

   ✘ Crown Court: sentences are more severe than in the Magistrates' Court.

F Preparations for summary trial

➤ The solicitor should:
- ensure that he has a copy of the custody record (see *Code C:2.4,* p 448).
- ensure, where identification is disputed, that he has a copy of the original description from which the identification was made, see p 444 and note points on p 502.
- obtain a copy of the charge sheet.
- interview the client and take a detailed statement and full instructions as soon as possible.
- interview witnesses: take a proof of evidence signed and dated by the witness.
  - When interviewing a prosecution witness, it is good practice to have an independent party present, and to write to the prosecution to let them know the interview has taken place; this avoids any suspicion of putting pressure on a witness.
  - During an interview, challenge the witness's version of events. (**Note:** 'preparing a witness' for cross-examination is forbidden.)
- visit the area of the alleged offence, and prepare plans if appropriate.
- seek expert evidence: if the client is LSC funded, obtain the LSC's authorisation for the expenditure.
- write to the prosecution asking for disclosure of the prosecution case.
  - In either way cases, the prosecution provides this before a mode of trial hearing (*CrPR r 21.3*). The prosecution does not *have* to disclose in purely summary trials, but a solicitor should request it.
  - *CPIA 1996 ss 1-21* and the common law contain the disclosure rules (see p 495). A solicitor should ask the prosecution for voluntary disclosure at this point as the main statutory disclosure will be *after* the plea.
  - details of any evidence the prosecution possesses which is favourable to the defence.
  - a record of any prosecution interviews with the defendant.
  - the names and addresses of witnesses the prosecution will not call.
  - a list of the witnesses interviewed by the police who the prosecution do *not* intend to call.
  - a statement of the defendant's criminal record. (This should be checked for inaccuracies.)
  - details of the criminal records of prosecution witnesses and co-defendants.
- put the prosecution case to the defendant, and note any comments he makes on it.
- decide whether witnesses should attend. (**Note:** where a witness will not need to be cross-examined, a statement submitted under *CJA 1967 s 9* will be sufficient, see p 508.)
- if a witness's presence is desirable, write to him asking for written confirmation that he will turn up at a specified time.
  - If this confirmation is not forthcoming, the solicitor should write to the relevant court officer using the unanswered letter as proof that the witness is unlikely to attend of his own accord.
  - If a JP is satisfied that a person is likely to be able to give material evidence (or produce any document or thing likely to be material evidence) at the summary trial **and it is in the interests of justice to issue a summons to secure the attendance of that person to give evidence** (or produce the document or thing), the JP issues a summons directed to that person requiring him to attend before the court at the time and place appointed in the summons (*MCA 1980 s 97*).

G Summary trial

Pre-trial hearings (MCA 1980 ss 8A-8D)

- MCA 1980 ss 8A-8D are intended ensure more efficient and uniform preparation of cases for trial in the Magistrates' Courts and to bring the powers of lay magistrates and judges in pre-trial hearings heard in the magistrates' courts into line with those of the Crown Court.

- The magistrates may hold a 'pre-trial hearing' before a summary trial (ie: where the accused has pleaded not guilty) at any time before it has begun to hear evidence from the prosecution at the trial.

- The court can make a ruling on:
    - any question as to the admissibility of evidence, *and/or*
    - any other question of law relating to the case.

- Before making a ruling:
    - the court must have given the parties an opportunity to be heard, *and*
    - it must have appeared to the court that it is in the interests of justice to make the ruling, *and*
    - if the defendant is not legally represented, the court must have asked the defendant whether he wishes to be granted a right to representation funded by the LSC as part of the CDS, and if he does, decided whether or not to grant him that right.

- There are restrictions on reporting matters at the pre-trial hearing.

1 Joinder

- Co-defendants tried on one 'information' for the same offence are tried together, unless there is a conflict of interest. The conviction of one does not prevent the acquittal of the other (eg: *Barsted v Jones* (1960) 124 JP 400).

- Defendants tried on separate 'informations' can be tried together if the defence agrees. But the court always has discretion to consider that as the facts are the same, or that as the offences are similar and related, a joint trial is 'in the interests of justice' (*Chief Constable of Norfolk v Clayton* [1983] 2 AC 473).

2 Defect in process

- If the defence is misled by an error in the 'information', summons or warrant, then it may seek an adjournment to rethink its case. It has no other remedy in these circumstances (*MCA 1980 s 123*).

CRIMINAL LITIGATION
Summary trial

3 Procedure (*MCA 1980 s 9 and CrPR Part 37*)

Steps

1. The charge is read to the defendant (unless summary trial has started from sending for trial/a mode of trial hearing where the charge has already been read to the defendant: *CPIA 1996*).

2. The defendant pleads 'guilty' (except if he has already indicated this on an allocation/mode of trial hearing) or 'not guilty'. He can alter this at any time before sentence.
   - ♦ If 'guilty', the court proceeds to sentence (and may hold a Newton hearing, see p 492).

3. The statutory disclosure procedure applies from this point (see p 495) and the disclosure of expert evidence procedure applies too (see p 510).

4. The prosecution makes an opening speech outlining the facts and issues (*CrPR r 37.1(1)*).

5. The prosecution calls evidence.

6. The legal representative of the defence must tell the court at this point that the defendant will give evidence, else the magistrate will give a 'silence warning' (see p 511) (*CJPO 1994 s 35*).

7. The defence may submit 'no case to answer' (see p 473 for a discussion of this) if *either*:
   a) there is no evidence to prove an essential element of the offence, *or*
   b) the prosecution evidence is so discredited under cross-examination *or* so manifestly unreliable that no reasonable tribunal could convict on it.
   - ♦ For the effect of 'adverse inferences' on a defendant's decision not to testify, see p 511.
   - ♦ The prosecution may reply to this submission.
   - ♦ If the submission is accepted, the case is dismissed, otherwise step 8 applies.

8. The defence may make an opening speech or may immediately move to calling evidence (*CrPR r 37.1(2)-(6)*).

9. If the defence evidence throws up unforeseeable surprises, the prosecution can seek leave to call more evidence.

10. If the defence did *not* make an opening speech, it has the right to address the court last..

11. The magistrates reach a majority verdict and then consider an appropriate sentence and costs.

> **Points of law at the trial**
> ➤ A magistrate's clerk can advise the bench on matters of law, but not of fact.
> ➤ If a point of law is raised at any stage, the other party always has a right to reply.

4 Costs

➤ **The defendant is acquitted (not LSC funded)** (*POA 1985 s 16(1)*): Costs are met from central funds, *unless* the defendant brought suspicion on himself by his own conduct (*POA 1985 s 16(7)*).

➤ **The defendant is acquitted (he is LSC funded)**: Costs are not met by central funds, but by the LSC. Any contribution the defendant has made may be refunded (*POA 1985 s 21(4A)*) unless there are exceptional circumstances.

➤ **The defendant is convicted**: Costs must be met by the defendant where the court is satisfied that he has the means and ability to pay (*POA 1985 s 18(1)*). (Costs must be met by the LSC if the offender is an assisted person, but may be subject to a RDCO, see p 21.) The court makes an order for a specified sum (*POA 1985 s 18(3)*).

CRIMINAL LITIGATION
Sending for trial and committal

H Sending for trial and committal

   I   Sending for trial or committal?
   II Sending for trial
   III Committal

I Sending for trial or committal?

▶ This section governs the next steps in the procedure when an accused is charged with an offence which is an either way offence or triable only on indictment.

Sending for trial or committal (before *CJA 2003 Part 6* is brought into force)

The accused is:

- charged with an **offence triable only on indictment** *and* accused is an adult
  → *CDA 1998 s 51* transfer for trial procedure applies

- accused is a child charged with a specified violent or sexual offence (*CJA 2003 s 224*) and it appears to the court that if he is found guilty of the offence, that an extended sentence to protect the public from harm (*CJA 2003 s 226(3), 228(2)*) would be necessary (*CDA 1998 s51A(3)(d)*)
  → *CDA 1998 s 51A* transfer for trial procedure applies (not covered in this

- charged only with an **either way offence** *or* accused is a child (but not a child as per CDA 1998 s51A, in the box immediately on the left)
  → Committal procedure applies

▶ Also, certain prosecuting authorities can avoid committal by giving a notice of transfer (*CJA 1987 s 4*).
   ◆ Eg: for offences of a violent/sexual nature where there is a child witness or serious/complex fraud.

Sending for trial or committal (after CJA 2003 ss 41-42 are brought into force) [not yet in force]

▶ *After CJA 2003, Part 6 (ss 41-42) is brought into force, committal will be abolished and all cases will be sent for trial [Not yet in force].*

II Sending for trial

➤ An adult before a Magistrates' Court who is charged with an offence triable only on indictment is immediately sent to the Crown Court for trial (*CDA 1998 s 51(1)*).

- ◆ The accused is sent for trial (*CDA 1998 s 51*):
    - for the indictable-only offence, *and*
    - for any either way or summary offence with which he is charged which:
        - appears to the court to be related to the indictable-only offence, *and*
        - (in the case of a summary offence only), is punishable with imprisonment or involves obligatory or discretionary disqualification from driving.
- ◆ Any other adult who is charged jointly with the accused with an either way offence which is related to the indictable-only offence, is also immediately sent to the Crown Court for trial of the either way offence (*CDA 1998 s 51*).
- ◆ A child jointly charged with the accused for the indictable offence is, if the court considers it necessary in the interests of justice, sent immediately to the Crown Court for trial (*CDA 1998 s 51*).

The above text will be replaced when CJA 2003 s 41 is brought into force [not yet in force]

➤ *An adult before a Magistrates' Court is immediately sent to the Crown Court for trial as per the 'sending for trial' box on p 467 (CDA 1998 s 51(1)).*

➤ *Where the court sends an adult for trial, it also sends him at the same time to the Crown Court for trial for any either-way or summary offence with which he is charged and which (CDA 1998 s 51(3)):*

- ◆ *(if it is an either-way offence) appears to the court to be related to the main offence for which he is sent for trial, or*
- ◆ *(if it is a summary offence) appears to the court to be related to the main offence for which he is sent for trial or to the either-way offence if that either way offence is punishable with imprisonment or involves obligatory or discretionary disqualification from driving (CDA 1998 s 51(11)).*

Note: If the adult has already been sent for a trial and subsequently appears or is brought before a Magistrates' Court charged with an either-way or summary offence, the court can also send him for trial for that offence at this later point, if these conditions above are fulfilled (CDA 1998 s 51(4)).

➤ *Where the court has sent an adult (A) for trial and another adult appears or is brought before the court on the same (or a subsequent) occasion who is charged jointly with A with an either-way offence and that either-way offence appears to the court to be related to an offence for which A was sent for trial, then the court sends the other adult to the Crown Court for trial for the either-way offence (CDA 1998 s 51(4)), together with any other linked offences as per the rules in CDA 1998 s 51(3) (CDA 1998 s 51(5)).*

➤ *Special rules apply if a child/young person is charged jointly with an adult (CDA 1998 s 51(7)-(9)).*

- ◆ *In general, a child jointly charged with the accused for the indictable offence is, if the court considers it necessary in the interests of justice, sent immediately to the Crown Court for trial (CDA 1998 s 51(7)).*

➤ *There are special rules also for cases involving children or serious or complex fraud cases (CDA 1998 s 51A-51D).*

CRIMINAL LITIGATION
Sending for trial and committal

Reporting restrictions (CDA 1998 Schedule 3) (Also CDA 1998 s 52A [not yet in force])

➤ It is unlawful to publish in the UK a written report or include for reception in the UK a report of any allocation or sending proceedings, unless a court orders otherwise.

➤ Defendant(s) may object to the lifting of reporting restrictions. If a lifting order is to be made, the court can only lift the restrictions if it is 'in the interests of justice'.

➤ However, the following matters may be reported:

- the identity of the court and the name of the justice or justices
- the name, age, home address and occupation of the accused
- in the case of an accused charged with an offence in respect of which notice has been given to the court under section 51B above, any relevant business information
- the offence or offences, or a summary of them, with which the accused is or are charged
- the names of counsel and solicitors engaged in the proceedings
- where the proceedings are adjourned, the date and place to which they are adjourned
- the arrangements as to bail
- whether a right to representation funded by the LSC as part of the Criminal Defence Service was granted to the accused or any of the accused.

Application for dismissal of main indictable offence

➤ After service of copies of the documents (but before arraignment), the accused can apply orally or in writing for the main indictable offence for which he was sent for trial to be dismissed (*CDA 1998, Schedule 3 para 2*).

➤ It is possible to obtain the attendance of prosecution witnesses for cross-examination if it is in the interests of justice to do so.

♦ *This will be repealed when CJA 2003 s 41 is brought into force.*

Mixed charges (*CDA 1998 Schedule 3 paras 6-7*)

➤ If the accused is sent to the Crown Court for:

- ♦ a main indictable offence *and* other either way offences:
    - if the accused succeeds in having the main indictable offence for which he was sent fo trial dismissed, then the Crown Court holds a plea-before venue hearing to ascertain if the either way offence should be tried in the Crown Court or the Magistrates' Court.
        - If the accused pleads guilty, then the court immediately proceeds to sentence.
        - If the accused pleads not guilty, there is a full mode of trial hearing (see p 460).
    - if the accused fails in having the main indictable offence dismissed, then the Crown Court considers that main indictable offence and the either way offence.

- ♦ an indictable offences *and* other summary offences:
    - if the accused is convicted on the indictable offence for which he was sent for trial, the Crown Court considers whether the summary offence is related to any of those indictable offences. If they are related, the court states to the person the substance of the summary offence and asks him whether he pleads guilty or not guilty.
        - If the accused pleads guilty, the Crown Court convicts him of the summary offence, but may deal with him for the summary offence only in a manner in which a Magistrates' Court could have dealt with him.
        - If the accused pleads not plead guilty, the powers of the Crown Court cease in respect of the summary offence and the matter goes for trial to the Magistrates' Court.

Ancillary matters

1 **Witness summons to ensure witnesses attend the Crown Court trial:** *CP(AW)A 1965 s 2* contains the rules for issue of a witness summons by the Crown Court. It applies when a person is likely to be able to give evidence likely to be material evidence (or produce any document or thing likely to be material evidence) for any criminal proceedings before the Crown Court, and it is in the interests of justice to issue a summons to secure the attendance of that person to give evidence or to produce the document or thing (usually to compel any witness with material evidence to attend trial who will not attend voluntarily). The *CrPR* govern the procedure which is very strict.

➤ Some of the rules that apply are:
- where a person has been sent for trial, an application for a witness summons must be made as soon as is reasonably practicable after service on that person of the documents relevant to that offence.
- a detailed affidavit is needed in support.
- evidence that the evidence sought is likely to be material in the criminal proceedings is needed in support.
- the court may also make a witness summons of its own motion.
- a Crown Court judge punishes disobedience of such a summons as contempt.

➤ (Committal only:) A Magistrates' Court which commits a person for trial must immediately remind him of his right to object, within 14 days, to a statement or deposition being read as evidence at the trial without oral evidence being given by the person who made the statement or deposition, and without the opportunity to cross-examine that person (*CrPR r 10.4*).
- The general rule, if the defendant does not object, is that all statements of a particular witness forming part of the committal bundle will be read at trial instead of the witness being called to give oral evidence.

2 **LSC funding:** The defence can apply for an extension of LSC funding to cover a Crown Court trial. It also confirms whether or not the defendant's financial circumstances are altered.

3 **Bail** (For committal the reference is: *MCA 1980 s 6(3)*): Bail is usually extended until trial. If the defendant is in custody, he can make a bail application.

4 **Fix a date for a PCMH:** Magistrates fix a date for a plea and case management hearing (p 476).

III   Committal

Note: Committal is due to be abolished when CJA 2003, s 41 and Schedule 3 is brought into force.

➤ Committal proceedings are the means by which a Magistrates' Court decides if there is sufficient evidence to send an accused to the Crown Court.

➤ There are 2 types of committal hearing, both in *MCA 1980 s.6*: *s 6(1)* committal and *s 6(2)* committal.

s 6(1) committal	s 6(2) committal
Committal **with** consideration of evidence	Committal **without** consideration of evidence

CRIMINAL LITIGATION
Sending for trial and committal

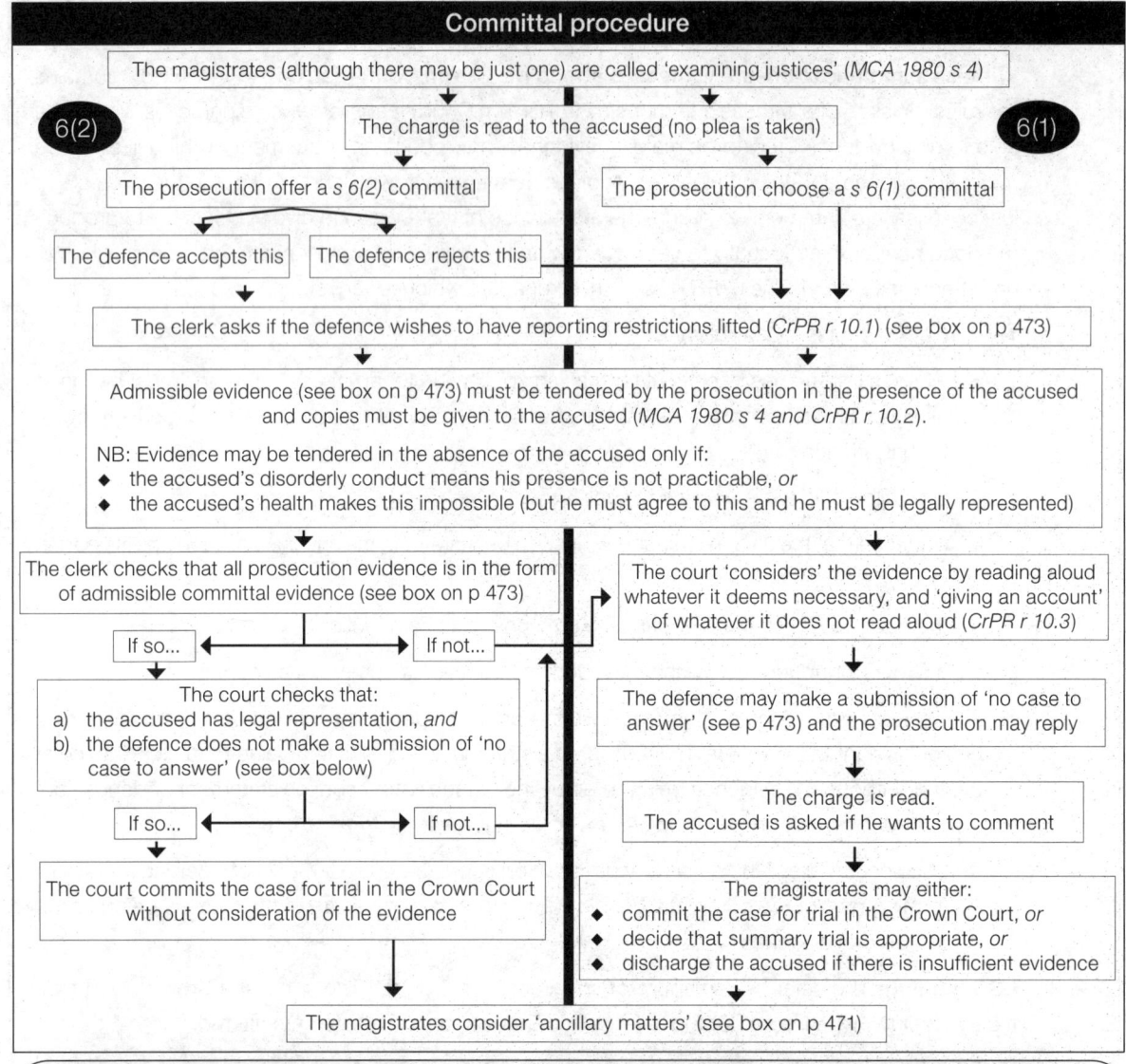

Which committal should be chosen?

➤ A *s 6(2)* committal is quicker and will usually be preferable.

➤ A *s 6(2)* committal can only take place if:

a) all evidence tendered by the prosecution at committal is (see p 473 for in-depth definitions):
- in the form of written statements, *or*
- in the form of documents or exhibits referred to in the written statements, *or*
- in the form of depositions, *or*
- in the form of documents or exhibits referred to in depositions, *or*
- any particular document allowed by statute, *and*

b) the defendant has a solicitor acting for him, *and*

c) the defence do not claim that the prosecution has insufficient evidence.

Prosecution reasons:	Defence reasons:
identification is at issue - the Attorney General has advised that *s 6(2)* is only suitable if the prosecution, defence and court are satisfied about reliability of identification evidence	• to submit no case to answer, *or* • to obtain publicity (it may help trace witnesses), *or* • to persuade a court to commit on a lesser charge.

472

Test for committal to the Crown Court

➤ The test is whether, having heard the case, there is sufficient evidence to put the accused on trial for indictment (ie: if a reasonably minded jury, properly directed, would convict on the evidence provided). If so, then the magistrates will commit the case to the Crown Court for trial.

Test for a submission of 'no case to answer'

➤ *R v Galbraith* [1981] 1 WLR 1039 - taken at its highest, could a jury convict on the evidence?
- This 'depends on the view to be taken of a witness's reliability, or other matters ... within the jury's province, and where *one possible view* of the facts is that there is evidence on which the jury could properly convict [and if all these apply, then a submission will fail]'.

Admissible committal evidence (MCA ss 5A-5D)

➤ Admissible committal evidence is evidence that is tendered by, or on behalf of, the prosecutor, *and* is:
- **a written statement**, *or*
  - this is a statement that:
    - purports to be signed by the person making it, *and*
    - contains a declaration by that person that:
      - it is true to his best knowledge and belief *and*
      - if tendered in evidence the person would be liable to prosecution if it contained anything he knew to be false or untrue, *and*
    - has been given together with any documents or exhibits it refers to (or copies have been given) (these must be inspectable if copies are not available) to each of the other parties before being tendered by the prosecutor, *and*
    - contains the defendant's age (but only if he is under 18).
- **a deposition**, *or*
  - this is a document that:
    - has been sent to the prosecutor after the *MCA 1980 s 97A(9)* procedure, *and*
    (NB: the *MCA 1980 s 97A* procedure is often used when an evidence statement has been taken from someone who may not voluntarily give evidence at committal and is made to do so pursuant to a witness summons, or is arrested to do so, see p 464.)
    - has been given together with any documents or exhibits it refers to (or copies have been given) (these must be inspectable if copies are not available) to each of the other parties before the inquiry as 'examining justices' begins.
- **documents or other exhibits referred to in written statements or depositions**, *or*
- **a documentary hearsay statement**, *or*
  - the prosecution must have signed a certificate that there is reasonable cause to believe the evidence may be properly used at trial.
- **any other document allowed by statute**.

> A document is anything in which any information of any description is recorded (MCA 1980 s 5A(6))

Reporting restrictions (MCA 1980 s 8)

➤ The press may report the names of defendants/witnesses, the charge and result of the proceedings.

➤ The press may not report evidence (to prevent a jury being prejudiced).

➤ A single defendant may ask that restrictions be lifted (eg: to obtain publicity to help trace witnesses).
- If a co-defendant requests, restrictions are lifted if it is 'in the interests of justice' (*MCA 1980 s 8(2A)*).

I Preparations for Crown Court hearings and trial

Between committal and trial

1. Make all relevant preparations as for summary trial (see p 464) *and get the committal bundle.*

2. Apply to the Crown Court or a High Court judge in chambers for bail, if necessary.

3. **Brief counsel** (see box below for '*Format of a brief to counsel*').

4. Ensure that the prosecution has turned over all relevant material (following the disclosure procedure, see p 495).

5. Ensure that witnesses can attend as planned.
   ➤ This is achieved by applying for any necessary witness summons (see p 471).

6. Exchange any expert witness statements with the prosecution as soon as practicable after committal (*CrPR r 24.1*)(see p 510).

7. Take instructions on mitigation.

8. **Obtain disclosure of materials unused by the prosecution** (a common law right and cf: *R v Ward* [1993] 1 WLR 619).

Format of a brief to counsel

1. **Heading:** case, title, court, relevant LSC funding certificate or fee, case number.

2. **List of enclosures**
   ➤ Eg: LSC representation order, list of previous convictions, bundle of witness statements, comments on witness statements, bail notice, indictment, custody record.

3. **Prosecution allegations**
   ➤ Direct counsel to specific allegations in the witness statements.
   ➤ Define facts which are not in dispute.

4. **Defence allegations**
   ➤ Give a brief statement of the relevant law.
   ➤ Apply the law to the circumstances of the case.

5. **Note any evidential problems**
   ➤ Character: Examine whether admission of character evidence will need to be adduced (see pp 499-501). (Rules for when convictions are spent are in *ROA 1974*.)
   ➤ Evidence: admissible as an exception to the rule against hearsay (ie: opinion, *res gestae*, etc).
   ➤ Confessions: point out any grounds for exclusion.
   ➤ Corroboration: note where this is needed, and highlight any suitable evidence, see p 502.
   ➤ Discuss briefly the reasons for and against the defendant testifying, see pp 499-501. State:
      a) why any difficulty is likely to arise, *and*
      b) any consequences which follow.

6. **Mitigation:** give any relevant information.

7. **Request:** 'Would counsel please advise ... and attend court on ... at ...'.

J Crown Court hearings and trial

A The indictment

➤ The prosecution is responsible for seeing that an indictment is drafted.

➤ An indictment is a statement of offences (called 'counts') with which an accused is charged.
- A 'count' is an individual charge.
- Each count in an indictment must allege only one offence (*IR 1971 r 4(2)*).

➤ The indictment must be preferred within 28 days of (*I(P)R 1971 r 5*):
- the date of committal (if there was a committal), *or*
- the date on which copies of the documents containing the evidence on which the charge or charges are based are served (if the accused was sent for trial).

➤ **Joinder:** Charges for any offences may be joined in the same indictment if the charges are founded on the same facts, or form or are a part of a series of offences of the same, or a similar character (*IR 1971 r 9*).

➤ 2 or more accused may be joined in one indictment.

B Procedure

A Plea and Case Management Hearing ('PCMH') is held (see flowchart on next page) - this includes arraignment. This also falls into the definition of a pre-trial hearing (see box left below)

Any pre-trial hearings are held to rule on:
- questions of admissibility of evidence, *and/or*
- questions of law

(*CPIA 1996 ss 39-43*)
NB: Stringent reporting restrictions apply to such hearings as for preparatory hearings

Any preparatory hearings may be held (*CPIA 1996 ss 28-38*) (see box on p 477)

The trial

Steps	
1	The prosecution makes an opening speech outlining the facts and the issues of the case.
2	The prosecution calls evidence.
3	The legal representative of the defence must tell the court at this point that the defendant will give evidence, else the judge will give a 'silence warning' (see p 511) (*CJPO 1994 s 35*).
4	The defence may submit that there is no case to answer. • The prosecution may reply to this submission. • If the submission is accepted the case is dismissed, otherwise proceed to the next step.
5	If the defence will be producing evidence other than just from the accused, they have a right to an opening speech, otherwise they do not.
6	The defence calls evidence.
7	If defence evidence throws up unforeseeable surprises, the prosecution can seek leave to call more evidence.
8	The prosecution delivers its closing speech to the jury.
9	The defence delivers its closing speech to the jury.
10	The judge sums up and directs the jury as necessary.
11	The jury must deliver a unanimous verdict. • A majority verdict (11:1, 10:2) is acceptable if unanimity is impossible after a reasonable time (minimum of 2 hours) (*Juries Act 1974 s 17(1)*).
12	If the jurors cannot agree on a unanimous or a majority verdict, a retrial may be held. The prosecution have discretion to ask for a retrial.

CRIMINAL LITIGATION
Crown Court hearings and trial

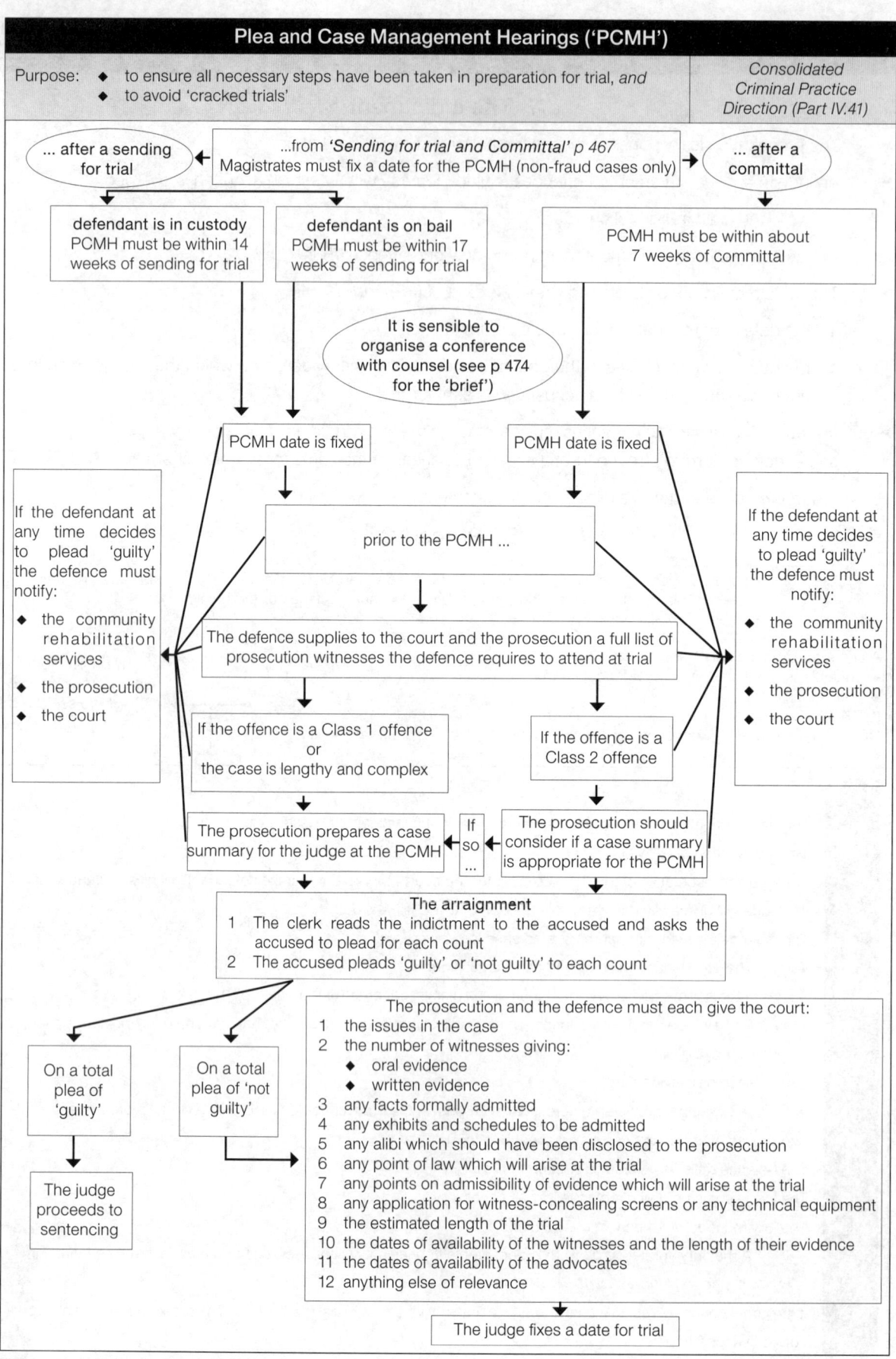

CRIMINAL LITIGATION
Crown Court hearings and trial

Preparatory hearings (CPIA 1996 ss 28-38)

➤ Any time after sending for trial/committal but before a jury has been sworn, a Crown Court judge may hold a preparatory hearing, if he decides that a trial will be so complex or so long or so serious that there will be a substantial benefit for one of the following purposes:
- to identify the issues likely to be material to the verdict of the jury.
- to assist the jury's comprehension of such issues.
- to expedite proceedings before the jury.
- to assist the judge in the management of the trial.
- considering questions as to the severance or joinder of charges.

➤ The hearing starts with arraignment (see p 476) (unless it has been done before, eg: at the PCMH).

➤ The powers of the judge at a preparatory hearing are (s 31):
- to rule on the admissibility of evidence.
  - There may be an appeal to the Court of Appeal (only with leave of the judge or the Court of Appeal) (s 35). No jury may be sworn until after the appeal is heard.
- to rule on a question of law.
  - There may be an appeal to the Court of Appeal (only with leave of the judge or the Court of Appeal) (s 35). No jury may be sworn until after the appeal is heard.
- to order the prosecutor to give a written statement of:
  a) the principal facts of the prosecution case, and/or
  b) witnesses, and/or
  c) exhibits, and/or
  d) a proposition of law on which the prosecutor will rely, and/or
  e) the consequences of the above.
- to order, *but only following any order to the prosecution to give a statement,* the defence to give the prosecution and the court a statement of:
  - its defence in general terms and the principal matters in dispute with the prosecution, and/or
  - written notice of objections to the prosecution case statement, and/or
  - written notice of points of law it might raise, and/or
  - written notice of points of admissibility of evidence.
- to order the prosecution to prepare the case in a form that the jury will understand.
- to order the prosecution to give a list of documents or matters with which it agrees.
- to order the prosecution to change its case if there are valid objections raised after the written statement ordered above.

➤ The judge must warn the accused of the consequences of later departing from the case outlined in the defence statement above (s 31(8)).
- The consequences are that at trial a jury may draw 'adverse inferences' following:
  - the judge's comment on this, and/or
  - other parties' comments on this (with leave).
  - NB: The judge must point out that the jury must have regard to the extent of departure from the case and any justifications for such departure (s 34).

Reporting restrictions (CPIA 1996 ss 37-38)

➤ There is no reporting allowed of the preparatory hearing (or an appeal from it) until after trial unless a judge authorises it. The following details are allowed to be reported however:
- the identity of the court and the name of the judge.
- the details of the accused and witnesses.
- the details of the offence(s).
- the name of counsel and solicitors.
- the details of any adjournment.
- the details of any bail arrangements.
- the details of whether LSC funded help was granted or not.

K Sentencing powers

NB: All sentences are subject to the statutory limits laid down for particular offences.

I	The purpose of sentencing	VI	Community sentences
II	General rules about increasing and decreasing custodial sentences	VII	Discharges
		VIII	General disqualification from driving
		IX	Motoring penalties
III	Custodial sentences	X	Ancillary orders
IV	Suspended sentences	XI	Summary of some youth sentences
V	Fines		

I The purpose of sentencing

➤ The purposes of adult sentencing are set out in statute by *CJA 2003 s 142*:

- punishment, *and*
- crime reduction, *and*
- the reform and rehabilitation, *and*
- public protection, *and*
- reparation.

Exceptions:
- where an offender is under 18 (there are separate purposes for the aims of the youth justice system set out in *CDA 1998*)
- where the sentence is fixed by law (eg: a mandatory life sentence imposed for murder)
- where offences require certain custodial sentences

NB: A surcharge is payable by an offender on conviction which contributes to the Victims Fund [not yet in force] (DVCAVA 2004 s 14 inserting CJA 2003 ss161A-161B)

II General rules about increasing and decreasing custodial sentences

➤ **Culpability and harm:** In considering the seriousness of any offence, the court must consider the offender's culpability in committing the offence and any harm which the offence caused, was intended to cause or might forseeably have caused (*CJA 2003 s 143(1)*).

➤ **Previous convictions:** In considering the seriousness of any offence, the court must treat each previous conviction as an aggravating factor having regard, in particular, to the nature of the offence to which the conviction relates and its relevance to the current offence, and the time that has elapsed since the conviction (*CJA 2003 s 143(2)*).

➤ **Offence while on bail:** In considering the seriousness of any offence committed while the offender was on bail, the court must treat the fact that it was committed in those circumstances as an aggravating factor (*CJA 2003 s 143(3)*).

➤ **Reduction in sentence for early guilty plea:** A court can reduce a sentence for an early guilty plea, to encourage defendants who are guilty to save court time and save victims and witnesses unnecessary trouble. The court must take into account when the guilty plea was made and the circumstances in which it was given (*CJA 2003 s 144*).

➤ **Racial or religious element:** A racial or religious element is treated as an aggravating factor which increases the seriousness (*CJA 2003 s 145*).

➤ **Disability or sexual orientation element:** A disability or sexual orientation element to any crime is treated as an aggravating factor which increases the seriousness (*CJA 2003 s 146*).

CRIMINAL LITIGATION
Sentencing powers

III Custodial sentences

A First custodial sentence

➤ The offender cannot be given a custodial sentence for the first time if he is not legally represented during the sentencing process *unless (PCC(S)A 2000 s 83)*:

- he was granted a right to representation funded by the LSC as part of the Criminal Defence Service but the right was withdrawn because of his conduct, *or*

- the offender has not applied for such representation despite previous opportunity to do so.

B Rules for prison sentences of less than 12 months ('Custody plus')
(CJA 2003 ss 181-182 [not yet in force])

➤ *See p 484 for details.*

C Intermittent custody (on pilot only)
(CJA 2003 ss 183-186)

➤ If a sentence of imprisonment of of 14 to 26 weeks has been imposed and the court deems it appropriate, if the offender consents, the custodial part of the sentence can be served intermittently by an 'intermittent custody order'.

➤ The custodial periods are served in short blocks of a few days at a time, while the licence period runs between the blocks (and may continue after the last custodial period).

- Only an unpaid work requirement, an activity requirement, a programme requirement and a prohibited activity requirement may be imposed.

➤ If an offender fails to comply with the terms of the community part of the sentence he is returned to custody and the Parole Board will decide when he is to be re-released.

D Racially or religiously aggravated offences
(CDA 1998 ss 28-32)

➤ *CDA 1998 ss 28-32* adds a set of racially or religiously aggravated crimes where the maximum penalty is greater where the 'racial' or 'religious' factor is proved. Where it *is* proved, the maximum penalty goes up.

- Eg: Where it is proved, the maximum custodial penalty (we deal here with indictment convictions only):

  - for grievous or actual bodily harm (*OAP 1861 s 20 and s 47*) goes from 5 to 7 years.

  - for common assault goes from 6 months to 2 years.

  - for criminal damage (*CrDA 1971 s 1(1)*) goes from 10 years to 14 years

  - for certain public order offences (eg: *POA 1986 s 4*) goes from 6 months to 2 years.

  - for certain sections of the *PHA 1997* goes up.

  NB: (*CJA 2003 s 145*)(see p 478) does not apply to these crimes.

E Discretionary custodial sentences

➤ A custodial sentence must be imposed if ...

a) ... the 'seriousness test' is satisfied, or ...

- Test: the court is of the opinion that the offence, or the combination of the offence and one or more offences associated with it, was so serious that neither a fine alone nor a community sentence can be justified for the offence (*CJA 2003 s 152(2)*).
  - Factors that can affect seriousness are:
    - information about the circumstances of the offence (*CJA 2003 s 156(1)*).
    - other factors listed on p 478.

b) ... the 'violent' or 'sexual' offence (defined in CJA 2003 Schedule 5) harm test is satisfied

- Test: a specified 'violent' or 'sexual' offence carrying 2 to 10 years and the court is of the opinion that there is a significant risk to members of the public of serious harm occasioned by the commission by him of further specified offences (*CJA 2003 s 227*).
  - Factors relevant for this are:
    - information about the circumstances of the offence, including any aggravating or mitigating factors (*CJA 2003 s 156(1)*).
    - other factors listed on p 478.
    - nature of offence, information about the offender, pattern of behaviour (*CJA 2003 s 229*).

➤ The length of a discretionary custodial sentence is dependent on 2 tests:

'seriousness test' term of imprisonment	'violent or sexual offence harm test' term of imprisonment	
◆ the shortest term (not exceeding the permitted maximum) that in the opinion of the court is commensurate with the seriousness of the offence, or the combination of the offence and one or more offences associated with it (*CJA 2003 s 153*)	◆ The greater of (*CJA 2003 s 227*): • the sentence here, or • 12 months	◆ an 'extension period' which must be added on for which the offender is subject to a licence and which is of such length as the court considers necessary for the purpose of protecting members of the public from serious harm.
	➤ The extension period must not exceed: ◆ 5 years in the case of a specified violent offence, *and* ◆ 8 years in the case of a specified sexual offence. ➤ Also, the term of the whole sentence taken together must not exceed the maximum term permitted for the offence.	

➤ The limits on length of discretionary custodial sentence are as follows:

- **Magistrates' Court:** maximum 6 months for any one offence unless an offence presents a lower maximum penalty (*PCC(S)A 2000 s 78*). *[To be replaced by: "maximum 12 months for any one offence unless an offence presents a lower maximum penalty (CJA 2003 s 154) [not yet in force].]*
  - The minimum is 5 days (*MCA 1980 s 132*).
  - There is a maximum of 6 months *[changed to 65 weeks by CJA 2003 s 155 [not yet in force]]* for 2 offences triable either way (*MCA 1980 s 133(2)*).
- **Crown Court:** up to the maximum set by statute for the offence. If none is set then 2 years on indictment (*PCC(S)A 2000 s 77*) *[to be repealed and replaced]*.

Time spent on remand (applicable to all sentences of custody)
➤ Time served on remand in custody is counted as time served as part of sentence unless remand was concurrent with an existing term of imprisonment or it is just in all the circumstances not to give effect to this (*CJA 2003 s 240*).

F Other mandatory rules on sentences

1 **Dangerous offenders** (*CJA 2003 s 225*)

- ➤ If ...
    - ◆ the offender is convicted of a specified sexual or violent offence (listed in *CJA 2003 Schedule 15*) carrying a maximum sentence of 10 years or more, *and*
    - ◆ the court considers that the offender poses a significant risk of serious harm,

    ... then a court may pass a sentence of imprisonment for public protection.

- ➤ Where the offence carries a maximum sentence of life imprisonment, the court must pass a discretionary life sentence if the seriousness of the offence justifies it.

- ➤ In all other cases the court must impose a sentence of imprisonment for public protection.

- ➤ When passing sentence the court must set the relevant part of the sentence that will be served in custody for the purposes of punishment and deterrence.
    - ◆ After the offender has served this relevant part then their release will be dependent upon the recommendation of the Parole Board.

- ➤ This sentence therefore provides for the indeterminate detention of those dangerous offenders who continue to pose a significant risk of harm to the public.
    - ◆ Release provisions are set out in more detail in *CJA 2003 s 230* and *Schedule 18*.

2 *Prison sentences of less than 12 months* (*CJA 2003 s 181*) *[not yet in force]*

- ➤ *In general, all prison sentences of less than 12 months must consist of a short period of custody followed by a longer period on licence, during which the offender has to comply with requirements fixed by the courts as part of his sentence.*

- ➤ *The term of the sentence must be expressed in weeks, must be at least 28 weeks, must not be more than 51 weeks in respect of any one offence, and must not exceed the maximum term permitted for the offence.*

- ➤ *A court may specify the number of days which an offender must serve in prison and the number of days on which he is released on licence (subject to specified licence conditions called a 'custody plus order').*
    - ◆ *The licence conditions are the same as the Community Order requirements (see p 489) but the requirements marked with a * cannot be imposed as licence conditions.*

- ➤ *The court must specify both the 'custodial period' and the 'licence period'. During the licence period the offender is to be subject to conditions specified in the 'custody plus order'.*
    - ◆ *The custodial period must be between 2 and 13 weeks.*
    - ◆ *The licence period must be at least 26 weeks.*

- ➤ *Where a court imposes two or more terms of imprisonment in accordance to be served consecutively:*
    - ◆ *the aggregate length of the terms of imprisonment must not be more than 65 weeks, and*
    - ◆ *the aggregate length of the custodial periods must not be more than 26 weeks.*

3 **Minimum 3 years for burglary** (*PCC(S)A 2000 s 111*)

- ➤ A convicted burglar must be sentenced to minimum 3 years for a third domestic burglary, unless particular circumstances relate to the offence/offender and would make it unjust in all the circumstances.

IV   Suspended sentences (CJA 2003 ss 189-194)

A   Imposition of a suspended sentence
(CJA 2003 s 189)

➤ A court which passes a sentence of imprisonment (or, for someone aged 18 to under 21, detention in a young offender institution) for at least 14 days but not more than 12 months (or in a Magistrates' Court, for at least 14 days but not more than 6 months) may suspend that sentence for between 6 months and 2 years while ordering the offender to undertake certain requirements in the community.

- ◆ The period during which the offender undertakes requirements is called 'the supervision period' and the entire length of suspension is called 'the operational period'.

➤ The custodial part of the sentence will not take effect unless the offender fails to comply with the imposed requirements or if he commits another offence within the period of suspension.

➤ The length of time the offender undertakes requirements may be less (but not more) than the entire period of suspension, but the supervision period and the operational period must each last 6 months to 2 years.

➤ The supervision period must not exceed the operational period.

➤ A suspended sentence may be combined with a fine/compensation order, but not a community sentence.

B   Imposition of requirements
(CJA 2003 s 190)

➤ The requirements that can be attached are the same as in the 'Requirements' box on p 489.

- ◆ Where the court imposes a curfew requirement or an exclusion requirement, it must also impose an electronic monitoring requirement unless electronic monitoring is not available in the local area or someone else whose consent is required (eg: a landlord) withholds that consent.

C   Review of a suspended sentence order
(CJA 2003 ss 191-192)

➤ The courts have a discretion to provide that a suspended sentence order be subject to periodic review at a review hearing. A review hearing is conducted by the court responsible for the order.

D   Breach and revocation of a suspended sentence order
(CJA 2003 s 193 and Schedule 12)

➤ If the responsible officer thinks that the offender has failed without reasonable excuse to comply with any of the community requirements of a suspended sentence order, the officer must give him a warning.

➤ If the offender fails again to comply without reasonable excuse within 12 months of the warning, the responsible officer must cause an information to be laid and the court may issue a summons, or if the information is in writing and on oath, issue a warrant for his arrest.

➤ If it is proved that the offender has breached the order (of if an offender is convicted of an offence committed during the operational period of a suspended sentence (other than one which has already taken effect)) then the court must consider his case and the court may:

- ◆ order that the suspended sentence takes effect with its original term, *or*
- ◆ order that the sentence is to take effect with a lesser term, *or*
- ◆ amend the order by imposing more onerous community requirements, extending the supervision period or extending the operational period.

Suspended sentencing powers (CJA 2003 Schedule 12)

Magistrates' Court	Crown Court
➤ Can issue a summons for an offender to appear before a court (or a warrant for his arrest) if the offender has failed to comply with any community requirements of the order in cases where the suspended sentence order was made by a magistrates' court (or which was made by the Crown Court and includes a direction that any failure to comply with the community requirements of the order is to be dealt with by a magistrates court). ◆ The summons will specify the court reviewing the order if the order contains provision for review. ➤ If the offender does not appear in response to a summons the court can issue a warrant for his arrest. ➤ If an offender breaches a suspended sentence by failing to comply with a community requirement (or by committing a further offence) there is a presumption that the suspended sentence will be activated, unless the court finds that it would be unjust to do so. ➤ If it activates the suspended sentence, the court can set a shorter term or custodial period for the offender to serve if it wishes. ◆ If the court finds that it would be unjust to activate the suspended sentence it can keep the sentence suspended but amend the order to make the community requirements more onerous or to extend either the supervision or operational periods. ◆ The court must state the reasons for choosing this option. ◆ It must also take into account the extent to which the offender complied with the requirements of the order and the facts of the subsequent offence. ➤ A magistrates' court can commit the offender to the Crown Court (including orders which were made by the Crown Court and include a direction that any failure to comply with community requirements is to be dealt with by a magistrates' court.) ◆ If the proceedings occur in the Crown Court the determination of breach is to be made by the court and not a jury.	➤ The Crown Court can issue a summons or warrant for the offender to appear before it where: ◆ the order was made by the Crown Court, and ◆ does not include a direction that any failure to comply with the community requirements of the order is to be dealt with by a magistrates' court. ➤ If the offender does not appear in response to a summons, a warrant for his arrest can be issued.

➤ When the suspended sentence is activated, the court must make a custody plus order (ie: it has to set the licence conditions that will apply on the offender's release from custody at the end of custodial period of his sentence). The court may decide whether the new sentence is to take effect immediately or after any other sentence that the offender is serving (subject to the rules affecting consecutive sentences).

V   Fines and other sums imposed on conviction (CJA 2003 ss 162-165)

➤ **Crown Court:** Where a person is convicted on indictment of any offence (except an offence where the sentence is fixed by law) the court can generally impose a fine instead of or in addition to any other sentence (subject to any enactment to the contrary) (*CJA 2003 163*).

➤ Before fixing a sum the court must:

- inquire into the offender's financial circumstances (*CJA 2003 s 164(1)*), and
- ensure the penalty reflects the seriousness of the offence (*CJA 2003 s 164(2)*), and
- consider the case circumstances, including the state of an offender's finances insofar as they are known, or appear to the court (*CJA 2003 s 164(3)*).

➤ If the offender is under 18, the parents must pay the fine (*PCC(S)A 2000 s 137*).

Methods used by the Magistrates' Courts to enforce payment of fines (or other sums)

➤ The Magistrates' Court may use the following methods to enforce immediate payment of the sum. The Court:

a) may order the offender to be searched for money to meet the fine (*MCA 1980 s 80(1)*),

b) if the offence is imprisonable, may order detention at a police station until 8am next day (*MCA 1980 s 136*),

c) on conviction (or after), may make a money payment supervision order specifying terms of payment and placing the offender in someone's care (usually an officer of a local probation board) who should advise and befriend the offender with a view to inducing him to pay and avoid imprisonment. No offender's consent is needed (*MCA 1980 s 88*),

d) may issue a warrant of distress to seize and sell the offender's goods to meet the sum (*MCA 1980 s 76*),

e) may order the offender's immediate imprisonment.

➤ If the offender fails to pay any sum imposed on conviction (eg: fines, costs or sums to be paid under compensation or confiscation orders) within the time allowed, the Magistrates' Court may issue a summons or warrant requiring the offender to appear or issue a warrant to arrest him and bring him before the court to conduct a means inquiry (*MCA 1980 s 83*). The Magistrates' Court may enforce payment by several methods (not detailed here).

- By *CA 2003 s 97* and *Schedule 5*, the court may:
    i) make an attachment of earning order,
    ii) make an order for deductions of benefits,
    iii) make collection orders to be enforced by fines officers (*see also FCR 2006*),
    iv) order vehicles to be clamped and sold to pay fines (*see also FCR 2006*).

- *In default of paying a fine, when CJA 2003 ss 300-301 come into force, magistrates will have the power to impose unpaid work or curfew requirements and can also disqualify for driving for up to 12 months [not yet in force].*

VI Community sentences (CJA 2003 ss 147-151, 177-180)

Note: a community sentence may not be imposed if a sentence is fixed by law (CJA 2003 s 150).

A Definition

➤ A community sentence means a sentence which consists of or includes (CJA 2003 s 147):

- a community order (see next page), or
- one or more youth community orders, ie:
  - a curfew order (PCC(S) 2000 s 163),
  - an exclusion order (ie: an order mandating that the subject of the order must stay out of a particular area) (PCC(S) 2000 s 40A),
  - an attendance centre order (PCC(S) 2000 s 163),
  - a supervision order (PCC(S) 2000 s 63(1)),
  - an action plan order (PCC(S) 2000 s 69(1)).

B Imposition of a community sentence

➤ For a community sentence to be passed:

- an offence should be serious enough to warrant one (CJA 2003 s 148(1)), or
  - Requirements forming part of the community sentence must be the most suitable ones for the offender and the restrictions on the liberty of the offender (eg: a curfew requirement) must be in line with the seriousness of the offence (CJA 2003 s 148(2)).
- *the offence itself does not warrant a community sentence but the offender has committed 3 or more offences, for each of which, he has received a fine in the past (CJA 2003 s 151 [not yet in force]).*

➤ If an offence is not serious enough for a community sentence, a fine, conditional discharge or absolute discharge would be appropriate.

➤ For certain orders a pre-sentence report is needed (CJA 2003 s 156).

C Breach and revocation of a community sentence
(CJA 2003 s 179 and Schedule 8)

➤ Non-compliance penalties (following a warning) are:

- imposition of more onerous requirements, or
- dealing with the offender for the original offence as if the community order had not been made, or
- if non-compliance is wilful and persistent, custody.

➤ If the defendant re-offends, re-sentencing is possible.

➤ Magistrates can revoke an order which they imposed.

➤ The Crown Court alone may revoke the order if it imposed the original sentence.

D Community Orders

➤ The following community orders (known as 'requirements') may be imposed (*CJA 2003 s 177(1)*).

- Certain requirements are subject to restrictions (*CJA 2003 s 177(2)*).

- If the court makes a community order that includes a curfew or exclusion requirement, it must also impose an electronic monitoring requirement unless electronic monitoring is not available in the local area or if someone whose consent is required (eg: a landlord) withholds it (*CJA 2003 s 177(3)*).

➤ The court must consider compatibility of the various requirements it proposes (*CJA 2003 s 177(6)*).

➤ The court should try to avoid any order which clashes with an offender's religious beliefs or with times of education and employment (*CJA 2003 s 217*).

Requirements (*CJA 2003 ss 147-151, 177-180, 199-223*)

➤ The court may impose on the offender one or more of the following requirements:

- **Unpaid work requirement:** unpaid work, eg: clearing canals, removing graffiti etc. (For between 40 and 300 hours.) (*CJA 2003 ss 199-200*).

- **Activity requirement:** certain defined activity at a defined place, time, for a certain number of days, eg: receiving help with employment or group work on social problems, etc. (For maximum 60 days.) (*CJA 2003 s 201*).

- **Programme requirement:** the offender must take part in an accredited programme on a certain number of days, eg: anger management course, sex offending court, substance misuse course, etc (*CJA 2003 s 202*).

- **Prohibited activity requirement:** the offender must not take part in a certain activity, eg: not contacting a certain person (*CJA 2003 s 203*).

- **Curfew requirement:** the offender must remain at a specified place for certain periods of time (From between 2 to 12 hours in any given day.) (*CJA 2003 s 204*).

- **Exclusion requirement:** the offender must not enter a certain place or area during a period specified (Order can last maximum 2 years.) (*CJA 2003 s 205*).

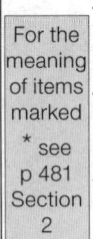

For the meaning of items marked * see p 481 Section 2

- ***Residence requirement:** the offender must stay at a specified place for a specified period (*CJA 2003 s 206*).

- ***Mental health treatment requirement:** As part of a community sentence or suspended sentence, the offender undergo mental health treatment for a certain period (*CJA 2003 ss 207-208*).

- ***Drug rehabilitation requirement:** As part of a community sentence or suspended sentence, the offender must undergo drug rehabilitation and testing (*CJA 2003 ss 209-210*).

- ***Alcohol treatment requirement:** As part of a community sentence or suspended sentence, the offender must undergo alcohol treatment (*CJA 2003 s 211*).

- **Supervision requirement:** The offender must attend appointments to promote his rehabilitation (*CJA 2003 s 213*).

- **Attendance centre requirement:** For offenders under 25 only, the offender must attend an attendance centre for a specified number of hours (Maximum once a day for a maximum of 3 hours on each occasion and for an aggregate maximum of 12 to 36 hours.) (*CJA 2003 s 214*).

- **Electronic monitoring requirement:** The offender must be electronically tagged (*CJA 2003 s 215*).

➤ The offender must be 16 or over for any of these (*CJA 2003 s 177(1)*) (although for anyone aged 16 or 17 convicted of an offence, this does not come into force until 4 April 2007) (*CJA(CN8)O 2005*).

VII Discharges (PCC(S)A 2000 ss 12-15)

➤ A court can issue a discharge if in the circumstances (the nature of the offence, the defendant's character), punishment is inexpedient.

- **An absolute discharge:** if the offender is morally blameless, but technically guilty.

- **A conditional discharge:** if the offender has a previously clean record, the offence is trivial, and the publicity and court appearance are sufficient ordeal.
  - A conditional discharge is for up to 3 years only.
  - If the offender commits an offence during this time, he may be re-sentenced for the original offence.

A summary of non-community sentence sentencing provisions (prior to CJA 2003)		
Penalty	Imposition	Effect
Custody	➤ Seriousness test ➤ Protect the public from violent/sexual offences	➤ Prison if aged over 21 ➤ If aged under 21, there are other options (see p 490)
Suspended sentence	➤ *Not* for those aged under 21 ➤ When the court has decided to imprison but there are 'exceptional' circumstances	➤ Court has discretion whether to activate the sentence
Fine	➤ Seriousness of the offence ➤ Circumstances of the case	➤ Consider the offender's financial circumstances when deciding to increase or decrease the fine

VIII General disqualification from driving

➤ If a person is convicted of any offence (except those mentioned in the point below), then the Crown Court or a Magistrates' Court may, in addition to, or instead of, dealing with him in any other way, order him to be disqualified from holding or obtaining a driving licence for such period as it thinks fit (*PCC(S)A 2000 s 146(1)*).

➤ The power to disqualify 'instead of' under *s 146(1)* does not apply to cases where a person is convicted of murder or where the sentence is imposed under (*PCC(S)A 2000 Chapter III*) (automatic life sentence for second serious offence) but the power to disqualify 'in addition to' still applies (*PCC(S)A 2000 s 146(2)*).

➤ The power is also subject to *PCC(S)A 2000 s 146(3)* ie: that disqualification under *s 146* may not be imposed unless the court has been told by the Minister that the power to make such an order is exercisable by that court.

IX Motoring penalties

1 Endorsement

➤ This is mandatory for i) dangerous driving, ii) aggravated vehicle taking, iii) careless driving.

➤ Conviction for 2 (or more) offences on the same occasion leads to an endorsement for the offence with the 'higher' number of points allowed. However, the court may wish to exercise its discretion and award more than just the points for the 'higher' offence (*RTOA 1988 s 28(4)-28(6)*).

➤ When a court makes an order for obligatory disqualification for 1 offence, it may not at the same time endorse penalty points for another offence committed on the same occasion (*Martin v DPP* (2000) 164 JP 405).

2   **Disqualification**

   a) **Obligatory** (for at least 1 year): for i) dangerous driving, ii) aggravated vehicle taking.

   b) **Discretionary** (for a period): i) careless driving, ii) taking a conveyance, iii) theft of a motor vehicle.

   c) **Under the penalty points system** (*RTOA 1988 s 35*)

   ➤ If the offender has no previous disqualification of at least 56 days (imposed within 3 years of the commission of the offence now being sentenced), the minimum period of disqualification is 6 months.

   ◆ If there is one previous disqualification, disqualification is for 1 year.

   ◆ If there are 2 or more previous disqualifications, disqualification is for a minimum of 2 years.

   ➤ Penalty points are dealt with first.

   ◆ If there are 12 or more penalty points from:

   • the current conviction (ignoring any order for disqualification for committing the offence) *plus*

   • points previously endorsed for offences within 3 years immediately before the commission of the present offence,

   THEN disqualification is obligatory.

   ➤ Points prior to a previous disqualification are ignored.

   ➤ The court will go on to consider discretionary disqualification if the driver is not automatically disqualified by having 12 points or more.

3   **Avoiding disqualification and endorsement**

   a) **Avoiding obligatory disqualification or obligatory endorsement**

   ➤ A 'special reason' is present.

   ➤ This is a mitigating circumstance (eg: a boomerang thrown across the windscreen).

   ➤ 'Special reasons' are connected with the commission of the offence, but are *not* personal to the offender (*Whittal v Kirby* [1947] KB 194).

   ➤ A 'special reason' is not anything which could constitute a defence to the charge in law.

   b) **Avoiding discretionary disqualification**

   ➤ *Any* mitigating factor relevant to the offence should be used to avoid discretionary disqualification.

   ➤ The factor may be *either* connected with the circumstances *or* personal to the offender. (For example, an obligatory situation or loss of job is relevant here.)

   c) **Avoiding disqualification under the points system**

   ➤ Disqualification is mandatory unless there are mitigating circumstances.

   ➤ All circumstances are relevant except ((*RTOA 1988 s 35(4)*):

   i) the triviality of the offence.

   ii) hardship (unless exceptional).

   iii) circumstances taken into account to avoid or reduce disqualification under the points system during the last 3 years.

   Note: i) a driver can have 7-12 points and escape disqualification.

   ii) disqualification wipes a licence clean of all the old points.

   iii) if 2 offences are committed simultaneously, both of which carry a point penalty, the court only adds the 'higher' of the penalties to the licence, unless it sees fit to order otherwise.

X Ancillary orders

1 Compensation order (*PCC(S)A 2000 ss 130-134*)

➤ The order is for the offender to pay compensation to a victim.

➤ Generally this order is *not* available for motoring offences (the victim can claim from the offender's insurers) (*PCC(S)A 2000 s 130(6)*).

➤ Magistrates' limit: £5,000 (*PCC(S)A 2000 s 131*); Crown Court: unlimited.

➤ The court has the power to make an attachment of earnings order to ensure that the compensation is paid (*CPIA 1996 s 53*). NB: Consent of the offender is required.

2 Forfeiture order (*PCC(S)A 2000 s 143*)

➤ Property in the offender's possession, or control, is forfeit by this order if the property is used for committing or facilitating the offence, *or* intended for use in connection with the offence, *or* held unlawfully.

3 Confiscation orders (seizure of proceeds of crime) (*PCA 2002 ss 6-91*)

➤ An order confiscates the proceeds of crime (*s 6*).

➤ Interest is payable on unpaid orders (*s 12*), with custody in default (*s 38*).

➤ May be made only in the Crown Court after a conviction in the Crown Court or the magistrates' court.
   ◆ Where the conviction takes place in the magistrates' court, a confiscation order can only be made if the defendant is either committed to the Crown Court for sentence or committed to the Crown Court for sentence and confiscation under *s 70*).

➤ An offender who gives reasonable grounds to believe that he is living off crime must account for his assets and will have them confiscated to the extent that he is unable to account for their lawful origin.

4 Restitution order (*PCC(S)A 2000 ss 148-149*)

➤ The order is to compensate, or restore to a victim, goods stolen from him.

5 Costs order (*POA 1985 s 18*)

➤ On conviction, 'just and reasonable' costs may be awarded to the prosecution (payable by the offender).

➤ On acquittal, if the defendant is not LSC funded, the court can order his costs to be paid from central funds. This is usual unless, eg: the acquittal was on a technicality *or* the defendant brought suspicion on himself by his conduct (*POA 1985 s 16*).

➤ On acquittal, contributions paid by a legally aided defendant may be repaid (subject to the above).

6 Deferment of sentence (*PCC(S)A 2000 s 1*)

➤ Passing a sentence may be deferred for up to 6 months.

➤ The offender must consent.

➤ The offender must comply with requirements set by the court (eg: see box on p 486) (*CJA 2003 s 278*).

➤ If the offender is convicted during the interval of another offence, he can be sentenced for both offences. The court will have the same powers as on conviction for the original offence.

➤ The power to defer a sentence is used to assess:
   ◆ the offender's conduct after conviction, *or*
   ◆ any change in the offender's circumstances (marriage, etc).

➤ The court specifies the conduct it expects, and the sentence it will impose if this is not complied with.

CRIMINAL LITIGATION
Sentencing powers

7 Committal to the Crown Court for sentence (PCC(S)A 2000 s 3)

▶ The offender must be aged over 18.

▶ The conviction must be for an either way offence *and* when:
  a) the offence (or a combination of associated offences) is so serious that a punishment greater than that which a Magistrates' Court is authorised to impose, is warranted, *or*
  b) the offence is a violent or sexual offence, and a custodial sentence is necessary to protect the public from serious harm, *or*
  c) the offender unexpectedly asks for previous offences to be taken into consideration (rare and usually the result of evidence, unknown at the mode of trial hearing, appearing during the trial.

> After CJA 2003 s 41 and Sch 3, paras 21-28 are brought into force, this power will no longer be available in cases where the Magistrates' Court has dealt with the case having accepted jurisdiction (whether as a contested case or a guilty plea) but will be limited to cases where a guilty plea has been indicated at plea before venue.

XI Summary of some youth sentences

Some youth sentences

No sentence of imprisonment may be passed on an offender under 21 (PCC(S)A 2000 s 89).

Age / Sentence	Under 21	20-19	18	17	16	15	14	13	12	Under 12
community sentence	━━━━━━━━━━━━━━━━━━━━━━━━━━━━━━ see p 485 ━━━━━━━━━━━									
detention and training order				━━━━━━━━━━━━━━━━━━━			only if a persistent offender			only if to protect the public from harm
	half the sentence is a period of training in detention; half is supervision in the community. imposed where a court could impose imprisonment if the offender was over 21. Orders may be for: 4, 6, 8, 10, 12, 18 or 24 months. (PCC(S)A 2000 s 100)									
supervision order				places the juvenile under the supervision of a local authority/ social worker / officer of a local probation board. Maximum 3 years. (PCC(S)A 2000 s 63)						
action plan order				this requires compliance with an action plan to address offending behaviour. It is imposed if it is desirable either to secure the offender's rehabilitation or to prevent the offender committing further offences. Maximum 3 months. (PCC(S)A 2000 s 69)						
reparation order				imposed to allow the offender to make reparation for the offence otherwise than by payment of compensation. Maximum work is 24 hours in aggregate. The consent of the offender is needed (PCC(S)A 2000 s 73).						
detention in a young offender institution		if convicted of an offence punishable by imprisonment if he was over 21. Minimum term: 21 days. Maximum term: the maximum term for the offence (PCC(S)A 2000 s 97).								
detention at Her Majesty's Pleasure				if convicted of murder and was under 18 at the time the offence was committed (PCC(S)A 2000 s 90).						
detention under (PCC(S)A 2000 s 91)				a) If the offence is punishable with minimum 14 years imprisonment *or* b) indecent assault on a woman or man *or*				As age 14-18 and also: c) death by dangerous driving, *or* d) death by careless driving while affected by alcohol		

Note: detention in a young offender's institution is due to be abolished when CJCSA 2000 s 61 is brought into force [not yet in force]

490

L Sentencing procedure and mitigation

> I   Sentencing Advisory Panel
> II Preparing a plea in mitigation
> III Newton hearing
> IV Pre-sentence report and drug test
> V   Court proceedings

I   Sentencing Advisory Panel

➤ The Sentencing Guidelines Council establishes sentencing guidelines (*CJA 2003 ss 167-173*).

- Every court must have regard to the sentencing guidelines in deciding on sentence.

- The Sentencing Guidelines Council also establishes guidelines for the allocation procedure (where magistrates decide whether an offence is more suitable for summary trial or trial on indictment).

II Preparing a plea in mitigation

Preparing a plea in mitigation

➤ The defence should present a plea in mitigation to reduce the severity of sentence and/or to persuade that a particular punishment is unsuitable and that another is more appropriate.

Steps

1 Make a realistic assessment of the likely sentence and consult the Sentencing Guidelines.

2 For likely custodial sentences:
- Consider whether the case is so serious that only a custodial sentence will suffice.
- Consider any relevant factors such as:
    - any early admissions, particularly with evidence of real remorse,
    - any practical steps taken to address addiction,
    - any youth and immaturity,
    - any good character, especially positive good character,
    - any family responsibilities and/or physical and mental disability,
    - whether it is a first custodial sentence.

Judges can give a defendant an advance indication of the likely sentence on a guilty plea (R v Goodyear [2005] EWCA Crim 888)

3 For **all types of sentence:** consider any relevant factors (*CJA 2003 s 166*) such as:

- the offender's age and history: youth or old-age may induce sympathy.
- the circumstances of the offence: provocation, stress, drug dependency.
    - Note: voluntary ingestion is *not* good mitigation.
- the effect of any increases in 'seriousness' or aggravating factors (see p 478 and p 480).
- subsequent behaviour:
    - remorse
    - guilty plea and the time and circumstances of this plea (*CJA 2003 s 144*).
        - There may be a discount on *custodial* sentences of up to a third (see the Sentencing Guidelines).
        - If the defendant has no choice but to plead guilty, there is still a discount given (*R v Forbes* [2005] EWCA Crim 2069).
    - **assisting police** - eg: naming others, revealing stolen property, confessing, saving police time.
    - **reparation** - voluntary rectification of damage and motive are important.

    Note: Character witnesses and letters of reference are admissible in a plea for mitigation.

III Newton hearing

▶ A Newton hearing is held after a guilty plea (*R v Newton* (1983) 77 Cr App R 13).

▶ Evidence is heard to ascertain the facts relevant to sentencing either because the prosecution and defence accounts of the facts differ greatly, *or* to resolve the respective liability of 2 or more defendants.

IV Pre-sentence report and drug test

▶ This is compiled by an officer of a local probation board or social worker.

▶ It *must* be ordered (if the offender is aged over 18) before (*CJA 2003 s 156(3)-(4)*):
- imposing a custodial sentence *unless* the court feels it is unnecessary, *or*
- making a community sentence unless the court considers it unnecessary.

NB: There are slightly altered rules for offenders aged under 18 (*CJA 2003 s 156(5)*).

▶ It *may* be ordered before imposing any other sentence, usually when it is anticipated that the accused will plead guilty and he is aged 30 or less.

▶ For offenders over 18, if the court is considering passing a community sentence, it may order a pre-sentence drug test to test for Class A drugs (*PCC(S)A 2000 s 36A*). *To be replaced by: "For offenders over 14, if the court is considering passing a community sentence or a suspended sentence, it may order a pre-sentence drug test to test for Class A drugs (CJA 2003 s 161) [not yet in force]."*

V Court proceedings

▶ For an offence triable 'either way', if proceedings have been in the Magistrates' Court until now, the court decides if it is appropriate to commit for sentence to the Crown Court (see p 490) (*PCC(S)A 2000 s 3*).

(Note: See box comment on p 490 regarding repeal of *PCC(S)A 2000 s 3*.)

- This also applies if the defendant pleaded guilty before the mode of trial procedure (*PCC(S)A 2000 s 4*).

Steps

1 The prosecution summarises:
- the nature of the offence.
- the offender's background and previous convictions.
- any other offences of similar or less serious nature to be taken into consideration (admitted by the offender). The offender may not be subsequently charged with these. A compensation order can be made in respect of these offences.
  - The offender signs a 'taking into consideration' form.

2 The pre-sentence report is presented to the court

3 The defence gives a plea in mitigation
- On a driving offence when disqualification is an issue, 'special reasons' for avoiding disqualification are given by the defendant on oath.

4 The judge passes sentence, taking into account sentencing guidelines

5 The court must state in open court the reasons for its deciding on the sentence (*CJA 2003 ss 174, 270*).

> *After CJA 2003, Sch 3, paras 21-28 are brought into force, despite the box comment on p 490, if a defendant is charged with a number of related either-way offences and pleads guilty to one of them at plea before venue and is sent to the Crown Court to be tried for the rest, the existing power in PCC(S)A 2000 s 4 to send the offence to which he has pleaded guilty to the Crown Court for sentence is retained.*

M Appeals

1. **From Magistrates' Court to Crown Court** (*MCA 1980 ss 108-110 and CrPR*)

    ➤ The defence only can appeal against conviction or sentence.

    ➤ Conviction:
    - if the offender pleaded guilty, there is only a right to appeal against a conviction if the plea was equivocal (ie: a non-genuine plea of guilty) (*MCA 1980 s 108*).
    - the Crown Court can remit an equivocal plea to the Magistrates' Court with a direction to enter a plea of 'not guilty'.

    ➤ **Sentence:** may be heavier or lighter, provided the magistrates would be empowered to impose it.

    ➤ Procedure:

    Steps

    1. Send a notice of appeal to the magistrates' clerk and the prosecution within 21 days of sentence or conviction (*CrPR r 63*).
        - The Crown Court can grant leave to appeal after this.
    2. **The appeal is heard by a Crown Court judge or a recorder sitting with 2 to 4 magistrates.**
        - If the appeal is against conviction, there is a rehearing following exactly the same process as for a summary trial (*SCA 1981 s 79(3)*).
        - If the appeal is against sentencing, the prosecution merely outlines the case facts, and the defence makes a plea in mitigation.
    3. The court can confirm, reverse or vary the magistrates' decision. It can also remit the matter (with its opinion) to the Magistrates' Court, *or* it may make any order it thinks just, exercising any powers the magistrates might have used (eg: concerning costs and compensation) (*SCA 1981 s 48*).

2. **From Magistrates' Court to Divisional Court** (the QBD of the High Court) **by way of case stated:**

    ➤ Grounds: the magistrates' decision is wrong in law, or exceeds their authority (*MCA 1980 s 111*).

    ➤ There is a hearing of legal argument (no evidence is called).

    ➤ The High Court may reverse, affirm, or amend the decision. It can also remit the matter (with its opinion) to the Magistrates' Court or the Crown Court, or it may make any order it thinks fit, exercising any powers the magistrates might have used (eg: concerning costs and compensation) (*SCA 1981 s 28A*). The High Court may also send the case back for amendment.

3. **From Crown Court to the Court of Appeal**

    ➤ Against conviction or sentence (*CAA 1968 ss 1,2,9,11 and CAA 1995*).

    ➤ On a question of law or fact, leave is required.

    ➤ The prosecution cannot appeal against acquittal (except in limited circumstances if new and compelling evidence and in the interests of justice) or sentence.

    ➤ The Attorney General may, with leave of the Court of Appeal, refer lenient Crown Court sentences for certain types of case to the Court of Appeal for review. The Court of Appeal passes the appropriate sentence in accordance with the Crown Court's powers (*CJA 1988 ss 33-36*).

    ➤ If the defendant is acquitted in the Crown Court, the prosecution can appeal on a point of law. The defendant stays acquitted, but the Court of Appeal will nonetheless rule on the point of law.

A summary table of appeals to higher courts		
Who appeals	Reason for appeal	Court where the appeal is heard
Appeal from the Magistrates' Court (*MCA 1980 s 108*)		
Defence only	Conviction	Crown Court appeal hearing
	Excessive sentence	
Defence *or* Prosecution	Ultra vires	Queen's Bench Division of the High Court for judicial review
Prosecution only	Lenient sentence	No right of appeal
	Acquittal	
Appeal from the Crown Court (*CAA 1968, CAA 1995*)		
Defence only	Excessive sentence	Court of Appeal
	Conviction unsafe (ie: law or fact)	Court of Appeal, with leave (full court may instruct CCRC (below) to investigate (*CJA 2003 s 313*)
Defence *or* Prosecution	Ultra vires	No provision for judicial review in the High Court
Prosecution only	Lenient sentence	Attorney General can refer the case to the Court of Appeal (Note: in the Magistrates' Court there is no such right) (*CJA 1988 Part IV ss 35-36*)
	Acquittal	Court of Appeal Limited right of appeal for certain specified offences only under limited circumstances, if new and compelling evidence and it is in the interests of justice to allow the appeal. The DPP must consent to such an appeal
	Question of law following acquittal	Court of Appeal The defendant *stays* acquitted, but the court can rule on the point of law anyway

▶ It should also be noted that the Magistrates' Court has power to hear 'appeals' from itself under certain circumstances (*MCA 1980 s 142 (as amended by ss 26-28 CAA 1995)*). However, this topic is not dealt with in this chapter.

▶ The Criminal Cases Review Commission ('CCRC') has powers to refer certain types of cases to appeal (*CAA 1995, Part II*).

N Disclosure

References are to CPIA 1996.

➤ *CPIA 1996 ss 1-21* contains a procedure for advance disclosure of evidence by both sides.

- Common law rules applying to the prosecution are disapplied (see box below).

NB: The schematic diagram below is a generalisation, eg: it does not cover the complete procedure for complex fraud and certain cases involving children

| A case is going to summary trial *and* after a plea of not guilty (*s 1(1)*) | A case is going to the Crown Court *and* after sending for trial (provided necessary notices have been served on the accused (see p 467)) or after committal for trial (*s 1(2)*) |

↓

Initial duty of disclosure by prosecutor (*s 3*)

The prosecution must give the defence (as soon as reasonably practicable after the not guilty plea/committal):
a) all material (or copies), it has that might reasonably be considered capable of undermining the prosecution case or of assisting the case for the accused, *or*
b) a written statement saying it has no such material

Note: 'Material' means material that came into prosecution possession in connection with this case only

↓

| No defence statement is given ← | If the prosecutor has complied or purported to comply with the initial duty of disclosure, the defence *may* give a voluntary detailed defence statement to the court and to the prosecutor (*s 6*) | If the prosecutor has complied or purported to comply with primary disclosure, the defence *must* give a detailed defence statement to the court and to the prosecutor (*s 5*) *[and, if the court so order, to any other accused to whom the court so orders (ss 5A, 5B, 5D) [not yet in force]]* |

The prosecution has an ongoing duty to disclose any new material that comes to light if it meets the same tests as for the initial duty (*s 7A*)

↓

Within 14 days of service of the prosecution notice of initial disclosure (unless extended by the court) (*s 5C, CPIA(DDTL)R 1997* and *DPP v Wood* [2006] EWHC 32) ...

↓

| ... The defence statement
... The defence must give a statement to the court and to the prosecutor stating (*s 6A*):
- the nature of its defence and particular defences on which he intends to rely, *and*
- on which matters of fact and law the defence disagrees with the prosecution and why, *and*
- details of any alibi and details of witnesses who can back up the alibi | ... *A notification of intention to call defence witnesses and experts*
... The defence must give a statement to the court and to the prosecutor stating (*ss 6C-6D*):
- the name and full details of proposed defence witnesses (or details of how to find them)
- the name and address of a proposed expert
[this box not yet in force] |

↓

NOTE: If the accused has not given a compulsory defence statement (under *s 5*) (or any update to it (*s 6B*)) *[or a notice of the intention to call defence witnesses (under s 6C) [not yet in force]]* a comment can be made by the judge and adverse inferences drawn at trial (see next page). The defendant must be warned about this at any pre-trial hearing (*s 6E(2)*).

↓

The defence may apply for a court order if it thinks prosecution ongoing disclosure has not been complied with (*s 8*)

↓

Trial

Changes to common law rules? (*s 21*)

➤ **Summary trial:** for *s 1(1)* disclosure, all common law rules relating to disclosure after the accused has pleaded 'not guilty' are abolished.

➤ **Crown Court trial:** for *s 1(2)* disclosure, all common law rules relating to disclosure after the accused has been committed for trial are abolished.

➤ The common law rules of disclosure continue to apply in the period between accusation (charge or summons) and a plea of not guilty/committal: R v DPP ex parte Lee [1999] 2 All ER 737.

Problems with ...

... the defence statement, notice of witnesses and trial

| 1. If the defence statement (under *s 5* compulsory disclosure) (*s 11*):
 ◆ is not given (under *s 5* disclosure), *or* | OR | 2. If the defence statement (under *s 6* voluntary disclosure) (*s 11*): | OR | 3. If the defence gives a witness notice out of time ('²') or later calls a witness at trial (other than himself) not adequately identified in the witness notice ('²') [not yet in force] |

◆ is out of time (according to the periods laid down by rules made under *s 12*), *or*
◆ does not give an updated defence statement, if relevant, or gives it out of time, *or*
◆ contains inconsistent defences, *or*
◆ is different from a defence later put forward at trial, *or*
◆ relies on a matter in breach of something he was meant to put into the defence statement ('¹')
◆ does not contain alibi details and details of those who will support that alibi, but such evidence is later used at trial

At trial (*s 11*):
◆ the court can comment on this
◆ any other party can comment on this (without leave. However, if ¹ applies and it is not a point of law or a point of authority, leave is needed). If ² applies, leave is also needed.
Note: it must have regard to the degree of any difference between the defence and the defence statement and the justification for any difference

The jury and the court:
may draw adverse inferences as to guilt (but cannot convict solely on this)

... time limits for disclosure

➤ All prosecution and defence disclosure must occur within time limits set down by the Secretary of State (under *s 12*).
  ◆ These time limits may be set as the Secretary of State sees fit (eg: the 14 day rule for defence disclosure, see previous page).
  ◆ There are various transitional provisions that say that if no regulations are made, the various stages of disclosure must occur 'as soon as practicable' after certain events listed (eg: prosecution disclosure is as soon as reasonably practicable after certain events such as a plea of 'not guilty' or committal for trial) (*s 13*).
➤ If the prosecutor does not comply with his time limits (*s 10*), then ...
  ◆ ... unless the accused would be denied a fair trial as a result ...
  ◆ ... this is not on its own an abuse of process leading to a stay of proceedings.

... confidentiality

➤ *ss 17-18* provide that any material disclosed by the prosecutor is confidential.
  ◆ Various new criminal offences are set out for breach of that confidentiality.

Prosecutor will not disclose material 'in the public interest' (*ss 14-16*)

➤ The prosecutor as a general rule must disclose all material.
➤ However, the prosecutor may apply to the court for non-disclosure if it would not be 'in the public interest'. The court may grant such an application.
  ◆ **In summary trial**, as long as it is before the verdict, the accused can apply at any time for a review of non-disclosure.
  ◆ **In other cases**, as long as it is before the verdict:
    • the court has a duty to keep any non-disclosure under review, *and*
    • notwithstanding the court's duty, the accused can apply at any time for a court review.
➤ If:
  ◆ a person claiming to have an interest in the material applies for a review of the non-disclosure, *and*
  ◆ he shows that he was involved in bringing the material to the attention of the prosecutor,
  ... *then* he must be heard before any order for non-disclosure is made.
➤ A third party who has material which has previously been inspected by the prosecution or which is in the possession of the prosecution, may be required to disclose this to the defence.
  ◆ This will be subject to a hearing if necessary on:
    • public interest, *or*
    • confidentiality.

O Evidence at trial

I	Evidential proof	V	Admissibility of evidence (all categories except hearsay)
II	Implications for 'character'		
III	Evidential safeguards	VI	Admissibility of evidence (hearsay)
IV	Witness's competence and compellability		
		VII	Inferences from silence at trial

I Evidential proof

A Burden of proof

➤ **The prosecution** must prove guilt 'beyond reasonable doubt'.

➤ **The defence** has an 'evidential burden' (ie: it must introduce necessary evidence before the court).

- Occasionally, a defence may need to satisfy the court on the balance of probabilities:

    a) insane automatism (*Bratty v AG for Northern Ireland* [1963] AC 386).

    b) insanity (*Sodeman v The King* [1936] 2 All ER 1138).

    c) diminished responsibility (*Homicide Act 1957 s 2(2)*).

B Proof by evidence

➤ **Everything must be proved *except*:**

- facts which are formally admitted by the defence and the prosecution (*CJA 1967 s 10*).

- where judicial notice is taken of a point of fact (eg: dogs bark, they do not quack).

- where judicial notice is taken of a point of law (eg: traffic must stop at a red light).

- circumstantial evidence (rebuttable): where there is an *inference* of fact drawn from *proven* facts.

    - Examples include:

        i) doctrine of recent possession: someone possessing goods illegally came by them illicitly.

        ii) doctrine of continuance: a given state of affairs continues (*R v Balloz* (1908) 1 Cr App R 258).

C Types of evidence

➤ **Oral evidence:** this carries most weight.

➤ **Real evidence:** this consists of objects (eg: weapons).

➤ **Documentary evidence:** this includes recordings and photographs.

- A document must be authenticated by demonstrating in what circumstances it was created.

- A copy is admissible (*CJA 2003 s 133*).

➤ **Written statements and depositions (see p 473):** any that were used at committal may be used at trial, as long as they have been signed by a magistrate.

➤ **Video recording evidence:** allowed in limited circumstances *[to be widened when CJA 2003 s 137-138 is brought into force [not yet in force]]*.

> A person giving oral evidence may refresh his memory from a document made or verified by him at an earlier time if (*CJA 2003 s 139*):
>
> - he states in his oral evidence that the document records his recollection of the matter at that earlier time, *and*
>
> - his recollection of the matter is likely to have been significantly better at that time than it is at the time of his oral evidence

D Finding the facts

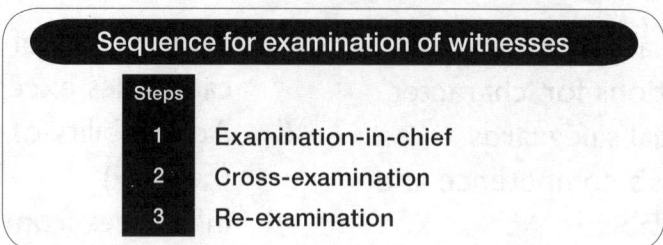

1 Examination-in-chief

➤ This is where a side calls its own witness and asks questions of that witness.

➤ A witness may refresh his memory from a contemporaneous document.

➤ No leading questions are permitted, except to obtain a rebuttal or denial of the opponent's case.

➤ Even if a witness gives unfavourable answers, the side which called the witness cannot contradict or discredit the witness *unless*:

- the witness is declared hostile. To achieve this, an application must be made to the judge (*CPA 1865 s 3*)). If this is done:
    - the party calling a witness may cross-examine him and ask leading questions, *and*
    - the witness can be confronted with statements made previously by him which are inconsistent with his testimony (see p 509).

2 Cross-examination

➤ After a side has called its witness for examination-in-chief, the other side may cross-examine the witness.

➤ The cross-examiner will seek to:

  a) put his view of the case to a witness, *and*

  b) extract useful information from the witness, *and*

  c) challenge a witness's credibility.

- The questions must be relevant to the evidence about the offence before the court.

- A witness's answer is *final* unless the witness:

    i) is biased (*R v Shaw* (1888) 16 Cox 503), *or*

    ii) has given evidence which is inconsistent with a previous statement (*CPA 1865 ss 4-5*) (see also p 509), *or*

    iii) has a relevant conviction (*CPA 1865 s 6*), *or*

    iv) has a reputation for untruthfulness (*Toohey v Metropolitan Police Comm.* [1965] AC 595).

3 Re-examination

➤ There may now be a re-examination by the other side after the cross-examination on matters brought up during the cross-examination.

➤ This may be done in an attempt to undo any damage from the cross-examination.

II Implications for 'character'

References in this section are to CJA 2003

➤ All common law rules governing the admissibility of evidence of bad character in criminal proceedings have been abolished (s 99). (This is subject to s 118 which preserves the common law rule that a person's reputation is admissible to prove his bad character.).

Meaning of 'bad character' (ss 98, 112)

➤ Evidence of a person's 'bad character' means **evidence of, or of a disposition towards, misconduct** on his part, other than evidence which:

   a) has to do with the alleged facts of the offence with which the defendant is charged, *or*

   b) is evidence of misconduct in connection with the investigation or prosecution of that offence.

   ◆ 'Misconduct' means the commission of an offence or other reprehensible behaviour.

➤ Evidence of a person's 'bad character' therefore includes evidence of previous convictions (cf. *R v Hanson, R v Gilmore and R v Pickstone* [2005] 1 WLR 3169), evidence on charges being tried concurrently, evidence relating to offences for which a person has been charged (but the charge was not prosecuted or acquitted), evidence that a person is racist etc.

➤ The Crown is able to lead at trial evidence of the defendant's bad character if the defendant has passed through one of the '7 gateways' (and the additional statutory requirements are met (*s 101*):

   a) all parties to the proceedings agree to the evidence being admissible, *or*

   b) the evidence is adduced by the defendant himself or is given in answer to a question asked by him in cross-examination and intended to elicit it, *or*

   c) it is important explanatory evidence, *or*

   d) it is relevant to an important matter in issue between the defendant and the prosecution, *or*

   e) it has substantial probative value in relation to an important matter in issue between the defendant a co-defendant, *or*

   f) it is evidence to correct a false impression given by the defendant, *or*

   g) the defendant has made an attack on another person's character.

   > ◆ The court must not admit evidence on these 2 items if, on an application by the defendant to exclude it, it appears to the court that the admission of the evidence would have such an adverse effect on the fairness of the proceedings that the court ought not to admit it.
   >   • The court must have regard, in particular, to the length of time between the matters to which that evidence relates and the matters which form the subject of the offence charged.

➤ The court must either direct the jury to acquit (or if it considers that there ought to be a retrial, discharge the jury) if (*s 107*):

   ◆ evidence of his bad character has been admitted under grounds c to g above, *and*

   ◆ the court is satisfied at any time after the close of the case for the prosecution that:

      • the evidence is contaminated, *and*

      • the contamination is such that, considering the importance of the evidence to the case against the defendant, his conviction of the offence would be unsafe.

➤ Offences committed under the age of 14 are only admissible if the offence for which the defendant is being tried and the offence for which the defendant was convicted under the age of 14 are both triable only on indictment and the court is satisfied that the interests of justice require it to be admissible (*s 108*).

Meaning of phrases used in grounds a to g above (ss 102-106)

Ground	Phrase	Meaning
c	Evidence is 'important explanatory evidence' if:	◆ without it, the court or jury would find it impossible or difficult properly to understand other evidence in the case, *and* ◆ its value for understanding the case as a whole is substantial.
d	'Matters in issue between the defendant and the prosecution' include:	◆ the question whether the defendant has a propensity to commit offences of the kind with which he is charged, except where his having such a propensity makes it no more likely that he is guilty of the offence ● This can be established by evidence that he has been convicted of an offence of the same description as the one with which he is charged, or an offence of the same category as the one with which he is charged. ■ This does not apply in the case of a particular defendant if the court is satisfied, by reason of the length of time since the conviction or for any other reason, that it would be unjust for it to apply in his case. ◆ the question whether the defendant has a propensity to be untruthful, except where it is not suggested that the defendant's case is untruthful in any respect. NB: Only prosecution evidence is admissible.
e	'Matter in issue between the defendant and a co-defendant'	➤ Evidence which is relevant to the question whether the defendant has a propensity to be untruthful is admissible only if the nature or conduct of his defence is such as to undermine the co-defendant's defence. ➤ Evidence is only admissable if: ◆ it is to be (or has been) adduced by the co-defendant, *or* ◆ a witness is invited to give (or has given) it in cross-examination by the co-defendant.
f	'Evidence to correct a false impression'	➤ The defendant gives a false impression if he is responsible for the making of an express or implied assertion which is apt to give the court or jury a false or misleading impression about the defendant. ◆ A defendant is treated as being responsible for the making of an assertion if: ● the assertion is made by the defendant in the proceedings (whether or not in evidence given by him), *or* ● evidence of the assertion is given and the assertion was made by the defendant: ■ on being questioned under caution before charge about the offence, *or* ■ on being charged with the offence /informed he might be prosecuted for it, *or* ● the assertion is made by a witness called by the defendant, *or* ● the assertion is made by any witness in cross-examination in response to a question asked by the defendant that is intended to elicit it, or is likely to do so, *or* ● the assertion was made by any person out of court, and the defendant adduces evidence of it in the proceedings. ◆ A defendant who would otherwise be treated as responsible for the making of an assertion is not so treated if, or to the extent that, he withdraws it. ◆ Where it appears to the court that a defendant, by his conduct (including appearance or dress), seeks to give an impression about himself that is false or misleading, the court may if it appears just to do so treat the defendant as being responsible for the making of an assertion which is apt to give that impression. NB: Only prosecution evidence is admissible.
g	'Attack on another person's character'	➤ A defendant does this if: ◆ he adduces evidence attacking the other person's character, ● ie: that he has committed an offence (whether a different offence from the one with which the defendant is charged or the same one), or has behaved, or is disposed to behave, in a reprehensible way; ◆ he asks questions in cross-examination that are intended to elicit such evidence, or are likely to do so, *or* ◆ evidence is given of an imputation about the other person made by the defendant: ● on being questioned under caution, before charge, about the offence with which he is charged, *or* ● on being charged with the offence or officially informed that he might be prosecuted for it. NB: Only prosecution evidence is admissible.

General rules about use of 'bad character' evidence

➤ A court, when considering the relevance or probative value of bad character evidence, must assume that the evidence is true (*s 109*).

- ◆ BUT when the evidence is so unreliable that no reasonable jury could believe that it was true, the judge does not have to assume the evidence is true.

➤ A court must give reasons for its rulings under these provisions (*s 110*).

- ◆ These must be given in open court and, in the magistrates' courts, entered into the register of proceedings, ensuring that a record is kept.
- ◆ This applies to rulings on whether an item to evidence is evidence of bad character, rulings on questions of admissibility and exclusion and any decision to withdraw a case from the jury.

➤ Bad character evidence that is admissible in relation to one charge in the proceedings is not automatically admissible in relation to another charge in the same proceedings, but must instead meet the provisions of this part of *CJA 2003* to be admissible in respect of that charge (*s 112(2)*).

➤ Nothing here affects the exclusion of evidence by *CPA 1865 s 3* (impeaching the credit of own witness by general evidence of bad character: hostile witness) (*s 112(3)*), see p 498.

Non-defendant's 'bad character' (*s 100*)

➤ Evidence of the bad character of a person other than the defendant is admissible if:

- ◆ it is important explanatory evidence, *or*
  - • This means that: a) without it, the court or jury would find it impossible or difficult properly to understand other evidence in the case, and b) its value for understanding the case as a whole is substantial.
- ◆ it has substantial probative value in relation to a matter which is a matter in issue in the proceedings and is of substantial importance in the context of the case as a whole, *or*
  - • In assessing the probative value the court must have regard to the following factors (and to any others it considers relevant):
    - ▪ the nature and number of the events, or other things, to which the evidence relates,
    - ▪ when those events or things are alleged to have happened or existed,
    - ▪ the nature and extent of the similarities and the dissimilarities between each of the alleged instances of misconduct where: the evidence is evidence of a person's misconduct, and it is suggested that the evidence has probative value by reason of similarity between that misconduct and other alleged misconduct,
    - ▪ the extent to which the evidence shows or tends to show that the same person was responsible each time, where:
      - i) the evidence is evidence of a person's misconduct, *and*
      - ii) it is suggested that that person is also responsible for the misconduct charged, *and*
      - iii) the identity of the person responsible for the misconduct charged is disputed.
- ◆ all parties to the proceedings agree to the evidence being admissible.

➤ **Leave of the court is needed except where all parties agree.**

III Evidential safeguards

1 Corroboration

➤ At common law, one witness is sufficient in all cases.

➤ By statute, corroboration (ie: independent supporting evidence) is required to convict a defendant of perjury (*Perjury Act 1911 s 13*) and speeding (except if the evidence is from a speed camera). The judge must tell the jury this.

➤ In other cases, where it is felt that further proof might be needed to support certain evidence, it is within the discretion of the judge to give the jury a corroboration warning, ie: the jury should be warned that further proof is desirable.

➤ Contents of a corroboration warning:

- A judge should point out to the jury why evidence is suspect, or identify corroborative evidence and non-corroborative evidence, as a warning that there is a danger in relying on the evidence.

- Magistrates warn themselves (!) - the defence can remind them in its closing speech.

When is a warning necessary?		
When corroboration itself is essential	When a corroboration warning is mandatory	When a corroboration warning is desirable
For charges of: • treason • perjury • speeding	There *used to be* a mandatory warning for the following 2 instances, but this has now been abolished by *CJPO 1994 ss 32-33*. However, a court may still give such a warning even though this is undesirable as it is contrary to the intention of the *CJPO 1994* (*R v Makanjuola*; *R v Easton*, [1995] 2 Cr App R 469) • An accomplice gives evidence • A victim of an alleged sexual offence gives evidence	• A prosecution witness has an interest in giving false evidence (eg: to preserve his own reputation or he bears a grudge) (*R v Cheema* [1994] 1 WLR 147) • A defendant tries to incriminate a co-defendant • A witness is shown to be unreliable (eg: a mental patient)

2 Disputed identification (Turnbull guidelines) (*R v Turnbull [1977] QB 224*)

➤ In a case where disputed identification of the defendant is the sole or a substantial issue, there is a danger of wrongful conviction unless the following procedure is complied with:

Steps

1 Evidence of identification is admissible if:
- the evidence is visual *and*
- on at least 2 occasions, the defendant was purported to be seen (eg: at the crime and at an identification parade).

2 The judge or magistrates must consider the soundness of the evidence by contemplating the following 6 factors:

1	the length of observation	4	conditions
2	whether the defendant was already known to the witness	5	distance
3	how close the witness's description is to the police description	6	lighting

3 If the identifying evidence is poor, then the judge or magistrates must order an acquittal.

4 If the evidence is sound, the judge gives the jury a **Turnbull warning**. He must warn the jury (or magistrates must warn themselves!):
- of the dangers of relying on identification evidence, *and*
- to consider factors 1 to 6 above in evaluating the evidence.

IV Witness's competence and compellability

Competent (meaning)	Compellable (meaning)
A 'competent' witness can lawfully give evidence	A 'compellable' witness can be required to testify

Unsworn evidence

➤ The following witnesses may not give sworn evidence (*YJCEA 1999 s 55*):
  - someone who has not yet reached 14 years old, *or*
  - someone who has not a sufficient appreciation of the solemnity of the occasion *and* the responsibility to tell the truth when taking an oath. (NB: 'sufficient appreciation' is assumed unless there is contrary evidence.)

Competent?

➤ Everybody is competent to give evidence except someone who (*YJCEA 1999 s 53*):
  - cannot understand questions put to him and give answers which can be understood, *or*
  - (as a prosecution witness) currently stands charged in the criminal proceedings.

Compellable?

Defendant as a prosecution witness	Defendant as a defence witness
➤ *Not* compellable (*CEA 1898 s 1*). (Also *not* competent - see above.)	➤ *Not* compellable (*CEA 1898 s 1*). ➤ His evidence is admissible against a co-defendant that he implicates. ➤ If he testifies, he must be called before any other witnesses for the defence (*PACE s 79*). ➤ If he decides not to testify, this can have adverse consequences, see p 511. ➤ The judge will comment adversely if the defence raises issues, but gives no evidence in support. ➤ The prosecution may comment on his refusal to testify (*CJPO 1994 Schedule 10 para 2*). ➤ A co-accused may comment freely on a defendant's refusal to testify.
Present spouse as a prosecution witness	**Present spouse as a defence witness**

➤ Compellable only if the defendant is charged with (*PACE s 80(3)*):
  • an assault on the spouse.
  • an assault or sexual offence on a victim aged under 16.
	➤ Compellable, unless the accused and the spouse are jointly charged) (*PACE ss 80(2), 80(2A), s.80(4), 80(4A)*).

Former spouse	
➤ Compellable (*PACE s 80(5)*).	

Is a co-defendant compellable?

➤ Whether a co-defendant is compellable to testify against a fellow defendant and the admissibility of his evidence depends on the co-defendant's plea as follows:

The co-defendant on a plea of...	
'guilty' (and therefore no longer on trial)	'not guilty'
Compellable	*Not* compellable
He is like any other witness and any statements made to the police, or a confession, will be inadmissible against the defendant as they will be hearsay	His confession, or statements made to the police, are only admissible against himself. (Evidence not made on oath by the co-defendant is not evidence against the defendant - it is inadmissible and must be disregarded)
A corroboration warning is not necessary (*CJPO 1994 s 32,* see p 502)	Some corroboration warning is desirable, see p 502
Cross-examinable on his record	Cross-examination: a defendant may be asked anything, even if it would incriminate him (subject to *CEA 1898 s 1(2),* see p 505)
Note: A defendant is innocent until he *pleads* guilty	**Note:** A defendant is competent as witness to his own alibi, or to authenticate a document

V Admissibility of evidence (all categories except hearsay)

Special measures and admissibility

➤ *YJCEA 1999 ss 16-33* introduces court powers to make special measures (eg: evidence by video link or from behind a screen) for vulnerable witnesses (eg: witnesses who are less than 17, or with a mental disorder, or who are in fear or distress). This evidence is admissible as if given normally.

➤ There are 7 primary types of *in*admissible evidence:

1 At common law

  ➤ The common law discretion of a judge to prevent an unfair trial is preserved by *PACE s 82(3)*.

  ➤ There is discretion to exclude evidence improperly obtained by the prosecution.

  ➤ Usually the discretion might be applied if the prejudicial effect on the jury of the evidence outweighs its true probative value.

  ➤ However, the discretion is very rarely exercised because as a *matter of law* much improperly obtained evidence is admissible. The following examples are admissible:

  ◆ evidence from the illegal search of a person (*Kuruma, Son of Kariu v The Queen* [1955] AC 197).

  ◆ evidence obtained by an agent provocateur (*R v Sang* [1980] AC 402).

2 *PACE s 78*

  ➤ The court has a general discretion to exclude evidence, if an admission of the evidence 'would have such an adverse effect on the fairness of the proceedings that the court ought not to admit it' given all the circumstances, including how the evidence was obtained.

3 Irrelevant evidence

4 Self-made evidence

➤ A witness may not support his evidence at trial by introducing a statement he made on a previous occasion.

➤ This is inadmissible *unless* it involves:

a) previous exculpatory statements to the police, *or*

b) statements that come under *res gestae* - 'circumstances of spontaneity or involvement in the event', so there is no possibility of concoction or distortion (see '*res gestae*' on p 510), *or*

c) evidence that rebuts the suggestion that the witness has recently fabricated his testimony.

} Admissible self-made evidence

5 Privileged evidence

➤ Privileged material is inadmissible and falls within these categories:

a) **legal professional privilege:** eg: client-solicitor communications, or those with third parties, in contemplation of proceedings (*Parkins v Hawkshaw* (1817) 2 Stark NP 239).

b) **against self-incrimination:** an answer which may lead to a criminal charge for a witness (*R v Garbett* (1847) 2 C&K 474, and *Evidence Act 1851 s 3*). However, this does not apply if a defendant elects to testify (*CEA 1898 s 1(2)*).

6 Public interest immunity

➤ Evidence that for reasons of public interest is inadmissible.

➤ Such reasons include:

- state interests (*D v NSPCC* [1978] AC 171).
- details of the prevention, detection and investigation of crime, eg: identity of a police informant, unless this is necessary to prove a defendant's innocence (*R v Turner* [1995] 1 WLR 264).

7 Similar fact evidence

➤ This is evidence that the defendant has committed offences before, similar to the ones now before the court.

➤ This is inadmissible because:

a) the prejudice created by such evidence outweighs any probative value it may have (*DPP v Kilbourne* [1973] AC 729), *and*

b) it is irrelevant, since irrespective of the number of similar crimes which have been committed, these crimes cannot connect a person with the crime in front of the court (*R v Miller* [1952] 2 All ER 667).

➤ However, if the prosecution can convince the judge/magistrates that in a particular case a) and b) are untrue *and* that the evidence is relevant, the judge/magistrates may rule that the similar fact evidence is admissible.

➤ An accused can *always* introduce similar evidence against a co-accused because the judge has no discretion to exclude it (*R v Miller* [1952] 2 All ER 667).

VI Admissibility of evidence (hearsay)

General principles

➤ *CJA 2003 s 114* removes the common law rule against the admission of hearsay evidence.

➤ *CJA 2003 s 114 (1)-(3)* set out the following circumstances in which a statement which is not made in oral evidence during criminal proceedings can be used as evidence of the facts stated within it:
   a) a statutory provision makes it admissible, *or*
   b) a common law rule preserved by *CJA 2003 s 118* makes it admissible (see box below), *or*
   c) all parties to the proceedings agree to it being admissible, *or*
   d) **the court is satisfied that it is in the interests of justice for it to be admissible** (*s 114(d)*).

➤ To allow the statement under ground (d) above, the court must have regard to the following factors (and to any others it considers relevant):
   - how much probative value the statement has (assuming it is true) in relation to a matter in issue in the proceedings, or how valuable it is for the understanding of other evidence ('first factor'),
   - what other evidence has been/can be given on the matter/evidence mentioned in the first factor,
   - how important the matter/evidence in the first factor is in the context of the whole case,
   - the circumstances in which the statement was made,
   - how reliable the maker of the statement appears to be,
   - how reliable the evidence of the making of the statement appears to be,
   - whether oral evidence of the matter stated can be given and, if not, why it cannot,
   - the amount of difficulty involved in challenging the statement,
   - the extent to which that difficulty would be likely to prejudice the party facing it.

> In deciding whether to admit hearsay, a judge must have regard to all of these listed factors but need not reach a conclusion on each of them (*R v Taylor* (2006) The Times 7 February)

Some definitions used in the first factor (*CJA 2003 s 115*)

'statement'	'matter'
• any representation of fact or opinion made by a person by whatever means; and it includes a representation made in a sketch, photofit or other pictorial form. NB: This changes the common law position.	• is a relevant matter only if one of the purposes of the person making the statement appears to the court to have been: • to cause another person to believe the matter, or • to cause another person to act or a machine to operate on the basis that the matter is as stated.

An extra power to exclude superfluous 'out of court' statements (*CJA 2003 s 126*)

➤ The court has a discretion to exclude superfluous out of court statements if it is satisfied that the value of evidence is substantially outweighed by the undue waste of time which its admission would cause.
   - The common law power for the court to exclude evidence if its prejudicial effect is out of proportion to its probative value and the discretion contained in *PACE s 78* is specifically preserved.

Statements by a machine (*CJA 2003 s 129*)

➤ If a statement generated by a machine is based on information input into the machine by a human, the output of the device is only admissible where it is proved that the information was accurate.
   - The common law presumption that a mechanical device is properly set/calibrated is preserved.

CRIMINAL LITIGATION
Evidence

> ### Hearsay notices (CrPR Part 34)
>
> ➤ A hearsay notice is required to admit statutory hearsay in court (but is no longer required for hearsay based on common law rules (eg: res gestae). A notice is needed if either party wishes to rely on:
>
> - *s 114(d)* (interests of justice), *or*
> - *s 116* (unavailable witnesses), *or*
> - *s 117* (business documents), *or*
> - *s 121* (multiple hearsay).

A Statutory hearsay (admissible)

1 Documentary hearsay: admissible

Witness statements (CJA 2003 s 116)	Business documents (CJA 2003 s 117)
First hand hearsay only	First hand and multiple hearsay
Oral or documentary	Documentary only
Admissible if:	Admissible if:

◆ The witness's oral evidence would have been admissible itself, *and*
◆ The person who made the statement is identified to the court's satisfaction, *and*
• This will enable the opposing party to challenge the absent witness's credibility (*s 124*).
◆ A party (or someone acting on his behalf) has not caused the unavailability of the declarant, *and*
◆ One of the following 2 conditions is fulfilled:
  1. the witness is unable to attend because:
  a) he is is dead, *or*
  b) he is unfit to be a witness because of his bodily or mental condition, *or*
  c) he is outside the UK and it is not reasonably practicable to secure his attendance, *or*
  d) he cannot be found although such steps as it is reasonably practicable to take to find him have been taken
or **2. through fear**, he does not give (or does not continue to give) oral evidence in the proceedings, either at all or in connection with the subject matter of the statement, and the court gives leave for the statement to be given in evidence.
• 'Fear' is widely construed eg: it includes fear of death/injury of another person or of financial loss
• Leave may only be given under ground e if the court considers that the statement ought to be admitted in the interests of justice, having regard to:
  ▪ the statement's contents,
  ▪ any risk that its admission or exclusion will result in unfairness to any party to the proceedings (and in particular to how difficult it will be to challenge the statement if the relevant person does not give oral evidence),
  ▪ the fact that a direction under *YJCEA s1999 s 19* (special measures for the giving of evidence by fearful witnesses etc) could be made in certain cases
  ▪ any other relevant circumstances.
	◆ The document or the part containing the statement was created or received by a person in the course of a trade, business, profession or other occupation, or as the holder of a paid or unpaid office, *and*
	◆ The person who supplied the information had or may reasonably be supposed to have had personal knowledge of the matters dealt with, *and*
	◆ Each person (if any) through whom the information was supplied received the information in the course of a trade, business, profession or other occupation, or as the holder of a paid or unpaid office.
	NB: A document prepared for pending or contemplated criminal proceedings or for a criminal investigation is only admissible if:
	◆ either of the '2 conditions' is satisfied, *or*
	◆ the person who supplied the information contained in the statement cannot reasonably be expected to have any recollection of the matters dealt with in the statement (having regard to the length of time since he supplied the information and all other circumstances).
	➤ The court may make a direction that a statement is inadmissible if satisfied that the statement's reliability as evidence for the purpose for which it is tendered is doubtful in view of:
	◆ its contents,
	◆ the source of the information contained in it, *or*
	◆ the way in which or the circumstances in which the information was supplied or received, *or*
	◆ the way in which or the circumstances in which the document concerned was created or received.

2 Written statements: admissible

➤ A statement defined as follows is admissible in trials (*CJA 1967 s 9(1)*).

a) the statement purports to be made by the signatory, *and*

b) there is a declaration that it is true to the best of the witness's knowledge and belief, and it was made in full knowledge of the danger of a prosecution for falsehood, *and*

c) a copy is served before any hearing on all parties *and* none object within 7 days of service.

} s 9 statement (non-disputed evidence)

3 Confessions: admissible

i) Confessions generally

➤ A confession is:
'any statement wholly or partly adverse to the person who made it, whether made to a person in authority or not and whether made in words or otherwise' (*PACE s 82(1)*).

➤ A part-confession is admissible in total. If there are periods of silence followed by periods of speaking, the whole is admissible.

➤ A confession from a co-defendant cannot be used by the other defendant if obtained in breach of *PACE ss 76* or *78* (see below) (*PACE s76A* inserted by *CJA 2003 s 128*).

  ◆ However, unlike for the prosecution, the co-accused only needs to satisfy the court on the balance of probabilities that the confession was not obtained in breach of *PACE ss 76* or *78*.

ii) Excluding confessions

➤ The following 3 points show ways to attempt to exclude a confession:

❶ *PACE s 76(2)*

  ◆ A confession is inadmissible *unless* the prosecution show 'beyond reasonable doubt' that the confession was not obtained in one of the following 2 ways:

  • by **oppression** of the person who made it, *or*

  • in consequence of anything said or done which was likely, in the circumstances at the time, to render **unreliable** any confession which might be made by him in consequence thereof.

  ◆ **Oppression:** the Court of Appeal has defined this as the 'exercise of authority or power in a burdensome, harsh or wrongful manner; unjust or cruel treatment of subjects ... the imposition of unjust or unreasonable burdens' (*R v Fulling* [1987] QB 426). ('Oppression' includes 'torture, inhuman and degrading treatment and the use or threat of violence' (*PACE s 76(8)*).)

  ◆ **Unreliability:** a breach of a *PACE* Code is, in itself, not sufficient. There must be a causal link between the breach and the unreliability. Demonstrative police misconduct is unnecessary.

❷ *PACE s 78* - see p 504.

❸ At common law - see p 504.

iii) The admission of evidence from an excluded confession

➤ Factual evidence gained from an excluded confession: Facts are admissible (*PACE s 76(4)(a)*).

➤ Expression: A confession is admissible as evidence that the defendant writes, speaks or expresses himself in a certain way, irrespective of whether the confession itself is excluded (*PACE s 76(4)(b)*).

4 Hearsay and previous statements by witnesses

➤ If a witness admits that he has made a previous inconsistent statement (or it is proved that he made one), it is not only evidence which undermines his <u>credibility</u> (as someone who makes inconsistent statements) but also evidence of the <u>truth</u> of its contents (*CJA 2003 s 119*).

➤ Other previous statements are also admissible as evidence of the truth of their contents (not only to bolster the credibility of the witness's oral evidence). This applies when (*CJA 2003 s 120*):

- A previous statement is admitted as evidence to rebut a suggestion that the witness's oral evidence is untrue, *or*

- A witness is 'refreshing his memory' from a previously written document. If he is cross-examined on the document and it is received in evidence, the statement will be evidence of any matter contained within it, *or*

- A previous statement is admissible as evidence of the facts within it provided the witness states that he made the statement and believes it to be true and one of the following applies:

  - The statement describes or identifies a person, place or thing (which includes objects such as a car registration number), *or*

  - The statement was made when the incident was fresh in the witness's memory and he cannot reasonably be expected to remember the matters stated (ie: this goes to the weight of the evidence, but should not make it inadmissible), or

  - The statement is a complaint by a victim of the alleged offence which was made as soon as could reasonably be expected after the conduct in question, and the witness gives oral evidence in relation to the matter. There is a further requirement for such a statement to be admissible which is that the complaint must not have been made as a result of a threat or a promise.

A note on multiple hearsay (*CJA 2003 s 121*)

➤ Multiple hearsay: where information passes through more than one person before it is recorded.

➤ Multiple hearsay is admissible in 2 circumstances only:

- under the exceptions for business documents (*CJA 2003 s 117*) or previous statements of witnesses (inconsistent or otherwise) (*CJA 2003 s 119-120*), *or*

- all parties to the proceedings agree, *or*

- the court uses its discretion to admit the statement.

  - The test for exercise of discretion is whether the court is satisfied that the value of the evidence in question (taking into account how reliable the statement appears to be) is so high that the interests of justice require the later statement to be admissible for that purpose.

B Common law hearsay (admissible) (unchanged by *CJA 2003 s 118*).

1   *Res gestae* (*Ratten v The Queen* [1972] AC 378): **admissible**

➤ *Res gestae* is:
- a statement by the doer of an act, which is related to the act and is contemporaneous with it.
- a spontaneous statement at the time of an event.
- a statement made at the time of an event, and which shows a state of mind, emotion or intention.
- an expression of physical sensation felt at the time.

➤ *Res gestae* is admissible if a judge can disregard the possibility that the statement was concocted or distorted (*R v Andrews (Donald)* [1987] AC 281).

➤ A classic example of *res gestae* is a dying declaration (*Mills v The Queen* [1995] 3 All ER 865).

2   **Opinion: admissible**

➤ Opinion is admissible if *either*:

    a) a witness recalls his personal perception at the time, *or*

    b) the evidence is from an expert witness. The opinion must be pertinent to the expert's expertise.
- If an expert is present, all can see copies of his report.
- If an expert is absent, leave of court is required to admit an expert's report (*CJA 1988 s 30(2)*).

➤ Advance disclosure of an expert witness's evidence is compulsory (*PACE s 81* and *CrPR r 24.1*).
- Leave of the court is needed if the evidence is not disclosed as soon as possible after sending for trial (*CrPR r 24.3*).

3   **Public information: admissible**

➤ Published works dealing with matters of a public nature (such as histories, scientific works, dictionaries and maps) are admissible as evidence of facts of a public nature stated in them.

➤ Public documents (such as public registers, and returns made under public authority with respect to matters of public interest) are admissible as evidence of facts stated in them.

➤ Records (such as the records of certain courts, treaties, Crown grants, pardons and commissions) are admissible as evidence of facts stated in them.

➤ Evidence relating to a person's age or date or place of birth may be given by a person without personal knowledge of the matter.

4   **Reputation or family tradition: admissible**

➤ Evidence of reputation or family tradition is admissible to prove/disprove the pedigree or existence of a marriage, existence of any public/general right or the identity of any person/thing.

5   **Admissions by agents: admissible**

➤ An admission made by an agent of a defendant is admissible against the defendant as evidence of any matter stated, or a statement made by a person to whom a defendant refers a person for information is admissible against the defendant as evidence of any matter stated.

6   **Common enterprise: admissible**

➤ A statement made by a party to a common enterprise is admissible against another party to the enterprise as evidence of any matter stated.

VII Inferences from silence at trial

▶ The following sections of the *CJPO 1994* can each adversely affect the defendant at trial.

s 35 CJPO 1994

The defendant (of any age) fails to give evidence at trial

↓

Sub-procedure for s 35

▶ At the end of the prosecution case, *unless the legal representative of the defendant informs the court that the defendant will give evidence*, the judge will ensure that the defendant knows that inferences may be drawn from his refusal to testify

▶ This procedure is covered by The Consolidated Criminal Practice Direction Part IV.44.

s 34 CJPO 1994

Situation 1: questioning before charge

a) The defendant had not yet been charged, *and*
b) was being questioned under caution by a constable, *and*
c) the constable was trying to discover whether, or by whom, an offence had been committed, *and*
d) the defendant failed to mention a fact he might reasonably be expected to mention at the time, *and*
e) the defendant later (at trial) relies on that fact in his defence

Situation 2: questioning at time of charge

a) At the time that the defendant was charged or officially informed he might be prosecuted for an offence, *and*
b) the defendant failed to mention a fact he might reasonably be expected to mention at the time

YJCEA 1999 s 58 says that no inferences from silence are permissible where a defendant had no prior access to legal advice

s 36 CJPO 1994

a) The defendant was arrested, *and*
b) with an object, substance or mark:
   i) on his person, *or*
   ii) in or on his clothing or footwear, *or*
   iii) in his possession, *or*
   iv) in any place in which he was at the time of his arrest, *and*
c) the constable reasonably believed that the object, substance or mark had something to do with the defendant participating in a specified offence, *and*
d) the constable informed the defendant of his suspicions and asked him to account for the object, substance or mark, *and*
e) the defendant failed or refused to provide an explanation

s 37 CJPO 1994

a) At the time that the defendant was arrested, *and*
b) the defendant was at a place where a constable reasonably believed that the person's presence might be to do with participation in an offence, *and*
c) the constable reasonably believed that the presence of the defendant at that time and place could be attributed to the defendant participating in a specified offence, *and*
d) the constable informed the defendant of his suspicions and asked him to account for his presence, *and*
e) the defendant failed or refused to provide an explanation

↓

Consequences of an adverse inference of silence

▶ In the Crown Court, arguments about the admissibility of the defendant's silence when previously being interviewed (ie: any case above apart from *s 35*) take place in the absence of the jury.

♦ The judge decides on admissibility and the jury decides whether inferences may be drawn.

▶ In the Magistrates' Court, the magistrates decide everything.

▶ The magistrates or jury can 'draw such inferences as appear proper' from the silence as applied to:

1 a submission of 'no case to answer' in a trial (see pp 465-466 and p 475).
2 determining the guilt or innocence of a defendant at trial.

Note: such inferences must not decide the matter alone - there must be other factors too (CJPO 1994 s 38).

▶ The defence needs to introduce evidence in order to put forward a 'good reason' for the defendant's silence, so as to avoid the 'adverse inferences' from the silence (*R v Cowan; Gayle; Ricciardi* [1995] 3 WLR 818 CA).

♦ This case also shows that *s 35* is not only meant to be invoked in exceptional cases.

P Forthcoming changes

- The Police & Justice Bill 2006 (PJB) is going through Parliament at the time of writing.
- The Bill is expected to achieve Royal Assent in late 2006, with provisions gradually brought into force during 2007.
- This page lists a few of the areas of the PJB which affect matters in this book.
- **PJB further details:** Details of the bill can be found in full at:
    - http://www.publications.parliament.uk/pa/pabills/200506/police_and_justice.htm

Police and Justice Bill 2006

- **Police bail and detention conditions:** PJB proposes to amend PACE 1984 on police bail and detention pending charging by providing for a police officer to attach conditions to:
    - bail issued at a police station before charge under PACE s 37(2) and 37(7)(b), and
    - bail granted by a constable elsewhere than a police station ("street bail") under PACE s 30A.
        - Currently, an officer may only attach bail conditions when a person has been charged or when a person has been referred to the CPS for a decision to charge.
        - PJB proposes enabling the officer granting bail to consider attaching conditions relevant and proportionate to the suspect and the offence.
            - The conditions that can be imposed must be necessary to secure that the person surrenders to custody, does not commit an offence while on bail and does not interfere with witnesses or otherwise obstruct the course of justice.
            - No recognizance, security or surety may be taken and no requirement to reside in a bail hostel may be imposed.
- **Conditional cautions:** PJB proposes to amend CJA 2003 s 22 on conditional cautions by making it possible to impose conditions which have the object of punishing the offender.
- **Crime and anti-social behaviour:** PJB proposes amending CDA 1998 by requiring local authorities to have a committee to scrutinise the way in which persons and bodies responsible for tackling crime and disorder discharge their functions.
- **Sentencing:** PJB proposes amendments to CJA 2003 so that the sentencing arrangements for prison sentences of less than 12 months introduced by CJA ss 181-182 are not applied to offences of absconding while released on bail, committed under BA 1976 s 6.

INDEX

Index 514

Index

Subject	Page

A

Abatement
    bill 78
    of gift 171
Absconding 459
Accounts
    abatements 78
    accruals 46
    agreed fees 74
    balance sheet 42-3
        partnership accounts 54
        pro-forma 50
    bank reconciliations 51
    bookkeeping *see* Bookkeeping
    cash account 69
    client account 69
    client ledger 69-71
    client money 61-3
        mixed payments in 63
        payment into account 62, 63
        withdrawals from account 62, 63
    controlled trust 61, 62
    costs 72, 73
    debts 45, 78
    deposits 75, 77-8
    depreciation 47
    disbursements 72
    disposal of fixed assets 47
    insurance premiums 76-7
    interest 77-8
        amount 68
        contracting out 68
        stakeholder money 67
        when paid 67-8
    interpretation 56
    see also Ratio analysis
    mortgages 75
    office account 69
    office ledger 69-71
    office money 61, 62
    partnership accounts *see* Partnership accounts
    prepayments 46
    profit and loss account 40-1
    ratios *see* Ratio analysis
    record keeping 66
    returned cheques 77
    Solicitors' Accounts Rules 1998 60-8
    trust money 61, 62
    VAT 73-4
    work in progress 44
Accruals 46
'Acid test' ratio 59
Acknowledgement of service 369

Action plan order 490
Activation of suspended sentence 483
Activity requirement 486
Ad item grant 157
Ademption 171
Administration (companies)
    appointment of administrator 298
        by company 298-9
        by court 298
        by directors 298-9
        by holder of floating charge 298
        notice of appointment 299
    effects 299
    Enterprise Act 2002 changes 297
    functions of administrator 299
    nature of 297
    procedure 300
    purpose 297
Administration (estates)
    ad colligenda bona 157
    apportionment 150
    appropriation 150
    chain of administration 170
    collecting in assets 160
    distribution 150
    final adjustments 162
    identification of beneficiaries 148, 165
    insolvent estates 163
    letters of administration 157
    litigation pending 157
    mentally incapacitated persons 157
    minors 157
    oath, filling in 159
    payment of debts 163, 164
    payment of legacies 165-6
        pecuniary legacies 166
        specific legacies 147, 148, 166
    powers in will 149-50
    receipt 150
    reimbursement 150
    remuneration 150
    solvent estates 164
    tax liability 161
    see also Probate
Administrative receivers 297
    debenture holders and 297
    see also Administration (companies)
Admissibility of evidence 504-5
    hearsay *see* Hearsay
Admissions 367-8
    of agents 510
    authenticity of document 406
    facts 406
    judgment on 379

Subject	Page
Advertising	3
Advice and assistance	19
Age	
discrimination	329
retirement	331
Agency	
admissibility of admissions	510
agreement	325
authority	323
company liability for agent	274, 275
distribution agreements	324
legislative rules	322
liability	323
marketing	322
non-disclosure	323
payment	323
principles	323
ratification	323
sales	322
termination	323
types	322
Agricultural property relief	102
Alcohol treatment requirement	486
Allocation to track	392-3
hearings	393
questionnaire	393
Alternative dispute resolution	335
Annual general meeting	264
Anti-social behaviour, demoted tenancy	235
Appeals	
civil	430
courts	430, 493
criminal	493, 494
Applications	
additional claims	374-5
content, form and procedure	372
contributions/indemnity	374-5
counterclaims	374-5
court	371
default judgment	377
freezing injunctions	382
further information	378
interim remedies	381-4
judgment on admissions	379
notice	372-3
search orders	382
summary judgment	376
telephone hearings	373
urgent, without notice	382
Arbitration	336
Arrest	
at police station	438
away from police station	438
citizen's	437
necessity	436
PACE Code G	435
powers of arrest	434, 435-7
reasonable grounds	436
reasons	437

Subject	Page
record of	437
release on bail	438, 450
without warrant	435
Articles of association	255, 258
Assessment of costs	
detailed	421
summary	420, 422
Asset turnover ratio	57
Assignment of lease	
consent of landlord	231
over commonhold unit	232
procedure	230
Assignment of reversion	232
Associated companies, stamp duty	128
Attachment of earnings order	426, 429
Attendance centre requirement	486
Attestation clause, wills	147
Auditor	273

B

Subject	Page
Bad character evidence	
attack on character of another	500
false impression correction	500
grounds for admission	500
important explanatory evidence	500
leave to adduce	501
matters in issue	500
meaning	499
non-defendants	501
probative value	501
see also Character evidence	
Bail	
absconding	459
appeal against conditions	458
Class A drugs	456
conditions	458
hearings procedure	455
imprisonable offences	456
misuse of controlled drugs	457
non-imprisonable offences	457
objections	457
police bail	512
refusal	456-7
release of arrested person	438, 450
remand	454
right to	455
sending for trial	471
surrender	459
Balance sheets	42-3
partnership accounts	54
pro-forma	50
Bank reconciliations	51
Bankruptcy see Insolvency	
Barristers see Counsel	
'Bed and ISAing'	138
'Bed and spousing'	138
Beneficiary	
children	165
class gifts	165

Subject	Page
identification of	148, 165
land held on trust for	194
Benefits code, income tax	84-5
Benjamin order	169
Bills	
client's remedies	23
conditional fee agreements	24
detailed assessment request	24
interest on unpaid	24
remuneration certificate	24
requirements	24
solicitor's remedies	24
Board meetings	
elective resolutions	259
first	259
minutes	272
quorum	272
resolutions	272
votes	272
Bona vacantia	152
Bookkeeping	
accruals	46
adjustments	40
balance sheet	42-3
partnership accounts	54
pro-forma	50
debts, bad and doubtful	45, 78
depreciation	47
disposal of fixed assets	47
double entry	36
payments in advance (prepayments)	46
payments in arrears (accruals)	46
profit and loss account	40-1
'T' accounts	36-7
balancing	38
trial balances	
mark up	40
partnership accounts	52
production	38-9
work in progress	44
Breach of contract	
damages	242
drafting claim	364
Briefs	412, 474
'Buildmark' policy cover	226
Business documents	410, 507
Business property relief	102

C

Subject	Page
Calderbank offer	385
see also Part 36 offers and payments	
Capital	
loan	129
share	278-9, 281-2
working	58
Capital allowances	
claimable	93
claimants	92
industrial buildings	92

Subject	Page
meaning	91
plant and machinery	92
use	91
Capital gains tax	
allowable expenditure	94
allowable loss	94
business medium choice	291
calculation	94-9
overview	116
chargeable gain	94
deceased's estate	161
disclaimers and elections	141
disposal identification	94
exemptions	95
hold-over relief	96, 98
indexation allowance	95
individuals	99
limited liability partnerships	99
partnerships	99
payment	116
instalments	99
personal representatives	99
rates	99
records	115
roll-over relief	96, 98
self-assessment	115
taper relief	97-8
tax due	99
tax return	115
taxable gain	95
trustees	99
Case management	342
automatic transfer	392-3
conference	400
consultation requirement	393
criminal litigation	452
directions	
fast track	398
multi-track	400
small claims track	394
documents for court	346-7
see also Electronic filing and documentation	
fast track	397-8
multi-track	399-400
pre-trial checklist	397
sanctions	344
stay of proceedings	393
time provisions	345
track allocation	392-3
Case progression officers	452
Cashflow ratios	59
Cautions (in criminal investigations), wording	439
Caveats	167
Certificate of incorporation	255
Cessate grant	157
Chain of administration	170
Character evidence	499-501
bad character	
attack on character of another	500

Subject	Page
false impression correction	500
grounds for admission	499
important explanatory evidence	500
leave to adduce	501
matters in issue	500
meaning	499
of non-defendant	501
probative value	501
Criminal Justice Act 2003	499-501
family tradition	510
reputation	510

Charges
- fixed ... 305
- floating ... 305

Charges Register ... 216-17
- indemnity ... 217
- rectification ... 217

Charities ... 195

Children *see* Minors

Citizen's arrest ... 437

Civil litigation
- acknowledgement of service ... 369
- additional claims ... 374-5
- additional liability ... 365, 370, 422
- admissions ... 367-8
- allocation hearings ... 393
- alternatives to litigation ... 335-7
- appeals ... 430
- applications
  - additional claims ... 374-5
  - content, form and procedure ... 372
  - court ... 371
  - default judgment ... 377
  - further information ... 378
  - judgment on admissions ... 379
  - notice ... 372-3
  - summary judgment ... 376
  - telephone hearings ... 373
- case management ... 342, 392-3
  - conference ... 400
  - fast track ... 397
  - multi-track ... 399-400
- civil restraint orders ... 344
- claim form
  - drafting ... 362
  - parties ... 361
  - procedure for issue ... 361
- commencement of action ... 357
- companies ... 355, 361
- conditional fee agreements ... 12, 22-3, 24, 337
- consent orders ... 380
- contract ... 334
- costs
  - assessment
    - detailed ... 421
    - summary ... 420, 422
  - at trial ... 419
  - client notification ... 417
  - default costs certificate ... 421
  - discretion of court ... 417-19
  - fast track trial ... 420
  - final costs certificate ... 421
  - fixed ... 419
  - forthwith ... 418
  - here and below ... 418
  - indemnity bases ... 417
  - in any event ... 418
  - in the case ... 418
  - interim costs certificate ... 421
  - no order for ... 418
  - of and caused by ... 418
  - orders ... 418
  - publicly funding client ... 422
  - reserved ... 418
  - security for ... 384
  - solicitor and own clients ... 422
  - standard basis ... 417
  - taxation *see* assessment
  - thrown away ... 418
- counterclaims ... 366
- county court ... 357
- declaratory judgment ... 380
- defence ... 366
- defence to counterclaim ... 370
- defendant's response ... 365-9
- depositions ... 413
- discontinuance ... 379
- discovery *see* Discovery
- documents for court ... 346-7, 360
  - service *see* service of documents
  - *see also* statements of case; statements of truth
- enforcing judgments
  - attachment of earnings order ... 426, 429
  - bankruptcy ... 426, 429
  - charging orders ... 426
    - over land ... 428
    - securities ... 428
  - debtor's means ... 424
  - execution against goods ... 426
  - interest on debts ... 425
  - international aspects ... 423
  - judgment ... 423
  - oral examination ... 424
  - orders ... 423
  - receiver appointment ... 426
  - reciprocal ... 423
  - seizure of goods ... 426
  - third party debt order ... 426, 427
  - tracing debtor ... 424
  - warrant of execution ... 426
  - winding up ... 429
  - writ of *fi fa* ... 426
- evidence
  - hearsay ... 409-10
  - notarial acts and instruments ... 410
  - opinion ... 408
- failure to attend trial ... 360

517

Subject	Page
fast track	397-8
allocation	392-3
costs	420
financing	337
foreign jurisdiction	337
further information	378
hearings	360
allocation	393
telephone	373
High Court	357
initiating proceedings	355-64
instructing counsel	412
insurers	355
interim payments	383
interim remedies *see* Interim remedies	
joinder of causes of action	355
joint claimants	355
jurisdictions, disputing	369
latent damage	334
litigation friend	351, 356
minors	356, 361
multi-track	
allocation	392-3
procedure	399-400
negligence	334
non-payment of fees	344
offers to settle *see* Part 36 offers and payments	
orders on initiative of court	342
overriding objective	341
overview of proceedings, early stages	340
particulars of claim	
compulsory matters	363
drafting	364
interest	363
parties	355-6
adding or substituting	350
on claim form	361
removing	350
service *see* service of documents	
see also individual parties eg minors	
partnership	355, 361
patients	355, 361
payments into court *see* Part 36 offers and payments	
personal injury	334, 337, 339
pre-action disclosure	339
pre-action inspection	339
pre-action protocol	337
pre-trial checklist	397
privileged material	405
public funding	422
public hearing	360
reply	370
rules of court	333
sanctions	
non-compliance with directions	344
non-compliance with protocol	337
non-payment of fees	344

Subject	Page
relief	345
security for costs	384
selection of court	357-9
transfers	358-9
service of documents	
acknowledgment	369
address	352
alternative	352
by claimant	353
by court	353
certificate of service	354
children and patients	352
companies	353
delivery to permitted address	354
DX	354
electronic communication	346-7, 354
fax	354
notice of non-service	353
partnerships	353
personal	354
postal	354
small claims track	
allocation	392-3
appeals	396
conduct of hearing	395
directions	394
experts	395
non-attendance	396
reasons for judgment	395
record of hearing	395
rehearing	396
representation	395
setting aside judgment	396
sole trader	355, 361
statements of case	348
adding or substituting party	350
amendments	349-50
counterclaims	366
defence	366
defence to counterclaim	370
further information	378
particulars of claim	363-4
removing party	350
reply	370
striking out	343
statements of truth	351
electronic filing and	347
stay of proceedings	393
striking out, statement of case	343
summary judgment	376
time	
limits	345
meanings	345
timetable for trial	360
track allocation	392-3
questionnaire	393
trade and professional schemes	337
transfer of court	358-9
application to set aside order	359

INDEX

C

Subject	Page
competition law claims	359
criteria	359
procedure	359
trial bundles	360, 411
trial preparations	411-14
trial procedure	415-16
viability of claim	334
witnesses	413
see also Electronic filing and documentation	
Civil partner	
home rights	
conveyancing	191, 216
intestacy	153, 191
notice	216
inheritance tax	102
Civil restraint orders	344
Client care	13
informed consent	8
Clinical negligence, pre-action protocol	337
Close companies	
close investment holding company	113, 114
definition	112
IHT on transfer of value	113
interest relief	114
participators	
attribution of capital gains to	113
expenses	113
loans to	113
taxation	113-14
Close investment holding company	113, 114
Coal Authority searches	222
Codicil	168
Commercial tenancies	
compensation	237
grant of new	238
security of tenure	236-8
termination	237, 238
Committal	
abolition	471
before trial	474
evidence	473
no case to answer	472, 473
procedure	472
reporting restrictions	473
for sentence	490
test for	473
with evidence	471, 472
without evidence	471, 472
see also Sending for trial	
Common enterprise, evidence of	510
Commonhold and Leasehold Reform Act 2002	239
Commonhold tenure	239
assignment of lease	232
new buildings	226
registration	239
Commonhold title	219
Commonhold unit information certificate	181

Subject	Page
Community Legal Service, funding legal help, civil	16-18
Community orders, requirements	
activity	486
alcohol treatment	486
attendance centre	486
curfew	486
drug rehabilitation	486
electronic monitoring	486
exclusion	486
mental health treatment	486
programme	486
prohibited activity	486
residence	486
supervision	486
unpaid work	486
Community sentences	
adults *see* Community orders, requirements	
breaches	485
definition	485
imposition	485
revocation	485
young persons	490
see also Community orders, requirements	
Companies	
agents	274, 275
annual accounts	270
annual return	271
articles of association	255, 258
associated, stamp duty	128
auditor	273
board	
control of	262
meetings *see* Board meetings	
business records as hearsay	410, 507
certificate of incorporation	255
chairman	273
charges	305
checks before establishment	255
choice of medium	290-1
civil litigation party	355, 361
competition *see* Competition	
conveyancing party	194
debentures	276-8, 283
directors *see* Directors	
director's report	271
dividends	283
documentation	256-8
establishment	255
insolvency	
administrative receiver	297
striking off	297
voluntary arrangements	301-2
see also liquidation	
liquidation	
compulsory	304
distribution of assets	304
fraudulent trading	305

INDEX

C

Subject	Page
recovery of assets	305
voluntary	303
wrongful trading	305
memorandum of association	255, 256-7
names	256, 257
alteration	257
objects	257
alteration	257
off-the-shelf	255
officers	273
pensions	331
private	255-85
procedures	284-5
public	286
registered office	256
reorganisations	128
secretary	256, 273
service of documents on	353
share capital	278-9
reduction	281-2
shareholders *see* Shareholders	
shareholders' meetings *see* Shareholders' meetings	
shares *see* Shares	
Societas Europaea	287-8
statutory books	256
ultra vires acts	274
winding up petition, shareholders	263
Companies Registry	255
Compellability of witness	503-4
Compensation order	489
Competence of witness	503-4
Competition	
agreements	
of minor importance	309
small	311
block exemptions	309
comfort letters	309
dominant position abuse	310, 313
European Union	308-10
enforcement	312
merger control	307
minor importance agreements	309
negative clearances	309
restraint of trade	310
restriction or distortion	308-9, 311, 313
restrictive practices	310
United Kingdom	
common law	310
Competition Act 1998	310-11
enforcement	313
Enterprise Act 2002	310
merger control	308
OFT	310, 311, 313
restraint of trade	310
restrictive practices	310
small agreements	311
transfer of court	359

Subject	Page
Completion	
arrangements	205
delayed	241
money	206
personal	206
place	206
post-completion	224, 226
postal	206-7
preparing for	205, 224
sale of part	224
statements	205
time	206
Conditional cautions	434, 512
Conditional fee agreements	12, 22-3, 337
bills	24
challenge by paying party	23
indemnity principle abrogation	22
road traffic cases	22
Conduct	
advertising	3
confidentiality, disclosure and	11-12, 496
conflict of interest	8-10
costs	15
discipline	
bodies	27
inadequate professional services	26
negligence	26
disclosure and confidentiality	11-12, 496
discrimination	13
financial services	28-30
Guide to Professional Conduct	33
human rights	34
instructions *see* Taking instructions	
Law Society Code of Conduct	2
legal aid *see* Legal aid	
professional ethics *see* Professional ethics	
referrals	3
Solicitors' Practice Rules	2
undertakings	25
Conferences (Counsel)	412
Confessions	508
Confidentiality, disclosure and	11-12, 496
Confiscation order	489
Conflict of interests	
acting for buyer and lender	10
acting for seller and buyer	10
conveyancing	9-10
gifts from client	9
taking instructions	8-9
Consent orders	380
Construction and engineering disputes, pre-action protocol	337
Consumer Complaints Service (CCS)	27
Consumer guarantees	318
Contingency fee agreements	22
Contracts	
conveyancing *see* Conveyancing, contract	
third party rights	322

INDEX

C

Subject	Page
Contributions/indemnity, applications	374-5
Conveyancing	
acting for buyer and lender	10
acting for seller and buyer	10
bankruptcy of seller	202
charities	195
chronology	174-211
civil partners	191
companies	194
completion	
arrangements	205
delayed	241
money	206
personal	206
place	206
post-completion	224, 226
postal	206-7
preparing for	205, 224
sale of part	224
time	206
conflicts of interest	9-10
contract	
amending	190
buyer approves	225-6
competition legislation	190
conditional	223
drafting	177-81
new buildings	225-6
sale of part	223-4
special conditions	180
standard terms and conditions	178-9
contract races	9
covenants	187
death of party	202
deposits	75, 77-8, 198
ED	211
electronic	211, 218
END	211
exchange	
consequences	202
methods	201
preparations	191-200
from attorney	214
from lender	214
Home Information Packs	183-4
land held on trust	192-4
beneficiaries	194
trustees	193, 213
leases *see* Leases	
married couples	191
mental impairment	195
minors	191
mortgages	199-200
discharge	211
ED	211
END	211
new buildings	225-6
pre-contract package	225
non-solicitors	31

Subject	Page
parties	191-7
personal representatives	194, 212, 213
plan colour scheme	173
planning difficulties	187-8
post-completion	224, 226
acting for buyer	208
acting for seller	208
formalities	208-11
pre-contract package	
assembling	182
contract drafting	177-81
sale of part	224
seller's title	177
purchase deed	
delivery	204
form	203
parties	203
plans	203
preparation	203-4
sale of part	224
signatures	203, 204
witnesses	204
Register	216-17
registration	209
compulsory first	209
electronic lodgement	211, 218
Land Registration Act 2002	209-10
period	209
qualifying estate	209
registrable dispositions	210
requirement	209
remedies	
compensation for delayed completion	241
contractual	242
notice to complete	240
vendor and purchaser summons	240
restrictive covenants	187
searches	
adverse entries	221
checklist	219-21
Coal Authority	222
HM Land Registry	222
Land Charges Registry	222
local authority	222
National Land Information Service	222
pre-completion	221
pre-contract	185, 220
preparation for exchange	197
validation insurance	220
water authority	222
surveys	189
taking instructions	
first interview	175-6
post-interview formalities	176
sale of part	223
title	
commonhold	219
documentation	185
documents retained by seller	215

INDEX
C

Subject	Page
freehold	
registered	218
unregistered	212-15
leasehold	
registered	219
unregistered	215
proving	215, 218
registered	185, 197, 216-17
freehold	218
leasehold	219
requisitions	202
root of	212
seller's, checking	177
unregistered	186
freehold	212-15
leasehold	215
undue influence	196
voluntary dispositions below market value	213
Corporate venturing scheme	107
Corporation tax	
allowable loss	106
calculation	104-8
capital profit	106-7
chargeability notification	119
charges on income	107
close companies	112-14
corporate venturing scheme	107
derivative contracts	109
disposal identification	106
exemptions	107
first accounting period	121
franked investment income	108
goodwill	106
income profit	104-6
information	120
intellectual property	106
large company	110, 121
loan relationships	105, 109
loss relief	109
mainstream	108
payment	121
profits	108
R & D tax credits	110
records	120
reliefs	107
remediation relief	104
replacement relief	107
roll-over relief	107
self-assessment	119-20
tax credits	114
R & D	110
tax return	119, 120
taxable gain	
calculation	107
identification	106
total profits	107
wasting assets	107
see also Distributions	
Corroboration	502

Subject	Page
Costs	
assessment	
detailed	421
summary	420, 422
at trial	419
civil litigation	417-22
client notification	12, 15, 417
default costs certificate	421
discretion of court	417-19
fast track trial	420
final costs certificate	421
fixed	419
forthwith	418
here and below	418
indemnity principle	22, 417
in any event	418
in the case	418
inter partes	15
interim costs certificate	421
no order for	418
of and caused by	418
orders	418, 489
publicly funded client	422
reserved	418
security for	384
solicitor-own-client	15, 422
solicitors' accounts	72
standard basis	417
summary trial	466
sums received on account	73
taxation *see* assessment	
thrown away	418
Counsel	
civil litigation	412
conference	412
criminal litigation	474
fee	412
instructing	412
Counterclaim	366
applications	374-5
defence to	370
Court of Protection	157
Courts	
civil appeal	430
orders on own initiative	342
Covenants in leases, liability	229
Criminal compensation order	336
Criminal Injuries Compensation Authority	336
Criminal Justice Act 2003, character evidence	499-501
Criminal litigation	
appeals	493-4
applications	
contributions/indemnity	374-5
counterclaims	374-5
at police stations *see* Police stations	
bail *see* Bail	
case management	452
case progression officers	452

Subject	Page
committal *see* Committal	
confessions	508
Counsel brief	474
Crown Court *see* Crown Court hearings	
disclosure	495-6
evidence *see* Evidence	
identification *see* Identification	
mode of trial	460-3
offences *see* Offences	
overriding objective	451
overview	432
remand	454
rules of court	451, 453
sentences *see* Sentences; Sentencing	
summary trial *see* Summary trial	
witnesses *see* Evidence; Witnesses	
Cross-examination	498
Crown Court hearings	
criminal	474-7
indictment	475
plea and case management hearing	475, 476
pre-trial hearings	475
preparation	474
preparatory hearings	477
procedure	475
reporting restrictions	477
Curfew requirement	486
Current ratio	59
Custody officer	447, 450
Custody plus	479, 483

D

Subject	Page
Damages	334
breach of contract	242
Dangerous or careless driving	450
Data protection	329
De bonis administrandum grant	157
De bonis non administratis grant	170
Debentures	283
administrative receiver appointment	297
authority to borrow	276
procedure	277
redemption	278
registration	278
remedies	278
searches	276
terms	277
type of security	277
Debtor days	59
Debts	
bad	45, 78
doubtful	45
judgment	425
late payment	318
payment	
insolvent estate	163
solvent estate	164
Declaratory judgment	380
Defamation, pre-action protocol	337

Subject	Page
Default judgment	377
Defence, duties	32
Defence (statement of case)	366
Defence to counterclaim	370
Demonstrative legacy	147, 148
Demoted tenancy, anti-social behaviour and	235
Dependants, provision from estate	168, 169
Depositions	413
Deposits	
agent, holding as	198
conveyancing	75, 198
interest	77-8, 198
solicitors' accounts	75, 77-8
stakeholder, holding as	198
Depreciation	47
Detention at Her Majesty's Pleasure	490
Detention at police station	
after charge	450
informing someone	449
Detention and training order	490
Detention in young offender institution	490
Directions	
fast track	398
multi-track	400
plea and case management hearing	471, 475, 476
small claims track	394
variation	453
Directors	
alternate	267
annual accounts	270
annual return	271
appointment	267
authority	275
board, control of	262
chairman	273
confidentiality of address	267
contracts	272
disqualification	269
duties	
administrative	270-2
care and skill	270
employees' interests	271
fiduciary	270
gratuitous compensation	271
liability	274
loans	272
loss of office	268-9
managing	273
meetings *see* Board meetings	
names on stationery	271
non-executive	267
numbers	267
protection of position	269
register	271
register of interests	270, 271
removal	
automatic	268
by members	268

Subject	Page
remuneration	267
report	271
service contracts	267, 271
shadow	267
statutory declaration	256
statutory restrictions	271
substantial property transactions	271
Disbursements, solicitors' accounts	72, 73-4
Discipline	
bodies	27
inadequate professional services	26
negligence	26
Disclosure	
before proceedings	402
civil litigation	32, 339
claim to withhold	401
common law rules change	495
confidentiality	11-12, 496
copies	401
criminal litigation	495-6
defence statements	496
documents	401, 405
duty of search	403
electronic	404
inspection	402
order for specific	402
procedure	403
prosecution duties	31
public interest immunity	496
standard	403
third party	402
time limits	496
see also Discovery	
Discontinuance	379
Discrimination	
age	329
disability	329
European workers	328
qualifications	328
race	329
sex	329
taking instructions	13
UK legislation	329
Disease and illness, pre-action protocol	337
Dismissal (from employment)	
unfair	330
wrongful	330
Disqualification of directors	269
Disqualification from driving	488
Distance selling	318-19
Distribution agreements	325
legislation	324
types	324
Distributions	
franked investment income	111
higher rate taxpayer	111
shareholders	111
tax credit	111
see also Corporation tax	

Subject	Page
Dividend cover ratio	57
Dividends	283
Documentary evidence	497
Driving disqualification	488
Drug rehabilitation requirement	486
Duty solicitors	
at police station	19
in court	21

E

Earnings per share	57
EIS investments	96, 98, 137
Elderly clients	
disposal of home	140
residential care	140
Electronic conveyancing	211, 218
Electronic discharge (ED)	211
Electronic disclosure	404
Electronic filing and documentation	346-7
online forms service	347
statements of truth and	347
Electronic monitoring	
community order requirement	486
suspended sentence and	482
Electronic Notification of Discharge (END)	211
Employment	
data protection	329
disability discrimination	329
discrimination	
EU equal treatment	328
UK legislation	329
equal pay	329
health and safety	329
illegal immigrants	330
pensions	331
personal data	329
qualifications	328
redundancy	330
starting a business	330
statutory rights	328-30
trade unions	328, 330
transfer of undertakings	329
unfair dismissal	330
workers	
equal treatment	328
EU law	326-8
families	326
free movement	326
residence rights	326, 327
working time	330
wrongful dismissal	330
Enforcing fines	484
Enforcing judgments	
attachment of earnings order	426, 429
bankruptcy	426, 429
charging orders	426
over land	428
securities	428
debtor's means	424

Subject	Page
execution against goods	426
interest on debts	425
international aspects	423
judgment	423
oral examination	424
orders	423
receiver appointment	426
reciprocal enforcement	423
seizure of goods	426
third party debt order	426, 427
tracing debtor	424
warrant of execution	426
winding up	429
writ of *fi fa*	426
Enterprise Investment Scheme (EIS)	96, 98, 137
European Company	287-8
European Convention on Human Rights	34
Evaluation	
expert	335
neutral	335
Evidence	
admissibility	504-5
hearsay *see* Hearsay	
admissions	
authenticity of document	406
facts	406
burden of proof	497
character	499-501
committals	473
common enterprise	510
confessions	508
corroboration	502
criminal litigation	433, 497
depositions	413
documentary	497
examination of witnesses	498
expert	414
family tradition	510
hearsay	409-10
hearsay *see* Hearsay	
identification *see* Identification	
memory refreshing statements	509
models	408
non-sensitive material	433
notarial acts and instruments	410
notice to admit facts	406
notice to admit or produce	406
opinion	408, 510
oral	497
photographs	408
plans	408
preparation of Schedules	433
privileged material	405, 505
proof	497
public information	510
public interest immunity	496, 505
real	497
reputation	510
res gestae statements	510

Subject	Page
retention of material	433
self-made	505
sensitive material	433
silence inferences	
at police station	441, 442-3
at trial	511
similar fact	505
statements and depositions	497
witness statements	407-8
see also Witnesses	
Examination-in-chief	498
Excluded confessions	508
Exclusion clauses	320-1
Exclusion requirement, community orders	486
Execution against goods	426
Executors	146
Expert determination	335
Expert witnesses	413, 414
content of report	414
joint experts	414
Extraordinary general meeting	264

F

Subject	Page
Facts, notice to admit	406
Family mediation	17
Fast track	
allocation	392-3
costs	420
directions	398
procedure	397-8
Fatal accident, drafting claim	364
Fees	
conditional	12
conditional fee agreements	12, 22-3, 24, 337
information to client	12, 15
quotations and estimates	12
solicitors' accounts	74
Financial services	28-30
financial promotion restriction	29
FMSA 2000	29, 30
general prohibition	29
investments	29
Law Society	30
regulated activities	29
Financial Services Authority	28
Fines	484
Fixtures, Fitting and Contents Form	179, 180, 182
Forfeiture order	489
Franchises	325
Fraudulent trading	305
Free movement of goods	314
Free movement of workers	
equal rights	328
families	326
mutual recognition	328
residence rights	326, 327
Freedom of establishment	243
Freedom to provide services	243
Freezing injunction	382

Subject	Page

Funding
    conditional fee agreements . . 12; 22-3, 24, 337
    contingency fee agreements 22
    see also Public funding
Further information application 378

G

Gas safety, duty of landlord 232
Gearing 58
General civil contract 19
General criminal contract 19
General family help 17
General legacy 147, 148
Gifts
    abatement 171
    ademption 171
    failure of 171
    from client 9
    lapse 171
    legacies 147, 148, 165-6
    substitutional 171
Goods
    execution against 426
    free movement 314
    see also Sale of goods and supply of services
Goodwill, corporation tax 106
Guarantees 318
Guardians 147
Guide to Professional Conduct 33
Guilty plea, sentencing and 478

H

Hearings
    allocation 393
    civil litigation 360, 373, 393
    rules 453
    telephone 373
Hearsay
    admissibility of evidence 506-10
    admissions by agents 510
    business records 410, 507
    civil litigation 409-10
    common enterprise 510
    common law 510
    family tradition 510
    general principles 506
    machine generated statements 506
    meaning 409
    memory refreshing statements 509
    multiple 507, 509
    notice 410, 507
    opinion evidence 510
    previous statements by witness 509
    procedure 409
    public information 510
    published works 409
    reputation 510
    res gestae statements 510

Subject	Page

    statutory 507-9
    superfluous out of court statements 506
    witness absent from court
        cannot be found 507
        dead 507
        fear 507
        outside UK 507
        unfit 507
    witness statements 507
    written statements 508
    see also Confessions
Help with mediation 17
Hold-over relief 96, 98
Home Information Packs 183-4
    home condition report 184
Housing disrepair, pre-action protocol 337
Human rights
    European Convention 34
    Human Rights Act 1998 34
    taxation and 142

I

Identification
    confrontation 446
    court 445
    disputed 502
    group 446
    matters to be explained 444
    parades 445
    photographs 446
    suspect known to police 444
    suspect not known to police 444
    Turnbull warning 502
    video 445
Income tax
    accounting date 88
    benefits code 84-5
    business medium choice 291
    calculation, overview 116
    deceased's estate 161
    deductions 81, 83-4
    employment income 83-5
    individuals
        private persons 80-7
        sole traders/partners 88-9
    limited liability partnerships 90
    loss relief 89
    overlap relief 89
    partnerships 90
    payment 116
    pensions income 83-5
    personal reliefs 87
    private service providers 86
    profits from property business 81
    profits from trade 80-1
    records 115
    savings and investment income 82
    self-assessment 115
    social security income 83-5

Subject	Page
statutory income	80-6
tax return	115
taxable income	87
total income	86, 87
trustees	87
types of income	80
Indemnity principle, costs	22, 417
Indictable offences	450, 462
Individual Savings Accounts (ISA)	137, 138

Inheritance tax
- agricultural property relief ... 102
- assessment ... 117
- associated operations ... 139
- business medium choice ... 291
- business property relief ... 102
- calculation ... 100-3
- charitable gifts ... 102
- civil partner ... 102
- close companies ... 113
- death
  - apportionment over estate ... 103
  - calculation ... 103
  - free estate ... 100, 101, 103
  - loss relief ... 101
- debts ... 102
- deceased's estate ... 161
- disclaimers and elections ... 141
- exemptions ... 102
- free estate
  - identification ... 103
  - valuation ... 103
- funerals ... 102
- gifts with benefit reserved ... 139
- liability ... 100
- lifetime chargeable transfer ... 100, 101
- non-interest in possession trust ... 137, 139
- payment ... 118
- potential exempt transfer ... 100, 101
- public benefit gifts ... 102
- quick succession relief ... 102
- reduced form IHT 200 ... 117
- reserved benefit gifts ... 100
- spouse gifts ... 102
- valuation
  - free estate ... 100, 101
  - transfer ... 101
- woodlands relief ... 102

Injunction
- application ... 382
- evidence ... 382
- freezing ... 382
- jurisdiction ... 382
- urgent application ... 382

Insolvency
- bankruptcy notice ... 216
- corporate
  - administrative receiver ... 297
  - liquidation *see* Liquidation
  - striking off ... 297
  - voluntary arrangement ... 301-2
- EU cross-border ... 306
- fraudulent trading ... 305
- limited liability partnerships ... 296
- partnerships ... 296
- personal
  - bankruptcy ... 294, 426, 429
  - bankruptcy notice ... 216
  - disabilities ... 296
  - distribution order ... 296
  - false representations by bankrupt ... 296
  - false representations by debtor ... 293
  - fast-track procedure ... 293
  - trustee in bankruptcy ... 295
  - voluntary arrangements ... 292-3
- preferences ... 295, 305
- statutory demand ... 294, 306, 335
- transactions at undervalue ... 295, 305
- winding up ... 429
- wrongful trading ... 305

Insolvent estates
- secured creditors ... 163
- unsecured creditors ... 163

Inspection ... 339, 404-5
- claim to withhold ... 401
- order for specific ... 402
- privilege ... 405
- witness statements ... 405

Instructing Counsel ... 412
Insurance premiums ... 76-7
Intellectual property, corporation tax ... 106

Interest
- cover ... 58
- deposits ... 77-8, 198
- on judgment debts ... 425
- particulars of claim ... 363

Interim payments ... 383
Interim remedies
- application ... 381-4
- consent orders ... 380
- discontinuance ... 379
- freezing injunctions ... 382
- interim payments ... 383
- search orders ... 382
- security for costs ... 384
- types of order ... 381
- urgent applications, without notice ... 382

Intermediaries ... 132
Intermittent custody ... 479

Intestacy
- *bona vacantia* ... 152
- civil partners
  - home ... 153, 191
  - redemption of life interest ... 153
- expenses ... 151
- extent of estate passing ... 151
- fund for pecuniary legacies ... 151
- order of entitlement ... 152

Subject	Page
spouse	
matrimonial home right	153, 191
redemption of life interest	153
statutory trusts	151
Intimate samples	447
Introductions	3
Investments, tax planning	137-40

J

Subject	Page
Joinder of causes of action	355
Joinder of charges in indictment	475
Joinder of parties	355, 475
Judgment	
on admissions	379
declaratory	380
default	377
enforcement *see* Enforcing judgments	
summary	376
Judgment debts	425
Judicial review, pre-action protocol	337

K

L

Subject	Page
Land	
charging orders over	428
VAT	124
Land Charges Registry searches	222
Land Registration Act 2002	
e-conveyancing	211, 218
registrable dispositions	210
registration under	209-10
Land Registry	
electronic discharge	211
electronic lodgement	211, 218
plan colour scheme	173
Land Registry searches	222
Lapse (of gift)	171
Latent damage	334
Law Society	
Code of Conduct	2
designated professional body	30
Guide to Professional Conduct	33
Search Validation Insurance Scheme	220
Leading questions	416
Leases	
assignment	
consent of landlord	231
over commonhold unit	232
procedure	230
of reversion	232
common law presumptions	228
Commonhold and Leasehold Reform Act 2002	239
contract approval	229
covenants liability	229
deed	229
definitions	227
drafting	227-8
gas safety	232
management schemes	228
post-completion	229
pre-contract package	229
procedure for grant	229
reversion assignment	232
see also Security of tenure	
Legacies	147, 148
payment	165-6
Legal aid/legal help *see* Public funding	
Legal professional privilege	405
Legal Services Commission *see* Public funding	
Legal Services Ombudsman	27
Letters of administration	157
attorneys	157
Licence	325
Limited liability partnerships	
agreement	251-2
capital gains tax	99
description	250
formation	250-1
income tax	90
incorporation document	251
insolvency	296
obligations and liabilities	
of members	254
to third parties	253, 254
under CA 1985 (as modified)	253, 254
purpose	250
stamp duty	128
taxation	254
written agreement	251-2
Liquidation	
compulsory	304
distribution of assets	304
recovery of assets	305
statutory demand	306
voluntary	303
wrongful trading	305
Listing questionnaire *see* Pre-trial checklist	
Litigation friend	356
statement of truth	351
Loan capital	129
Local authority searches	222
Loss relief, corporation tax	109

M

Subject	Page
Management schemes, flats	228
Matrimonial home rights	
conveyancing	191, 216
intestacy	153, 191
notice	216
Mediation	335
family	17
help with mediation	17
Medical negligence, pre-action protocol	337
Medium-sized business/company, definition	93

Subject	Page
Memorandum of association	255, 256-7
alteration of name	257
alteration of objects	257
objects	257
Mental health treatment requirement	486
Merger control	
European	307
United Kingdom	308
Minors	
beneficiaries	165
civil litigation party	356, 361
conveyancing	191
litigation friend	351, 356
Part 36 offers and payments	389
service of document on	352
Mitigation	491
Mode of trial	460-3
advising client	463
allocation procedure	461
Money laundering	
acquiring, using and possessing	4
arranging	4
concealing	4
defences	4, 5
failing to disclose	5
keeping records	7
reinterpretation after *Bowman*	6
tipping off	6
verifying identification	7
Moratorium, CVA small company	301-2
Mortgages	199-200
discharge	211
ED	211
END	211
solicitors' accounts	75
stamp duty	128
Motor Insurers' Bureau	335
Motoring penalties, disqualification	488
Multi-track	
allocation	392-3
directions	400
procedure	399-400

N

Subject	Page
Name of company	256
alteration	257
Name of partnership	244
National Land Information Service (NLIS)	222
Negligence	334
clinical	337
Negotiation	335
Neutral evaluation	335
New buildings	
'Buildmark' policy cover	226
buyer approves contract	225-6
commonhold	226
NHBC pack	226
post-completion	226
pre-contract package	225

Subject	Page
Newton hearing	492
NHBC pack	226
No case to answer	472, 473
Non-intimate samples	448
Notarial acts and instruments	410
Notice	
agreed	216
bankruptcy notice	216
civil partnership home rights	216
excluded interests	216
matrimonial home rights	216
to admit facts	406
to admit or produce documents	406

O

Subject	Page
Offences	
dangerous or careless driving	450
either way	460-3
indictable	450, 462
summary	450, 462
Offer to settle *see* Part 36 offers and payments	
Office for Client Relations	27
Office of Fair Trading	310, 311, 313
Office for Professional Regulation	27
Opinion evidence	408, 510
Oral examination, enforcing civil judgment	424
Orders *see individual orders*	
Overriding interests	217

P

Subject	Page
Part 36 offers and payments	
acceptance	388
at trial	391
before proceedings commence	389
Calderbank offer	385
clarification	387
form and content	385-6
funds in court	388
minors	389
patients	389
prior to judgment	390
time of acceptance	388
time of making	387
Participators *see* Close companies	
Particulars of claim	
compulsory matters	363
drafting	364
interest	363
Partners	
income tax	88-9
obligations and liabilities	246
personal liability	247
limitations	247
Partnership accounts	
appropriation accounts	52-3
balance sheet	54
current accounts	54
revaluation of assets	54

INDEX
P

Subject	Page
trial balance	52
Partnerships	
agreement	245
capital gains tax	99
choice of medium	290-1
civil litigation party	355, 361
continuance	90
conversion to company	289
dissolution	248-9
distribution of assets	249
formation	244
income tax	90
insolvency	296
limited liability *see* Limited liability partnerships	
names	244
obligations and liabilities	246
recovery from	246
service of documents on	353
sole trader conversion to	289
Patients	
civil litigation party	355, 361
Part 36 offers and payments	389
service of document on	352
Payment into court *see* Part 36 offers and payments	
Pecuniary legacy	147, 148
payment	166
Penalty notices	434
Pensions	
employees	331
income withdrawal	331
lifetime allowance	331
retirement age	331
state	331
Personal data	329
Personal injury	334, 337, 339
criminal injuries	336
drafting claim	364
insurance	336
pre-action protocol	337
provisional damages	384
Personal representatives	
breach of duty	169-70
capital gains tax	99
choice of grant	157
collecting in assets	160
conveyancing by	194, 212, 213
conveyancing to self	212
death	170
debts paid from wrong property	169
delegation	149
dependants	169
leaseholds	169
liability	170
missing beneficiaries	169
operation of business	149
powers in will	149
release from liability	170
relief from liability	170

Subject	Page
solicitor's duty to	154
statutory powers and rights	160
statutory trusts	151
tax liability of estate	161
Trustee Act 2000 powers	149, 150
unknown creditors	169
unreasonable delay	169
Planning law	187-8
Plea before venue hearing	470
Plea and case management hearing	471, 475, 476
Police bail	512
Police and Justice Bill 2006	512
Police officers, witnesses	413
Police powers	
arrest	435-6
cautions	439
conditional cautions	434, 512
penalty notices	434
reprimands	434
Police stations	
arrest at	438
arrest away from	438
cautions	439
charges	447
custody officer	447
detention	
after charge	447
before charge	440
informing someone	449
identification *see* Identification	
interviews	
inferences from silence	441, 442-3
legal advice	441
recording	441
safeguards	440
investigations, Code of Practice	433
legal advice right	441, 449
PACE codes	434
retention of material	433
samples	
intimate	447
non-intimate	448
safeguards	447
silence at	441, 442-3
solicitor's role	448
voluntary attendance	440
Powers of arrest	435-7
Pre-action protocols	337
after first meeting	339
non-compliance sanctions	337
procedure	338
Pre-sentence reports	492
Pre-trial checklist	397
Pre-trial hearings	465
Crown Court	475
Preferences	295, 305
Prepayments	46
Private service providers, income tax	86

Subject	Page
Privileged material	405, 505
inspection	405
public interest immunity	496, 505
Probate	
applicants	158
application	156-9
chain of administration	170
de bonis administrandum grant	157
de bonis non administratis grant	170
dependant's claim	168, 169
failure of gift	
abatement	171
ademption	171
lapse	171
grant of representation	
additional evidence required	168
application	156-9
caveats	167
choice of grant	157
citation to propound will	167
citation to take or refuse	167
codicil validity doubted	168
due execution affidavit	168
failure to take oath	167
knowledge and approval affidavit	168
lost will	168
objections	167
plight and condition affidavit	168
uncertain interpretation	168
immediately after death	155
lost will	168
oath	
filling in	159
swearing	156
personal representatives *see* Personal representatives	
solicitor's role	154
see also Administration (estates), ; Intestacy; Wills	
Professional ethics	
civil litigation disclosure	32
conveyancing with non-solicitors	31
criminal law	31-2
duties of defence	32
duties of prosecution	31
Guide to Professional Conduct	33
Professional negligence, pre-action protocol	337
Profit margin	57
Profitability ratios	56-7
Programme requirement	486
Prohibited activity requirement	486
Property Register	216
indemnity	217
rectification	217
Proprietorship Register	216
indemnity	217
rectification	217
Prosecution, duties	31

Subject	Page
Public funding	
civil	337
certificate	18
Community Legal Service funding	16-18
costs	422
exclusions	16
family mediation	17
financial restrictions	17, 18
full representation	17, 18
general civil contract	16
general family help	17
help at court	17
investigative help	17, 18
legal help	17
merits restriction	18
representation	17, 18
criminal	19-21
advice and assistance	19
police questioning	19
advocacy assistance	20
duty solicitor in court	21
financial restriction	19, 20, 21
general criminal contract	19
merit restriction	19, 20, 21
representation	20-1
sending for trial	471
payments	
from Legal Services Commission	65
from third party	65
Public interest immunity	496, 505
Public issue of securities	132
Public limited company (plc)	
advantages	286-7
conversion to	287
disadvantages	286-7
Purchase deed *see* Conveyancing	

Q

Qualifications, mutual recognition	328
Quick succession relief	102
Quorum	
board meetings	272
shareholders' meetings	266

R

R & D tax relief	110
Racial discrimination	329
Racially aggravated offences	479
Ratio analysis	
'acid test'	59
asset turnover	57
cashflow	59
current	59
debtor days	59
dividend cover	57
earnings per share	57
financial risk	58
gearing	58

Subject	Page
interest cover	58
profit margin	57
profitability	56-7
return on capital employed (ROCE)	56
stock turnover	59
working capital	58
Re-examination	498
Rectification	242
Redundancy	330
Referrals	3
Register of directors	271
Register of directors' interests	270, 271
Registered office	256
Registration	
commonhold tenure	239
debentures	278
Religiously aggravated offences	479
Remand	454
sentencing and time spent on	480
Remediation relief	104
Remedies see Interim remedies	
Reorganisations	128
Reparation order	490
Replacement relief, corporation tax	107
Reply (statement of case)	370
Reporting restrictions	
committal	473
Crown Court preparatory hearings	477
preparatory hearings	477
sending for trial	469
Reprimands	434
Reputation, evidence of	510
Res gestae statements	510
Rescission	242
Residence	
European workers	326-7
permanent	327
temporary	327
Residence requirement, community order	486
Residential care, disposal of home	140
Residuary legacy	147, 148
Resolutions	
board meetings	272
shareholders' meetings	265
Restitution order	489
Restraint orders, civil	344
Restrictions	216
Restrictive covenants	187
Retainers	
authority	14
responsibilities	13
terminating	14
Retirement age	331
Return on capital employed (ROCE)	56
Risk ratios	58
Road traffic cases	
conditional fee agreements	22
insurers as party	355

Subject	Page
Roll-over relief	
corporation tax	107
EIS investments	96, 98
incorporation of business	96, 98
replacement of qualifying assets	96, 98
VCT investment	98

S

Subject	Page
Sale of goods and supply of services	
consumer guarantees	318
distance selling	318-19
exclusion clauses	320-1
late payment of debts	318
Sale of Goods Acts	316-17
terms implied by statute and regulation	315
Samples	
intimate	447
non-intimate	448
safeguards	447
Search	
disclosure duty	403
order	382
Searches see Conveyancing	
Securities	
charging orders over	428
stamp duty reserve tax (SDRT)	131-2
Security for costs	384
Security of tenure	
assured shorthold tenancy	233, 235
assured tenancy	233, 235
commercial tenancies	236-8
compensation	237
grant of new	238
termination	237, 238
commonhold	239
demoted tenancy	235
possession	
commercial tenancies	236-7
residential tenancies	234, 235
purchase of freehold	234
residential tenancies	233-5
right to buy	234
Sending for trial	467, 468-71
application for dismissal	470
bail	471
mixed charges	470
plea before venue hearing	470
plea and case management hearing	471
public funding	471
reporting restrictions	469
witnesses	471
Sentences	
action plan order	490
community	
requirements	486
youth sentences	490
compensation order	489
confiscation order	489
costs order	489

Subject	Page
custodial	
custody plus	479, 483
dangerous offenders	481
discretionary	480
first	479
intermittent custody	479
licence conditions	483
mandatory	481
time spend on remand and	480
youth	490
deferment	489
detention at Her Majesty's Pleasure	490
detention and training order	490
detention under PCC(S)A 2000	490
detention in young offender institution	490
discharges	487
driving disqualification	487
factors decreasing sentence	478
factors increasing sentence	478
fines	484
forfeiture order	489
motoring penalties	487-8
reparation order	490
restitution order	489
supervision order	490
suspended	482-3
Sentencing	
committal for sentence	490
court proceedings	492
drug tests	492
guilty plea and	478
mitigation	491
Newton hearing	492
Police and Justice Bill 2006	512
pre-sentence reports	492
purpose	478
racially aggravated offences	479
religiously aggravated offences	479
seriousness test	478, 480
time spent on remand	480
violent and sexual offence harm test	480
Sentencing Advisory Panel	491
Service of documents	
acknowledgement of service	369
address	352
alternative	352
by claimant	353
by court	353
certificate of service	354
children and patients	352
companies	353
delivery to permitted address	354
DX	354
electronic communication	346-7, 354
fax	354
notice of non-service	353
partnerships	353
personal	354
postal	354

Subject	Page
Sex discrimination	329
Shareholders	283
agreement	262
becoming a member	260
common law actions	263
control of board	262
register of members	260
removal of directors	268
rights	260-1
safeguards	263
taxation	282
unfair prejudice actions	263
winding up petition	263
Shareholders' meetings	
AGM	264
EGM	264
formalities	266
notice	264
proxies	266
quorum	266
resolutions	265
voting	266
Shares	
allotment	279
buy-back conditions	281
dividends	283
earnings per share	57
financial assistance for purchase	282
fully paid	278
issue of new	279, 281
partly paid	278
pre-emption rights	279
redeemable	281
transfer	280
transmission	280
types	278
Silence	
at police station	441, 442-3
at trial	511
legal advice	441, 442, 443
Similar fact evidence	505
Small business, definition	93
Small claims track	
allocation	392-3
appeals	396
conduct of hearing	395
directions	394
experts	395
non-attendance	396
reasons for judgment	395
record of hearing	395
rehearing	396
representation	395
setting aside judgment	396
Small company, definition	93
Societas Europaea	287-8
Sole trader	
choice of medium	290-1
civil litigation party	355, 361

INDEX

S

Subject	Page
conversion to partnership	289
income tax	88-9
Solicitors' accounts	
abatements	78
agreed fees	74
bad debts	78
cash account	69
client account	69
client ledger	69-71
client money	61-3
mixed payments in	63
payment into account	62, 63
withdrawals from account	62, 63
controlled trust	61, 62
costs	72
sums received on account	73
deposits	
conveyancing	75
interest	77-8
disbursements	72, 73-4
insurance premiums	76-7
interest	
amount	68
contracting out	68
stakeholder money	67
when paid	67-8
mortgages	75
office account	69
office ledger	69-71
office money	61, 62
public funding	
payments from LSC	65
payments from third parties	65
receipt and transfer of costs	64
record keeping	66
returned cheques	77
sums received on account of costs	73
trust money	61, 62
VAT	73-4
Solicitors' Accounts Rules 1998	60-8
Solicitors' Disciplinary Tribunal	27
Solicitors' Practice Rules	2
Special measures, vulnerable witnesses	504
Specific performance	242
Stakeholder, holder of deposit as	198
Stamp duty	
associated companies	128
calculation	126-9
deferral	129
dutiable instrument	126
exemptions	128-9
heads of charge	127-9
limited liability partnerships	128
loan capital	129
mortgages	128
payment	130
penalties	130
reliefs	128-9
reorganisations	128

Subject	Page
stampable consideration	126
Stamp duty land tax (SDLT)	
calculation	133-5
chargeable consideration	134
chargeable transaction	134
collection	136
effective date of transaction	133
land transaction identification	133-4
notifiable transaction	136
penalties	136
reliefs	135
Stamp duty reserve tax (SDRT)	131-2
intermediaries	132
public issues	132
Statements of case	
adding or substituting party	350
amendments	349-50
counterclaim	366
defence to	370
defence	366
defence to counterclaim	370
drafting	348
further information application	378
particulars of claim	363-4
practice rules for	348
removing party	350
reply	370
striking out	343
Statements of truth	
electronic filing and	347
form	351
litigation friend	351
signature	351
Statutory demand	294, 306, 335
Stay of proceedings, civil litigation	393
Stock turnover ratio	59
Striking off, insolvency of company	297
Striking out, statements of case	343
Substantial property transactions	271
Summary judgment application	376
Summary offences	450
linked to indictable offences	462
Summary trial	
costs	466
defect in process	465
joinder	465
pre-trial hearings	465
preparations	464
procedure	466
Supervision order	490
suspended sentence	482-3
Supervision requirement	486
Surrender to bail	459
Surveys	
full structural survey	189
housebuyer's report and valuation	189
valuation	189
Suspended sentences	
activation	483

Subject	Page
breach, revocation or amendment of order	482
electronic monitoring	482
imposition	482
imposition of requirements	482
review	482

T

Taking instructions
- acceptance ... 12
- acting for buyer and lender ... 10
- acting for seller and buyer ... 10
- advertising ... 3
- client care ... 13
- conflicts of interest ... 8-9
- conveyancing *see* Conveyancing, taking instructions
- discrimination ... 13
- fees ... 12
- gifts from client ... 9
- informed consent ... 8
- introductions ... 3
- money laundering ... 4-7
- referrals ... 3
- retainers
  - authority ... 14
  - responsibilities ... 13
  - termination ... 14

Taper relief ... 97-8

Tax credits
- abuse ... 114
- corporation tax ... 111, 114
- large companies ... 110
- R & D ... 110

Taxation
- assessment
  - capital gains tax ... 115
  - corporation tax ... 119-20
  - income tax ... 115
  - inheritance tax ... 117
  - self- ... 115, 119-20
- capital allowances ... 91-3
- capital gains tax *see* Capital gains tax
- close companies ... 112-14
- close investment holding company ... 113, 114
- corporation tax *see* Corporation tax
- distributions *see* Distributions
- income tax *see* Income tax
- inheritance tax *see* Inheritance tax
- limited liability partnerships ... 254
- payment
  - capital gains tax ... 116
  - corporation tax ... 121
  - income tax ... 116
  - inheritance tax ... 118
  - instalments ... 99, 118
  - stamp duty ... 130, 136
- planning
  - anti-avoidance ... 140, 142
  - death of client ... 141-2

Subject	Page
disclaimers	141
during lifetime	137-40
human rights	142
variations	141
self-assessment	115, 119-20
shareholders	282

- stamp duty *see* Stamp duty
- stamp duty land tax (SDLT) ... 133-6
- stamp duty reserve tax (SDRT) ... 131-2
- VAT *see* Value added tax

Taxation of costs *see* Assessment of costs
Telephone hearings ... 373
Tenancies *see* Leases; Security of tenure
Third party debt orders ... 426, 427
Third party rights, contract ... 322
Time limits, variation ... 453
Tipping off ... 6

Title
- absolute ... 218, 219
- documentation ... 185
- documents retained by seller ... 215
- freehold
  - registered ... 218
  - unregistered ... 212-15
- good leasehold ... 219
- leasehold
  - registered ... 219
  - unregistered ... 215
- possessory ... 218, 219
- proving ... 215, 218
- qualified ... 218, 219
- registered ... 185, 197, 216-17
  - freehold ... 218
  - leasehold ... 219
- requisitions ... 202
- root of ... 212
- seller's, checking ... 177
- unregistered ... 186
  - freehold ... 212-15
  - leasehold ... 215
- *see also* Conveyancing; Land Registration Act 2002

Tomlin order ... 380
Track allocation ... 392-3
Trade dispute schemes ... 337
Trade unions ... 328, 330

Trading
- distribution agreements ... 324
- franchise ... 325
- fraudulent ... 305
- free movement of goods ... 314
- licence ... 325
- wrongful ... 305
- *see also* Competition; Sale of goods and supply of services

Traffic accidents
- first client meeting ... 339
- insurance claims ... 335, 336
- uninsured drivers ... 335

Subject	Page
untraced drivers	335
Transactions at undervalue	295, 305
Transfer of undertakings	329
Trial	
civil litigation	415-16
closing speeches	416
leading questions	416
mode of trial determination	460-3
opening speeches	415
sending for	467, 468-71
silence at	511
summary *see* Summary trial	
Trial bundles	
civil litigation	360, 411
making up	411
Trustee Act 2000	149, 150
Trustees	
capital gains tax	99
income tax	87
Trusts, non-interest in possession	137, 139
Turnbull warning	502

U

Subject	Page
Ultra vires acts	274
Undertakings	
enforcement	25
from non-solicitors	31
steps before giving	25
Undervalue transactions	295, 305
Undue influence, conveyancing	196
Unpaid work requirement	486

V

Subject	Page
Value added tax	
capital goods scheme	125
flat rate scheme	122
land, option to tax	124
mandatory registration	122
penalties	125
solicitors' accounts	73-4
supplies	
exempt	123
rated at 5	123
types	122
zero rated	123
Venture Capital Trust (VCT)	137
roll-over relief	98
Victims Fund	478
Voluntary arrangements	
consequences	301
corporate insolvency	301-2
small company moratorium	301-2
Voting	
board meetings	272
shareholders' meetings	266
Vulnerable witnesses, special measures	504

W

Subject	Page
Warrant of execution	426
Wasting assets	107
Water authority searches	222
Wills	
additional evidence required	168
administrative powers	147
alterations	145
attestation clauses	147
capacity	144
caveats	167
class closing rules	147
codicils	168
common clauses	146-7
dependant's provision from estate	168, 169
destruction	145
disposal of remains	146
distribution powers	150
divorce	145
drafting considerations	147-50
executor appointment	146
failure of gifts	171
formalities	144
guardian appointment	147
intention	144
knowledge and approval affidavit	168
legacies	147, 148
payment	165-6
lost	168
marriage	145
personal representatives *see* Personal representatives	
plight and condition	168
revocation	
clause	146
dependant relative	145
express	145
implied	145
Trustee Act 2000	149, 150
validity requirements	144
see also Intestacy; Probate	
Witness statements	407-8
inspection	405
Witnesses	
cannot be found	507
civil litigation	413
competence and compellability	503-4
dead	507
depositions	413
ensuring attendance	413
examination	498
expert	413, 414
in fear	507
outside UK	507
police officers	413
purchase deed	204
sending for trial	471
special measures	504

Subject	Page
summons	413
unable to attend court	507
unfit	507
vulnerable	504
Woodlands relief	102
Work in progress	44

Subject	Page
Working capital	58
Working time regulation	330
Writ of *fieri facias*	426
Wrongful trading	305

X–Z